Psychotherapy and Counselling for Depression

Third Edition

Paul Gilbert

SAGE Publications
Los Angeles ▪ London ▪ New Delhi ▪ Singapore

First published 1992
Reprint four times
Second edition published 2000
Reprinted four times
This third edition published 2007

SAGE Publications Ltd
1 Oliver's Yard
55 City Road
London EC1Y 1SP

SAGE Publications Inc.
2455 Teller Road
Thousand Oaks, California 91320

SAGE Publications India Pvt Ltd
B 1/I 1 Mohan Cooperative Industrial Area
Mathura Road, New Delhi 110 044
India

SAGE Publications Asia-Pacific Pte Ltd
33 Pekin Street #02-01
Far East Square
Singapore 048763

British Library Cataloguing in Publication data

A catalogue record for this book is available
from the British Library

ISBN 978-1-4129-0276-2
ISBN 978-1-4129-0277-9 (pbk)

Library of Congress Control Number 2006935792

Typeset by C&M Digitals (P) Ltd., Chennai, India
Printed in Great Britain by The Cromwell Press Ltd, Trowbridge, Wiltshire
Printed on paper from sustainable resources

To my long enduring family for all your love and support, and my clients who have tried to educate me

Contents

Preface to the First Edition

Cognitive therapy began in America some thirty years ago. Since that time, it has seen enormous developments in the client groups treated and in its therapeutic approach. Two areas that have seen important changes to the early formulations are a renewed focus on the therapeutic relationship (e.g. Beck et al., 1990; Safran and Segal, 1990) and an increased focus on interpersonal cognitive processes (e.g. Bowlby, 1980; Liotti, 1988; Safran and Segal, 1990). Both these concerns are a main focus in this book. In 1988 Trower et al. published *Cognitive-behavioural Counselling in Action* (London: Sage). They outlined the basic techniques and issues of the cognitive approach. The present volume, for the 'Counselling in Practice' series, is designed to build on their introduction. It explores interpersonal counselling with a particular client group – depressed people.

The aims of this book are to focus on the interpersonal themes in counselling depressed clients, including those of the therapeutic relationship. The book is divided into two sections of four chapters each. Chapter 1 addresses issues of the nature of depression and the therapeutic relationship. Here I try to capture something of the nature of the depressive experience and focus on important counsellor skills. Chapter 2 explores the central issues of interpersonal approaches, the basic domains of relationships and how these are affected in depression. Chapter 3 outlines the basic premises of the cognitive approach and why cognitive counsellors are particularly concerned with the construction of internal meaning, ways of attributing causes to things, and basic attitudes and beliefs. Chapter 4 explores the many ways of conceptualising therapeutic interventions and challenging dysfunctional thoughts and attitudes.

The second section aims to build on these concepts, and lead the reader through a step-by-step approach to the process of counselling the depressed person. Counselling scenarios are given to illuminate specific points and highlight types of intervention. Most of these scenarios are not derived directly from taped interviews (although some are) but from notes made at the end of sessions. They are not meant to represent exact scenes but rather to indicate and highlight issues. All client names have been changed, and minor alterations introduced in the history, to avoid identification. Chapter 5 outlines the issues that arise during the early parts of the therapy, and how to engage and agree shared understandings and goals of counselling. Chapter 6 explores the kinds of issues that arise in the middle of counselling, as the counsellor and client engage in deeper explorations and seek opportunities for change. Chapter 7 looks at some special problems that arise in depressed clients. Special attention is given to shame, guilt, envy and idealising which often figure prominently in depressive experience. Chapter 8 explores termination issues and offers some personal reflections.

Preface to the Second Edition

In the time since I wrote the first edition of *Counselling for Depression* things have changed, including gaining more experience in working with depressed people, who are the greatest teachers. Also our own research efforts on submission, escape and defeat behaviour have been illuminating in a number of ways (e.g. Allan and Gilbert, 1997; Gilbert and Allan, 1998). For example, we have found that many (but by no means all) depressed people feel unable to escape from the things that cause them pain. These may either be their relationships, dashed hopes and aspirations, relationships or physical illness. Depressed people can suffer a constant bombardment of negative thoughts, feelings or conflicts, from which escape seems impossible. So they often feel defeated and overwhelmed by their negatives. Therapy can help reduce that bombardment and help the person develop more internally supportive relationships, more helpful coping behaviours, and elicit more support in the external world.

The outline of the book is similar to the first edition but some chapters have been extensively rewritten and updated and there is an extra chapter devoted to interventions. Chapter 1 discusses the nature of depression and the importance of various aspects of the therapeutic relationship. Chapter 2 has been rewritten to accommodate new understandings and findings in research on depression. The typical backgrounds, themes of depressive thinking and various coping behaviours that often can be ineffective for depressed people are covered. Chapter 3 outlines some of the basic premises of the cognitive approach to depressive disorders and notes how depressed people tend to 'dwell' on various negative thoughts, feelings and negative scenarios of the future. Chapter 4 explores the different processes for cognitive behavioural interventions for challenging the various negative thoughts and behaviours. Chapter 5 offers insight into challenging negative cognitions in specific ways and in particular internal shaming cognitions. I also cover in more detail the importance of developing inner warmth.

Part 2 begins with Chapter 6, which outlines some of the ways to begin the counselling process for the depressed person. Chapters 7 and 8 then focus on special issues that are likely to arise in counselling depressed people. Because this book is focused on interpersonal themes, these two chapters give examples of working with specific problems. Chapter 9 gives an overview of the types of intervention discussed, explores termination issues and basic therapeutic relational issues that can arise in counselling. In particular we finish by exploring some of the beliefs and thoughts of counsellors when they try to help depressed people.

This edition also contains new appendices to help guide you in identifying negative thoughts, questions to challenge them, and how to work with thought forms.

As for the first edition, this book is not designed for people with no training or experience in counselling. We anticipate that people using these techniques will have undergone proper training in counselling and that the approaches outlined

SAD, and some are linked to bipolar disorder. SAD has some atypical symptoms, including a seasonal onset (usually autumn and winter) with relief in the spring and summer. Depressed mood is associated with increased appetite, especially for carbohydrates, weight gain and *increased* sleep. This is an important distinction since exposure to bright light has been shown to be a promising, effective and quick treatment for this condition (Dalgleish, Rosen and Marks, 1996; Kasper and Rosenthal, 1989).

Evolutionary and functional approaches: Medical approaches to classification remain wedded to symptom studies. However, evolutionary approaches start by trying to understand the functions of symptoms and underlying defensive mechanisms that have been activated (Nesse and Williams, 1995). Gilbert (1984, 1992) suggested that some depressions are linked to attachment disruption and may activate the protest-despair defensive strategy (Bowlby, 1969, 1980), while competitive defeats activate a defensive strategy to cope with interpersonal conflicts and hostile others. Recently, Keller and Nesse, (2005, 2006) found that symptoms of crying, sadness and seeking social support were linked to interpersonal losses, while anhedonia, fatigue, guilt, pessimism and rumination were linked with failed efforts to achieve certain goals. Gilbert, Allan, Brough, Melley and Miles (2002) found that feelings of defeat were highly linked to anhedonia. We will explore these ideas, that different forms of depression are linked to different person – environment interactions in Chapters 5 and 6. A complicating fact here is that there are only a few basic emotion systems, and so it is the way that they are patterned in different states of mind that is at issue, a theme we will explore in Chapter 2.

The assessment of depression

There are many ways of assessing depression and, as we have seen, depression can be subdivided into various types (see Nezu, Nezu, McClure and Zwick, 2002 for a comprehensive overview). In addition to assessment of symptoms, assessment will often focus on the following key areas.

Psychological

1   What does the client think and feel about him/herself? Especially important is attributional style (a tendency to self-blame), shame, and social comparison (feelings of being less able, or less competent than others or different in some way).
2   What does the client think and feel about the future?
3   In what ways are certain styles of behaviour, such as avoidance and ruminations, contributing to the depression?
4   What are the client's current life circumstances? Do they feel defeated in their life goals?
5   How long has the client felt depressed?
6   Is the depression a change from his/her normal mood state or an accentuation of more chronic low mood?
7   Is there loss of enjoyment of previously enjoyed activities (e.g. sex, meeting friends, going out)?

8 Does the client see their depression in psychological and/or relationship terms, or is there a belief that they are physically ill? Strong beliefs in physical illness can make some counselling difficult.

9 How trapped does the client feel and what thoughts do they have in that regard (e.g. assess risk of self-harm)?

10 How does the client view their resources to cope? What outside sources of help are there, and how might these be utilised in the counselling?

Social

1 Are there any major life events or upsets that might have triggered the depression, accentuating or maintaining it?

2 What are the client's perceptions of social relationships? Have there been major losses? Is the home environment aggressive or neglectful? Are there conflicts with family members – parents, in-laws, spouses/partners or children? Does the client have feelings of hostility to others (that maybe they feel unable to express or work through), entrapment, and/or feelings of being let down?

3 What are the sources of social support, friends and family relationships? Can the client use these if available or have they gradually withdrawn from social contact?

4 Does an unstimulating or socially isolating social environment play a role (e.g. young mothers struggling to cope with young children and lacking adult company and sharing interests)?

5 Are there major practical problems that may need other sources of help (e.g. social work for accommodation problems or advice for financial problems or job seeking)? Practical problems can sometimes be overlooked.

6 Are their problems in the work domain (e.g. being out of work or bullying at work)?

Biological

1 Is there sleep disturbance (early morning waking, waking after being asleep for a short period and/or difficulties getting to sleep)?

2 Are there major changes in appetite and weight?

3 How serious is fatigue and loss of energy?

4 Psychomotor changes, especially agitation and retardation, should be noted. If a client is very slowed up and finds it difficult to concentrate, this can hamper counselling. Severe retardation and lowered concentration may be a poor prognostic indicator for some counselling.

5 Would a trial of anti-depressant drugs help to break up a depressive pattern? Most studies suggest that anti-depressants do not interfere with counselling and are indicated if the depression is severe. The National Institute for Clinical Excellence (NICE, 2004) does not recommend anti-depressants for mild depression.

There are a host of physical disorders, including thyroid dysfunction and diabetes onset, that can involve fatigue and mild depression. Hence, all cases should be medically screened for such, especially if fatigue is a major symptom. Sleep disturbance is now known to be a major problem in depression, linked to both fatigue and suicidality (Cukrowicz et al., 2006).

Measures

The most commonly used, and well-researched, self-report scale for depression is the Beck Depression Inventory (BDI; Beck, Rush, Shaw, and Emery, 1979). This scale not only allows the therapist to gain an overall impression of the *patterns* of symptoms, but also can be used to monitor recovery. Some therapists spend time discussing responses on the BDI with clients (Beck et al., 1979). The therapist may then ask which of the symptoms causes most distress, with the aim of coming back to them at the end of the session and targeting the symptoms with some specific interventions. However, be aware that this scale is copyright. Alternatives include the Depression, Anxiety and Stress Scale (e.g. Lovibond and Lovibond, 1995). Other measures use clinical rating scales and interviews of various forms. Good general overviews of measuring instruments for depression can be found in Berndt (1990), Ferguson and Tyrer (1989), Katz, Shaw, Vallis and Kaiser (1995), Nezu, Nezu, McClure, and Zwick (2002), and Peck (2004).

As noted, therapists are also interested in the other affects (or emotions) of depression. In some cases it can be anxiety. Various anxiety conditions often become worse when a client is depressed. In some of these cases helping the anxiety lifts the depression. For other cases treating the anxiety helps the depression. Other affects may include strong hostility or passive, unexpressed anger (this is often noted from the non-verbal behaviour of the client), envy, guilt and shame. There are some suggestions in the literature that men tend to be more aggressive/irritable at least in the early stages of their depression.

Risk

For any depression it is important to assess risk arising from the depression. Risk can take many forms. It may relate to the fact that people are avoiding work and are at risk of losing their jobs, or are having difficulties in their relationships which puts them at risk of losing a relationship or being neglectful or aggressive (e.g. to children). In some cases individuals may be very self-neglectful and not attend to basic self-care. A key risk is of course from self-harm. Self-harm can relate to forms of self-hurting and mutilation (where there is no intention to die), used as a form of emotion regulation (Babiker and Arnold, 1997). However, self-harm can also be very directed at desires to die (as an escape from depression (Baumeister, 1990)) and individuals who are impulsive can kill themselves as an impulsive act. There are a series of risk factors that should be kept in mind when assessing depression and its associated difficulties (Hawton, 1987; MacLeod, 2004). The factors that may increase the risk of a suicide attempt are:

- personality disorder, especially with poor impulse control
- use of alcohol to escape problems
- being young, male and unemployed
- a history of previous self-harm
- living alone and social isolation
- major life events of losses and exits
- illnesses that involve reduced capacities and/or chronic pain
- family disputes and high expressed emotion
- anniversaries of losses

- sudden separations (e.g. from a keyworker)
- a suicide in the family.

These are common risk factors that should be borne in mind when assessing risk. Leahy and Holland (2000, pp. 30–4) offer a useful checklist for assessing risk. In addition, of course, there are a number of psychological risk factors which, in the context of the above risk factors, increase overall risk. Fazaa and Page (2003) found that high self-criticism elevated suicide risk, and Apter, Horesh, Gothelf and Lepkifker (2001) found that being unwilling to engage in self-disclosure distinguished suicide attempters from non-attempters and was significantly linked to the seriousness of the attempt. Sleep quality and nightmares have also been linked to suicidality (Cukrowicz et al., 2006). Although many people, even when not depressed, can have thoughts of suicide, if a client has started to work out how they could do it and make plans this elevates risk. Risk is elevated again if the person has the means to carry out their plans. Depressive cognitions that are associated with a chronic sense of hopelessness, poor coping skills and chronic sense of entrapment, with strong desires to get away, are psychological risk factors.

Unresolved traumas from the past, high levels of shame and low self-esteem can increase risk. Recovering from a severe depressive illness can also be a time when suicide risk increases. The general thought here is 'I can't go through that again'. This is particularly true for bipolar depressions, who have a high risk of suicide as they slip into depression. This is more than hopelessness because there is a 'fear and dread' of the future.

When working with people who are suicidal it is important to gain support and advice from other professionals and work out a clear treatment plan which can vary from admission, through to specific problem solving and support. The treatment plan may also involve an agreement that if a depressed person feels they cannot resist their suicidal feelings they should call their general practitioner, a crisis service or maybe the counsellor. In a counselling session, patients can find it helpful to work through problems with a counsellor in a step-by-step fashion, breaking problems down and developing a plan to work with them. Smaller, more manageable, steps are usually better. Counsellors can also help people look at 'reasons for living' which can easily go unnoticed when in a depressed state. It is important to de-shame the feelings of wanting to kill oneself but at the same time buying time and enabling the person to see that they haven't always been depressed and the depression can be resolved.

The Beck Depression Inventory (Beck et al., 1979) taps suicide risk and indicates a potential danger requiring further exploration. A combination of a desire to harm self and hopelessness are warning signs. For further explorations of assessing and working with suicidal clients, see Grollman (1988), Hawton (1987), Hawton and Catalan (1987), MacLeod, (2004), and Williams (1997).

How common is depression?

Much depends on the definition of depression and the precision of the diagnosis, but the short answer is it is *very* common; worldwide many millions of people are suffering depression at any one time. The World Health Organisation suggests that depression will soon become second only to cardiovascular disorders as the most common health burden in the world today. Indeed, for women aged 15–45 years, it is far and away already the most common health burden. In general, some estimates suggest that as many as one person in four or five will have an episode of depression warranting treatment at some point in their lives, although this may be a conservative figure depending on social class and other social demographic variables (Bebbington, 2004; Bebbington, Katz, McGuffin, Tennant, and Hurry, 1989).

Taking into account definition and diagnostic concerns, Bebbington (2004, p. 14) suggests that: 'My best guess is that the annual prevalence rates of ICD depressive episode may be around 4% and that of DSM – IV depressive disorder around 5%.' It should be noted, however, that women suffer depression twice to three times that of men. Care should be exercised in noting how men and women present when distressed, because males may have more denial and present with more anger (Cochran and Rabinowitz, 2000). Thus one should be aware of gender differences (Hankin and Abramson, 2001; McGuire and Troisi, 1998b). Also rates vary greatly with social group, with poor and high unemployment areas having considerably higher rates of a range of health problems including depression (see Melzer, Fryers and Jenkins, 2004). Ostler et al. (2001) found depression differs between GP practices and that around 48.3% of this variation could be accounted for by poverty and socio-economic status. Although detection and treatment are slowly improving, at least in western countries, many depressed people go undetected in their communities and even those who are detected may not receive adequate treatment (Bebbington, 2004).

Not only is there a vast epidemic of misery, which affects individuals and their families, the resulting economic costs are estimated in many millions of pounds (NICE, 2004). Sadly, there is no sign that, with our increasing wealth, depression rates are reducing. If anything, competitive and materialistic societies tend to have increasing rates of depression (Arrindell, Steptoe and Wardle, 2003; Kasser, 2002), with serious concerns that depression may be on the increase, especially for younger cohorts (Fombonne, 1999; Klerman, 1988). There are many possible contributing reasons for this, including demographic changes, lifestyle changes, dietary changes, increased use of drugs with depressive side-effects, and social stresses of various forms (Gilbert, 1992, 2004; James, 1997). A counsellor who makes depression a special source of study will have no shortage of cases.

The course of depression

Posternak and Miller (2001) explored the course of depression in 201 patients on waiting lists: 20% had improved within the first two months and by six months 50% had improved. This remission rate is related to a variety of factors such as life events and depression severity. This remission rate should be kept in mind when looking at data from research trials. As many as 20% of cases may have a chronic course, that is, the person can remain depressed at varying levels of severity for two years or more (Scott, 1988). Some clients suffer acute episodes that are superimposed on milder chronic conditions (McCullough, 2000). Andrews (1998) has linked chronic depression in women to a history of sexual abuse.

Relapse and reoccurrence

About 50% (in some studies it is higher) of clients with diagnosed depression will relapse or have a subsequent episode. Age of onset can predict relapse vulnerability with those having onset before the age of 20 the more vulnerable group (Giles, Jarrett, Biggs, Guzick and Rush, 1989). With second and third episodes, risk of relapse climbs to 70% and 90% respectively (NICE, 2004).

The sources for relapse are many and include life events such as losing one's job, a stressful job that one feels trapped in but goes back to after recovery, ongoing financial strain, poverty, poor social supports, lack of a confidante, and criticism from a spouse (Belsher and Costello, 1988; Hooley and Teasdale, 1989); underlying psychological vulnerabilities such as low self-esteem and self-critical styles (Murphy, Nierenberg, Monson et al., 2002); and unresolved issues of early abuse (Andrews, 1998; Hammen, Henry and Daley, 2000). Hankin and Abramson (2001) note that some depression-related events can be independent of self-actions (e.g. collapse of the stock market and financial or job loss) but others are linked to them. For example, some personality dispositions reduce the probability of developing close supportive relationships and increase the probability of relationship break-up and conflicts – which are linked to depression. Linked to both personality disposition and vulnerability to depression is cognitive style (reflecting certain attitudes and attributions). Iacoviello, Alloy, Abramson, Whitehouse and Hogan (2006) found that negative cognitive style, after controlling for baseline depression, affected the number of episodes (relapse), the severity of the episode and chronicity (see also Alloy et al., 2006). Monroe and Harkness (2005) suggest that once a person has become depressed their physiological systems are sensitised to more severe shifts in mood state in the face of stressful life events (a kindling theory). Both the cognitive-focused, and the physiologically-focused approaches see differences between first and subsequent episodes, with subsequent episodes being easier to trigger via a *spreading activation* of negative thinking and stress states – that is (and this is a concept we will return to) we need to think of various patterns of activity in multiple systems that produce depressed *brain states*.

Given the high relapse risks, there is now work exploring how to reduce relapse. Hollon, DeRubeis and Seligman (1992) suggest that depressed patients treated with cognitive therapy may be at less than half the risk of relapse than are patients treated with pharmacotherapy alone. Mindfulness cognitive therapy (Segal, Williams and Teasdale, 2002) was specifically designed for working with the second and third relapse-vulnerable group. Certain types of behavioural therapy may also reduce the risk of relapse (Klein et al., 2004). Studies have also sought to explore medication dose and maintenance in relapse prevention (NICE, 2004).

Treatment resistance

NICE (2004) notes that some patients are treatment resistant. This is defined as not having responded to adequate trials of two or more anti-depressants at an adequate dose for an adequate time. But there is also resistance to psychological therapies. In regard to the latter, resistance may relate to the degree of how embedded and trapped people are in unsupportive or critical environments or the length of time it takes for some patients to develop a trusting therapeutic relationship, and feel sufficiently low-shame to begin to engage in the process of change. Some clinical studies 'advertise' in local media for depressed people for their trial. It is very unclear how these people differ from NHS depressed people who may be too shame prone or not motivated to answer 'advertisements'. I have treated a number of chronic and treatment-resistant depressions with a history of abusive experiences, where the first few months can be spent in helping the person form the relationship and begin to engage. Although professionals are under increasing pressure to fit therapies into a relatively short number of specific sessions (which were designed for clinical trials), these may be far too short for some people. Moreover, even though short-term (16–20 session) focused therapies can be effective for some patients, still 40% and over show little response or only a partial response. Further study of this group of patients is needed (McCullough, 2000). There are, for example, debates over which components of a therapy (e.g. the focus on thoughts or behaviours) are the most effective and relapse preventive (Dimidjian, Hollon, Dobson et al., 2006).

Treating depression

There have been many different treatments suggested for depression, including drugs and ECT, and a plethora of psychosocial interventions. NICE does not recommend anti-depressants for mild depression, although rightly or wrongly general practitioners may continue to use them if they see them as helpful for chronic stress and/or sleep difficulties. These debates are ongoing in the medical profession as I write this. In regard to psychological therapies, there are many forms, including psychodynamic, marital and family therapy, social skills training, affect therapy, interpersonal therapy, cognitive therapy, behaviour therapy and various hybrids and combinations. (For an overview of various therapies, see Beckham and Leber, 1995; Power, 2004.) This book will focus primarily on working with individuals. For a discussion of family and marital counselling, see Beach and Jones (2002); Clarkin, Haas and Glick (1988); Gotlib and Colby (1987); Prince and Jacobson (1995).

Poor prognostic indicators for basic counselling include: severe depression such that the client struggles to engage, serious difficulties for the client in forming a therapeutic contract; difficulty in articulating thoughts and feelings; high defensiveness; an entrenched belief that they are suffering from a physical illness, serious personality disorder and clear evidence of cyclical depression. These kinds of difficulties may require alternative interventions or at least other interventions to run in tandem with the psychological approach. Psychological therapies for these people require specialist interventions.

At the risk of repetition, therapists should always be aware that all depressed states have biological effects, and some are related to hormonal/biological changes (e.g. thyroid, diabetes, chronic fatigue, the menopause, head injury, etc.). There is concern that some depressions have become over 'psychologicalised', missing important physical causes (Goudsmit and Gadd, 1991). In the social domain, poverty, poor social conditions, lack of social support and negative life events also increase the risk of depression, while positive life events are associated with recovery (Brown, 1989). Consequently, the approach here endorses the

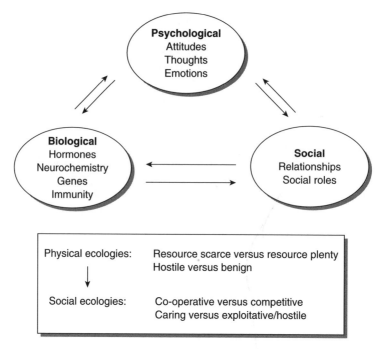

Figure 1.1   Biopsychosocial and ecological interactions

From Gilbert 2004: 103, reproduced with permission from J. Wiley and Sons

biopsychosocial model of depression (Gilbert, 1984, 1995a; Vasile, Samson, Bemporad et al., 1987). This model is concerned with different levels of functioning rather than simple models of causality. We now turn to this.

Biopsychosocial approaches to depression

Twenty years ago. L. Eisenberg (1986) noted that there was much in psychology and psychiatry that was either 'brainless' or 'mindless' science. This was not to perpetuate some 'dualism'. Rather the opposite. It was a call for a better science of mind and psychopathology that recognised a systems approach. This is to get away from reductionism – that depression can be reduced to a change in brain chemistry, the emergence of core beliefs or avoidance behaviour – and rather to see it as involving interacting, complex patterns of dynamic systems. Depression involves a number of complex and disabling symptoms, as noted above. It is vitally important to recognise that when people are depressed they will have disturbances at many levels of their being. Figure 1.1 outlines a simple general biopsychosocial approach.

This model suggests that there are a range of biological factors that can impact on our moods and thoughts, on the one hand, and social relationships on the other. There is good evidence that at the physiological level certain brain chemicals called 'neurotransmitters' are disturbed. Serotonin, noradrenalin and dopamine are especially implemented in depression. These affect our ability to feel positive emotions (joy, happiness and pleasure) and take an interest in things (e.g. food and sex). They also affect negative feelings and emotions like anxiety, anger and shame.

It is also clear that depression is associated with increased activity in 'stress systems' – as if stress systems are in over-drive. For example, many depressed people have elevated cortisol – a stress hormone. Good reviews of these studies have been given by Numeroff (1998) and more technical accounts for those who want to know more can be found in Thase and Howland (1995), Thase, Jindal and Howland (2002) and Cleare (2004). The point is that the physiological changes that accompany depression will obviously affect (and are part of) moods, behaviours and abilities such as memory and concentration.

In the psychological domain people not only feel bad, but they tend to see themselves, their future and the world, negatively (Beck et al., 1979). Increasing attention has also been given to the behaviours associated with depression, such as avoidance and rumination (Dimidjian et al., 2006). As we shall see in this book, thoughts, behaviours and memories are often specific targets for therapy work. These processes clearly impact on physiological activity and social relationships.

In the social domain, depressed people may have various life difficulties and social relationship problems (Brown and Harris, 1978; Brown, Harris and Hepworth, 1995). Different types of person – environment interactions may link to different symptom profiles (Keller and Nesse, 2006). Social relationships and desired social roles can play a major role in vulnerability, onset and recovery (Champion and Power, 1995). Marital conflicts are highly associated with depression both as cause and consequence of depression (Beach and Jones, 2002). Generally, supportive and loving relationships are conducive to well-being and recovery, while critical, neglectful and hostile ones, and social isolation, are not.

The importance of emergence

At each level of our being there is self-regulation. Thus each cell of our body can self-regulate, each physiological system – the cardiac and immune systems – can self-regulate. They do this of course at various levels of complexity and in ways that interact with other systems. Clearly, systems at 'lower levels' influence and pattern systems of organisation at higher levels (e.g. genes influence/build physiological systems that constitute the living bodies of animals – whether they are fish, rabbits or humans). They build the basic infrastructures for the brain that will enable people to have sensory systems, basic motivations and emotions, and be able to think in certain ways. However, higher levels of organisation can also influence lower levels of organisation. For example, if we live in a war-torn world this creates intense stress. This stress affects our physiological systems and our feelings and motivations. We now know that stress can even affect gene expression – how genes get turned on and off. The origins of that war may be from centuries earlier, as in the case of religious wars. So a conflict that began centuries ago can affect gene expression in us today!

You can see that if I ask a depressed person from a war-torn country why they are depressed, there is a whole variety of possible answers: from the history of their culture, to their own personal experiences, to how their minds and bodies react to certain events; to how their genes have built them so that they react in certain ways. To argue that one level of explanation is 'better' than another is to completely mis-understand emergence. We are all psychobiological patterns of organisation moving through time, experiencing our 'being in the world'. My job as a psychotherapist is to try to engage with a person's psychobiological pattern and explore together if there are ways that the 'pattern that gives rise to the experience of suffering' can be altered. If they experience my connection with them as sharing and caring, this may help; if we can alter behavioural patterns, this may help; if we can change the meanings, beliefs and interpretations, this may help; if we can help them with life events (e.g. get a job or resolve relationship conflicts), this can help.

Although we can isolate and study these domains, as outlined in Figure 1.1, separately, *states of mind* and *brain states* (Gilbert, 1984) are emergent phenomena from complex interactions. For some people genes are important factors in vul-nerability to depression – and different types of depression have different genetic loadings. But genes do not operate in a vacuum. We now know that gene – environment interactions are complex and give rise to different phenotypes from which vulnerabilities emerge (Caspi and Moffitt, 2006). So physiological vulnera-bility to depression can arise from many sources. For example, early physiologi-cal maturation in the womb can affect temperament, and the way in which we engage with others, from the first days of life (Harper, 2005). Our social relation-ships can affect how genes are expressed. The physiological effects of interactions (e.g. if they are calming or stressful) influence which genes can get turned on and off (Harper, 2005). Our social relationships can also have a major impact on how our physiological systems mature. For example, memory systems, and emotional regulation systems in the frontal cortex, can be affected by early abusive experi-ences (Gerhardt, 2004; Schore, 2001). Hence, there is a very clear interaction between our experiences of the self-in-the-world and physiological maturation. Our social relationships also shape our attitudes about the world we live in, our expectations about ourselves, and our sense of self-identity (Chapter 6). These attitudes, beliefs and styles of interpreting events affect our physiological systems and our social behaviour.

Families, and the interactions between parents and their children, will be severely affected by whether the family is living in a peaceful, supportive envi-ronment or a war-torn or crime-ridden poor area. *Physical* ecologies (e.g. whether we are able to move outside into attractive areas, or be trapped in dark rooms or a crime-ridden block of flats) influence our states of mind and our relationships. *Social* ecologies are related to the typical beliefs and patterns of social groups. These loosely can be regarded as the cultural domain, and the cultural domain has a major impact on people's vulnerability to mental health problems and their help-seeking behaviour.

The background or early vulnerability factors interact with current life stres-sors. For example, a negative life event may increase the production of stress hor-mones. Stress hormones can affect concentration, attention and planning, making problem-solving and 'balanced thinking' difficult. As this happens, our thoughts and emotions are affected and we focus more on negative events which further increases the production of stress hormones. A negative event may trigger underly-ing negative beliefs (e.g. of being worthless, useless or unlovable). As these beliefs seem 'more true', they increase stress and that releases more stress hormones and increases the symptoms of stress (e.g. poor sleep and poor concentration). This adds to feelings of exhaustion and of being 'inadequate'. Or a belief like 'I am boring – people will get fed-up with me' may lead to reduced social behaviour and further feelings of aloneness, all of which affect the stress hormones.

In their seminal work, Brown and Harris (1978) found that in a community sample of women, depression was often associated with *vulnerability factors* (such as low self-esteem and low intimacy with a spouse) and *provoking agents* (such as various losses and threats that have long-term consequences). They suggest that events that reduce a person's sense of value and self-esteem are particularly important in depression (Brown, 1989). Social loss events that are experienced in some way as humiliating or shaming, and from which the person feels unable to escape, have been found to be more depressogenic than loss events alone (Brown et al., 1995). The linkage between life events, social relationships, self-esteem and sense of control over life's difficulties is often central in depression (Becker, 1979).

Life events and coping styles will vary in regard to gender, age and ethnic group. For example, women are more likely to be the primary child-carer, including following the breakdown of a relationship (i.e. a single parent). They are more likely to get trapped in the home with young children and suffer role strain (Brown and Harris, 1978). In some social groups women are placed in highly subordinate positions. Older age groups will be more subject to losses such as grief and changes in physical health, and for some loss of their own home requiring movement to a nursing home. Some studies suggest that depression rates are very high in these contexts (Laidlaw, 2004).

So it is useful to think of depression as sequences of *interacting processes that create complex biopsychosocial patterns that can spiral a person downwards*. All interventions, be they drugs, psychological or social support, are aimed to break into the *spiral* of depression and web of interacting processes. The point about this is to suggest that there are constant, complex multi-layered interactions occurring within us, affecting our mental state.

Different kinds of therapy will tend to target different elements of those domains. For example, biological treatments tend to target the biological domain, whereas psychosocial interventions tend to focus on the psychological and social domains. Social interventions tend to target people's interactions with their environment (e.g. helping people to find work, to sort out finances or child support, to find more conducive living places). However, each treatment should ripple through to affect other domains. Drug treatments will affect people's style of thinking and behaviour, while psychological treatments have physiological impacts (Cozolino, 2002; Linden, 2006). Thus therapists need to be aware of working with 'a person' who has a historical context to their depression, lives within a certain social context, and be mindful and respectful of their history, culture and social context.

Conceptualisation

Considering depression in this multifaceted way can be helpful when it comes to an individual formulation (Chapters 8 and 9). The kind of biopsychosocial model outlined here was first proposed by Brown and Harris (1978), and in my view remains a very useful approach. We can begin the model by identifying three key domains that can give rise to depression. These are: *early vulnerability factors, current vulnerability factors* and *provoking events*. These are given in Figure 1.2.

Early vulnerability factors can involve a range of things that we have already noted, such as genetic vulnerabilities, and difficult early life experiences. These individuals can be vulnerable in a variety of ways, which can be accentuated in the context of current vulnerability, such as social isolation, bullying, conflicts in the marriage or at work. As Brown and Harris (1978) suggest, these kinds of vulnerabilities typically 'load the gun'. However, in the context of a major life event, which has major long-term consequences, such as losing one's job, it can provoke a spiral down into depression. The importance of this way of thinking about depression suggests that depression is not a black and white issue, present or absent, but can exist in degrees, and depressions can wax and wane. A provoking event may be what accentuates a mood difficulty such that a person crosses a threshold and reaches a diagnosis. The diagnosis might come when a certain number of symptoms are manifest, but the vulnerability factors may exist before that and may have been eroding the person's well-being for some time.

In this type of model vulnerabilities can interact such that some individuals who have had traumatic backgrounds find it difficult to form relationships or hold down jobs, and therefore their lives tend to be plagued by a variety of life events that are linked to their interpersonal coping styles (Hankin and Abramson, 2001). Shahar, Henrich, Blatt, Ryan and Little (2003) found that in a large group of adolescents (n = 860), self-criticism predicted less positive life events in girls. They suggested that self-critical or self-reassuring styles impact upon what one elicits from the social and non-social environment. Thus life events are not necessarily independent of the personal style of engaging in the world.

Looking at the next level we can see that as a depression gets going, there is an accentuation of the physiological systems of stress, the psychological and especially the experiential aspects, such that people begin to experience and evaluate themselves, the world and their future in a negative light. Typically, their coping behaviours are problematic; they may quickly run out of ideas of what to do to help themselves. Or they may ruminate about why things have gone badly for them rather than focusing on coping and trying to improve their situation. Commonly running out of coping options can lead to avoidance and then feelings of being trapped and becoming overly focused on feeling defeated and on escape/avoidance. Sometimes, escaping from an abusive environment is helpful, at other times escaping from relationships doesn't lead to better times, or may make things worse and people regret it once they are no longer depressed. This level is the level of *spreading activation* of depressed brain states.

This constellation of background variables, personality, coping style and availability of social and physical resources texture the shift down in mood, making it unique in some ways to each individual person, yet also part of our mammalian and human heritage with common identifiable features, such as anhedonia, sleep disturbance and fatigue.

Because depression is such a multifaceted experience, we can see that there are a range of interventions or relieving factors that may well be helpful for the person. The psychotherapist will obviously focus primarily in the psychological domain and so this book will be focused on that, rather than on other elements of

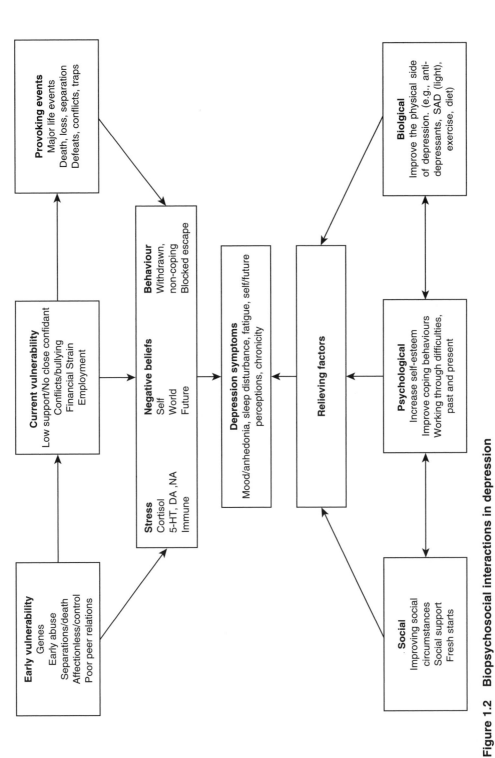

Figure 1.2   Biopsychosocial interactions in depression

From Gilbert 2004: 105, reproduced with permission of J. Wiley and Sons

treating depression. It is important, however, to think about how a client can use therapy to produce changes in their life (e.g. in their social relationships) which are conducive to the healing of depression. Paying attention to diet, or getting more exercise can be important too. Counsellors should be aware of these other evidence-based interventions. The key point, then, is this focus on the *whole person*, even while one is going to be working primarily in the psychological domain.

Using this book

NICE guidelines point out that people working with depression should be familiar with the *complexities* of the disorder and skilled in an evidence-based approach. In addition to being aware of NICE guidelines, two excellent handbooks of depression are by Gotlib and Hammen (2002) and Power (2004). I highly recommend these if you are going to make depression a serious study. In regard to keeping up with therapies, this is a little more tricky than it appears because approaches like Cognitive Behaviour Therapy (CBT), for which there is good evidence, are changing and evolving all the time in the light of new research on psychological processes and interventions. There are also increasing versions of CBT: some focus on more behavioural aspects, some on cognitive, and yet others on emotions or social relationships. In fact, it is becoming increasingly untenable to think about treatment in terms of 'schools' rather than process and problem-focused approaches (e.g. intervention for avoidance behaviour, rumination, self-criticism). The issue here is that many therapies are becoming multi-modal (Lazarus, 2000) and more research aware. Nonetheless, despite problems in the evidence base for a range of therapies, and major debates about the value of methods to investigate therapeutic interventions (e.g. randomised control trials and meta-analysis, use of people who answer advertisements), NICE (2004) draws attention to the evidence for *focused* therapies that have been designed for mood disorders, especially those of CBT and IPT (Interpersonal Psychotherapy).

This book is *not* designed as a manual-like approach to treating depression, as one might follow if doing a controlled trial. Rather, it is a process-orientated approach that tries to marry an understanding of processes that underpin depression with ideas of how to help depressed people. Clearly, your skills in basic psychotherapy and counselling and the modes of intervention, be these cognitive behavioural, interpersonal or emotion-focused, will have been learnt by you elsewhere. What this book will cover is some issues related to conceptualising mood disorders (because we have to develop our interventions by better understanding the processes underpinning depression), the formulation and focused interventions that can be helpful to people with a variety of unipolar depressions. An added aspect outlined here is a focus on compassion – and this book will build the argument for why this is important – the key elements of compassion, and how to being a compassion-focus to your therapy.

Conclusion

Depression is common. It can vary from mild to severe and from a relatively short-lived to a chronic condition. Depression sometimes ends in suicide. The depressed client can also have serious effects on their children and family. Therapists who have worked with depression for any length of time will be familiar with its misery, varied disguises and destructive potential. In working with depression one first tries to bridge into the depressed person's internal experience and need 'to feel understood'. This can offer the first sparks of new hope and break into demoralisation. The ability to understand a depression is related to the preparedness of the therapist to see the person as a historically and socially contextualised being and not just as a set of symptoms requiring intervention. It also requires us to see depression as linked to our common humanity that we, like other animals, have the potential for depression.

In December 2004 The National Institute for Clinical Excellence published their guidelines for the treatment of depression. Their document provides a wealth of information on: the symptoms of the various forms of depression, causes of depression, rates of depression, ethnic, social and gender variations, the social costs of depression and treatment mode recommendations. It also outlined the stepped care model for developing service for depressed people. Therapists working with depressed people should be familiar with this document, and its updates. In the light of treatment recommendations there are efforts to improve access to psychological therapies. Time will tell how this will eventually work out.

2 Multi-Level Systems in Depression

Over thirty years ago Akiskal and McKinney (1973, 1975) referred to depression as a final common pathway. In their classic papers they pointed out that not only does depression vary in form and experience but a variety of different, interacting factors, for different people (such as genes, early and current relationships, life events, thinking and coping styles, and drugs) can operate in different patterns for different people. As we saw in the last chapter, this type of approach underpins the biopsychosocial approach to depression. As counsellors and psychotherapists, however, it is the way we understand the 'inner experience' of depression (as more than just focused on 'symptoms') which enables us to develop our working alliance, build formulations and agreed interventions with depressed people. Many people who have studied depression suggest that what sits at the heart of the experience of depression is a sense of threat and loss, and that depression can be seen as a form of self-protection to threat and loss.

However, depression is related to different combinations of different types of threat. For example, Jane got depressed because she became too anxious to take up a university place and had money problems. Though depressed, she dearly *wanted* to go. She remained very *interested* in going to university but felt a failure in not being able to conquer her anxiety. Tim got depressed because he started to feel that what he was doing with his life was meaningless. He was a talented artist but his family had 'pushed' him on an academic route and then into law. Although earning good money, he hated it and felt trapped by the need to keep the money coming in. Things that he had been interested in and had enthused him lost their appeal – even sex. Karen was a live wire and found lots to be interested in but she got overburdened, burnout and felt like a failure. Sue got depressed when she had a baby. She spent years in and out of psychiatric clinics, and was told she had 'biological' depression and would need drugs for most of her life. It tuned out that her mother had been seriously sexually abused and was a poor carer for her. Her psychological therapy was a long and painful one. These cases suggest subtle but important differences in how our motivations, energy and emotional systems work that are still not well understood. Drug companies tend to assume all depressions are the same simply because they have similar symptoms, such as low mood, loss of pleasure (anhedonia) and other symptoms. Although there are commonalities of course, different depressions can be associated with different physiological profiles, different types of thinking and behaviours, different life histories and current stresses. Psychological therapies should individualise treatments for the unique difficulties of each person.

Nonetheless, as a rule of thumb it is when positive feelings are toned down and we lose the desire or confidence to engage with and go out into the world that depression sets in. So in the rest of this chapter we are going to look at evolved regulators of our emotion systems and why so many of us can lose positive affective tone and with it various abilities to feel pleasure from things. Understanding these basic affect processing systems and their functions can shed important light on the basic experiences of depression. In our days of quick fixes for complex problems it is useful to look at the complexities.

The multidimensional mind

Not only are there different types of depression, with different pathways into it, there are also many different theories and therapies for depression (Power, 2004). To the beginning therapist and counsellor this can be confusing. So how does one decide the best approach? One way is to look at research evidence for various types of therapy, which is the approach taken by various national guideline groups. Although obviously important, there are dangers to this if we lose track of the fact that each depression is unique to the individual.

What is emerging throughout the field of psychological therapies is that therapies need to be based and developed on our increasing *scientific* understanding of human psychology and how the mind works. Cognitive and behavioural therapies were among the first approaches that tried to be evidence-based and were linked to the scientific understanding of how we actually process information in different mood states. However, researchers from a range of different approaches (in evolution, neuroscience, social and developmental psychology and psychiatry) have been pooling their knowledge, leading to increasingly complex models of how the mind works and processes information, such as through parallel processing systems that can compete with each other. Therapists are developing therapies that target sub-components of our processing systems, such as types of memory, attention, behaviour and rumination (Brewin, 2006; Dalgleish, 2004; Harvey, Watkins, Mansell and Shafran, 2004; Lee, 2005). We now know, for example, that our threat systems, which evolved millions of years ago, can easily override more (recently evolved) competencies for rational thoughts; we can have powerful distressing intrusions at times when we wish to concentrate; we have memory lapses when we need to remember; our sensory and verbal memories may not cohere; we can experience negative emotional shifts when we want to be happy.

The emotional self and the reasoning self

What recent research has indicated is that we need to conceptualise the mind, not as a single processing system, but rather as a multi-mind (Ornstein, 1986). In fact over two thousand years ago the Buddha recognised that our minds are unruly, prone to flights of passions, emotions and desires. Without attention training (mindfulness) we can be 'taken over' by these passions and emotions. Shortly after, the Stoic philosophers in the Mediterranean drew attention to the conflict between emotion and reason and that human competencies for reason should be used to regulate the emotions. Even today these issues of training attention (mindfulness) versus training of reason (cognitive approaches) are still with us and seen as sources for helping us relieve depression and other emotional difficulties.

These early thinkers put their finger on a fundamental issue that is still a source of much research and debate. The modern version is that the brain has evolved slowly with various basic emotions and motivational systems that guide animals (and us) to important survival and social-reproductive goals. Our capacities for reasoning evolved in the service of these (see Chapter 5). This was less to regulate them but rather to more successfully pursue them. Birtchnell (2003) suggested that as a consequence of our evolution we have two types of self: one that is concerned with reasoning, meta-cognition, self-identity formation and generating meaning; and one that is focused on basic motives and emotional systems (e.g. to defend against threat, find love and friendship, and sexually reproduce). These two 'types of self' vary in terms of their conscious/non-conscious processing systems and priorities. They can work together or be in serious conflict. Indeed, because self-identity (which, as we see in Chapter 6, focuses on the sense of the self one 'is' and 'would like to be') may be in conflict with the more emotional and motivational priorities of the 'emotional brain' we can suffer in various ways. Moreover, reasoning and self-identity can be used to justify and give meaning to decisions made non-consciously by our emotional brains (Haidt, 2001).

So concepts and ideas pertaining to innate potentials for the construction of meaning have become increasingly prevalent. For example, Coon (1992, p. 1) opens his introductory text on psychology with this graphic depiction:

> You are a universe, a collection of worlds within worlds. Your brain is possibly the most complicated and amazing device in existence. Through its action you are capable of music, art, science, and war. Your potential for love and compassion coexists with your potential for aggression, hatred ... Murder?

What Coon, Birtchnell and many other researchers suggest is that we are not unified selves, despite our experience of being so. Rather, we are made up of many different possibilities for the creation of meaning. Our brain is a mixed multi-layered system with old and new evolved components (MacLean, 1985). As Ornstein (1986, p. 9) pointed out:

> The long progression in our self-understanding has been from a simple and usually 'intellectual' view to the view that the mind is a mixed structure, for it contains a complex set of 'talents', 'modules' and 'policies' within ... All these general components of the mind can act independently of each other, they may well have different priorities.
>
> The discovery of increased complexity and differentiation has occurred in many different areas of research..., in the study of brain functions and localisation; in the conceptions of the nature of intelligence; in personality testing; and in theories of the general characteristics of the mind.

So there has been increasing recognition that many human difficulties may be due to the *way* information is processed in multiple, parallel processing systems. These multiple systems have different priorities, can be riddled with conflict and compete (Dalgleish, 2004). For example, a distinction has been made between propositional and implicational cognitive systems (Power and Dalgleish, 1997; Teasdale and Barnard, 1993), which, at the risk of oversimplification, relates to rational versus emotional reasoning respectively. As Teasdale (1997, p. 146) notes, at the propositional level, thoughts such as 'I am worthless' are simply statements of belief – propositions about properties of self as an object. At the implicational level, however, such a statement represents a rich activation of affect and memories associated with experiences of being rejected or shamed.

There is also increasing evidence that some cognitions are products of very *rapid* information processing systems that are designed for speed rather than accuracy. Epstein (1994) and Epstein, Lipson, Holstein and Huh (1992) call these *experiential* systems. These experimental processing systems often have *built-in biases* because they are designed to motivate and emotionally direct animals, and this is because over time they have been conducive to survival and reproduction (McGuire and Troisi, 1998a). These fast-track processing systems (modules) use heuristics, take short-cuts to reach conclusions quickly, use crudely integrated information, are reliant on affect and how something feels, are preconscious and often rely on earlier experience and conditioned emotional responses (Power and Dalgleish, 1997). They are highly affected by self–other interpersonal schema that can affect self-judgements outside consciousness (Baldwin and Dandeneau, 2005). Hence, certain emotional and mood states utilise *fast-track* modes of functioning and are reliant on more primitive, earlier evolved appraisal-response systems (modules), possibly encoded in limbic and sub-limbic areas (Panksepp, 1998).

We can depict these various ideas with a simple model that considers the interactions between fast and automatic systems and slower, more consciously controllable ones, as given in Figure 2.1. This is no more that a rule-of-thumb outline. We do know, however, that genes, conditioning, diets and exercise, disorders such as thyroid and diabetes can all impact on physiological processes that affect mood states and styles of thinking. Equally, our moods affect, and are affected by, the way we reason about things. It is the interactions that are key and for a full understanding of depression these different aspects of our functioning are kept in mind. The ways we might try to change a process affecting brain states and automatic processes, such as with diets and exercise, treating diabetes, or exposure for conditioned emotional responses, are obviously different from those of a (say) cognitive approach that focuses on consciously available thoughts and behaviour styles. Thus we are always trying to work holistically.

Domains of our multi-minds

There are many ways we can explore the multiple levels of our minds and their implications for depression. My own approach is to start by thinking about how our minds were designed by evolution to do certain things and secure certain goals. This is to focus on evolved psychological systems, and consider how these systems interact. I suggest that there are at least four domains of functioning that can be delineated (Gilbert, 1984, 1989, 1993, 1995a, 2005a).

1. Basic threat and safeness processing.
2. Role-seeking and forming.
3. Symbolic and meta-cognitive abilities.
4. Identity-forming that depends on abilities for certain types of self-awareness, and which gives rise to a sense of self 'who is', 'who can', and 'who wants to be'.

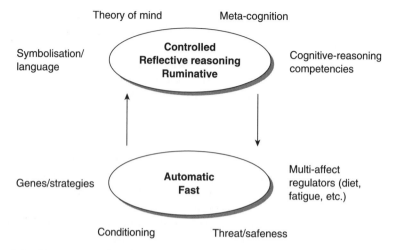

Figure 2.1   Processes affecting automatic and controlled interactions

The suggestion I will offer here is that depression represents certain patterns of organisation of these various domains. So this chapter will give a brief overview of these aspects of our minds. Later chapters will explore each domain in more detail. Armed with these insights we will have something of a road map to explore the complexities of depression and how to tailor interventions for individuals. We will be able to see how to weave cognitive, existential, behavioural, emotional and relational aspects together and have insight in why helping depressed people engage in self-compassionate attention thinking, behaviour and feeling can be helpful (Chapter 11). Indeed, as we will see as our story unfolds, compassion-focused work is now core to how I work with depressed people. The first point to make clear is that depression is a problem of threat and threat processing. *Threat is at the core of the depressive experience.* If you miss this fundamental fact about depression, and *only* look at depression as related to beliefs or cognitions, then therapy and the therapeutic relationship can become problematic.

Basic threat processing and its links to negative affect

We can begin the story of the evolution of brain design by noting that all animals, from simple bacteria to fish, to mammals to humans, must have some way of deciding what is safe and what is not. This is a basic design feature of all living things. No behaviour can be activated without some attention to this. No matter how clever we become, threat and safeness are always major concerns (Baumeister, Bratslavsky, Finkenauer and Vohs, 2001). Indeed, we often use our intelligence to cope with threats and make the world safer or more conducive to our needs and wants.

So all animals must have some way of deciding what is safe and what is not, and ways to do this are basic to the design of all living things. When threats arise animals need to be able to respond appropriately. If one confronts a predator, then the best thing may be to become anxious and to run. If someone tries to take something from you, thwarts you or treats you unfairly, then the best thing might be to feel anger and express aggression and threaten them. If confronted by a more powerful person, then the best thing might be to be anxious and submit. If one comes across a noxious substance, then feelings of disgust that make us pull back and keep away might be useful. If one has eaten a noxious substance, then the best thing might be to vomit.

Baumeister et al. (2001) have reviewed a substantial body of evidence to suggest that the brain is highly threat-sensitive because to miss a major threat (e.g. predator or aggressive other) can have a far more serious outcome than missing a possible positive one, such as a food source or mating chance. We have more processing systems devoted to threat events than positive ones; in ambiguous situations we look for threat cues first and pick up on threat cues quicker than positive ones. Negative/aversive memories can be more powerful than positive ones in many contexts. Thus the brain operates the rule of *better safe than sorry* (Gilbert, 1998b).

LeDoux (1998) has pointed out that we have evolved at least two brain pathways for detecting, decoding and responding to threats. One is through the fast-processing system in thalamic–amygdala systems that triggers a stress response. They are highly sensitive to sensory signals. For example, walking along a path one sees something move on the path and jumps back with the immediate thought it is a snake. The thought is automatic, generated from the subcortical brain. These subcortical brain systems are highly sensitive to learning/conditioning (Rosen and Schulkin, 1998). Another route for processing threat (especially important for humans) is a slower pathway via the cortex that may dampen and reappraise the threat ('I thought the shape on the ground was a snake but actually it is a piece of old rope') or may amplify a threat via beliefs, or even create new ones (e.g. beliefs in the supernatural).

Once a threat is detected there is a menu of options (Gilbert, 1989, 1993, 2001a; Marks, 1987) for coping and responding located in fast-acting systems. We have a range of emotions (e.g. anger, anxiety, disgust) and behaviours (e.g. fight, flight, expel, submit) to help us cope with *different types* of threat. These systems and potentials have been designed *to protect us*. They have evolved over many millions of years, are found in many other animals and are part of innate brain design. So another way of looking at this is to suggest that anxiety (escape, avoid), anger (attack) and disgust (expel, avoid) are part of the brain's protection strategies. A strategy is a basic detection–response pattern or innate rule that runs the programme of 'if A do B; if C do D etc.'. These strategies are threat-focused and safety-seeking. Emotions then offer forms of innate knowledge about certain signals (Greenberg, 2002; Loewenstein, Weber, Hsee and Welsch, 2001).

We can put a little more detail into this story by noting that some *protective* strategies automatically increase activity (to help us run away or fight) but other forms involve automatic (outside conscious control) deactivation or demobilisations (Beck, Emery and Greenberg, 1985; Gilbert, 1989, 1993, 2001a). Moreover, some protective strategies are designed for social use. For example, submissive behaviour is a bad idea when faced with a lion or having eaten bad food; running or vomiting is better. But submissive behaviour can be useful when confronted by a powerful other person who can understand and respond to our submissiveness by not attacking further. So threat-alerting and safety-seeking strategies can be active or passive, social or non-social and rapidly activated (Gilbert, 1989, 1993, 2001a).

Once we understand these basic protective strategies that are coded deep in our brains then the next question is how are they turned on and off? One answer is that there are natural cues that turn them on and off, but also learning, and (in humans) the way we 'think' and give meaning to events, can turn them on and off (Beck, 1987; Beck et al., 1985; Gilbert, 1984, 1992, 2004). We will consider learning and our thoughts in relation to threats later. Note that when (say) anxiety is turned on a whole pattern of responses in our brains and bodies is activated (e.g. heart rate speeds up, cortisol is released from the adrenal glands) and these responses are also associated with ways of thinking.

Many of these defensive components are operated through 'old' brain areas such as the amygdala. This picks up on sensory cues which stimulate the activation of memories and alerts the cortex to possible dangers and the need to 'check out'. If a threat arrives, the hypothalamic–pituitary–adrenal axis (HPA) and sympathetic and parasympathetic nervous systems are brought into action to prepare and facilitate the body to take defensive actions. There is now a lot of evidence that many of the components of the (fast automatic) defensive systems are highly activated in depression. This is noted in studies showing raised sensitivities in the amygdala, increased outputs from the HPA, such as cortisol, and changes in the sympathetic and parasympathetic nervous systems in depression (Numeroff, 1998). Low serotonin is also involved in increased sensitivities to threat and negative affect and some depressions are associated with low serotonin. Such findings in the *brain state* patterns in depression help to explain why a number of elevated threat emotions (increased feelings of anxiety, anger, irritability, disgust, sadness and dread) are common in the experience of depression (see Thase, Jindal and Howland, 2002, and Davidson, Pizzagalli and Nitschke, 2002 for comprehensive reviews). Siegle, Carter and Thase (2006) found that depressed people showed raised sensitivities in their amygdala, meaning that they are highly threat-focused. Interestingly, this sensitivity also predicted response to cognitive behavioural therapy. What this therapy may do is to work on forms of threat processing and help people to bring their sense of threat into balance. The take-home message is that *depression is a state of raised threat processing.*

A key point for the psychotherapist is that experiences of depression *emerge* out of these brain state patterns (Gilbert, 1984, 1992). Moreover, threat closes us down and narrows attention to focus on the threat and defensive actions. If you are running from the lion, you do not need to focus on how beautiful the trees are that you are running past. Brain states of threat, then, *will narrow our attention and thinking* as we shift to a 'better safe than sorry' style of processing (Gilbert, 1998b; Tobena, Marks and Dar, 1999). Brain-state concepts help us to understand some of the cognitive problems of depression in terms of poor concentration, black and white thinking (one cannot risk ambiguities), attention to threat and the negative, the faster recall of negative memories, and loss of abilities for certain types of problem solving.

Defence, protection and safety-seeking versus safeness

A key distinction to note, because it is a basic aspect for much of the approach outlined later, is the distinction between defence, protection and safety-seeking in contrast to safeness (Gilbert, 1989, 1993, 2005a). There are different levels of these basic processes. First, *safety-seeking* pertains to defensive behaviours such as fight, flight, avoidance, immobilisation, submission and returns to a 'safe base' that are triggered by specific stimuli or events. These are designed for *protection* or damage limitation in threatening contexts. They can be automatic and easily conditioned (Rosen and Schulkin, 1998).

When we anticipate a threat we can *make plans* to avoid it. Agoraphobia is a classic case of anticipating threats, including anticipating becoming overwhelmingly anxious and then not going out. However, many depressed people predict that they will not be able to cope with certain things and engage in avoidance behaviour. Planned safety behaviours may also be carrying tranquillizers in one's pocket (Salkovskis, 1996a, 1996b). These directly regulate activity in threat systems in that, if successfully enacted, a person may feel relatively safe. However, any block to the safety strategies can reactivate the threat system. In contrast, when desensitised to fear/threat, certain stimuli no longer trigger the same threat response because the person is processing *the threat itself* in a different way. Thus the network of safety strategies, such as remaining vigilant to the possible threat, and being ready with defensive safety behaviours, is deactivated. In this context one can feel relatively safe even in the presence of (what were) threatening stimuli. One may even come to enjoy them (e.g. an agoraphobic may come to enjoy going out, a depressed person may come to enjoy socialising again where before it had seemed too threatening). In childhood the transition from (natural) fear and safety behaviours to those of feeling safe with exploration and engaging depend crucially on parental soothing and social referencing (Schore, 1994, see also Chapter 5 in this volume). The therapeutic relationship and tasks may play a similar key role in how a client makes the journey from threat evaluations (e.g. of internal anger or acting assertively) and safety behaviours, to explorations, coping and coming to feel 'safe with' (Gilbert, 1989; Holmes, 2001).

We should note, however, that once a fear has been learnt it does not disappear. Rather, when someone learns that a feared situation is in fact safe, new pathways are formed (e.g. in the frontal cortex) that overlay or regulate 'fear' ones. Hence in some cases, if these new pathways are compromised for any reason, then old fears, behavioural habits and states of mind can return. Unfortunately, we cannot explore all the implications of the new findings here except to say that they offer a way of thinking about relapse sensitivities (Monroe and Harkness, 2005). Moreover, it may explain why, as people become depressed with a raised stress hormone such as cortisol, which affects the frontal cortex, they can have a return of earlier acquired fears.

The third level of threat is related to safety beliefs. Salkovskis (1996a, 1996b) points out that if someone thinks they are going to have a heart attack and sits down or backs off from a situation, then they may attribute the absence of the heart attack not to a misinterpretation of the sensations in their body, but to their safety behaviours. So they believe that sitting down or backing off is what saved them. They do not learn that the actual sensations in their body, though unpleasant, are not major threats. Therapy is therefore focused on helping people change these beliefs (see Thwaites and Freeston, 2005 for a discussion).

Safety beliefs (and assumptions) in depression are a little more complex because they are often focused on *social* threats and because they may have had some basis in fact in childhood. For example, a belief like 'only if I work hard and achieve a lot will people have any interest in me and not abandon me' or 'only if I am submissive and put others first will they like me' or 'only if I do not express anger will people not reject me' implicates a threat and how to deal with it. So if they find others do like them, they attribute this not to their likeability but to their safety behaviours, for example, of being submissive. And of course if they have occasions of expressing anger or not being submissive and run into conflicts with others, they attribute this not to normal conflicts in relationships but to their need to reinvigorate their safety behaviours – often feeling more resentful in the process.

The essence of the story is therefore that for many disorders, including depression, threat-focused protection and damage limitation efforts and various safety beliefs are common. As we will see in later chapters, these safety strategies can operate at *automatic* levels (e.g. the innate defences for coping with loss of control, separation and social defeats), at the *behavioural* level of avoidance, and at the more *social-cognitive* levels related to self-presentation and self-identity. The key point is that the depressed person cannot create a feeling of safeness and soothing. Unlike most anxiety disorders, in which sufferers can get relief if they are out of the threat context, depressed people cannot, and the sense of failing and dread live with them constantly. If the experience of (or lack of) safeness is important for depression, then we need to look at this in detail.

Safeness and the positive emotions

Depression also involves toned down positive emotions that affect both fast-automatic and slower systems of processing. Some positive emotions evolved to encourage us to seek out and consume things that are conducive to our survival, reproduction and prosperity (Panksepp, 1998). Fredrickson (1998) noted that positive emotions and moods have been less studied than negative ones and that there are some major differences between positive and negative emotions. Positive emotions tend to focus on enhancements, broaden attention, help us to recover from stress and negative life events and have far less specific actions (compared to negative affects) associated with them. Indeed, there is now evidence that positive emotions have numerous impacts on cognitive and social processes (Ashby, Isen and Turken, 1999; Fredrickson, Tugade, Waugh and Larkin, 2003). Fredrickson (1998) and Gilbert (1989) suggest that positive emotions build and consolidate relationships and increase approach behaviour via signalling interpersonal safeness. When we feel safe our brains are organised in different ways with different attention-focusing strategies, and more integrative ways of processing information (Gilbert, 1993).

If depression is related to a problem in positive affect, then we need to try to see how positive affect works and its links to feelings of safeness and contentment (Gilbert, 1989). When we do this there are some surprising and deeply illuminating new findings about positive affect systems that shed considerable light on depression. First is the finding that there are *two types* of positive affect system (Depue and Morrone-Strupinsky, 2005). One gives us a sense of drive and vitality to seek out rewards and positive things, but another positive affect system operates when we have consumed and no longer need to seek things (turns off seeking and drive) – we are content. Both systems have been 'borrowed' and used by evolution

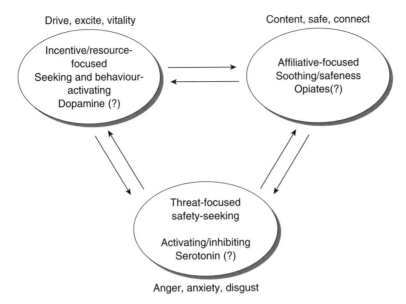

Figure 2.2   **Types of affect system**

From Gilbert 2005a: 26, reproduced with permission from Routledge

to regulate behaviour in regard to social relationships. Not only can relationships activate us – we seek them out and get a real buzz when starting a new love relationship or when we are chosen to be on the team – but the contentment systems have also evolved into a system that registers care, love and affection signals (Carter, 1998; Wang, 2005). When social signals of affiliation and love trigger this system, we feel soothed by the support, kindness and care of others. The care of others can be soothing and calming. These feelings are strongly linked to feelings of contentment, safeness and well-being, and regulate both drive-seeking and threat systems. Although the neuroscience is complex, and these systems are in constant states of co-regulation, a simplified model of these three affect systems is given in Figure 2.2.

So our questions are: How are these systems constituted? How do they interact? And how are they functioning in depression?

Activating systems

As noted, one type of positive affect system is focused on doing/achieving and anticipating rewards/successes. This system maybe dopaminergic and is arousing and activating (Depue and Morrone-Strupinsky, 2005; Panksepp, 1998). Humans, like other animals, are motivated to seek out certain types of resource, for example seeking out food and sex and the things that are associated with or lead to them. To seek these we must be motivated, energised and activated, searching our environments for them (Panksepp, 1998). When this kind of positive affect system is aroused we feel activated and are anticipating rewards and pleasures.

Drugs such as amphetamine affect this system and emotions are experienced as energising and activating. In everyday life when we seek out things we would like to do or have, do things that give us a sense of achievement, or when we look forward to things, this system is involved. Attention can also be narrowed by this system, such as when we become fixated on the goal or incentive we are pursuing. Now for some depressed people this system seems to be toned down and they may struggle to experience energy, vitality or motivation in doing things. When we help people do things that bring a sense of achievement we are hoping they get a burst of positive emotion or, in behavioural terms, will be able to increase their positively rewarding behaviours. Indeed, some behavioural theories are actually called behavioural *activation* (Martell, Addis, and Jacobson, 2001). However, while these are helpful, some clients also need help to develop another type of positive affect which is *not* about activating but about soothing.

Soothing systems

Neuroscience has revealed that we have a very different type of positive affect system that runs with the activating system and partly regulates it. This affect system is particularly linked to the enjoyment, appreciation and pleasure of consuming things and may underpin feelings of satisfaction and contentment. These feelings are linked to neurohormones such as oxytocin and opiates (Depue and Morrone-Strupinsky, 2005). Clearly, it is important that once we have achieved something, we can relax and *enjoy* it. To consume and enjoy something means we are not under threat and are not seeking. Thus, these systems must be toned down.

Evolution often makes use of systems that are already available, puts them to new uses and modifies them. It turns out that this opiate system, associated with contentment, has been adapted during the evolution of attachment behaviour and with a hormone called oxytocin. This system has become responsive to the way a mother bonds with, cares and soothes her child. Mother soothing/caring behaviour also activates these systems in the infant, calming the infant, and providing the experience of safeness. So this system is also especially linked to social soothing such that social signals of affiliation and care have the qualities of soothing, and it involves neurohormones such as oxytocin and opiates (Carter, 1998; Depue and Morrone-Strupinsky, 2005; Panksepp, 1998; Uväns-Morberg, 1998). Signals and stimuli such as stroking, holding, voice tone, facial expressions and social support are *natural* stimuli that activate this system (Uväns-Morberg, 1998; Wang, 2005). Drugs such as heroin can stimulate this system, and the positive feelings are less ones of activation and being energised and rather those of being calmed, soothed and a sense of well-being. They may come with feelings of connectedness to others, feeling safe and content.

Depue and Morrone-Strupinsky (2005) link these two different positive affect regulating systems to different types of social behaviour. They distinguish affiliation from agency and sociability. Agency and sociability are linked to control and achievement-seeking, social dominance and the (threat-focused) avoidance of rejection and isolation. So when people are seeking these social outcomes they need drive and energy. Blocks on the path to these goals can be experienced as threats. In contrast, affiliation and affiliative interactions have a more calming effect on participants, alter pain thresholds, the immune and digestive systems, and operate via an oxytocin-opiate system. There is increasing evidence that oxytocin is linked to social support and buffers stress; those with lower oxytocin having higher stress responsiveness (Heinrichs, Baumgartner, Kirschbaum and Ehlert, 2003). So evidence points to the possibility that this oxytocin-opiate system is particularly linked to soothing and calming and regulates the production of the stress hormone cortisol (which, as we have seen, is often raised in depression) (Carter, 1998; Depue and Morrone-Strupinsky, 2005; Field, 2000; Wang, 2005). It can therefore be regarded as part of a safeness contentment system (Gilbert, 1989, 1993, 2005a). Problems from a toning down of this affect system may be linked to feelings of actual and emotional aloneness, feeling disconnected and cut-off from others.

Some depressed people have a lot of difficulties in feeling content, safe and socially connected. They may see life as a constant battle to keep going, achieve, avoid errors or keep up. They can have a puritanical view that there is something wrong with sitting back and simply enjoying things, or doing things simply for the pleasure of doing them. Relaxing and having fun makes them anxious. Some people do not feel soothed by another's kindness or praise because this is associated with ideas that the other is out to use them in some way or they don't deserve it.

We can use these insights in therapy by sharing them with depressed people. I tend to talk to people about the three circles of affect and direct attention to how their drive and threat systems may be overactive and interactive (e.g. 'I drive myself to achieve so that I can avoid criticism and rejection but maybe I need to work on soothing and contentment'; see Chapter 11). People who come from neglectful or abusive backgrounds may have few experiences of feeling soothed by others and such feelings can be frightening to them (Gilbert and Procter, 2006).

Interactions

Now we do not need to be over-focused on the neurobiology of these systems, but rather have an appreciation that we may need to address *different types of positive affect* in depression. So, to re-cap, Figure 2.2 suggests that we have a *threat system* that is set to detect and respond to threats. This system will link to various safety/defensive-focused emotions such as anxiety, anger and disgust, ways of focusing attention, thinking, and behaviours. It can be easily activated because like many animals we often operate on a 'better safe than sorry' rule (Gilbert, 1998b). It can easily turn off positive emotions. For example, if while having an enjoyable lunch in the park an escaped tiger suddenly appears, it is not useful to go on enjoying lunch in case you become its lunch. What you need is a fast-acting system that turns off all concern and positive interest with lunch and that is energised to run.

All our systems in the brain are operating *with mutual influence on each other*. They operate as interacting systems. This is why it is better to think in terms of organising patterns rather than of single systems. The key point here is that being able to enjoy things and feel safe is not just about low activity in a threat system but depends on a certain type of positive affect system and signals (Gilbert, 2005a). Toning down positive emotions can occur naturally when we are confronted by certain evolutionary meaningful threats that we feel unable to cope with. We will look at what these are in the next chapter, but they include loss of control, social losses and defeats (Beck 1987; Gilbert, 1984, 2004). These events activate what I call *psychobiological response patterns* in our brains because we have evolved to be able to respond to such threats in protective ways (Gilbert, 1984,

2006a). So the key point is that different depressed people will have *different patterns* in the organisation of these basic affect systems; for example there will be individual differences related to genes and learning. However, in essence, the potential for lowered mood (toned down positive affect systems) with reduced motivation, feelings of emotional aloneness and difficulties in feeling soothed, with a focus on the negative, can be seen as a *psychobiological pattern of primitive protection strategies* in the context of certain stressors. The next questions are what triggers them, how do they become dysfunctional, and what will tone down negative affects and tone up positive ones? These are the concerns we will address throughout this book. For the moment though, let's look deeper into the experience of depression and see if evolution can offer clues as to why depressed people experience the world in the way they do. Let's shift levels and look at another function of our minds: co-creating social relationships.

Role-seeking and forming

In addition to being able to distinguish threats from safeness, all animals must be able to engage in a variety of social behaviours that are conducive to their safety and reproduction. To put this another way, they need to relate to others in certain ways. To do this they must have *special* processing systems that can send and understand signals that are sent from their own kind in order to co-create different types of relationship (roles) with them (Buss, 2003; Gilbert, 1989, 1992, 2005a, 2005b). So, for example, certain signals displayed by others will indicate a potential sexual partner; different signals may indicate that the other has aggressive intent. These signals need to be picked up quickly and appropriate responses engaged. Many animals, from fish to humans, clearly have abilities to understand social communication and do not require high-level cognitive systems. Being receptive and affected by social signals and communication from others is thus a design feature of our brains such that certain signals affect our physiological states (Cacioppo, Berston, Sheridan and McClintock, 2000). If it were not like this, the new infant would have to learn that her mother's touch and voice tone is a signal of safeness; we would have to learn what is sexually stimulating. Though learning is important, we have innate processing systems that give meaning to these signals and organise our brains into certain patterns (Buss, 2003; Gilbert, 1989).

Major social relationships

There are various key roles that we are motivated to co-create with others, because over evolutionary time being able to co-create these roles has been good for survival and reproduction (Buss, 2003; Gilbert, 1989, 2005b). These include the following:

- *Care eliciting*, which is crucial in the early phase of life. As we mature, our needs for different types of care change, and the signals that help us feel cared for change too. However, being able to feel cared for, able to be soothed by the caring behaviours of others, and knowing that there are others around who care about us and our well-being can be central to feelings of well-being (Mikulincer and Shaver, 2004).

- *Care-giving* involves motives to be caring and various competencies to be sensitive to the needs of others and respond to those needs appropriately (Fogel, Melson, and Mistry, 1986; Gilbert, 2005a).
- *Co-operation* involves motives to share with others, forming reciprocal alliances, feeling part of a group with a sense of belonging, being valued and accepted by others (Baumeister and Leary, 1995).
- *Competing-ranking* involves motives to win competitions/conflicts for resources and social positions and subdue competitors. Competitions need not be aggressive but require one to present self in such a way that others choose in one's favour. We *win* the affection of potential lovers, friends or employers, we get that research grant, we win in contexts where others are going after the same things. Competition in attraction (in contrast to subduing) contexts involves awareness of what others are offering (social comparison) and trying to out-perform them to impress an audience with which one wants to relate or be associated (Gilbert, 2005b), for example 'choose me because I am better than him/her'.
- *Sexualities* involve being motivated to form sex relationships and engaging with others for such unions.

The motive to co-create a role is called a biosocial goal. The strategic ways of thinking and the detailed plans to secure a biosocial goal – a particular role – are called a *social mentality* (Gilbert, 1989, 1992, 2005a, 2005b). The activation of a biosocial goal with its appropriate (social mentality) processing systems creates *patterns of activation* in the brain. So, for example, you see someone whom you care about in distress. A caring-giving mentality organises brain patterns to enable us to be sensitive to others' distress, and generate feelings (e.g. sympathy), thoughts and behaviours to be helpful. In contrast, you see someone you do not like and/or want to compete with or see them as an enemy. In that context the care-giving aspects are turned off or toned down and we focus on how we can get an advantage over others and even on how we could hurt them. If we were too affected by sadness and sensitivity at the distress of our enemies, then this might inhibit our aggressive actions and we could be harmed by others who wish to hurt us. Of course in the modern world this natural turning on and off of brain systems by social contexts and beliefs is exactly why we have the serious problems we do, because once people are seen as threats, compassion for them typically goes by the wayside. So we have to work hard to think these issues through and change our perspective. The key point to note (and it is a concept we will return to many times) is the way patterns of brain pathways are organised – with some elements turned on and some turned off or toned down according to the goal and social role.

Threat, safeness and social roles

How do threat and safeness relate to social roles? The answer here is that these roles are so basic to our survival and well-being that to pursue them and then fail is a major threat. This suggests that each social mentality is organised to create an inner representation of self and other, and then alert threat systems to certain types of event. This is outlined in Table 2.1.

First, we can note how each social mentality represents the self in one aspect of a role and the other in the complementary role – the 'self as' and the 'other as'. When we are in a care-seeking role, for example, we see ourselves as needing

Table 2.1   Link between biosocial goals (care-seeking, care-giving, co-operation, rank/status, sexual) and social mentalities

Social roles	Self as	Other as	Monitoring threat/safeness
Care-seeking	Needing, Seeking	Providing, Alleviating	Availability, Access
Care-giving	Providing, Alleviating	Needing, Seeking	Distress in other, Empathy
Co-operation	Sharing, Belonging	Sharing, Belonging	Similarity, Cheating
Rank/status	Power comparing	Power comparing	Relative power, Talents, Abilities
Sexual	Attracting, Attracted	Attracting, Attracted	Attractiveness

Innate motivational (seeking) systems with a range of emotional and cognitive processing systems that link to a 'sense of self' – A self as …

Adapted from Gilbert, 1992: 140, reproduced with permission from Psychology Press

something from others and we target searches and generate behaviours to elicit what we need from them. We are attentive to the signals that others are *accessible and available* to us. When others behave towards us with caring, we can feel cared for and soothed by them (safe). However, when the monitoring system picks up that others are not accessible or available (or even hostile), then this activates the threat systems and sets in train a sequence of protective and safety strategies (see Chapter 5). Similarly for co-operation. When we are seeking acceptance from others and a sense of belonging and being valued, if others send signals that they do accept and value us, then we feel safe. However, if they send signals that we are not accepted and we are at risk of exclusion, rejection or even persecution, then the threat systems come online. It is the same for competition and social ranking. If our efforts result in wins, we can assert and defend ourselves (and avoid being put in relatively powerless and unwanted subordinate positions) – we feel pleased. In the attraction areas, if others choose in our favour (our lovers choose us, our friends have an interest in socialising and sharing with us, we pass our exams or get those research grants), we feel on track and safe. In contrast, if we cannot defend ourselves and are subject to others' put-downs and bullying, this is a major threat. Or if, in the attraction competitions, others always choose for someone else (your desired lovers, friends, employers reject you), then even though they may not be hostile you end up in a rather subordinate position with limited power to influence the minds of others in your favour. As such your control and abilities to co-create various important relationships become increasingly limited – that is a major threat. Now in depression threat processing is key and most depressed people are in states of threat because these efforts at creating desired social roles are compromised.

These roles also form the basis for *human social needs*. In other words, from the day we are born *we need others to prosper*. The human brain is highly attuned to what others are doing and feeling in relation to ourselves and their actions literally help shape and organise psychobiological patterns in our minds. Major threats to our basic social needs for care and support activate our threat and protection systems such that we feel angry, anxious or sad – and at times suffer a lowering of positive affect.

Also note that social mentalities can blend together. For example, one person may use others as only sexual objects. Another may care for and cherish his/her sexual partners. Yet another may be frightened of sexual behaviour or their inner sexual fantasises. As we see in Chapter 5, issues of assertion, feeling inferior to others, feeling unable to elicit from others desired social resources, feeling isolated and cut off, feeling under pressure to prove oneself to others, and feeling that we do not have what it takes to win the everyday competitions of social life, are rife in depression.

Looking at it in this way raises important questions about depression. If someone feels a failure or worthless, then how much is this related to thinking styles and how much to having developed a highly competitive way of trying to win their social place? These are not, of course, mutually exclusive aspects. However, it is the fear and threat associated with failure in key social roles that are central and the therapist needs to be sensitive to those fears. We seek to understand the long-term hopes of some people's efforts to find the way to win a valued social place, and despair of feeling unable to. A 'thwarted emotional needs' approach to depression also matters because we need to ask questions of our competitive cultures. Not only are modern cultures fragmenting of social communities that offered a sense of social place and belonging, but we can only ponder if there are cultural processes that are pushing people to judge themselves in more and more harsh, competitive terms – of winners and losers, haves and have nots, valued and shamed. No only does this affect the construction of individual identities, it also affects the kind of societies we build – those that focus on caring and supporting each other (in line with our evolved human needs) versus those of gaining competitive advantage (Arrindell et al., 2003).

Symbolic and meta-cognitive abilities

Most mammals will seek and respond to care from others, grow up to form sexual relationships/roles and friendships, and be wary of more dominant animals on the basis of signals and cues in their environment. Their emotional lives are tied in directly to how they behave and how others behave towards them. They do not, as far as we know, worry that if they are too fat their sexual partners will go off them, or that they are at risk of a heart attack. Human evolution, however, has resulted in an amazing ability to *internally represent the world in conscious images, fantasies, language and symbols* (Malik, 2000; Singer, 2006; Wells, 2000). We can get sexually turned on by seeing something sexual (say) on the television, but also in the privacy of our own homes via our own (purely internally generated) fantasies and images. Note that our own thoughts, images and fantasies can run the psychobiological programme that sends a flush of sexual excitement through us. So our thoughts and images, that we create in our own minds, can activate basic evolved physiological systems and patterns in our brains. This is what makes our thoughts/images and ruminations so powerful – and is the essence of the cognitive model – that our thoughts, images and fantasies are not physiologically neutral but have powerful physiological effects (Beck et al., 1985).

Note also that we are symbol-using animals. We can become happy by passing our examinations and gaining a degree, or feel loved when our partner remembers our birthday. Now a university degree has no natural meaning itself. Rather it is a symbol that conveys meaning about one's ability, and will link to more evolutionary important roles about one's acceptability to others, sense of belonging (I can now become a doctor or lawyer or counsellor) or competitive advantage. To fail the degree carries *meaning* about one's relative social standing and chances of fulfilling future goals. These meanings are derived in part by how we value things (and these are linked to cultural processes) and the implications we derive for their success or failure.

In addition, we have meta-cognitive abilities that allow us to reflect on and give meaning to things; for example, my increasing heart rate means I need to get fit or that I am going to have a heart attack. We will feel different things according to the interpretation. 'Because Sally did not phone me last night this means she was tired, or (more negatively) wants to reject me for someone else.' Hence we can run simulations and make predictions in our minds and then react as if they are true. This kind of thinking can activate basic threat systems (Wells, 2000). Some of these interpretations will be influenced by emotional memories (Brewin, 2006). As we see in later chapters, these ways of thinking and interpreting things and events are a focus for cognitive working.

The use of language also plays a key role in the creation of meaning. For example, we communicate our meanings, feelings and intents through both verbal and non-verbal channels (Lock, 1999). We can be told we are lovable, useless or bad. This conveys meaning of how we 'exist in the mind of the other' and then we might feel happy, anxious or depressed at 'hearing' such messages. Our interpretation of that verbal message is key of course – we might see a critical comment as coming from a subordinate, or might think they are just in an angry mood and dismiss it. Although the way we think in language and communicate in (symbolic) language offers complex layers to information-processing and meaning-making, these abilities do not change our basic human needs, especially for social connectedness.

In so far as language is the main way of communicating what we feel in therapy, then it is important to note that language is not always an easy medium in which to express feelings. There are two aspects to this. First, depressed people may struggle to put their feelings into words. The translation of an affective state into words is not easy and some people may be very unpractised in talking about feelings, or even frightened to do so. Moreover, feelings are often mixed, entangled and confused and confusing. Imagine you work hard on a piece of work and your boss criticises it. You may have a flush of anger with a thought, ('that's unfair'), a flush of anxiety (I am not doing well) and a tearful feeling of wanting reassurance. You will then have to 'choose' which feeling to go with or how to keep a certain self-presentation. Crying, for example, might threaten your self-identity and you might be angry or feel ashamed with yourself if you do. You will have to be pretty emotionally competent to be able to recognise, organise, label, verbalise and control all these mixed feelings. When patients shut down and say 'I don't know what I feel', what they are often referring to is feeling overwhelmed by too many mixed, conflicting and confusing feelings. Sometimes, under this pressure, they dissociate and close down. Therapists who think that there are simple emotions with simple chains of thought can get lost here. It is preferable to explain the complexity of mixed emotions and normalise the experience in a non-shaming way – that part of the therapy is to help them to explore the tangle of feelings (Greenberg and Watson, 2006). At other times a 'don't know what I feel' response is about shame and fear of revealing.

The second problem with language and verbal reports of feeling is that people will generate thoughts to fit the feeling. We use our thinking to justify and make sense of what we feel – even when this may not be a true reason for what we feel. In other words, we can have feelings, derived from our fast, automatic processing systems that then the controlled-reasoning systems try to make sense of. We now know that some of our thoughts are explanations for what we feel. Moreover, the true reasons for some feelings may not be in consciousness; we can create meanings that fit with our feelings but these may not be accurate reasons for our feelings (Haidt, 2001). There is increasing evidence that the ways in which we interpret signals can be outside conscious awareness. There is now a quickly expanding research literature on non-conscious processing (Baldwin, 2005; Hassin, Uleman and Bargh, 2005). One example of this is when people are very self-critical they may believe that they either deserve it or it is a true reflection of themselves. In fact, self-criticism is often based on fear and can be a form of safety behaviour (Gilbert and Irons, 2005; see Chapters 9 and 12 in this volume). Taking that view directs attention to the fear of giving up self-criticism rather than focusing on the evidence for or against it – an idea we will explore in detail later.

Identity-forming

Developing a self-identity depends on abilities for certain types of self-awareness, and gives rise to a sense of a self 'who is', 'who can' and 'who wants to be'. Our 'sense of self' emerges from the choreographies of the other aspects of our minds and is shaped via social relationships in which the self is embedded. Wanting to become a famous tap dancer is probably unlikely in the deep Sahara; wanting to be a feared terrorist is unlikely in a Buddhist monastery. Self-identities emerge to fit the social environment and in particular to cope with the socially constructed roles, threats and opportunities in that environment. We thus develop our self-identities, the person we will aspire to be, through our relationships. When we get depressed we may often feel that those self-identities and aspirations, which are the vehicles to form helpful relationships, have been compromised or threatened and we can feel 'just not up to it'.

Animals do not have a sense of self-identity that they consciously wish to groom and develop as far as we know, but humans clearly do. Our identities will focus on evolutionary important roles, such as 'I want (and will work hard) to be accepted by others, to be valued rather than rejected, to gain respect among my peers, to be helpful to others'. If our identity and sense of who we are seems to convey to us that we are not able to co-create these roles – 'I am unlovable, bad or inadequate' – then this is a threat and activates the various threat and protection systems. So our self-identities are very much linked to the social reputations we wish to create (Buss, 2003). Our self-identities can also help (or hinder) us in coping with urges and threats. For example, I might be hungry but choose to override this because I want to lose weight, to get fit, improve my attractiveness or sense of control – these are important for my self-identity. Or I might feel very anxious about something but do it anyway because I believe this will help me overcome my anxiety or I do not want to be (or be seen to be) a coward.

Complexities

These four domains of functioning are intimately linked in very complex ways, bridging between automatic and controlled processing systems. For example, our interpretations are both reflections of our physical states *and* help create and regulate certain states of mind and psychobiological patterns. If I am in a state of anger, then I will have angry thoughts, but angry thoughts can also accentuate my anger (I can be angry at getting angry, depressed at getting depressed) and may activate memories of other times I have been angry or depressed (Brewin, 2006). Moreover, if I am angry at work (another NHS change!), I might stay in this state when I get home and feel irritable with things at home (the non-eliciting situation). My anger at home may lead to me feeling even more angry with myself because I do not want to be angry at home and feel I am not controlling myself. So my own anger is a threat to my self-identity (the person I want to be) and my desired social role at home (being loving and relaxed).

However, the key idea to convey here is that while we have a complex psychology for symbolic thinking, meta-cognition and forming self-identities, what lies at the heart of us are basic threat-protection strategies, and human (social) needs, with abilities to form certain types of relationship with our fellow humans. It is when these are thwarted that our threat systems come online and can take us into some dark areas of feeling. Our brains have evolved slowly and our threat systems and ways of dealing with threats evolved long before our more complex cognitive talents, such as our abilities for language and symbol use self-reflection and self-awareness. It is when these different systems of functioning (our primitive threat systems that simply do what they are designed to do, and our higher cognitive systems) interact that we become vulnerable to a whole array of psychopathologies, and depression can be dysfunctional.

This kind of thinking can help therapists because it enables them to work at different levels of functioning. One can work with thoughts, meta-cognitions and ruminations and behaviours that are stimulating basic threat systems and maintaining unpleasant feelings. One can explain to patients how our thoughts stimulate our emotions. However, we can also think about underlying human needs and how these have become thwarted. Moreover, focusing on social threats and losses enables the therapist to understand the possible root causes of some depressions.

The importance of strategies and 'if-then' rules

Before we explore how and why the loss of control and the social aspects of our lives can be such powerful regulators of emotional states we need to consider the concept of *strategies*. In part this is because these are extremely important when it comes to working therapeutically. Strategies can be understood as 'if-then' rules. First, we should note that evolutionists use the concept of strategies in a slightly different way from psychotherapists. For example, evolutionists might focus on the fact that the breeding strategies of turtles, who lay hundreds of eggs and then leave their offspring to survive as best they can when they hatch, is different from those of the mammals, who have few offspring but care and protect them. These are species-specific strategies. However, strategies can also operate on psychobiological response patterns that are context-sensitive, such as the timing of sexual maturation in helpful (later onset) versus hostile environments (earlier onset) (Belsky, Steinberg and Draper, 1991). Strictly speaking, these relate to *phenotypes* of strategies. An example of a phenotypic variation in a breeding strategy may show itself in the changes in emotion and behaviour that a woman experiences over her menstrual cycle. Some women can experience major shifts of mood and behavioural engagement or withdrawal over the course of the cycle related to how likely she is to conceive.

Strategies can also refer to 'if-then' behavioural rules. In many animals these are signal sensitive and automatically run systems in the brain that generate psychobiological response patterns. As these patterns take shape they create *brain states* where thoughts, memories, feelings and action tendencies are patterned and organised in certain ways (Gilbert, 1984). If a predator appears, *then* activate anxious arousal, focus attention, turn off positive affect/interest and run or freeze. *If* another sends a sexual signal, *then* explore, feel randy and engage in courting. *If a* dominant threatens you, *then* submit and withdraw, and stay vigilant of their whereabouts. Animals can run these strategies (that pattern brain states) because of innate knowledge and innate systems for certain types of learning that enable context-appropriate behaviour. In humans, learning and conditioning affect our 'if-then' strategies and these can operate both in and outside conscious awareness.

Learning

Conditioning is a powerful way we learn and enact 'if-then' rules. For example, if a light has been paired with a shock, an animal learns that the light means there is a shock coming. So the rule becomes: '*If* the light appears, *then* become anxious and try to escape'. To put this another way, the light can activate a similar psychobiological 'whole organism' response pattern as the innate stressor, a painful shock. Conditioning (the association between event and stimuli) is a very direct form of learning and requires no cognitive mediation (Gray, 1987; Timberlake, 1994). In contrast, cognitive therapists focus on learning that results in core beliefs, schema or modes (Beck, 1996). Modes are interconnected sets of ideas, emotions and physiological patterns that are fused together. For example, if a child has been rejected and told they are unlovable, this may become a schema or mode that organises much of how that child engages with the world and others, but it will also involve the emotional experience of *feeling* unlovable that is rooted in emotional memory systems. Modes are similar to concepts of brain states (Gilbert, 1984).

Whichever way we learn, be this via direct conditioning, through social referencing or by people telling us things and treating us in certain emotional ways, what learning does is to pattern our brains so that we are ready to respond in certain ways the next time an event happens. Part of what this learning does is to set up the contingencies for when to activate threat and protection strategies and when to feel safe. In terms of depression, there are two protection strategies (for social loss and defeat) that interact but are especially linked to threats and losses in the social domain. Understanding these strategies and how they can influence behaviour, thinking, feeling and physical states can help us understand more about the experiences that emerge in depression. This is the theme for our next chapters.

The implication of this is that our (protection) strategies, and the way our minds and bodies are organised to cope with certain threats, are complex combinations of innate and learnt 'if-then' rules, and these rules are acquired in different ways. 'If-then' rules can be guided by memory that affects the whole organisation of a person. Imagine a child who is physically abused. When her father 'attacks', she activates an automatic defence of rapid arousal, fear, submission and freezing. Later in life her boss comes to work in a bad mood and criticises her. She suddenly experiences a rapid onset of intense fear and freezing. Her boss apologises but that night she has a panic attack. The next day she is full of anxiety and cannot go to work. Her husband does not understand it, nor does she, because she does not connect the incident with the 'return' (reactivation) of the psychobiological states of early childhood. She becomes tearful, sensing that she wants some kind of loving protection from others (just as she did in childhood) but cannot articulate these feelings. She ruminates about why she feels so bad and that maybe she is losing her mind. She is diagnosed with depression. I see her and explain that this is not her fault but that her protection strategies have been reactivated. I explain that in many ways there is nothing wrong 'with her' but that unfortunately in times of threat like this sometimes threat systems are highly (re)activated, and positive affect systems shut down as protection. These protection strategies are being run by her *automatic* systems. So we can explore ways to work with these painful 'states of mind'. In therapy we work with her painful childhood memories as sources of her psychobiological patterns and brain states and help her develop compassion for herself, and work with her thoughts, feelings and behaviours as they emerge in the here and now.

Our experience and memories of others and 'if-then' rules

Evidence now suggests that some automatic 'if-then' rules can be non-conscious, are linked to complex associations between self and others, and affect psychobiological states. For example, *if* others express disapproval, *then* respond with withdraw or shame/submissive defences. These have been explored in a research programme by Baldwin and colleagues (for reviews see Baldwin 1992; Baldwin and Dandeneau, 2005). In one early study, students were asked to generate research ideas and were then subliminally primed by being flashed a picture of either an approving or disapproving face of the departmental professor. This was presented so fast they knew something had been flashed up on the screen but it was too fast to know what it was. Those primed with the disapproving face rated their ideas more unfavourably than those primed with the approving face. *Self-evaluation* was non-consciously linked to approval/disapproval of another (see Baldwin and Dandeneau, 2005 for reviews of this work).

The way we deal with setbacks (and how threatened we feel) is significantly related to the accessibility of internal representations of others. Baldwin and Holmes (1987) found that people who were primed with thinking about a critical relationship, and who then failed at a laboratory task, showed depressive and shame-like responses of blaming themselves for their failure and drawing broad negative conclusions about their personality (i.e. a typical shame response). Conversely, individuals who were instead primed with a warm, supportive relationship were much less upset by the failure and attributed the negative outcome to situational factors rather than personal shortcomings.

Kumashiro and Sedikides (2005) gave students a difficult intellectual test. They were also asked to visualise either a close negative, close neutral, or close positive relationship. Those who visualised the close positive relationship had the highest interest in obtaining feedback on the test even when that feedback reflected unfavourably on them. Baldwin and his colleagues (see Baldwin and Dandeneau, 2005) have demonstrated that a key variable determining *self*-evaluative styles in certain contexts is the accessibility of other-to-self (others as critical or reassuring) and self-to-self (self-critical or self-reassuring) schemas and role relationships that are activated. Attachment theorists have also shown that the way people respond to various interpersonal threats (i.e. the degree of anxiety and anger they may feel) is related to internal working models of attachment security that affect automatic processing (see Mikulincer and Shaver, 2004, 2005 for reviews). These studies suggest that the degree to which people are able to rapidly-automatically access warm and supportive (in contrast to condemning and critical) other-to-self and self-to-self scripts and memories has a central bearing on emotional and social responses to negative, self-defining events, and abilities to cope with failures and setbacks. To put this another way, Baldwin suggests that most of our self-schema are actually emergent from representations of self-other interactions – that is they are interpersonal. In the model presented here positive memories of others are coded in, and give ways to activate, our soothing systems (see pp. 30–31).

The take home story from this work seems to be that people's automatic threat responses (which can follow 'if-then' rules), *including their self-evaluations and feelings* to setbacks and failures, are significantly influenced by the accessibility they have to memories, schema and potential psychobiological patterns elicited by how helpful or rejecting other people are or have been. Importantly, these interpersonal schema and emotional memories also become key co-ordinators of the three basic affect systems we noted above. Having schema and memories of others that are helpful means we have access to soothing systems when stressed, whereas having memories of others that are hurtful means that when stressed we may access these memories, and consequently feel more threatened and have less access to reparative positive affect (e.g. soothing) systems (see Brewin, 2006).

Putting levels together

This chapter has suggested that there are multiple specialist systems that have evolved over millions of years (Buss, 2003; Gilbert, 1989). We started with basic threat and safeness systems, then noted how mammals are motivated to create social roles and how success or failure in these roles activates threats and safeness. For humans, there are multiple ways we can create and internally represent 'self in roles' and form 'interpersonal schema'. These can affect us at conscious and non-conscious levels. However, humans, like other animals, are slow-growing, maturing beings who are undergoing radical changes in the patterning of brain systems as they grow and mature, and are laying down sensitivities to this or that

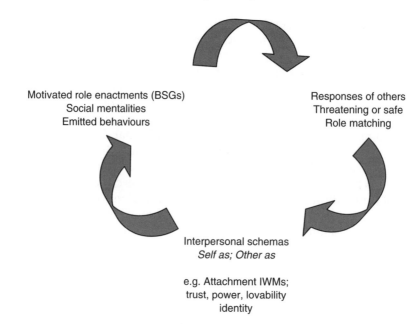

Motivated role enactments (BSGs)
Social mentalities
Emitted behaviours

Responses of others
Threatening or safe
Role matching

Interpersonal schemas
Self as; Other as

e.g. Attachment IWMs;
trust, power, lovability
identity

Figure 2.3   Motivated social goals, social mentalities and the emergence of interpersonal schema

BSG = Biosocial goals
IWM = Internal working models

threat, and forming mental representation of them as they do so. This is depicted in Figure 2.3.

To understand the emergence of different states of mind we can start with what humans are motivated to do. The brain is as complex as it is because it has evolved ways to navigate animals in their environment so that they can distinguish threat from safeness, respond with appropriate responses to different kinds of threat, seek appropriate foods, build appropriate living quarters (burrows or nests) and co-create a number of social roles conducive to survival and reproduction. These motivating systems give rise to emitted behaviours that impact on others. In the social domain, the distress of the infant brings soothing from the parent; our early exploration and assertive efforts meet with rewards or punishment from parents/ teachers; our efforts to form friendships meet with acceptance or rejection. The responses of others are key to whether we code experiences and our efforts to co-create roles as successful or likely to fail or be punished. From here emerge the interpersonal schema that code for 'self as' and 'other as'. These internal representations then affect how we will continue to seek out and shape our efforts in pursuit of various biosocial goals (in evolutionary terms they shape our phenotypes). Threat-filled, early life experiences can shift people to various forms of safety strategies to try to head off threats in the future. When these safety strategies do not work, are blocked or create more problems, people can become very threatened and suffer depressions.

Crucial in psychotherapy, therefore, are the stories of how people have experienced their efforts to be loved and accepted, how they choose and win the competitions of everyday life, and what they have made of their successes, losses or defeats. We learn what people have hoped for, or what they have given up on and closed down and may now be fearful of reclaiming. So when people change in therapy they do not just change their thoughts, behaviours or emotions also change but the patterns of motives that underpin their self-identities. They may shift from avoidance to engagement; they may learn to assert themselves more or less; they may become able to tolerate the grief and pain of acknowledging early neglect or abuse; and they may become more concerned with compassion values rather than competing, more forgiving rather than vengeful, and gentle rather than harsh. If people can learn 'I do not need to be threatened by this any more', new possibilities open up. When we feel safer in the world then our minds are freed to organise and reorganise our basic social goals in new ways, – which are key to our well-being (Gilbert, 1993). Although not all therapies would articulate these processes in this way, most aim to help people feel safe rather than threatened, to engage with life rather than avoid it, to drop unhelpful safety behaviours and beliefs, and to reach out to others rather than to shut them out. It is not just treating a panic disorder or depression that is central to well-being, but rather what this liberates them to do in their lives.

Conclusion

This chapter has outlined some basic research findings that can help us to understand the basis of depression and also how to design interventions. We are slowly moving away from single-model theories and therapies to much richer ideas about 'how our minds work', the nature of depression, and interventions based on research. Having insight into these findings will help make sense of the approach that will be taken here – which is basically to tone down threat systems and tone up positive ones. By understanding the innate and learnt regulators of these affect systems, and our social role-creating systems and needs, we will be in better positions to try to design our interventions for individuals, based on compassionate understanding of human struggles and our common humanity.

The turn of the nineteenth century was a time of Darwinian ideas, which linked us to other animals. In literature there was a fear of the 'beast within' – the mind of Frankenstein, and Jekyll and Hyde. It was a time of increasing acknowledgement of our bloody and violent history and of atrocities committed. Early therapies addressed issues of savage passions and inner conflicts, and argued that culture and the rule of law were but thin veneers (Ellenberger, 1970). The world of science got us thinking that our minds are like a scientist at work, testing and confirming theories. In our love affair with computer analogies, we can reduce people and their difficulties to those of information processing systems and devices, with errors in processing. However, the evolved realties of our minds require us to address our underlying human motives and needs and to see that when these are thwarted various pathologies are more likely. The most basic of all needs is for people to relate to each other to create feelings of connectedness and safeness. As we will note in Chapters 5 and 6, our human evolution probably owes much to that. The savage passions noted by some psychodynamic theories and the negative schema of cognitive theories are often the result of trying to cope with threat and a lack of safeness. When this happens, our minds get caught up in protection strategies, some of which take us into the darkness of depression – the subject of our next two chapters.

3 The Brain, Threats and Depression

Given the symptoms of depression and its physiological profiles it is easy to see depression as a disorder, dysfunction, deficit or illness. However, is it possible that we have evolved brains that under certain circumstances *are designed* to tone down positive emotions, reduce motivation and give us feelings of depression? If we only think of depression as something gone wrong, then we may miss the fact that actually we all have the potential for some forms of depression because our brains have evolved to generate the psychobiological patterns of low mood in certain circumstances. So research has focused on the hunt to understand how our brains have evolved and what regulates emotions, feelings and moods. We now know that: (a) emotions and moods influence information processing, especially the assessment of threat and safeness, and (b) research has shown that certain types of threat are major regulators of mood and emotions. This book will return *again and again* to the notion that depression is about threat processing and the activation of protection strategies, because this will orientate us in our understanding of depression and how we approach psychotherapy and counselling. Also it will become clear why compassion is a key antidote to threat processing (see Chapter 11).

Emotions and moods affect information processing

Research on moods and emotions suggests that they provide important sources of information that *guide* behaviours, attention and subsequent thoughts (Izard, 2002). Indeed, there are now many studies where people have been subliminally primed with an emotion (e.g. by showing disgusting or frightening pictures but below the level of awareness) and then their cognitive styles are assessed. Our thinking is pulled by the aroused emotions (Haidt, 2001; Hassin, Uleman and Bargh, 2005). For example, once we become anxious, that mood and brain state affects how we engage with the environment over a certain time period. In other words, if one's immediate response to a threat is anger (and this may be a conditioned emotional response), then not only will the anger come with various action tendencies but it will also come with dispositions to attend and evaluate things in a certain way. Lerner and Keltner (2001) call this *appraisal tendency*. Within this paradigm researchers have suggested that moods are also ways in which the brain orientates itself in regard to evaluating degrees of threat and safeness. Hence good moods are indications to the animal that the environment is relatively safe and previous actions have been successful. However, bad moods indicate that the environment may not be safe and certain future actions may not be successful. Moods can then be both a consequence of a particular interaction between animal and environment and can also influence the way the environment is processed and actions are enacted. In a recent study, Chartrand, van Baaren and Bargh (2006) found that individuals could be primed with negative or positive words and the subsequent mood change affects information processing.

Threats as major regulators of mood

If moods are linked to the internal generation of brain state patterns, which enable animals to recognise and cope with either safe or threatening environments, then we would expect depression to be a basic threat-coping strategy. Threats should, in some contexts, trigger mood drops and threats should be central to the cognitive and behavioural focus. This is indeed the case. However, low mood evolved to cope with certain types of threat.

The threat of losing control

Frustration   The first typical response to losing control over something you want is frustration. Frustration is an aversive state closely linked to anger whose function is to increase effort. The brain picks up that there is a mismatch between what one is trying to achieve (or wants) but that there are blocks and hindrances in the way and this increases arousal and anger to try to make us force through. Think of all the many areas of our lives where feelings of frustration can erupt if things don't go our way – from driving on blocked-up roads, to our personal relationships. When I played competitive cricket it was when we had an important game and were losing that tempers could become frayed. Whatever you did you must not drop that vital catch! Whether it is a rat whose path to a food source is blocked or a highly symbolic action in humans that requires us to give meaning to things, like playing cricket, frustration operates on the emotional brain in much the same way. Many people find that small dips in mood states are triggered by frustration. As mood goes down, much then depends on what is activated in the person as to how far and for how long that mood goes down – this is referred to as a spreading activation.

Frustration 'tolerance' shows up early in children, although again there are individual differences in temperament related to the ease of frustration activation and tolerance. It is not the case, of course, that anger-frustration is the only response to not getting what you want or being confronted by threats you can't control. If you don't get the job you want, and worry about how you are going to pay the mortgage, then you are likely to feel anxiety. If you think you deserve the job and they choose a less able candidate than you, you may feel cheated, and vengeful feelings may enter one's mind. Depressed mood can also come from not getting things you think you want (e.g. the love affair, that well-paid job). Evidence suggests that if you think your frustration, and not being able to get what you want, is due to some personal inadequacy and has major implications for future goals, then you are more likely to get depressed, than if you think it is just bad luck and temporary, and with a bit more effort or luck you can win through.

To a brain that wants to get its own way frustration is perhaps one of the most destructive emotions if not carefully handled. There is much in Buddhist teaching that is really about the dangers of being overly committed to getting control over things (one *must* have what one desires) and these 'attachments' to desires are the source of frustration and disappointments that can bring misery to self and others; hence the value of forms of 'detachment.' Rational emotive therapists also place a lot of emphasis on frustration tolerance and the 'musts' in our thinking (Ellis, 1977a, 1977b; Gilbert, 1992). This was also a profound insight by the Buddha all those years ago and yet we live in a modern world where we are taught to want more not less, to work faster not slower, to compete more vigorously not less vigorously, to be self-focused not other-focused. We live in a world where a sense of deserving and entitlements can only add to our sense of frustration. Frustration activation and tolerance, then, are as much products of social contexts and personal learning as they are about mechanisms in our brains for coping with blockages. Nonetheless, frustration is one of the evolved solutions that comes with brain mechanisms for dealing with blocks to our goals and desires – and it is relatively non-specific.

Many depressions are related to *a build up of stressors and frustrations* which can exhaust stress systems. Sometimes there can be one major stressor that then just overloads systems. For example, Jon had been under stress at work trying to meet time pressures. He felt he was just about on top of things and then one day he 'lost' days of work as a result of a computer virus. His main feelings were intense anger and frustration. Two days later he woke up early feeling 'very unwell', shaking, anxious and depressed. I have also met people with chronic fatigue who note that if they become very angry and frustrated, within a day or two they can suffer a relapse. Psychological factors can be important, such as rumination and cognitive style. So are social factors such as social supports that can soothe us. Also important is the way intense frustration affects physiological systems to produce changes in brain states.

Stress   In recent years there has been growing interest in how one aspect of the stress/defence systems is working in depression. This system is called the hypothalamic-pituitary-adrenal system (HPA) that we noted in the last chapter. Sitting at the base of the brain are two small but very important areas called the hypothalamus and pituitary. When the brain detects and responds to threats and losses, the hypothalamus sends a signal to the pituitary (by release of a hormone called corticotropic releasing hormone (CRH)). The pituitary picks up the message from the hypothalamus and signals to the adrenal glands (which lie just above the kidneys). The message to the adrenals is sent by release of a hormone called adrenocorticotrophic hormone (ACTH) into the blood stream that tells the adrenal glands to increase the release of the stress hormone cortisol. So the hypothalamus signals to the pituitary and the pituitary signals to the adrenal glands and the basic message is 'we are under threat – mobilise for action.' When we experience stress this system is activated.

'Stress' is a word that is sometimes used to refer to external events, sometimes a subjective state (one is suffering from stress) and at other times a coping style (Hobfoll, 1989). A stressful event can include just about any type of event, from loss of a job, or valued relationship, a shortage of resources, or interpersonal conflict. Much depends on the value we place on things. 'Stress' is a generic term to imply that the animal or person is confronted with something that is exceeding their resources. The physiological effects of stress take us to an important fact about the organisation of our defence systems. As someone becomes stressed there are changes in their physiological state and as these state changes manifest, the threshold for the whole menu of defensive responses (thoughts, feelings, behaviours and accessible memories) alters. Consider, for example, that someone who is stressed and depressed over a lost love affair can also experience lower frustration tolerance, more social anxiety, and develop a fear of the dark or become hypochondriacal. How often have you found that if you feel down, then you can lose confidence in a lot of things, not just the things you feel down over. Last week playing with the kids was great fun, this week, with your job on the line, it's a pain and you shout at them. Thus we get what we might call *ripple effects* or knock-on effects because of the patterning effects in our brains.

We cannot, however, just rely on a stress hormone such as cortisol to tell us about stress. Cortisol can go up when you fall in love or when you exercise. In some depressions, especially those associated with early life abuse, there can be blunted cortisol responses to stress. Thus any physiological process must be understood in terms of how it is patterned with other processes (Wang, 2005).

Chronic stress   Stressors linked to depression can be from major life events or a build-up of ongoing smaller ones that exhaust us. If we cannot resolve or escape a stress, then there is a risk that it will become chronic. Cortisol is an important hormone released at times of stress but it also circulates in the body all the time in 24-hour cycles or waves. This hormone does some useful things. It mobilises fat for use as energy, is an anti-inflammatory, affects the liver and it may also increase the sensitivity and detection of threats. It may also help in the reorganisation of information processing systems. Having a blunted cortisol response might make new learning more difficult. Unfortunately, *prolonged* stress elevation of cortisol is bad for us. It is bad for the immune system and can cause undesirable changes in various brain areas, which affect memory, other cognitive functions and emotions (Bremner, 2002). Indeed, we know now that if our stress hormone cortisol stays high for too long it starts to affect the brain and may actually cause shrinkage in certain areas such as the hippocampus and frontal cortex (Sapolsky, 2000). Problems with memory and concentration can be symptoms of excessively high cortisol levels. Cortisol also affects the mood chemicals such as serotonin, dopamine (linked to drive) and the opiates (linked to soothing and feeling safe). And becoming hyper-sensitive to threats (which cortisol enables) is not necessarily useful because our attention and thinking can become narrowed and over-focused on the negatives. Then cycles of negative thinking, feeling and physical change get locked into a downward spiral.

Research has revealed that many depressed people have hyper-active HPA systems with elevated cortisol levels (Numeroff, 1998). There is a substance called dexamethasone which normally suppresses the production of cortisol for 24 hours or so in non-depressed people. However, if we give this to depressed people, we find that they can show what is called *early escape,* that is dexamethasone does not suppress their cortisol. This means that their HPA system overrides the inhibiting effects of dexamethasone and continues to produce high rates of cortisol, that is the stress system is in over-drive.

So we have a stress system that may be useful for dealing with short-term threats and losses but can become a real disadvantage in the long term. Our stress system can be physiologically harmful (Bremner, 2002; Sapolsky, 2000). When we look at evolutionary aspects we might wonder how evolution could have allowed such a poor design – to have allowed stress systems that can actually cause damage to other bodily processes. The answer is that it is an evolutionary *trade off*. In fact, all defensive systems have a range of triggers, intensities, frequency and duration over which they are adaptive, and outside this range they may not be. This means that we need to look to things that might too easily trigger our stress–defence systems and/or keep them turned on. In the later chapters we will look at how our early life can be a source for sensitising the stress system such that it is easily triggered. We may live in new environments where getting away from stressors is more difficult than it was millions of years ago. Equally important is that our capacities for symbolic representations and meta-cognitions of ourselves and our future may have introduced a new ingredient. The way we think and ruminate on things may produce cortical feedback on to the stress system. The more we dwell on the negative feelings of being worthless and inadequate, the future is dark and how bad we feel, the more the stress systems may get locked into unhelpful feedback. This is one of the key ideas in cognitive approaches to therapy – to help people with their thinking and to engage in coping actions rather than dwell on the negative (Gilbert, 2000a). For the moment, though, let's think about another aspect of stress that will be essential for whether our stress systems settle quickly or not. Can we control the stress on us?

The loss of control: helplessness

A very major regulator of threat and positive affect systems is linked to abilities and options to *control* stress. The central requirement when confronted with a threat or a stressor is that you will have to do something. But supposing you cannot? You would like to find a solution or back out of the stress you are in but your routes out are blocked, or far too much depends on you to keep going. Can animal studies help us here? Well in fact many theories of depression have focused on what happens if you stop animals engaging in their adaptive defensive-coping behaviours – when they want to escape but they can't, when you make them helpless.

The *learned helplessness theory* of depression was developed from studies on animals who were subjected to uncontrollable aversive events (Seligman, 1975). What happened was this. Animals were placed in a learning box with a barrier to jump. Their side of the box was electrified and when a light came on, five seconds later, a weak but unpleasant shock went through the floor. Normally a rat or dog would quickly learn to jump the barrier into the safe side, eventually getting so good at it that they showed little anxiety and jumped the barrier as soon as the light came on. However, Seligman first restrained the animals, so that they could not escape and they received shocks they could not control. He then released them and found that many failed to learn to jump the barrier. Many (but not all) became passive and did not explore their environments; they huddled in the corner when the light signalling a shock came on. Seligman and his colleagues had found an extraordinary defensive response to loss of control – a tendency to shut down and become inhibited when one encounters threat that one cannot control. They called it *learned helplessness*. Seligman (1975, pp. 53–4) reasoned that:

> When a traumatic event first occurs, it causes a heightened state of emotionality that can loosely be called fear. This state continues until one of two things happen; if the subject learns that he can control the trauma, fear is reduced and may disappear altogether; or if the subject finally learns he cannot control the trauma, fear will decrease and be replaced by depression.

Seligman went on to apply these findings to a range of things, including ideas about how people develop beliefs about their abilities to control things in their lives, and how some people will persist and others give up quickly. There were studies of genetic differences in how quickly different animals show this learned helplessness pattern (Peterson, Maier and Seligman, 1993; Weiss, Demetrikopoulos, McCurdy et al., 2000).

There were also studies of the chemical changes in the brain in learned helplessness states and how these related to clinical conditions like depression. It has been found, that if animals are subjected to stressors they cannot control, then stress hormones rise and key neurotransmitters such as serotonin, dopamine and opiates start to get depleted. Basically they are used up faster than they can be made. As this happens, pathways start to change in the brain and receptors that are involved in how neurones signal to each other also change, becoming super-or sub-sensitive. The brain is toning down, cutting back on motives that require energy, reducing desires to go out and/or try to actively escape. Although, as we shall see shortly, this is not a full explanation of human depression, learned helplessness revolutionised our way of thinking about many of our depression-linked behaviours.

Seligman thought that this was *learned* behaviour but Joseph Weiss, a neurophysiologist, was doubtful (Weiss et al., 2000). He thought that the passivity of helplessness was caused by chemical changes in the brain. There were two findings that suggested this. First, if you take the animal away from the scene, and let them recover from their ordeal for 48 hours or so, when you bring them back they can learn to jump the barrier. If they had *learnt* that they were helpless, they would not have forgotten this in 48 hours. Secondly, if you give animals anti-depressants, which stops their neurotransmitter systems from depleting to the stress, they again did not show learned helplessness. Yet, if it was learning, then they should have done. So it looked like this state of helplessness was mediated by changes in the brain rather than (just) learning as such.

Since that time the interaction between chemical changes and learning has become more complex, and it is certainly true that humans can develop beliefs that they are helpless and nothing they do will work (Peterson et al., 1993). Confront them with a stress and they immediately feel down and assume they will fail. They find it difficult to generate ideas for solutions and are relatively inflexible in their thinking and problem solving (partly because threat narrows attention and coping). There is also evidence that these states and psychobiological response patterns that emerge with helplessness are *conditionable* and easily triggered by cues and signals that are associated with lack of control (see Gilbert, 1992, 2004 for a review). This can also be seen in terms of a 'kindling' of response patterns, and relates to the spreading activation aspect of depression and subsequent episodes (Monroe and Harkness, 2005). So we only need to pick up certain cues for that sinking feeling to get going and our psychobiological response patterns start shifting to prepare for a 'no-control' situation. However, the evolutionary implications were often implicit rather than explicit. What we have here is an *evolved strategy and regulator for demobilisation* in the context of threats and punishments one cannot control. Hence, just as we have brain systems for activating anxiety or anger/aggression, so there are brain systems for passivity and demobilisation in the context of chronic stress.

Incentive disengagement

At about the same time, during the 1970s, that Seligman was working on learned helplessness, other psychologists had started to find that if you block an animal's ability to achieve a *positive* goal it will show reductions in behaviour. If you stop an animal from (say) getting to a food resource, it gives up trying, and then later, when the blocks are removed, it can still show less inclination to go and get the food. This became known as *incentive disengagement theory* (Klinger, 1975, 1993). This theory suggests that 'depressed activity' serves the function of disengaging an animal from unobtainable incentives and goals (i.e. to give up). In other words, one's own behaviour can be a threat to the extent that one wastes time and energy in pursing the unobtainable. So, for example, you want to form a relationship with Jane or Fred but it is a no go – they don't fancy you. If you keep going, when the chances of success are low, then you will miss out on other options (people). The more you value the resource you are going after the more you will try, but also the more depressed you'll become when you fail. The idea is that our efforts (drive systems) need to be regulated so that our positive, searching and seeking motivations can be turned off to stop us from pursuing the unobtainable. Without such regulation, animals could remain engaged in useless pursuits for the desired but unobtainable. What we have here, then, is an evolved rule/strategy that says 'try to achieve your goals but give up and disengage if the costs of pursing them exceed a certain point'. This is to say, we have built-in regulators of behaviour that are attuned to the evaluated costs in the pursuit of goals and tone down drive in certain contexts.

Nesse (2000; Nesse and Williams, 1995) has developed this view into *resource allocation theory*. He suggests that depression (which is a form of demobilisation) has no single function but that mood tracks the propitiousness of situations in order to adjust resource allocation (e.g. energy and investment – thus activity in the drive systems) in activities so as to maximise long-term pay offs. When times are bad (or people believe they are) depression is a kind of 'sit tight and hunker down' strategy that inhibits investment in poor pay-off activities. There is much evidence of course that people's moods do vary if things are going well (obtaining adequate rewards) or badly for them (Morriss and Morriss, 2000; Nesse, 2000) and depression can remit with improving social circumstances (Brown, Adler and Bifulco, 1988). Perceptions of hopelessness, pessimism and behavioural inactivity are seen as manifestations of this 'hunker down – things are not good right now' strategy. Thus there seem to be some built-in regulators of behaviour that adjust physiological processes, giving rise to changes in motives, emotions, thoughts and behaviours according to circumstances (see also Allen and Badcock, 2003).

Blocked and ineffective defences

There is a large literature on coping behaviour and depression (see Lazarus, 1994, 1999; Martell, Addis and Jacobson, 2001; Perrez and Reicherts, 1992). Basically, when confronted with stressors we have two coping tasks. First, to try to deal with the *external* problem(s) (problem-focused coping) and, second, to cope with the *internal* emotions (anxiety, anger and depression) elicited by the meaning of the stressful event (see Carver, Weintraub and Schierer, 1989 for an outline and mea- sure of typical coping behaviours). To cut a rather long and complex story short, as people become depressed they tend to engage in less external problem-focused coping and focus on trying to control internal painful emotions. Moreover, the ways they try to cope with emotions, such as using alcohol, avoidance, or exces- sive help-seeking, can often make things worse. For this reason problem solving and solution-focused therapies, such as breaking down problems, going one step at a time, engaging rather than avoiding the problem, or learning new skills to deal with problems, are often helpful for depressed people.

There is, however, an evolutionary angle on the way we can conceptualise cop- ing difficulties in depression and link problematic coping to increased activation of threat-stress and the toning down of positive emotions. This is related to a con- sideration of how we *naturally* tend to defend ourselves when confronted by threats and losses. As noted, all humans and other animals have a basic, innate menu of defensive behaviours for dealing with threats. These include flight and escape (e.g. running away from a danger), avoidance, fighting back, submitting and backing down or giving up if the odds are overwhelming, and seeking out help and protection from others (Gilbert, 1993, 2001a). Most of these were designed by evolution for short-term use. But like physical defences of diarrhoea and vomiting, what are helpful and adaptive for short-term use may become mal- adaptive in the long(er) term. In the last few years our research (Gilbert, 1984, 1992, 1993, 2004) and others (Dixon, 1998) have suggested that depression can often involve heightened desires to engage in defensive behaviours, but not being able to. In essence, depressed people can suffer from *blocked, arrested and ineffective* defences. I have found that exploring these with depressed people can illuminate the processes and conflicts that depressed people face. Let's look at each in turn.

Blocked escape and entrapment

Sometimes a key theme in depression is one of *entrapment* (Gilbert, 1992). Entrapment is obviously a form of 'loss of control' but unlike control theory it focuses on the heightened escape motivations that can dominate some people's ruminations. Indeed, an over-focus on escape can block out ways to positively solve problems, and people do not consider (and sometimes do not want to con- sider) how to improve their current situation – they just want out. People who are very *flight*-motivated in their marriages may not want to try to improve them, especially if they carry a lot of anger. So trying to focus on 'positives' before escape motivation is assessed and explored can be problematic. Entrapment may arise in a relationship, whether intimate (e.g. a marriage, family) or social-public (e.g. work), that one cannot get out of but would very much like to. For example, a person would like to leave a neglectful or abusive spouse or a job but for economic reasons, guilt, fear of the spouse's reaction or fear of aloneness they are unable to leave. A sense of being stuck in an undesirable situation and not being able to move from it is more common in depression than is sometimes recognised. Brown, Harris and Hepworth (1995) have shown that entrapment is a more powerful predictor of depression than loss alone. In a major study, Kendler, Hettema, Butera, Gardner, and Prescott (2003) also found that entrapment was significantly linked to depression. Gilbert, Gilbert and Irons (2004) found that entrapment was a common experience in depression and depressed people often ruminated and fantasised about escaping (although less commonly made plans to do so). In animals too, defeats are far more problematic if animals cannot escape and get away from powerful others.

Gilbert and Allan (1998) explored feelings of entrapment that were both externally focused (feeling trapped and wanting to escape from relationships or situations) and internally focused (wanting to escape from inner pain, feelings and thoughts). In regard to inner states, depressed people often feel trapped by their depression and by their loss of energy (Gilbert and Gilbert, 2003). The data suggest that many depressed people feel very trapped and are highly motivated to escape but feel unable to (technically called *arrested flight*).

When people are highly motivated to get away from their feelings (e.g. pain of depression) or outside stressors but feel trapped and can see no way out, suicide becomes a risk. Indeed, Baumeister (1990) referred to suicide as a kind of escape from the self (see also Williams, 1997). There are also many clinical observations that when very depressed people make the decision to kill themselves, and they feel sure the pain will end and that they can get away, then their mood lifts. Indeed, it is clinically important to spot an unexpected shift in mood in some depressed people for this can indicate the person may intend to kill themselves.

It can be very useful to explore with a client feelings of desire for (strength of and fantasises about) escape. They may, however, be ashamed to tell you. For example, a depressed young mother may feel too guilty and ashamed to admit that part of her feels overwhelmed by the demands of motherhood and that she would like to leave it all behind. Or a person may have very ambivalent feelings about leaving a marriage. In my experience, giving space to explore feelings of wanting to escape can have many benefits. Moreover, one can simply explain escape motivations as natural and normal responses to stress because our threat systems are going for quick solutions, as they are designed to do: 'this is not your fault, it is part of brain design'. This helps clients to recognise that they can discuss these feelings in a non-shaming way. It can help to explore whether these feelings are part of the depression, and will recede with the depression, or precede the depression. Moreover, sometimes the very real dilemmas of whether to give up on, leave or stay in a relationship may be central to recovery. For example, in emotionally and physically abusive relationships a woman may feel that it is her fault that the problems exist and this self-blame keeps her in that relationship, but if she can escape she may give up self-blaming (Andrews and Brewin, 1990).

Sometimes depression becomes stuck while people remain stuck in these dilemmas and the counsellor can offer support through a difficult and painful life transition – especially if escape or ending (getting out of) a relationship/job is the preferred option. At other times, if people learn to be more assertive and control the demands on them, then desires to escape subside. It is important, though, that counsellors aid the client to explore the dilemma and not put any pressure on them to go one way or another.

Jane was married to a man who had problems recognising her feelings and expressing his own. In their early years she liked him as a 'quiet type' but later felt he could not offer her emotional closeness. She felt increasingly trapped and fantasised about finding someone who would 'love her emotionally'. Her emotional withdrawal and depression made her husband feel insecure and he became jealous – further accentuating their problems. This difficulty required marital help (Beach and Jones, 2002). Jane learnt to be more reassuring of her husband and focus on other positives in the relationship, while her husband learnt how to be more emotionally attentive and express feelings of his own and of affection. Sometimes people feel trapped because their communications and fears increase each other's insecurities. For example, David was a highly paid executive but hated his job and the pressures of the job, and his critical, hard-driving boss. He often felt very suicidal – that this was his only 'escape'. However, in therapy he worked on his self-identity that 'he should always be a top provider' for his family and children's education. With the family's help and support (he had difficulties feeling that he could be loved or worthwhile as a person if he was not achieving for them), he decided to resign and 'down-size'. Once he was able to see this not as a 'personal defeat' or sign of weakness he was able to work on it. A year later, though still anxious about money, he 'felt better than he had in years'.

Escape and avoidance behaviour shows itself in other ways too. If one asks clients why, for example, they go to bed or don't get up, they may reveal that it is not only because they feel tired but also because they are avoiding and escaping from the demands of the day. Often depressed people will openly admit that this is 'hiding' behaviour motivated by strong desires to escape. Such desires may well be `driven' by various negative beliefs, but whatever the source, the key issue is that escape motivation is highly aroused but does not bring relief. Indeed, such behaviour can often leave a person feeling worse. In this sense the defensive behaviour is ineffective. Helping people to act against their desires to escape and avoid, and become active can be useful (Martell et al., 2001). Looking at this from the stress point of view, we might explain that while the escape strategy is running there is high stress, as if the amygdale and HPA systems are in over-drive, but the avoidance behaviour does not bring relief. This kind of stress overheats the system and contributes to physiological disruption.

In regard to internal entrapment, the depressed person may be unable to distract themselves from painful feelings and worries. Sometimes they feel they would like to escape from their feelings and thoughts – to be internally at peace. Mindfulness training may be especially helpful for them. It is also not uncommon to find some depressions beginning with a physical health problem from which the person feels they cannot escape or recover. A sense of being trapped in (and wanting to escape from) a diseased or crippled body can be powerfully depressogenic. Key questions to ask clients are: Do you have strong feelings of wanting to escape or hide from . . .? Do you ever think that you would just like to run away? How trapped do you feel in your current situation? Have you ever thought of ways to escape? What are they? What stops you?

Need for space

Sometimes people need a temporary escape. A common theme in depression is a need for space. Sometimes people can feel overwhelmed by the demands and responsibilities on them and they need some temporary respite. Desires to escape can sometimes be linked to lifestyles where a person has no personal space. This is particularly common in women who have various degrees of 'role strain' – trying to cope with children, work and marriage. Carers of dementing relatives may have needs to get away and have space. There can, however, be much shame around such desires (e.g. 'I am a bad person to want to put my mother in a home') (see Martin, Gilbert, McEwan and Irons, 2006). Helping a person create time for 'personal space' can be very helpful, especially if they can learn to do it without feeling ashamed or guilty.

When general practitioners or counsellors advise mildly depressed people to take a holiday there is an intuition that 'getting away' from stressful situations can be helpful. It can allow the stress system to settle down and help bring new perspectives. If people do feel better when they do this, it is important that recognition is given to how their current situation is increasing their stress. At other times this kind of intervention does not work. For example, if the problems are in the family relationships, then taking a holiday with the family can make things worse. Some people cannot 'switch off', but instead worry about what is happening back home or at work. And, of course, some people may not have the resources for holidays or the support networks to get respite. So counsellors have to be sensitive to the issue of space from whom or what.

When people become excessively fatigued and depressed about being 'tired all the time', it is not uncommon for them to be exhausted and poor at taking time out or having respite. There may be very practical reasons for this (e.g. the demands of family and work). However, these folk can also be highly driven and work themselves to a frazzle. They may have unrealistic expectations of what they should be capable of, compare themselves negatively with those who seem to achieve a lot, and drive themselves hard. Helping people to see they may be exhausted and may need quite a long time to recuperate, and sometimes medications, can be a tough lesson for them. Such people are especially vulnerable to feeling defeated and (more) depressed by their loss of energy. The linkage here is: high demands or personal drive → becoming exhausted → feeling defeated and unable to reach goals → feeling more defeated and more depressed. Key questions to ask are: Do you feel that you would like to take time out and get away, at least temporarily, from your current situation? Do you feel you have enough personal space in your life? What stops you from making more space for yourself?

Arrested fight and anger

When we are stressed we can activate *a range* of negative emotions, for example both flight and fight can be activated as defences. There is a good deal of evidence that many depressed people experience increases in their anger and irritability (Gilbert, Gilbert and Irons, 2004; Riley, Treiber and Woods, 1989). However, again this anger may be either arrested (not expressed) due to a self-identity concern (anger is bad or shameful), fear of others' responses, wanting to protect others, or, if it is expressed, it is too aggressive, 'tantrum or rage-like' (rather than assertive) or ineffective and can make things worse. However, it can be useful to explore with clients the degree of their anger and what they do about it. Some depressed people just feel more generally irritable and on 'a short fuse'. We can explain this as a sad symptom of depression but not evidence of personal badness. Others are 'embittered' and have a strong sense of being treated unfairly or unjustly. Such folk may ruminate on their anger and desires for revenge. Constantly dwelling on a sense of injustice but not being able to do anything about it not only increases a sense of powerlessness (lack of control) but also probably keeps the stress system in a high state of arousal. Some depressed people are unaware of their anger, are frightened of it and have learnt to avoid processing it – it is non-conscious to them. We will explore examples later in the book. For all such anger difficulties, working with their anger may be important (Gilbert, 2000a). In fact, I have seen a number of people who presented with depression but the main affect that was problematic was their anger. Key questions to ask are: Do you feel very irritable inside? Do you find you are quick to anger? How do you express anger or discontent. Do you feel a sense of injustice – like life has treated you unfairly and you'd like revenge somehow? What stops you expressing your anger or discontent?

Submissive behaviour

Submissive behaviour is a basic form of defensive behaviour that is many millions of years old (Gilbert, 1992, 2000b). Many animals can exhibit submissive behaviour, especially when they are under challenge from more powerful others. In humans, beliefs in personal inferiority and being subject to criticisms and attacks can trigger submissive behaviour. There is now good evidence that many depressed people either have a history of taking submissive positions in relationships or become submissive as their mood goes down (Allan and Gilbert, 1997). A sense of being in a one-down, subordinated position and under the control of others can arise from abusive or neglectful relationships. The key point is that a sense of inferiority and weakness can activate internal inhibition, social anxiety, reduce explorative behaviour and inhibit assertiveness (Gilbert, 1992, 2000c).

Submissiveness can often be associated with a type of approval-seeking behaviour, by being excessively accommodating to others. The basic belief here is: 'In order to be loved and avoid abandonment I must accommodate myself to others – be for them what they want me to be' (Young, Beck and Weinberger, 1993). Clearly this limits the degree to which a person can feel free to explore or express their own needs, preferences and desires in relationships. This submissive inhibition of self can lead to further feelings of inferiority, a loss of power and limits assertive behaviour and entrapment (Gilbert, 2000b). There is now good evidence that depression is associated with submissive behaviour (Gilbert, 2004).

Not uncommonly, depressed people can feel resentful at their own submissive behaviour (angry submission). They may back down and may put the needs of others first but resent it. So they either lack the skills to act assertively or are too frightened to act assertively. Key questions to ask are: Do you tend to back down if you are in disagreement with others? Are you frightened to stand up for yourself? Do you feel resentful if you have to back down or go along with others when you don't want to? What stops you from being more assertive?

Arrested help-seeking

Help-seeking is another common defensive behaviour, and in children it is the most typical way to cope with threats and things that are overwhelming. Knowing that there are people who can help, support and understand you when in a crisis can be very soothing. In Chapter 5 we will note that receiving help and knowing we are cared for is important in maintaining the tone of the soothing positive affect system. However, some depressed people do not seek help or, if they do, they are ignored or rejected. For example, some people become depressed because they simply don't have access to support (Brown and Harris, 1978). Others avoid help-seeking because they are ashamed to admit they can't cope or are depressed – depression can be seen as very unattractive to others. Yet others avoid help-seeking because they think that it won't help them. And yet for others gaining help makes them feel obligated to the help provider and in a one-down subordinated position.

There is an affect and process that is associated with help-seeking and help-eliciting–which is grieving and expression of sadness. When we cry we send signals of distress, we tear up and curl our heads. From an evolutionary point of view this means we cannot attend to outside threat. It is adaptive, however, in that it activates caring behaviour in others. It is in part the experiences of others as caring when we grieve that can be helpful. Depression often involves major disturbances in the grieving process. Some people are not able to grieve because they feel overwhelmed by the feelings; they feel ashamed or expect to be rejected. For some, the inability to grieve freezes up certain affect systems and people note that they have difficulties in feeling certain feelings for self and others (Gilbert and Irons, 2005). As we will see later, when people start to be self-compassionate and give up treating themselves harshly, grief and sadness can emerge. They begin to really recognise how painful their depression is and has been, and how alone, unloved or unvalued they have felt for so long. Jane, for example, was adopted into a harsh family and after a beating would lay at night looking at the stars fantasising that her biological mother was out there and she would come one day to take her away. When she began to work on these memories she was overwhelmed by crying and sadness – feelings that despite previous therapy she had not processed before. I would just sit quietly with her or speak softly to her, empathising as best I could. When she recovered from the depression that had haunted her most of her life she thought this experience and working through had had a profound effect on her recovery.

Grief can be the first sign that depressed people are beginning to work with these feelings and reactivate the social soothing system. The therapist's ability to tolerate and be gentle with grief is key to the process for it allows people to process these memories and feelings in the context of a caring supportive signals in a relationship which will lay down different affect memories (Brewin, 2006), which, as we see in Chapter 5, are related to attachment systems. Other depressed people, however, find it difficult to stop crying or feeling sad, and here the therapeutic task may be different.

Finally, the way people seek help can impact on the help others are prepared and able to give. They may focus on their depression, complain or be aggressively sulky and this drives others away (Segrin and Abramson, 1994). Help can come in different forms. For example, some people may be good at offering practical help but not good at listening, sharing, or validating a person's feelings and offering basic comfort. Not uncommonly in some depressions it is feeling validated, valued and comforted that people seek. Sometimes people find themselves in conflict between wanting support from a loved one and being angry with them, and this conflict results in a kind of inner paralysis. Because of their anger, the support that is offered does not seem to be helpful. Key questions to ask are: Do you have people around who you feel can help, understand or support you? Are you able to acknowledge a need for help? How would you like to use help? What stops you from seeking help? If you cried in therapy, how would that be for you?

A model for problematic innate defences

Our innate defences were designed for short-term use, and operate deep in our brains. They can become problematic because of the complexities of modern life (e.g. marriages, working in paid jobs, living on run-down estates) and our complex human psychology (e.g. cognitive-reasoning, symbol-forming systems, self-identities, and moral dilemmas) that can now regulate them. As a result, these simple defensive strategies and psychobiological response patterns become compromised, blocked, arrested and ineffective. When this happens we can feel the urge to act on them, pushing us from the inside, but if we are not able to act on them adaptively they can add to our stress rather than resolving it. This can put us into chronic stress situations, and keep the threat processing systems toned up and increase the risk of depression. These processes can be delineated in a simple model (Figure 3.1) that indicates how they impact on us. Part of what therapy involves is thus helping people to understand them and either adaptively act on them or learn alternative, more helpful ways of coping with life's difficulties.

Keep in mind that although people can feel hopeless, in this model it is the emotion of 'fear and dread' that can be crucial. In suicide, people do not just feel hopeless but can have a 'fear and dread' of the future; the feeling of 'I just can't face that again'; or 'I just can't go through that'. People who commit suicide to escape pain or shame or the return of depression fall into this group (Williams, 1997).

Conclusion

Many therapies will focus on people's thoughts, emotions or behaviours but may not explain to people why the way they are thinking/feeling and wanting to behave is in part a reflection of underlying protection-defence systems that have evolved in our brains. When patients begin to understand why they feel as they

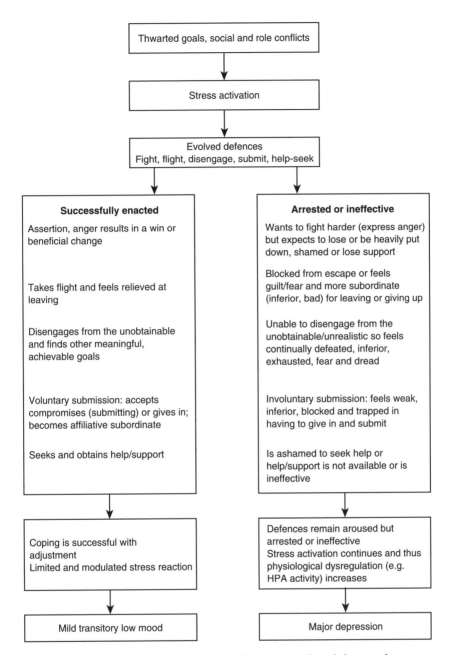

Figure 3.1   Linkages of evolved defences with stress-related depression

Adapted from Gilbert, 2001b

do, this can help to develop the therapeutic tasks of change. It helps to de-personalise and de-shame depression and allows people to become mindful of what the different systems in their brains are 'feeding into consciousness' and textures of self-awareness. Our conscious minds may be only too aware of the pain of entrapment, despair or defeat, the conflicts in our minds, and can ruminate on them, but of course these systems did not evolve just to give us a hard time but to motivate and de-motivate certain actions for self-protection.

Thus, the key to this way of thinking has been the way threat systems and different types of positive emotion systems have different functions and interests. Depression is a toning up of threat sensitivities and a toning down of the positive ones. This can happen because evolution has plumbed these systems in us. They are designed to be run and be activated, *not* come what may, but to be sensitive to physical and social contexts. In humans, part of the context that triggers them lies in (compromised) efforts to co-create desired social relationships, and our symbol-using and self-identity-forming systems.

The counsellor who uses this kind of approach may explain that to get out of depression means finding ways to think and act that help resolve protection strategies. Thus the counsellor tries to help the person pay close attention to their thoughts and feelings and consider alternatives, and also to (re)engage the world and make efforts to open up to others or socialise rather than withdraw and hide – at times we must act to override our primitive protection strategies. So sometimes clients will need to learn how to be more assertive or try harder, sometimes to change tactics or change their goals, sometimes how to bow out gracefully without feeling a personal failure, and often how to be accepting and kind to themselves. Fear and dread are often part of feeling depressed. The shared idea is to try to gently teach our minds to recognise but also override or tone down the protection strategies that are now not useful to us and are the source of considerable pain and despair.

4 Behavioural Approaches: Action Matters

Behavioural theories focus on the outputs and behaviours of living systems and the contexts in which behaviours are emitted. To some extent they endorse the importance of thinking about ourselves and other animals as systems and patterns of psychobiological organisation (Timberlake, 1994). For the behaviourist, if you change the patterns of outputs/behaviours, then this can change the internal organisation and patterns of systems. Crucially, therefore, it is important to focus on the behaviour in context. In the last chapter we focused on loss of control, passivity, avoidance, and various arrested defences such as escape and anger. It is these problematic coping behaviours, that arise in the context of threat, that behaviourists view as key to depression. The behaviourist focuses on direct experience and less on cognitive mediators of experience. To learn to drive, give a talk, or overcome (say) agoraphobia, one must 'do it' – that is act against the fear. The same can be true for depression: action can be a powerful regulator of moods. Thus before exploring social relationships and interpersonal schema (Chapter 5) and cognitive processes (Chapter 6) in depression, this chapter will focus on behavioural approaches. This will enable us to note how behavioural approaches are often weaved into other focused therapy approaches and can be central to them.

As outlined elsewhere (Gilbert, 1992), there are two basic behavioural approaches to depression. One approach focuses on what is called *classical conditioning* emotional memory and the linkage between emotions. The other focuses on the outputs or functional behaviours of a person and the way these may be reduced, become focused on avoidance, or tend to elicit criticism and punishment from the environment. Both these approaches see some depressions as *natural* consequences of certain types of learning and life events. They are less focused on placing the source of depression *inside* the person in terms of faulty cognitions or neurophysiological problems but on the way the person *interacts* with the world (Martell et al., 2001). Behaviourists suggest that changing behaviour directly also changes various cognitive parameters, including beliefs and expectations of self-efficacy (Bandura, 1977). It is recognised that the generalisation of change outside the therapy session requires behavioural change. An analogy might be that one can read all there is to read about cars (have insight) but never be able to drive and remain fearful of doing so unless one practises the actions. Thus, one needs experience.

Conflicts

Psychoanalytic perspectives regard various behaviours as symptoms of psychopathology and as indicators of a deep, underlying, often unconscious, conflict. If the behaviours are changed without resolving this conflict, symptoms will change their form (due to a diversion of energy), but the individual will not be restored to healthy functioning. Behaviourists, on the other hand, regard behavioural symptoms, either as a sample of the disturbance, or as the actual disturbance itself. They do not, it is said, look for underlying conflicts. This polarisation of perspectives is unhelpful and misleading. In fact, behaviourists also regard much neurotic behaviour as originating from *inner conflict* (Gray, 1979). These conflicts, however, may or may not be available to consciousness, but relate to approach-avoidance conflicts, problems of conditioned anxiety, and perceived response-outcome contingencies. After all, many animals can have approach-avoidance conflicts but this does not mean they are conscious of them. Thus a lot of behavioural approaches to depression implicitly, if not explicitly, are focused on depression as a problem of threat and safety-seeking behaviours.

Wolpe's conditioned anxiety model of depression

In 1971 Wolpe presented a classical conditioning theory of depression, suggesting that depression was a consequence of conditioned anxiety. Unlike many of the behavioural models, Wolpe draws sharp dividing lines between normal, neurotic and endogenous depression, and limits his analysis to the neurotic depressions. He maintains that depressive neurosis should be regarded like other neuroses, which are fuelled by *conditioned anxiety*. He defines neurosis as persistent, unhelpful habits acquired by learning in an anxiety-generating situation or succession of situations. Thus, Wolpe suggests we should turn our attention to the older forms of experimentally induced anxiety, which, as he correctly maintains, tend to get forgotten these days. Wolpe's key idea is that in situations of anxiety there are reductions in positive (reinforceable) behaviour. Wolpe's observation of the relationship between conditioned anxiety and the cessation of positive reinforceable behaviours is an important one. Indeed, the learned helplessness model (Seligman, 1975), explored in the last chapter, relates to stressors that are anxiety-inducing, which, over time, reduce positive affect. Wolpe also directs attention to the emotional and behavioural consequences of strong approach–avoidance conflicts.

Wolpe (1979) offers a neat sub-classification of neurotic depression along the lines of differently acquired conditioned anxiety responses. He suggests four sub-types of depression:

1. Depression as a consequence of severe and prolonged anxiety that is directly conditioned.
2. Depression as a consequence of anxiety based on erroneous self-devaluative cognitions.
3. Depression as a consequence of anxiety based on an inability to control interpersonal behaviour.
4. Depression as a consequence of severe or prolonged responses to bereavement.

If anxiety and dread are prominent in depression (which research shows they often are), then many of the behavioural techniques for anxiety control can be helpful (e.g. relaxation and exposure and desensitisation; see Clark, 1999). However, some depressed clients do not find relaxation exercises helpful. This is because, in depression, the client can be highly focused on internal negative ruminations and thoughts. It is often more helpful to use various forms of activity that require their attention to be outwardly directed. In other words, work with what is helpful to the individual. It is also helpful to be familiar with ways of helping people with social anxiety as this can be a common complication in depression (e.g. see Bates and Clark, 1998; Beidel and Turner, 1998).

Depression also often involves anxiety about possible self-initiated behaviours such as acting more assertively with bosses, spouses, children or friends, or leaving a difficult marriage or changing a job. Indeed, this is why the behaviours can be inhibited and arrested (see Chapter 3). *Anxiety* over taking the steps to change (e.g. making life changes) can be a key reason people feel or become trapped. To this we can add the idea that some people have conditioned anxiety to a variety of internal stimuli, such as to feelings of anger or vulnerability (see below). Wolpe suggests that in the absence of counter-conditioning of these habits of responding (working directly with the anxiety underpinning some forms of avoidance), they will not dissipate over time. I like this model because it emphasises the importance of anxiety that can underpin and be a vulnerability factor for depression. Some other models of depression under-emphasise this fact. It also points to key interventions to address anxiety.

The importance of approach-avoidance conflicts

Wolpe touched on but did not fully address the key issue of approach-avoidance conflicts. We need to understand approach-avoidance conflicts because they can be *central* to some depressions. Suppose you teach a rat to run up a runway for (say) food when there is a square above the entrance, but if there is a circle above the entrance then the rat will get a mild shock if it enters. The rat runs when it sees the square and avoids when it sees the circle. No problem. But suppose you gradually make the square and circle difficult to distinguish by making it more elliptic. Under these conditions you have created competing behavioural action tendencies that seek to regulate each other. Now the rat, who was happy running for or avoiding food if it needed to, becomes confused and highly aroused and disorientated. It may engage in circling behaviour, bizarre stereotypic behaviours and even self-biting, all of which are indicators of high stress activation in physiological systems. The more hungry the animal (the more it wants the food resource) the more disturbed its behaviour. Remember there is no problem when it knows what to do – to run or avoid. What this shows is that psychobiological systems become disorganised as they compete with each other for expression, and difficult to regulate when there are strong approach-avoidance conflicts. *Inner* conflicts over what to do can be intensely stressful! Gray (1979) gives an excellent review and discussion of the behavioural studies on these aspects.

Now some depressions are riddled with internal approach-avoidance conflicts: should I stay in this loveless marriage for the children and financial security, or strike out on my own? Should I leave this job where I am bullied or overworked and tired and give up my salary or stay and keep the mortgage going? Should I take a less stressful job and spend more time with the children, but lose being able to live in this house or take holidays? Should I take a new job that means moving from my social network or stay where I am? Should I express my feelings and risk rejection or suppress them and be subordinated? Whichever way you go there is positive and negative outcome. Depressed people may not be fully conscious of the intensity of their conflicts, especially if they have closed down. The counsellor can help here and explore the advantages and disadvantages of different behaviours (Beck et al., 1979). Sometimes people are ashamed of their conflicts. For example, I worked with a man for some time before he told me he was having an affair but was unsure whether to leave his wife.

People can also dissociate in these conflicted states. For example, Jon felt increasingly overwhelmed at work. One day he found that rather than go to work he had driven to the coast and walked along the beach. He had little conscious awareness of how he got there but described his mind 'as if in a fog'. Later Jon was able to reflect that he could not leave his stressful job because he felt he would be letting his family and work mates down. To think about and think through leaving his job was 'a very frightening prospect'. In the end, helping him reduce his over-developed sense of responsibility, learning to share problems rather than 'bottle up' helped him cope much better at work. The point is that approach-avoidance conflicts can disorganise our minds – just as they can for the poor rat noted above! Then problem solving becomes very difficult because we just can't 'think straight', and then we need another, less disorganised mind to help us resolve them and sooth us. So some difficulties in problem solving can be related to 'brain' disorganisation as a result of conflicts and hard dilemmas.

Also note that when people suffer depression they start to become acutely sensitive to conflicts over competing actions. Should I go to the shops now or wait for the gas man? Even small decisions can seem like mountains. As one person told me, "I get into 'I'm not sure' mode and procrastinate – like my decision-making abilities have gone". Normalise this as a common but distressing symptom of high stress and depression.

We will discuss attachment issues in the next chapter but we can note here that people who come from secure attachment backgrounds, and can use others as sources of help, soothing and talking through, knowing there are others who will support them whatever they decide to do, are much better placed to face and resolve approach-avoidance conflicts. Those from insecure backgrounds are more likely to either act impulsively or get stuck with things going around and around in their heads, becoming highly disorganised, stressed and depressed.

Another source of conflict that can produce disorganisation is conflicts between strong, different *emotions* and action tendencies. The classic is, of course, love and hate. Conflicting thoughts and dilemmas are also common in depression, and not being able to resolve them can be a source of chronic stress. It can help to write these down with people so that they can begin to see clearly what they are (often depressed people have a hazy ideas about their conflicts) and explain how conflicts can stress us in certain ways.

Ferster's model of behavioural adjustment

In 1973 and 1974 Ferster published two important papers on depression outlining the applicability of both classical and operant models of learning to depression. Many other behavioural therapists have borrowed from this source. Ferster made clear that we always need to understand the *functions of behaviour*. Two people may take an overdose – one wanted to die, the other was drunk and thought he was taking painkillers for a headache. Like most behaviourists before and since, Ferster stresses the avoidance behaviours associated with depression and how these can become reinforced (e.g. via short-term relief) but make things worse in the long term. He suggests that these difficulties often arise when people are called to make adjustments to their behaviour to cope with disturbances/changes in their way of life. He suggests that failures in adjustment behaviour may be related to negative perceptions of reinforcement contingencies. He highlights three such difficulties. Depressed people may have:

- a limited view of the world. In this situation the depressed person may be unable to see which behaviours are appropriate for reinstating adequate levels of reinforcement. They may sulk and complain but have little insight into what behaviour on their part would bring the required reinforcement.
- a lousy view of the world. In this situation the depressed person may be aware of what behaviours are required but fears the aversive consequences of such behaviour. In other words, their passivity is under aversive (e.g. anxiety) control by its potential negative-reinforcing properties.
- an unchanging view of the world. In this situation it is not so much a lack of perception, or a fear of aversive consequences, but a lack of skills. In other words, the behavioural repertoire is not sufficiently developed or comprehensive to be able to adjust to significant changes in reinforcement and life events. Ferster likens this view to a kind of development arrest (similar to, but not identical with, psychoanalytic concepts of fixation).

Repressed emotions

Another key idea of Ferster's is that for some people, some emotions/desires are under conditioned inhibitory control. Ferster (1973) pointed out that if a child's expression of anger or affection-seeking is constantly punished, this will generate anxiety and fear of punishment. Thus the inner stimuli/feelings of anger or affection-seeking will be associated with fear. Eventually the arousal of anger or affection-seeking automatically elicits a conditioned fear/anxiety response. In this context, the child may gradually become unaware of feelings of anger or affection-seeking feelings in situations where these could be useful. Instead they are only aware of the secondary conditioned anxiety to stimuli, and not feelings of anger or affection-seeking motives and feelings. This can have serious consequences for the child's abilities to recognise certain emotions and mature them in helpful ways. Consider Jane, who saw her mother as powerful and critical but also 'always right/clever'. Jane idealised her and relied on her for help. Jane felt that she herself was physically unattractive. Jane was able to recall how her mother would often tell her that she had an awkward body, and that 'everything you wear looks like a rag on you'. Although these 'put downs' were clearly a source of shame (and she internalised these judgements), Jane was at first unaware and then very fearful of acknowledging anger to her mother for shaming her, or that her mother could be wrong.

To begin to consider these alternative possibilities can be intensely threatening, especially if 'the other' is more powerful and can inflict harm on us for rebellion or defiance (Gilbert and Irons, 2005). Her healing of shame emerged with seeing her mother as *not* always right, acknowledging and processing her anger at her mother and her fear of her mother's counter-attack or punishment (like a dominant on a subordinate), letting go of her dependency, and learning to cope with the changed dynamic of the daughter–mother bond. Healing shame can often require changes in our inner representation of others, processing feared and conditioned emotions, revisiting and working with shame-trauma memories, reducing submissive defences and becoming more able to defend/maintain a sense of self from external and internal (memory-linked) 'attacks'. These may be key to alterations in *self*-evaluations. We will explore this more fully in later chapters.

As noted throughout this book, anxiety and anger are often two key emotions that can be problematic for depressed people and can require careful attention. For some people anger and expressions of anger are feared and there are problems in learning to behave assertively. Thus, for Bob the situation was, feeling anger with others, fearing expressing this anger, negative self-evaluations for feeling angry, acting submissively and then feeling more resentful and angry. Karen had a high need to be liked, also feared expressing anger and would put on 'her smiling face' but would ruminate and brood on anger. Kim would be submissive to others' requests (because she wanted to be liked), take on too much, get stressed and irritable, and sometimes felt like exploding inside. She would be angry and irritable with her children and then collapse in tears, feeling herself to be a bad person. She wanted to run away from all the demands on her and 'it would be better if she killed herself'. She would then become very frightened that she might act on her suicidal feelings. All these people also had bad and frightening dreams, not realising that some of the aggression in these dreams was related to their own anger.

Emotions-focused therapists have discussed how we can fear certain emotions, such as anger, and acting in dominant (stating our claims) rather than submissive ways, and that therapy can be a time to overcome this fear and process these feelings by tolerating them (Greenberg and Watson, 2006). Learning to work with and tolerate avoided or repressed feelings is highly compatible with a behavioural approach. Normalise anger, and our fear of it, e.g. noting films like *The Hulk* and seeing it as a common if unpleasant feeling. Learning anger tolerance, helping people understand how anger rumination is problematic and learning more helpful appraisals, assertive behaviours (and coping with anxiety of assertiveness, especially the fear of not being liked) can be important in helping some depressed people.

Go beyond emotions

While behaviourists may focus on the conditioning of behaviours or emotions, and the way one emotion can act as a conditioned stimulus for another, we can go beyond this. What are conditioned are *psychobiological response patterns*. These patterns of positive affect (as toned down) and negative affect (as toned up) can be easily elicited by certain cues. That is to say certain cues may come to activate various patterns and protection strategies. As part of the pattern, emotions, thoughts and emotional memories may be activated in parallel with each other. Which 'bits' of the pattern become conscious and which bits do not is a complex research question (Hassin, Uleman and Bargh, 2005). For the therapist working with complex cases, understanding the power of conditioning, and the way associations in the mind (right down to the neural level) can be elicited in fast-acting ways, can be useful to thinking about mood states.

Using imagery

There is a long history to the use of imagery in psychotherapy, and imagery can have a powerful effect on emotions and our psychologies (Singer, 2006). Feelings of anger for people in the past can be worked through using re-living and imagery procedures. For example, Hackmann (2005) offers examples of how people can work through memories (e.g. of feeling angry with parents for certain behaviours) and (in imagery) deliver assertive messages.

In cases where anxiety is high, it is useful to have clear insight into anger images and fantasies. Then you can develop alternative images and fantasies with clients that they can practise in the feared situation. You can practise generating new internal video-like scenes. For example, one depressed client who was afraid of the dark had an image of being attacked but imagined herself as helpless. This had come from her early life when her mother was very physically aggressive and where passivity and covering up *really was* the only way to reduce the attacks. Hence we taught her to practise imagining fighting back. She had never thought of this possibility but it proved a very helpful intervention in her case, especially when she had seen the connection between her passivity images and problems in her childhood. It is actually quite difficult not to think of something, hence advising clients 'not to think' about their automatic thoughts or to 'put things out of their minds' does not work. It is better to find alternative thoughts or images (see Hackmann, 1997).

Key points

1. Behaviourists focus on the *functions* of behaviour and these can be highly individual to a person.
2. Approach-avoidance conflicts and painful dilemmas can increase stress and disorganise our minds, making 'clear' thinking difficult – people can feel as if their minds are 'in a fog'.
3. Many depressive behaviours are forms of *safety behaviours*, such as submissiveness and avoidance or unhelpful ways of trying to regulate (avoid) problematic emotions, interpersonal situations or contexts.
4. Emotions and 'fear of emotions' are common internal problems that need to be addressed in depression. It is therefore important to have a good understanding of how anxiety and anger operate and can conflict for the depressed person.
5. Learning how to accept, tolerate and work with emotions, and reduce depression-related behaviours, is central to many types of behavioural approach.

Perrez and Reicherts' stress coping model

Perrez and Reicherts (1992) developed a very helpful model to classify many elements within the behavioural model of coping. Key to their model is the relationship between the objective aspects of situations and subjective experiences. Their overview is given in Table 4.1.

Tabel 4.1   Objective distinctive characteristics of stress

| 1. | Loss | The removal of a desired source of reward or positive reinforcement (e.g. loss of a relationship). |
| 2. | Punishment | The occurrence of an aversive situation (e.g. an attack, road accident). |

Objective dimensions of situations

1.	Valence	The inherent stressfulness of situations.
2.	Controllability	The inherent opportunities for control within a situation.
3.	Changeability	The probability that the situation will change by itself, that is via its own dynamics (e.g. the weather).
4.	Ambiguity	The degree to which a situation is inherently lacking in sufficient information to enable clear meaning of the situation to be ascertained.
5.	Reoccurrence	The inherent likelihood of reoccurrence of the stressful situation.

Subjective dimensions of situations

1.	Valence	The subjective meaning of a situation/event that contributes to its stressfulness, but is individually determined.
2.	Controllability	The subjective appraisal of personal ability to control the stressful situation.
3.	Changeability	The subjective appraisal that the stressful event will change by itself, that is without the person taking any action.
4.	Ambiguity	The subjective appraisal of ambiguity and uncertainty of the situation.
5.	Reoccurrence	The subjective appraisal of the reoccurrence of the stressful situation.
6.	Familiarity	The extent of personal experience with such a situation.

Source: From Perrez and Reicherts, 1992: 26, with kind permission from Hogrefe and Huber

In their research they found that depressed people underestimate the degree to which they can change situations, operate usefully on a stressor, influence outcomes (controllability), and the degree to which situations are themselves changeable (changeability). They point out that adaptive coping *is always individual* and relates to a person–situation interaction. For example, if stresses are unchangeable (e.g. the firm where one works closes down, and one loses one's job, or one has a major illness), then the key coping strategy is to adapt to the event while exploring possible new behaviours for adapting. This may involve developing new skills for new types of work, or learning illness-coping behaviour. If a stressor is likely to change by itself (e.g. getting the flu), then the behaviour is to rest and wait for the situation to improve. If one knows that situations are unstable, then passivity can be useful. For example, if one is dealing with a volatile person who calms down quickly, it may be useful to wait until they have calmed down before discussing things with them. If there is a lot of ambiguity in a situation, then searching for more information is helpful. If one has a lack of knowledge, then seeking information and help from others can be useful. If one requires the help of others (e.g. brain surgery), learning how to trust others (e.g. your surgeon), and let others be in control, can be helpful. Sometimes, avoidance is important, for example, avoiding foods you know make you ill, or keeping away from people who bully you. Sometimes, depressed people who have very major conflicts with parents can feel better if they learn to emotionally disengage and distance themselves.

The point about this is therefore that acceptance, avoidance, passivity, active engagement and information-seeking can all be useful in certain contexts. One cannot identify adaptive coping outside the contexts and people's own individual needs and coping styles.

Behavioural Activation Therapy

Behavioural Activation (BA) Therapy is outlined by Martell, Addis and Jacobson (2001). This approach, pioneered by the late Neil Jacobson, has increasingly good evidence to support it. As Martell et al., (2001) note, however, behavioural activation is not the best of names because at times the counsellor helps a person reduce certain behaviours. This approach is a development of previous behavioural approaches described above. A recent study (Dimidjian et al., 2006) has shown BA to be highly effective for depressed people, especially those with severe depression, and it may be more effective than those focusing on cognitions. However, rumination, a key cognitive target, was in the BA rather than CT intervention. Behavioural activation does not focus on the content or validity of thoughts or rumination, but their utility and helpfulness. It thus explores distinctions between helpful and unhelpful processes.

BA suggests that the counsellor should develop a good, shared understanding of the following:

1. The activating context in which a depression arises – what was happening in a person's life that triggered depression.
2. The way the context and life event(s) elicited certain understandable but unhelpful, coping efforts and behaviours to adapt to the context and stressor they experienced.
3. How those behaviours (called secondary problems, such as avoidance and rumination) can themselves become sources of depression.
4. How things are now (e.g. current life stressors, relationship quality, coping behaviours).
5. Agree a formulation based on the behavioural model.
6. Agree on an approach that targets efforts to develop a new repertoire of behaviours and coping strategies.
7. Acknowledge (and work with) the fact that shifting to new behaviours can be difficult.

The BA approach focuses less on (but does not ignore) people's interpretation and thoughts about things but focuses more on understanding the functions of certain depression-linked behaviours and how to enact specific anti-depressant behaviours. Key questions include: How would you behave or cope with this situation if you were not depressed? How might you advise someone else in your situation?

Behavioural approaches to depression focus on helping people to see how depression has altered their styles of behaviour (e.g. they may have become more limited and avoidant). Like other behavioural approaches, BA rests on the idea that our feelings and thoughts are significantly influenced by our interactions with the social and non-social environment. BA also follows a key behavioural idea that changing behaviours and increasing rewarding and rewardable behaviours are key to mood change.

Helping people change their behaviours sometimes means giving up unhelpful and ineffective defences and safety behaviours. For example, avoidance, where someone stays in bed a lot, may be a key target for change. Gradually learning to plan activities in a step-by-step way can be helpful. Or it may be the person has to build more 'personal space' into their lives if there are many competing demands on them and forms of role strain. This can involve coming to terms with the fact that we are all limited and are not inexhaustible. One might note that, like a bank account, if one keeps taking money out without putting anything back in, then sooner or later one runs out of cash! So the key idea is what a person is putting into their lives that can act as rewards and reinforcers.

Lifestyles

There are a variety of lifestyles that can contribute to depression. Exploring sleep and 'sleep hygiene' can be useful (Espie, 2006). The patient should stay up until tired and avoid catnaps during the day, avoid laying in bed ruminating (e.g. if not asleep after 15 minutes, get up and do something), avoid alcohol as a way to get to sleep because sleep quality is 'poor', and avoid (complex) mental activity before bed. The value of a balanced diet is important (e.g. reduce coffee intake if this is high or stop relying on sweet snacking). Discuss how inactivity increases depression (metabolic slow down) but *exercise* and focused activity can reduce it. They could consider going to a gym. Are there people whom they might go with? These simple suggestions can be a core around which a client can feel they are exerting more control and are helping themself.

Problem solving and solution-focused approaches

Because depressed people get exhausted or disorganised (e.g. via approach-avoidance conflicts and stress), they can feel overwhelmed with their problems; it just seems like one big black mass of difficulties. Problem solving involves discussing and recognising this. One way to approach this is to break problems down into specific difficulties. For example, one might develop a problem list and then think about prioritising the problems. Prioritising can have two aspects: one is based on the importance or difficulty of the problem, the other is based on how easy it might be to deal with. Both of these need to be considered because one shouldn't assume that one goes for the most difficult problem first (because that is a top priority). Success at solving the easier problems can sometimes spin off into having confidence in dealing with the more difficult ones. Think through what people may need to help with the problems and then the steps for getting that help or some solution. As noted by Perrez and Reicherts' (1992) approach, if the problem is irresolvable, then it is how to accept, come to terms and live with it.

If more information is needed, then consider how to find out, and who to ask or seek help from. Breaking things down into small steps can be helpful to depressed people who can struggle to think like this, that is planning steps to coping.

Scheduling activities — including positive ones

Some clients find it very difficult to carry out certain tasks because their ability to plan ahead has been affected by the depression. Scheduling activities can be taught in the counselling session and worked out in a collaborative way. You can write down the days of the week and then break each day down into morning, afternoon and evening (see Appendix). Then help people plan activities for each session of the day. Clients can learn to schedule in activities on an hourly basis through each day (e.g. 9 am get up and have breakfast; 10 am go to the shops and buy groceries for the week; 11 am phone a friend and visit, etc.). If people feel overwhelmed, then maybe a couple of straightforward tasks can be planned, for example even getting out of bed at a certain time and making something to eat. One client had enjoyed digging in his garden but had stopped doing this, so we planned five minutes increasing to ten minutes of digging a day. One client suffered from loneliness and therefore we scheduled that he should visit friends on as many evenings as possible. People can rate the degree of mastery and pleasure of these activities on (say) a 1–5 scale of low to high.

It is important to focus on the do-able and build from there. One might use the motto of 'challenging but not overwhelming'. Activity planning can be very helpful but, again, while some clients take to this easily and find it helpful, others do not. So work with the individual and do not 'force' techniques on clients because the books recommend them as options. It is useful to focus on these as *behavioural experiments* (Bennett-Levy, Butler, Fennell, Hackmann, Mueller and Westbrook, 2004).

Activities should also include things that the person may find rewarding. If the person schedules too many boring activities (e.g. doing housework because they feel they ought to), then although they may have a sense of achievement, this may not be enough to keep them going. Doing difficult or boring things can be matched by trying to schedule in more positive things. So one aspect is to try to increase the number of rewarding activities in the day – even if at first these are only minimally rewarding.

Changing what one does, how one does it and how one thinks about it

Helping people to become more engaged with their depression and trying to enact certain behaviours, even though they don't feel like doing so, can be very helpful for some people. However, there are some depressed people who are very good at acting despite what they feel. These individuals may have been trying to put a brave face on things and to keep going for years. The behavioural therapist should spend some time exploring this, otherwise people can get the idea that you are simply trying to 'push them back' into their old ways of coping – which is to keep going regardless. Sometimes one might say:

Your depression may be your brain telling you that you need time out. What we can explore is what works for you and what does not. Although doing more can be helpful, we need to think about 'more of what'. Rushing around to please others or live up to others' expectations may not be so helpful. Finding out what you genuinely want to do, what kinds of things help *you* feel a little better, what you enjoy and what you would like your life to have more of is what we are interested in. This might seem frightening at first so it is a step-by-step approach. It is working out what you feel would be helpful – rather than doing things because you feel you must or ought to but then feeling resentful or exhausted.

Time spent exploring the difference in just increasing activities because that seems sensible compared to being genuinely focused on self-healing can be time well spent. Indeed, clarifying this distinction (which may take a number of sessions) can itself help depressed people work out their own views and desires at a time that they feel lost about what they feel or want. In Chapter 11 we will note that we can focus on compassionate behaviour by helping people to choose and work with their activities with warmth and encouragement. This can also help with 'contentment'.

New role enactments and social skills

Some depressed clients have difficulties in certain interpersonal skills, for example assertiveness (Argyle, 1984; Arrindell, Sanderman, Van der Molen, Van der Ende and Mersch, 1988). In these cases instruction and behavioural practice may be helpful. One can give reading material (e.g. Dickson, 1982) or arrange to attend assertiveness training classes. Same-sex groups can be especially helpful. This can often be better than trying to do it all in individual therapy. In a group, the client will have an opportunity to practise with others, and share experiences. Here the counsellor is trying to enlarge the client's opportunities for new learning. However, skills sometimes do not generalise outside the counselling situation. Various negative thoughts may inhibit this. Hence some clients are skilled (know what to do) but are inhibited if anxiety has not been addressed.

Related to social skills is the identification of how a person would like to behave socially. This can be to act assertively or in a more caring way. In these situations one may talk about the role, the skills that are necessary and the blocks to their enactment. For example, a depressed man wanted to show more affection to his children but felt embarrassed to do so. He was worried about being seen as a sissy and his actions being misunderstood as sexual. Simple discussion of this issue and some normalisation, sharing of the fears and information on the role of physical touch, was helpful. In another case, a depressed woman wanted to show more affection to her children but often felt she did this out of shame rather than genuine concern. Also, after an argument she found it difficult to reconcile with them, without feeling she was giving in. However, she wanted to repair the relationships between them. So we talked about the shame, based on her thoughts that she 'was not good enough', and about the value of reconciling behaviours. I used examples from chimpanzees to show the importance of reconciliation. She thought that if she instigated reconciliation she was saying she was in the wrong and was admitting defeat. Via cognitive restructuring and behavioural training she was able to make changes.

Long- and short-term goals for change

Some clients may have difficulties at generating *steps to change* and may disqualify small steps (e.g. disqualifying the positive). It is also quite useful to check out the *fantasies* of getting/being better. Sometimes these can be quite unrealistic and over-idealised. The client may have a belief that one day they can be magically better and never be unhappy or frustrated again. The slow progress of getting better, and dealing with the frustration of two steps forward and one back, all need to be worked through.

Working with an individual, couples, families or groups

Although we are focusing mostly on individual work, the counsellor should also have skills in recognising the need for working with couples, families, and in groups (Beach and Jones, 2002). One simple question to ask is: Would you like to work on this problem with your partner/family? Then work out the advantages and disadvantages. Sometimes new interpersonal understandings and skills are more easily achieved in helping people work out their problems with others. So although there is not the space here to outline in any useful detail how to work with couples, families or groups, the counsellor should at all times consider the need for and value of these (Beach and Jones, 2002; Gotlib and Colby, 1987), and when to refer to others to do them. (For further discussion of these issues and others related to the social domains of depression, see Milne, 1999).

There are many therapies that use various elements of the behavioural approaches but blend them into other approaches, creating new generations of hybrid therapies. What they have in common is a focus on *actions* as part of the treatment approach. Some also recommend forms of exposure and acceptance to help work with conditioned emotions. Traditional cognitive behavioural approaches to depression (e.g. Beck et al., 1979) are also hybrid therapies and we will focus on the more cognitive aspects later in the book. The point here is to note that there are various ways of working with behavioural aspects of depression.

Dialectic Behaviour Therapy

Dialectic Behaviour Therapy (DBT) was originally designed for patients with borderline personality disorders (Linehan, 1993). It is a biosocial theory which gives due regard to the emotional dimensions of difficulties that are regulated in specific brain areas. Thus, it fits very well with the biopsychosocial view outlined in Chapter 1. I want to introduce it here because it has a number of elements which are very helpful for working with depressed people and it is increasingly being applied to a range of disorders other than borderline problems. Marra (2003) has written a very helpful workbook for depressed and anxious clients covering the basics of this approach for depression.

Like many other therapies today, it is a hybrid therapy that integrates various treatment modalities but targets them at specifically identified areas. Linehan suggests that while behaviour and cognitive therapy can be helpful, there is a tendency to focus on *changing* thoughts, behaviours and feelings rather than coming to terms with, accepting and tolerating them (see also Hayes, Follette and Linehan, 2004; Hayes, Wilson, Gifford, Follette and Strosahl, 1996). Hence, the dialectical aspect of DBT is the way that any process of change can involve a balancing of opposites such as approach-avoidance conflicts. Thus, there is often a conflict between the threats and fears of changing versus the threats and fears of not changing, and similarly for positive outcomes. It is holding the tension of opposing forces that can be key to the process of working through difficulties. Conflicts can exist in many domains, such as what we feel to be true or what we feel we wish to do versus what our logic and rational mind suggest. Conflict can also exist between different emotions and emotional systems (e.g. we can love and be angry with somebody at the same time), and of course conflicts can be associated with approach-avoidance and painful dilemmas (see pp. 65–66). This leads into what Linehan (1993) has called 'Wise Mind', which is the skilful blending of emotion and reason, within wider and contextualised frames of reference (see also Greenberg, 2002).

Like other behaviour therapies, exposure is a prominent aspect of the approach. Linehan (1993; Lynch, Chapman, Rosenthal, Kuo and Linehan, 2006) introduced a number of ideas from Buddhist and Zen philosophies on the value of developing *mindfulness*. Mindfulness, however, can be used in different ways. For example, it can be about developing attentiveness 'in-the-moment' to both the outside world and felt experience as it emerges in the mind (Hanh, 1991). An excellent self-help book focusing on mindfulness, that comes with a CD, is that of Brantley (2003) – it is well written and simple to follow, yet with detailed, mindful exercises. Although sometimes seen as a distraction technique, this is incorrect. Rather, it is to see how thoughts and emotions can cascade through us, but with focused attention we don't need to be pulled in and lost in them. We become aware of them and allow them to ebb and flow without (meta-cognitive) engagement. Sometimes this is related to cultivation of the observing mind, and noting that when we feel things, there is a part of self that *observes* our reactions. Attention to the 'observing mind' can help us to become mindful. Linehan (1993) acknowledges this aspect but in addition suggests that it can be used to be *more fully* in the experience. To become mindful is to notice all the textures of an experience and become more observant in the here and now (Lynch et al., 2006). Dysregulated emotion is often related to fear of engaging with emotion or feeling overwhelmed and using avoidance to cope. Thus, mindfulness is used to help tolerance, and also to begin to develop emotional regulation skills.

DBT also uses the *function analysis approach to behaviours* and what is called 'chain analysis'. Chain analysis is a way of looking at the steps in the lead-up to a difficult emotional change, or problematic behaviour, in very precise (micro) detail. It is to help the person to see how one behaviour, thought or emotion tends to trigger another. This can be written out like stepping stones. Depressed people can begin to discern where they could take different steps in a chain.

Acting against or in opposition to an emotion is another key behavioural component of DBT. Here the person notes their usual behaviour in certain emotional states or situations and works out how to work against those old styles. For example, when anxious I avoid, so this time I will try to tolerate the anxiety and engage rather than avoid. I feel overwhelmed and avoidant when thinking of writing this letter, so this time I will give myself (say) ten minutes to engage with the task I am avoiding. This is key to BA too. If one is trying to help the person gain new evidence, for example that we can, rather than cannot, do a task, or that things can turn out better than we hoped, this is called a behavioural experiment (Bennett-Levy et al., 2004).

The therapist also works on the processes of commitment to change and the processes that can interfere with therapeutic tasks. This involves a form of motivational interviewing where the advantages and disadvantages of actions are explored and time is given to the dilemmas of change. Hence, in general DBT teaches emotional tolerance and acceptance, has a dialectical focus, including a focus on dilemmas, works in a micro-analytic way with specific behavioural and emotional episodes (what, when, how), teaches engaged mindfulness, helps people to use reasoning skills in the service of richer emotional awareness and living, teaches various problem-solving and social skills, teaches how to work against unhelpful emotions and avoidance, and identifies therapy-enhancing and therapy-interfering behaviours. DBT also views the therapeutic relationship as extremely important because it provides the emotional context for working with difficult feelings. DBT therapists are encouraged to judiciously share personal experiences in order to form a shared bond and sense of common humanity with the person they are working with.

There is considerable evidence that this approach helps the patient groups for which it was designed, that is people with borderline and self-harming difficulties. However, it is an extremely comprehensive and well worked out therapy and recently has started to be applied to mood disorder (Marra, 2003). Therapists interested in DBT could usefully explore this approach with some profit. Compassionate mind-focused therapy, as discussed in Chapter 11, fits comfortably with DBT. However, it is far more focused on the neuroscience of soothing and the generation of self-soothing is one of its targets (see Chapter 11).

Cognitive-Behavioural Analysis System of Psychotherapy

A major sub-group of people with depression have chronic depression. Cognitive-Behavioural Analysis System of Psychotherapy (CBASP) was designed for this group of patients (McCullough, 2000). It integrates a number of different approaches (and regards itself as an integrative therapy) but is highly focused on changing behaviour, especially interpersonal behaviour. The key focus of this therapy is on coping behaviour, understanding the effects of a person's behaviour on others and developing better interpersonal relationships that are more conducive to well-being. It is highly structured and focuses on the experience of interpersonal relations (including those in the therapeutic relationship), micro-analysis of interpersonal relationship episodes and teaches communication and problem-solving skills. Depressed people learn how they can be caught up in repetitive interpersonal cycles which lead to adverse outcomes for themselves and others. Increased awareness of the steps in these cycles and how depressed people can identify them and begin to act differently at 'decision' points is key to the therapy. So this therapy focuses on the importance of social relationships as regulators of moods and that people who have difficulties in creating positive relationships with others are going to be cut off from a major source of soothing as well as generating a major source of threat.

Keller, McCullough, Klein et al. (2000) found that a combination of nefazodone and CBASP was highly effective for this group of patients, with a 73% response rate. This was higher than the 48% response rate in either drug or psychotherapy condition alone. This study was used in the NICE (2004) guideline. Klein et al. (2004) explored the value of CBASP as a maintenance psychotherapy and found that CBASP significantly reduced rate of relapse.

Interpersonal Psychotherapy

Another approach that focuses on very specific elements of the depressed person's problems, with guided work on those difficulties, is Interpersonal Psychotherapy (IPT), developed by Klerman, Weissman, Rounsaville and Chevon (1984). Once again this is a hybrid therapy, highly influenced by the American social psychiatrist Harry Stack Sullivan, who worked in the 1950s, and also attachment theory (see next chapter). IPT emphasises how to cope with being depressed, the role of (social) life events, the nature of significant relationships (mostly in the present, but also with some consideration of early relationships), grief, and the interpersonal behaviours a person uses to gain and maintain relationships and resolve conflicts (see also Markowitz, 2004; Markowitz and Weissman, 1995). This model proposes various specific triggers for depression: grief and loss, interpersonal role transitions, role conflicts and social skills deficits. The model outlines various therapeutic interventions for dealing with each source of difficulty. In many trials it is fairly equivalent to other focused therapies and is now an evidence-based treatment for depression (Markowitz, 2004; NICE, 2004).

The Five Areas Approach

Another example of a focused approach to depression was developed by Chris Williams (this is called the 'Five Areas Approach' (Williams, 2001)). It was designed to increase accessibility to cognitive behavioural approaches for mild and moderate depressions, avoid complex language such as 'dysfunctional assumptions' and 'selective abstraction' and to be used in busy out-patient clinics. It was also developed as part of an NHS commissioning process (Wright, Williams and Garland, 2002). The five areas are:

1   Current life difficulties, including relationship and practical problems.
2   Thinking difficulties, including concentration problems and the negative focus of thinking.
3   Mood and emotional regulation difficulties.
4   Depressive behaviour and changed activity.
5   Physical feelings and symptoms, such as sleep disturbance.

Clinician and client list these five areas and then explore the specific difficulties within each area. There is then an agreement on prioritising and developing targets for change. Short-term targets are those that can be enacted very quickly within the next days. Medium-term targets can be achieved over weeks and long-term targets might be six months or a year ahead. Targeting is designed for focused work and to approach one or two difficulties at a time. Each of these five areas do not have any special new therapy behind them but essentially pull on standard CBT practice but in a very practical and language-friendly way. This approach is now being explored in regard to guided self-help and further information can be found on the NHS website (www.livinglifetothefull.com).

Conclusion

Behaviour therapies focus very much on the outputs of people and on their interactions with the environment. Some focus *relatively* less on internal processes (BA) while others have extensive ways of working with thoughts and feelings (DBT). Many focus on social behaviour. Conscious and unconscious conflicts are important too in the theory but are different from those suggested by psychodynamic theorists (see Ferster, 1973). Behaviour therapies focus on micro and functional analysis. Not only do we need to know the purpose of a behaviour, but we need to understand its eliciting elements in detail. This is why behaviour therapists focus on very specific themes in the depressed patient's experience and behavioural styles.

As you can see, all of these therapies are what we call 'focused' therapies because they have a structure to them and bring specific 'techniques' to bear in working with specific difficulties. This is somewhat different from psychodynamic therapies. Currently, research is underway to see how specific versus non-specific therapies compare in the treatment of depression. We should be careful, of course, because people may improve for a variety of reasons that are not necessarily about the therapy techniques, or at least people can improve for reasons other than those that the therapists think they do.

Behavioural therapies can look straightforward, but looks can be deceptive. Skilful behavioural therapists blend their work in a very friendly and open way, encouraging and supporting patients on their journey into new ways of living. Indeed, it is often not only the understanding of the behavioural processes that are key but the interpersonal engagement which facilitates the depressed person to feel encouraged to try new things.

One can see how the behavioural approaches counteract many of the threat aspects we discussed in the last chapter. They will help people to regain control, identify positive life goals, address blocked escape and blocked anger responses, teach appropriate help-seeking and good emotional communication with others. Hence, people are less likely to feel trapped and blocked in their lives. In my view, it is because behavioural approaches can tone-down these protection strategies, and their arrested fight/flight profiles, that low mood is ameliorated.

Blending these ways of working into skilful counselling and therapy takes time and practice. Many of these basic interventions are not achieved in five minutes but can take hours of work and repetition. They offer powerful means by which we can engage a depressed person's self-experience and help them shift out of these states of mind. However, clients are not socially decontextualised and the environment can be a powerful recruiter of negative self-beliefs and behaviour (Milne, 1999).

5 Human Social Needs and Roles: Attachment, Social Connectedness and Defeat

Exploring the impacts of stress, loss of control and arrested and blocked defensive behaviours on physiological (e.g. stress), emotional (threat, drive and soothing) and behavioural (e.g. avoidance, passivity and withdrawal) systems can take us a long way to understanding the experience of depression and its psychobiological response patterns. However, humans are relationship-building animals and relationships have major effects on psychobiological states. Depression can arise when certain basic *human social needs* for affection, emotional support and sense of belonging are thwarted and blocked, or, as we saw in the last chapter, people are not able to generate these relationships. If it is loss of control over *social* resources (and the means to acquire them) that is key to depression, then this may help us understand the various relational themes that emerge in depression, such as feeling emotionally alone, struggling to have a sense of connectedness to others, feelings of inferiority, feeling a failure or a burden. Hence, this chapter will explore various *special* protective-defensive strategies, and patterns of psychobiological organisation, for coping with certain types of *social relationship* threat and loss.

The basic proposition in this chapter is that there are *two (or possibly three) different but overlapping defence strategies* for coping with different types of interpersonal threat. The threat of disconnection and loss of support from caring others is linked to threat in the care-seeking mentality and to a protest-despair defensive strategy (Bowlby, 1969, 1973, 1980) – marked by grief-like symptoms of sadness, crying, separation anxiety, yearning, and feeling alone. However, the social world can also be a threatening place where people actively reject, shame, bully, humiliate, are aggressive and harmful. When people have more malevolent and/or fear aspects to social relationships (and interpersonal memories) this is more likely to recruit the competitive mentality (focused on the relative power of others). The defensive strategies for coping with powerful and harmful others *that one cannot get away from* activate different defensive patterns of 'shut down' with intense submissive behaviour. At times the experience of hostility (one cannot get away from) is carried in *self-criticism* and people can feel beaten down by their own self-criticisms (see Chapter 6).

Competitive defeats can also arise when people have built their goals around the competitive mentality of gaining competitive advantage, striving to avoid inferiority and impress others. They often have a sense of personal defeat and failure if defeated in life goals. There is evidence that these different types of threat (social losses versus achievement failures) are linked to overlapping but also different types of depressive symptoms, with competitive defeats involving more anhedonia, shame and pessimism than social losses alone (Keller and Nesse, 2005, 2006). As we will note below, however, many studies do not clearly distinguish *'other as absent'* versus *'other as threat'*. Moreover, these strategies for self-protection (protest-despair and defeat, low rank) often merge into each other. This is partly because both defensive strategies are organised through the same three emotion and motive systems outlined in Chapter 2, and because many vulnerabilities are linked to early experiences of both a lack of soothing attachments, and threat and harms from others in attachment relationships. Thus these defences interact.

Attachment and the care-seeking mentality

As we saw in Chapter 2 the contentment and soothing positive emotion systems have evolved to be intimately linked to social signals of affiliation. How might this have happened? Consider that many life forms have very high mortality early in their lives. Even on such a life-conducive planet as ours, the struggle for life is so fierce and risky that the vast majority of species that have ever existed (over 99% of them) are now extinct. Predation, diseases, starvation and changes in a species' ecology are responsible. However, there are various basic solutions (strategies) to some of these threats. One is mass production. For example, sea turtles will lay hundreds of eggs and then leave them to it. Assuming the nest has not been discovered and they not are eaten before they hatch, they emerge from the eggs and dash to the ocean as fast as they can, but the predators from the air, land and sea are waiting. In fact only about 1–2% make it to adulthood to keep the species going. All over the world, for the species that lay quantities of eggs, the genes of these species (information for building their hosts) survive simply because of the numbers of their hosts.

There is, however, another solution to this problem. Produce fewer offspring, but (a) don't harm (eat) them, and (b) offer them some protection in early life. Even a small amount of care provided either pre-birth (e.g. making nests out of harm's way) or post-birth (nest guarding) offers big advantages. The more a species protects its young from the threats to life, by defending them against predators, the more it creates *safeness*. Mammalian milk also contains powerful anti-bodies to help the infant fight infections. In this social context what evolves are brain systems for 'seeking closeness' to the parent and looking to them to provide resources (Bowlby, 1969; Geary, 2000). Over time these evolve into increasingly elaborate care-eliciting and care-giving strategies. The *care-eliciting and seeking mentality* (see pp. 35–36) is constituted with the appropriate, specialised mental abilities to be motivated to seek care, recognise a need for care, signal distress in its absence and be responsive to its presence (Gilbert, 1989, 2005a). Indeed, by the time we get to humans, our infants are the most helpless and the most dependent on others for survival. Moreover, the mother–infant relationship becomes the major way the emotional and physiological states/patterns of the infant are regulated. In particular, the mother acts as a soothing agent/stimulus for the infant, calming the baby when distressed. Even the way our brains mature and the way they are organised become highly influenced in the infant–parent interaction (Gerhardt, 2004; Schore, 1994; Siegel, 2001).

This is the basis of attachment theory, developed by John Bowlby (1969, 1973, 1980). He suggested that humans, like many other mammals, have innate seeking systems that are attentive to certain cues of protection from others. Moreover, because these cues are associated with safeness, they regulate 'stress systems' and enable us to feel safe and connected to others (Gilbert, 1989, 2005a; Wang, 2005). So important is access to a protective agent that loss of access to them (usually the mother) is recognised by the brain as a major threat. In social mentality theory the focus is on the attributes of the care-seeking systems and attachment is an outcome (Gilbert, 1989). When we are in loving interactions, the care-eliciting/seeking mentality is functioning to be sensitive to these signals and patterning appropriate brain states – that is pleasure, happiness, exploration, soothing and well-being via the relationship. As Bowlby made plain, certain stimuli and cues will turn on the *threat focus* of care-seeking mentality, certain stimuli will turn off the threat focus and there are certain innate defences that are activated when the care-seeking mentality cannot find the signals it seeks to reduce threat.

Protest-despair strategies

Exploring how we have evolved to respond to lost attachments (care providing others) will help us to understand *the experience* of some depressions. Humans, like other mammals, need others to care for them as infants and children. For many mammals, including humans, for most of our evolution, separation from mother put juveniles at risk from a variety of dangers. While the mother is present, she signals safeness and access to a source of support. She also provides food and comfort and will help the infant calm down if anxious and upset. So she regulates her infant's threat-stress system with soothing and care because the infant cannot do this for itself. In fact we now know that these interactions impact on a wide variety of physiological systems and affect their maturation (Hofer, 1994).

In her absence the world becomes threatening and the child shows a *protest-despair* reaction, which is part of a *normal* evolved protection strategy. Protest involves distress, anxiety, crying and seeking to connect again with mother. It is designed to engage in urgent searching and to *signal/communicate* distress (e.g. distress calling and crying) to elicit help, protection, and support via reunion to a caring other; that is, the signal is designed to impact on others. This may be called *yearning*. This protection 'protest' strategy can be turned off when soothing cues arrive (Bowlby, 1969).

Things may not turn out so well, however. Suppose the efforts of protest do not result in the return of the mother or the input of soothing signals from her. This is potentially very dangerous. For most mammals, a distressed/searching young individual on its own is in danger of attracting predators, getting lost and/or exhausted and starving. In such contexts, sitting tight and waiting for the parent to return may be the best protection strategy for survival. Despair is a form of behavioural deactivation when protest does not work. Drive and seeking systems are toned down because this aspect of the protection strategy is designed to *stop signalling and moving* about in the environment (to hunker down) when not to do so is dangerous (Allen and Badcock, 2003; Bowlby, 1969, 1973; Gilbert, 1984, 1989). So protest can involve anxious drive and seeking behaviour whereas despair closes those behavioural systems down. Studies of the physiological effects of separation have indicated significant overlaps with the physiological changes in depression (Hofer, 1994; Panskepp, 2005; Reite and Field, 1985).

There is an important aspect of this which can be easily missed. In some contexts our own behaviour can be a threat and safety behaviours are to stop us doing things. If you wander around in lion country, without a care in the world, you could have problems. So anxiety stops us from doing this. Pain alerts us to injury and enables us to protect the damaged area. Demobilisation and despair can be looked at like this. They are internal behavioural controls to stop us engaging within threat-filled environments. And because it is a safety-protection strategy, it too, like anxiety (LeDoux, 1998), can be triggered in fast-emotional brain systems and/or via slower cognitive routes. Moreover, it is quite possible for both protest patterns and despair patterns to be subject to conditioning. So we should not think that only responses like salivation, or emotions like anxiety or anger, are subject to conditioning and fast activation. Basically, any protection psychobiological response pattern that has innate ways to organise our minds can be similarly conditioned. Thus pathways into some depressed patterns can become highly sensitised (Monroe and Harkness, 2005; Perry, Pollard, Blakley, Baker and Vigilante, 1995). If you have been following the arguments put forward so far, about the power of conditioning and the sensitisations of brain pathways (Chapters 2 and 4), and the importance of accessibility of interpersonal schema for coping with stress (Chapter 3), then you will see how depression can link to various forms of spreading activation when the individual is confronted by certain cues. Basically, some people have a very 'easy' triggering of protest-despair strategies that organise brain states.

So protest-despair are *protection strategies* that are wired into our brains and can get switched on under certain conditions. The ease of activation of these strategies, their intensity and ease of being turned off are linked to genetic differences and learning (Caspi and Moffitt, 2006; Suomi, 1999). Thus some people can slip into despair psychobiological patterns far easier and more intensely than others. When activated in a self-aware species like ourselves, protest-despair 'brain states' can fuel feelings of being cut off from others – disconnected, alone and vulnerable. Sometimes depressed people express this as feeling there is a barrier between themselves and others; they feel totally disconnected from the social world, as if in a dream. Such a feeling might indicate problems in a particular type of social positive affect system, such as the affiliative-soothing system. They may ruminate on these feelings, try to work out why they feel like this, self-blame, feel more inferior, become convinced that others do not care about them or would wish to exclude them, and thus feel more disconnected. The reason they 'feel' so bad, can't sleep, lose interest in food or sex, and so forth is because the brain has switched into a specific defensive psychobiological response pattern. You do not feel bad (only) because of your thoughts. Had evolution not plumbed this kind of defensive psychobiological response pattern into us, then we would not feel it. Your thoughts might trigger, accentuate or maintain this 'hunkering down' protection strategy, but such strategies, with their patterns of motivations, emotions and behaviours, are part of evolved brain design. Moreover, they can generate painful *archetypal* feelings that one's very life is in danger and that one is beyond help or rescue – out of reach, completely lost. Helping depressed people think that these are frightening but also innate and archetypal (and maybe linked to early memories) can help depressed people understand their depression in new ways.

Social connectedness

Protection and support from others matter greatly throughout life and not just in intimate relationships. Another reason relationships matter is that many primates, and especially humans, are very dependent on others for their survival. Over millions of years those not well accepted and integrated into their groups fared poorly. Helping others who are in distress or incapacitated is part of our primate evolution. For example, consoling behaviour has been observed in non-human primates (de Waal, 1996). Archaeological finds of Neanderthals and early humans have found evidence that people with deformities and badly broken bones survived – something that was unlikely unless others cared for them (Mithen, 1996). At one time in our evolution we might have been as low as several hundred humans in the world and we only made it into the species we are because we helped each other, cared for each other and shared information. So humans have innate needs to belong, feel connected, to be valued by others and participate in sharing relationships (Baumeister and Leary, 1995; Gilbert, 1992, 2005a). The social mentality involved here is less focused on intimate care and more on the abilities to co-operate with others. Thus the *co-operative mentality* provides the appropriate psychological systems for recognition of, and sensitivity to, signals that others accept and value us, and they will build co-operative, sharing and mutually supportive relationships with us (Gilbert, 1989, 2005a, 2005b). Studies on social connectedness suggest three factors related to: isolation, relational connectedness and collective connectedness (Cacioppo, Hawkley, Rickett and Masi, 2005). People who score low for social connectedness are more lonely, have higher depression scores, are physiologically more stressed, and more orientated to making threat interpretations (Cacioppo et al., 2005). To feel isolated, not valued or wanted is a major threat, picked up by the co-operative mentality, and our brains can respond to this by activating stress systems and protection strategies (Allen and Badcock, 2003; Gilbert, 2001a, 2001b). Indeed, MacDonald and Leary (2005) and Panskepp (2005) have given a fascinating account of how social losses, exclusions and rejections can work through brain mechanisms that overlap those of pain.

Not only do people spend much of their time thinking about other people's feelings towards them and have special cognitive systems for thinking about what others are thinking (called theory of mind, see Chapter 6), but many of our goals are orientated towards trying to earn other people's approval and respect, and be accepted in groups. If you think about how you would like your lovers, close friends, counselling peers, patients and bosses to see you, it will mainly be to value you and see you as desirable, helpful, talented and able. If you can create these feelings in the mind of others, then three things happen. First, the world *is safe* and you can know they will not attack or reject you because they value you. Secondly, you will be able to co-create meaningful roles for mutual support, sexual relationships and sharing. Thirdly, receiving signals from others as valuing and caring of you has direct effects on your physiology and soothing system (Cacioppo et al., 2000, 2005; Gilbert, 2005a, 2005b; Wang, 2005). One reason for this is that these signals affect the affiliative, social co-operative system which has soothing effects (Depue and Morrone-Strupinsky, 2005). To be seen as undesirable, unhelpful, untalented and unable, risks loss of all those benefits and is a major threat. There is now very good evidence that critical relationships, where people or children are labelled negatively, greatly elevates the risk of depression, even if the verbal labels carry no direct physical threat (Teicher, Samson, Polcari and McGreenery, 2006; Wearden, Tarrier, Barrowclough, Zastowny and Rahil, 2000). Also, *to believe* that we are seen in this way can be as bad as actually being seen that way, and to become self-critical is also highly linked to depression (Gilbert and Irons, 2005). So important are our social needs to feel safe, accepted and valued by others that people will even risk their own lives and serious injury in order to avoid shame and exclusion. As we will see in the next chapter, this is why shame (related to feeling unattractive to others and looked down on) can be a major (threat) issue in some depressions. Basically, criticism and shame activate threat systems and cut us off from sources of soothing and affect regulation.

If we now think about the 'depression experience', be it in intimate or friend-ship types of relating, many depressed people have a sense disconnection from others and can feel emotionally alone. There can be many external reasons for this, such as social isolation, for example in asylum seekers who have lost or been cut off from their families and social networks, or those living in neglectful or abusive relationships. Brown and Harris (1978) have shown that the lack of someone to talk to about feelings and problems is a major vulnerability factor for depression in women. In fact, social losses and lack of emotional support have long been linked to depression (Brugha, 1995). Not only do signals of social affiliation affect our feelings of well-being, but they have very direct effects on stress systems. Recall that oxytocin-opiate activity, linked to social support, regulates the stress HPA systems (Heinrichs, Baumgartner, Kirschbaum and Ehlert, 2003). These signals can operate outside conscious cognitive systems and can affect our emotional states. A friend whose husband had gone away for a few days had an aggressive interaction with a neighbour and felt very distressed about it. She was not able to sleep and felt very anxious and tearful, with desires to sell up and leave. She tried to use some of her 'cognitive' techniques to calm down and this helped. However, once her husband came home and she spoke with him and shared her distress she felt considerably better. She was amazed how quickly his presence calmed her. My reflection to her was that his presence and support acted directly on her (emotion) soothing systems.

This, of course, suggests key therapeutic efforts (see Chapters 7 and 11). First, one needs to validate and empathically understand these feelings of disconnection and aloneness, and see them as linked to our human nature and need to feel connected, valued and cared about by others (Leahy, 2005). With listening and empathic skills, the counsellor can bridge into this feeling of isolation – the feeling that that there is no one who can help them. This often shows up in fantasies of fear. For example, a depressed doctor told of his fear of making a mistake or missing something and then being taken to court. When he imagined this he was always facing the 'prosecution' alone and could not imagine any strong allies coming to his aid. These feelings of being left alone to cope with punishing others, who would not 'take his side', may be echoes of earlier memories because when children are punished or abused by a parent they *are* often 'alone'. Siblings or another parent may be too frightened themselves to come to their aid. So, early traumatic memories of rejection and/or abuse are often coded with feelings *of facing it alone* with no help or rescue. Clearly, therefore, it can be important to explore these with some depressed people if, when they feel threatened, they feel

'I am alone with this – there is no one who can help me'. Experiencing a therapist as highly orientated to help them can offer a powerful, helpful, emotional experience that can be coded as alternative memories and beliefs (Brewin, 2006).

Emotional memories

Emotional memories can be viewed through this way of thinking and link to the work of Baldwin and others that we explored in Chapter 2. For example, if we grow up in a rejecting and abusive home, then we will have heightened emotional memories of threat. These may become linked to a basic orientation to the world where our threat systems and protective, psychobiological response patterns are easily activated (Perry et al., 1995) and we can suffer intrusive, aversive memories (Brewin, 2006). Alternatively, we can dissociate from trauma, not be able to recall details of abusive events but can experience a reactivation of powerful protection strategies in the presence of certain cues (Reinders, Nijenhuis, Paans, Korf, Willemsen and den Boer, 2003). The point then is that, be they consciously available to us or not, our threat system can be loaded with aversive memories and conditioned (protective) responses. In contrast, if we grow up in a world where others love and care for us and are rarely threatening, then we will have had many experiences (and emotional memories) of being soothed and feeling content and connected to others. So our soothing systems will have many emotional memories (and rehearsed psychobiological response patterns) to call on when stressed. In essence, our soothing systems are more robust and able to regulate drive-seeking and threat systems. We grow up knowing that not every setback or bump in the road is a major threat. If we grow up feeling that others will turn against us, are unreliable, or that only if we achieve, assert dominance or prove ourselves 'worthy' to others can we defend against the threat of rejection or criticism, or can earn a safe place among our peers, then things are rather different. It is not easy to feel accepted, connected and safe 'as one is' – in part perhaps because we do not have many accessible emotional memories of such (Baldwin, 2005; Brewin, 2006).

Therapists from different schools and approaches have begun to utilise concepts from attachment theory to help formulate client problems (Guidano and Liotti, 1983; Holmes, 2001; Liotti, 2007; Safran and Segal, 1990). There is a large body of evidence that early relationships with parental figures, siblings and friends result in the development of *internal working models* of relationships (Bowlby, 1969, 1973, 1980; Gilbert, 1984, 1992, 2004; Guidano and Liotti, 1983; McCann, Sakheim and Abrahamson, 1988; Mikulincer and Shaver, 2004, 2005) or *relational schema* (Baldwin, 1992, 2005; Safran, 1998; Safran and Segal, 1990). Internal working models or relational schema are sets and patterns of basic ideas, beliefs, memories and expectations about the self and about others, and typical styles of interaction that are linked together through emotions. These internal working models can provide resilience if they are reasonably positive about self and others (Masten, 2001). However, if people have beliefs and emotional memories of others as being neglectful, absent and abusive, and self as being criticised and inadequate (shamed), then they carry vulnerability because they can be *reactivated* in times of stress.

At risk of repetition, the take-home story from this work seems to be that people's automatic responses (which can follow 'if-then' rules), *including their self-evaluations and feelings* to setbacks and failures, are significantly influenced by the accessibility they have to memories and schema of how helpful or rejecting other people are or have been (Baldwin and Dandeneau, 2005). Hence, we are beginning to build a picture of the kinds of protection strategies that are activated in depression and the routes (e.g. 'if-then' rules) that can play consciously and non-consciously in people's minds. This research simply suggests that the way we think and feel about ourselves, and the ease of activation and strength of our protest-despair strategies to setbacks and failures, are influenced by the conscious *and* non-conscious representations of how helpful, caring or rejecting or hostile others are. It is by no means the only influence, of course, but an important one. These internal representations are powerful regulators of the ease of activation, intensity and duration of protest-despair strategies.

Warmth is different from protection

Warmth involves a number of qualities such as tenderness, gentleness, kindness and concern. It is conveyed in various communication channels, such as facial expressions, holding, touching and voice tones. While Bowlby focused on attachment via accessibility and availability of parental figures, Rohner (1986, 2004) directed attention to the warmth dimension of parent–child interactions (Gilbert, 1989, 2005a). MacDonald (1992) also distinguished a protection-based attachment system from a warmth and affectionate one. He suggests that:

> While attachment as a mechanism for protection from danger is virtually a pan-mammalian system, close intimate relationships characterized by warmth are not. The only plausible explanation for the existence of the human affectional system is that it evolved as a mechanism for underlying close family relationships, parental investment and mate choice. (MacDonald, 1992, p. 757)

Field (2000) has reviewed the growing body of evidence on the beneficial effects of holding, stroking and touching during development. As Sapolsky (1994, p. 92) observed:

> Touch is one of the central experiences of an infant, whether rodent, primate, or human. We readily think of stressors as consisting of various unpleasant things that can be done to an organism. Sometimes a stressor can be the *failure* to provide something to an organism, and the absence of touch is seemingly one of the most marked of developmental stressors that we can suffer.

Studies of rats, monkeys and humans have shown that they grow up considerably calmer if they are regularly handled or stroked (Field, 2000). This is not just about offering protection but is stimulating soothing systems. Although Bowlby (1973) was well aware of the soothing functions of parenting, distinguishing between these two (protection and warmth) systems allows insight into why one can have attachment in the absence of warmth or affection, and provide affectionate care for others (e.g. care of the dying) in the absence of (a desire for) attachment. Dominant animals and humans may be able to protect their infants from dangers and threats in a way that subordinates cannot, but this does not mean they provide more warmth. People may form attachments based on submission or appeasement to 'not very warm others', if they seem the best bet for protection. People can form attachments and even feel devoted to people who are actually very cold and potentially harmful (e.g. Hitler). This is attachment via protection where the attachment behaviours function to stop the dominant turning against them, and also the dominant offers some protection from external threats. Many leaders have found that if you raise people's fears and then offer yourself as a rescuer or protector, people may follow you. Indeed, anxiously attached people use appeasement as an attachment/security device (Sloman, 2000). Choosing partners because they appear strong or capable of being protective can backfire if these people turn out to be abusive. One of my clients freely admitted that she was attracted to her partner precisely because he was jealous and she knew he would not let any one 'mess with her'. It was only later, as she became more self-confident, wanted to find a job and make new friends that his jealousy became a problem.

If warmth is a special dimension of attachment and social connectedness, that can stimulate the soothing system and give different feelings of safeness (Rohner, 2004), then what do we mean by 'warmth'? We can suggest that warmth has at least three key attributes. First, warmth provides signals of care and investment that are *soothing* and switches on the recipient's 'safeness' internal organisation (Gilbert, 1993). The signals are expressed in voice tones and facial expressions and various care-focused and concerned behaviours. Second, warmth can involve a sharing of positive affect between individuals that stimulates *liking*, affection and feelings of connectedness. Third, warmth is more likely when individuals feel safe with each other. Individuals who are easily threatened and become defensive may struggle to feel or express warmth (see Gilbert, 2005a for a more detailed discussion).

The key point, then, is that warmth/soothing and protecting are different aspects of social behaviour that can 'pull' on attachment systems in different ways and regulate positive affect and threat systems in different ways. Ideally, they operate together, especially in intimate relationships. Not only are our parents, partners and friends warm, but we can rely on them coming to our aid if we need them. The problem is that protection without warmth, or warmth without protection can cause difficulties. This may raise serious issues in how we relate to our children. For example, the fear of being accused of sexual abuse means that teachers are not supposed 'to touch' children; they have to use sun cream sprays rather than rub-on creams, and holding or cuddling distressed children can be problematic. In our increasingly threat-focused and competitive world, are we losing sight of human needs? The data on touch (and lack of it) should raise our concerns (Field, 2000).

The early years: why they matter

It is sometimes said that cognitive and behavioural therapies are not concerned with the past. This is an over-generalisation and much depends on the case or specific theory – as we will explore later. It is true that for many psychological problems detailed work with past memories is neither necessary nor sufficient for change, and that working with people's *current* beliefs, experiences, coping behaviours and states of mind is central. But what has gone before affects what comes after and in some cases attention to the past may be *vital*, especially since some depressed people can suffer from intrusive aversive memories (Brewin, 2006; Reynolds and Brewin, 1999). Indeed, at times opportunities to re-evaluate the meaning of past events, and grieve past losses and traumas, may be crucial for change to occur. One of the reasons for this is that appropriate grieving and working with trauma can alter certain processing systems and affect brain organisation (Cozolino, 2002). Also helping people recognise the origins of their depression-related thoughts, beliefs, feelings and ways of coping can be very useful in helping people change and grow.

Many therapists, including cognitive therapists (Beck, 1967) have long suggested that negative styles of thinking, beliefs and feelings (e.g. I am unlovable; I am a failure) arise from early experiences with parents, peers and others. Early acquired negative beliefs may not be observable when a person is well. They may be latent but can be reactivated by life events or stress states. Over recent years there has been development of these ideas and an effort to gain a clearer understanding of how our early relationships shape adult styles of relating, beliefs and 'if-then' rules, and how we face life difficulties (Masten, 2001; Mikulincer and Shaver, 2004, 2005; Safran, 1998). A key finding is that latent beliefs and 'if-then' rules (which cognitive therapists call assumptions) can be emergent from learning experiences that actually shape the way our brains have become organised (i.e. our phenotypes). This is because we now know that early experiences can have a profound effect on the way our brains, potential brain states and psychological abilities mature (Gerhardt, 2004; Schore, 1994; Siegel, 2001; Teicher, 2002).

Increasingly, psychotherapists are understanding how our responses to situations are linked to complex psychobiological patterns that are constantly being created and re-created in our minds. These patterns emerge with the interaction between genes, life experiences and learning. From the first days of life (and even in the womb) our physical development is influenced by the mother's mental state and hormone profiles. When we are born we are acutely sensitive to social stimuli. Even babies of a few hours old can respond to the mother's voice and touch. The mental state and motives of a mother (what is going on in her mind) is translated into a range of behaviours, such as how she talks/sings, looks at, strokes, touches and holds her infant, and her ability to empathically reflect and resonate with her infant's feelings and mental states. The process by which the mind of the mother is able to influence the mind of the infant, through a process of empathic resonance, is called intersubjectivity (Trevarthen and Aitken, 2001) – that is intersubjectivity is related to the moment-by-moment co-regulation of participants as they experience the feelings of others directed at them. Co-regulating interactions, related to empathic communications, can also occur in psychotherapy (Stern, 2004).

The co-regulating 'dances' of mother and infant have important effects on the infant's mind/brain, helping to choreograph the infant's brain maturation as it forms new neuronal connections at a rate of many tens of thousand a day (Gerhardt, 2004; Schore, 1994; Siegel, 2001). The mother is literally affecting *patterns of neuronal connections*. Especially important is how early caring experiences stimulate various cortical areas (e.g. in the right hemisphere and prefrontal cortex). These systems are important for emotion regulation, forming internal representations of self and others, and influence the ease of activation (and soothing) of protection strategies. Later, the way others, as socialising agents (especially the primary carer), understand and empathise with the child's emotions and behaviours, has major impacts on the child's ability to understand and regulate their own emotions, behaviours and personal characteristics, and link these to self-processing and self-defining systems (Schore, 1994). So abused/rejected children, in contrast to loved and stimulated children, develop different psychobiological infrastructures in their brains, out of which emerge different patterns of organisation.

People can be vulnerable to accessing more intense protest-despair psychological response patterns because they have been sensitised to experiences of separation, rejection or bullying early in life (Perry et al., 1995). Even if you carry genetic sensitivities to depression, good quality early care can go a long way to developing brain organisations that reduce the risk of depression (Caspi and Moffitt, 2006; Caspi et al., 2003). Suomi (1999) crossed fostered infant monkeys with this genetic vulnerability to high-caring, responsive mothers. They found that their outcomes were positive, with some genetically vulnerable infants growing to become very sociable and often gaining high rank via affiliations (Suomi, personal communication). Taylor, Way, Welch, Hilmert, Lehman and Eisenberger (2006) have shown that early care interacts with genetic sensitivity to depression. Early care may affect how genes are expressed. Early care significantly reduces risk of depression via changing phenotypic profiles.

Good parenting has usually meant that one's feelings were validated and so one is more likely to understand them and not feel ashamed or conflicted over them (Leahy, 2001, 2002, 2005). Being validated, listened to and heard is *key to feeling safe and soothed*. However, if you have had a number of experiences of separation and rejection, or your parents were not able to be available to you, or could not stimulate the positive affect systems of soothing, then you are more likely to develop neurophysiological patterns that underpin an *insecure attachment*, with expectations that others will reject you and you will be alone, or your feelings seem confusing, wrong or bad. As we get depressed these psychobiological response patterns, with their emotional memories, can edge their way back into our minds (Brewin, 2006). Once again, in discussing this with clients we stress this is 'not their fault'. As we will see later, some people have spent a lifetime trying to keep these painful feelings and brain states, associated with feeling alone, rejection or being bullied (experienced in childhood), at bay. Unfortunately, those very coping efforts (safety behaviours), such as always trying to please others, being submissive, hiding one's anger or seeking high achievement to prove one's value to others, can increase the risk of dropping into depression if they don't work – we fail and then are back to feeling rejectable and defeated. People can cope better with failures if they have access to schema of others as warm and supportive (Baldwin and Dandeneau, 2005; Kumashiro and Sedikides, 2005). The way neurophysiological patterns are created and re-created in you will thus depend on how your brain has matured and the kinds of information (e.g. schemas, 'if-then' rules and memories) it contains.

The themes of our story so far are that early life experiences affect gene expression and the psychobiological infrastructures of our brains, out of which emerge dispositions for different types of social engagement and affect regulation, which in turn create and re-create psychobiological response patterns. Contained within the patterns are memories, if-then rules and schema of self and others. These help code the world as safe or threatening and regulate the innate protection strategies (protest-despair, defeat, helplessness) that can take us into the deep feelings of depression – represented as heightened negative emotions and toned-down positive ones. Thus, as noted over twenty years ago, depression is a brain state with various psychobiological response patterns (Gilbert, 1984, 1992). Psychotherapy is a way of entering and altering these patterns with depressed people (Cozolino, 2002; Linden, 2006).

Styles of parenting

Kessler and Magee (1993), in a large epidemiological study, found that childhood adversities are related to both onset and recurrent episodes of depression. In a follow-up study of 121 student women, Hammen, Henry and Daley (2000) found that women with a history of childhood adversity needed less stress to trigger depression than those without childhood adversity. There is now much evidence that early stress affects sensitivities in stress systems (Teicher, 2002). Goodman (2002) has given a helpful overview of the link between certain styles of threat-related early rearing and various vulnerabilities to depression. Lack of any kind of parenting, as in studies of Romanian children in orphanages, has shown just how detrimental these experiences are. Although early adoption may help with cognitive deficits, it is unclear the degree to which emotional vulnerabilities are offset. As noted by Goodman (2002), and earlier editions of this book, many different parental rearing styles and their links to psychopathology have been studied over the last thirty years – far too many to be concisely reviewed here. Thus I will just pick out some common ones that reoccur in working with depressed people. One often needs a handle on these details to conduct a full assessment and build this into a comprehensive formulation.

The absent other
As noted above, we need to distinguish problems associated with the absent other; that is where the parent does not act a soothing agent, from those of threat where the parent or others inflict harm leading to fear of the other.

Parental unavailability   These individuals may have experienced parental separation and abandonment. Sometimes this is through parental illness, death or divorce. This theme can also be a major issue in those who were adopted, fostered or were in care as children (Verrier, 1997). For such people the search for (and conflicts about searching for) the biological parent(s) can be intense and it can be useful to link them up with various adoption agencies and support groups who can discuss and help them in their search. Parental unavailability can arise from work pressures on parents, and children struggle for attention from parents who are tired and stressed. Many parents have noted that when they can give their children good quality time and engage with their play and shared tasks, minor emotional or behavioural problems settle down. The degree to which television and computer games can be a substitute for shared play and tasks is a concern.

Parental inaccessibility   Parents may have been physically present but not able to act as a care provider or give emotional support. They may have been unable to help their child learn about their feelings, validate them and feel secure with them (Leahy, 2001, 2005). Koren-Karie, Oppenheim, Dolev, Sher and Etzion-Carasso (2002) explored three types of maternal interaction: positively insightful, one-sided, and disengaged. Positively insightful mothers tried to see their child's experiences through the *child's eyes*, and accounted for them being a child. The mother makes an effort to understand the *child's* feeling and motives, and explore them (i.e. they have 'concerned empathy'). The one-sided mother is keen to care for her child but has preset ideas of what a child needs and a 'undimensional' view of the child. The researchers think this could lead to inconsistent care. These mothers impose care rather than empathically work out feelings with the child. Disengaged mothers are characterised by lack of emotional involvement. Even thinking about what might be going on in their child's mind was novel to them and not something they found pleasant. The researchers think that these disengaged mothers would have avoidant children. As one might expect, the positively insightful mothers had the most secure children. Koren-Karie et al. (2002) have shown that the way a mother is able to empathically attune to her infant has a major impact on the maturation of her infant. Some depressed people describe their parents as cold, distant, disinterested or neglectful. Despite having made repeated efforts to form emotional links with the parent they have not been able to (Bowlby, 1980).

Needy parents   Some people have children so that there is someone around who will love them. They use their children to boost their inner sense of lovability or to give them a purpose in life. They can put great pressure on the child to act in this way for them. A dependent parent may try to turn their child into a carer, using shaming or guilt along the way.

Anxious parents   Some parents are extremely anxious of their own safety and those of their children. Rather than being a source for soothing and calming for the child, they are more likely to alarm the child. Some of these children can go on to become easily alarmed themselves, especially by minor difficulties such as physical illness, where they are prone to ruminate on possible dangers to the self.

Depressed parents   There is now evidence that depressed parents (like other parenting styles) can have detrimental impacts on their infant's development. This is partly because the infant's brain is innately attuned to the voice and face of the mother. If the mother is unable to interact with her child in ways that convey soothing and affection, this leads to problems in the development of certain positive affect systems in the child and emotional delays (Gerhardt, 2004). The child can grow up in a rather joyless, gloomy and unpredictable world.

Key to some of these experiences (and noted in other parental styles) are recall of a lack of physical affection in the forms of kisses, cuddles and hugs. Recall that the physical behaviours of affection, often associated with warm, affectionate facial expressions and non-verbal communications, are major stimulators of the soothing and affiliative positive affect system (Carter, 1998; Wang, 2005). Some depressed people have a yearning to be hugged and 'wrapped up and enfolded, and protected'. These feelings can at times feel overwhelming and activate intense sadness and grief-like feelings that are difficult to process and can generate feelings of shame.

From these life histories the underlying experience can be that others are not there for them; they can have emotional memories of being alone and feeling isolated from others, and their feelings are confusing and potentially overwhelming to them. These themes can also be present when the focus is on actual threat from the parent.

The other as threat

Abuse and bullying   There is increasing concern and research on the impacts on children who witness domestic violence and emotional abuse. These create very threatening and unsafe environments and model unhelpful ways of dealing with conflicts. We should also be mindful of the possibilities of severe early neglect and abuse, both physical and sexual, in those presenting with complex depressions. Some children are even threatened to be killed by their parent. An excellent review of the research in this area can be found in Bifulco and Moran's readable and disturbing book, *Wednesday's Child* (1998). Their data make clear that abuse undermines people's ability to cope with stress and increases vulnerability to depression. All forms of physical, sexual and emotional abuse can be highly damaging to our psychobiological maturation, development of basic trust and capacity to form intimate relationships (Gerhardt, 2004; Teicher, 2002). These early traumas also affect the maturation of the stress and emotional regulation system. Andrews (1998) reviews how abuse increases proneness to various forms of shame and chronic depression. It is important that counsellors not familiar with working with abuse cases should seek advice, supervision and possibly pass the client to someone experienced in this area of work. The therapeutic skills needed will often exceed those outlined in this book.

In a recent major study, Teicher et al. (2006) explored the pathogenic impacts of verbal, physical and sexual abuse. Although considerable attention has been given to sexual and physical abuse, these researchers found that verbal abuse (being shouted at and called names in hostile emotional tones) was highly linked to subsequent depression and anxiety. Verbal abuse not only makes the other highly threatening, but also has a major impact on the sense of self and shame-proneness (see Chapter 6). People from these backgrounds can be vulnerable to depression and other disorders in a number of ways. First, because these experiences are traumatic, some depressed people can have dissociated trauma memories. These would easily activate certain types of defence (e.g. suddenly feeling frightened with loss of positive emotional tone) but the person may not be able to link such to their past in any clear way (Nijenhuis, van der Hart and Steele, 2002). Moreover these experiences can make people insensitive to touch (Nijenhuis et al., 2002) and presumably insensitive to signals of caring and affection. Indeed, signals of caring may be alarming and become associated with approach-avoidance conflict (Liotti, 2000, 2002; see also Chapter 11 of this volume).

There is another aspect to early abusive experiences that is especially important for the social defeat and social rank model discussed shortly. First, of course, one may not be able to get away or escape perpetrators, and thus one is in an arrested flight context (see Chapter 3). Secondly, perpetrators expect and enforce intense subordination – one has to submit to them and endure whatever it is they want to do to you. This of course sets up the experience of powerlessness and the various defences of 'shut-down' and dissociation that go with it.

There are in fact a range of parenting styles that can increase arousal of threat systems and code these in emotional memories, where the child is in a highly frightened and subordinate position (Perry et al., 1995). These styles are common in the life narratives of some depressed people.

Parental criticism and control   Parents who are excessively autocratic and controlling and/or excessively shaming in their efforts to force their children to comply, often produce people who are extremely sensitive to shame and being criticised by others. There is now much work showing that high expressed emotion (high criticisms and intrusive control) are vulnerability factors for a range of disorders, including depression (Teicher et al., 2006; Wearden et al., 2000). Later in life they can 'hear the harsh voice' of the parent in their heads, which may come as intrusive feelings and emotional memories (Brewin, 2006; Reynolds and Brewin, 1999). These children often grow up uncertain about authority figures, and whether they will be helpful or condemning.

Parental competitiveness   Some depressed people experience their parents as demanding excessively high standards of them and shaming them or withdrawing from them if they don't achieve these standards. Parents who 'shout at their children from the touch lines' in sport and shame them for not being good enough are often highly competitive and use their children as extensions of their own need to succeed and prove themselves. Another aspect of competitive families can be where parents compete *with* their children. Parental criticism can sometimes be an effort on the parent's part to show they are superior (e.g. as mother) to their child. Such children can grow up feeling inferior to their parents. Learning that one's parents always see themselves as superior to you can undermine self-esteem and has been linked to postnatal depression (Arieti and Bemporad, 1980a). Another theme in competitive families is where one parent (usually but not always, the father) may compete with the children for the other parent's attention, creating atmospheres of rivalries and jealousies. Insecure, jealous men, who themselves have come from neglectful backgrounds, can cause serious problems in some families – bullying their wives and children.

Parental favouritism   Some children feel they were less favoured or loved than a sibling(s) and can have an acute sense of inferiority. This may be seen to be because they had a certain personality, or gender or lacked the talents of the favoured sibling(s). Some evidence suggests that recall of parental favouritism, and of being a less favoured child is associated with depression (Gilbert and Gelsma, 1999). Such children can become adults who feel that they have to constantly compete for affection, but that they are not good enough to succeed (unless one can do something special) and they may experience problems of envy and shame.

Unpredictable parents   Some depressed people experienced their parents as highly unpredictable. Sometimes they are loving and sometimes aggressive. This can produce approach-avoidance conflicts (Liotti 2000). This pattern can be especially noted where parental mental illness has been a problem. Liotti (2000) pointed out that parents who have not resolved their own trauma (e.g. abuse) can have problems in feeling comfortable with caring and responding to a child's distress. They can send conflicting signals (both threat and safeness-approach) to a child that leads to confusion and conflict in internal working models. Liotti (2000) suggests that coding a parent as both safe and frightening are sources of disorganised attachment. As for other parenting experiences, such children can become highly sensitive to the moods of others, and can find it difficult to rely on or trust others.

Turbulent parents   Some children grow up in turbulent households of constant conflicts and where one or both parents often threaten to leave (Bowlby, 1980). These create very unsafe environments and atmospheres of high stress. Such children are not only at risk of being dragged into the parents' conflicts or forced to take sides, but live under constant threat of abandonment and become very sensitive to other people's moods. Witnessing domestic verbal abuse and violence is a known vulnerability factor for depression (Teicher et al., 2006). Sometimes these children become appeasers, having taken on the role of trying to calm others down. At other times they may try to avoid dependence on, or closeness to, others because it is too risky.

Recalling childhood experiences

There are many scales that measure people's recall of how their parents acted towards them, and although there is a risk that some of these can be affected by current mood and emotional states, Brewin, Andrews and Gotlib (1993) suggest they are fairly reliable indicators of early background. The caution to this is that some people are dissociated from these early traumatic experiences and have poor recall (Liotti, 2007; Nijenhuis et al., 2002). Nonetheless, many of the self-report scales that have focused on recall of parental behaviour, have found that low affection and high control are common in depressed people's backgrounds. Scales that measure active rejection and shaming, however, often find this factor the more pathogenic. In our own work, we have been interested not so much in how people recall *the actions of others*, but the typical emotional memories of how they felt as children. We developed the Early Life Experiences Scale (ELES) that focused on recall of being frightened and fearful in one's family, subordinated and having to be submissive, in contrast to feeling valued. We found that feeling afraid and submissive as a child was linked to depression (Gilbert, Cheung, Wright, Campey and Irons, 2003). Ongoing work in our department suggests that recall of one's emotional state as a child may mediate the link between parental behaviour and depression. Thus there are important individual differences in how children react and cope with adversity and it may be the emotional memories of how one felt (internal experience of self) that are especially important (Mikulincer and Shaver, 2004).

Adjusting within a family and peer groups   Different children cope differently with the same family stresses due to temperament, position in the family, family dynamics and availability of alternative sources of care/affection. It is important to note that child–parent relationships take place in wider systems of relating, such as extended families, sibling relationships and peer groups. These can soften (e.g. developing good relationships with a grandparent) or accentuate problems. Children can also react quite differently to threats. For example, when Jane's father left them, her mother 'fell part'. Her older sister became angry and acted out, often drinking, having tantrums and getting into trouble. Jane, however, aligned herself with her mother, becoming her support and 'a good girl' who never expressed her feelings. This brought angry contempt from her sister, with whom she had previously had a good relationship and had loved and looked up to. She noted that 'when father left something inside me died'. If she had negative feelings for others she would often hide them, but if she felt positively and tried to be 'good', she felt others would envy her and be contemptuous. Note the issue of conflict (see Chapter 3). Clearly, you cannot understand these complexities unless you understand something of the family dynamics. For Jane there was a lot of grief and anger to work through.

Summary

So the above themes, then, offer variations on parental styles (and there are others). Three key themes arise for such experiences: (a) growing up feeling alone and disconnected, (b) being and feeling frightened and subordinated; (c) having to compete for attention and to be valued. How people have adapted to cope will be unique to the person. It is in this individualised understanding of patterns that the therapist and client gain insight and build the formulation (see Chapter 9). As you can imagine, these early life themes are not mutually exclusive and in fact combinations are more the rule than the exception (Teicher et al., 2006). Moreover, some coping efforts may lead the child to behave in exactly the opposite way. For example, a child with a very fussy and anxious mother may become very cavalier about risks. A child with a very demanding parent, who has high expectations, may give up, 'drop out' and be an under-achiever. So these are only examples and guides. Each individual *is unique* in how they cope with their early life. By the time a person comes to therapy they will exhibit influences from the past, family and peers, plus their own coping efforts.

Attachment styles of relating

As a result of our early experiences, research suggests that there are four basic interpersonal styles that emerge in childhood and are carried through into later, adult life. Some of these result in major difficulties in adjusting to loss, role conflicts, and role transitions later in life. These styles have been summarised by Collins and Read (1990), although various others are also noted (Cassidy and Shaver, 1999: Mikulincer and Shaver, 2004). We will note these styles in detail here because they can emerge in the patient-therapist relationship (Liotti, 2007; see also Chapter 7 of this volume). Thus a therapist can 'look-out' for them.

Secure attachment
These individuals are able to get close to others or cope with distance. They are comfortable with depending on others and with others depending on them and

rarely worry, in the normal course of events, about abandonment or getting too close and intimate. They have a basic trust in themselves and in others. In counselling they develop trust fairly easily, are open, but also recognise boundaries.

Anxious attachment
These individuals feel that they cannot get close enough to others and are very sensitive to cues of rejection or abandonment. They often crave physical affection. They often worry that their partners and friends may leave them or ignore them. Their need for constant reassurance of their lovability and acceptance sometimes drives others away and can show up as clinginess, possessiveness, jealousy and other anxious forms of attachment and relating. They are more likely to be emotionally expressive.

Avoidant attachment
These individuals prefer distance and are uncomfortable if others get too close. They do not like to be dependent on others nor for others to be dependent on them. They often find that their partners wish for them to be closer but this call to intimacy is frightening to them. They are often distrustful of others' motives and are sensitive to being hurt and/or controlled in relationships. They are the least emotionally expressive and may be subject to strong shame. Goodman (2002) notes work that suggests this style may offer some protection to emotional dysregulation. Recent work suggests that avoidant styles may be of two forms related to dismissing (I don't need others) and being fearful (I need others but they are too frightening to get close to).

Ambivalent and disorganised attachment
These individuals show mixtures and oscillations of anxious and avoidant behaviour. If others get too close they are worried about being controlled and 'swamped' and show avoidant patterns. If others are too distant they are worried about abandonment and aloneness and show anxious patterns. In borderline clients this oscillation can be marked and is sometimes referred to as disorganised attachment (see Liotti, 2000, 2002). Again, notice the importance of inner conflicts between motives, emotions and protection strategies (see Chapter 3).

Whether or not these classifications are adequate to deal with the range of abusive experiences that children can be subject to is a point for research. Nonetheless, these basic self–other relational styles may reflect psychobiological patterns of reactivity, influence the experience of connectedness and relatedness with others (Mikulincer and Shaver, 2004) and may be acted out in the therapy (i.e. some depressed patients appear anxious and needy, others are withdrawn, distant or hostile, and yet others oscillate between these two styles). Liotti (2000, 2002, 2007), Safran (1998) and Sloman (2000) have written on how these attachment styles affect the therapeutic relationship and interventions. It can be useful to have some shared view with your client of past relationships and how these may impinge on their current relating style, including that of therapy. You can focus on the fact that these can be automatic protection efforts.

Given what we know about the linkage of early background to vulnerability this indicates a need for a detailed case history and ways to contextualise the depression (see Chapter 9). This is not because you are going to 'ruminate together' on how bad the past was, but rather to 'empathise and make sense' of vulnerabilities, thoughts and feelings, de-shame (I often focus on people's safety efforts 'so you see thinking/feeling like this makes sense and is not your fault' language) and build this into your mutual formulation with the client. Moreover, although psychiatric classifications separate post-traumatic stress disorder and depression, many people with complex depressions have had a variety of repeated emotional traumas and losses (e.g. lack of affection and frightening early experiences) that need to be addressed.

Social competition, bullying, rank and defeat states

We have touched on two themes above that now need to be considered more fully. First is the fact that it is not just loss or separation and 'feeling alone' that textures some people's early experiences, but also that others were more powerful, highly threatening and hurtful. Second, it is often about feeling valued, wanted and included rather than being an outsider that textures depressive experience. Although some depressed people seek care-providing intimacies, others are seeking co-operative relationships and ways to feel socially included and 'desired;' that their contribution (and attributes) matter to those around them. Protest-despair was evolved to cope with absences of protective others. So we can ask: What kind of protection strategy do we have for coping with powerful and threatening others when they are all too present and intrusive? Have we evolved different types of 'shut-down', inhibition, protection strategies in these contexts? Second, what kind of protection strategy do we have for coping with being excluded or allotted low rank such that others do not have much interest in us? This takes us to the crucial issue of *power relationships*, the experiences of power-lessness and *competitive* behaviour (Gilbert, 1984, 1992, 2000b). To gain insight into these protection strategies requires us to look first at the way animals engage in, and cope with, aggressive conflicts.

The aggressive side of competition

We can start by thinking about aggressive competition in general. Territorial animals come into conflict at certain times, such as during breeding or when other animals encroach on another's territory. Spacing regulates aggression. Group-living mammals, however, are never far away from each other and may compete for resources. This 'closeness of living' means that conflicts can break out at any time. How is aggression managed in such a context? Most mammals compete for resources and some will win and some will lose. Most contests in nature are not fights to the death like the gladiatorial games (and the fact that humans can push conflicts this far is a subject in its own right). Rather, nature has come up with some clever social strategies to avoid everyone fighting to the death over each contest for resources. Animals have ways to *socially compare* themselves to others and work out if they are likely to win a contest or not. Those who believe they are unlikely to win, avoid the conflict and thus give up trying to gain control over the resources, be this for sex or food resources. If they are unsure, they may engage in ritualised displays and fighting until one backs down. The loser then simply runs away or expresses submissive, 'you have won and I recognise you are more powerful' behaviour and that's the end of the contest (Gilbert, 2000b; Price, 1972; Price and Sloman, 1987).

The upshot of this is that an animal in social contexts, where others are more powerful than itself, and anything it does to gain control of resources will activate the more dominant and powerful to threaten it, has a problem. If it remains confident and positive in mood and optimistic, and does not down-grade its approach and 'go-getting' behaviour, it is going to get into rather serious social conflicts and difficulties. Higley et al. (1996) have shown that in monkey groups, those who cannot regulate their 'go-getting' and challenging behaviour suffer a large number of injuries and greater mortality. Hence, at times positive emotions that underpin drive and go-getting, and negative emotions that increase anxiety and social wariness need to be regulated in regard to the social context. Basically, the subordinate needs to be cautious rather than confident, and be ready to express submissive behaviour should it inadvertently activate the dominant to attack it. Even a certain type of eye gaze from a subordinate can activate the more dominant animal to attack/threaten. In humans, too, the social power dynamic is key to how conflicts are engaged in and handled, with subordinates being more wary of and inhibiting anger, and dominants being more expressive of anger (Fournier, Moskowitz and Zuroff, 2002). There is now good evidence that subordinates in many groups, that are competitive and unsupportive, have higher levels of stress (e.g. as measured by cortisol), are more inhibited, submissive and less 'go-getting' and less confident, compared to the dominant ones (Sapolsky, 1989, 1994). Following a threat, a subordinate's blood pressure and cortisol response can be higher and take longer to return to baseline than that of the dominants (Sapolsky, 1989, 1994).

So subordinates have innate strategies for coping with low rank, defeats, and the presence of more powerful threatening others, in their environment. The defeat model of depression is based on the original ideas of John Price (1972, 2000; Price, Sloman, Gardner, Gilbert and Rohde, 1994). Originally, a defeat was seen to occur when an animal made an 'up rank' bid but lost the competition. However, now we can see a defeat as occurring from potentially any hostile attack, provoked or not, that results in activation of subordinate's defences of increased fear and submissive self-protection. In fact dominants may attack (bully) subordinates in unprovoked ways because this maintains the stress (cortisol) of the subordinate, may maintain low serotonin and dopamine that keeps the subordinate in a 'subordinate brain state' (and compliant) and mitigates against a challenge to them. Additionally, being the victor boosts their own serotonin and dopamine. The induced signals of submissiveness may help relax the dominant (Gilbert and McGuire, 1998). When dominants are put behind one-way mirrors so that they can see their group but others cannot see them and so do not submit to their threats, their serotonin levels fall (Gilbert and McGuire, 1998). Is it possible that for humans who cannot self-regulate (boost their serotonin and opiates) through love, affection and caring will seek alternative, more bullying ways to do it? I will leave that thought with you.

Price noted that defeat states in animals and humans have characteristic patterns. First, defeat states are activated as *a protective strategy*; that is to say many animals show defeat-like profiles of becoming inhibited and withdrawn after losing a hostile encounter. As noted above, some of our safety and protection strategies are to stop us behaving in certain ways where our own behaviour can get us into trouble. So second, defeat states are internal regulators that stop us engaging in certain behaviours or thinking and feeling (e.g. optimistic and energised) in certain ways. Defeat states readjust the ambition of the animal downward and make them inhibited, non-assertive, lose confidence and be wary of others. They protect the animal to the extent that it does not keep challenging more powerful others who will simply continue to injure it. Moreover, when the dominant sees that the other is 'not challenging and is inhibited', it may lose interest in threatening it. In humans, too, once we know an opponent is defeated we might lose interest in attacking further. In courts of law or in child–parent conflict, showing submissiveness and shame will affect the court or parent differently compared to displays of aggressive defiance (Keltner and Harker, 1998). Thus part of the function of such strategic displays is to de-escalate conflicts and attacks from others.

So defeat can induce psychobiological response patterns that have various functions. The technical term for this is the *involuntary defeat strategy* (IDS) (Sloman and Gilbert, 2000). Social defeats are now used as animal models of depression. Findings show that animals can show major and long-lasting changes in their physiology and behaviour following a social defeat (Gilbert, 2000b, 2006a). Once the IDS is triggered, it will organise psychobiological responses that show up in patterns of brain activity, behaviour, emotions and (in humans) styles of thinking (Levitan, Hasey and Sloman, 2000, p. 102–3). In some studies of animals, defeats produce such powerful physical changes and 'giving-up' profiles that the animal becomes highly immobilised and dies. Defeat states are also likely to be open to conditioning and can be easily reactivated in certain contexts.

Bullying

We have established that under aggressive threat from more powerful others there is an automatic strategy to shut down and become submissive. In the normal course of events subordinate animals can at least keep out of the way of aggressive others, but a child cannot – they are, to all intents and purposes, *trapped*. Experiencing these hostile relationships will code for others as not just unavailable but threatening. Liotti (2000, 2002) has pointed out that hostile parents also produce serious approach-avoidance conflicts in attachment systems. As we have seen in Chapter 4, these can produce disorganisation of various systems. Also, of course, we know that some vulnerabilities to depression are rooted in early abusive experiences.

It is not just bullying parent–child relationships that are linked to depression vulnerability. Abbott and Williamson (1999) found domestic violence was highly related to depression in women. Bullying and rejection by peers at school and work is also a well-known predictor of depression. Gibb, Abramson and Alloy (2004) found that recall of peer victimisation made an independent contribution to cognitive styles that are linked to depression. Indeed, aversive peer relationships, that give rise to feelings of being shamed, rejected, and/or an outsider, can powerfully influence people's sense of social connectedness.

The key message is that in the context of powerful hostile others, who are threatening and attacking, there is a protection strategy that activates threat processing and tones down *positive affects*. This will be associated with intense fear of the powerful other(s) and can induce a highly demobilised state. When the protection strategy is turned on people may feel a loss of energy and drive, and a focus on their inferiority and powerlessness. For people who have emotional memories of intense fear of others, as a result of abuse, these memories, and their associated fears, can be reactivated in depression and texture dreams (Cukrowicz et al., 2006). They are common in shame-focused depressions (see Chapter 6). Keep in mind, though, that when abuse is early or highly traumatic a person may experience the reactivation of the protection strategies but not be able to link these to, or be able to process, early memories (Nijenhuis et al., 2002).

Subjective experiences of inferiority and defeat

Even in hostile environments subordinates are not necessarily depressed. There are important individual differences in susceptibility to severe defeat states that are subject to research (Gilbert, 2000a). One fact may be the degree to which subordinates can relate and identify with each other, and form social connectedness through stories, rituals and religious beliefs (Scott, 1990). In my boarding school I and a few others were frequently caned and slippered for relatively minor offences by an abusive 'master' (as they were then called) but *together* we saw these canings as badges of honour. Beatings or verbal abuse given to a child or a partner trapped in their own home would be quite different. It is the individualised (me alone) *socially disconnected* sense of defeat and inferiority/subordination that is most closely linked to depression. In humans, the *subjective* experience of *personal* inferiority in defeat is therefore crucially important. For example, Ehlers, Maercker and Boos (2000) point out that many victims of torture may feel defeated and sign false confessions, but may not feel *inwardly or personally inferior or defeated* in the sense that one has lost autonomy or *self-identity*. Mental defeat, however, is defined as, 'the perceived loss of all autonomy, a state of giving up in one's mind all efforts to retain one's identity as a human being with a will of one's own' (Ehlers et al., 2000, p. 45). They found that mental defeat, in this context, was associated with feelings of total subordination, such as feeling merely an object to the other, experiencing a loss of self-identity, being prepared to do whatever the other asked, and not caring if one lives or dies. Those who experienced mental defeat had more chronic post-traumatic stress disorder (PTSD) symptoms and higher depression. Ehlers, Maercker and Boos (2000) indicate that refusing to feel *personally* inferior to one's torturers (e.g. one is morally superior to them) might help to limit mental defeat. Gilbert (1992, pp. 209–17) noted these themes (of feeling controlled by others and not caring if one lives or dies, of feeling one has lost one's identity) to be common in some depressions. In cases of severe abuse, children may have these experiences too.

Buchbinder and Eisikovits (2003) found that women often feel shame and self-blame in the context of a powerful, hostile spouse and is one reason women do not leave violent and abusive relationships. Andrews and Brewin (1990) found that when women were in an abusive relationship they tended to self-blame for the violence but once they had escaped (and were safe) they blamed the abuser.

Sharhabani-Arzy, Amir and Swisa (2005) found that in the context of domestic violence self-criticism significantly increases the risk of post-traumatic stress disorder and depression. As we will see in Chapter 6, these are typical defensive styles of people when they are in highly subordinate positions with threatening others.

Self-bullying and defeat   Helping people understand the power of defeat, especially in the context of put-down and bullying, or being overwhelmed by tasks, can link to another important concept – that of *internal harassment*; that is, our own self-criticisms can act like a form of *self-bullying* and can be so constantly in our heads that we can come to feel beaten down and defeated by them (Gilbert, 2004; Whelton and Greenberg, 2005). This will be a key theme in later chapters. If the world appears to turn hostile and rejecting, and inside oneself one is critical and condemning, then in essence there is nowhere to go – there is no place, inside or out, that is safe or soothing. This is why, as we will note later, helping people to become self-compassionate can be helpful – we create an internal space and place where they can try to activate some inner soothing (Gilbert and Procter, 2006). We will look at these aspects and their relationship to self-criticism more closely in later chapters.

Note, however, that *everything can change if dominants are friendly* and supportive of a subordinate's efforts to progress. Indeed, one of the major changes in human social behaviour is that dominants can help and support subordinates (e.g. caring, teaching and training them). Hence, the soothing system can play a key role in hierarchical social groups (recall this responds to social affiliation cues and regulates stress). The point is that it is not being subordinate that is the issue but how threatening or supportive, more powerful others are (or are seen to be). Having looked at the aggressive side of conflicts and hierarchical competitions and controls, we can turn attention to another aspect of the competitive mentality and its link to depression – competing for a social place.

Competing for positive attention and avoiding inferiority and rejection

Not all sensitivities to defeat states are the result of experiencing others as aggressive and hostile. Nonetheless, themes of inferiority and powerlessness still texture the experience of self. Is there another competitive aspect that can give rise to these feelings? We have seen how important social relationships are for making the world safe and soothing, and for regulating our psychobiological patterns. Moreover, they are essential for social tasks such as mating, rearing offspring and the tasks for survival. Thus the adaptive advantages of various *positive* relationships mean that the use of aggression and threats to dominate others to get what one wants is tempered by the need to compete for social place, by stimulating positive feelings in others about the self – to be attractive to them. If we can do that, then others will engage and co-create sharing, supportive relationships with us. High-quality social relationships are powerful survival and reproduction-related resources and animals and humans will compete for them. What happens if they try to win them or co-create them with others but fail? Can the IDS be triggered for coping with these types of social defeat?

Table 5.1   Strategies for Gaining and Maintaining Rank-Status in Social Roles

Strategy	Aggression	Attractiveness
Tactics used	Coercive Threatening Authoritarian	Showing talent Show competence Affiliative
Outcome desired	To be obeyed To be reckoned with To be submitted to	To be valued To be chosen To be freely given to
Purpose of strategy	To inhibit others To stimulate fear	To inspire, attract others To stimulate positive affect

From Gilbert and McGuire, 1998: 112, reproduced with permission of Oxford University Press

The competitive dynamic to this is rooted in the fact that people can choose whom they will associate with. Will others choose you as a friend or lover, to be on the team or an employee? How can you entice others to choose you? Do you have qualities that they would find useful or desirable? What happens if others (you think) have these qualities more than you? Aggression may still be useful if one can limit the choices of others and/or in some way enforce compliance out of fear; and this, of course, is far from uncommon in human relationships. Aggression is risky, however, in that it can increase the chances of conflict and injury and also withdrawal and defection by others. So an alternative strategy is to display qualities of the self *that attract* others and stimulate their approach behaviours towards the self. These two social systems for social engagements are presented in Table 5.1.

So to obtain a place in a network of co-operative relationships one needs to be valued by others. Gilbert (1989, 1997) suggests that people have evolved mechanisms to monitor their attractiveness to others. This is called their *social attention holding potential* (SAHP). SAHP can be positive (e.g. I am attractive to others because I have 'these' aspects/characteristics, and people have a positive interest in me) or negative (e.g. I am unattractive because I have 'these' aspects/characteristics and people are disinterested or have a negative opinion of me). SAHP can be role-focused; thus it can be high in one role but negative in another (e.g. friends like my helpfulness, but academic colleagues think my work is seriously flawed). The more I wish to compete in a certain domain (e.g. seek academic acceptance), the more vulnerable I am to shame and feeling defeated in that domain or competition). Santor and Walker (1999) used this paradigm and found that we tend to value qualities about ourselves, and link them to self-esteem, if we think they are qualities that *others will* value in us.

Self-esteem and social rank

Low self-esteem has been referred to as *involuntary subordinate self-perception*, linking it to a competitive dynamic and focus (Gilbert, 1992). If we look at this more carefully, it is often only in certain competitive domains that depressed people have low self-esteem. So they see themselves as inferior and lacking in competencies to achieve goals. But if you ask them about other qualities of self that are caring or morally focused, such as whether they are honest, try to be reliable, are kind and supportive of others, then they commonly see themselves positively on these traits, sometimes even superior to others. Whether they are or not is another matter.

Price (1972, 2000; Price et al., 1994) was one of the first to link self-esteem to competitive behaviour and suggest that low self-esteem can be linked to a subordinate strategy. This strategy guides attention to the power of others, alters the threshold for social threat detection and submissive defences, and regulates confidence and 'go-getting'. Gilbert (1992) suggests that it also accentuates self-monitoring (such as not doing things to stir up criticism or attacks from others) and facilitates self-blame (Gilbert and Irons, 2005).

It has often been thought that mood is key to confidence. However, Gilbert, Allan, Ball and Bradshaw (1996) found that confidence and estimates of one's ability and success on an intelligence task were related more to social comparison than to mood. We now know that social rank also impacts on how people think, behave, their characteristic emotions, and their social confidence (Keltner, Gruenfeld and Anderson, 2003). If you prime people, with being higher social rank, this is associated with more abstract thinking (Smith and Trope, 2006). So the degree to which you see yourself as dominant or in an unwanted subordinate position affects attention and information processing.

From a different paradigm, Leary, Tambor, Terdal and Downs (1995) coined the term *sociometer* to describe an inner sense of one's social connectedness. The sociometer is linked to self-esteem which in turn is linked to the felt security in one's primary relationships. Thus people suffering low self-esteem are believed to be estimating their sense of social connectedness (in my view their social attractiveness and SAHP) as relatively poor or fragile. Murray, Griffin, Rose and Bellavia (2006) note that people with low self-esteem often believe they are less loved by their partners than they are. Moreover, they found that within couples, for low self-esteem people (but not high self-esteem people), feelings of being loved and accepted by partners were higher on days when their professional lives were going well. These data suggest that it is in the competitive dynamic and people's sense of 'having to earn their place' as opposed to having 'unconditional acceptance' that is key. Unfortunately, to have one's sense of love and acceptance overly linked to one's competitive successes can increase vulnerability to depression. Indeed, one sees this clinically quite often. For example, in a recent depression a high executive could not imagine that his family could love him if he lost, or did poorly at, his job. Although depressed people may see themselves as having traits of kindness and honesty, they may believe (perhaps incorrectly) that others do not value these – that is, these traits do not make them desirable and give high SAHP. The difference between feeling 'a nice' person and 'an effective' person needs more research.

Baumeister, Tice and Hutton (1993) suggest that self-esteem reflects two different underlying social strategies. High self-esteem was related to social enhancement and seeking out opportunities to develop and grow. Low self-esteem, however, was a threat-focused sense of self and focused on damage-limitation efforts. Experiences of self-esteem may vary as to how far one feels confident to pursue goals, or needs to be highly focused on damage limitation. Damage limitation is probably also linked to shame proneness (see Chapter 6). When people have fragile or vulnerable self-esteem this may be because they can go for an enhancement strategy when they feel safe, but they easily feel threatened and then they switch to a damage-limitation strategy (Gilbert and Irons, 2005). Moreover, their self-esteem may be overly focused on competitive winning of approval and validation from others rather than growth (see below).

Our perceptions of social rank and social place (where we stand in relationship to others and whether others are friendly or highly judgmental and discerning choosers) therefore exerts powerful effects on a variety of psychological processes. Helping some depressed people recognise that perceptions of low self-esteem may be part of an *involuntary* protection strategy (that may be linked to memories of powerful, critical others), and thus they can be fearful of raising it, helps people make sense of why they 'hang on' to it. It is not (just) cognitive processes that drive and maintain low self-esteem, but perceptions of one's social position, fear of others and safety strategies.

Striving to avoid inferiority

If people cannot rely on more powerful others or friends being accepting, helpful and supportive, and/or they see themselves as needing to constantly impress and win others' approval in roles, and earn their social place, then life is seen as a constant competition, where exclusions, rejection or put-downs can occur at any moment. Rather than feeling safe in one's network of co-operative relationships they are more threat-focused. Ongoing work in our department has shown that striving and competing to *avoid inferiority* (which is different from wanting to be superior) and fear of failure (Gilbert, 1984) are significantly linked to depression.

The idea that feeling under pressure to strive and compete to earn one's place and avoid inferiority is related to psychopathology, is not new. Alfred Adler (1870–1937) suggested that such striving could develop to compensate for an inferiority complex. More recently, Dykman (1998) suggested that there are two main motivations behind achievement, which he calls *growth*-seeking versus *validation*-seeking. Growth-seekers enjoy challenges and their ability to learn and mature through challenges and mistakes. Validation-seekers, however, feel under constant pressure to prove themselves as likeable and acceptable to others. Validation-seeking, as ways to improve the self and stabilise self-esteem, is highly linked to depression vulnerability. He also suggests that validation-seeking is a defensive coping strategy that develops in the context of critical and perfectionistic parenting. Thus it can be linked to shame and to damage-limitation strategies. In a series of studies Dunkley and colleagues (e.g. Dunkley, Zuroff and Blankstein, 2006) explored various measures of perfectionism and suggested two underlying factors: the first is setting and striving for personal standards; the second is striving to avoid criticism/rejection from others – the latter were labelled 'evaluative concerns'. Dunkley et al. (2006) found that it is the evaluative concerns dimension that is linked to various psychopathological indicators including depression.

Social rank, competition and depression

Over the last twenty-five years, although I believed that learned helplessness (loss of control) and protest-despair models are good models of depression, I did not think they accounted for all of the *felt experiences* of depression – especially those linked to feeling inferior and worthless, social anxiety, submissive behaviour and the intense feelings of being defeated. They did not fully address the issue of social power, bullying, the feelings of needing to strive, nor the way different societies vary in the degree to which they accentuate competitive behaviour and undermine social connectedness, and have higher rates of depression and other mental health problems (Arrindell et al., 2003; Wilkinson, 1996). Psychological models must address these issues (and questions of social justice) and not see problems in coping or thinking as personal deficits (rather than linked to protection strategies). So, since the 1970s my own research interest has been on how depressed people get caught up in competitive (archetypal) dynamics, become focused on competitive ways of thinking about the self (e.g. social comparison), defences to competitive defeats, and see themselves in relationship to others in regard to their relative power and social standing. Many helpful conversations with John Price, depressed people, and research evidence also convinced me that *social power* is often involved in depression and is key to the experience of it.

So my own research has focused on how people (especially those from insecure backgrounds) *compete* for their social place, for social acceptance and for desired relationships – for friends and sexual partners – and can be sensitised to defeat states. (For reviews, see Gilbert, 1992, 2004, 2005a, 2006.) When people are insecure they can easily flip into a *competitive mindset and mentality*. In this mindset/mentality our psychobiologies, strategies and 'if-then' rules for engaging with the world become organised in certain ways. People feel *driven* to strive and compete, to prove themselves worthy of other people's attentions, and avoid being inferior and rejected. They worry about other people's negative opinions of them. So they often *compare* themselves to others, are worried that they don't match up (are not good enough), consider other people to be better at coping than they are, and that people will look down on them and see them as subordinate and/or not worth bothering with. They may struggle to assert themselves, defend their spaces, boundaries and self-identities, and struggle with anger. There is now a lot of evidence that when people are depressed they feel threatened by the fact that they compare themselves unfavourably with others and see themselves as subordinate to others (Gilbert, 2004). So for me clues to the nature of depression and other emotional and behavioural difficulties come from studying social threat and the psychology (and psychobiology) of subordination and inferiority (Gilbert, 1984, 1992, 2000b; Gilbert and McGuire, 1998). Throughout history it is always the subordinates (be these the defeated, women, children or slaves) who have not had a voice (the dominants speak for or about them), and we are apt to pathologise their experiences as they struggle as best they can to protect themselves (Scott, 1990). Indeed, when people are subordinated their control over the social environment is significantly reduced, and subordinates have a greater risk of a number of psychological and physical disorders (Wilkinson, 1996). Hence different people are sensitive to 'failures' in various roles that are linked to self-identities, social position/control and social connectedness. But this is how evolution is and we should be cautious about concepts of illness (Nesse and Williams, 1995) or 'deficits', which can be shaming and themselves a way of 'inferiorising' others (Gilbert, 1998a).

I stress again, however, that inferiority itself may not be a problem if people are happy with their social position, or believe that those more able or powerful than themselves are friendly and helpful. We are all familiar with the fact that if someone more knowledgeable helps us in a supportive way to see where our thinking is wrong or how we can improve things, then this can be helpful, comforting and our minds are open to change. However, if others simply use our errors as a way of putting us down and shaming us, then that is upsetting and we get defensive. If we do not trust others to be sharing, helpful and non-hostile, then we can envy their power in destructive ways (Gilbert, 1992). Envy is an emotion of social competition and can be a problem in some depressed people (see Chapter 14). So it is *involuntary* inferiority, when this increases the risk of rejection and criticism or blocking our social goals, that is key. People often don't strive to be superior to others (though some do), but to avoid inferiority and falling out of the orbit of helpful, supportive relationships and hopes of 'being chosen and included'.

If some depressions are linked to competitive behaviour (a competitive mentality; Gilbert, 1989, 1992, 2005b) and to the triggering of an *involuntary defeat strategy with its psychobiological response patterns*, then we would expect to see depressed people feeling defeated and knocked down, feeling inferior to others, seeing others as critical rather than supportive, believing that others look down on them (see them as subordinate), behaving submissively in conflicts, showing demobilisation of hope and confidence, being in high states of stress, experiencing loss of energy to try things, and engaging in avoidance and flight behaviour. Sounds familiar? Indeed, each aspect is positively correlated with depression (for a review see Gilbert, 2004).

Our research has found that feeling defeated is a more powerful predictor of depression than hopelessness (Gilbert and Allan, 1998). Gilbert, Allan, Brough, Melley and Miles (2002) also found that feeling defeated was highly associated with anhedonia – the loss of positive drive-related affect. Depression is commonly associated with feeling that we are losing in the social tasks, goals and competitions of life. In a major study of twins, Kendler et al. (2003) found that life events that involved dimensions of humiliation, in the form of losses of status and social standing (social defeats), were important predictors of onsets of major depression. Brown et al. (1995) have also shown that 'humiliating' life events are centrally related to depression and more so than loss events alone. As noted above, defeat states can knock out the seeking and drive systems; for example, defeats affect the serotonin and dopamine system and can have long-term effects on psychobiological states. Defeat affects opiate and soothing systems too (Gilbert, 2004, 2006a).

When people feel overwhelmed they will often voice this as feeling defeated or saying that 'things have got *on top* of me' or feeling 'squashed/crushed.' Use of this type of language indicates the feeling of being 'pushed down' in some way, of experiencing a defeat, while descriptions of feeling washed-up, no good, inferior, inadequate and worthless indicate the social and hierarchical nature of their thinking and feeling. So understanding the systems that can be activated in defeat states is important because this colours how people experience and speak about depression – at least in western cultures which are competitive and focus on individual striving, personal control and achievement. Being able to recognise that some of these feelings may be experienced because key defensive strategies have been triggered can be helpful and can act as a bridge to the intense emotional feelings of depression. Seeing them as partly linked to innate systems (this is why many depressed people think and feel the same way) can help a person de-personalise their experience, stand back from it, develop a form of social connection through our shared humanity and suffering (Neff, 2003a), become mindful and note 'so this is what my defeat strategy is enticing me to think' – as it does for other depressed people. When discussing evolutionary aspects with clients we seek to help make sense of their feelings, and that it is not their fault. Also we seek to help them recognise that depression is sadly a common experience and that when we are depressed the thoughts and feelings are similar the world over. One may feel alone or 'the only one' because this is what the protection strategy is about. However, it is not true because such experiences of depression are common. Such insights into depression, along with insights into the behaviours and thoughts that accentuate depression and make it difficult to deal with, set the platform for the person to rise to the task of taking responsibility to try to work against the depression.

Interactions of social loss and defeat

The protest-despair strategies and the defeat strategies both operate through the three affect systems we noted in Chapter 2, generating varied and *complex patterns* of brain activity (Sloman, 2000; Sloman, Gilbert and Hasey, 2003). In a major meta-analysis of subordinate stress in monkeys, Abbott, Keverne, Bercovitch et al. (2003) found that cortisol levels in subordinates were predicted by two key variables: first, the rates of conflicts and stressors experienced and, second, subordinate opportunities for affiliative kin and supportive interactions. This is intriguing because affiliative interactions may stimulate oxytocin-opiate systems and these can inhibit cortisol and lower stress (Carter, 1998; Heinrichs et al., 2003). Thus the role of affiliative relationship in helping to cope with conflicts and defeats seems clear. It is when we feel rejected *and alone* that defeats can have serious impacts on our threat and positive affect systems. Even an uncontrollable event, such as facing death, does not inevitably lead to depression, especially in the context of feeling loved and cared for, which can be linked to spiritual beliefs as sources of comfort, and act as a buffer against depression (Aldridge, 2000). All this fits with a large literature that shows the value of social support both as a buffer for depression and an aid to recovery (Brugha, 1995; Gilbert, 1995b). Thus people's abilities to be able to elicit support, respond to support and be internally self-supportive and caring are key processes regulating affect systems. The interaction between seeking connectedness and control over social resources and defeat are illuminated in a number of key themes in depression that often pre-exist the depression.

   The interaction between affiliative strategies and competitive ones can also be looked at developmentally (Gilbert, 2002, 2005a). Derived from the pioneering work of attachment theorists and researchers, we can suggest that infants experience a social world in which others create safeness and stimulate warmth, or fail to do so. When parents are unable to create safeness, or are themselves threatening to the child, the child's defences (anger/fight, anxiety/flight, submission/appeasement, and anxious clinging) are often activated (Perry et al., 1995). The world becomes a dangerous place. The *social mentalities* best suited to cope with this danger are those that enable the child to focus on attending to the power of others, to their harmfulness or neglect/abandonment. If others are more powerful than you, and are unreliable, potentially hostile or need to be impressed to notice you, then there are various *competitive and rank-focused* strategies one can use (Gilbert, 2002, 2005a).

Up-rank and autocratic strategies

These involve being self-focused, quick to spot threats from others and (at times) use bullying tactics to make others wary of you. These individuals can be highly competitive, autocratic and may do well in competitive societies. They appear to close down the biosocial goals and social mentalities that seek safeness through trying to create affiliative climates and mutually supportive caring relationships, mostly it seems because they don't trust them, value them or do not feel soothed by them. They can focus on their drive/achievement systems for good feelings – being self-reliant, strong, autonomous, gaining the competitive edge. They can be perfectionist, fearing criticisms that could undermine their sense of control and status. They can be highly self-critical (see Chapter 6). On the way up they may be highly status/rank-conscious, try to impress the higher ranks and to out-compete peers for approval, validation and special attention. Some can be highly submissive to those above them but rather unkind and demanding of those below (Keltner et al., 2003). Vonk (1998) called this 'upward licking and downward kicking'. If they get depressed, they may prefer to self-medicate or use non-relational therapies such as drugs, and are vulnerable to suicide. Feelings of yearning for affection and protection, or possibilities of becoming dependent, can be frightening for them.

Down-rank strategies

Some people see others as more powerful than them but have hope that they *can* form affiliative relationships with the more powerful for protection, soothing and access to resources. These individuals are socially orientated to be submissive, to use appeasing behaviours and have various social and separation anxieties. They may find self-assertion, handling conflicts, anger and self-autonomy problematic.

These strategies are not mutually exclusive and they have been described in numerous other ways (e.g. in terms of attachment strategies see Sloman, 2000; Liotti, 2000; and see Chapter 6). Wolfe, Lennox and Cutler (1986) discussed the complex dynamic and conflicts of social goals in relationships between 'getting along' with others in contrast to 'getting ahead' of them. It is known that in some cultures sharing and non-self-promotion is key to social integration, and self-promotion is shamed – the exact opposite of competitive societies (Arrindell et al., 2003). However, the theme that has been noted here is that up-rank and down-rank strategies reflect heightened sensitivities to rank and hierarchical relationships and in different ways show heightened competitive concerns. What links them is the fear of shame and being devalued – the subject of the next chapter. Whatever safety strategies one uses, the bottom line is that if they do not work they reactivate fundamental insecurities and bring online automatically protection strategies that tone-down positive affects and tone-up negative affects.

The imagined powerful other

As noted above, humans have evolved in hierarchical groups, with fear of more powerful (especially male) others. This can show up in a variety of archetypal experiences in depression, particularly in societies that have monotheistic religions. In these societies God is normally seen as a dominant male who can act like a loving father or as a judge who can punish or exclude for disobedience. As Porter (2002) outlines, many depressed people in centuries past and in the present have been tormented by the idea that they have sinned and now are 'worthless in the eyes of God'. Indeed, the Book of Genesis is the story of expulsion from paradise as a result of committing an offence and being shamed. Depressed people can sometimes discuss the experience of depression as feeling as if they have been 'expelled'; they see themselves as outsiders and feel worthless. Religious depressed people can feel as if God has abandoned them, has turned against them, is disappointed or angry with them. In contrast, individuals who experience their Gods as loving, benign and forgiving may be less vulnerable to depression (Aldridge, 2000; Cacioppo et al., 2005). It is quite likely that these experiences reflect underlying schema of self–other relationships. It would seem that if there are cultural narratives about Gods and our relationships to them, then these can texture the depressive experience. They are recruited into the way we make meaning of the (archetypal) feelings of being alone, cut-off and subordinated, or under the eye of a potential hostile dominant who will punish subordinates for not conforming in certain ways. Human depression is therefore highly linked to how we think we exist in the minds of others (see Chapter 6). In psychotherapy, these archetypal experiences will not be uncommon, particularly in the more severe depressions.

Resilience

Resilience is an important process in understanding why life events and hassles do not tip some people into depression (Masten, 2001) or why people recover from setbacks fairly quickly (Diener, Lucas and Scollon, 2006). Although there are many aspects to resilience, such as developing secure attachments, with positive self–other schema, current social support systems, helpful styles of thinking and problem-solving abilities, one aspect is that resilient people feel connected and integrated with others (Cacioppo et al., 2005). They are less likely to have grown up focusing on rank and power issues and are more likely to have a relatively positive view of how they exist in the minds of others. Thus they are less likely to access the competitive mentality (which pulls thinking and feeling in certain ways) when things go wrong. A setback is a set-back and not evidence of loss of status, inferiority, vulnerability to shame and rejection and thus control over social relationships. The depression-prone person, however, easily shifts into seeing themselves as a failure, inferior, looked down on by others and defeated, and thus experiences the defeat protection strategy.

Looked at this way, in terms of protection strategies and phenotypes, helps us move away from 'depression as deficit', which can be shaming. If people have certain genetic sensitivities because evolution has scattered these genes in populations, and/or if people grow up in abusive or neglectful families, then their brains are organised to cope with threatening environments. These are not deficits but (genotypic and phenotypic) adaptations. Thus in our therapies we are helping people adapt in different ways, maybe even trying to change phenotypes. We can therefore talk to people about different types of adaptation rather than in terms of maladaption, thinking errors, or problem-solving deficits. This will affect our orientation to therapy, our language and concepts and styles of interacting.

Conclusion

This chapter has suggested that over the many millions of years of mammalian evolution the 'brain' has evolved to seek out certain types of relationship (e.g. care and support) and compete for social place in various ways. Failures in these efforts can constitute major threats and we have evolved a range of protection strategies for coping with such social threats. Both the urgency of trying to control social threats and the sensitivity and ease of access of protection strategies can be linked to early learning and childhood adversity. Depression can be seen as the activation of particular kinds of protection strategy that involves toning down positive emotions and motives and becoming highly sensitive to, and focused on, threats rather than rewards. As threat systems come online and positive affect systems go offline, attention narrows and thinking and feeling follow the negative path. Helping people see depression as due to the activation of primitive protection strategies of various types can help to de-shame these feelings. We feel what we feel in part because we are running basic innate (archetypal) programmes. This is no different from when we 'feel' anxious' – we are activating anxiety systems in the brain (Beck et al., 1985).

So, therefore, the *internal experiences* of depression are shaped partly by the activation of the protection strategies, partly by emotional memories and past personal experiences that code for beliefs, and by current events. The feelings of emotional aloneness are reflections of the activation of protest-despair strategies in our brains, while the feelings of inferiority, shame, defeat and shut-down are linked to the protection strategy that originally evolved to cope with competitive defeats and with being a threatened subordinate. The protection strategies, coded deep in the brain, can 'pull' thinking and feeling in certain ways. Feeling defeated and having all feelings of hope squashed (which is what the defeat strategy does) is to live in a dark and terrifying place. Helping depressed people understand what can colour their internal experience (it is, if you like, archetypal) can help to de-personalise it. We can have a sense of sharing this experience with millions of others by virtue of our common and shared humanity and evolutionary journey. This can help set up the therapy focus for working on depression as 'threat'-related and to 'turn off or tone down these self-protections systems'. The degree to which genes contribute to the severity and ease of activation of these 'shut-down' states is unclear, but genes are not coding for depression as such but protection strategies. Understanding these processes offers the research platform for why compassion-focused therapy can be helpful for some depressed people – the topic of Chapter 11.

6 Thinking, Self-Awareness, Social Goals and the Role of Shame in Depression

Imagination

Humans differ from other mammals in a myriad of ways. Although chimpanzees may share nearly 99% of our genes and have many social goals in common with us (to be free from pain and form attachments, friendships and sexual relationships) and can suffer anxiety and depression, they are not 99% human. We differ from them in the most profound ways by virtue of our abilities to use language and symbols, and to think, reason and imagine (domains 3 and 4 in Chapter 2). Along with these abilities has come a special kind of self-awareness about the world we live in, and how we exist within it. These competencies give rise to an awareness of being 'a self' and creating 'a self-identity'. The question is: How do these abilities influence our basic protection strategies?

From these qualities of mind we have evolved into a species that lives in two worlds: the world 'as is' and the world 'as imagined' (Singer, 2006). Chimpanzees may feel the pain of loss of a loved one, or the misery of defeat, but they probably do not imagine how they would feel if such were to happen, or what their future will be like. They may solve problems, and may even be able to use symbols to a degree, but they are locked into a 'world as is'. Human imagination, with our new forms of awareness and abilities to reason, however, means that we do not just experience emotions through the success or otherwise of our goals, but also from our imagination. Wells (2000, p. 30) puts it this way, noting the evolutionary benefits of evolving a capacity for imagination to anticipate and cope with threats:

> In adaptational or evolutionary terms, the presence of a cognitive mechanism for facilitating the acquisition of plans for dealing with threat, without the need to repeatedly encounter the threat, would bestow on the individual a survival advantage. Imagery provides a 'virtual world' for programming procedural knowledge that avoids the dangers of on-line behavioural practice during exposure to actual danger.

Imagination, then, is a kind of internal simulator, an onboard virtual reality system. As Wells points out, imagination is often dynamic and we can change what happens in it; imagine 'what would happen if …'. We can run lots of different simulations. We can make the most elaborate plans in our imagination by linking our behaviour to outcomes. Sometimes they remain as just fantasies that we know we have little hope of coming true; at other times they are put into actions. In our imagination we can anticipate the fun of a holiday, the acclaim and life change if we achieve a goal (e.g. pass an exam) and the lost opportunities if we fail. We use our imagination to deliberately stimulate physiological patterns (e.g. a sexual fantasy), and can enjoy such pleasures alone in our rooms. Darker imaginations, however, can stimulate the physiological patterns of more unpleasant emotions. There is a two-way flow between imagination and emotional arousal. Stimulate an emotion and the imagination may follow; accentuate emotions and imaginations are filled with their themes. Because we live in two worlds, 'the world as is' and 'the world as imagined', our imagination can be a source for enjoyment or fear and despair. Although a crude simplification, approaches like behavioural ones and mindfulness help us engage in the world 'as is', while cognitive and emotion-focused ones concentrate on the world as imagined, and our inner representations. As we will be exploring a variety of these interventions in later chapters, we need to explore these aspects in some detail.

The abilities to imagine (literally meaning image-ing the world) enable us to be creative. If we work on this flint stone we can fashion it into a spear head, or imagine and build a new house extension. Imagination allows us to write books and make movies with complex characters, storylines and plots. This is a great ability for problem-solving and planning how to secure goals. Our imagination is also a place for questions. We can look to the stars and wonder what they are. If a loved one dies, we imagine what might have happened to them: Is there another place where they might exist? Is there a chance of seeing them again? Religion would be impossible without this imagination for in it we create imaginary worlds that go beyond our direct experience (Bering, 2002). Because we can form inner representations of the world we can build theories about causes (this happened because …) and make predictions (if I do X, then Y will happen, if I do A, then B will happen). Because we can internally represent the world we can hold a model of the world in mind and 'play' with our models. From these we can derive *attributions*, *expectations* and *implications*. We can think about *causes* for feelings. For example, if I get anxious giving a talk, I might think 'this is perfectly normal in these situations and will settle' or I might think 'this is too much anxiety; I am anxious *because* there is something wrong with me'. I can also reason about the *implications* of my anxiety: 'If I am anxious, others will be friendly and understanding – or rejecting'. I might also think about the best thing to do to cope. Cognitive therapists (Beck et al., 1979, 1985) focus on these forms of thinking which are called meta-cognitions (Wells, 2000).

All these form the basis of what we can call *beliefs* and *assumptions* about the world and our place in it. Although we can use our imagination in a variety of ways, its primarily evolved function arose because it helped us achieve evolutionary important goals for survival and social relating. Many of the things we find meaningful are meaningful because they are linked to these goals. Although some philosophers and therapists see meaning and meaning-creating as key to the human mind (Malik, 2000), we should not lose sight of the basics of social relating and social connectedness as one of our most fundamental sources of meaning. We have evolved our imagining and thinking abilities because they gave us extraordinary flexibility in how we navigate, plan and think ahead to achieve various social goals and avoid dangers and threats.

The problem with the imagination is that while it can inspire us and provide ways of solving problems and planning we can also be easily thrown into despair by it. The depressed person's inner world is inhabited by a loss of control over social connection and in which they cannot imagine change. Whether it is because of current life events, the re-surfacing of painful emotional memories or getting exhausted and burnt out, our imaginations can be taken over by defeat and social disconnection protection strategies. We find ourselves textured by unpleasant feelings that ripple through our bodies and our attention is attuned to them and the negative. At a subjective level we lose contact with a sense of meaning, purpose and hope. If only our imagination were not so powerful we might not get stuck here; stuck where our imaginations and thoughts stimulate feelings and our feelings maintain our thoughts and imagination (Beck et al., 1979; Beck et al., 1985). So the therapist attempts to make contact with this inner world of the depressed person and raise the possibility of new engagement; raise the possibility of learning to think, feel and behave in different ways, to imagine 'what it might be like if....'. Our role as psychotherapists is to enter the patients' inner world of shut down protection and gently coax them into exploring alternative worlds; to help them see that their depression is related to the activation of protection strategies that have their origins in our evolved and personal past; to share the task of gently testing out our imaginations and beliefs (e.g. of 'whatever I do cannot work') and treat their depression with understanding and compassion rather than hatred and avoidance.

Meta-cognitions and self-identities

Self-identity goals

There is a large and growing literature on self-identity which is yet to be integrated with the cognitive therapies. Here, however, we can only focus on a few key themes but further reading can be found in Leary and Tangney (2003).

While basic beliefs and the ways we imagine the world are key to our emotional reactions to things, so are our goals. For example, I might choose to override my basic feelings in order to achieve a network of goals. I do not run away when anxious about giving a talk *because* I want to learn to cope with anxiety *because* I want to be able to give talks. I want to give talks *because* I want to share my ideas. I want to share my ideas *because* I want to belong to a certain group, develop friendships and alliances, and make a contribution that is useful and valued. The more our sense of belonging and being valued depends on doing well the more anxious we might become. Or consider that you might feel very hungry but don't act on this feeling because you want to look slim (or attractive, or get healthy, or prove to yourself you can control your impulses (some hope in my case!)). You do not act on anger because you do not want to hurt the person who has triggered your anger. Although you might fancy a student, you do not act on this because it would upset your spouse/partner and violate a self-identity goal of 'not exploiting others'. There is thus a self who reacts quickly to things or has a push of motivation and a self who seeks to regulate those feelings and action tendencies to fit with more basic goals and a self-identity. Freud talked about these aspects in terms of primary (id-based, source of desires, urges and fantasies) and secondary (the reality principle) process thinking. Today, however, we talk in terms of motives and emotions systems, self-identity formation and self-regulation

(Mahoney, 2003). Self-identity goals – how I wish to locate myself in relation to others, 'the kind of person I want to be' – thus become key regulators of emotions and motives. As we will see shortly, these self-identity goals can play a crucial role in some depressions. Although, as we will explore in later chapters, helping people to think, behave and imagine their worlds differently can be very helpful, it is also useful and important to have a shared view of people's goals.

We can look at this issue from an evolutionary view. This suggests that self-conscious self-identity rides on a sea of underlying motives and strategies that must be organised to fit local conditions. Because humans have to operate in, and learn from, the social domain, one of the organising systems that aids this is the creation of a *self-identity*. Thus a self-identity is a vehicle (an evolved solution) for the organisation of the competing potentials that lie within us. Animals may not need one because they rely on more automatic systems in their interactions. But for a symbolising self-aware mind, that has meta-cognitive abilities, and which can regulate more primitive desires, there would be just too much *flexibility* and competing possibilities for thought and actions. Without some sense of 'a self and a self-identity' we could be overwhelmed by possibilities of 'being' (McGregor and Marigold, 2003). Many psychologists now see 'the self' and self-identity like this, as a motivated organising system that co-ordinates memories, emotions, beliefs and other processes for a cohesive securing of goals (e.g. see Conway and Pleydell-Pearce, 2000 for a review). We need a cohesive sense of self: who we are and where we are going (Swann, Rentfrow and Guinn, 2003).

Our self-awareness and abilities to imagine enable us to create a self-identity as an internally constructed model of 'the self as is'; a self with needs, desires, preferences, likes and dislikes; a self that can be threatened in certain ways; a self as one wants to be (and does not want to be); a self that wants to be known/valued/respected (by self and others) via the roles one enacts; a self that imagines and hopes. As Taylor (1989) says, a self-identity allows us to decide what we should value or not value in our 'self' (e.g. certain feelings and thoughts), and what we should aspire to and *train* ourselves for. As he points out:

> To know who I am is species of knowing where I stand. My identity is defined by the commitments and identifications which provide the frame or horizon within which I can try to determine from case to case what is good, or valuable, or what ought to be done, or what I endorse or oppose. In other words, it is the horizon within which I am capable of taking a stand. (Taylor, 1989, p. 27)

Self-identities help us to fit local conditions/ecologies. In hostile environments men tend to have self-identities based on being aggressive, tough and fearless, while in benign environments they might be 'to be peaceful and helpful' (Gilmore, 1990). A self-identity guides our thoughts in pursuit of evolved basic goals (e.g. for sex, status, power, affection, etc.). A self-identity provides consistency and regularities to actions that build a sense of coherence to our 'self' and, via regular actions, build reputations in the minds of others (e.g. we are someone to be trusted or loved or someone to be feared). Threats to a self-identity, coming from within or without, can feel dangerous because they threaten a loss of coherence, control and predictability (Swan et al., 2003). As we will see shortly, depression can represent a collapse of one's self-identity; one has become a shamed self, a failing self, a rejected self; a self that cannot control emotions; a self that is conflicted and paralysed; a self that is unable to secure important goals of social connection and control. (See also Champion and Power, 1995).

External and internal threat

Having such a rich inner world of imagination and sense of self introduces a new dimension to threat and threat processing. Threats that come from external causes can be subject to conscious reasoning and problem solving. We can seek out others to court their advice or help in solving a problem. We can ask other people questions and pull on their knowledge – 'how do you think I should cope with this?' On the other hand we can see others as threatening and unhelpful. Crucially, however, our abilities to create inner worlds and a sense of self create another source of threat: that which emerges from within us. Chimpanzees do not worry that a pain might be a cancer, or this elevated heart rate could be an oncoming heart attack. They do not ruminate on the fact that this or that emotion might overwhelm them. They do not experience certain emotions, such as anxiety, anger or sexual fantasies, as threats to their self-identity or conclude that these indicate something bad about them. They may feel 'depressed' but may not have a higher order self-awareness of being depressed, nor worry or ruminate on the reasons and implications of being depressed. They cannot contemplate suicide as an escape and then be fearful that such an urge could take them over. To put this clearly, we can feel threatened by what we consciously experience as emerging and being triggered in our own bodies and minds. This is because we have a particular type of self-awareness and a way of seeking out and creating meaning for all 'things' that appear in consciousness. While many people can become depressed because of external threats, they can also become depressed because they feel that they may lose control over internal threats and aversive feeling states.

Internal feelings, fantasies, and states of mind can be so aversive that we can engage in experiential avoidance (Hayes et al., 1996). Safety and protection strategies now take on a new life. They can be planned actions to keep us away from feared situations or used to avoid internal aversive states because we feel we cannot bear them. A number of therapies now recognise that our efforts to avoid certain feelings can be problematic and require us to learn acceptance and tolerance of them (Hayes, Follette and Linehan, 2004; Hayes, Strosahl and Wilson, 2004; Linehan, 1993).

Living in the mind of others

If our self-identities evolved for, and are used primarily in the service of, securing social goals and relationships, then there is another meta-cognitive ability we need to look at closely. It turns out that our meta-cognitive abilities attend to what is emerging not only in our own minds but also in the minds of others (Fonagy and Target, 2006). In order to better develop social roles we have also evolved ways of thinking about what other people are thinking and feeling. This is called *theory of mind* (Byrne, 1995, 1999; Decety and Jackson, 2004; Malle and Hodges, 2005; O'Connell, 1997), and may emerge from neonate abilities for intersubjectivity

(Trevarthen and Aitken, 2001). With theory of mind abilities one can think about someone else – what motivates *their* behaviour, what they might value, what they know and what they don't know – and we can *think* how to manipulate them to like us or be wary of us. We can think of linked inferences: 'I believe that you believe, that she believes …'. Our abilities to reason about other people's states of mind and intentions give us a great advantage in social relating. Whiten (1999, p. 177) argues that: 'Reading others' minds makes minds deeply social in that those minds *interpenetrate* each other.' To put this another way, I can model/imagine how I exist in your mind for you, and how you exist in my mind for me.

Consider a friend has had a car accident and when you phone them up they are irritable and short with you. 'Look,' he says, 'I don't want to talk to you right now.' Our emotional brain may respond to that signal with a feeling of hurt and the thought, 'I was only trying to help.' If one gets lost in that emotional reaction we might further think/imagine 'they do not really like me'. We are thus self-focused on self-protection and may 'personalise' the remark. But supposing one can think: 'gosh he is really upset. That is understandable, as he is probably very shaken up. Thus his response is due to his state of mind and nothing much to do with me.' Although cognitive therapists note this as an attribution, it is much more than this. It is related to what Peter Fonagy has called 'mentalising': the ability to stand back and imagine the mind of the other in a non-egocentric way. People with borderline difficulties struggle with these abilities, making them more vulnerable to egocentric emotional reactions (e.g. they would get upset or angry by the phone call because they can't mentalise very well) (see Bateman and Fonagy, 2004; Fonagy and Target, 2006 for a fascinating outline of a mentalisation-based psychotherapy for people with borderline difficulties). Depressed people also can have problems with mentalisation, especially when they become threat-focused. When we have empathy and can reason/think/imagine about another person's state of mind (put ourselves in their shoes), we can feel quite differently about someone putting the phone down on us.

The interchange between minds can go both ways. I can assume that what is in my mind is also in yours, but also how I experience your mind may change my own. For example, self-consciousness may have evolved because of the advantages it gave us in reading other people's minds by having insight into our own. Certainly, we often operate on the assumption that 'if I see this as red, others will too', or 'if I feel good or bad about this event, others are likely to too'. If we use our own minds to judge what is in the minds of others this is called *projection* – we literally project our feelings and thoughts about things into the minds of others; that is we make assumptions that they think and feel as we do. Indeed, as Nickerson (1999) notes, if we could not assume that other people are more or less like we are ourselves, they would become like aliens. It would be horrendously difficult, if not impossible, for us to work out how to interact with them. Thus our theory of mind, on which we base our knowledge of others, *must start* with the idea that others think and feel much as we do and then we have to change/update our views/models about them as we discover otherwise. This updating skill comes with the maturation of various cognitive abilities and experience, that are crucial to theory of mind and hence recognition that others may not know or feel as we do. This updating (understanding differences between us and other people via use of theory of mind abilities) is not always achieved adequately and some people have difficulties in understanding that others do not know what we know, or feel as we feel (Nickerson, 1999).

Projection is common in psychotherapy where, for example, a patient who feels ashamed of a certain thing, assumes the therapist will experience shame towards them too if they reveal it. Sometimes this is based on a transference belief. For example, 'my father shamed me for this so my therapist will too'. The patient does not experience the mind of the therapist as it might in reality be – kind, supportive and de-shaming. Indeed, it is working against such projections that can be important in the therapeutic relationship. Empathy and experiencing empathy, however, involve a standing back from projections and assumptions to experience the mind of the other on their own terms. We are open to be influenced in new ways by the mind of the other. We shall look at this further in regard to the therapeutic relationship (see Chapter 7). The point here is that the ability to create a self-identity arises from evolved competencies for self-awareness and an ability to think and imagine in certain ways. However, the kind of self-identity we have, what we aspire to and how we come to understand and feel comfortable or threatened by our inner world (of innate passions and feelings) is largely scripted by our social relationships, that is how we experience the self through the minds of the others (e.g. 'because I appear lovable from how you relate to me, then I can feel lovable'). Out of our social relationships come the way we pursue certain social goals and create an identity for pursuing them.

The narrative mind

Cognitive therapists are apt to talk in terms of cognitions and beliefs and use computer metaphors. We must be cautious here because a 'cognition' can be poorly defined and is not reducible to information processing. Your computer and DNA are both information-processing systems; your threat systems (e.g. a collection of cells in your amygdala) will process information rapidly but these do not have cognitions as such. Cognitions emerge from information processing and appear in the mind as thoughts. We have a similar problem with meaning. Because physiological systems react to stimuli, for example, a moth flies towards the flame, we cannot say that the flame has meaning to the moth. Meaning is more than reactions. The concept of meaning is linked to a more abstract and creative process and requires a form of consciousness. Meaning and meaning-making are creations not a reaction. One way we create meaning is via the way we fit events to cohere with self-identities and goals. One process by which we give meaning (via fitting events and interactions to self-identities and goals) is via *narratives*.

External narratives emerge from the flow of interactions (real and imagined) with others. They are located in social discourse and require interaction with others. Through that process we may come to adopt certain beliefs or, in the sharing of ideas and discourse, discover things about ourselves we were unaware of, or come to articulate a view and become clearer about our own views and attitudes to things (e.g. It wasn't until I started talking to Sam that I realised how angry I was about this or that). *Internal narratives* occur inside our heads, that is, they are forms of self-talk and self-to-self relating ('I am pleased I did that', 'oh that was a stupid thing to do'). So the mind is not generating isolated thoughts or beliefs but scripts and narratives about self and others from which meaning emerges. Thus we can make sense of events by placing them in a context that links them with other events and tells a coherent story. Our stories reflect our basic views of the world. For example, if my child dies, as an evolutionist I may see this as being 'typical of this harsh world', whereas a religious person may see it as 'God's will'.

Narratives are linked to beliefs, of course, but they are more dynamic and changing processes; they provide insight into the ways that we create meaning and develop beliefs. I recall a famous psychologist once saying: 'I am never sure what I think about something until I have discussed it or written on it. Evidence may change my mind but so will the views of others.' Because our narratives take in the 'narratives' in the minds of others, it is into this flow of narratives that we enter as therapists. Although highly simplified, such views underpin those of the constructive approach to psychotherapy – where the creative acts of meaning through narratives are key (Mahoney, 2003).

Self as object

Chapter 2 discussed the importance of our high-level self-awareness in creating the experience of 'self-as-object'. In part, this emerges from our mind as made up of multi-component systems. We noted that we can have positive or negative views about all aspects of the self, including the physical self (our looks, textures and bodily functions), how the self performs in roles (performing competently or failing), and internal experiences within the self (e.g. dreams, emotions and fantasises). This capacity to observe and 'judge with feelings' (e.g. pleasure in self or frustration with self) creates what was called 'internal looping' where, for example, one part of the self can become critical and another part of the self responds to that self-criticism in a self-to-self relationship. This is important because self-criticism involves one's frustration and anger being directed at the self. Then another component system responds to that attack as a threat and engages subordinate defences. We will explore this further shortly.

Rumination

Another spin-off of our higher-level self-conscious abilities, which gives rise to various meta-cognitive abilities, is rumination. There is evidence that 'holding' various negative thoughts in mind, with focused attention on them, is detrimental to our moods and well-being. There has been increasing research on depression exploring the role of repetitive thoughts (rumination) about one's depression and symptoms. Rumination may affect the intensity and duration of depression (Nolen-Hoeksema, Marrow and Fredrickson, 1993). Ruminating about the causes and consequences of depressive symptoms and feelings may interfere with adaptive problem solving, enhance negative thinking and be a powerful process that maintains depression (Davies and Nolen-Hoeksema, 2000). Ruminations may go some way to explaining gender differences in depression (Nolen-Hoeksema, Grayson and Larson, 1999). Ruminators also use social networks less well than non-ruminators and have difficulties sharing problems (Nolen-Hoeksema and Davis, 1999), possibly because of shame (Cheung, Gilbert and Irons, 2004). (Depressive rumination can also focus on anger and revenge (Gilbert, Cheung, Irons and McEwan, 2005)). Rumination can be a key target for therapeutic work, as we note later.

The struggles of the pre-depressed person

Given that meaning-making, with forms of self-awareness and theory of mind, are core to being human, how are these linked to depression and the protection strategies disussed in previous chapters? Vulnerability to depression comes from many sources that include genes (Caspi and Moffitt, 2006), early life adversity (Bifulco and Moran, 1998), brain maturation (Schore, 2001), styles of thinking (Alloy et al., 2006), life events (Kendler et al., 2003), and social support (Brown and Harris, 1978). However, most vulnerabilities manifest into depression via social interactions. Indeed, everywhere we look, from the way we have evolved to secure various social goals and create certain types of relationship (Buss, 2003; Gilbert, 1989), the way the security or threat in relationships affects our physiological state (Cacioppo et al., 2000; Schore, 2001), the way our minds have evolved to form self-identities that fit social conditions (Leary and Tangney, 2003), and competencies such as theory of mind (Byrne, 1999), we find we are deeply embedded in a network of relational patterns (Whiten, 1999). It is thus the internal organisation of our goal-seeking self, in a particular social world, that textures the depression experience. Indeed, research has given us a number of clues to the fact that some depressed people are vulnerable to depression because of the way their self-identities and goals are con-structed and because of their efforts to *protect* themselves from social disconnection and defeat. We have touched on these in Chapter 5, noting, for example, that inse-cure attachment is a major vulnerability factor for depression.

When trying to help depressed people we can focus with them on their styles of reasoning – that as a depression gets a hold they focus on threats and losses (in their attention, attributions and implicational reasoning, and efforts to control their emo-tions); they ruminate in unhelpful ways and shut-down with behavioural avoid-ance. For some depressed people this is sufficient to get them going again and learn skills that will put them in good stead for the rest of their lives. But there are other depressed people who have lost hope and feel invalidated by life, have a fractured self-identity and feel alone. So we are not simply mind mechanics but need to engage with people's narratives and life goals (Leahy, 2005). When we do this, we hear repeated stories of *struggles* to find meaning and social connection. A key dimension of life goals is to be valued and accepted, and avoid shame.

Self-psychology

In the last chapter we focused on attachment theory and the importance of inse-cure attachment as a vulnerability to threat. Self-psychology, as developed by Heinz Kohut (1913–81) (1971), also offers useful ways of thinking about depres-sion, and people's struggle to find social connection, and illuminates how protection strategies can become activated. In my view, it can dovetail into new ideas on self-identity (Leary and Tangney, 2003), memory activation in distressed states (Brewin, 2006), interpersonal schema theory (Baldwin, 2005) and also conditioning theory (Gilbert, 1992). It can also help link some of the concepts of 'living in the minds of others' discussed above. So, in the next few sections we will look at Kohut's ideas. Some of these ideas were not original to him and he was not good at recognising his sources. For example, Kahn (1985, 1989) notes that Kohut and Carl Rogers were at the same university (Chicago) for ten years. Although they do not seem to have acknowledged each other, they were nonetheless probably aware of each other's ideas. Others have suggested that Kohut was influenced by Bowlby. Elsewhere (Gilbert, 1992), I have compared these two theorists. (See Banai, Shaver and Mikulincer, 2005 for research on the approach).

Kohut argued that there were certain kinds of internal experience and needs that needed to be understood and recognised in the client. These were: (a) the need to feel valued and approved of by others (*mirroring*); (b) the need to have others whom the client can turn to and feel comforted and protected by (*idealising*); and (c) the need to feel like others (*belonging*). If we think about this in terms of the emotion systems that I outlined in Chapter 2, all pertain to feeling safe and connected in the world and thus may influence the soothing system.

Mirroring

Mirroring may begin from the first days of life when a mother smiles and coos at her baby. This automatically activates positive affect systems in the baby which show in the baby's facial and other body movements of pleasure. The baby experiences positive feelings to the facial expressions and voice tone of the mother (Trevarthen and Aitken, 2001). The need to be valued and approved of continues to emerge with a child's early exhibitionist behaviours (the 'look at me, mummy/daddy, watch me do this' behaviour).

When a parent mirrors pride to the child ('well done, that's very good'), the child internalises a good and vigorous sense of self. For example, parents often express positive affect to their child's growing abilities to walk and talk and later to draw and solve problems (e.g. 'walk to mummy, that's right. Oh well done. What a clever boy/girl'). If a child shows off or demonstrates an ability, and the parent praises the child, then the child experiences themself as able and good. Note that not only will the child experience the parents as approving (they have generated a positive affect in the mind of the other), but the child will also experience themself as approved of and attractive; that is to say there are positive emotions generated in the self about the self.

Kohut called these internal experiences of self 'self-object experiences'. Such terms are less used today (outside psychodynamic therapy) and instead we focus on positive self-referent memories and schema (Baldwin, 2005). The key point though is not what we call them but recognition that the child feels good about themself because of the *positive affect coming from the parent towards them*; that is, it is via the positive affect that the child has stimulated in the parent by their own behaviour, and seeing this expressed in the facial and other displays of the parent, that creates positive self-feelings. In terms of love, the child not only experiences themself as loved but also *lovable* (Gilbert, 1993, 2003). This mirroring search goes on throughout life as we seek to be valued and earn the 'pats on the head' from others. We can see how this links to theory of mind and how we develop expectations and beliefs about how others will see and experience us and relate to us.

We now know that lack of these important positive emotional reflections and interactions can have serious impacts on the maturation of the child's brain – because the child needs these inputs to stimulate their positive affect and various cognitive systems and link them to a sense of self (Gerhardt, 2004; Schore, 1994; Siegel, 2001). So if children are deprived of positive affect directed at them and/or parents repeatedly ignore developmental milestones, then problems can arise. Not only can this affect brain maturation, but people who have had few mirroring experiences in childhood can enter life feeling highly motivated to try to elicit mirroring from others. This is because without these signals the world feels unsafe.

Parents can also be shaming. If a child displays behaviours that the parent criticises or is angry about or expresses a 'disgust face' ('don't do that, you look stupid'), then the child experiences having activated negative emotions in the mind of the other (Lewis, 1992). The negative emotion in the parent may now resonate back to the child so that the child experiences themself as bad, shameful or ineffective to influence the positive attentions of others; that is experienced as a threat.

Morrison (1984) notes Kohut's distinction of *defensive self-structures,* which mobilise efforts to conceal deficits in self, and *compensatory self-structures,* which mobilise efforts to make up for a weakness in self – literally to compensate. Morrison offers a complex but interesting idea that depression often results from the inability to maintain compensatory structures. A compensatory structure in cognitive therapy terms is like a core belief of: 'if I can achieve this standard, then people will love and respect me; I can compensate for other deficits or previous experiences'. In my view we should add 'and then I will be accepted and the world is safe'. There have been many therapists who have seen depression as resulting from people's failed efforts to try to win approval or acclaim to make up for feelings of inferiority or unlovability (see Chapter 5). Thus, depression can emerge when an individual simply cannot achieve the ideals which are necessary (be it via a relationship or personal effort) to lift self-esteem (to feel competent and lovable) and restore a sense of self-cohesion, vigour and safeness. Morrison notes similarities with Bibring's (1953) concepts (that depressed people are trying to live to certain ideals such as never being aggressive, always being hard-working), but unlike Bibring he places shame as a central affect. For Kohut, problems with anger and depression are usually secondary to feeling unsafe and failures in feeling valued and positively mirrored. (This is quite different from other object relation therapists who see anger as a primary impulse; see Russell, 1985).

Idealising

This relates to the fact that the child needs to rely on others. When those to whom the child looks up to react with helping and caring responses, the child feels soothed, safe, secure and loved, and develops basic trust. When this is not the case, the child feels that there is no one there for them and is unable to feel soothed in the presence of strong negative emotions (sadness, anxiety and anger). Subsequently, as an adult, the person might resort to various defensive measures (e.g. drinking) to try to soothe themself when under stress rather than obtaining help and support from others. They may be distrustful of the counsellor, expecting to be let down in some way. This way of thinking has a lot in common with attachment theory (Gilbert, 1992). Kohut (like Bowlby) talked about soothing but in his day did not know that our brains have a special soothing system (see Chapter 2).

The counsellor can empathise with the needs of the client in their wish to have some 'strong other' come to the rescue and make things better. Thus the counsellor can recognise a client's yearning for rescue, their fear of abandonment and aloneness and being beyond rescue, beyond help. Hence, if a client says, 'Can you help me? I feel so desperate', the counsellor should *not* say 'Well, it's up to you', or 'I can only help you help yourself'. Rather, the counsellor could *reflect feelings* and point to the collaborative journey of therapy. Possible responses are: 'When we feel depressed or are in pain it can feel a very lonely and isolated experience and we can desperately want to find someone who will help us and alleviate that pain (i.e. reflecting feelings). Let's look at your problems together and see what you find helpful.'

Belonging

This relates to a child's need to feel at one with others, as part of a group or relationship, rather than an outsider and cut off from others. There is much evidence now that this is an important and powerful motivation for humans (Banai et al., 2005; Baumeister and Leary, 1995). Again, a counsellor can empathise and recognise a possible yearning to belong to a group and feel part of a social situation. Sometimes this shows itself in a desire to be meaningfully engaged with others. A policeman who had had to retire due to injury felt he was 'no use to anyone any more and a burden'. His depression was relieved when he found a new occupation and undertook charity work, where he felt he could make a useful contribution and work on projects. Feelings of belonging and being able to make contributions are important for many people. The counsellor's empathic connection to this need can be important.

Kohut's theory of depression is well summed up by Deitz (1988). Basically, depression results when a client has lost the external inputs (e.g. relationships) or the internal positive dimensions of self-experience that maintain positive feelings about the self. We might also see this as related to the activation of different types of emotional memory (Brewin, 2006); that is, when depressed, we can't remember what it feels like to feel well, or we can't remember that we can feel competent and able. Our negative memories and feelings have preferential access. The goal of counselling is to facilitate and develop contact with internal positive self-feelings (i.e. positive experiences and memories of self). To put this another way, it is to help rebuild a positive self-identity and develop positive life goals, or, in cognitive terms, positive self-schema and attributes that bring back or develop representations of self as having worth and being able, rather than of being worthless and unable. Indeed, Deitz (1988) notes that these ideas are similar to cognitive notions of self-schema.

In a way, Kohut's view of depression is that it is nearly always secondary to a painful sense of disappointment; disappointment that life has turned out the way it has; that others are not as loving or reliable as was hoped; that plans have not come to fruition; that one cannot feel connected to others or find a meaningful place in the social world. Somehow one has not made it. This is a position that was portrayed brilliantly in Arthur Miller's play, *Death of a Salesman* (for a further discussion of this, see Baker and Baker, 1988). It is important to help the person to articulate their sense of disappointment and to reflect on the sources of this disappointment, sometimes of unrealistic aspirations, misinterpretations or unmet needs.

These themes that self-psychologists focus on come up time and again in many writings by other therapists. The language may differ, and the way they work with them may differ, but there is growing agreement that some chronically depressed people have been struggling to find social connection and meaning for a long time. Whether we focus on thoughts, behaviours or emotions as a route out of depression, as therapists we need to convey our understanding of the *struggle* in depression. It is in the context of struggle to secure social goals, find positive self-identities, and efforts to feel safe, that depressive protection strategies can be activated. One of the key aspects of self that carries risk for the loss of a positive self-identity and social goals is shame.

Shame

In the last chapter we explored in detail protection strategies related to unwanted inferiority/subordination and social disconnection in potentially hostile/rejecting social environments. If there was one self-conscious emotion that would capture the essence of these, it is *shame*. Shame is essentially a self-conscious emotion, associated with being inferior and socially rejected (Kaufman, 1989). Shame is a key problematic emotion associated with human self-consciousness, and our need for a self-identify that helps us achieve social goals (Gilbert and Andrews, 1998; Gilbert, 2003, 2007; Tangney and Dearing, 2002). We can feel shame intensely pre- cisely because we have the abilities explored above. Although other animals can be socially anxious and engage in submissive behaviour and avoidance – which shame involves (Gilbert and McGuire, 1998; Keltner and Harker, 1998) – it is prob- ably only humans who experience shame, because shame is about self and self-identity. Shame is not so much the distance from the ideal self or falling short of standards, but closeness to the *undesired self* (Ogilvie, 1987), a vulnerability to rejection or ostracism; being an object for derision. Exploring the psychodynamic idea that shame is about failure to live up to ideals, and using qualitative methods, Lindsay-Hartz, de Rivera and Mascolo (1995, p. 277) found that:

> … most of the participants rejected this formulation. Rather, when ashamed, partici- pants talked about being who they did *not* want to be. That is, they experienced them- selves as embodying an anti-ideal, rather than simply not being who they wanted to be. The participants said things like. 'I am fat and ugly,' not 'I failed to be pretty;' or 'I am bad and evil,' not 'I am not as good as I want to be.' This difference in emphasis is not sim- ply semantic. Participants insisted that the distinction was important.

Based on a review of the evidence and current theory, Gilbert (1998a, p. 22) sug- gested that it is the:

> … inner experience of self as an unattractive social agent, under pressure to limit possible damage to self via escape or appeasement, that captures shame most closely. It does not matter if one is rendered unattractive by one's own or other people's actions; what matters is the sense of personal unattractiveness – being in the social world as an undesired self; a self one does not wish to be. Shame is an involuntary response to an awareness that one has lost status and is devalued.

As noted then, whereas we seek to elicit positive feelings (e.g. liking and desires to associate with the self) in the minds of others (this makes the world safe), when we feel shame there is a belief that we will or have stimulated negative feelings (contempt, ridicule, disgust or disinterest) in the minds of others, and, as a consequence, this will lead them either to not wish to form useful relationships with us, to disengage, actively reject the self or even attack the self (all of which make the world threatening). When shame is internalised, individuals may have similar evaluations to part of themselves, that is certain aspects of the self activate feelings of self-directed anger, contempt or hatred rather than feelings of acceptance and pleasure.

Shame involves:

1. *A social or external evaluative component.* This relates to what we think is in the mind of others about ourselves. Beliefs are that others see the self as inferior, bad, inadequate and flawed; that is, others are looking down on the self with a condemning or contemptuous view and will 'disconnect' from or harm the self (Gilbert, 1998a).
2. *An internal self-evaluative component.* This involves the self-judgemental beliefs and feelings that one *is* inferior, inadequate or flawed. Many of our self-attacking thoughts (e.g. I am useless, no good, a bad person, a failure) are in essence shaming thoughts and negative self-evaluations (Gilbert, 1998a; Tangney and Fischer, 1995).
3. *An emotional component.* The emotions and feelings recruited in shame are various but are all from the threat-defence system, and include: anxiety, anger and disgust in the self and self-contempt (Tangney and Fischer, 1995). There is no separate emotion for shame but it is how these primary emotions are textured in the self-identity system.
4. *A behavioural component.* There is a strong urge to adopt a submissive profile, hide, avoid exposure and run away, or (when anger is the emotion) retaliate against the one who is 'exposing' the self as inferior, weak or bad (Lewis, 1992, 2003; Tangney and Fischer, 1995).
5. *A physiological component.* Shame is now known to be one of the most powerful activators of stress responses in social interactions (Dickerson and Kemeny, 2004).

Given that going for counselling and therapy are often times when we will have to 'open up, be honest and discuss the painful things of life (our failures and traumas)', it is not surprising that therapy can be a time of the most acute experiences of shame. Thus, when working with shame we keep in mind two basic facts of human psychology. First, we are all highly motivated to conceal negative information about the self and try to promote positive self-presentations to others (Leary, 1995). Second, acts of concealment may aid self-presentation but can also be highly detrimental to health (Pennebaker, 1997). Shame motivates concealment but concealment inhibits the assimilation of negative information about this self and has detrimental physiological effects (Pennebaker, 1988, 1997; Pennebaker and Becall, 1986). If people can work through experiences that they have not shared before and develop new meanings, this can be highly therapeutic (Pennebaker, 1997). Shame is also a key reason why people feel and remain disconnected and isolated from others. There are also gender differences in how shame affects men and women and is expressed and played out in therapy (Osherson and Krugman, 1990).

Shame plays a key role in a variety of problems, including depression, anxiety, violence, eating disorders and personality disorders (Gilbert, 1997, 1998a; Gilbert and Irons, 2005). Shame can be focused on many aspects of the self. For example, we can feel ashamed of our *bodies* (as is common in some eating disorders, but also in the more typical feelings of being too fat, the wrong shape, of getting old and of disfigurements or various bodily functions; Gilbert and Miles, 2002), our *feelings* (e.g. anger or sexual desires), *traits or abilities* (feeling stupid), and our *behaviours* (e.g. lying or losing control, being submissive or running away and avoiding things out of fear). Shame can significantly interfere with therapeutic relationships, especially when people try to cover up what they feel ashamed about, or have been unable to process or work through emotional episodes heavy in shame (Miller, 1996). Shame can result in important experiences going undisclosed. For example, adult survivors of child sexual abuse can go through counselling without the abuse being addressed (Jehu, 1988, personal communication), and there is an important relationship between shame, sexual abuse and chronic depression (Andrews, 1998). Shame can also produce powerful feelings of helplessness in both counsellor and client. Issues of 'stuckness' can sometimes hint at underlying shame. Here are some examples of shame.

Donna had a difficult third session where she started to discuss abuse. The therapist felt she had been supportive but Donna didn't come back. Subsequently, the therapist discovered that having revealed this history, Donna could not face the therapist again. Sometimes a 'successful' session uncovers shame and this is a dangerous time for avoidance. Therapists can warn patients of this and ask if this might be an issue for them.

Growing up in a very religious household and social group, David had long worried about his sexual orientation (related to religious beliefs) and had kept it hidden from his friends and parents. In doing so, he felt cut off from others, different and bad, and found it desperately painful to discuss in therapy. He just wanted to be 'rid of it'.

Janet had put on weight due to medication and was now 'disgusted' with her body. 'I feel trapped in a horrible alien body' she said, and could not stand for her husband to see or touch it. This added further to her shame for she felt she was failing as a wife and greatly missed their previous sexual life.

Sandra felt exhausted by the birth of her child and at times had feelings of wanting to run away and even of harming her baby son when he didn't stop crying. She could not tell anyone for she felt they would think she was mad and bad.

Although behaviourists have explored avoidance in detail in depression, they rarely focus much on the complexities of shame – one of the major reasons for avoidance. Depression is especially likely if life events elicit a sense of shame (Andrews, 1998; Gilbert, 1992, 1998a, 2004) or humiliation (Brown et al., 1995). For some depressions, shame themes and issues have been around a long time and the person has never really had a robust sense of themselves as attractive, acceptable, able or intrinsically lovable. In post-traumatic stress disorder, shame can play a major role, especially if people are ashamed of how they reacted or have coped (Lee, Scragg and Turner, 2001).

External shame

Recall above that we distinguished between external threats and internal threats. This distinction is important when working with shame. *External shame* relates to the feelings we can have when we think others are looking down on us. That is, in the mind of others we believe we create a self that 'in their minds' is undesirable or rejectable. Thus shame has often been called the emotion of exposure (Lewis, 1992, 2003). When we are sensitive to external shame, and being shamed, our attention is *outward* on what is going on in the minds of others. When working with shame always follow (seek out) the basic threat – not only what the depressed person thinks others will think, but what they think others will *do* (e.g. criticise, ignore, reject or harm). The reason for this is that it is the basic threat that will link you to protection strategies. A simple question of 'so what is the basic threat, or greatest fear here…?' can help. Other therapists might ask: 'What do you see as the worst thing that will happen?' where threat is implied rather than the specific focus and language.

Depressed people may not reveal many things about themselves, not because they do not know about them, but because of how they will exist in your mind *if you* know about them. Think about just how much of yourself, including your thoughts and fantasies, you hold back on for fear of what others will think if they knew what goes on in your mind. So external shame is highly linked to fear of negative evaluation by others. Provided you can keep others from seeing the undesired aspects of self, then you may not be too threatened, although there may be fear of discovery. This kind of shame is common in many disorders and is a *trans-diagnostic* problem. People can worry about how others are viewing them and whether they might do or say something that courts their ridicule ('gosh, he looks odd'), criticisms and rejection. A lot that is written on social anxiety (which animals have) is actually shame anxiety (which animals don't have).

Stigma

External shame relates to fears of stigma. For example, a person might have come to terms with the fact that they have had a mental illness, or a homosexual orientation but can worry that others will reject them if they find out. Pinel (1999) coined the term 'stigma consciousness' to refer to concerns that one will be rejected because one has been located as belonging to a stigmatised group. Thus women, people from different ethnic backgrounds, those from poor or uneducated backgrounds, or those with mental illness or physical disabilities may fear rejection because they are seen as belonging to a 'stigmatised' group. They fear they will not be judged on their own merits but seen as 'one of them'. So the key aspect is that people can have major fears of how they exist in the minds of others in regard to a 'group identity' and this can lead to a host of safety and defensive behaviours. These include a high attentional focus to what others are thinking and feeling about them and efforts to conceal or compensate.

It is very common to find people are ashamed of being depressed and depressed about being depressed. They may believe that depression (and their fatigue and lack of motivation) is evidence of being weak and that others will look down on them or dismiss them as not up to it – a neurotic. Also, because depression can involve loss of the ability to engage in pleasurable activities and constant fatigue, depressed people can feel very unattractive to others. They may feel they are boring or a 'drag' to be with – that they are unattractive.

Types of approval-seeking and shame sensitivity

Seeking reassurance, admiration (mirroring) and approval are typical ways we cope with shame. A need for approval (being valued) is a very human need and not a pathology. In the last chapter we noted that the need for social inclusion and being valued, related to feeling safe, and having confidence that one can co-create advantageous roles. So most humans want to be seen as attractive to others: to be *chosen and desired* as a friend or lover, to be selected for a job, and to be welcomed into a group (Gilbert, 1997, 2003; Leary, 1995). And social support (receiving signals from others around us that we are loved, valued and approved of) can have powerful physiological effects. So, as with many of the themes discussed here, it is often a matter of balancing our capacity (and skills) to gain approval and support from others, while at the same time being able to cope with conflicts and criticism and maintain some sense of our autonomy. Nonetheless, the type and amount of approval one needs from others, and one's feelings about one's 'approval rating' (one's SAHP, see p. 103) are common themes in how depressed people think about themselves. That is, some people are highly prone to depression if the supplies of approval dry up or turn to rejection and criticism.

Seeking intimacies

Many therapists have suggested two basic approval-seeking strategies in the pre-depressive person. The first is focused on forming close attachment bonds that will provide care and protection from a more powerful other. Arieti and Bemporad (1980a, 1980b) called these forms of vulnerability pursuing the *dominant other*; the existential therapist Yalom (1980) called them the pursuit of *the ultimate rescuer*; Beck (1983) calls them *sociotropic*; Blatt, Quinlan, Chevron, McDonald and Zuroff (1982) and Blatt and Zuroff (1992) refer to them as *anaclitic* and *dependent*; attachment theorists refer to them as *anxious attachment* (Mikulincer and Shaver, 2004). In the last chapter we suggested that these are linked to down-rank/subordinate protection strategies. In the pre-depressive phase they tend to be anxious and demonstrate a fair degree of submissiveness in their social behaviour to *avoid shame and rejection*. Such safety behaviours (e.g. clinging, avoidance of expressing anger and self-preferences, and submissiveness) can actually make relationships more problematic. These safety behaviours can become a focus in therapy. Depression and a sense of powerlessness arise when people feel they cannot secure this highly valued goal, and feel a sense of shame (e.g. being weak and unlovable). Loss of important relationships activates protest-despair strategies and people find themselves feeling tearful, anxious (lack of soothing relationships) and aimless.

While there is general agreement on this 'attachment' strategy, as a vulnerability style for depression, there is less agreement on the second type of strategy. The second strategy has been related to seeking to impress others with one's abilities and talents and needing high levels of mirroring-type approval. Arieti and

Bemporad (1980a, 1980b) suggest that these folk are less interested in close, intimate forms of relating than in achieving 'lofty goals' that others will admire. Blatt et al. (1982) and Blatt and Zuroff (1992) suggest that these people are perfectionist and self-critical, while Beck (1983) thinks it is a struggle for autonomy that is key. As noted in the last chapter, we suggested that these may be up-rank strategies, focused on striving to avoid inferiority by adopting certain standards. Living up to group norms, excelling and being validated (be this in behaviours, talent or appearance) is a common theme in depression (Dykman, 1998; Gilbert, 2005b).

Sometimes people can have a chronic sense of 'not being good enough' and that criticisms and rejection are just around the corner. In Dunkley, Zuroff and Blankstein's (2006) model such people have 'evaluative concerns' and can be perfectionist to avoid criticism from others (see p. 105). Their drive systems can become over-activated and they may push themselves hard (e.g. working long hours), shunning play and more intimate goals. The buzz of pleasure (and security) they get from success may become addictive, and positive affect regulation becomes narrowed to such activities alone. Loss of energy, burn out and not being able to keep going, or needing to take time out threaten their life goals, and self-identity. They are more likely to conceal feelings of vulnerability and desires to be loved and comforted. This is partly because anything that threatens their path to success and being in control threatens them with the experience of *shame*.

As good as others? The role of social comparison

Both these strategies are linked by their focus on social comparison. Our inner sense and experience of self can be strongly influenced by how we compare ourselves with others. In fact, social comparison is one of the oldest forms of social cognition and even animals engage in it. For example, an animal has to work out if it is stronger or weaker than a potential opponent before it decides whether to fight or flee (Gilbert, Price and Allan, 1995). The theme of social comparison (in how people derive their self-worth and make judgements about it) is common in depression. There are two types of social comparison, *superior–inferior* (related to hierarchy) and *same–different* (related to belongingness or connectedness; Gilbert, 1992). Indeed, many of our emotions and behaviours, and even life goals, are affected by how we compare ourselves with others and, in general, depressed people compare themselves very unfavourably, seeing themselves as both inferior to others, and different or alienated (Brewin and Furnham, 1986; Gilbert and Allan, 1998; Swallow and Kuiper, 1988). (For a good general overview of social comparison in relation to health, see Buunk and Gibbons, 1997). For these reasons shame is closely linked to the experiences of inferiority and subordination (see Chapter 5).

Sally consistently felt her friends were better mothers than she was; they seemed better organised and less irritable with their children. We had been working on her thoughts and one idea (behavioural experiment) was to talk in detail with a friend. She was surprised to learn that her friend had similar concerns and got irritable and tired too. Sally came to therapy greatly relieved with a new set of ideas (narratives) that mothering is hard and 'it's not just me who *struggles* at times'. This conversation softened her sense of 'being the only one with these difficulties and feeling inferior'.

Parental favouritism can make people acutely aware of social comparison issues, as can some of the competitive dynamics of school and peer groups. Kate was depressed about her appearance. She said that since her school days she had been aware of there being a 'hierarchy of attractiveness', where the prettiest girls got more attention and seemed to be happier. She had spent many years feeling bad (shame) because of her negative social comparisons with others, which were reinforced by images presented in the media. She had a strong belief that only by moving up the hierarchy of attractiveness could she be accepted by others and then feel confident and be happy. There is evidence now that 'attractiveness' is of great benefit in securing many social outcomes (Etcoff, 1999).

Patterns

If you follow the approach I have been taking here, then the focus is on patterns and narratives in the mind. Most depressed people will have various patterns of these two strategies and express them in different ways in different relationships. For example, I have encountered some men who are rather tyrannical at home, but are submissive and clingy at work with the boss, or who can be tyrannical at work and docile at home. How you experience a depressed person in your therapy room might be different from how their family experiences them.

The different patterns of vulnerability may also reflect gender differences, with women tending to be more sociotropic, with anxious attachment and low-rank strategies. This is not necessarily genetic but social, in that women tend to be socialised to, and occupy, more low-rank positions. As social pressures build in competitive societies, the patterns of depression in women may change too, becoming more 'male-like' in their need to compete and prove their worth.

If we keep in mind that depression is related to threat, then shame-threat that results in feelings of inferiority, exclusion and rejection is common to many types of depression. Although there are different strategies for coping with the threat of social disconnection, unwanted subordinations, and exerting control over social relationships, external shame-threat (being devalued in the minds of others) is a common theme.

The internal world of shame-threat, self-criticism and terror

Beck et al. (1979) suggested that the stream of depressed, negative thinking focuses on three key domains: the self, the world and the future. In regard to thoughts about the world, and especially the social world, we covered these aspects above. This noted various cognitive systems that are set up to monitor and evaluate how we experience ourselves as 'living in the minds of others'. The external world is not just a place of objects and things, but also of other minds. Thus we focused on certain interpersonal needs (for mirroring, protection and comfort, approval, achievement, social acceptance and belonging). These make us acutely sensitive to (external) shame. In this section, we are going to consider the internal experience of the depressed self, that is self-to-self relating. In terms of the multiple levels outlined in Chapter 2, these are domains 3 and 4. As Beck et al. (1979) noted, the depressed person experiences a stream of negative self-focused thinking that may or may not be in the forefront of consciousness. Such negative thoughts and feelings are often threat-focused, and patterned by threat-processing systems.

How we experience ourselves and how components that make up our brains interact, can give rise to negative experiences of self – a self in conflict. This is a potentially vast area to explore so we will keep our focus on shame and, in particular, internal shame – the way we can experiences 'ourselves' and relate to ourselves with anger, fear and/or disgust. A key to much depression-related psychopathology is that we have lost contact with a cohesive and desirable sense of self. The separation between what we think and feel about ourselves and what we think others think and feel about ourselves is in a constant dynamic flow, so this separation of processes needs to be held loosely. Nonetheless gaining insight into the power of internal shame, and especially the self-critical and self-attacking aspects of internal shame can be helpful in working with depressed people.

Internal shame: the bad-punishable self

Internal shame is the shame we feel about the self. It relates to the way we attend to and judge various aspects of the self and then try to control, subdue, avoid, conceal, compensate for, or even get rid of those aspects. In external shame we try to avoid such aspects of ourselves appearing in the minds of others: 'I don't want you to see this about me or see me this way.' Internal shame is about our own feelings: 'I don't want to see myself like this or I don't want to be like this. *I* am ashamed and rendered unattractive in *my own* eyes by my own attributes, thoughts, feelings or behaviours.' As noted, we can feel ashamed of our *bodies,* our own *feelings, fantasises or thoughts*, or by our *traits or abilities* and our *behaviours.*

These internal shames are, of course, threat-focused and have a history to them (Kaufman, 1989). We are not born ashamed but learn to be ashamed. Of all animals, we are the most dependent on care in early life. Our brains grow and mature rapidly after birth, and our neuronal connections and sense of self (self-identity) are shaped by life experiences. This is why we spent some time exploring attachment and learning styles in the last chapter. There is now considerable evidence that abuse of various kinds (sexual, physical, emotional and verbal) lays down foundations for a sense of being a 'bad self' (Andrews, 1998; Bifulco and Moran, 1998). These can be coded in conditioned emotional memories that are not always easy to articulate. Importantly, though, they can texture inner creations, including our dreams.

Terrors and dreams   Cukrowicz et al. (2006) have found that depression and suicidality are linked to sleep disturbances and insomnia and one aspect of these is nightmares (clear indications of threat-focused processes at work). Beck (1967), in early research, found that depressed people often have masochistic (i.e. submissive) themes in their dreams. However, these themes are often about having done something wrong and then being punished, persecuted or even killed. Jane had a critical mother and throughout most of her life had a 'nagging feeling' that she had done something wrong and was bad in some way. She 'knew' that this was irrational and probably related to her mother's behaviour but the feeling did not go away. When she was depressed she had a terrrifying dream. She dreamt that in a 'past life' she had been a torturer and now her depression was a punishment. Psychodynamic therapists might view this as guilt/fear over hostile impulses towards her mother. Perhaps, and she was not averse to such possibilities. However, what made more sense to her was the feeling of being bad; and having done bad things (and being a torturer would be very bad in her own self-definition) for which she is to be punished was a form of emotional memory played out in her dreams. It made sense to her because she noted that 'as a child I often felt I had done something terrible that my mother would have a rage over'. And of course if mother was 'raging,' then whatever it was would have the emotional feel of being terrible/bad – after all your mother does not rage over minor things! So the dream was like an echo of these memories of having done something bad and then being punished. Working in imagery–telling mother 'your rage is completely unacceptable. You do this to me because you are out of control and need help. I am sorry you are so messed up but that is not my fault' – was helpful (see Hackmann, 2005). Lee (2005) advocates a careful cognitive analysis of the 'credentials' of the person who was hostile to the self (e.g. are they loving, a good judge of character and had your interests at heart), to help the person see that the accusers are not reliable judges (see below on the issue of rebellion).

Some years ago Lewis Wolpert made an excellent documentary series for BBC2 on depression, following his own depression. In one programme, Chris Brewin interviewed a man who had had a rejecting and aggressive father. He too recounted a powerful dream. He and others were dressed in Ku Klux Klan robes and he knew he was about to be executed. When one of the people pulled back his hood he saw it was his father. In our dreams, the terrors can be highly embellished, related to deep archetypal fears (e.g. to be punished or killed). Dreams like these may tell us something about internal threat-focused scenarios that the brain is 'running'. Psychodynamic therapists talk of internal *persecution* fantasises and fears. In my view, these are related to emotional memories and safety strategies, including fear of one's own natural retaliation/revenge strategies.

There are many kinds of hurtful and blaming experiences that can leave children with emotional memories of punishment for wrongdoing (as labelled by a parent) and feeling they are bad. These are coded as interpersonal and interactional scenes. David's father would have rages and beat him. Through much of his life he had this 'background feeling' that something could go wrong or he could make a serious mistake at any moment and then 'something very bad would happen'. Sally came from a problematic family (her mother had been abused and suffered emotional instabilities, getting angry and blaming or becoming withdrawn). When Sally got depressed she was also slightly paranoid, feeling that the police would come to her door and blame her for something terrible and take her away. You can hypothesise all kinds of associations here – such that as a child she wished someone (e.g. the police) had *taken her mother away* and made her safe. However, it is important to stay with felt experience, which is the sense of being bad and having done something wrong – that is shame.

Carole was caught up in an abusing family over which there was intense secrecy. The abuser was also an intensely cruel man whom everyone in the family feared and appeased. She had gone though fifteen years of psychiatric treatment and never revealed it. Even though the abuser was dead, she felt he could haunt her. It was many months before she started to indicate this. When she started work on these memories she was overcome with terror and wanted to apologise to 'him' for saying anything. She became tearful and wanted to stop therapy, feeling there was no one who could protect her. Gradual exposure to her fears, behavioural experiments and assertive responses were helpful and offered a therapeutic support. Carole was also afraid of openingly revealing and acknowledging her own hatred of him. The point here is that sometimes internal shame memories are associated with intense fears of persecution, can produce highly dissociated states (as a result of conflicts to attack and submit), but these can be missed if one does not carefully look out for them.

Different therapists will explain these difficulties in different ways. Cognitive therapists, for example, will point to types of core beliefs ('I am bad'), self–other schema and modes (Beck, 1996). My own view is in terms of conditioned emotions that are coded as interpersonal memories (Baldwin, 2005; Brewin, 2006: Greenberg and Watson, 2006). Because these memories are those of threat and punishment, linked to experiences/feelings of being to blame for being bad, and because depression activates threat systems and threat processing, these can come back to texture the experience of depression and activate protection strategies. Psychiatric classifications that separate post-traumatic stress disorder (PTSD), depression and anxiety, as if they are different disorders, are unhelpful here because these kinds of depressions can be rooted in traumatic memory. However, unlike PTSD trauma memories, which tend to focus on one or a few intense events, these kinds of trauma are of multiple events and basic relationship styles, especially of a hostile dominant enforcing subordination. Telling people that they have a 'disease' called depression and need drugs can, for some people, simply fuel these feelings that there is something wrong with them. Although drugs can be very helpful for some people, one needs to be very sensitive in how one explains their possible use.

Cognitive behavioural therapists have made major inroads into understanding the nature of trauma memory (Brewin, 2006; Dalgleish, 2004; Lee, 2005) and developing exposure-focused treatments (Clark and Ehlers, 2004). Hackmann (2005) outlines the importance of, and ways of working with, early memories and helping people de–sensitise and give new meaning to them. In compassion-focused therapy (see Chapter 11 of this volume; Gilbert and Irons, 2005), people are taught how to develop compassion for these feelings and memories. We develop compassion for the fear of being bad and punished, and compassion for feeling vengeful as a defence. So although these experiences can be represented in the language of core beliefs ('I am bad'), one must work with the *conditioned emotions* (see Chapter 4; Hackmann, 2005). The take-home message is then that deep shame-based feelings can be rooted in trauma memory where intense threat (e.g. from a parent) was associated with being (told one was) bad and blame-worthy. The emotional experience textures self-schema and self-identity, and our theory of mind focus. Moreover, these memories are likely to affect the psychobiological organisation of the person.

The inner world of emotions and our fears of them

It is well known that we can develop secondary emotions to primary emotions due to how we interpret them (Leahy, 2002; Linehan, 1993). People can become anxious of getting anxious if they think their anxiety will have a major harmful outcome. They then develop safety behaviours to avoid feeling anxious and attribute the non-occurrence of the threat to the safety behaviour (Salkovskis, 1996a). However, we can feel threatened by the emergence in us of a range of emotions and fantasises. As Freud suggested, the inner world can become threatening to our sense of self, although nowadays we have different ways of thinking about threats emerging from within.

Because we have abilities for self-awareness and self-identity formation, we can experience a range of internal stimuli (emotions and fantasies) as threatening. This threat can be to the physical self (this anxiety will put my heart rate up and kill me) or shame-focused on a self-identity and social roles (this anxiety means I am a weak person; it will overwhelm me, or get out of control, and/or others will see this and reject me).

Leahy (2001, 2002, 2005) pointed out that people can develop a range of negative threat reactions to their own internal stimuli of emotions/motives/desires and fantasies – that is, these internal experiences constitute threats. There are many culturally related stories about this fear of 'the emergence of the beast within', as depicted in films like *The Hulk*, horror films and stories of Dr Jekyll and Mr Hyde. We are fascinated by these because they tap basic archetypal fears in us. Carl Jung called these 'the shadow'. These threats are linked to beliefs that certain emotions/desires/fantasies might be overwhelming and take control, are confusing, would be shamed by others, and by beliefs in thought-action fusion (if I think or feel it, it is as bad as doing it). Safety behaviours can involve trying not to think about certain things, avoiding situations that elicit certain feelings, hiding feelings from others, denial or dissociation. Leahy makes clear that the therapist's role here involves containment and psycho-education on the complexities of our evolved and socially shaped emotional lives; that we can have multiple and conflicting feelings/desires (because of parallel processing systems) to the same event (e.g. can be angry with someone we love), normalising (i.e. 'it is understandable that you feel threatened by this because … '), exposure and validation. Therapist empathy and warmth are crucial so as not to activate shame ('I am stupid to think like this; my therapist thinks I am immature with my emotions'). This requires the therapist to be empathically attuned with the patient, have an appropriate understanding of emotions and feared material (e.g. a patient can have sadistic revenge fantasies that are feared), and feel safe enough with their own emotions and 'shadow material' to act as a *soothing* agent. The therapist helps clients (re)code their inner world as safe to the extent that, while some emotions/fantasies are unpleasant or strange, they are normal to our humanity, and are manageable once we accept them, no longer fight to suppress or deny them, or label ourselves negatively as a consequence of having them. They can in fact be important sources of information that need to be addressed (Greenberg and Watson, 2006). Jung believed that 'shadow material' could be a source of vitality and creativity if approached in certain ways and integrated in the mind.

Conditioning   We can look at these difficulties in another way based on conditioning. For some depressed people, therapists will be aware that some emotions/desires are under conditioned inhibitory control (Ferster, 1973; Gilbert, 1992).

As we explored in Chapter 4 (pp. 67–68), Ferster (1973) pointed out that if a child's expression of anger or affection-seeking is constantly punished, this will generate anxiety and fear of punishment. Thus the inner stimuli/feelings of anger or affection-seeking will be associated with fear, until the arousal of anger or affection-seeking automatically elicits a conditioned fear/anxiety response. In this context the child may gradually become unaware of feelings of anger or affection-seeking, where these could normally be useful. Instead, they are only aware of the secondary con-ditioned anxiety to stimuli, and not anger feelings or affection-seeking. This can have serious consequences for the child's abilities to recognise certain emotions and mature them in helpful ways.

Shame commonly underpins problems of becoming sensitive to one's internal emotions that can seem confusing. Recall that humans are highly motivated to try to create positive feelings in the minds of others about the self – in part because this makes the world safe and in part because it facilitates opportunities to develop positive relationships with those who are conducive to our prosperity (e.g. friendships and sexual partners). Shame, as we noted, is about becoming the undesired self – the self one does not want to be. Thus one reason why people avoid distressing emotions is that to process those feelings takes the self to where it does not want to be – a shamed and vulnerable self. Therapists may need to explain and explore these aspects with their clients and normalise these feelings.

Self-criticism

Driscoll (1989) pointed out that self-criticism has many functions, e.g. to stop us making errors or to drive us on. One can relate to one's self (or parts of self) in the same way as one relates to others. For example, one can like or dislike oneself, be helpful and take care of oneself or ignore one's needs. We can forgive ourselves errors or become intensely frustrated and *self-critical and attacking*. This type of self-to-self relating emerges from our ability to have self-awareness, meta-cognitions, form a self-identity and to be able to view self as 'object'. There is now much evidence that self-criticism pervades many disorders, especially depression, and has been a focus of many therapies (Blatt and Zuroff, 1992; Gilbert and Irons, 2005; Gilbert and Procter, 2006; Zuroff, Santor and Mongrain, 2005). Zuroff, Koestner and Powers (1994) found that the degree of self-criticism in childhood is a predictor of later adjustment. People with psychosis who hear 'condemning voices' can take the fact that the voice knows their deepest secrets and fears as evi-dence that the voice is omnipotent. They mistake the internal (self-to-self) sham-ing systems for an external shaming-attacking system.

Self-critical depressions can be difficult to treat with standard therapies (Rector, Bagby, Segal, Joffe and Levitt, 2000). Depressed self-critics can be motivated to escape negative feelings with suicide and use more lethal means (Fazaa and Page, 2003). Self-critics can also be critical of others, particularly if they have been criti-cised; that is they show strong tendencies to retaliate and defend their status aggressively (Santor and Zuroff, 1997). Self-criticism affects abilities to form affil-iative relationships. Zuroff, Moskowitz and Cote (1999) found those high on dependency needs are submissive and inhibit hostility to others. Self-critics, on the other hand, can behave in hostile *and* resentfully submissive ways, are relatively poor at validating others, and have problems developing affiliative relationships. Perhaps given this, or in addition to it, Dunkley, Zuroff and Blankstein (2003, p. 235) suggest that self-critical perfectionists experience chronic dysphoria 'because they experience minor hassles in catastrophic terms and perceive others as condemning, unwilling or unavailable to help them in times of stress'. Irons, Gilbert, Baldwin, Baccus and Palmer (2006) found that self-criticism and lack of abilities to be self-reassuring mediated the link between recall of aversive rearing by parents and depression in students.

Repeatedly, we come back to the way various aspects of depression, including self-criticism, are linked to experiences and expectations of others – because it is not the failure itself that is usually the threat but the internal negative representation of what others will do that is the threat to humans. The point for depression is that depressed people, who have both high external shame (see others as quickly condemning with emotional memories of such) (Baldwin, 2005) and internal shame, are in deep trouble. When things go wrong for them or they make mistakes, they experience both the internal world and the external world turning hostile and condemning them. There is no safe place to go. The ability to soothe the self by focusing on positives, activating positive emotional memories or being able to look to others for help, are all cut off. If defeat strategies can be activated by attacks, then our own self-attack may be enough to activate this strategy.

A key problem with self-criticism is that one cannot get away from it. Because it exists on the inside there is no concealing it from one's own inner eye. People often feel trapped with their own self-attacking thoughts and would like to escape from them (Gilbert and Allan, 1998; Gilbert et al., 2003). The combination of processes, of feeling inferior to others, high self-criticism, feeling trapped and wanting to escape from one's internal self-criticisms was explored in an important study by Sturman and Mongrain (2005). They studied 146 graduate students who had experienced at least one episode of depression and were given structured clinical interviews. They also measured levels of self-criticism, social comparison style, feeling trapped by external events and feeling trapped with one's own negative thoughts. Self-criticism was significantly associated with feelings of being trapped with one's negative thoughts ($r = .60$) and feeling inferior ($r = -.44$; the minus indicates that the lower the score the more inferior you feel). A key finding was that feeling trapped and inferior significantly mediated the link between self-criticism and major depressive episodes. Thus as these researchers suggest, a self-critical style may develop for a variety of reasons but its linkage to feelings of inferiority and also being motivated to get away from one's own self-attacking are key to depression. The fact that one can't get away from these internal self-attacks, and the feeling of inferiority may also link to feeling alone and beyond rescue. They are also a form of constant *internal harassment and bullying* that is stressful.

Gilbert, Birchwood, Gilbert et al. (2001) looked at a similar process in comparing depressed people with critical thoughts and people with psychosis, who hear hostile, condemning voices. Depressed people were asked to identify the content of their critical thoughts and in most cases they were highly derogatory and shaming. For both depressed people, in regard to their thoughts, and voice hearers in regard to their voices, there was a clear association between the dominance and power of these thoughts/voices and depression. Moreover, the more trapped and flight motivated they were to these thoughts/voices, the more depressed they were. The correlation between feeling trapped with one's critical thoughts and depression was $r = .56$. The correlation between wanting to escape from one's critical thoughts and depression was $r = .45$.

Beaten down by one's own criticism

People can feel *internally harassed*, bullied, put-down, and defeated by their own negative and self-attacking thoughts and feelings. Greenberg and his colleagues (1990, p. 170) have indicated two aspects of this internal self-relationship that often come together to produce depression:

> Based on our clinical observation, it appears that depression is much more likely if a person's weak/bad, hopeless, self-organisation is triggered, than if the critical self and negative cognitions alone are activated. It is much more the person's response to the negative cognitions and their inability to cope with the self-criticisms, than the cognitions and criticisms alone, that lead to depression. People are unable to counter or combat the negative cognitions when the weak/bad helpless state has been evoked. This is when depressed affect emerges.

In my view it is when self-criticism activates the inferiority-subordinated-defeat protection strategies, with their closing down and narrowing of attention aspects, that is the problem here; that is to say our own self-put-downs, as internally generated signals, can stimulate protection strategies that evolved to cope with hostile others. Evidence for this comes from a variety of sources. Whelton and Greenberg (2005) measured students' levels of self-criticism with the Depressive Experiences Questionnaire. They then asked each student to sit in one chair and spend five minutes imagining themselves sitting in the other chair, and to criticise themselves. They were then invited to switch chairs and respond to the self-criticism. Those high in self-criticism often *submitted* to (agreed with) their own self-criticisms, expressed shame and submissive postures (slumped with head down, eyes averted) and sad faces, and felt weak and unable to counteract their own self-criticisms. In other words, submissive and defeat-like profiles were activated *to their own attacks*. Low self-critics found it easy to dismiss their criticisms.

Why people can't cope or defend themselves against their own self-criticisms, and feel beaten down by them, is related to a range of factors that include the intensity, focus and type of self-criticism. Self-criticism is a form of self-to-self *relationship*, where one part of self finds fault with, accuses, condemns or even hates the self. In our research (Gilbert, Clarke, Kempel, Miles and Irons, 2004), we have found there are two functions of self-criticism. One is to goad a person on – to try harder and avoid making mistakes, to self-correct and self-improve. A sense of defeat arises when the person simply feels unable to keep going at this. The other form of self-criticism is to hurt the self because of self-disgust or hatred, with a wish to try to get rid of parts of the self. Improving self-critics do not necessarily dislike or hate themselves but feel they must 'keep' their self-criticism as a way to ensure self-improvement. Nonetheless, the relentless barrage of self-criticisms is depressing. Part of the role of the counsellor is therefore to help the client (a) to recognise the degree and extent of internal self-downing and negative self-talk (e.g. 'I'm a failure, I'm boring, I'm useless'); (b) think about why they self-criticise (the functions; emotional memories); and (c) to change this negative self-to-self relationship talk to a more nurturing, accepting and compassionate self-to-self relationship (Gilbert and Irons, 2005; see also Chapter 11 this volume).

Self-criticism as a safety strategy

Over a century ago the philosopher Nietzsche (1844–1900) suggested that no one blames themselves without a secret wish for vengeance. Freud (1917) adopted this same idea in his essay on 'Mourning and Melancholia', when he argued that depression is anger turned inward (Ellenberger, 1970). This happens because to express anger to others that one is dependent on could hurt or drive them away. This can be looked at in a different way in relationship to submissive safety strategies and power dynamics (Gilbert, 1984). If someone is much more powerful than you and they are threatening or critical of you, and you cannot get away from them, then what is the best defence? If you blame them and express your anger this could get you into even more trouble. A submissive defence would be to self-monitor and try to ensure you do not do things that excite their anger, and to self-blame if you do (if you blame them they will be more angry!). One blames self in part because when we are self-monitoring, trying to control our outputs/behaviours so as to avoid anger from the others, if they are angry, then it must be because of our outputs/behaviours. By blaming our outputs/behaviours we can see where we 'went wrong' and try harder next time.

My daughter Hannah, who is an anthropologist, drew my attention to these processes at a cultural level, noting that this style is common in some religions, especially where Gods are seen as powerful and potentially hostile. Once we have constructed these powerful Gods who can control the world, and the benefits and misfortunes to befall us, then the next thing is to bring them onside as helpful agents. If we can do this, then they won't send the diseases or famines. So maybe a few sacrifices or obedience to laws will appease them. If things go wrong – harvests fail and diseases kill one's children – people often do not blame their Gods and defect, but wonder what they might have done to upset them and how they can atone. Even more submissive appeasement and sacrifice, perhaps? These are highly focused safety behaviours. As in other forms of safety behaviour and beliefs (Salkovskis, 1996a), if the diseases do not come and life seems good, then this is explained because the Gods are happy with us or favour us. And so the beliefs are maintained. The reason for noting this here is to point out that self-blame is not (just) a cognitive distortion or even a pathology as such, but operates as a safety behaviour in individuals, and even for whole societies. It is linked to power dynamics.

Self-criticism and self-blame, as defensive/safety (appeasement) behaviours, which are linked to efforts to calm the self and *the other* in conflict situations, were discovered by Forrest and Hokanson (1975). They investigated the propensity for depressed and non-depressed people to use self-punishing behaviours in response to interpersonal conflict (confederate aggression). They measured physiological arousal to conflicts, and how arousal changed depending on how a person responded to the challenge on them. One of their measures was rates of self-administered electric shock in response to aggressive behaviours from others. They found that baseline rates of self-punishing responses were much higher for a depressed compared to a non-depressed group. They suggested that this indicates a previously established repertoire (self-attacking) for dealing with aggression *from others*. They also found evidence that self-punishment, or the emission of a friendly (appeasement) response, in the face of aggression from another, had significant arousal-reducing properties for depressed but not for non-depressed people. In other words, self-attacking and appeasement could reduce the arousal associated with confrontation in the depressed, but not in the non-depressed group. Forrest and Hokanson (1975, p. 355) state:

> The experimental findings indicate that the greatest plethysmographic arousal reduction takes place in the depressed group when a self-punitive (or friendly) counterresponse is made to the aggressive confederate. The nondepressed group exhibited comparably rapid reductions only following an aggressive counterresponse.

This led them to suggest that:

> ... depressed patients have learned to cope with environmental and interpersonal stresses with self-punitive and/or non-assertive behaviors and these behaviors have been successful in dealing with normal day-to-day existence. At times when situational stresses become great this limited behavioral repertoire may be invoked to a degree that may seriously impair adequate functioning and these people may manifest a clinical depressive or *masochistic* episode. (p. 356, italics added)

The idea that self-blaming is a safety behaviour was also explored by Trower, Sherling, Beech, Horrop and Gilbert (1998). They asked socially and non-socially anxious people to interact in a conversation with a confederate on a video. The confederate, however, broke conversation rules by interrupting and changing the subject. When later watching the video, non-socially anxious students blamed the confederate for these rule breaks while the socially anxious people blamed themselves. Social anxiety is a well-known vulnerability factor for some depressions and these data fit with those of Forrest and Hokanson (1975). A self-blaming style will clearly increase the disposition to feel shame in some contexts.

It is also known that subordinate monkeys will often return and approach dominant animals who have threatened or harmed them, expressing submissive behaviours as they do so, until the dominant pats, or strokes them and indicates reconciliation (called reverted escape). It is a way the subordinate can reduce hostile intent in the dominant. Further discussion of submissive defences as ways to calm both self and dominants can be found in Gilbert (2000b).

The emotions of internal shame and self-criticism

Shame and self-criticisms are not just negative thoughts but are experienced with powerful emotions. Cognitive therapists often focus on the consequence of negative thoughts (e.g. feeling depressed), not on the emotion *of the thoughts themselves*. However, it is the emotion *in* the self-critical thoughts that seems most linked to emotional difficulties. An easy way to elicit the experience of emotion in shame and self-criticism is to ask 'when you focus on your self-critical thoughts what is the main emotion in them – how do you feel or hear them in your mind?' A number of studies have found that shame is associated with anger to self and others, and can be ruminative and destructive (Gilbert and Miles, 2000; Tangney, Wagner, Barlow, Marschall and Gramzow, 1996).

Power and Dalgleish (1997) suggested that self-disgust underpins shame. Lewis (1992) suggests that shame can occur when parents show a disgust face to the child's behaviour; that is, the child experiences having generated disgust in the mind of the parent. In my view disgust is involved in some problems of self-criticism and shame, but not all. The affect of disgust evolved to deal with expelling and avoiding noxious substances. Disgust is about the body, bodily excretions and contaminants. When people have disgust-focused shame it is usually on some aspect of the body, and is felt to be internal. The desire is to destroy, get rid of, expel and cleanse oneself (Gilbert and Irons, 2004). Although there is little research evidence, disgust-shame seems common for those who have suffered sexual abuse. In these experiences people can feel that there is something 'horrible' about them and they want to expel it or cut it out. This is why body shame is prominent in these cases (Andrews, 1998). Contempt is related to disgust but the focus is on being a very low rank. It is associated with terms such as 'pathetic'. Disgust and contempt feelings about the self are also related to self-hatred (Gilbert, Clarke, Kempel, Miles and Irons, 2004).

The differences between feeling an 'inadequate' self, a 'bad' self and a 'horrible' self or a 'contemptible' self are both subtle and important because they indicate different emotional textures to self-experience and may require different therapeutic interventions (Gilbert and Irons, 2005). If one only works with core beliefs or schema, these subtleties can be missed. Self-compassion-focused therapy was developed in part to work directly with the emotions *in* the self-criticism (Gilbert and Irons, 2004; see also Chapter 11 in this volume).

Self-criticism is thus a complex process with different origins, different foci, and different emotions. Also there can be major fears in giving it up. Self-improving self-critics hold on to self-criticisms because they see them as a route to avoid errors and push themselves on. Some hold on to them because they are an established safety behaviour. Those with disgust-based self-disliking and self-criticisms do not want to accept themselves as they are because they are focused on trying to rid themselves of feelings of disgust and contempt. Learning to 'accept' feelings of fear and anxiety or even depression (Hayes et al., 1996; Linehan, 1993) may be easier than working with feelings of self-disgust. Counsellors who follow a *functional* analysis approach will be well placed to explore these variations with clients and not be lulled into thinking they are only the result of cognitive 'distortions' or 'errors of reasoning'.

A model for shame

The potential to feel shame evolved because we are a self-aware and self-identity forming species. We seek social validation to feel safe, fit in and belong, compete for social place and engage with others to form advantageous social roles. How our efforts turn out and what we do if we cannot feel safe in the minds of others can be depicted in a simple model (see Figure 6.1).

From the first days of life we need others to care for us, for not only will that influence our survival but also such inputs (along with genes) will actually shape

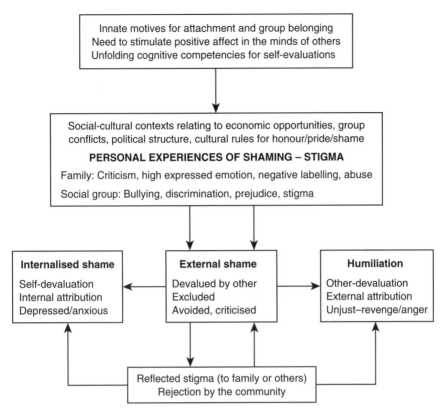

Figure 6.1   An evolutionary and biopsychosocial model for shame

Adapted from Gilbert, 2002: 34, reproduced with permission from Routledge

the kind of brain we will mature; the self we will become. Key to such is the generation of positive feelings in others we can elicit about the self. We are born with unfolding motives and competencies (e.g. self-awareness and theory of mind) to mature into complex social beings, able to co-create and navigate and narrate our self-identities to fit local, social ecologies.

At the next level are the social processes that impinge on *personal* experiences. Children are subjected to parental rearing practices that can be caring, soothing and loving, or hostile, critical, abusive or neglectful. These early experiences will lay down affect-based memories of others as helpful or not, caring or threatening (Kaufman, 1989), and interpersonal schema that will come to regulate self-organising systems (Baldwin, 2005). As noted above, key to this can be shame-filled memories that texture the experiences of self being bad or having done something wrong. In the wider social domains of peers, individuals may experience their reference groups as accepting and supportive or bullying. Peer bullying can be a common experience for shame, especially when bullying involves exclusion and ridicule – attacks on one's attractiveness and social standing (Hawker and Boulton, 2000). As for group dynamics beyond close peer relationships, the social contexts can be experienced as prejudicial or discriminatory on the basis of ethnicity, gender, physical attributes (e.g. deformities) desires (e.g. homosexuality) and talents (or lack of talents). Moreover, individuals can fear being shamed and stigmatised, not necessarily because of their personal abilities as such, but because of fear of being classed as belonging to a stigmatised group – being 'one of them' (Pinel, 1999). Thus, the social contexts for shame arise from local, historical, cultural and ecological conditions that influence personal interactions and provide the backdrop on which people seek to mature and satisfy their social needs and shape their identities. Cultures that are unjust and/or drive competitions between people, and create gross disparities of power, and haves, have nots and have lots, create greater domains for shame and have raised rates of mental ill health and crime (Arrindell et al., 2003; Wilkinson, 1996).

The centre of this model is therefore *external shame*. It is when the world is seen as unsafe (and others will be rejecting) that people will engage in defensive strategies. If the chosen defence is submissive (and this can be triggered in the first instances non-consciously), this will go with high levels of self-monitoring, self-attribution styles and efforts to try to regulate expressions and minimise harm from others (Gilbert and Irons, 2005; Gilbert and Miles, 2000; Keltner and Harker, 1998). Such individuals tend to focus on their relative inferiority and relative (lack of) power to resist others, and blaming self can be safer than blaming powerful others (e.g. one's Gods or parents) who can retaliate (Gilbert, 2005a). This does not mean that shamed people, who adopt submissive defences, do not feel anger for, as noted above, they can do – both to themselves and others.

An alternative defence to social threats, however, is to express aggression, particularly in environments where submissiveness is likely to cause even more difficulties and threats. This can be seen as an externalising *humiliation* response, which focuses on 'the other as bad', with desires for revenge (Gilbert, 1998a). The essence of the humiliation response arises with anger as the automatic defence to a put down, slur or rejection. In street language, it is to be 'dissed', and the need to develop a reputation of someone who is not to be 'messed with' (Ahmed and Braithwaite, 2004). Humiliation and shame are not be mutually exclusive and people can move between them. People with shame may come to recognise anger at others who have harmed them, and people who express humiliation may come to acknowledge fears and vulnerabilities that are kept out of consciousness with anger. Key to whether people can shift position and acknowledge warded-off emotions depends on how safe they feel with others when exploring them (Greenberg and Watson, 2006).

Finally, we can note that in cultures where shame and honour systems are intimately linked to the behaviours of one's associates, issues of reflected shame/honour (how, for example, my family's or group's behaviour can shame me and my behaviour can shame them) become prominent, and then the defence and repair of shame are linked to the power dynamic of the relationship and cultural scripts for honour and the repair of honour (Lindisfarne, 1998).

This descriptive process model places centre-stage the importance of how we have experienced, and currently experience, 'the mind of others' and their behaviour towards us in various domains, both intimate and social. In this model, shame cannot be detextualised from the social dynamics in which it exists, nor from our evolved needs for social safeness, and to engage others in various social roles (for a more detailed exploration, see Gilbert, in press a).

Life is hard

We noted in Chapter 1 that poverty is highly linked to depression. While the psychological aspects of depression are important, we should not underestimate the fact that for some people *life is hard* and simply exhausts their resources to cope. We must avoid simple notions that if someone gets depressed it is something *inside* them that has gone wrong (be this becoming more negative in their thinking or a change in brain chemistry). If we are to do anything on the epidemic of depression, then attention to social factors is paramount. So at times we may be trying to support and boost people's coping resources with guided support, empathic 'being with' and problem-solving help. Nonetheless if people feel they are doing a good job in difficult circumstances they may be spared shame and depression. It is when people feel that they cannot cope, and in spite of life hardships (that are not their fault) there is something wrong with them or they should be coping better than they are, or that they are losers and failures – that this is associated with depression. We can ponder how cultures fuel these beliefs and experiences.

Conclusion

This chapter has been a long one because we have tried to pull a lot of different threads together. It has pointed out that we are a species that, like other species, pursue various social goals. Unlike other species, however, we have evolved a complex set of abilities for types of self-awareness, meta-cognition, theory of mind and need for coherent self-identities that are culturally appropriate. We are a species deeply dependent on others from the first days of our lives. All our new abilities evolved because they helped us better adapt to the social world in which we live, and as these abilities evolved so did the social world we need to adapt to. Our needs for love and abilities to give love and care make us capable of bringing new ways of being into a world that can be harsh and indifferent to suffering. However, we are also something of a tragic species because our self-awareness cannot easily free itself from the motives and strategies (for love, protection, acceptance, belonging, revenge, despair) that evolved long ago. Our emotions act as guides to goals that are still primitive in design and our protection strategies can powerfully pattern the internal organisation of our minds. The tragedies of wars and mental illness owe much to the way our minds find it difficult to follow the rational and compassionate when threat-protection patterns are activated. We can act, dictated by our feelings, even when we know it is irrational to do so.

As for psychotherapy, we can ask why psychotherapy exists at all? How can the mind of one person have such an impact on the mind of another? There is one reason only – that we have evolved minds that are highly sensitive to the relationships in which they are embedded. This is shown in our needs for attachment, protection and nurturance, intersubjectivity, and in our need for other minds to help us mature, develop and regulate our own, and shape our self-identities – right down to the way our genes are expressed. It is against this backdrop of evolved design that the psychotherapists can work in the way they do – to use their mind to heal and help the minds of their clients. So psychotherapy of many forms seeks to offer hope, to find ways to exert some control over the primitive; to face our anxieties with courage; to not act or judge ourselves and others as our emotions tell us to; and to find ways of thinking, feeling and behaving that turn off (in this case) the pain of depressive protection strategies.

PART II

Processes for the Therapeutic Journey

The first six chapters explored various ways of conceptualising depression. With this knowledge we are now able to explore the processes involved in working with depressed people, starting with the importance of developing a *therapeutic* relationship and working alliance.

7 The Therapeutic Relationship and Working Alliance

The therapeutic relationship is a meeting and interaction of minds. It is thus an emergent and co-constructed relationship. Although there is now general agreement that the therapeutic relationship is a major ingredient for successful therapy, there are different views of how the therapeutic relationship exerts its impact (Freeman and McCloskey, 2003; Liotti, 2007; Norcross, 2002). Zuroff and Blatt (2006) outline four possible routes by which the therapeutic relationship exerts its impact. For example, in some client-centred approaches it is believed that it is the way the therapist creates safe conditions for the patient to explore their inner world that produces change, rather than any specific technologies.

A second view, common to psychodynamic approaches, is that it is what goes on in the mind of the therapist, as they engage the mind of the patient, that is crucial to change. Especially important is the therapist's ability to be aware of the reactions that they trigger in their clients (transference) and what emerges inside themselves (countertransference). These are seen as pointers to the client's difficulties. How the therapist works with these dynamic interactions and co-constructions affects the emergence of unconscious material and thus insight and progress.

A third view, more common to cognitive behavioural therapists, is that the therapeutic relationship is important because a trusting and helpful relationship sets the platform for *collaboration* on the tasks of therapy. The 'potent' aspects of therapy are in the new learning (e.g. via understanding thought–emotions links and practising thought change, engaging in behavioural experiments, exposure, and practising anti-rumination strategies).

A fourth view is that a positive relationship is the product of (such) helpful interventions. As people feel better, they feel positively towards their therapists. Thus it is change that predicts the experience of the therapeutic relationship, not the other way round. While there is some truth to this, the evidence is that the quality of the early therapeutic relationship is also predictive of outcome in depression (Zuroff and Blatt, 2006). The story is that relationship processes are non-linear (not a simple A causes B), but reciprocal and dynamic.

Deeper insights into how the therapeutic relationship works, through 'mind-to-mind' interactions, will come from: a better appreciation of our minds as evolved for a range of specialised social interactions; studies of 'theory of mind' and inter-subjectivity in the therapy context (Fonagy and Target, 2006; Stern, 2004; Trevarthen and Aitken, 2001); understanding social referencing and social interaction processes (Miranda and Anderson, 2007); better recognition of the roles of non-verbal communication (Dreher, Mengele, Krause and Kämmerer, 2001); non-conscious processing of relationships markers (Baldwin, 2005); and the way the interpersonal schemas of the therapist and depressed person are activated in their co-constructed interactions in the relationship (e.g. a highly self-reliant therapist will interact with depressed people in a different way from, say, a dependent therapist (Leahy, 2007)).

If we take it that part of the depressed person's mind is under the influence of protection strategies, then the therapist's role is to act in a variety of ways to try to engage with these strategies, and tone them down. Hence, part of the therapist's role is to guide a depressed person into, and through, domains of experience that they may be fearful of, or find distressing or have erected a range of (disorder maintaining) safety strategies in order to help them cope. Often, with relatively straightforward cases, this is not too difficult. Kind, supportive interactions, focused psycho-education and guided problem solving, and behavioural and cognitive work are highly effective. For others, with more chronic difficulties, and those caught in painful life dilemmas or from problematic backgrounds, things can get trickier. For some, the prospect of change may involve risks (e.g. to a relationship or way of life), fears of change to a self-identity, fear of loss of control and, for some people, terrors and confronting shame. Indeed, the therapist may be confronted by the patient's experience of threat (and lack of safeness) in specific domains (Gilbert, 1993). In the context of confronting threats, the therapist can be called on to enact a multitude of roles: as educator, mentor, coach, validator, boundary setter, soother-reassurer, morale-enhancer, inspirer, container, safe base, encourager, as well as being simply a fellow human being with whom to share painful experiences.

The therapeutic relationship is a place for the co-generation of interacting patterns of: minds meeting minds and physiologies influencing physiologies. What the depressed person expresses to you may sadden you, anger you or alarm you, and how you react to these emerging experiences will impact back on the depressed person's mind and physiological patterns. For these and other reasons, therapists draw attention to our need to be 'mindful' in the present moment in the therapy process (Katzow and Safran, 2007; Morgan, 2005).

However a person got to be depressed (e.g. via early life history, life events, thinking and problem-solving styles), once in that state they are caught in 'protection strategies' that have evolved to tone down positive affect, and now pervade their lived experience with loss of vitality (drive), and loss of the ability to feel connected and safe in the social world; they feel shut down, cut off and alienated (Liotti, 2007). How can we enter this world and try to turn positive systems back on again? How can we help the person (and these brain systems) feel safe enough to let go their various protection strategies and engage with life? Whether you are a therapist who focuses on thoughts, behaviours, relationships, or 'meaning and purpose', if you cannot make contact with these basic affect systems and ignite new life in them then your efforts may stumble.

Creating safeness and a safe base

The requirement to create a safe base where work can be undertaken is common to many therapies (Holmes, 2001). So our tasks are, first, to try to create safeness *with us* by an orientation of basic friendliness and openness, voice tones, facial expressions (using smiles and half smiles), offering a coffee/tea, and acknowledging fears of attending. These are all to put the person at their ease with ourselves. Then we have to make it safe enough to explore and tell the story, and over time safe enough to explore shame or frightening material and engage in the tasks of therapy. We also try to convey that their material will be 'safe' in our minds and not hurt or damage us, and not turn us into persecutors. A depressed person's fear of hurting, overwhelming or dragging the therapist into a world of hopelessness is more common than is often acknowledged (O'Connor, 2000). So we try to convey that we are safe with our own feelings and can 'take care of ourselves'. Because people have theory of mind processing, they will be monitoring these aspects in you. This can be especially important for people who have spent their lives worrying about what others think about them and trying not to be a 'nuisance' to others or fear that what they are ashamed about you will also recoil at.

The next domain of safeness is to help the depressed person feel safe enough exploring inside their own heads; safe enough to move from protection and various forms of emotional avoidance to exposure, exploration and engagement. Beliefs about their internal emotions can be key here (Leahy, 2002). Whether our focus is on mindfulness, guided discovery or forms of exposure, nearly all therapists agree that avoidance of certain feelings and behaviours can cause problems.

Whether people avoid certain behaviours because of the emotions they will stir up, or from fear of the consequences or fear of failure, we try to create sufficient safeness to start to take risks and explore new behaviours and learn new coping skills. In this context, it is not just reducing negative and avoidance aspects but also discovering and acting on life changes that are related to the person's *positive* life goals.

So there are various domains of safeness that the therapist and depressed person seek to co-create. These help move the person on from the closed-down protection strategies that have taken them over, to experience the mind of another as a robust, helpful and caring mind, to move forward with new understanding about how our minds work and engage in ways that promote well-being. There are various skills that can help us in these endeavours.

Process

Successful therapuetic relationships are rooted in three key issues. These are: (a) *the bond* formed between the counsellor and client; (b) *the goals* and objectives of the counselling process; and (c) *the tasks* and activities carried out by the counsellor and the client to reach desired goals (Bordin, 1979; Dryden, 1989b). The nature of these changes as therapy progresses (Hardy, Cahill and Barkham, 2007). Problems in counselling are sometimes due to difficulties in one or more of these. For example, a client may fear you, not trust you, or (due to shame) may not be open with you. Or it may be difficult to agree on how counselling should progress; that is the tasks and work of the therapy (e.g. monitoring thoughts in cognitive therapy, or free association in psychoanalytic therapy, or working with the family in family therapy). It is useful to develop an agreed formulation and set of goals (see Chapter 8), but this can change or the client may agree submissively but not really commit to them. Establishing bonds and a commitment to engage in agreed tasks and goals can take time, but it is time well spent. This is achieved by helping the client explore fears and the reasons for having a go at certain tasks (e.g. coming regularly, or practising a task outside the session), and gently exploring the advantages of making efforts at change. Depressed people commonly think that a task might not be useful, or that even if useful, they will not be able to do it, they will fail and be shamed. One normalises such fears and stresses that tasks are like experiments – have a go and see what happens.

Sharing an understanding of the goals and tasks of therapy and gaining agreement to move forward in a particular way is called the *therapeutic contract and working alliance*. If counselling is not going well, it is useful to revisit issues of the therapeutic relationship and contract. It may be that problems here are stopping you and your client *working together*.

The therapeutic relationship is like the boat you sail in on a journey that passes through certain stages (Hardy et al., 2007). Egan (2002) outlined a general model for counselling which is applicable to most approaches. These stages include:

1   *The present scenario.* This is the first stage in the counselling process. Here the counsellor focuses on the basic tasks of inviting the client to tell their story, gaining insight into current difficulties and developing an appropriate relationship.
2   *The preferred scenario.* This marks the second stage. Here the counsellor negotiates and clarifies the goals, aims and objectives of counselling with the client. This is often helped by a clear and agreed formulation. Here also are the positive goals for what the client would like to happen and how they would like it to be. The therapist acts as both a source of hope and guidance and a reality coach.
3   *Getting there.* Here the counsellor and client focus on the tasks of achieving the goals and objectives that have been agreed, and moving towards termination.

Each of these stages may be further subdivided, taking into account such things as resistances and blocks to change (Leahy, 2001, 2004). Various approaches to counselling move through these stages with a particular focus on the interpretations, evaluations and beliefs of clients and also key behaviours, such as social or emotional avoidance or low rates of activities. From a review of the research literature, Hardy et al. (2007) outlined a model of the changes that take place in the beginning/early, middle and end stages of therapy. Key ingredients of the therapeutic relationship will differ according to the stage of therapy; for example, helping a person become engaged with therapy early on versus how to work with painful difficulties in the middle of therapy.

Qualities of the therapy relationship

Freud thought that the therapeutic relationship should facilitate free association and in this way allow unconscious material to be revealed for the therapist to interpret. Various key developments in the relationship (such as the transference, for example) occur during this process (Miranda and Anderson, 2007). However a number of early therapists shifted away from a focus on unconscious material. One of these was Carl Rogers (1957). He was one of the first counsellors to emphasise the qualities of relationship between counsellor and client as a source of healing. He suggested that if the counsellor created the right relationship for the client, they would be able to discover ways to help and heal themselves. He argued that the 'best' therapeutic relationship should have three basic elements: (1) accurate empathy; (2) congruence, genuineness and 'counsellor realness'; and (3) unconditional positive regard. These qualities are likely to create safeness.

It is known that the background and personality of the therapist contribute to the building of therapeutic relationships (Gilbert, Hughes and Dryden, 1989; Leahy, 2007). Much has been written on the nature of accurate empathy and what this entails (Goldstein and Michaels, 1985), and we shall return to this below. These qualities, which Rogers helped to identify, have now been adopted as key ingredients to all therapeutic relationships (Kirschenbaum and Jourdan, 2005). In addition, there has been discussion of what is sometimes called 'counsellor realness'. This means that the counsellor should act in a genuine way and not mask feelings or pretend. However, others think that there are limits to the non-masking of feelings in counselling and doubt the value of expressing (at least some) negative feelings to clients (Kahn, 1985), especially with depressed clients. In general, there should not be 'a counselling persona' that one puts on when one sees the client. Nor should the counsellor slip into a detached and technique-orientated mode of relating. The client's awareness that the 'person' of the counsellor is 'with them' in the session provides an important interpersonal experience (Greenberg, 2007). This experience is a moment-to-moment high level of attentiveness to the client and the interaction (Stern, 2004). This is particularly important for depressed people because they often feel separate and cut off from others and think that others cannot be bothered with them or will not understand them.

The therapeutic atmosphere should be one of warmth and safeness that encourages exploration and engagement, rather than one of technique-focused detachment (Leahy, 2005). The counsellor tries to provide an atmosphere of genuine care and concern rather than a 'job-orientated role'. These experiences, in Rogers' view, were both necessary and sufficient to enable the client to find within themself the solutions to their own problems. However, relationships are of course co-constructions and even the most empathic therapist may not be experienced as caring by some people. It is more accurate to say, therefore, that it is how the therapist and client work together, such that the patient is enabled to come to experience the mind of the therapist as caring, sharing and understanding, that is crucial. However, for some people even these experiences can feel alien and threatening (Gilbert, 2005a). Using a social mentalities approach Liotti (2007) has pointed out that clients can shift in their role-creating, moving between care-seeking, cooperative and competitive roles. The way the therapist recognises this 'shifting' and responds can be important to the outcome and process.

Although Rogers did not discuss this in depth, the physical environment can also be important to clients and should be both relaxing and as consistent as possible. Some clients can become confused if counsellors change the rooms in which they are seen regularly or move furniture around. This can be a problem for NHS staff who sometimes have to see people in whatever room is available. Much may depend on the nature and severity of the depression.

Key issues 7.1   The therapeutic relationship

1   The counsellor recognises the basic ingredients of a therapeutic relationship and how it differs from other forms of relationship.
2   The counsellor understands the process of therapy and the role of bonds, tasks and goals and the co-constructed nature of these.
3   The counsellor understands therapy as a journey for both parties that changes over time.
4   The counsellor offers time and space for exploring and the 'invitation' to talk.
5   The counsellor shows openness, genuineness and positive regard, and is non-judgemental.

Micro-skills

One of the major innovations that Rogers helped to stimulate interest and research in was 'micro-skills', that is specific, identifiable elements in the interaction between counsellor and counsellee (Ivey and Ivey, 2003). Before beginning any type of approach (be this cognitive, behavioural or psychodynamic), counsellors should have a good grounding and understanding of these. Below we can look at some of the more central ones, but see Ivey and Ivey (2003) for a comprehensive discussion.

Attentiveness

Learning to attend and *really* listen to what clients say, and the way they say it, is a skill. There are two types of attentiveness: one is externally focused on the client, and the other is internally focused on the thoughts and feelings emerging in one's own mind. External attentiveness involves a variety of attending behaviours, such as appropriate eye contact, observing non-verbal behaviour and active listening, noting voice tones, the ways clients say things, changes in the subject matter and the emotional textures in the narrative (the counsellor is absorbed and curious at the patient's experience/story). The counsellor may observe the non-verbal behaviour of the patient, such as subtle changes as the story unfolds (e.g. shame patients may begin to look down and curl their head into their chest when narrating a shame-filled experience). Other non-verbal pointers can be clenching the fist, or jaw when discussing events. Careful attention to 'the person as a whole' (not just the verbal content but body postures and voice tones) gives a fuller picture of possible internal processes. Clearly, however, the eye contact of the therapist should not be staring or threatening. Research into non-verbal communication, both from the patient and the therapist, is revealing complex interactions that can affect outcomes (e.g. see Dreher et al., 2001).

Internal attentiveness involves a form of mindfulness. Katzow and Safran (2007) suggest that mindfulness involves learning to attend, in a non-judgemental fashion, to one's own internal processes. This enables the therapist to become aware of their thoughts, feelings, and actions *as they emerge* in the present moment. It involves cultivating an attitude of open curiosity about one's inner experience as it unfolds, with an ability to let go of one's preconceptions as they arise when sitting with a client. The counsellor should be non-judgemental and non-self-critical of thoughts and feelings that emerge from within them, but equally they should have sufficient internal capacity to hold on to those thoughts and feelings without acting them out.

Non-verbal behaviour

Research is only just beginning to explore the impact of non-verbal behaviour in counselling, but it is profound (Dreher et al., 2001). Facial expressions and body posture help to convey a sense of 'being with' the client. Non-verbal behaviour helps to set the emotional climate of counselling and the conditions of warmth. One tries to be relaxed, warm and welcoming yet not too laid back or detached. If we have to meet someone in authority, or someone we may need to help us (e.g. your family doctor), we commonly make our first impressions from their non-verbal behaviour – how they look at us, their facial expressions and general manner. A key concern of a client is: 'Do I feel safe and comfortable with this person? Do they seem to be somebody I can talk to and confide in?'

Open and closed questions

Open questions are invitations for the client to tell their story and explore their own meanings. For example, after initial introductions there might be an invitation such as: 'I wonder if we might start by you saying a bit about what has brought you here today'. Cognitive therapists use a style of open questions called Socratic questions that use words like 'what' and 'how'. For example, the classic cognitive question of 'What was going through your mind?' is an open question. Other examples are: 'What did you make of that?' 'How did that affect you?' Closed questions are aimed at eliciting more specific information and are more commonly used for a diagnosis: 'How long have you been depressed?' Can you tell me how you are sleeping?', 'Are you taking any medication?' Closed questions do not invite the client to articulate or narrate their own meanings and (outside diagnostics) should be used sparingly. Many novice counsellors are good at closed and directive questions but less skilled with open questions, which are the real bedrock of counselling.

Minimal encouragers

Often clients may require prompts and small interjections that encourage further revelation. These can be non-verbal, such as nods or other head and eye movements, or verbal prompts such as 'Hmm', 'Ah-ha', etc. Subtle prompts may call forth different types of information from more direct questions which can be controlling or directive. Sometimes it is useful to encourage exploration with simple words like, 'Because?', 'And?' or 'So?' This is short for 'you think this happened because . . .?', 'You see that as important because . . . ?'. (Non-verbal behaviour and voice intonation are important here: a 'because' can sound hostile rather than a position of interest). These help the person to link ideas and allow the discussion to flow more naturally. At other times the counsellor can encourage exploration with more open questions: 'Can we look at this more closely?', 'Can you say more about that?' Also, if the counsellor does not understand what the person is saying or meaning, then it is helpful to say so, for example, 'I'm not sure I understand that. Can you help me by explaining further?', or 'Can we go into that a little more?' etc.

Reflecting feelings

Sometimes feelings are implicit in a message and the counsellor can draw attention to them. This requires attentiveness to *the way* a message is conveyed, for example:

Client: When Sally invited me in for a coffee after the dance I just had to turn her down. At that point I wanted to get home as quickly as possible.
Counsellor: Sounds as if her offer made you pretty anxious.
Client: Absolutely. I found my stomach turn over in case she wanted me to stay the night and all.

However, the same statement given in a different way and in a different context may prompt a different reflection of feelings:

> *Client:*   When Sally invited me in for a coffee after the dance I just had to turn her down. At that point I wanted to get home as quickly as possible.
> *Counsellor:* Sounds as if her offer made you irritated.
> *Client:*   Absolutely. She knew I had a busy day the next day and that I was really tired, and there she was making more demands on me.

Reflecting feelings enables the counsellor to convey their understanding and awareness of the client's internal view and experience. However, the counsellor might follow this up with a statement like 'So you thought that Sally was making demands on you'. The counsellor would be cautious not to reinforce the idea that it was only Sally's request that produced the affect. Rather, the counsellor would direct attention to the client's interpretation of Sally's behaviour and (later) that maybe this interpretation is open to an alternative (theory of mind) view. Thus, although counsellors reflect feelings, in the early stages they may *float* an idea that other interpretations are possible. For example 'Is it possible Sally had other thoughts in her mind when she asked you to stay over?' However, the counsellor must balance these in such a way that the client does not feel they are being *invalidated* or that their view is wrong. Reflecting feelings is thus primarily a way of the counsellor indicating that they are picking up key emotional experiences from the client.

Paraphrasing

Paraphrasing also enables the counsellor to convey understanding, but here the focus is on content. This is not to be confused with simply repeating what the client has just said in parrot fashion (sometimes mistaken as an empathic response). Rather, it is designed to show 'being with' the client and understanding the meaning in the message.

> *Client:*   After the relationship broke up my car went wrong so I was stuck at home and just had time to brood. The bills were piling up and I've just put them to one side. Now they are threatening to cut off my electricity. I just can't get things sorted out.
> *Counsellor:* So your time to brood on the lost relationship has made it difficult for you to keep on top of things and that is another source of stress for you.

Summarising

Summarising is similar to paraphrasing in its basic skill but takes larger chunks of meaning, follows long(er) periods of exploration, and focuses on core theme(s). For example:

> *Counsellor:* Given what you have been saying about your family and recent events, you perceive that no one has shown much interest in your difficulties and this has led you to think that you are rather unimportant and uncared for. Given how you have talked about your life this seems a common theme for you – feeling unimportant and uncared for.

A counsellor might start summarising with, 'Can I just check with you that I have understood you. It seems to me that from what you have been saying …'. Summarising is used in many different ways. It is often helpful in taking a history and can be a form of crystallisation, to help a client and counsellor focus on *recurrent patterns/themes in the client's life, events and styles of explanation of events*. It is useful to summarise frequently, to clarify with the client a shared understanding. Sometimes novice counsellors do not summarise enough. Done well, summarising helps build the overview summary which is the basis for the formulation (see Chapter 8). Also hearing someone else verbalise what one (as client) has been saying can provide new insights.

Whatever specific model of counselling one engages in, counselling requires the counsellor, at the outset, to be proficient in these basic micro-skills. Practice and supervision are important to help 'craft' these aspects and to understand and gain empathy for their use and timing in the sessions. However, it is the basic empathic concern that will help here rather than attempts to apply them mechanically (e.g. I must get in at least four minimal encouragers, a couple of paraphrases, and four or five summaries, etc.).

Getting it wrong

No one is perfect, and we can often get it wrong. We make an intervention that seems to change or interrupt the flow of the dialogue and the client becomes silent or looks away. Such non-verbal signals are important to note. Sometimes a simple acknowledgement or even apology is helpful.

Counsellor: I note that when I said [. . .] that you were silent and looked away. Maybe I misunderstood you. Did anything go through your mind just now?

Or:

Counsellor: When I said we need to look at your thoughts about this event you looked hurt – like maybe I am being insensitive or not really understanding. What went through your mind?

Client: Well you think my problems are all because my thinking is wrong – that it's all my fault.

Counsellor: I am really sorry to have given that impression. I was just interested in the meaning you had about this event [pause]. But I wonder if you often have that thought that I see it as 'all your fault' for thinking wrongly?

And what happens if you are exploring a sequence of thoughts that seem to be leading nowhere or are getting confused?

Counsellor: I wonder if we can pause here for a moment. I am not sure about what is going through your mind but I am thinking we need to take stock here. Can we back-track a bit and try to pick up the key threads again?

If you get into a hole, stop digging. Misunderstandings, confusions and/or therapeutic ruptures are *common* and counsellors should be quite prepared to focus non-defensively on them (Katzow and Safran, 2007). When you do this you are modelling a capacity to be open, able to make mistakes, get confused and deal with these openly without shame. This is partly what collaboration means – working together, 'working and struggling together', openly sorting out confusions and misunderstandings. Although some clients with certain types of difficulty will find your imperfections a source of anger, others will benefit greatly from your openness and non-defensive style. Of course, I am not suggesting that you become submissive; only that you are open.

Non-defensive countertransferences

To the best of your ability try to be non-defensive. Consider this:

> *John:*   (angrily) I have been coming here for some weeks now and don't feel a lot better. Are you sure you know what you are doing and we are on the right track?

The feelings this will generate in a counsellor are called *countertransference*. There are various types of countertransference. A common one is related to the ways an interaction activates threat and safety strategies in the therapist (Leahy, 2007). For example, while some counsellors might see the above complaint as an opportunity to explore the person's sense of disappointment, or check if they *are* on the right track, for others it is seen as a threat to their competence or control, with a rapid threat reaction of anger or anxiety. Defensive counsellors who feel threatened may try to defend themselves in various ways. If internal shame is activated, attention is directed within, and the counsellor becomes self-conscious, feels unsure of themself, has a flush of anxiety, self-blames and may defensively monitor what they say. When external shame dominates the counsellor's thoughts and feelings, attention is directed outwards – to what is going on in the mind of the client or what a possible supervisor may think if John complained to them. They may worry that the client would rather see somebody else and wants to reject them as a counsellor. Various safety strategies, such as explaining, apologising, becoming more technique-focused, rather than staying with the feelings, can be enacted to try to appease the client and prove that the therapist can be helpful. Another counsellor might experience their threat in externalising anger and a sense of humiliation. They may show this in their non-verbal communications and even blame the client: 'Well I think you need to work harder on your homework!' Or they may have the thought: 'Well if you don't like it here go somewhere else and let me work with somebody who appreciates me!' Burnt-out counsellors may feel indifferent and imply a 'come if you want or don't. What do I care?' attitude.

These are not uncommon experiences and we will have them at certain points with certain clients. By learning to be internally attentive we can spot these reactions in ourselves and not act them out by switching off from the client or rushing in to try to find new techniques. When I was newly qualified one of my first clients said she thought she might kill herself. I had an immediate flush of anxiety and thought of being blamed for being a negligent or a bad therapist. I recall almost suggesting to the client: 'Please don't kill yourself because it will go badly for me if you do'. She must have taken pity on me and did not. One cringes now but if we are open to our own fears and worries, then we can work with them rather than be ashamed of them. So now I might try to reflect feelings and contact the despair behind the client's concerns. So one response to John's comment above might be:

> *Counsellor:* Given how depressed you feel, it is very disappointing to come here hoping for help and feeling it is not helping. I guess that puts you back to feeling alone with it.
>
> *John:* Yeah. I have always felt no one really understands me or could help me.
>
> *Counsellor:* So this feeling is coming from a very lonely place. (Pause to allow the client space to recognise that you recognise their underlying feelings.) Well let's put our heads together and see if we can work out what it is you think is not helping and what you think would help. (Here the counsellor now tries to bridge into the client in a collaborative manner.)

Or alternatively, if you know the key themes in the client's style of thinking, you might say:

> *Counsellor:* Given how depressed you feel it is very disappointing to come here hoping for help and feeling it is not helping. Does that connect with other feelings in your life where you have had high hopes of people being helpful to you and they seem to let you down?

As a rule of thumb I often try to explore *the threat and fear* behind the anger. The point about this is to try to stay with the patient's feelings and their meanings rather than get pulled into being defensive and feeling rushed or attacked. Therapists have ways of steering patients away from things that are upsetting, especially if the patient is upset with the therapist (Dalenberg, 2004). Counsellors should try to avoid taking on a burden of 'getting the patient better'.

Silence

Silence is golden, as the song says, and sometimes it is. Therapists should be cautious of 'filling the spaces' during silences because this can be intrusive, dominating and interferes with learning how to tolerate certain emotions and memories. In other words, therapy does require at times spaces and silences for reflection, being with and learning to tolerate painful feelings. Also a silence can be a time when we are simply 'with' the depressed person in that moment of feeling; that we are fully present (Greenberg, 2007). We are not trying to rush away from it because we find it unbearable, or being pushed into doing or saying something because of what *we* feel. You can use your own experience to reflect that sometimes when you are feeling down or confused it is not helpful to have someone who gives you no space to reflect or be with your feelings, or keeps asking you questions. Working collaboratively, it is useful to discuss this.

> *Counsellor:* Sometimes when we are trying to work things out in our own mind it is helpful to have space and silence. Rather than me asking you about 'what is going through your mind?', can we work out how you would like me to be with you at these times? So this is to say I am here for you when you feel ready to explore or think things through together.

In other words, the depressed person and counsellor agree *some shared process* of how to work with silences. However, with shame-prone people, who can simply close down, *not* filling the space can also be unhelpful. This is because the patient has become stuck in a shame-frozen state, feels highly scrutinised by the therapist, concerned with what is expected of them and their own frozen state. Attention has switched from working on a specific emotion or memory to a concern with what is in the mind of the therapist and their social presentation. To work collaboratively means to talk about silences: what they might mean, what is going through the mind of the patient when they occur, when they are useful because they offer space 'to be with' and explore one's feelings, and when they are not because the patient has switched to ruminating about what the therapist is thinking and expecting of them, and feeling under shame-linked scrutiny.

Key issues 7.2   Core skills

1   Attentiveness to verbal and non-verbal behaviours in both counsellor and client.
2   Attendant behaviour of listening and observing.
3   Minimal encouragers.
4   Reflecting feelings.
5   Paraphrasing.
6   Open and closed questions.
7   Summarising.
8   Awareness of therapeutic ruptures and the (non-defensive) reparation process.
9   Use of silences.

Empathy and sympathy

Although much has been written on the nature of accurate empathy, and the influence of training (Goldstein and Michaels, 1985), the role of empathy in counselling has had a chequered history (Duan and Hill, 1996). Confusion reigns in this area because there have been many different definitions of empathy, including empathy as a cognitive skill, a feeling state and personality disposition. It is recognised that the counsellor should attempt to form an empathic relationship with the client, enabling the client to feel understood and accepted, and to explore painful feelings.

A short while ago a counsellor, recently back from a training course, told me they had been taught that sympathy was unhelpful in counselling. I think there is a mix up with pity and sympathy. In fact, sympathy is important in counselling, but we need to clarify the difference between sympathy and empathy. These have been well researched by Eisenberg (2002). She articulates these as:

1. The situation in which an individual feels the same emotion as another or understands what is in the mind of another: this is neither self-centred nor other-directed, and is *true empathy* or emotional contagion.

2. The response of one to the distress of the other, which need not match the other but is focused on the *well-being* of the other. This is labelled *sympathy*. Sympathy is more closely associated with altruism. In sympathy we are emotionally moved by the other's distress.

3. A self-centred response related to anxiety, worry, shame or guilt rather than sympathy: this is labelled personal distress. *Personal distress* is related to self-focused threat processing.

Table 7.1 offers a way of comparing and contrasting empathy and sympathy.

Table 7.1   Comparing sympathy and empathy

Sympathy	Empathy
Involves a heightened awareness of the suffering or need of the other. Something to be alleviated. The focus is on the other person's well-being	Involves a heightened awareness of the experiences of the other (not necessarily suffering) as something to be understood
Behaviour is on relating, acting for the other, or alleviating (or mediating responses)	Behaviour is on knowing, conceptualising, understanding
Is relatively automatic	Is effortful and depends on capabilities to use imagination
The self is emotionally moved by the other	The self reaches out to the other
The other is the vehicle for understanding and some loss of identity may occur	The self is the vehicle for understanding and never loses its identity

From Gilbert, 1989: 174, reproduced with permission of Psychology Press

Consider a client who is crying and giving strong signals of emptiness and loneliness. Our empathic feelings are close to how the client actually feels: empty, alone and maybe tearful. Our sympathetic feelings are those that elicit care and concern to reach out to the person, help alleviate the pain, to rescue or reassure them that it's going to be okay. To have these feelings can be helpful, but to act on those feelings may not be helpful and the person may need to learn how to work with and tolerate such pain. However, without sympathy and caring interest the client may feel the counsellor is detached.

Empathy and theory of mind

Empathy is closely related to 'theory of mind' (which we discussed in Chapter 6) but not identical to it (Decety and Jackson, 2004; Völlm, Taylor, Richardson, Corcoran, Stirling, McKie, Deakin and Elliott, 2006). 'Theory of mind' relates to the way we make inferences about the internal causes of other people's feelings and behaviours, and assess 'what is going on in their minds' – what they are thinking (Byrne, 1995). Thus we can attribute intentions, desires and feelings to people's actions and mental states (Malle and Hodges, 2005). For example, Sally did this because – she was feeling sad; to get back at John; because she was confused; she misheard John, etc. Although attributions are clearly an important aspect of theory of mind, we also have to have some concepts of 'minds' and how they work. This skill develops with age.

Theory of mind-based empathy uses imagination. We imagine what it would be like to be in the life context of the other person. Sometimes this imagination blends with self experiences and can activate emotions. For example, hearing of the death of a loved child brought to mind my imagined feelings if one of my children died. Sometimes the imagination lacks affect qualities. For example, although we might imagine what it is like to break a leg, we do not feel any pain from the imagination of it.

Empathic resonance and understanding

Recent research has shown that we can understand the feelings of others because their emotion cues stimulate similar patterns of neuronal firing in ourselves – as if we were experiencing the emotion. This is believed to happen via mirror neurons. For example, when we watch a sad or exciting film, we can feel sad or excited ourselves. This is called empathic resonance (see Decety and Jackson, 2004 for a review of this work). Empathic resonance can go both ways in therapy. It is partly via the automatic simulation of affect in the mind of a therapist that enables the therapist to tune into and understand the feelings of their clients. Equally, a client's attention to the emotion displays, expressions and voice tones of the therapist can influence the internal simulations of the depressed person.

Empathy also has an intuitive aspect that relates to a kind of creating an impression, not just to attributions of intentions, and putting oneself in the shoes of the other. However, we can make mistakes here. Book (1988) offers some common mistakes in empathy. Consider one of his examples.

> A Holocaust survivor raged against the rudeness to which he felt subjected at work. His Jewish counsellor responded, 'It really makes me angry when I hear that. What the hell's the matter with them?' The client responded, 'That's what I'm telling you. They're all a bunch of butchers.' (Book, 1988, p. 422)

In this example the counsellor was responding from his own frame of reference. When we are too much in our own frame of reference we tend to project our own feelings and thoughts on to the other. For example, suppose it is my wife's birthday. Now if I use projection I would buy her what I would like (e.g. a new guitar) – the problem is she doesn't play. To be empathic is to buy her a trip to, say, Paris because this is what *she* would like. Counsellors should be aware of these distinctions between theory of mind, empathy and projection, and thus always check with the client on shared understanding.

There can also be difficulties in our efforts to express or demonstrate empathy. Here is another example from Book (1988, p. 422):

> A first-year resident, when verbally assaulted by a paranoid client, responded, 'I'm glad to see you can get your anger out.' The client hesitated, looked perplexed, and then angrily roared, 'You bastard! To be so happy that I am this upset!' When asked about his comment, the resident stated, 'I was just trying to be empathic.

In this example the counsellor had confused a genuine desire to help the patient feel safe to express his anger with empathy. Book (1988) gives many other examples of confusions between genuineness, unconditional positive regard and empathy, including hearing but not really believing that a client can mean what they say, or making subtle alterations in the client's statement that actually changes the meaning.

In empathy, one listens and attends to both what is actually said and expressed, and what is not. One notes possible hidden shame and resentment, the fear of loss or the disappointment that lies behind a self-attack. A client's rage can often hide a deep sense of loss, being devalued and marginalised. An empathic response helps the client make contact with those feelings and their internal self-judgements (Greenberg, 2007). Another misunderstanding of empathy is filling in the blanks or finishing a client's sentence for them. This can be experienced as an intrusion. Instead, the counsellor can respond so as to help the client fill in their own blanks. Thus, as Book (1988) says, empathy may be understanding what the client is going to say, but being empathic is not saying it. A good measure of empathy is whether or not it enables clients to deepen their understanding and continue with their narrative. A genuine empathic response from the counsellor is not necessarily perceived as such by the client, and therefore Miller (1989) refers to the 'therapeutic empathic communication process'. This is a multi-stage model involving a counsellor's recognition of the client's internal experience (via the client's verbal and non-verbal cues), the sending of signals of recognition, and the client's ability to recognise and internalise such signals (i.e. I understand, I show you I understand, and you understand that I have understood). Empathy is a way of being with, or an 'in-tuneness to', the client, not simply a skill to be 'brought to bear'. As Margulies (1984) pointed out, empathy requires a 'sense of wonder', curiosity and caring interest (Gilbert, 1989). Interest alone can appear detached. Caring alone can involve more sympathy and too vigorous an effort to 'get the client better'.

Empathy for what a person wants or needs

Various schools of therapy doubt that the qualities of accurate empathy, positive regard and genuineness are, by themselves, sufficient to produce change (Zuroff and Blatt, 2006). Clients may need to learn about the way their own thinking, coping efforts and behaviours can contribute to their difficulties (Beck et al., 1979; Linehan, 1993). However, because there are various models of the sources of suffering, and the nature of human needs, these will impact on your orientation to the nature of human needs in your clients. Wong (2006), for example, has given a comprehensive and important account of how the issue of needs, such as the need for social connection and meaning, underpins a long history in the humanistic and existential psychotherapies (see also Mahoney, 2003; Yalom, 1980). Many of these ideas reach far back into various philosophical traditions on the nature of human suffering and needs, and counsellors would benefit from being acquainted with them. A number of these ideas have filtered though into other schools of therapies. Your model of therapy (e.g. psychodynamic, humanistic, cognitive or behavioural) will influence your thoughts on what a person needs to do or learn, to help with their depression; that is the process, tasks and goals of the therapy. However, it is the empathic skills of the therapist that enable them to do this collaboratively.

Different people will be at different levels of emotional and cognitive abilities. So the therapist must be sensitive to these and not engage in ways that are beyond the person's current abilities. Indeed, it is the empathic abilities of the therapist that enables them to deliver their therapy in ways that patients can use (or digest).

Validation

Because we are a social species, a common need is validation of our feelings from others. This validation helps to de-shame our feelings felt to be shameful. Many clients may wonder if their negative feelings are valid – maybe *they should* pull themselves together or should not feel what they do feel. This can be the case for past events as well as the present. As we have seen in the section on shame (see Chapter 6), this requires the counsellor to be empathically attuned with the client, have an appropriate understanding of emotions, and feel safe enough with their own emotions and 'shadow material' to act as a *soothing* agent (Gilbert, 2005a). The counsellor helps patients see that, while some emotions/fantasies are unpleasant or strange, they are normal to our humanity, and are manageable once we accept them, no longer fight to suppress or deny them, or label ourselves negatively as a consequence of having them (Leahy, 2002; Neff, 2003a).

It can be useful to be clear with the client that they may be feeling what they feel for protection-focused or other understandable reasons. In my own work I tend to look at the possible adaptive significance of threat and safety strategies (or advantages) of negative feelings (Nesse, 1998). For example, a client may say 'I shouldn't get so depressed or anxious over these events. I am blowing them out of all proportion.' To this I might say 'Well sometimes our feelings are there because we evolved to act on them quickly. Our emotional brains do that kind of thing. They can make us biased in our thinking in all kinds of ways but *that is not your fault.*' Once this is heard, then we say 'Well let's look at these biases and see if we can change the perspective'. The key point is that given the way the client sees and evaluates situations, their feelings are understandable and not evidence of personal weakness or stupidity. Indeed, this can be the first step towards helping people understand and accept feelings without self-criticism, and develop a collaborative relationship.

Validation can also be important in the relationship. Many clients will have experienced others as not being straight with them or covering up. For example, half-way through a session a client said:

Client. You know you look tired and not really here today.

Now, one could be defensive and say 'What makes you say that?' Or 'Well I am trying my best' and feel guilty, or not respond to it at all. Or one might deflect it by asking 'what is going through your mind?' But first it is important to validate the client's experience if it is true.

Counsellor. You know you're right, I am feeling tired today (smiles). You are very observant.

Your smile offers a non-verbal signal that this is okay to say and acknowledge. You might then follow up with more exploration of the feelings and meanings of this. In this particular case, noting my tiredness had triggered beliefs in the client that she should not 'burden me further'. This led to an important discussion of how she was very sensitive to others' feeling states and fears of being a burden.

Some clients may have fantasies about the counsellor and this can also be explored. A client may feel that the counsellor might see them as a hopeless or demanding case, or may have sexual desires for them, or they may have sexual desires for the counsellor, or yearnings for a closer attachment. Bailey (2002) suggests that clients often want a particular form of 'kinship' relationship with their therapist, either family-like, attachment-based or psychological/kinship-based (see also Liotti, 2007). These *transference* ideas and fantasies can be helpful to work with, but disruptive to the collaborative relationship if not addressed (Watkins, 1989a). So the counsellor needs to work sensitively so as not to act in a rejecting way while maintaining clear boundaries. For example, Sally 'fell in love' with me. Painfully she revealed this. My response was to de-shame it. 'Therapy like this can stir up very strong emotions and you have shown a lot of courage in revealing this. Sadly, this must be a very painful feeling for you because your yearnings cannot be taken further here. To yearn for somebody you are unable to develop that kind of relationship with is very painful.' In some ways yearning for someone who was out of reach made those feelings safe but also part of the problem. However, slowly we were able to connect her yearnings for me to those for the father she never had and how the therapy was re-enacting this experience. So, for such feelings, we de-shame them, validate them (as understandable and painful) and then gently bring the person back to the boundaries and basic work of therapy and the issues at hand.

Some depressed people can have *envious* fantasies about the counsellor, imagining how well adjusted they are, how easily they cope, that they never get depressed or rageful, or how happy their lives are compared to their own. Normalising these can be helpful but also needs sensitive handling. The most difficult to validate can be clients who are envious, angry and contemptuous. No matter what you do, they see it as not good enough and unhelpful. In my way of thinking envy, anger and contempt are related to deep feelings of threat, so I need to help the client explore these (Smith and Kim, 2007). Commonly, there have been chronic failures in the past by others to care. Burns (1980) suggests that it is useful to find something you can agree with in the patient's complaints and empathise with their anger. This avoids getting into battles with people.

However, sometimes people can experience being helped as threatening. This is because they are defensively self-reliant, and recognising others as helpful opens a range of other feelings that they are defended against. Sona, for example, constantly complained that no one could help her. I acknowledged that that might be one possibility and we could consider the reasons for it. However, there could be other possibilities, such as a fear of being helped. She thought that was a very odd idea. So you might say: 'Okay, so just as a thought experiment let's think about the kinds of fears someone in your situation from your background might have about being helped. We can brainstorm the fears and list them together.'

It can take time to elicit such fears over a number of sessions, but these are common ones: I might realise that I need others (loss of pride and sense of self-identity); I might realise that I need others and become dependent on them; I might realise that my hope of being helped was that the other person would somehow (unrealistically) magically cure me, or that there is no 'ultimate rescuer' (with a loss of hope); I might have to work with deep fears of vulnerability and risk of shame; I might realise that underneath my rage is deep sadness and fear of aloneness. There are others. Now these are, of course, fears that may relate to various beliefs that can be worked with to reduce their 'all-or-nothing' nature (threat beliefs are often all or nothing in form; see Gilbert, 1998b).

One should not assume that clients are prepared to reveal their central problems simply because they have presented themselves for help. For example, a client mid-way through counselling, when a central issue of aggressive, envious fantasies had been discussed, said:

> *Client:*   You know, when I first came here I knew in my heart what I needed to talk about but just felt too ashamed to say. As we went through our first session I knew it was pointless because I couldn't tell you about it. That's what made me feel hopeless about this counselling. During each session we got close and I backed away and afterwards got so angry with myself and you for avoiding the issue.

The client had expected that the counsellor would condemn these feelings, as had occurred in childhood. However, the client had also hoped I would have been more pushy and almost force them to confront the issues. I accepted the client's anger for not being able to deal with it earlier and said simply that these feelings had been very painful for her to carry alone. So feelings of hopelessness can arise because the client has a secret agenda but is too fearful to reveal it. Yet they can also feel angry because you don't have enough telepathy to pick it up! This is why the approach should be gentle and why trust is something that grows. The problem is that early on the client has no experience of the counselling on which to make such judgements and so it is not helpful to try to reassure the client with platitudes. Most clients are not reassured by a therapist whom they think does not really know what's going on in their mind, because they haven't told them.

The point about this way of working with anger or contempt is that all the time the therapist is focused on the fact that the surface feelings and behaviours are often protection strategies (anger and contempt are threat emotions from the *threat* systems) and the therapist's work is to help the person recognise and work with these. Try not to take a patient's contempt as personal; validate it as protection; stay curious as to what it means and what it would mean if they gave up their angry contempt (i.e. the disadvantages of change). Try not to placate or avoid it as it may be a central problem to their depression. Recognise, however, that it is difficult to engage early in therapy until some kind of relationship has been developed. Be empathic to the empty world of someone who simply looks down on everyone and can find no affiliative soothing. These people are often very poor at being kind to themselves as well!

Validating and encouraging people's *positive life goals* and hopes are also important. They may under-value or disqualify their positive attributes or previous successes, or see them as a fake or luck. They may pour scorn on their efforts to get well rather than recognise their courage and struggle. When people are living with critical others who are invested in maintaining the submissive orientation of the client, validating their movement to more assertive or self-focused behaviour can be important. As Jane got better she wanted to get a job and possibly train as a teacher. However, her husband wanted her to stay at home and was scornful of her desires due to his own insecurities. Validation means coming to see his criticisms as related to his insecurities (and that may require marital work (Beach and Jones, 2002)) but that Jane's goals were expressions of her increasing confidence and important.

> **Key issues 7.3   Empathy and validation**
>
> 1   Empathy involves attentiveness to the verbal and non-verbal affective messages emanating from the client.
> 2   It is non-judgemental.
> 3   It encourages exploration, especially of core areas and life themes and is sensitive to blocks and/or fears.
> 4   It is focused on knowing, understanding and sharing rather than helping and alleviating (as in sympathy).
> 5   Empathy is reflective and thoughtful and involves effort, unlike sympathy which can be immediate, automatic and is relatively effortless.
> 6   It is flexible and avoids the client feeling 'pinned down or exposed'.
> 7   Validation helps the person de-shame their feelings and work with them.

A compassion-focused therapeutic relationship

Our understanding of the psychology and brain processes involved in empathy and sympathy has moved on considerably since Rogers' days (Decety and Jackson, 2004). These new ways of thinking need to be incorporated into our understanding of the therapeutic relationship. One way of providing a framework for this new information is to focus on the role of *compassion* in the therapeutic relationship. In fact, efforts to understand the nature of compassion stretch back thousands of years. Not only was it central to Mahayana Buddhist practice (Leighton, 2003), but many philosophers, going back to Plato and Aristotle, saw it as key to moral and caring behaviour (Nassbaum, 2003). For example, Nassbaum (2003, p. 306) suggests that over 2000 years ago Aristotle suggested that compassion 'is a painful emotion directed at the other's misfortune or suffering'. Moreover, she suggested three key cognitive elements to Aristotle's view. These are summarised as:

> The first cognitive element of compassion is a belief or appraisal that the suffering is serious rather than trivial. The second is the belief that the person does not deserve the suffering. The third is the belief that the possibilities of the person who experiences the emotions are similar to the sufferer. (Nassbaum, 2003, p. 36)

Nassbaum also notes that we can feel compassion for a person who may not appear to be suffering at that moment (e.g. someone who has lost insight due to brain damage or is in a coma) because we understand what they could have been and what they have lost, even if they do not. This is also key in the process by which we can have compassion for someone who has no insight into what they could become. Buddhist compassion is based on the idea that we suffer because we are ignorant of how our minds really are. Such compassion can underlie forgiveness, as in Jesus' famous statement 'forgive them for they know not what they do'. Compassion can thus relate to having knowledge that the other does not have, but if they did have it this could help them.

   We cannot go into the history of compassion or these philosophical ideas here, but simply note that compassion is a complex process, and has been recognised to be so for a long time, including that it is key to human well-being. It is perhaps surprising that with a few exceptions (Davidson and Harrington, 2002; Glaser, 2005) compassion has not been a central focus of study. Although most therapists and counsellors will agree that counselling should be a compassionate process, there can be some vagueness about what this actually means (Glaser, 2005). Certainly it involves a kind, warm and open disposition to the client, but it is far more than that. In the last twelve years I have tried to develop a practical model of compassion that specifically articulates core components of compassion and can be used in therapy (Gilbert, 2000a, 2005a; Gilbert and Irons, 2005), but this should be seen as 'work in progress'.

Compassion is a complex, multifaceted process and different therapies have slightly different views of it. As noted, there are a range of therapeutic models that articulate what are believed to be key healing ingredients in the therapeutic relationship, such as accurate empathy, positive regard, mirroring, and validation, which can form the basis for compassion (Gilbert, 1989; Gilbert and Leahy, 2007; Kirschenbaum and Jourdan, 2005; Lynch et al., 2006; Norcross, 2002). Some therapists, however, have specifically focused on compassion as a therapeutic process (Glaser, 2005). For example, McKay and Fanning (1992), who developed a cognitive-based self-help programme for self-esteem, view compassion as involving *understanding*, *acceptance* and *forgiveness*. Compassion is a key quality of mind to develop if one follows a Buddhist tradition and this involves being open to other people's suffering, a recognition that all living things are vulnerable to suffering and a strong desire to alleviate suffering (Leighton, 2003; Neff, 2003a). (See Chapter 11 for a more detailed discussion of self-compassion.)

One view of compassion is that it is linked to caring behaviour and evolved from our capacities to look after, nurture and care for others, especially children and kin. My approach to compassion is rooted in social mentality theory, which is an evolutionary-based approach to social motivation and social competencies (Gilbert, 1989, 2000c, 2005a, 2005b; see also pp. 34–35 of this volume). This suggests that compassionate behaviour evolved out of the *care-giving mentality*. As such it utilises and *patterns* a variety of motivational, emotional and cognitive competencies that are care-focused. These organise our minds in certain ways and thus we call it compassionate mind or mentality, and refer to compassionate *mind* training rather than see it as a focused schema (Gilbert and Irons, 2005). The components are linked together in what I have called the *compassion circle* (see Figure 7.1). Problems in any one of these components can compromise compassion.

Care-concern for the well-being of the other (client)

The first element is that there has to be a *motivation* and desire to be helpful and to care. In Buddhist psychology this is the desire to alleviate suffering, but this must be done 'skilfully' with knowledge on the causes of suffering and the means of its alleviation. The evolved motivational elements for compassion are to be found in the evolution of altruism and nurturance (Decety and Jackson, 2004; Gilbert, 1989, 2005a). When we think about compassion as linked to nurturance, then we can think beyond the focus on distress and suffering and include factors that are conducive to well-being and that harness our potential. Altruism makes possible a genuine desire to help others, alleviate suffering and engage with

**Components of compassion
from the care-giving mentality**

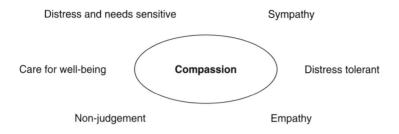

Distress and needs sensitive   Sympathy

Care for well-being   **Compassion**   Distress tolerant

Non-judgement   Empathy

**Create opportunities for growth and change with
warmth**

Figure 7.1   The compassion circle

Adapted from Gilbert, 2005a: 52, reproduced with permission from Routledge

others to foster development change conducive to their well-being. Fogel, Melson and Mistry (1986, p. 55) define the core element of care–nurturance as: 'the provision of guidance, protection and care for the purpose of fostering developmental change congruent with the expected potential for change of the object of nurturance'. They also suggest that nurturance involves *awareness* of the need to be nurturing, *motivation* to nurture, *expression* of nurturing feelings, *understanding* what is needed to nurture, and an ability to match nurturing with *feedback* from the impact on the other of nurturing. Nurturing, then, needs to be skilfully enacted using various competencies that facilitate caring behaviour. Problems with any of these competencies can interfere with compassion in a (therapeutic) relationship.

However, when a depressed person experiences these processes/motives occurring 'in the mind of therapist' – that is the mind of therapist is orientated towards them in a compassionate way – this may activate the social safeness and soothing system. Recall that this system may be toned down in depression, accounting for feelings of aloneness and being cut off from others. The experience of genuine caring interest from the therapist may send signals to this system that can activate it again or at least stimulate it, even mildly. As this system begins to come online, this may create opportunities for new learning and conditioning. The depressed person may experience the 'caring mind' of the therapist in association with their painful feelings, which helps to soothe them. This is clearly a research question.

Keep in mind, though, that for some patients experiencing a compassionate other can be frightening and associated with negative beliefs (e.g. it is weak, people can't be trusted, or people are nice to you so they can exploit you). People can feel that if you get close to them and really understand them, then you might find out negative things about them and that will turn off your caring interest and turn to shame and loss. People who have been abused can experience 'caring' as threatening because others took an interest in them only to abuse them. For some people the first experiences of caring activate sadness, which can be intense and feel overwhelming. Indeed, a lot of work in compassion-focused therapy is precisely on these fears and negative beliefs (Gilbert and Irons, 2005). The therapy specifically targets this affect system and such beliefs.

Distress sensitivity

This requires the micro-skills noted above and refers to how a therapist notices, attends and processes the patient's verbal and non-verbal behaviour (Gilbert and Leahy, 2007). Therapists trained in different schools of therapy will attend their 'listening ear' in different ways. Being sensitive to what is going on inside the client requires the therapist to be skilful in engaging with the client so that they can tell their stories of their distress, as they understand them. Therapists may hear things that are deeply distressing and clients may be upset in the telling. Therapists have ways of steering clients away from things that are upsetting. If I feel myself becoming defensive or autocratic, the chances are I have stopped hearing the client, and am less sensitive to their distress, and I have slipped into a competitive, defensive or controlling mentality and style. Therapists need to be internally attentive to this possibility (Bennett-Levy and Thwaites, 2007). Therapy with high shame-prone clients, who may 'hide' their true feelings and distress from the therapist, cannot be engaged with as if it is a technical or mechanical operation (Leahy, 2005). Shame-prone therapists who easily become defensive may be problematic for shame-prone clients. (see Pope, Sonne and Greene (2006) for an important exploration of these issues).

Sensitivity to a client's needs is related to understanding what will help them recover, grow and mature. These needs may emerge in the process of guided discovery and therapeutic work. Indeed, helping clients articulate positive life goals and needs can be an important therapeutic aim. Needs, however, are not the same as unhelpful 'musts' but a recognition of what it is that is conducive to our well-being. What knowledge you bring to the task of alleviating suffering will depend on your models of therapy.

Sympathy

I have addressed the issue of sympathy above. Recall that it is an emotional connection, we are emotionally 'moved' by the distress in the other.

Distress tolerance

DBT and other acceptance-focused therapies (Hayes, Follette and Linehan, 2004; Hayes, Strosahl and Wilson, 2004; Linehan, 1993; Lynch et al., 2006) have focused on the way in which clients may need to learn distress tolerance and acceptance as well as how to change. Generally, it is the focus on the patient that has been the primary concern. However, it is also an issue for therapists and not enough time is spent on exploring this aspect, or the needs that therapists have (see Pope et al., 2006). DBT stresses that therapists working with complex cases require a team approach to be supportive. When working with complex depressions, especially with suicide risk, it is important for you to feel supported by a team and not vulnerable to 'persecution' if things go wrong. Also, a team approach helps you to feel you are on the right track with your client and pulls on their knowledge, insights and support. So what can also help *you* tolerate difficulties is to obtain helpful supervision with somebody you can be open with and discuss your own positive and negative feelings, rather than cope alone. Indeed, compassionate behaviour is about how we look after ourselves and attend to our own needs. The value of focusing on therapists' emotional tolerance is an under-researched but key element in psychotherapy; the ability of the counsellor to tolerate both the distress in their clients and also their own feelings that their clients generate inside them.

It is important to be open and moved by the stories and feelings of patients but at the same time not to try to turn off one's own distress by acting as a rescuer or engaging in some kind of heroic effort. Learning to tolerate distress, simply being with it, may be an important element in the client's maturation process. This is, of course, not always the case and the therapist will need to make a clear distinction in their mind between feeling distressed, avoidance, and 'working with', as opposed to a pointless ruminative process.

Shame-prone clients who operate with beliefs about inferiority and incompetence can sometimes generate these feelings in the counsellor. For example, a client may say that they feel hopeless and want to kill themself, or they may suggest the therapy is not helping them or that the counsellor is not caring enough, understanding enough or talented enough. These will stir emotions in a counsellor but if they can learn to tolerate and contain the feelings inside themselves with a watchful mindfulness, then this can help the client feel contained. This is quite different from a submissive or an appeasing approach to a client's anger and may require the counsellor to enquire more deeply about these feelings. So distress tolerance is really about how we tolerate, accept, contain and work with distress and fear in both our clients and in ourselves.

Empathy and living in the mind of the therapist

I have discussed the various aspects of empathy above. However, there is another aspect to it. This is the way a depressed person comes to 'live in your mind'. There are various reasons why, when a session is over, you find yourself reflecting or ruminating on clients. You may worry about some clients and can experience intrusions (i.e. concerns and worries about them pop into your head). Sometimes this is because they have triggered your threat systems and you are worried that they might kill themselves in between sessions, or have a major blow up at home, or simply how they are coping with something that was difficult for them. Or you may be confused about them and are not sure if you are on the right lines or if you should be doing something different in therapy. Some people seem to have ways of 'getting inside you'. Frankly, if you have chosen to be a counsellor or therapist, then you have agreed to let people and their problems live in your head – at least at times. Again, supervision and sharing can help here and it is useful to reflect on why you are thinking about them outside the therapy. It is useful to have times to reflect on them when alone; you might review a session after it has finished, or think about a session to come so that you can get yourself into a desired state of mind.

So the way you reflect on your therapy, and the people you are trying to help, the supervision you seek and how you prepare for a session are all ways in which your mind is given over to thinking about them in their absence. These can be important processes in the therapeutic relationship.

Non-judgement

The essence of unconditional positive regard is to hold a non-judgemental position. This can sometimes be difficult when, for perfectly human reasons, we may find ourselves not liking our clients or worrying about our clients. The key therapeutic stance, however, is observational rather than judgemental. This non-judgement should extend to yourself too. Very self-critical therapists can do things in the therapy to try to ward off their own self-criticisms.

Being non-judgemental is a therapeutic stance, not a legal or moral one. There can be key issues around areas such as abuse or illegal behaviour. In these situations you need to seek advice from psychotherapists who work in these areas and are knowledgeable about how to deal with such issues. However, as therapists we are trying to understand the processes involved in a person's problems, to see things through the eyes of the client.

Empathy is a key element in being non-judgemental. Recognising that with a different set of genes, learning experiences or life contexts we could be in the position they are, is to recognise our common humanity (Neff, 2003a). This can be a little scary at times. I take the view that we do not choose our genes, or the families we are born into, or how our brains are shaped or our self-identities. If I had been born in Rome 2,500 years ago I might be looking forward to the gladiatorial games this weekend – which to my current mind is appalling. These thoughts raise complex questions about the notion of agency, self-determination and responsibility that we cannot explore here (Wong, 2006). We can, however, recognise that we are all caught up in the dramas of life, having brains that have evolved over millions of years, and we are trying to do the best we can. This sense of *common humanity* allows us to connect with the other person, not as a set of difficulties to be solved, but as a suffering, struggling individual. In DBT, therapists are encouraged to share some of their own stories (Lynch et al., 2006) and form bonds via links to our shared, common humanity. There are, of course, problems if such is not done judiciously or with care. So the point here is that to take a non-judgemental stance is to stay empathic and mindful – and that is not always easy.

Warmth

Warmth is a difficult quality to identify because a major part of it relates to the non-verbal communications and interpersonal styles between counsellors and clients. Warmth is related to affection but it is not affection. Warmth has qualities of openness, gentleness and humility about it. Warmth probably also relates to confidence and relatively low anxiety. When we become anxious or irritated, then warmth probably suffers. When we feel interpersonal warmth from others, we are also more likely to feel safe with that person. I am sure we have all seen counsellors who, perhaps because they feel unconfident or for other reasons, find being relaxed and warm with their clients difficult. They can say the right things but in a rather stiff and cold way. The development of warmth can sometimes come from taking a mindful and compassionate attitude. Although depression is a serious and sad situation, this does not mean therapists have to be grim and joyless. Indeed, your ability to smile, at times be playful, and share humour appropriately can help to create warmth and safeness. These interactions may also stimulate the soothing systems in your clients if done appropriately. As noted in Chapter 5, warmth involves sharing positive and affiliative emotions as well as negative ones. Warmth, then, is the context in which the other aspects of compassion can flourish and without it compassion can be difficult.

Conclusion

This chapter has focused on the therapeutic relationship. We have seen that the relationship is an emergent co-creation via interactions, where the counsellor brings to the relationship mirco-skills and types of knowledge. These include forms of attention, paraphrasing, summarising, and validation that go to building the formulation and agreeing tasks and goals in a collaborative manner. In addition, what goes on in the counsellor's mind and the way they use 'theory of mind' skills, empathy and sympathy and avoid projection and defensiveness play key roles in how the relationship will develop and work. All these are skills which develop over time, with experience and supervision.

Research on the nature of sympathy, empathy, theory of mind, intersubjectivity, and mutual influence has moved ahead since Rogers first articulated the key ingredients for the therapeutic relationship. One framework that may be useful to integrate both the old and the new findings on interpersonal processes, and orientate our focus, is with a compassion focus. Understanding the components of compassion and how they depend on, and mutually influence each other, can offer one way of thinking about the therapeutic relationship.

Compassion-focused therapy draws on what is important in any therapeutic relationship (Norcross, 2002). It is an approach that simply emphasises the key components of what, in any situation, is the 'compassionate way to be or thing to do'. It focuses on the idea that experiencing compassion in therapy and in the therapist will impact on the depressed person's soothing systems. Feeling listened to, heard, valued and understood can be key to soothing. This may then help people start to feel safe and accepted, and from this base find the courage to engage with their life problems. However, some people will find therapist compassion frightening because it reactivates attachment systems and triggers aversive memories (Gilbert, in press b; Liotti, 2007). Nonetheless for the more straightforward cases a compassion focus is soothing.

8 Beginning the Therapeutic Journey with the Depressed Person

Therapy goes through various stages where the nature of the therapeutic relationship and the tasks undertaken change (Hardy et al., 2007). There are, for example, some things that happen early and others that occur later.

Early themes

1 Developing rapport (getting to know each other) and creating safeness.
2 Exploring possible fears, concerns and expectations of coming for counselling.
3 Exploring the story with open questions, curiosity, reflection and summaries, and eliciting key themes and styles:
   (a) taking a historical perspective;
   (b) working in the here and now.
4 Assessing the symptom profile of depression and possible risks.
5 Developing a shared understanding and meaning that leads to:
6 Discussing the nature of depression.
7 Developing an agreed formulation.
8 Explaining your model for working and why.
9 Discussing possible tasks and goals of the therapy.
10 De-shaming depression.

These set up the first stages of counselling that provide a platform for focused working.

Later themes

1 Developing the formulation further.
2 Agreeing and engaging with the tasks of therapy.
3 Increasing awareness of the relationship between thoughts, feelings and behaviour.
4 Exploring how to generate and practise alternative ways of thinking, feeling and behaving.
5 Independent practice and behavioural experiments.
6 Identifying and working in-depth with specific problems (e.g. self-criticisms).
7 Identifying and working with sticking points.
8 Preparing for leaving counselling.
9 Reviews and maintaining learnt skills.

Developing rapport

As we noted in Chapter 7, the first tasks of therapy are building your relationship and creating a sense of safeness with your client. Keep in mind that these go on throughout counselling. It commences when the person enters the room and it is still important when it comes to saying goodbye. Beginnings are taken up with getting to know the client and the nature of the current difficulties, but also the client needs to get to know you. Different depressed people move through these stages at different paces and they often overlap (Liotti, 2007).

Fears and concerns in coming to counselling

When many of us seek help for the first time there are various hopes and fears of the first attendance. One can create an opportunity to discuss various thoughts and feelings the depressed person may have about coming to counselling: what are their explanations and expectations? After initial introductions, the counsellor may discuss the nature of the referral or the way the person came to take up counselling. Early in the first interview you might then ask various questions. For example, one might ask: 'Before we start to discuss things in more detail, I wonder if we could look at what has been going through your mind about coming here today.' Here are some typical thoughts and feelings that might arise:

1 I was told to come (by general practitioner, spouse, friends).
2 I thought I had to do something.
3 I do not want to have to take drugs.
4 I want you to tell me what to do.
5 It's pointless, there is nothing to help me.
6 I doubt that you will understand me (shame theme).
7 I expect you'll tell me it is my fault and to pull myself together (shame theme).
8 You might discover I am a weak or bad person or a hopeless case (shame theme).
9 I want to come but my spouse does not. (Hence, there may be various relational problems that could affect the work.)

One acknowledges these concerns but suggests that these are things that can be addressed as you go along. Until the client has some experience of you and your work together they have little to base their judgements on. Sometimes the counsellor may suggest the possibility of bringing a spouse or family members to counselling at some point in the process. Some find this helpful but some depressed people want their therapy to be 'for them' and not include others, especially early on. They may feel too confused and need time to work on their own thoughts and feelings. It may also be preferable to set up marital work with another therapist. Whatever the fears and doubts about engaging in counselling, the counsellor tries to clarify them and bring them into the open, but does not engage in detailed discussion because, at this point, the client will have no evidence to judge how they are going to get on with you, how the counselling will be structured, or how useful it will be. If the depressed person has strong fears or doubts about coming for counselling, the counsellor may say something like: 'These are very understandable concerns. At this point, since it is early days, perhaps we could see how this session goes and review the situation as we go.' Be friendly and open in your manner. The idea is that if you can have one session this will help you build a sufficient alliance to keep them interested. Other behaviours that help to develop rapport with the client and to overcome the fears of coming for counselling are those core skills outlined in Chapter 7.

Key issues 8.1   Beginning the process

1   Keep in mind the power issues of counselling and try to create a safe place (e.g. friendly and open but don't deny the power issues).
2   Be aware of shame in being depressed and (possibly) in feeling a need for counselling. Address this but also be aware that a client might have secret things they wish to talk about but are too ashamed to do so.
3   Recognise a common fear that the therapy may not work for them.
4   Give an opportunity to discuss fears of coming to or undertaking counselling.
5   Avoid providing false reassurances or making control statements (e.g. you must trust me).
6   Be aware that trust builds from experience.

Exploring the story

At the start of obtaining the story the counsellor invites the client to tell their story with the use of Socratic discussions (see Chapter 9). Below we will use the example of a depressed person we will call Peter. As for all material discussed in this book, this is for demonstration purposes and is a mixture of various others.

Counsellor: We have spoken a little about your feelings of coming to counselling and the symptoms you are experiencing. Perhaps we could start to look at what's been happening to you recently.

Peter: Yeah. Things seem to have been piling on top of me. I feel washed up, like there is no point any more.

Counsellor: How long has that feeling been with you?

Peter: Oh, I don't know, maybe a year. Maybe longer.

Counsellor: What about before that? Looking back two years, how were you feeling then?

Peter: Well, not like this. Things seemed to be going okay then.

Counsellor: So you have been feeling low for about a year, but before that things seemed okay.

Peter: Yes.

Counsellor: Has there been anything that has happened over this year that seems to be related to this feeling low?

Peter: Well, there isn't one thing. It's a number of things.

Counsellor: A number of things? Could you tell me about them?

Peter: We were hoping to move to a new house about a year ago and then we ran into financial difficulties. Then there was a problem at work. I didn't get the promotion I was due and all our plans started to slip away. My wife and I started to argue and I got pretty irritable. It seemed nothing was going right for me.

[The client then explained various life events and how they had happened.]

Counsellor: So you have had a pretty rotten time recently. There seem to have been a number of major disappointments for you. I guess you must be pretty exhausted by it all.

Peter: Yes, you could say that.

Once the counsellor has a general idea of life events (which in reality can take a lot longer than outlined here), they may wish to focus the discussion. This helps set out a problem list and to work with the person's priorities. Keep in mind that problems are usually both external and internal. For example, this might be a list for Peter.

External	**Internal**
Got stuck in career and want promotion	Feel out of control of emotions and moods
Conflicts with wife and less affectionate relationship	Losing motivation, tired
Financial concerns	Self-critical
Want to move house	General sense of disappointment

Be sensitive when developing a problem list because some depressed people can look at a list like this and feel overwhelmed and worse. Stay collaborative, ask: 'Would it help if we jotted down some of your key worries and concerns?' Ask about priorities.

Counsellor: Looking at each of the disappointments, which one seems to have affected you most?

Peter: Well, right now it is my relationship with my wife. We were quite close early on like, but now we seem to be drifting apart. In a way I know it's me. I think I've messed it up if I'm honest.

Counsellor: So it's your relationship with your wife that is your key concern right now?

Peter: Yes, we argue a lot. She doesn't understand how I feel about things. She tells me we'll be okay and that I am making mountains out of molehills. I try to explain but she doesn't want to listen.

Counsellor: Okay, maybe we could make that a priority to think about and work on – or do you feel there is something more urgent for you?

This is a rather common theme in depression and tells the story about feeling misunderstood and not receiving empathy from loved ones. Here we see the client oscillating between 'I've messed it up' and 'She doesn't want to listen'. The counsellor should also be alert to the possibility that the client may fear that the counsellor will turn out to have a similar attitude (i.e. they won't really listen, or will not become an ally). This theme needs empathic handling. If one rushes in too fast with techniques, the client can get the idea that 'Just like others, the counsellor thinks I am being irrational or neurotic'.

Sometimes clients can present with a more angry style. For example, 'I keep trying to explain how I feel to others, my GP and so on, but they don't seem to listen/understand'. One response might be: 'So you feel that people whom you are looking to for help, don't listen to you. That must feel quite upsetting.' In other words, some kind of reflection and validation of feelings of frustration can be useful. Unhelpful responses are: 'Well you haven't told me' or 'I can't help you until you tell me your difficulties'. These are defensive responses by the counsellor.

Let us return to Peter who has conflicts with his wife. The underlying theme is feeling that others do not appreciate his internal struggle and difficulty. At this point the counsellor has a choice. The counselling may become focused on historical data, or proceed to explore the meaning of the wife's behaviour for the client. Let us look at both options because you may need both if you are to develop your formulation.

Taking a person's history

In depression, that is anything more than mild, one needs to have an overview of a person's background. In fact, most approaches to formulation for depression assume that you have some insight as to the origins of people's core beliefs, basic threats and safety strategies (Tarrier, 2006).

> *Counsellor*: If I understand you, some of your depression now revolves around the thought that your wife doesn't listen to your worries and fears, which is a key issue for you right now. I wonder if we could just look at that in more detail for a moment. Have you had these kinds of ideas before, in other relationships?
>
> *Peter*: Well, thinking about it, it has often seemed that way. As a child my parents had a lot of financial problems and were always rowing and there was never much time for us kids. I mean they tried and all that, but if we had problems they didn't really want to know.
>
> *Counsellor*: Hm, this early feeling of others not *having time for you*, and it being tied up with money difficulties, may be important. Could we stay here a little and see how things were for you as you grew up?

When you take a full history you can then explore systematically the following key relationships:

1. Relationship with mother.
2. Relationship with father.
3. The relationship between mother and father.
4. Relationships with siblings.
5. Peer and school relationships.
6. Early dating relationships.
7. Marital relationships.
8. Relationships with children.
9. Other significant relationships (e.g. with grandparents, uncles, aunts or teachers).
10. Relationships with peers.
11. Work history.
12. Major hobbies and sources of enjoyment.
13. Major ambitions and life goals.
14. Typical ways of coping with stress.
15. Major life events in the recent past and earlier.

History-taking not only enables the counsellor to get to know their client in the context of their life histories, but also offers a person a chance to tell their story and to know that the counsellor has an overview of key themes in their lives. Moreover, it starts the process of linking things together and making sense of why the client is depressed and why now. Also, in the process of discussion, this can settle a person and they become more comfortable in talking. However, stay sensitive to the client, as for very depressed clients one might first work with more practical issues.

As you move through the life history, you will be constantly checking on two things. First, repetitive patterns (e.g. of rejection, neglect, abuse or over-protection, or needing to look after significant others). Second, you are interested in *meanings, attitudes* and *beliefs* that may have developed in these relationships by asking questions such as: What did you make of that? What did that mean to you? What sense did you derive from that? What did you conclude from that? For example:

Counsellor: What was your relationship with your mother like?
Peter: Well, I felt sorry for Mum. She had too many problems. Dad wasn't that interested really. He was more in the background. He worked hard and then spent a lot of time with his mates down the pub. He'd whack us if we were naughty but not show much interest.
Counsellor: So you saw your mother as a fairly lonely person, somewhat withdrawn?
Peter: Yes, I think she was probably depressed.
Counsellor: How do you think growing up with a depressed Mum and distant Dad has affected you, your beliefs about yourself and others. What do you think it might have made you sensitive to?

If you are focusing on a safety strategies approach you would be interested in how Peter talks about sensitivities he may have picked up from his childhood and how he has learnt to try to avoid them (i.e. key fears and safety strategies). Or you might be interested in key beliefs and assumptions (see Chapter 9). Peter went on to reveal various ideas that others were generally unavailable to him, that his fears and concerns were not taken seriously and, importantly, that nobody could see things from his point of view. There was also a relative lack of physical affection. Peter has a complex attachment style. We were able to crystallise this basic theme as lack of recognition and that he had been very concerned through his life to gain recognition and validation. Gaining recognition through work and from higher status males was important to him and you might note how this linked to a distant father. So it began to make sense how the problems at work (failing to get the promotion), and those with his wife, were related to the underlying theme of lack of recognition/validation and the associated disappointment. In Chapters 5 and 6 we spent some time exploring different attachment styles and how these give rise to different vulnerabilities. For example, the depressed person may have learned various strategies to cope with abusive, rejecting or demanding parental styles: (a) to be submissive and avoid trouble; (b) to try to achieve in an effort to impress others and win approval; (c) to put the needs of others first at the expense of themselves (perhaps more common in women); (d) to be aggressive and ensure that they control others (perhaps more common in men).

Other key issues can involve sibling rivalry and competitiveness (Gilbert and Gelsma, 1999). Obtaining an outline of basic experiences, key emotional memories, and attitudes to significant others will be important for it helps you and your client begin to comprehend how their depression may be related to basic emotional memories, attitudes and experiences that existed before the depression (Brewin, 2006; Gut, 1989; Safran, 1998; Safran and Segal, 1990). Sharing these experiences can aid rapport and heighten the experience of being understood, of having shared something of one's life with the counsellor. Sometimes acknowledgement of the basic themes in a life history can arouse strong emotions. For example, consider Susan discussing her relationship with her mother:

Susan: My mother was cold. If we hurt ourselves she would say not to be a 'sissy' and to get a 'grip'. I can't really remember her ever hugging us that much or showing that she cared. If I see things on the TV where a mother and child get together and love each other or something, it really fills me up.

Counsellor: [Pausing and watching to see if this idea is starting to activate significant feelings for the client, the counsellor gets the feeling there is something she is struggling with] Maybe that feeling of 'filling up' taps into something you would like, a kind of recognition of some deep hurt?

Susan: [Eyes beginning to water] Oh yeah, [pause] yeah.

Counsellor: [Pause and gently] Could you tell me what is going through your mind right now?

Susan: Your words of deep hurt. Like it is real deep, maybe too deep.

Counsellor: Too deep?

Susan: Yeah, too deep.

Counsellor: Like it's beyond reach?

Susan: Yeah, I guess so.

Counsellor: That's sounds like a hopeless, empty feeling.

Susan: [Cries and nods].

In this situation the counsellor has used empathy and been able to tap into a theme of emptiness and loss that is very charged with emotion. However, the hopelessness aspect is related to ideas of it being too deep and beyond reach or rescue. Later Susan changed this to 'beyond repair'. This example demonstrates that even in the first session, if one explores historical data, one may tap highly charged emotional memories and beliefs.

It is possible that a client might reveal a horrific story (say, of abuse) with little or no emotion. Here the counsellor notes the absence of emotion and may draw attention to this later. However, working with what has been called 'split off' emotions and feelings is more complex than we can outline here (see Greenberg, Rice and Elliott, 1993; Greenberg and Watson, 2006).

In exploring these issues the client can begin to build a picture of how previous experiences have led to basic themes and issues of self-identity. Recall that during the historical exploration the counsellor asks 'What did this mean to you?'. Here one is interested in how the self-identity has developed. Let us stay with the case of Susan:

Counsellor: You were saying that you felt your mother rarely hugged you, and this has given you the feeling that maybe things are beyond repair. Would it be okay to focus on that feeling for a moment and tell me what you have concluded about yourself?

Susan:	Now or then?
Counsellor:	Well, both really. Let's think about then, like when it was happening to you.
Susan:	I'm not sure. I saw that other parents seemed to hug their kids and wondered why it was different at home. I guess in the back of my head I began to think maybe there was something wrong with me.
Counsellor:	Something wrong with you?
Susan:	Like she didn't love me because I was unlovable.
Counsellor:	Did you have any ideas about what it was that might be unlovable about you.
Susan:	[*Pauses and looks down*] I've never mentioned this to anyone before, but you know I was the second girl and I sometimes thought that maybe they wanted a boy rather than another girl.

At this point in our work together we note that Susan has introduced two new ideas: (a) lovability, and (b) gender. Now the counsellor could check on the evidence. For example, because her mother didn't hug her, why did that mean she didn't love her? Or, look to see if she thought her sister had been treated differently. This could be unempathic, however, and runs the risk of implying an invalidation. If you take an evolutionary approach, as I have done here, you would not do that because you would take it that the *experience* of being loved is linked to certain kinds of signals (especially those of physical affection). Whether her mother loved her or not is less important than the fact that Susan did not recall experiencing certain signals of being cared for and loved. It may be that her mother did love her but had a problem with the expression of affection. So keep in mind it is the emotional experience that is key. So the counsellor notes this connection, continues to explore self-ideas and feelings, and later offers a crystallisation and empathic validation.

Counsellor:	So you had the impression that because your mother didn't hug you that much and you saw it was different for other kids, that maybe this was because she didn't love you. And you also had the idea that maybe this was because she had wanted a boy rather than another girl.
Susan:	Yeah, that sounds close to it. Yeah.
Counsellor:	Gosh, Susan, that must have been a very lonely and sad experience for you.

Later it was possible to look at 'evidence' and discover that her mother was equally distant from her sister. There was little evidence that her mother wanted a boy. However, her sister had coped with the mother's distance differently, leading Susan to feel more inadequate *in comparison* with her sister.

At this stage we have engaged historical data to explore basic key themes in self–other relationships. This is part of developing rapport and also exploring the basic life themes of the person's story. It helps clients feel understood. Clients are not a set of disconnected problems or schema to which one can apply techniques *ad hoc*. Rather, one needs to have a sense of the whole person, since people live with their history and make sense of the present by virtue of what has happened in the past.

Working in the present

Part of working with the present is obtaining some overview and current problem list (see p. 175). One of the things on Peter's problem list was self-criticism. You can anticipate self-criticism is going to be a problem for the majority of your depressed clients and it is important to gain information on how the client evaluates the self. To help here one can focus on a specific example and explore how various ideas are linked together. This is called inference chaining (see Chapter 9). In this example we can focus on shame, and we do this by exploring self-evaluations.

> *Counsellor*: Peter, this theme of recognition is obviously important to you. However, I wonder what goes through your mind about yourself when others don't seem to recognise your feelings in the way you might wish.
>
> *Peter*: I'm not sure I understand what you mean.
>
> *Counsellor*: Right. Well, let's think about a particular example. Let's imagine that tonight you try to talk to your wife and she doesn't show the interest you would like. What will go through your mind?
>
> *Peter*: Hm, I think I feel something like, she doesn't really care that much. I am being a nuisance to her and shouldn't feel this way. [*external shame theme of 'being a nuisance' in the mind of his wife*]
>
> *Counsellor*: You shouldn't feel this way?
>
> *Peter*: Yes.
>
> *Counsellor*: What do you say about you? What are your feelings about you as a person?
>
> *Peter*: I feel maybe *I am* making mountains out of molehills. Then I think, God, I must be weak and stupid for getting into such a state about things. If I'm honest, part of me starts to dislike myself and feel pretty worthless, inadequate, but like I'm trapped. [*internal shame theme of being 'pretty worthless and inadequate'*]
>
> *Counsellor*: So then you have two sets of ideas and evaluations, one about others and one about you. First is the idea that your wife doesn't recognise you and may see you as 'a nuisance' and that feels upsetting and disappointing. You interpret this as evidence that maybe she doesn't care. But also because you feel unrecognised this makes you feel down and when you feel down you feel weak, stupid and worthless. Is that how it is?
>
> *Peter*: Yeah. I feel pretty much a failure really.

What has happened here is that the counsellor has taken a specific example of the problem, set it up for detailed exploration and elicited the typical (shame) constructions that Peter makes. If one has access to historical data then one might see this as a repeating theme. Note how the counsellor spells out the different self–other evaluations (by saying `You have two sets of evaluations, one about you and one about others').

You can now move to thinking and working on a formulation (outlined in Chapter 9). To begin with a formulation can be quite simple and straightforward, provided it captures an agreed understanding with the possibility of filling in more detail as you go along.

Sharing therapeutic goals and developing the therapeutic contract

Sharing therapeutic goals and developing the therapeutic contact means establishing with the client an agreed focus for work:

Counsellor: So far, Peter, we have talked of some of the things that are bothering you right now and have looked a little at your early life. We have drawn up a formulation and overview of these together. Do you think working on some of those issues would be helpful?

Peter: What do you mean?

Counsellor: Well, you mentioned that you get disappointed and angry when your wife does not recognise your feelings and that you then begin to get angry at yourself. Suppose you could learn another way of dealing with this situation that didn't lead you to feel bad about you or think of yourself as weak, would that be helpful?

Peter: Oh, yes, of course. If I could cope better I would be happier.

Counsellor: So that might be a useful start. Perhaps one goal of our work together might be to see if we can help you cope in a different way at home?

Thus, beginning to share therapeutic tasks and goals involves hypothesising 'what would be helpful'. Asking questions like 'Do you think it would help you if . . .' or 'What do you think would be most helpful to you right now?' allows the client to begin the process of thinking how to work towards change. It is of little use if the counsellor heads off in a direction that has not been agreed with the client (e.g. well I suggest we do this, or you do that). Although depressed clients often appear compliant, compliance is not the same as collaborative work. It is the skill of the counsellor to help guide the client towards goals that are workable and seen as helpful, and to recognise the difference between compliance and collaboration. Sometimes this takes considerable therapeutic effort.

In a case like Peter's we would be cautious about moving too quickly to consider the idea that his wife does not care, without first attending to self-attacking and self-experience. For example, imagine that you feel others have not treated you well. You would want to find someone who, although they may not agree or disagree, shows empathic understanding of your feelings and does not rush into trying to convince you that you are being over-sensitive. Later, when you feel better about yourself, it will be easier for you to recognise this, if it's true. Nevertheless, the way Peter comes to experience his wife as not caring for him will need to be addressed. We can validate the experience without agreeing with the 'facts'. As Peter reduces shame and self-blaming and sees some of his anger as linked to earlier relationships, he is more able to think about his actual relationship with his wife and that maybe he *is* difficult to relate to when depressed. High shame can make it difficult for people to take objective views because of the sense of self-condemnation. So they bounce between feeling 'there is something wrong with me for getting upset with my wife; it is my fault' and 'if only people would understand me better'. Helping shame-prone (self-critical) people recognise that interpersonal problems are usually complex, related to dynamic patterns of co-constructions, and co-constructions are products of what we each bring (from the past) to the relationship, and are thus multi-causal rather 'your fault – my fault' polarities, can take time. Developing compassion can be very helpful here.

Key issues 8.2   Sharing and basic themes

1   Explore the current events that have led up to the depression and which may be continuing.
2   Look at the most difficult situation, or the client's priorities.
3   When working with historical data, explore past significant relationships of the client and how these took on certain meanings.
4   Attempt to identify basic interpersonal styles and beliefs, and safety strategies.
5   Note critical events (past or present) that stir up strong emotions and try to illuminate key self–other beliefs, clarifying these with the client.
6   Note possible areas where there is an absence of affect and a detached attitude.
7   When working in the present, create inference chains and separate and clarify key self–other beliefs (see Chapter 9).
8   Keep clear in your mind *external* concerns (what others are thinking or problems in the outside) and *internal* concerns (such as self-criticisms or being overwhelmed by feelings or mood states).

Explaining the therapeutic rationale

As one moves through the first few sessions, and normally around the time of sharing therapeutic ideas, tasks and goals, the counsellor will introduce the client into the rationale of their approach. Cognitive-behavioural counsellors see this as important because it enables the client to understand and take an active part in counselling and to make the therapeutic tasks and goals clearer. A simple state-ment such as 'We are here to talk about your feelings' is not enough. There can be problems if the counsellor gives the impression that they know what is going on, what to expect and the stages counselling will take, but the client is left largely in the dark. Also, clients are helped if they learn that there are things that they can do to help themselves and that the counsellor will offer guidance on this. Whatever model is used in counselling, it is important that clients should be informed as to the kind of process it will follow. Introducing the model can go something like this:

> *Counsellor*:   We agreed just now that if you could find ways of helping you tackle difficulties in your relationship without 'attacking yourself' this might be helpful to you. Can I show you one way we might approach this? [*At this point the counsellor explores the client's interest*] We will focus on the meanings you give to events. A simple way to show this is for me to write an example with you and then look again at your current situation.

Following this, one takes a pad and pencil and, if necessary, moves one's chair to be at the side of the client. The counsellor may offer various examples of how thoughts can affect feelings (see Chapter 9). The counsellor may then draw out two or three columns and run through some simple example. Following this, check that the client understands the approach. Does it make sense? Often, the simple act of sitting next to the client and engaging in a shared task helps the sense of collaboration. However, if a person is very depressed this may be inappropriate, or if the client gives off various nonverbal signals of disengagement then one has to slow it down. So, while you are sharing your model, attend to the client's verbal and nonverbal behaviour and check on any thoughts they might be having (e.g. it is too logical, it won't help my feelings, I want to talk more). However, assuming that the client agrees, one then move to the client's example.

> *Counsellor*:   Okay, Peter, you have mentioned that problems with your wife seem to be central right now. One way we can explore this is to begin to make sense of how you think about these interactions. So we can write down together the typical sequence of events, thoughts and feelings.

For Peter it went like this:

Telling my wife

Triggering events	Beliefs and fears	Feelings/behaviours
She doesn't understand about my money worries; tells me not to worry	*External focus* If she cared for me she would try to listen to me.	Angry, depressed, withdrawn
	Key fear: She is fed up with me and maybe is becoming distant – neglect theme	
	Internal focus I have to take responsibility. I must be a weak sort of person for not being able to cope	
	Key fear: I am not worth caring for – worthless	

In helping clients write thoughts down in this way a number of things are happening. First, it helps to crystallise those half-formed ideas in the mind and to clarify meaning. Secondly, it helps in the process of shared understanding, and offers a focus. Thirdly, and rarely mentioned in the literature, there is a behavioural exposure aspect to this approach in that the thoughts and their feelings are subjected to repeated exposure, and desensitisation. Fourthly, keeping the 'internal' and 'external' conceptually separate makes the focus on change easier.

Increasing awareness

The inference chain and emotions in Peter's case
One can increase awareness of thought-emotion links with the idea that internal meanings (thoughts and personal constructions) are fuelling the dysphoric emotions. This is an educational aspect. Hence one may stop at this point and draw out the inference chain and emotions in a circle. The circle for Peter is shown in Figure 8.1.

Figure 8.1   Peter's circular inference chain

Counsellor: Do you see how this sequence of events and ideas drive this circle around, such that you end up feeling worse until eventually you withdraw and go to bed. We could probably draw another circle that puts in the fact that when you withdraw, your wife also withdraws more, and so again things get worse for you.

Peter: Now that you draw it out like that it seems so clear. That's exactly what happens. But I still can't see how it's going to change.

In this case, writing down and drawing has helped Peter clarify some issues. At these times one can check on the level of agreement and the possibilities of 'yes but' thinking.

Counsellor: Okay, Peter, this is an important part of our work together, to gain more understanding of what goes through your mind, why, how you then act and how what goes through your mind and how you act – though very understandable – can make things unintentionally feel worse.

Key issues 8.3   Sharing and explaining the therapeutic process

1   Once a key set of dysphoric attitudes has been identified, use questions to explore what might be helpful (e.g. 'What would it be helpful to change?', 'Would it help if you could . . .?', etc.).
2   Gain the client's co-operation in targeting certain thoughts or behaviours (i.e. agree therapeutic goals).
3   In depressed clients, look for shame and the self-attacking and self-undermining thoughts.
4   Be clear about how you are to *work together*. Write things down, offer examples.
5   Use various procedures (e.g. writing down an inference chain and drawing circles of interacting thoughts and behaviours).
6   Prepare the client to begin to do this kind of work for themself.

Moving to alternative conceptualisations

To help develop alternatives for thinking and behaving we can work off the circle or go back to the chain. As noted many times, self-attacking is often triggered by disappointment. It is important to help clients recognise this and reconsider and recognise their genuine emotions.

Counsellor:	What we can do now is to see if there are other ways that you might cope differently with this situation. Like we can experiment with some ideas, is that okay? Let's start with the idea that you are worthless. How does your wife not listening to you make you, a human being, worthless?
Peter:	Well, it doesn't I guess, it just feels that it does. [*Here the client has shifted the idea of worthlessness into a feeling so the counsellor can use this*]
Counsellor:	Looking at it now, although understandable, does that feeling seem reliable?
Peter:	Well, logically no not really, but then that's how I feel.
Counsellor:	Well, right; you do feel bad for understandable reasons, but suppose it was something other than worthlessness. What else might this bad feeling be?
Peter:	[*Thinks for awhile*] Lonely, disappointed. [*Pause*] Empty, I guess.
Counsellor:	Can you be in touch with those feelings for a moment?

The counsellor then stays here and explores images, feelings or memories, enabling the client to gain deeper insight into how disappointment and emptiness launch the self-attack. Sometimes early life memories of being put-down or neglected come to mind. This helps to link the current work with past themes and emotional memories.

Counsellor:	Can you see how, when you feel unrecognised and disappointed and lonely, this triggers anger and also a self-attack and makes you think that you're worthless?
Peter:	Hm. Sort of.
Counsellor:	Well. Let's stay here a while. What is your self-attacking trying to make you do? [*We are thinking if Peter can see the function of the self-attacking*]
Peter:	To make me pull myself together.
Counsellor:	And if you could do that, then…?
Peter:	I would not feel so bad and get into these states.
Counsellor:	And then…?
Peter:	I could keep going and would stop being depressed.

Now at this point the counsellor does not want to keep firing questions so it is best to summarise by saying something like:

Counsellor:	So you see the self-criticism is trying to bully you out of your depressed state and then you won't feel bad, and then you won't upset your wife, and she and other people will not criticise you for feeling depressed and irritable, and then people will like you again. You see it all makes sense but the problem is that this effort to bully yourself out of depression and label yourself worthless actually makes you feel worse not better.

We discussed this for a while so that Peter gradually saw his self-criticism as trying, in a strange way, to protect him. The self-criticisms arose from his fear of behaving in ways that courted criticisms from others. We also noted that it deflected attention from another emotion – one that he had felt on and off for a long time – that of loneliness.

> *Counsellor*: Okay, so suppose we were to change that idea of worthlessness and stay with lonely and disappointed. How would that feel?
>
> *Peter*: [*Pauses, thinking*] I would still feel upset but maybe not so angry with myself.

Later the counsellor might add:

> *Counsellor*: Well, it is possible that you learned to self-attack when you felt lonely and unrecognised as a child. Perhaps we can make some changes in this and help you develop a more accepting, caring and compassionate attitude to yourself. It seems to me that the one time you need to care for yourself, you put the boot in, a kind of kicking you when you're down.
>
> *Peter*: [*Client smiles*] Oh, yeah, I've always been good at that.
>
> *Counsellor*: Okay, so one of the things we can do together is to see whether this lonely feeling may be partly linked to echoes and emotional memories of your childhood. When these feelings of loneliness and not feeling understood are triggered, they trigger a range of other feelings, such as anger, but also efforts to control them by being self-critical and closing down. This is a way you have tried to protect yourself from them and cope.

You can see that we are clarifying the link between feeling invalidated, feelings of loneliness and the safety behaviours of withdrawing, anger and self-criticism. Peter has not been able to understand or work on his feelings of loneliness but rather has tried to *avoid* them. It is the counsellor's ability to validate these feelings of loneliness, de-shame them and make them central to the issue that will enable Peter to acknowledge these as underlying issues that he can learn to work on and tolerate. As Peter learns to self-validate and be compassionate to his long-lived feelings of loneliness (and never really feeling accepted) he can reduce his self-attacking and anger. This is likely to need repetition many times since, for Peter, there is a long history of the experience of feeling a lack of recognition (and affection) triggering the self-attack. Also note that sometimes we need to help clients experience specific feelings more deeply (Linehan, 1993). In these cases anger at self becomes a secondary emotion to disappointment and loss, especially in depression, and this linkage will need further work (see Wolf, 1988). The counsellor's empathy for the disappointment will be important in the healing process. Thus, clear insight into the linkage of the feelings of disappointment and anger at the self is helpful. So one can provide further opportunities for reflecting the client's experience of disappointment and loneliness, and make the first inroads into developing self-compassion (see Chapter 11) with a simple intervention.

> *Counsellor*: Let's think more about this idea of worthlessness. Now sometimes we might call this 'black and white' thinking, or 'either/or' thinking. Like if my wife recognises me, I am okay, if not, I'm worthless. That is very harsh on you. Suppose you had a friend and one day he comes to you with a rather similar story, what would you say to him?

Peter: I'd understand his feelings, I think.
Counsellor: So you wouldn't say well, 'I'm sorry my friend, your wife doesn't share
                your fears therefore she doesn't care for you. You should be able to
                cope, therefore you are worthless.'
Peter: [*Smiles*] Oh, no, I wouldn't say that.
Counsellor: [*Smiles*] Would you think it?

Sometimes people would think harshly of others, although they would not say so, and this needs to be recognised. The counsellor's response here can be, 'Well, you are certainly consistent. But if you did say it, how would your friend feel?', again getting across the idea that the attack leads to feeling worse.

At this point one again has a choice. We can continue to work the theme of worthlessness in various ways. We might talk about different parts of the self, pointing out that we are made up of multiple bits, feelings, competencies, abilities and so forth, and that the client is globally rating themselves negatively due to one situation or theme. We may talk about putting all one's eggs in one basket, and so on. In role reversal one might say, 'How might you help a friend who has a similar experience?' The counsellor would like to help him see that because his wife does not listen to his money worries as he would like this does not mean that she does not care for him or that he is worthless.' Of course there may be major marital problems, but this does not seem the case here.

Re-attribution training can also be used. For example, can Peter generate alternative explanations for why his wife does not wish to listen to his worries? When Peter was asked this he said it was his wife's attitude to things. Her approach was: 'If you can't change it, worrying only makes it worse.' She did not like ruminating, while Peter was something of a ruminator. Thus we had an alternative explanation for his wife not wishing to focus on his money worries. This technique therefore involved Peter stopping to think 'Maybe she just sees things differently' and 'Maybe she is worried too, but deals with it in a different way'. As we note later, spend time *really focusing* on this idea. Peter might close his eyes and really imagine this, allowing him *to feel* this alternative. In a sense we have introduced him to a more complex 'theory of mind' way of thinking. Rather than get caught up in automatic reactions, he can step back and think that his wife has different ways of thinking and coping and this is not a reflection of her love or otherwise for him. She may express her own fear in certain ways and her own care for him in certain ways.

So he learns to be more in touch with his feelings of loneliness when he feels invalidated, disappointed and stressed. As we progress through the therapy, Peter acknowledges and learns to compassionately tolerate those feelings as echoes from the past; that they are understandable and not his fault. This reduces self-criticism and develops possibilities to be more open to the difference in coping between himself and his wife (see Chapter 11). This softens his anger and sense of disappointment with her.

By the end of this intervention session, however, Peter will have an agreed set of alternative ideas to call on in situations of *disappointment*. Sometimes one can write these out on a flash card, on one side of which are the typical depressing thoughts, and on the other the agreed alternatives. Clients often like this because it links them back to the counselling situation when they are on their own, and triggers memory of the session, especially the therapist's validation.

> **Key issues 8.4   Moving to alternative conceptualisations**
>
> 1   Look for and clarify the negative self-beliefs and self-attacking in the depressed client's style.
> 2   Help the client to recognise the situations and feelings that often precede self-attacking (e.g. disappointment).
> 3   Be empathic to these feelings of disappointment in depression, which often centre on evaluations of how others treat the client or goals that are not being met.
> 4   Note ideas like 'I must be or have to be recognised, otherwise it is unbearable and I am a worthless person'.
> 5   Use a variety of approaches to interrupt the disappointment → self-attack → self as worthless sequence (e.g. look at the evidence, focus on black and white thinking, or use the friend technique).

Monitoring internal feelings and cognitions, and role enactments

A major aspect of all therapies is to increase 'awareness' outside the counselling situation. There are a number of ways of doing this. One is to show clients the value of writing things down and practising thinking through alternatives. We might call this 'becoming your own compassionate therapist/helper'. Some clients take to this very easily and find it helpful, others do not. Sometimes it is helpful to write out flash cards that they take out whenever they feel themselves slipping. This acts as a prompt. Sometimes making audiotapes of sessions helps. It is helpful to explore for any *disconfirming* ideas they might have. For example, a client would see the value of the flash card during counselling but when alone would discount its validity: 'I can't change my ideas that simply'. The intervention here might be: 'Well, perhaps that is true but let's try for a while and see how it goes. What have you got to lose?'

Cognitive counsellors often talk about developing the *observing self* (Beck et al., 1985). Hence the counsellor can suggest that: 'One part of the self that we are trying to develop is your observing self and your self-awareness. If we can help you identify ideas and images as they pass through your mind, then we might have a better handle on helping to change or cope with them.' Or if you are using mindfulness, 'to see thoughts as thoughts that with practice we can let pass'. Teaching self-awareness and increasing the activity of the observing self helps put a buffer between the thoughts and the affects associated with them. We explore these themes more fully later.

Doing work outside the session and alternative role enactments

Helping depressed people make changes in their actual social behaviour is more important than waiting for it to happen. This is key to many behavioural approaches (see Chapter 4). This is the value of independent work, which can be set up in a number of ways. Again, it is engaging the client's collaboration that is important, not their compliance. With compliance they may go through the motions of the work but not really engage in it. At the end of the session one gives a summary of what has taken place. This might be written down for the depressed client to take away and reflect on. Let's think about Peter. This is what a brief summary might be like.

Counsellor: We are coming to the end of the session now and I would like to go through what we have shared together. You started by telling me that things seem to have been worse for you over the past year, and that this is associated with a number of disappointments and financial worries. We looked a little at your early life and found that you have often had the feeling that others didn't really have time for you. This is linked to feeling lonely and not understood. We then looked at a specific area that is causing you distress right now and this was to do with your relationship with your wife. Here we noted two key themes. The first theme is that you feel your wife does not care for you because she tells you that you are making mountains out of molehills. This triggers feelings of aloneness again and anger. The second theme is the idea that because of this you are weak and worthless. We also explored how these ideas go around in your mind, making your distress even greater. [*Pause*] Is that a fair summary of some of it?

Peter: Yes, I think so.

Counsellor: Okay, Peter, given what we have discussed, can you think of anything you might like to try out between now and the next time we meet?

This involves helping clients to plan their own work out of session. This again is aimed at encouraging the client to collaborate actively in the process of change.

Peter: From what we have discussed, I guess I could practise not putting myself down when my wife doesn't want to hear about my problems.

Counsellor: How could you do that?

Peter: By being more aware, as you say, of my disappointment and not attacking myself when I feel disappointed or lonely.

Counsellor: Yes, let's see if that is helpful. Otherwise you have two problems. One is the disappointment and the other is the attack on you. [*Counsellor points to the circle and watches to see if Peter is thinking about it*] So over the next week, can you keep a note of the situations that arise when this circle seems to be activated? Note down your feelings and thoughts and how you tried to cope with them. To the best of your ability, try to be kind and understanding of your feelings. We can explore that in more detail in the coming weeks.

However, the counsellor is also aware that helping Peter make changes in his social behaviour would be important both for him and the quality of his marriage. Thus, the counsellor explores the possibility of Peter taking on new roles within the relationship. In the case of role enactments it is helpful to enable the client to predict the social consequences of their behaviour (McCullogh, 2000).

Counsellor:	You were also saying earlier that you and your wife get into arguments about things, especially your view on money, and you both withdraw from each other. Would it be worth trying not to engage this subject right now as it is such a bone of contention?
Peter:	Oh yes, if I could stop doing that it would be much calmer at home. It really winds her up.
Counsellor:	Well, shall we try for a week and see how it goes? To the best of your ability avoid talking 'money' at home. You can bring your worries about money here and we will look at them together.

Here the counsellor has attempted to bring some relief to the marital situation by making the counselling the focus for his fears and worries. This is aimed at setting a new style in the relationship. It is also a behavioural experiment. At some point the partner might be invited to the counselling but at the moment it is helpful to see if Peter can make changes himself. There may also be various resentments that will have to be worked with but these will come later.

The other area one might focus on is how they could share more *positive relations*. Could Peter take his wife out, for example, to a film or on a walk? What were the things they *enjoyed doing* in the past? Note that depression affects both the sufferer and the partner so how could they try to reintroduce positive activities. Thus increasing the level of mutually rewarding activities can be helpful. The counsellor can discuss how the depression can cause problems in a marriage against one's true desires. Thus, looking at how a client might instigate a more positive role relationship can be important. But, of course, this depends on the case, and the client has to have a basic desire to continue the relationship. In cases where there is much resentment, and a desire to terminate (escape) the relationship, then working on shared activities may be counterproductive at first. There may be too much anger with the spouse to make this an attractive idea, at least early in counselling. In these situations the couple may need to be brought together for marital counselling. In Peter's case, the loss of the previously good relationship was another source of disappointment. Helping him focus on how he could improve it again was helpful to him and helped him feel more in control.

Key issues 8.5   Working outside the session and alternative role enactments

1 Help the client to recognise that self-monitoring is part of 'the work' and also a useful life skill.
2 Teach the client to monitor and test out thoughts with kindness between sessions and review this with them at the beginning of each session.
3 Help clients plan their own independent practice and behavioural experiments.
4 With depressed clients, these behavioural experiments often involve developing more rewarding social behaviour (e.g. seeing friends, or relating in a different way to a spouse or partner).

Conclusion

This chapter has touched on various 'techniques' that we will explore in more detail in subsequent chapters. In the early stages of working you are trying to help the person feel at ease, to tell their story, and build the beginnings of a shared formulation and approach to working. In this chapter we have explored how these are built into an unfolding process. Sometimes these can take a few sessions to agree. Ideally, by the end of the first few sessions the client will have an overview of their depression, have worked a little on shame issues if they are a concern, and begun to develop insights into how they might cope in new ways. The more complex the case, the longer these things take to build up.

The key is to stay collaborative and open, but at the same time to guide people through the formulation to show how life themes link together in the nature of their core beliefs and safety strategies. In the next chapter we look more closely at the detail for doing this.

9 Thoughts, Beliefs and Safety Strategies: Constructing Formulations

This chapter explores in more detail the processes of therapy and how to build towards a formulation. We can begin by noting that most of us will have had some experience of at least mild low mood. As we enter into these mood states we note that our thoughts tend to be pulled towards negative ways of thinking. These ways of thinking can be triggered by many things – recovering from flu and feeling tired, a falling out with friends, lovers or children, failing to get the desired job, a build-up of various hassles in life and feeling overwhelmed. For the most part, however, we move out of these mood states by redirecting our efforts, seeing them as a natural shifting in mood that will pass, and gaining support from others.

However, for some people these shifts in mood can be easily triggered, become more intense or long-lasting or cannot be quickly overcome. So a key question becomes why are some people more vulnerable to depression whereas others are more resilient (Masten, 2001)? There are many answers to this question, including genetic disposition, early life history, the basic beliefs we develop about self and others, specific life events, getting trapped, not being able to feel we can recover from defeat and losses, the serious and long-term implications we derive from these events, our (avoidant) coping efforts, our access to social support, or our tendencies to ruminate. All come down to the fact that certain patterns of thinking, feeling and behaviour are triggered or become activated in depression-prone people.

Cognitive behavioural therapists suggest that although depression is related to life difficulties, the way we think about these difficulties and our coping efforts can play a major role in the nature of our depression (Beck, 1976). One common recipe for depression is to derive very negative conclusions with long-term implications about the self, world and future, ruminate on these conclusions, avoid our problems rather than try to solve them and withdraw from various activities (Beck et al., 1979; Sacco and Beck, 1995). For some people mild depression starts them on a slide into deeper depression because of these processes.

For example, Sam and Mary break up and Sam's thoughts are: 'Mary does not want to go out with me any more (event). This is because she does not like me any more (interpretation). This means I am unlovable (negative self-judgement) and can never be happy (negative long-term implications). With this mindset Sam tells his friend and his friend says 'Stop dwelling on it and come out for a drink'. Sam thinks: 'My friend does not understand me, there is no point talking to him, and I don't want to go out with people who don't understand me and are just making small talk.' So he stays at home feeling isolated, misunderstood and ruminating. Another person may experience the break-up in less extreme terms and think: 'Yes, my friend is right.

I need to get my mind off the relationship for a while and try to refocus on other things in my life. If I dwell on it I am only going to make myself miserable.' So to the same upsetting event two people may respond very differently.

When working with depressed people it is therefore important to explore how they think *and feel* about themselves, the world (including relationships) and the future, how they engage with others as social supports and their coping behaviours. Our therapeutic efforts may thus be aimed to help the person think, understand and feel about things in alternative ways, develop anti-rumination strategies and help them develop new coping behaviours. As we shall see later, depending on the nature and complexity of the depression, *this does not mean* we ignore people's feelings/emotions or unresolved problems from the past. However, these will emerge in the process of the work.

There are some basic concepts in the cognitive-behavioural approach to counselling which involve the following.

1 *Automatic thoughts* are the immediate ideas and interpretations that spring to mind. In depression they are often self-evaluative and/or focus on negative implications for the future.
2 *Styles of rumination* relate to how people get caught up in cycles of self-devaluing thoughts and dwell on hopelessness, feelings of aloneness, defeat and/or entrapment.
3 *Rules and assumptions* are the ideas and beliefs that guide our lives and set us in particular styles of living. For example, I must be successful; I must be approved of; other people should be nice and not aggressive or selfish. Rules can relate to ideals. Assumptions are 'if-then' rules. 'If people see I am depressed, *then* they will think I am flawed and will not want to relate to me.'
4 *Core beliefs and self–other schema.* Core beliefs are basic ways that one sees the world, self and others. We have a core belief that 'the world is round not flat' (as they thought in days past). We also have core beliefs *about others* and base these on direct experience and our understanding of 'other minds' (e.g. others are trustworthy, nice but ineffective, or out for themselves). We also have core beliefs *about the self* that link to our felt internal experience and self-identity: 'I am nice but weak', 'I am strong and independent', 'I am successful', 'I am a failure' etc. *Self–other schema* relate to the internal organising systems that form the basis of our self-judgements and experiences on the one hand, and our judgements, expectations and experiences of other people on the other. Note that these are not equivalent in the sense that a core belief about the world can be learnt (and changed) in a totally different way from a schema about the self, which is derived from emotional experiences of how others have treated the self.
5 *Safety strategies* and coping behaviours are ways people have learnt to rapidly detect threat ('better safe than sorry') for self-protection and adopt 'best effort' safety behaviours to cope and prevent threats. Safety beliefs also relate to explanations of why bad or worse things have not happened, and what one must do to prevent them.

Automatic thoughts and automatic reactions

Automatic thoughts, as the name implies, are those interpretations/ideas/ thoughts that come automatically to mind; they are our pop-up thoughts. In a way they are 'thoughts without thinking'. I prefer to think of automatic *reactions* because our thoughts often come with emotions and action tendencies that seem fused together and when we focus on thoughts we are choosing to focus on *one aspect* of our reaction to events. In fact, research suggests that it is often difficult to separate emotion from cognition as the brain processes information as units of information. We now know that once an emotion has been triggered it will tend to pull attention and processing in line with that emotion (Haidt, 2001; Power and Dalgleish, 1997; see also Chapter 3 in this volume).

So automatic reactions are the reactions that 'flush' through us without much conscious thought. They are the immediate, consciously available reactions; they require little or no effort and seem plausible. They are not arrived at through reflective reasoning. In depression they are often self-evaluative and future-directed. Automatic thoughts and reactions are not necessarily in clear/syntactic language and can be poorly formulated, using fragments of grammar. Also, it is common for them to occur in images or inner scenes, daydreams or fantasies (Beck, 1976; Gilbert, 1992; Hackmann, 1997). Keep in mind, too, that what can become triggered in depression are psychobiological response patterns that begin to organise the brain to engage in protection strategies – especially those of protest-despair or 'shut down'.

Some clients will take negative views of their automatic reactions to things and can be ashamed of them. For example, they may see themselves as weak for getting anxious or bad for getting angry. It is important to explain that automatic reactions are often triggered before we have a chance to regulate them and are often activated without much thought. This is because part of our brain (e.g. the amygdala) likes to operate fast. If, however, we take a compassionate view of our reactions, we can learn to work with them, understand them, not fear them, and in that way have more control (see Chapter 11). Just becoming angry with ourselves for feeling certain things, telling ourselves not to think or feel certain things or that we are stupid, or trying to avoid certain feelings/reactions, does not usually help. So as counsellors we try to help people to see why their automatic reactions – although they may be undesirable – are understandable and are linked to our history, key fears and concerns, and that the brain often rushes into feelings and actions because this is how it is designed to work.

Linking thoughts and feelings

To use the cognitive model in a formal way requires providing a clear rationale for the therapy (Beck et al., 1979; Blackburn and Davidson, 1995; Sacco and Beck, 1995; Tarrier, 2006). For example, a person can be shown the cognitive model by using examples highlighting the relationships between events, thoughts and emotions. The counsellor may write down three columns A, B, C. A stands for an *Activating event*, B stands for *Beliefs* and C stands for *Consequences*. This is called the triple-column technique.

A	B	C
Activating event	Beliefs/appraisals Interpretations	Emotions Behaviour Biology

The counsellor may then use the example of a lover or friend who does not phone or some other example. First, a counsellor may say:

> One way we can work together is to understand that the way we see certain things affects what we feel about them. It's about the meaning of things to us. I would like to show you an example of how this works. Imagine that a friend or lover was going to phone you tonight, but then they didn't. I will write that down in the A column. Now it is possible that we might have various different feelings about that. We could be angry or irritated, anxious or sad, or stay calm. I will write those down in the C column. Now let's think about the kind of meanings and thoughts that would go with each feeling and I will write these down in the B column.

If possible, the client is encouraged to do this with you and generate thoughts/images. Ask: What is likely to be in your mind if you felt angry? What is likely to be in your mind if you felt sad, and so forth? So the result might look like:

A (Activating event)	B (Beliefs and meanings)	C (Emotions/Behaviours)
Lover has not phoned as he/she promised.	They don't love me enough to remember and care.	Sadness
	They are so thoughtless. I bet they went off down the pub. How dare they.	Anger
	They are usually reliable. Something must have happened to them.	Anxiety
	I guess they were busy or could not get to a phone.	Calm

The counsellor may use this type of example to indicate how the interpretation of an event is associated with emotional, behavioural and biological changes. To show how the meanings also affect *behaviours* the counsellor would then say: 'What might you *do* if you felt sad?', 'What might you do if you felt angry?' and so on. These can be written down with the emotions in column C. Although we are separating cognition and emotion here, recall that they are often fused together, so you can explain to people that this separating 'meanings' from feelings is somewhat artificial but offers a useful window through which to work on our reactions to things.

This type of event may lead us to *imagine and fantasise* about the possibility that the lover has lost interest, or does not care enough to remember, or is out with someone else. Sometimes these fantasies are felt like *intrusions*. We would like to put things out of our mind but our mind keeps coming back to them. It is important to normalise this and work on ways to cope with intrusions. We may also construct scenarios of seeing the lover in some particular place (e.g. a pub) and imagine them having a good time, laughing, drinking, etc. These images and video-like scenes we play in our minds can be very painful, but it can be difficult to stop them intruding. We may enter into internal *elaborations* and amplifications of our thoughts and fantasies. For example, having decided that our lover has forgotten because they decided to go somewhere else (e.g. down the pub) and are out having a good time, we may start to rehearse in our minds an argument or what we intend to say the next time they do phone. We may even rehearse something that we know in reality we would not carry out due to fear of being rejected/disliked, or because of moral concerns. However, if we had an image that something bad had happened (e.g. a road accident), then our whole set of imaginations, feelings and thoughts would be different.

Two other areas are important: *context* and *history*. In regard to context, if the lover is on an oil rig where phones keep breaking down compared to being at home or having a mobile phone, then these contexts will affect the probable interpretations. As for history, if it is very uncommon for the lover not to phone, this will have a different impact than if it is common. Further, if a person has suffered, say, frequent abandonments in the past, then an evaluation that 'the lover is about to abandon me' will make a lot of sense even if (in this case) it is inaccurate.

Explanation of the cognitive model should be conducted in a compassionate way and the use of gentle humour during the example sometimes helps to relax a client. It is important to check with the person that they see the validity of this approach. When this has been agreed the counsellor can then say:

> Okay, now let's use the same kind of approach to the kinds of problems you are having. Can you give me an example of an event that has upset you in the past week? Right now, we are mainly interested to understand what this event meant for you.

This is then written down under A. The emotions/feelings and behaviours elicited are written in column C. Then the counsellor says: 'Now let's look at what was going through your mind at B, to see if we can understand what meanings are associated with those feelings and behaviours at C.' The most salient aspect of automatic thoughts and reactions is their *core of meaning*. An important procedure of cognitive therapy is therefore thought catching; teaching how to recognise depression-related thoughts as they occur and, as we explore in depth in later chapters, how to work with them.

Key issues 9.1   Automatic reactions and thoughts

1   They are triggered by events which may be external (e.g. criticism from another person) or internal (e.g. an emotion or spontaneous memory or change of brain state).
2   They are immediately available and just jump or pop into the mind; they require little or no effort and appear to be spontaneous.
3   They occur in shorthand, often as images, or an 'essence' of meaning and may be poorly formulated in language.
4   They follow no clear sequence as in logical reasoning or problem solving.
5   They can be difficult to turn off, especially in the presence of emotional arousal.
6   They often seem plausible and reasonable to the client, although they may be far-fetched (e.g. catastrophic).
7   They can arise in spite of evidence to the contrary.
8   People often need to train themselves to be attentive to (thought catching) and monitor their automatic thoughts.

Types of Socratic dialogue discussion and questions

To enable people to begin to explore their meanings and interpretations of things in more detail requires that we engage in a form of discussion and dialogue that is called *Socratic*. The most basic questions are those that are curious and invite reflection and exploration: 'What went through your mind?' or 'What is going through your mind?' These are both examples of open questions which enable the client to focus more clearly and avoid vague descriptions of 'it', 'always', 'something'.

Other common questions are:

- What would happen if ...?
- What would happen then/next?
- What does that lead you to think/believe?
- What conclusions do you draw from that?
- What do you think this means?

To get at more specific self–other schema and 'theory of mind' processing you might ask:

- What do you think other people thought?
- What do you think was going through their minds?
- What might others want to do?
- What do you conclude about yourself?
- What were you thinking about yourself?
- What do you think they were thinking about you?

To work with historical data you might ask:

- When was the first time you thought/felt this way and what was happening? (elicit images and memories)
- Do you often have that view?
- How often have you felt/thought this way?

The counsellor can ask the client how *strongly* they believe something by giving it a percentage rating, for example: Out of 100 how strongly do you believe this? One can also ask about *frequency*, for example: How commonly do you tend to think like this?

As a rule of thumb, 'what' questions encourage the person to explore the nature and implications of their thoughts/interpretations. That is the *Socratic* part. The implications the counsellor is particularly interested in are those related to the pursuit of long-term goals and rules for living, idealisations, hopes and key fears/threats, schema or self-views, and ideas about significant others. In other words, what does this thought or idea imply? How might it be linked to a key fear (e.g. of rejection or defeat)? One can also note that underlying issues of shame can block this kind of exploration.

Another form of questioning seeks to explore a more causal form of thinking. In this case the questions follow a 'why' set of questions, or less often a 'how' set of questions:

- Why do you think that?
- Why do you think that happened?
- How do/did you reach that conclusion?
- How do you think other people would see you because of that?
- How do you think other people will react to you?

Although cognitive counsellors sometimes use 'why' questions, Egan (2002) argues that 'why' questions can be experienced as threatening. People may feel they have to justify their thoughts and feelings. Thus they should be used cautiously or when you have established a good working relationship with the client.

Yet another set of questions seeks to enable clients to make predictions:

- What are you likely to feel when you think this way?
- What happens when you behave this way?
- How do others respond to you when you behave this way?
- What are the advantages and disadvantages of thinking/behaving this way?
- What would be the advantages and disadvantages of making this change?

Helping clients predict the consequences of their ways of thinking or behaving, and predicting what would happen if they changed, is important in counselling, as we shall see later. Again, it should be emphasised that the purpose of these kinds of questions and discussion is *guided discovery* – to give form and clarity to vagueness. Hence, the counsellor should be aware that sometimes clients may not actually address the question but remain vague or answer a different question. Thus, the counsellor wants to enable the client to focus on the question that has been put. These questions are designed to help the client gain a clearer idea of what is going through their mind, the core essence of the meaning. They are not just to satisfy the curiosity of the counsellor.

When exploring an inference chain with such questions it should be conducted in the manner of a *collaborative friendly venture*. It is not an interrogation. The style of the interaction should be one of caring interest (Gilbert, 1989). The counsellor should avoid just 'firing off' questions, one after another, and intersperse questions with gentle reflections and paraphrases. It is a focused *discussion*. One tries to foster in the client a desire to explore and discover (guided discovery), yet also convey a sense of safeness. Be attentive to your non-verbal communication, voice tone and pacing. Counsellors need to be sensitive to the current state of the client. For example, if a client has a desire to share painful feelings and be understood, has serious shame problems or is very inhibited, then there is little point doing highly focused work. Cognitive therapists use these Socratic-type questions in two basic ways (Sacco and Beck, 1995):

1 To *probe* the ways people are reasoning – to explore their basic constructs – to illuminate the links in the chains of their reasoning, and illuminate key fears and concerns.
2 And later to stimulate people to *reflect* on this reasoning and see if it holds good. Here one may help the client gain evidence for or against their judgements, consider compassionate alternatives or try out various homeworks and experiments to test out their theories and ideas. This is called *collaborative empiricism*. This is explored more fully in later chapters.

In general, Socratic questioning involves:

1 Seeking information that a person can (is able to, or is prepared to) give.
2 Helps to direct attention and focus on the nature of the problem.
3 Moves from the specific to the more general so that the person:
   (a) gains increasing insight into their general/basic beliefs and key fears.
   (b) begins to see how thoughts, feelings and action tendencies can be linked together.
   (c) develops the skills to change key conclusions and beliefs, and work on key fears.

Let's look at a hypothetical example: Jane was a depressed single parent who was trying to start a new relationship with Dave. However, she was cautious and doubtful of his feelings for her and very attentive to cues of rejection.

Counsellor:	Jane, you were saying that this weekend has been particularly bad for you. Can you remember any particular event that seemed to start it off?
Jane:	I guess it was Friday night. Dave had said he would come over but then he phoned to say that he would not be able to make it as he had to go down to London to pick up some work.
Counsellor:	How did you feel about that?
Jane:	I was very disappointed and went to bed. I just switched off. Everything seemed pointless.
Counsellor:	So that was very disappointing and upsetting when you had obviously been looking forward to seeing him. [*Note reflecting feelings here with a gentle voice tone and acknowledging the upset feelings*] What went through your mind?
Jane:	Hm … something like, here we go again. I am obviously not that important to him. He has better things to do. Maybe he would prefer not to be coming over.
Counsellor:	So you thought he'd prefer not to come over. Did you have any thoughts about why that might be the case?
Jane:	Yes. I got to thinking that maybe I am not really that much fun to be with. He probably thinks I am a rather boring person and does not want to get too involved with a single parent with kids. I began to think that sooner or later he would pull out of the relationship and I'd end up alone again.
Counsellor:	I see, so when Dave didn't come over that was a huge disappointment and upset and in that state of mind you began to think that there were things about you that he was rejecting, like being a single parent and that you felt you were boring.
Jane:	Yes.
Counsellor:	Suppose for the moment that Dave does pull out of the relationship. What would go through your mind then?
Jane:	I'd think that everything is empty and there is no point. Life is very hard on one's own.
Counsellor:	That feels very desperate. [*Pause*] What would you feel about you?
Jane:	Oh, that this is typical. I am a loser and better just accept that. It's pointless to try to make meaningful relationships. I get this sense of being unlovable somehow, you know like deep down there is something wrong with me. So I am going to be on my own. That really makes me depressed. Everything seems so empty.

In this case we see that the disappointment and feelings of disappointment are linked with a number of more depressive and implicational thoughts about self as boring, being unlovable and a key fear of being destined to be alone. Note how Jane has also experienced a separation, closed-down protection strategy and psychobiological pattern and her thoughts get pulled into focusing on threat (loss of Dave). The counsellor listens for *key words* that may *act as markers* for underlying beliefs and *key fears* (e.g. boring, empty, pointless, alone). Sometimes one might say: 'Let's explore the worst. Let us for the moment suppose that X has happened. Now what is going through your mind?' Very often in depressed clients the worst is about being abandoned, rejected, worthless, pointless and powerless, that is it is about basic threats. Recall that these are key themes in our innate and archetypal protection strategies (see Chapters 5 and 6).

Sometimes if clients find it difficult to put thoughts into words, a counsellor might ask a client to imagine a situation and talk about the inner picture in their minds. One person who was having difficulty expressing his thoughts about his depression in language was asked to describe a picture. After some reflection he said: 'It's like I can see this party going on and I'm standing in the garden or somewhere. It's very cold, maybe snowing and very dark. I know that no matter what I do I will not be allowed in, but must stay outside just looking in and being on my own.'

Inference chains and guided discovery

Once clients understand the linkage between thoughts, interpretations and feelings it is then possible to begin to deepen the exploration by searching for some underlying, deeper meaning or more global or extreme evaluations and *core beliefs* and fears. One of the most common forms of this type of work is called *inference chaining or laddering*. This technique is one of *guided discovery* – not interpretation.

Inference chains are the ways our thoughts and interpretations are linked together. An inference chain follows an 'if A then B' form of reasoning. In other words, the client associates one idea or outcome with another. Usually a subsequent inference is more global, extreme and emotionally laden. For example: 'If my friend ignores me, *then* it means they do not like me. This is because I am a boring person. If I am a boring person, *then* I am unlovable. If I am unlovable, *then* I will never find a loving relationship and will be alone and depressed forever.'

A note of caution: One of the most common mistakes people unfamiliar with the cognitive model make is to assume that CBT suggests people actually think like this – in these steps. Maybe sometimes, but not usually. A downward arrow technique is *not* to explore the process of thinking (steps in our thinking) but the content. Cognitive therapists point out that what is usually triggered first is the core belief, schema or basic threat or conditioned emotions, *that then* directs subsequent thinking. However, the depressed person may only be aware of the later aspects of their thinking and not the full nature of a core belief, conditioned emotional reaction or key fear. Beck et al. (1979) note that to articulate a core belief might take much hard work and reflection, even though these are sources for automatic thoughts. If they are associated with traumatic memories, then this can take time (see below). So the downward arrow technique is to help reveal the more core beliefs, threats or fears.

Procedures

Eliciting an inference chain is a kind of directed (as opposed to free) association. The counsellor is active in the use of Socratic questions, and does not go beyond what has been said. To explore an inference chain requires a preparedness to suspend efforts to modify thoughts as the exploration unfolds. Some counsellors may jump in too quickly with their own interpretations or ideas, for example 'Do you think you are thinking this because …?' or 'Isn't this because …?', or the counsellor engages in guessing. Ideally, the counsellor tries not to suggest ideas but to let the person discover them for themselves – this is called *guided discovery*. Cognitive counsellors believe that self-discovery works better than interpretation, hence the importance of the Socratic 'what' or open questions. By Socratic we mean a type of discussion which invites further exploration. Let's look at the lover example again (p. 195). One sequence or pattern of thoughts might relate to sadness and depression. Another sequence or pattern might relate to anger.

Activating event	Thoughts		Emotions/behaviours
Lover has not phoned as they had promised	1	They don't love me enough to remember	
	2	They are losing interest in me	Sadness
	3	This is because I am not attractive or desirable enough	Behavioural withdrawal
	4	Most people get bored with me when they get to know me	
	5	I will never find someone who loves me	
		Key threat. Alone and loveless	
	1	I bet they went off down the pub	Anger
	2	They are thoughtless/unkind	Criticise them and try to control them
	3	This is typical of men/women. They are completely unreliable	
	4	I am not going to be treated like this. Just wait till they do phone	
		Key threat. Losing control over others' behaviour	

Note how these reactions flow around together, moving upwards and downwards in the process. For example, the person may notice the phone call not coming and start to feel lonely and anxious, and then the thinking moves upward as she reasons about why she is lonely and the reasons for no phone call. Similarly for anger, the person may begin to have a feeling of mild irritation and then start thinking in various ways. The point about this is to keep in mind that 'thinking/feeling interactions' are rarely linear. Therefore, explain this carefully to clients, especially when you write things out and draw them in linear ways. As mentioned throughout this book, many of our processing systems are processing information in a parallel rather than in serial fashion.

A note about core beliefs: Among these thoughts are reflections of *core beliefs* such as: 'Most people get bored with me when they get to know me. I will never find someone who loves me.' For anger they are: 'This is typical of men/women. They are completely unreliable.' Core beliefs are usually developed in childhood and help organise, structure and give meaning to events (Beck et al., 1979). They are believed to be stable and people will endorse their beliefs regardless of mood state. However, core beliefs are often emergent from people's basic fears and how they have learnt to cope. The 'sad' core beliefs reflect fears of abandonment and preparing for it. The 'angry' core beliefs reflect fear of not being able to control the other and using aggression as a means (coping tactic) to do that. Anger might also *function* to deflect attention away from the self (e.g. helplessness or shame that maybe they are not as attractive to the other as they think they are). So we must always have *a functional analysis to core beliefs* and not take them at face value. This is especially so if you are going to work with them as linked to protection strategies and safety behaviours.

Some clients can be ashamed to admit what they are thinking and counsellors should be very sensitive to this for a number of reasons. First, because the client may tell you what they think *you* want to hear, or they may not reveal too much of what they are actually thinking (because they feel ashamed or silly to admit it). Sitting in a counsellor's room in the cold light of day may make the thoughts seem irrational and silly. I suspect we all have thoughts that we would not necessarily find it easy to admit to someone else! The problem is, however, that the people who conceal and have difficulties in being honest about feelings and thoughts tend to be more vulnerable to various forms of psychopathology and can be more difficult to help than those who are more trusting and open. Second, because in the early stages clients often have an eye on what *you* might be thinking about them, one cannot be sure that what the client offers as their negative thoughts are actually the ones causing most distress. So one needs to keep an open mind ready to change track as more information becomes available and trust develops. This is one reason cognitive therapists put a lot of emphasis on *guided discovery*. However, for high shame people this is more complex than it seems, especially so if 'discoveries' are deeply threatening to a self-identity. Shame-prone people can be very sensitive to this and will express beliefs such as a fear of 'what you will dig up' – not only what you'll discover about them but what they themselves might discover.

Third, some clients might not be able to articulate clear thoughts and may not know exactly what they are thinking because they are not used to putting complex feelings into words. They may not be used to talking about their internal worlds or have had little opportunity in their lives to reflect on or discuss with others their thoughts and feelings. For example, Stiles and colleagues have developed assimilation models of therapy whereby people move from denied or warded-off material, hard-to-verbalise feelings, to gradual awareness and then become able to give new meanings to internal fantasies and feelings (e.g. see Honos-Webb, Stiles and Greenberg, 2003). It is now recognised that clients who have these difficulties can be difficult to help in short-term therapies, and that the counsellor will need to be aware that *short-term* cognitive forms of counselling probably work best for people who can articulate thoughts and feelings, are reasonably open, and have some capacity for internal reflection.

Complex chains

Dryden (1989c) articulated the importance of complex chains, that is, how one set of ideas and conclusions sets off another set of ideas and conclusions, or how one theme triggers another. This is a common problem in depressed clients. They may say things like 'My head is full of so many thoughts' or 'Everything is just zooming about inside'. For example, a person became angry because she thought that someone was deliberately doing something to hurt her. However, the experience of anger led to fear, with the thought, 'If I get angry I may get out of control. If I get out of control I will look silly and be humiliated.' So she believed she would not say anything, but then was resentful with the thought, 'Why do I never stand up for myself and let others push me around. I am a weakling.' Hence thoughts about being hurt and pushed around, thoughts about looking silly, and thoughts about herself as a weakling were all tied up together.

In such cases the counsellor attempts to help the person stay with one theme at a time. Dryden (1989c) points out that if a person gets highly emotionally aroused, it may be very difficult to get out of this cycle with cognitive restructuring. A depressed person may say, 'I understand the ideas but when I get really low I can't get out of it'. Sometimes distracting physical activity, like running or digging the garden, and at other times working on graded tasks, can be helpful. Relaxation can be *un*helpful, especially if this increases the focus on self and rumination on negative thoughts. Hence distraction, which involves some motor activity, or redirecting attention (as in compassion work, see Chapter 11) can be more effective.

It is important to explain that depression will pull us towards inactivity but it is worth experimenting to see whether if we make an extra effort to become active, this can be helpful. Hence laying in bed ruminating on all those thoughts buzzing about in one's head will make us feel worse so we can try getting up and being active. In DBT (Linehan, 1993) this is called opposite action. As we will explore in later chapters, there are other approaches to this difficulty, especially learning how to be more self-compassionate and developing compassionate images to focus on.

Specificity

Cognitive therapy for depression seeks to be very specific about the events (antecedents) and eliciting situations. Depressed clients can be vague about things that trigger mood changes and may need to work to become more focused. When this happens it is sometimes possible to arrive at a list of specific situations that trigger negative affects, thoughts, beliefs and key fears. Specificity helps to target interventions and also to focus the client on the fact that things can become manageable and controllable. However, brain state and mood shifting can occur for a whole variety of reasons (e.g. it can be common after flu, linked to the menstrual cycle, or when we are fatigued), so we are not implying that interpretations always cause depression. Rather, it is exploring thoughts and interpretations that are linked to, and accentuate, depression.

Thought catching

Automatic reactions can emerge with, and in a flow of, other feelings and thoughts. For example, if a friend or lover said they would phone us and then the telephone does not ring we may find ourselves becoming anxious, sad or irritated, but our awareness of our *thinking/reasoning and thoughts* may be hazy or poorly recognised. In the back of one's mind might be ideas that the person does not care enough to phone on time and that 'this is typical of the people one meets; you can never rely on anyone'. Or we might think 'something terrible has happened to them'. Hence, sometimes we need to *train ourselves* to tune into these background thoughts and bring them into clear consciousness. Hence a depressed person may need to train themselves to *attend* to their automatic reactions, interpretations and thoughts so as to sharpen their focus and make them subject to more detailed analysis, communication and open to alternatives. The client can be taught to say to themselves: 'Okay I am feeling sad or angry about this so how am I actually seeing it?; What am I saying to myself?; What is my key fear here?' This is called *thought catching*. Clients are taught how to attend to changes in moods or feelings, to become attentive to these changes and explore for personal meanings in that mood change. They can also try to identify events around these changes.

Another way to think about this is to help people become more 'mindful', learning to develop a form of inner attention to what emerges in the mind (Linehan, 1993). For those therapists who teach mindfulness, the idea is often not to try necessarily to change what one thinks but change how one relates to one's automatic thinking by developing an observant curiosity (Hayes, Follette and Linehan, 2004). We come to see our automatic reactions as exactly that – automatic reactions – that can be seen as things 'emerging in the mind'. But we can train ourselves not to be pulled into depressive spirals so readily.

Writing thoughts down

To help people become skilled at thought catching they can be taught how to *write things down* – to take time out to explore their thinking in relationship to their feelings. Thought catching and focusing are key aspects of the cognitive approach because the typical way people interpret situations will be a focus for therapy.

Clients can be shown how to use various thought recording forms – and there are many types of them (Beck et al., 1979; Gilbert 2000a; Greenberg and Padesky, 1995; Leahy and Holland, 2000; Sacco and Beck, 1995). Examples of these are given in the appendices. I tend to work on a few thought forms collaboratively in session first and then invite the client to try for themselves. This then becomes part of the work out of session. Some clients take to this readily, others do not. So it is important to have a clear understanding of this in the therapeutic contract. The advantage of writing things down is that it slows thinking, helps people reflect and also to take a more detached observational orientation to their thoughts and feelings. However, developing 'writing down' with clients should occur when they have enough insight into the process of the approach to be able to also write down alternatives for themselves to their thoughts – a process we will explore in later chapters. It is not helpful just to write down negative thoughts.

Internal and external worlds

Another way to think about core beliefs and key fears in depression is that they relate to fear/concerns about the outside world *and* the inside world (Beck et al., 1979, 1990). If you have a threat and fear-focused approach (as I do), then rather than there being one bottom line or key fear *there are nearly always two*: what the outside will do to you (i.e. how others will be with you), and secondly, what this will stir up inside you and how you will cope with what is stirred up in you. A third might be how the outside world will then respond to your reactions (with kindness and understanding or rejection). Suppose a student fails an exam. The externally focused fear (or bottom line) is that others will look down on him, be critical or rejecting (i.e. social disconnection and social put-down). Because the world is seen as threatening, these social threats will activate protective strategies such as self-blaming and feelings of heart-sink and anxiety.

Failed the exam	
External concerns/threats	**Internal concerns/fears**
Others will think I am not bright enough to do this May think I have not worked hard enough/lazy	Doubt my own abilities Will want to give up Loss of hope for outcomes Feel a failure (self-critical)
Key fears: Others will reject me, see me as inferior and not be helpful. Will wish to distance themselves from me	*Key fears*: Will feel overwhelmed with depression, won't be able to cope with these internal feelings, will do less and waste my life

The key fears may also be linked to a reactivation of emotional memories (e.g. of a critical father). Moreover, different coping behaviours will be directed to the different fears. Our student might deal with the external threat by social avoidance and feel ashamed about asking for help, and the internal threat of unpleasant feelings by drinking or taking drugs to feel better and to 'switch off his mind'.

Self-monitoring and guided discovery can help to illuminate these two foci of our key fears, threats and concerns. It is helpful to clearly distinguish external from internal concerns/fears because this makes working with them easier – rather than letting them run into each other. It also helps to clarify people's thinking about 'what I think is in the mind of others about me (what they are thinking and feeling about me), and what I think and feel about myself'. Careful clarification of these can show how we often adopt our self-evaluations from what we think others think (or have thought) about us. If you use the triad of negative views of self, world and future (Beck et al., 1979) then you could have three such columns: my key *fear about myself* (things emerging in me, such as feelings that are overwhelming); *fear about others or events* (what others will do or how the world will treat me); and *key fears about my future* (I will fail and not achieve goals or get out of depression).

Types of feeling in relation to negative thoughts

We have seen that negative thoughts are often associated with negative feelings; that there is a linkage between B and C. However, recall the thoughts of Jane who, when Dave did not come over for the weekend, said 'Oh, this is typical. I am a loser and better just accept that. It's pointless to try to make meaningful relationships ...'. Such thoughts made her more depressed. And of course if she does stop making efforts, then this may make her situation worse. Or she might decide that she can be happy even without a man in her life. But what might be the emotions of the thoughts themselves? What is the *emotional tone* associated with the delivery or generation of the thoughts?

Counsellor:	When you think like that, Jane, what is the emotional tone of the thoughts? I mean, how do you actually say them in your mind?
Jane:	How do you mean?
Counsellor:	Well, you could say them to yourself in a matter-of-fact way, or in an anxious way or an angry way. What way do you say them?
Jane:	[Pauses] Oh pretty angry I guess. Like if only I could be different then the relationships might work out.
Counsellor:	So when you 'kind of' hear these thoughts in your mind they are angry?
Jane:	Oh yes – I feel very angry and frustrated with myself.

Now self-attacking and self-criticising in depression are rarely neutral but, as the term 'self-attacking' implies, are often fired with disappointment, anger or contempt. It is *the emotional tone of the delivery of self-evaluative thoughts* – and anger or contempt is common – that can be important (Gilbert, Clarke, Kempel, Miles and Irons, 2004; Whelton and Greenberg, 2005). In later chapters we will see how it can be useful to focus on the emotional tone of thoughts and help people to become more self-compassionate, caring and supportive (Gilbert, 2000c; Gilbert and Irons, 2005). Indeed, it is important that when people consider alternatives to their depressing thoughts they *do not* do so with another form of self-attacking, for example 'Come on, stop being so irrational. Get your head together. Now what's the evidence – stupid!' Or 'you know activity will help you, so get out of bed you lazy person!' Whatever alternative thoughts the client might try to generate, or whatever coping behaviours/activities they try to engage in, always check that their orientation is one of trying to be *kind, caring and supportive* – one cannot bully oneself out of depression. We will explore this important point in chapter 11.

Cognitive biases

The strength of an emotion or mood dip can often be associated with the global evaluations – the 'key threat' at the end of the chain – and the nature of these evaluations (i.e. this would be terrible and unbearable). These, however, are not necessarily in clear consciousness. As clients link ideas together there can be various *biases* in their thinking. Depression naturally pulls us to be more negative – it is *naturally* part of what negative moods do. When we get depressed we may focus on certain negative details and exclude positive alternatives. Or we may 'jump to conclusions'. For example, 'this relationship has failed so *all* will fail' or 'I failed at this examination so I will *fail everything'*. Or 'I will *never* be a success'. As the mood worsens, thinking becomes more black and white and extreme. Beck et al. (1979) suggest that there are particular types of bias in the reasoning and automatic thoughts of depressed clients:

1 Arbitrary inference – drawing a negative conclusion in the absence of supporting data.
2 Selective abstraction – focusing on a detail out of context, often at the expense of more salient information.
3 Over-generalisation – drawing conclusions over a wide variety of things on the basis of single events.
4 Magnification and minimisation – making errors in evaluating the importance of, and implications of, events.
5 Personalisation – relating external (often negative) events to the self when there is little reason for doing so.
6 Absolutistic, dichotomous thinking – thinking in polar opposites (black and white) such as something is all good or totally bad and a disaster.

All these are typical of threat-related 'better safe than sorry' thinking (Gilbert, 1998b). Others have added egocentric thinking (i.e. 'People must think the same way I do') and the telepathy assumptions (i.e. 'People should know how I feel without me having to tell them'). Some of these biases are not original to cognitive therapy. For example, black and white thinking is one form of 'splitting' in object relations theory. Also, it has become apparent that human reasoning in general often involves these styles of reasoning (Gilbert, 1998b; Hollon and Kriss, 1984) and that depressed clients are not untypical in this. In fact, evolutionary and social psychologists have shown that most of the time we operate complex biases in our thinking (Tobena et al., 1999). The way we reason about our own behaviours in comparison to others, or our children compared to those of strangers, or our in-groups compared to out-groups, or those we love compared to those we don't, all these are domains where biases (usually self-serving biases) in thinking are common. So it is the focus and content that is more important, not whether we are always completely rational. There is also an evolutionary aspect such that under stress it is common for us to start to 'imagine the worst, become highly attentive to threats, and threat-biased in our thinking (Gilbert, 1998b). Such styles of thinking actually may have had adaptive functions. This is called *better safe than sorry thinking*. However, it can also become highly maladaptive.

Try to avoid the language of 'cognitive distortion' or 'faulty or maladaptive thoughts' because depressed people may not understand these terms in the academic way we do – as defensive biases in reasoning. It is easy for them to think that you are implying that their thinking is wrong and they are being irrational. This can lead to 'should' thoughts, which can be more depressing, and denial of feelings: 'I should not think like this. I am being silly/irrational.' Counselling is *not* to show people they are being illogical or irrational but rather to see the links between their thoughts and feelings, and how they may have become stuck in understandable but unhelpful ways of thinking (Salkovskis, 1996a). Although biases occur in thinking in various mental states, in some cases depressed people may actually be more accurate than non-depressed people (Taylor and Brown, 1988). The counsellor can help the client recognise that cognitive biases are

understandable (e.g. because of past history, stress and human natural tendencies to think in certain, often irrational ways), and the 'pull' of mood and brain state shifts on thinking. This will help the client become orientated to the hard work of not taking their thinking at face value and to consider alternatives. So it can be useful to explain to clients that this is the *depression* style of thinking. (And there is a style of thinking associated with anger and a different style associated with being happy, and yet a different one associated with anxiety, etc.) Most people tend to think in a certain way as they become depressed, just as most of us tend to get a higher temperature when we are sick, or shiver when we are cold. However, there are things we can do to bring our temperature down or to get warm again, and so we can find alternatives to our threat-defensive thinking.

Dwelling and ruminating

It is useful to help people distinguish between those thoughts/feelings that are truly automatic and those a person dwells on and turns over and over in their minds. Dwelling and ruminating on negative thoughts can drive people further into depression and they can spend a long time focused and repeatedly indoctrinating themselves with their negative thoughts and feelings. It is almost as if they have addictive qualities. To help people recognise the difference between automatic thoughts and repetitive ruminations, you can ask: How much time do you spend thinking this way? Once the rumination cycle starts up, how do you break out of it? What do you think happens to your feelings when you dwell on them? Note also the *feeling* in rumination. For example, self-critical rumination may be accompanied with a constant feeling of anger and frustration with the self and these inwardly directed feelings accentuate depression. It is then possible to show how those thoughts and feelings can spiral down together by drawing out circles, as we explore in later chapters (see p. 184 and p. 228).

Key issues 9.2   Exploring personal meanings

1   Help clients to recognise the link between feelings and thoughts.
2   Introduce them to the basics of thought-feeling catching and thought-feeling monitoring.
3   The use of certain types of question, such as when, what, and how questions, help the client to clarify what is going through their mind.
4   These questions are aimed at facilitating guided discovery. They should be discursive and not an interrogation.
5   Sometimes the counsellor can ask about mental images and/or pictures rather than rely on spoken words. At other times the counsellor can explore using the client's fantasies, such as 'Let's imagine that …'.
6   Depressed clients often have various sets of thoughts that become complex chains with interacting themes. At these times the counsellor tries to be specific by following one theme or idea at a time.
7   Explore with clients the differences in automatic reactions in contrast to rumination.
8   Distinguish between key, basic internal and external fears.

Rules, attitudes and assumptions

Life rules can be regarded as the instructions or assumptions that relate to happiness and avoidance of pain and unpleasantness (e.g. 'To be happy I must be loved' or 'I must be successful to avoid rejection', and so forth). Certain rules and attitudes have been developed into the dysfunctional attitude scale (DAS) (see Blackburn and Davidson, 1995, pp. 211–14 for a copy of this scale). Here are some typical dysfunctional attitudes from the DAS:

(4)   If I do not do well all the time, people will not respect me.
(11)   If I can't do something well there is no point in trying.
(16)   I am nothing if a person I love doesn't love me.
(23)   I should be upset if I make a mistake.
(25)   To be a good, moral, worthwhile person I must always put the needs of others first.

Dysfunctional attitudes relate to various domains and social themes, such as perfectionism and approval (e.g. 'People will probably think less of me if I make a mistake', 'If a person asks for help it is a sign of weakness'). Much work has now been conducted with the DAS in depression (Sacco and Beck, 1995). It has been found that depressed clients score significantly higher on the DAS than non-depressed people. However, so do many client groups and dysfunctional attitudes are not specific to depression. DAS scores correlate with neuroticism (Teasdale and Dent, 1987). It has also been found that the DAS is mood sensitive and subject to changes in mood state. Importantly, the ease of reactivation of dysfunctional assumptions (e.g. by mild shifts in mood state) is related to depression vulnerability and relapse risk (Siegle, Carter and Thase, 2006). As noted in Chapter 3, sometimes the trigger can be frustration. So depression vulnerability is related to the activation of depressive cognitive styles which in turn are linked to key fears and protective strategies (see Chapters 5 and 6).

Traps, dilemmas and snags

Ryle (1990) has explored cognitive and other therapeutic ideas and placed them in a helpful framework. He has suggested that repetitive themes (called traps, dilemmas and snags) arise in various forms of psychopathology, especially depression. These set up various (approach–avoidance) conflicts, increase arousal and lead to confusion.

Traps are negative assumptions leading to various forms of behaviour, the consequences of which reinforce the assumptions (e.g. 'I am boring to others, therefore they won't be interested in what I have to say, therefore I won't say anything'). The result is the person behaves in a boring way and people lose interest in them.

In *dilemmas,* a person acts as though available solutions or possible roles are limited to polarised alternatives (false dichotomies). Often we are unaware that this is the case (e.g. 'Either I express my feelings (but then get rejected), or I conceal them (but then feel resentful). If I love someone then I must give in to all their wishes'). This is related to black and white thinking and uses the 'if-then' style of thinking. When feeling trapped, dilemmas can revolve around these black and white dilemmas: 'Either I leave this relationship and am miserably alone or I stay and have to put up with it.' Such thinking can lead to feelings of there being 'no way out' and entrapment (see chapter 3).

Leahy (2002) has also written on how various beliefs about emotions – that certain emotions/thoughts and fantasies can be experienced as shameful, incomprehensible or overwhelming – can lead to this kind of thinking. In my view, they are related to forms of 'splitting' and they often lead to internal battles within the self. For example, one part of self tries to please others and another part of self just feels exhausted and resentful at having to be at others' beck and call. Or one part of self feels furious with, say, the therapist, but another part of self is terrified of this being revealed.

Snags are appropriate goals or roles that are abandoned (a) on the (true or false) assumption that others would oppose them, or (b) independently of the views of others as if they were forbidden or dangerous. Again key beliefs often underpin this (Leahy, 2002). The depressed individual may be more or less aware that they act in this way and may relate this to feelings such as shame. Cognitive therapy uses the advantages–disadvantages approach to explore this aspect (e.g. 'If I get better I might be more assertive, but then I might not like myself or become more like my (disliked) mother'). Snags manifest themselves in the 'yes but' styles of thinking. Depressed clients often engage in 'yes but' responses. Never underestimate the possible snags some clients may feel about recovery! Snags can represent high ambivalence about change which is central in motivational interviewing.

Key issues 9.3   Dysfunctional attitudes

1   Dysfunctional attitudes are often generalised 'rules for living'.
2   They can be over-rigid and generalised and can involve concepts like always, never, must, should, have to. Dysfunctional attitudes lack flexibility.
3   They are dysfunctional because they keep us from our goals or lead to poor role enactments (e.g. 'the more I have to be close to someone, the more this may drive them away' or 'I believe that I must never fail so I withdraw and don't try at all').
4   They can lead to various traps, snags and dilemmas.
5   In depression they tend to be focused on the themes we outlined in earlier chapters and on various roles (e.g. 'I must be caring, I must be loved, I must gain respect').
6   Dysfunctional attitudes are linked to basic self-experience (e.g. 'I feel bad if a rule is broken, but good if successful'). The occasional positive reinforcement of them may maintain them.
7   They are linked to basic hopes in the future (e.g. 'If I am loved, then I will be happy', 'If I am successful, then I will be good – a somebody rather than a nobody').
8   They are often culturally reinforced (e.g. 'Men should be individualistic and achieve', or 'Women should be always loving and caring').

Safety behaviours and safety strategies

I have spent a lot of time emphasising that all living things are orientated to try to protect themselves from harm and injury. Humans are no different. Indeed, we come into the world, like other animals, with a range of potential emotions (e.g. anger, anxiety and disgust) and behaviours (fight, flight, submission) that will warn us about, and help us cope with, threats and dangers. There are also automatic tendencies for mood to dip in the context of loss and defeat (Gilbert, 1992, 2006a). These automatic safety strategies can be triggered in depression and it can be useful to talk to clients in these terms so that they can think about depression as part of an *evolved protection system* in their brain.

However, we can think about safety behaviours and strategies in a different way. For example, children who have been neglected or abused will develop beliefs that others are threatening. It is a perfectly understandable safety behaviour, then, not to get too close or too trusting of others. Their belief fits with the *safety strategy* of 'stay away from others who could harm you'. Unfortunately, while this makes perfect sense, it can also be very unhelpful because it means that individuals struggle to learn to discern the safe from the unsafe person, have problems developing genuine intimate and caring relationships because any sign of conflict triggers their automatic safety strategies, and thus makes it difficult to (learn how to) work through and tolerate all the ups and downs of such relationships. For example, Kate came from a critical background and had developed a withdrawing, submissive way of coping with threats from her parents. She found it very difficult to be assertive with people, especially with men. And she certainly had not learnt to express her own needs to them. Whenever they appeared assertive or aggressive she would automatically adopt submissive behaviours and withdrawal. This is understandable because she had learnt to keep herself *safe* from her father's anger by engaging these behaviours. Indeed, submissive behaviour is a perfectly understandable safety behaviour in the context of feared other people. So rather than discuss this in 'maladaptive' terms, it can be helpful to outline with the client how their behaviour and ways of thinking are often related to their *best efforts to stay safe*.

Unfortunately, these automatic safety strategies now have unforeseen, unintended and undesirable consequences. So before we try to change things it is helpful to validate people's efforts. Thus, talking to people about how they try to *protect* themselves from bad things happening can be very helpful. This avoids any discussion about core beliefs or schema being maladaptive or distorted (see below). Rather, for clients who become easily anxious, aggressive, submissive or avoid/withdraw, they can conceptualise these difficulties as 'their protection system' working overtime and being constantly on 'red alert'. We can thus validate their efforts. This helps to de-shame people and also gives them a focus for thinking about how to change their behaviours.

As noted below, in the formulation it is therefore useful to think about people's characteristic ways of seeing and dealing with things that threaten them. Recall that threats will be linked to emotional memories (Brewin, 2006). From this the counsellor can begin to think about the way in which behaviours and cognitions can become locked together in vicious circles. These are completely unintended consequences and the therapist can talk to the client about how they are partly linked to 'our best efforts to protect ourselves'. We will explore this shortly when considering formulation.

Self-other schema

'Schema' relate to central and basic *organising* systems for knowledge about the self and others. These are built up through life as the result of interpersonal experiences. They are seen as composites of memories, emotions, action tendencies and cognitions. Self–other schema can at times be put into single words that describe personal attributes: 'I am …', 'the other is…'. They can be highly *emotionally* charged and represent core aspects of identity – the basic sense of ourselves and others. Their emotional 'power' can be elicited in interpersonal relationships. Figure 9.1 offers a simple outline.

History of relating experiences
Parents
Siblings
Peers/friends
Teachers/bosses

	Self as...	Other as...
Positive	Able, loving, caring, trusting, friendly, worthy, competent, attractive, good, etc.	Able, loving, caring, trusting, friendly, worthy, competent, attractive, good, etc.
Negative	Unable, unloving, incompetent, hostile, neglectful, bad, selfish, ugly, etc.	Unable, unloving, incompetent, hostile, neglectful, bad, selfish, ugly, etc.

Figure 9.1   Self–other schema

There are, of course, other domains linked to self-identity, such as 'How I think others see me' (e.g. as able, kind, etc.), and 'How I want others to see me'. Cognitive therapists also make a distinction between conditional and unconditional self–other schema. A conditional view is 'I am good if …', whereas an unconditional view is 'I am bad regardless (i.e. there is nothing I can do to make me into a good person)' (Beck et al., 1990). In uncomplicated depression episodes it is believed that there is a switch from previous (usually) positive schema of self and others (or self-organisation and identity) to the activation of negative schema (e.g. 'I used to feel okay about myself but now I feel a failure'). This is important because it is believed that stored in long-term memory is a set of positive schema and positive emotional memories (Brewin, 2006). So working at the level of automatic thoughts and attitudes, reattending, reattributing and refocusing one's thinking, will help to reactivate these positive schema and memories which do exist but have become latent in the depression (Beck et al., 1979; Blackburn and Davidson, 1995).

In complex and long-lasting depressions, especially those associated with so-called 'personality disorder', positive schema and memories of self, or the affection and help of others may not exist, or at least may be very fragile even at the best of times (e.g. a person may have rarely felt okay about themselves and always felt subordinate/inferior and vulnerable; others have rarely been caring and supportive). Hence, techniques to reactivate and tap into a person's premorbid level of functioning are ineffective because there is rather little positive schema (in long-term memory) to tap into. Therapy that deals with these difficulties then becomes much more one of developing something 'anew'. This takes much longer, and requires a different focus, especially on the importance of the therapeutic relationship (Gilbert and Leahy, 2007). Hence it is important to gain some idea of the person's premorbid level of functioning. The main issue here is one of, 'how much in the way of growth, new schema and emotional memories does the person need to develop?' A number of therapists take the view that in some cases we grow out of our psychopathologies, and the issue of maturation and new learning (rather than reactivating positive schema) is a key issue in therapeutic change (Gilbert, 1995a; Safran, 1998). These developments greatly enrich the cognitive model and offer up new ways of working therapeutically (see Gilbert and Leahy, 2007; Kuehlwein and Rosen, 1993; McCullough, 2000; Snyder and Ingram, 2006).

Another way schema are used is to depict key themes that reoccur in people's difficulties. For example, it may focus on issues of mistrust or abandonment and it is quite easy from here to look at core beliefs around these themes (Young, Beck and Weinberger, 1993; Young and Klosko, 1993). The argument is that if a schema is triggered it will orientate people's attention and ways of thinking in a schema-congruent way. So, for example, a person who has an 'abandonment' schema may be inclined to interpret ambiguous situations or normal interpersonal conflicts in terms of other people's wish to abandon or reject them. Hence, they emotionally respond to that situation in an excessive way. Helping people recognise their schema can be a way of helping people recognise their points of 'vulnerability'.

Cautions with schema

Concepts of schema have been used by many therapists and they are very useful heuristics (Young, Beck and Weinberger, 1993; Young and Klosko, 1993). However, they should not be used to imply that there is 'some negative schema' sitting inside an individual (e.g. 'You have this problem because you have an x schema'). Also, they should not be used tautologically (e.g. 'You don't trust people because you have a mistrust schema or you are frightened of abandonment because you have an abandonment schema'). Rather, schema are about the way in which emotions and thoughts are *organised and patterned* around certain themes; they are not entities that sit in the brain. Although it can be helpful for the therapist to think in terms of schema, in my view, it is equally useful to think of clients' key themes that relate to some of the domains of threat (Gilbert, 1992). In this way potentially any theme and any pattern is possible and one doesn't have to 'diagnose' specific types of schema. Schema concepts should not be used when clients can feel potentially shamed by them. So if you use schema ideas, use them compassionately to discuss 'understandable' sources of vulnerability.

I make this point because in supervision one sometimes hears therapists using the concepts of schema almost as if it is a medical diagnosis. This is not the way they are intended to be used. In their self-help book, for example, Young and Klosko, who have developed 'schema therapy', never use the term 'maladaptive schema' but rather the term 'life traps' (Young and Klosko, 1993). So ensure your use of language and use of concepts is not technically focused and shaming, but is facilitative.

Another caution is that evidence increasingly suggests that the concepts of autonomous self-schema are not supported by the data. There are many reasons to believe that our construction of self and self-schema are only useful in the context of the social relationships in which they are embedded. For example, in numerous research studies Baldwin has shown that self-evaluation is consciously and non-consciously linked to what we think others think of us (see Baldwin and Dandeneau, 2005 for reviews). This is why we are careful to distinguish external from internal threats. So once again we see that the reasons people may give for certain types of feelings are not necessarily accurate (Haidt, 2001). Indeed, when people focus on negative characteristics of self, it is always worth thinking that this can be defensive. Also consider that our minds have multiple ways of processing information which can conflict with each other. Also recall that approach-avoidance conflicts and dilemmas are common in depression. They can activate complex interacting chains of thoughts and feelings, giving the experience of 'many things rushing through one's mind' and a sense of fragmenting and falling apart (see Chapter 4).

Key issues 9.4   Self–other schema

1   There are basic core self–other belief structures (e.g. I am. You are).
2   The counsellor can explore whether there has been a major shift from previous positive self–other views of self to negative schema, or an accentuation of negative self–other schema.
3   Once activated, these schema tend to be self-perpetuating and defended against change; that is, the person distorts information to maintain them (e.g. by personalisation and focusing on the negative/threat).
4   In some clients, although their schema are negative, they are also safety-focused, by being familiar – what is known and predictable.
5   When a schema is activated, it tends to generate high (usually) defensive arousal and trigger defensive responses (anger or anxiety and fight/flight/avoidance, etc.).
6   Our basic self–other schema often come from early life.
7   Thus they may be difficult to articulate in language but are 'experienced' as feeling states.
8   Sometimes a client feels and behaves 'as if' negative schema are operative even though they may not be able verbally to label the schema.
9   Typical triggers of depressive schema are lack of recognition or control, defeats, and actual or potential losses of valued relationships.

Conceptualisation and formulation

Let us now try to put these various aspects together in the process of *formulating* a person's difficulties. The issue of formulation is not without controversy (Bieling and Kyken, 2003). While therapists may think it is important to do it in certain ways with certain concepts and language, clients may have other ideas – so stay with guided discovery and do not try to 'diagnose' or locate thinking 'errors' inside people. This can be shaming. Tarrier (2006) offers an excellent review of the formulation process.

We can conceptualise a case of depression as representing an interaction of genes and previous life history that gives rise to the development of: key fears and areas of vulnerability; aversive emotional memory; self–other schema and basic attitudes and assumptions. These lead to basic interpersonal and role-creating styles, expressed or repressed needs, and key safety strategies that guide social and other behaviours. These are what clients bring to each situation in their lives and colour their impenetrations and meanings they give to those situations. Thus when critical incidents arrive they can activate people's key fears and vulnerabilities and a predictable set of automatic reactions will unfold, including of course feelings and thoughts. Formulation 1 (p. 216) is an example of a person who had critical parents who were high fliers. They had high expectations of their son, struggled to deal with shame themselves and thought that any failing on their son's part showed them in a bad light too. Mother was described as a somewhat cold, detached but efficient woman and father an ambitious and envious man.

This scenario is not untypical in achievers. By conceptualising a case in these terms it is possible to have an overview which acts as a kind of map. You can use these headings to *gradually* build up a shared formulation with your client. In Chapter 8, recall that for Peter we started in a more simple way. As you build your formulation the pieces of the jigsaw must be agreed both in terms of their importance and how they fit together. Both you and the client can then keep a copy – but be free to change it in the future if needs be – nothing is written in stone. This helps clarity in understanding and also in negotiating interventions.

A safety strategies approach

Another way problems can be formulated is with a safety strategies approach. Although this kind of approach is more typical in anxiety (Salkovskis, 1996a) than depression, it has a lot to offer our understanding of mood disorders – and other problems too (Tarrier, 2006). For personality disorders Beck et al. (1990) focus on: views of self and others; core beliefs; key threats; safety strategies; and affect. This fits well with an evoluationary focus that suggests that we (like other animals) adapt to our environment to try to cope with threats and secure key social and other goals. In the process of adapting to our environments we will come to use a range of basic innate and planned defences. A basic or innate defence is, for example, becoming anxious if a powerful other person threatens us, or we are suddenly confronted by a large, aggressive dog. These are relatively automatic and subject to conditioning. Planned defensive behaviours are when we make decisions to, say, avoid anyone (or dogs) who could be aggressive. If we are fearful of rejection, then we may develop a range of strategies such as always trying to be nice to people and trying not to be aggressive or

Early experiences

Parents only paid me any attention if I was successful and achieved things.
Failures led to punishment, neglect or being ignored and feeling a
disappointment to them.
I learned to feel disappointed in myself if I failed.

Core emotionally textured sense of self and others

Self as

Not good enough, a failure, a
disappointment, lacking.

Others as

Fickle, rejecting, powerful,
critical, demanding.

Basic attitudes and rules for living

I have to show others that I am
competent and try hard.
I have to achieve things to maintain
my sense of self-worth.
Without success, I will be ignored and not
respected or attended to.
Without success, if people got too
close to me they would discover I am empty.

Roles and safety behaviours

I constantly try to demonstrate competence.
I do not assert myself.
I use submissive behaviours to try to avoid
attacks or rejections from others.
I do not express emotions unless I can ensure
others are accepting.
I impress others with my success/abilities/
personal qualities to avoid rejection.

**Critical incidents and situations
triggering depression**

Lack of recognition, validating attention.
Failures of various kinds at
college, work, etc.
Entrapments (e.g. my need to
earn money means I cannot
pursue qualifications).

Negative thoughts and reactions

It's my fault I am not successful.
I am not good enough. I am useless.
I will never make it. It is all too difficult.
There is no point in trying.
Others will not like or respect me.
I have no control over my life.

Depressed symptoms

Loss of energy.
Increased performance anxiety.
Strong wish to escape, hide.

Social behaviours

Withdrawal from others.
Angry/irritable with others.
*Reduced positive social
interactions.*

Formulation 1   Cognitive-Focused Formulation

too pushy. However, we can also fear *internal* stimuli and avoid certain feeling states. For example, if we believe that we can get anxious and lose control or have a heart attack (internal stimuli and processes) in certain situations, then we may want to carry valium. Or we might try *to avoid* those situations where certain inner emotions are activated (see Leahy, 2002). Once a person has had a depression they can be highly vigilant to a depression coming back and be desperate to avoid depression emerging inside them again. In some cases a suicide can be triggered by the feelings of fear and dread of a returning depression and 'not being able to go through that again'. Some people drink, take drugs or self-mutilate to try to turn off and cope with unpleasant internal feelings. Internal defences are also complex and automatic and can involve repression, denial of feelings and dissociating from feelings (Greenberg and Watson, 2006).

That all seems understandable, except that our defensive strategies can lead to all kinds of unforeseen, unintended and undesirable consequences. Even worse, we might then become angry with ourselves when we find ourselves behaving defensively. We might get cross with ourselves if we are nice when part of ourselves would rather be more assertive. Cognitive therapists might focus on the fear of rejection and the beliefs that underpin that. Although obviously important, it can also be useful to formulate problems in terms of safety strategies. So let's explore a formulation couched in these terms. We can begin with a person we will call Jane given in formulation 2 (p. 218). As in all cases I outline, in order to avoid identification, this is a composite of a number of people.

Historical influences   The formulation begins with recognising and discussing historical influences. Jane's mother had suffered a number of miscarriages before Jane was born and Jane felt that her mother was very 'fussy' and over-protective. She was also very critical and controlling. Jane understood that some of this was related to her mother's anxiety about being a mother. Her parents did not have a close relationship. At meal times there would either be silences or they would avoid each other. Conflicts were either avoided or could blow up in frightening ways. She experienced her father as often (but not always) a cold and difficult man to please. She felt that 'he just needed to look at you and you'd wish the ground to open'. It would seem that he would often have a 'disgust face' when showing his disapproval. However, when he was nice she liked being with him. She acknowledged having an 'approach-avoidant' relationship with him and always trying to work out what kind of mood he was in. Jane got on well at primary school but was somewhat shy and was bullied at secondary school. One day the bully would be nice and the next she would be ridiculing and unkind. In consequence Jane has many *emotional memories* which were focused on shame, feeling unsafe and being alone. These included others being very threatening and critical to her and herself feeling very small, vulnerable and powerless. So, we have experiences and memories of others and of self that are coded in scenes and imagery fragments associated with emotions.

Key fears   When the therapist has this type of historical background they can then ask the client how they think this background has influenced them and in particular what key fears and concerns they may have carried forward in time.

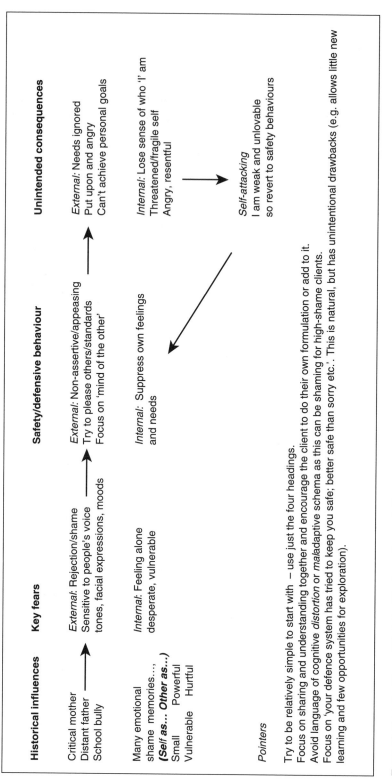

Historical influences

Critical mother
Distant father
School bully

Many emotional
shame memories....
(Self as... Other as...)
Small   Powerful
Vulnerable   Hurtful

Key fears

External: Rejection/shame
Sensitive to people's voice
tones, facial expressions, moods

Internal: Feeling alone
desperate, vulnerable

Safety/defensive behaviour

External: Non-assertive/appeasing
Try to please others/standards
Focus on 'mind of the other'

Internal: Suppress own feelings
and needs

Unintended consequences

External: Needs ignored
Put upon and angry
Can't achieve personal goals

Internal: Lose sense of who 'I' am
Threatened/fragile self
Angry, resentful

Self-attacking
I am weak and unlovable
so revert to safety behaviours

Pointers

Try to be relatively simple to start with – use just the four headings.
Focus on sharing and understanding together and encourage the client to do their own formulation or add to it.
Avoid language of cognitive *distortion* or *maladaptive* schema as this can be shaming for high-shame clients.
Focus on 'your defence system has tried to keep you safe; better safe than sorry etc.'. This is natural, but has unintentional drawbacks (e.g. allows little new
learning and few opportunities for exploration).

Formulation 2   Threat/Safety Strategy Formulation

Jane was able to suggest that she was very sensitive to people rejecting her and being critical. She noted that when there is a slightly critical 'atmosphere' she has a rapid increase in arousal and can notice her heart beating rapidly. Further exploration suggested a high sensitivity to people's voice tones and facial expressions. When she was criticised as a child she felt completely alone. Even today she felt that the feelings of rejection are associated with 'feeling that I have to cope on my own in a hostile world'. Thus, the social anxiety and the abandonment anxiety are fused together. Thus we have external fears (others becoming critical and rejecting) and internal fears of the return of feeling alone and frightened.

Safety and defensive behaviours   Having ascertained historically critical episodes and emotional memories, focusing on key fears and *specific* stimulus-related sensitivities, the therapist can now discuss the fact that when we have such anxieties and worries *it is only natural* for us to try to defend ourselves from that happening. So I asked what did she think her ways of defending herself were, to try to stop the frightening things (e.g. being criticised and rejected or when conflicts blew up resulting in painful silences) from happening. After some discussion, she reflected that she tends to be non-assertive, finding it difficult to articulate (and at times even to know) her own needs. She feels that she deals with conflicts by trying to appease other people. Another key safety behaviour, designed to head off possible criticism, rejection and thus an (automatic) reactivation of feelings of social and abandonment anxiety, is to try to please others and meet their expectations or standards. As part of this strategy she needs to be very focused on what is going on in the 'mind of the other'. Hence, she tries to 'second guess' people and is very sensitive to other people's moods. Because she has a number of unprocessed fears and fear memories from the past, Jane tries to suppress these feelings by keeping active and busy. She believes that if she can do things right, then people will be happy and she can feel safe. She is frightened to think too much about the experience of feeling emotionally alone and so avoids it, unless depressed, and then it 'all floods back'. The therapist clarifies with her that so far all of this makes perfect sense and is a relatively natural and understandable way to cope with these key fears.

Unintended consequences   We can now discuss that although these safety strategies can work to a degree, they can have unintended and undesired consequences. So, we then explore these together. After some discussion Jane was able to articulate these. She felt that at times she was so busy trying to please others that she didn't know 'who *she* was'. She found her head confused, with various conflicting feelings. She felt that her sense of self (i.e. self-identity) was quite fragile and easily threatened. This had stopped her from taking on challenges in life that her talent probably would have been suited to. Also, she admitted, if she was honest, that there were times when she felt very angry inside. The way she dealt with this anger was to withdraw and go quiet. She said 'I just shut down inside'. She feels her husband tries to be supportive but she blocks him out because she is so confused as to what is happening inside of her. She then 'hates herself' for doing this because 'blocking out others is what my parents did to me'.

Self-attacking   When she gets into these states of mind of feeling angry, confused and frightened, she begins to dislike herself intensely. She feels weak, unlovable and bad, and at times feels other people would be better off without her. She tries to tell herself to 'pull herself together', stop being selfish and self-focused and get on with her life. Eventually she 'pulls around' and returns to her safety strategies. Self-criticism has many different functions (Driscoll, 1989) and thus it is important to conduct a functional analysis on it and explore its link to safety strategies. For Jane it was partly to force her back into her safety strategies.

Feedback   We were then able to discuss how part of her self-criticism emerged out of her fears of rejection, which pushed her back into her traditional safety behaviours and thus set up a vicious circle. Moreover, we were able to explore how, when she experiences the world this way, both the external world (what the world and others will do to her) and her internal world (how she thinks and feels about herself) turn hostile. In fact, there is nowhere inside her or outside her that gives her any feelings of support, kindness, reassurance or warmth. When I mentioned this, her eyes became tearful: 'I guess that is true. I never really felt safe or part of things.'

You can see here that the focus has been on early life experiences and key emotional memories, key fears, safety behaviours/strategies and their unintended consequences. It is in fact very common for depressed people to become very self-critical and angry with themselves when they confront the unintended consequences of their safety behaviours. It is important therefore for therapists to be gentle at this point and to help the client *validate* their key fears and safety behaviours as being their best efforts and that the unintended consequences are genuinely unintended and *not their fault*. In fact, in compassionate mind work, which we will explore shortly (see chapter 11), this can be a very important insight. Moreover, when the therapist is helping the client to appreciate that the unintended consequences are not their fault, the voice tone is very quiet, gentle and soothing. Not uncommonly, this may elicit a tearful response from the client, who has never really had an opportunity to see their difficulties this way. If you are going to engage in a compassion-focused therapy it is helpful to have some kind of formulation like this because this is your 'spring board' into a compassionate focus. Without awareness that our safety behaviours often generate unintended (not our fault) consequences, the client may struggle to develop a compassionate focus and may get stuck in self-blaming and a deep sense of shame. This shame can come from both how they have lived their lives up to now and also as echoes of how people have treated them in the past.

Interestingly, Jane had done some limited work with a cognitive therapist and unfortunately this seems to have reinforced her view that her thoughts were 'irrational' and she should look at the evidence. The therapist had focused on 'the evidence' for and against being small and vulnerable now (as an adult) or emotionally alone. In our work together we focused on processing memories of being alone and frightened as a child. This is because these operate like trauma memories and in behavioural approaches one must 'open' those memory systems, experience affect, while working on new experiences of feeling safe in the therapy (Brewin, 2006; Clark and Ehlers, 2004; Lee, 2005). So we spent time accessing these memories and being compassionate with them. After one painful session, Jane noted that she had known (in her head) she was frightened as a child but had not really 'been in touch' with those feelings or recognised just *how* frightened she had been and alone she had felt. She returned the following week to say that although she had been very upset by the previous session, over the past week she had felt 'strangely more at peace with myself' and that 'somehow it all made sense to me' as to 'why I get so depressed'. Thus, as Salkovskis (1996a) makes clear, CBT is not about showing people that they are being irrational, but that they have got stuck and trapped in understandable but unhelpful ways of trying, as best they can, to get safe.

When to formulate and in how much detail

Let's backtrack a bit here. Formulation helps guide you to your interventions but it is also clearly linked to your model. In Chapters 5 and 6 I have outlined why some depressions are rooted in trauma and unprocessed trauma memories. Of course these give rise to schema and core beliefs but it is the functioning of the threat and safety-seeking systems that are crucial. Moreover, some traumas, such as growing up in cold or aggressive or competitive households, activate innate and archetypal fears that pull on innate defences (e.g. protest-despair, and even fears about one's very survival) which can be experienced as overwhelming. Explaining the nature of these fears and innate (archetypal) processing systems, and working with emotional memories, can be very helpful for some depressed people. Moreover, it helps to establish a base, from which to develop positive life goals, which safety strategies may have prevented.

The process by which you get to these formulations, however, can be in *small* steps. Remember that you are always collaborative, sharing people's own views of their depression. Thus, as in Chapter 8, we may start to formulate with a summary. We might say 'Given what you have been saying, it seems that ...' and then 'One way of thinking this through together is for us to draw it out. We can start with ...'. With some depressed people one can formulate quite quickly and in some detail, but for others it may take a rather long time and it is much more basic and 'bare bones'. Very depressed people will not cope with the more complex types of formulation – they are far too detailed at this time. Moreover, you may have to do some basic work on behaviours to lift the depression a little, instil hope and develop your therapeutic relationship before going into areas that are painful for the person. So you have to tailor formulation and working together to just a few key ideas, for example, by simply noting that: 'When we get depressed our bodies close down and focus on how bad we feel. As we focus on those thoughts, we naturally feel more depressed. If we can act against these feelings this can sometimes help us feel a little more in control and better' (Martell et al., 2001). However, the above has offered more detailed information than we covered in Chapter 8, on the processes of therapy (e.g. Socratic discussion) and the key constructs (such as eliciting core beliefs and safety strategies) that guide your formulation. Keep in mind, though, that the more detailed formulations and development of therapeutic tasks may take time to evolve. In the first instance formulation is aimed at how you are going to focus your interventions.

A caution in regard to threat memory   Keep in mind that discussing painful feelings and memories can be upsetting and the therapist can give clear validation and understanding for how hard it can be to discuss things. When you are formulating using a safety strategies approach, you are trying to link people's safety behaviours to early or current threatening or distressing life experiences. However, we now know that some people will just not be able to focus on this because it is too threatening, it is relatively unprocessed and they just do not have the capacity for reflecting on their pain. So, for example, they may say they can remember being hit as a child but not have much detail and rather shrug their shoulders at it. On the other hand, if they are criticised or threatened they might show quite major physiological responses. People will have their experiences of threat coded in the amygdala, which co-ordinates physiological responses to threat, but the verbal and event memory may be poorly developed. So keep in mind that for some people this may be a complex area to work with. Nonetheless, if people can begin to slowly work with and assimilate these memories, then, as in other trauma work, this can be very helpful (Brewin, 2006; Lee, 2005). However for some people with disorganised attachment this can take some time (Liotti, 2000, 2002) and one must only work at a pace and intensity that depressed people can work with.

Conclusion

This chapter has articulated a variety of ways in which you can begin to think about and structure therapy with depressed people. We started with the idea that people's interpretations of things are important aspects of mood and mood regulation. These interpretations influence our automatic thoughts and reactions to events. When we derive long-term negative conclusions about things, we are prone to ruminate in ways that often accentuate the mood shift. We also explored how people's automatic reactions are linked to a network of memories, meanings and major fears and concerns. These include those associated with abandonment, rejection or loss of control, which were the subject of previous chapters. So these processes address the way in which moods themselves operate, and help you to explore what's going on in a person's mind when they are depressed.

However, we recognise that we are all human, with human needs, feelings, hopes and desires, yet we are also unique by virtue of our genes and life experiences. Thus, our interpretations and vulnerabilities to mood shifts do not come out of the blue. They are shaped by: (1) our individual genes, and innate and archetypal systems that are guiding us to goals that require certain inputs, and will defend us in various ways; and (2) by our personal experiences that shape us into the people we are. Together, these give rise to us as people with key hopes, desires, fears and concerns, basic rules for living, self–other schema and a range of safety strategies. It is these processes that people bring with them into new situations, and form the lens by which they interpret and cope with situations.

Finally, we noted that we try to capture these different processes in our formulation, which is both unique to that person's story and also a form of psychoeducation. By this I mean we are giving the person a framework on which they can hang various ideas so that their feelings and thoughts make sense to them. The way you formulate, however, is collaborative, based on joint, guided discovery, using the person's own language and styles. It is also related to how you are going to work with a person and this is true for whatever school of therapy you choose to engage with. This chapter has given two compatible (and not mutually exclusive) but different styles of formulation; one based on a fairly traditional cognitive approach but with safety strategies added, and the other based more fully on a safety strategies and behavioural approach. The latter, in my view, facilitates an important de-shaming process and sets therapy up for the development of a compassionate approach to change. We will elaborate this approach in Chapter 11.

10 Helping People Engage and Change: Some Basic Principles

Working with the biopsychosocial approach (Chapter 1), you may discuss with depressed people the nature of depression – that when we are depressed there is a physiological aspect to our depression (e.g. our stress systems may be overactive, and we may be physically exhausted), a psychological aspect related to how we see ourselves now and in the future (including health worries), and a social aspect related to current social relationships and external life problems. You can outline how these domains interact, for example, how life events can disturb the stress system, leading to poor sleep and tiredness, and pull our thoughts and feelings into a negative frame of mind. We might also note that dwelling on negative thoughts is also physiologically powerful and stress-inducing. The key point is to help clients recognise that depression affects us at *many* different levels, that these levels interact and create brain states. Hence the holistic nature of counselling work.

Explain and de-shame

Some people are ashamed of feeling depressed or struggling to cope. Some people are unaware that depression can make them *feel* unwell or very tired. Thus it is helpful to explain and de-shame depression. For example, one might say:

> When we are under a lot of stress, or stress has gone on for some time, this can use up various chemicals in our brain and body. Also we may produce a lot of stress chemicals. In effect, we become emotionally and physically exhausted and depressed. Various systems, like our sleep and energy systems, can be disturbed. When this happens our minds can shift towards very negative conclusions and feelings about things. When we feel exhausted we can want to withdraw from things. This is not your fault, it is the way we can be when we are very stressed.

Of course, not all stress results in depression and caution is needed not to over-diagnose stress states as depression. For some people we can draw out a 'stress tree'. Here the trunk is labelled stress-depression. At the end of each branch can be an identified stressor or life problem. This type of discussion offers a view of why they may *feel* so bad. It provides a language of talking about *exhaustion* and it cues them in to the fact that depression changes the way we think about things, feelings, body states and our behaviours. It is also de-shaming. The counsellor can also explain that depression, and some of our behaviours, such as avoidance, can be *natural* protective consequences from emotional exhaustion and feeling depressed. Some people like a label, for example 'depression', because it helps them recognise that they do have a problem and also that there are ways to recover. Other people find it stigmatising but may work with a concept such as emotional exhaustion. Check that the person is with you on this approach. Then suggest that over the next few sessions, as you both share the nature of the difficulties in more detail you will be working out an agreed plan to tackle these difficulties.

Collaboration

Sharing difficulties and developing a joint plan is called collaboration (Beck et al., 1979). Collaboration is a two-way process. Not only should clients collaborate in their own therapy process, but the counsellor should collaborate with their clients – being sensitive to their issues, fears and abilities (Liotti, 2007). This means three things:

1   Continually check with the client that you have a mutual understanding. Keep an eye on helping them become involved in and committed to the process of change. This may involve helping the person become actively engaged in the explorative process, in planning their own independent home practice, for example, rather than passively waiting for the counsellor to 'come up with the answers' or what they should do.

2   Part of the work centres on sharing painful feelings, hopes and fears; validating people's experiences; identifying key problem areas and brain storming coping options; becoming more self-aware of the links between thinking, feeling and behaviour; learning how to stand back from depressive thoughts and generate alternatives; tackling rumination; processing emotions that might be avoided; learning affect tolerance and acceptance where appropriate; planning and engaging with behavioural experiments; exploring the value of anti-depressant behaviours; and developing self-compassion.

3   Change may be difficult without the client being prepared to *practise* and try working at developing new ways of thinking and behaving (Bennett-Levy et al., 2004; Martell et al., 2001). Some types of practice can take courage and fortitude and require the counsellor to work on motivations, noting that this effort can be hard and may not bring immediate relief. As Beck et al. (1985) and Leahy (2001) note, sometimes we help people do things that are hard to do in the short-term to gain longer-term benefits.

Thus in many ways the counsellor acts as *a personal mind coach*. Collaborative approaches require the counsellor to be sensitive to the interpersonal style of the client and the therapeutic relationship (Leahy, 2007; Liotti, 2007). While procedures for the above are relatively easy to describe, *their simplicity is often deceptive.* For example, once a procedure has been used, such as developing alternatives for styles of reasoning or beliefs, this may need to be *practised* and used *many* times before the client takes it on board. In fact, even the most obvious of beliefs (e.g. 'I am a failure') can take many hours of work before the person gradually gets the hang of the idea that performance and personhood (performance evaluation and self-evaluation) need not be equated. It can take some time before a person comes to see that self-blame can be a safety behaviour that they might be frightened to give up. One needs to be patient and persistent and often use the same procedures over and over again. When one reads in the books about various alternative thoughts that clients might generate, what is sometimes not said is that these can be the product of hours of careful work, emotional exploration, looking at it in this way and then that, and a lot of practice in working with depressing thoughts. So there can be much work to be done in terms of repeating interventions, exposure, trial-and-error learning, developing new skills and gaining confidence in those skills, working through disappointments, finding hidden blocks, and so forth.

Early stages

Instilling hope   In the early stages of therapy one tries to facilitate some hope through validation of the pain and fear of depression, listening and taking a keen interest in their stories – explanations that make sense to the person – de-shaming, noting (and triggering memories of) times when they did not feel so depressed, offering the therapy as an opportunity to explore and see what might be helpful (i.e. what have you got to lose by coming along for a while and see what happens).

Consider the use of self-help materials   Some depressed people find it helpful to read about other people's depression and ways of improving. The judicious use of self-help materials can be useful. These can be provided by recommending self-help books or websites (see Appendix). Make sure you are familiar with these before recommending them.

Fear of getting better and of not getting better   These are common fears, or at least fear of what needs to be achieved to get well. Validate the fear as understandable and show that you have a real appreciation of it. So the question is, how to take on the fear(s) in a compassionate way. If fear of change dominates the picture, then practice can be sabotaged. It may be useful to use the advantages–disadvantages procedure to explore this (see Chapter 12). In some cases of depression this issue can take a lot of work.

Helping people find their own way   Much of what we are trying to do is help people articulate and work on goals that are important to them (Mahoney, 2003; Wong, 2006). Sometimes people are unclear on these goals or doubt their own judgements. For example, one person decided he wanted to try another type of therapist while working with me. However, the other therapist said CBT would not help with emotions and to give it up. In my view, this is destructive and envious. My approach is to say: 'It is important that you feel free to contact anyone you like for help. Our job here is to help you feel what is in your own heart and use that freedom for your benefit; use your own experience and test out ideas and see what *you* think.' If you take this kind of stance you are demonstrating a non-judgemental position, avoiding competitions with other therapists and making clear that the exercise of freedom to choose is not always easy.

One of the reasons people may not 'know their own heart' (and you get a lot of 'don't knows') is because there are many conflicts, mixed feelings and dilemmas. We are open to that (as acceptance) as a fact of life and this can be hard and confusing. There may be no one 'rational thing' to do but a gradual working out of gains and losses of different courses of action.

Shame in the therapy process   When people try to practise things on their own – for example to 'catch' their thoughts 'as they arise' or become mindful of their thoughts and body states, or generate alternatives and schedule activities – they may feel they do not do so well. Many depressed people feel they (will) fail at these and therefore have a sense of shame. We should be very sensitive to the issue of shame in independent practice and clarify (often many times) that independent practice is not like being at school where one will get marks for 'good' work or might court the counsellor's disapproval or contempt for doing things poorly. Mindfulness, for example, involves learning to pay attention in a non-judgemental way, and to observe – there is no other outcome than that. The idea, then, is not to do these things '*to make* you feel better' but to be open-minded enough and 'have a go and see if they are helpful'. This is why Bennett-Levy et al. (2004) call them 'behavioural experiments'. And of course, like all of us, what might work today might not tomorrow and we need to do something different depending on the context (Perrez and Reicherts, 1992).

Sometimes depressed people can get angry and frustrated because try as they might they can't make the 'therapy work' for them. The sensitive counsellor will explore these things. For example, Sally had trouble writing down her thoughts. While in the therapy she could understand them but at home alone it was more difficult. This left her feeling frustrated and useless, and that the therapy might not work for her. She was also fearful to reveal her frustration at the therapy. However, she revealed enough for us to work on these themes and especially her fear (and shame) of failure (see Gilbert, 1998c for further discussion).

Many of us hope that counselling or therapy will act quickly to relieve our pain. We all like a quick fix for pain. So it is easy to see that some people will become disappointed if the things they try do not bring immediate relief or as much relief as they hoped for. Helping clients understand that therapy can be hard work and that learning new skills is time consuming and involves effort can be an important (if painful) first step (Leahy, 2001, 2004). This can be especially so when clients are trying to cope with their depression by avoidance and numbing, because starting to engage with things can bring back some pain. Counsellors themselves must also come to terms with this and not abandon efforts if they are not at first successful. Many analogies can be used here, such as building up muscles one has not used for a while or getting physically fit. At first the exercises may hurt more than they give benefit but if one stays with them they can be successful. This, of course, does not mean that one does not try to instil hope early on (Beck et al., 1979) or one is overly focused on the 'struggle' of therapy to the point the client thinks it is bound to be too hard and they cannot do it. Rather, it is to go step by step and validate the efforts needed (Gilbert, 2000a).

Agenda setting   We can help people set agendas and outlines for the work in the session to unfold. Hence at the beginning of each session it is often helpful to form an agenda for the session. This involves monitoring thoughts and feelings about the previous session, checking mood, checking on practice, and deciding the crucial areas to be covered in the session to come. However, the counsellor needs to be careful since some clients can hold back issues until well into a session. So at all times the counsellor needs to remain flexible. Also, if one is too rigid the client may rely on the counsellor and not bring their own material. A simple question of 'what would you like to focus on today?' can start the ball rolling.

All these themes bear centrally on the issue of *collaboration*. We collaborate to help the depressed person find *their* way out of depression. Of course, we have various ideas and will work with a model of depression (I tend to focus on safety strategies). However, we do not impose it but share it. The art of good therapy is *guided discovery*, finding out what makes depression worse and what heals it (Beck et al., 1979).

Procedures

Helpful procedures for working with depression are listed below, but these must be set within the context of a supportive therapeutic relationship. None of these is in any sense a magical change process, but rather they represent ways of working to be conducted in the atmosphere of 'caring interest' and an empathic relationship. There are a number of counselling issues which tend to be associated with good outcome:

1   Role structuring and creating a therapeutic alliance.
2   Developing the therapeutic contract and commitment for change.
3   Conducting behavioural analysis (what happens when, how, etc.).
4   Negotiating treatment objectives (what are we trying to achieve? Is there agreement on this?).
5   Executing treatment tasks and maintaining motivation.
6   Monitoring and evaluating progress.
7   Programming for generalisation beyond the counselling situation (e.g. teaching anti-depressant lifestyles and behaviour).
8   Preparing the client for the termination of counselling.

Some of these aspects can be broken down into specific tasks of therapy.

Monitoring and recording

Understanding your model   It is important that the depressed client understands your model and its aims. You can use examples to demonstrate the links between thinking and feeling (e.g. the lover who did not phone example in Chapter 9), or explore ways in which avoidance behaviour can make difficulties worse (see Chapter 4). Clients need to understand how and why you are working in the way you are, to have *shared* understanding, rather than thinking: 'Well, I guess the counsellor must know what they are doing.' The client's engagement in understanding helps to bring them into the counselling process.

Exploring personal meanings   It is useful to explain that meaning is always a personal issue related to many things, including our history, current life contexts and desires, hopes and fears. Some of our deeper meanings can be implicit rather than explicit (Haidt, 2001). While some meanings can be articulated, others may be difficult to talk about. Clients do not walk around with well-articulated

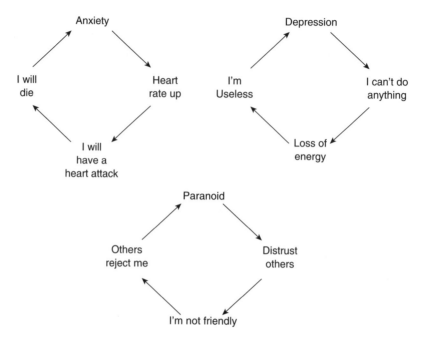

Figure 10.1 Examples of feedback loops

attitudes and core beliefs in their minds. Indeed, Beck et al. (1979) note they may take considerable reflection and thought to work out and articulate. Meaning is often not coded in language so it may need to be worked with in different ways (e.g. pictures, images or re-enactments). Metaphor is another good way to help convey meaning. Hence, although one will try to put things into spoken and written language, this does not mean that the thoughts that are associated with distress occur in the best-spoken English.

How behaviours, emotions and thoughts interact – the process of diagramming In developing the therapeutic contract and commitment for change it is helpful for depressed people to gain insight into how their thoughts and behaviours may increase rather than reduce their difficulties. Making diagrams of summaries with a client gives a visual overview (for more complex formulations and diagrams, see Blackburn and Twaddle, 1996). Diagramming is especially helpful to show positive recursive feedback, which can be drawn as circles (see Figure 10.1). For example: 'I feel depressed; when depressed I can't do anything; when I can't do anything I feel useless; when I feel useless I get more depressed; when I get more depressed I do less'. This kind of diagram then gives an opportunity for a behavioural experiment to explore whether the client is prepared to try to see if doing more helps, even though they feel depressed.

Discussion can centre on where best to intervene and help make predictions for certain thoughts and what would happen if they changed. So we help clients identify their own typical feedback loops and how to break into the circle. For example, 'If you could stop putting yourself down when you feel unable to do things, would this be helpful? What would be the advantages and disadvantages of giving up putting yourself down?' This enables depressed people to gain an overview of the issues and helps them understand the role of cognitions and behaviours in depression and how to change. The counsellor may constantly note that these types of spiral are very common in depression because *depressed mood is designed by evolution to make us withdraw*, 'so we need to plan how to compassionately act against or in spite of them'. If we have hurt a muscle, and it has stiffened up, we might have to do stretching exercises that may hurt a little to get things moving again (see p. 184).

Self-monitoring, mindfulness and the observing self Self-monitoring is designed to help clients become more aware and attentive to their flow of thoughts, emotions and behaviours as they arise, the meta-cognitions ('this means …') that follow, and the links between them. For example, a person wakes up and feels tired and then (meta-cognitively) thinks 'Oh gosh, today is going to be a hard day if I feel like this', and may then feel angry – 'why am I always so tired?'

Learning to pay attention to the flow of thoughts, how one thought can lead to another and how easy it is for our minds to get caught up in a flow of thoughts and feelings is sometimes called 'becoming mindful' (Germer, Siegel and Fulton, 2005; Hanh, 1991; Linehan, 1993). There are many ways to help people become mindful and aware of how chaotic our minds can be. Brantley's (2003) book is excellent in this regard and goes into far more detail than we can here (see also Marra, 2003). One way is simply by encouraging the depressed person to become aware of their thoughts, feelings and emotions and behaviours as they arise in the present moment. That is, we teach 'thought catching' and explain that thoughts can rush by so quickly through our minds that we might not fully notice them but they can affect what we feel. We might say that if we learn to be attentive to our thoughts and feelings, we might notice changes in our mood and sometimes, if we reflect on that, we might notice certain events or thoughts. So we have to *stop and reflect and pay attention*.

One way to help people recognise how easy it is for our minds to wander all over the place is with a simple, brief relaxation exercise. You can do it with the client. As you go through the exercise close your eyes or look to the floor so that the client does not think you are staring at them. You might then say:

> For the next minute let's just focus on our breathing and the feel of the breath as it enters through the nose, moves down into the lungs and then outward through the mouth.

At the end of that minute you can then reflect on the experience:

> Did you notice anything about your thoughts? How they slipped off this way and that? What kind of thoughts went through your mind? What other things (e.g. sounds or sensations) did you notice other than those of the breath? Did your body feel (un)comfortable or were you self-conscious? Were there thoughts of 'am I doing this right?'?

I might offer one of my own: 'You know I noticed the door banging downstairs and was wondering why they don't get that fixed.' After discussing this you might say:

> So you see our minds can be quite chaotic, looking forward and backward, distracted here and there. When we practise mindfulness we simply learn to notice 'this rushing' of thoughts and intruding sensations. That's it! Nothing more – just notice them without trying to stop or change them – we just gently and with kindness bring our minds back to focus on our breathing or whatever sensory aspects or action we are engaged in. Learning to be mindful can be helpful because we notice how easy it is for our thoughts to get caught in a flow of ideas. When we are depressed this flow is often into dark places because that is where our protection strategies will pull us. So one thing we can do is simply to notice the *thoughts arising*, stand back from it and watch a *thought or emotion arising* as a thought or emotion rather than a reality.

Some depressed people can find even a short relaxation exercise stressful and so one might use a focus on an object. In our group work we sometimes use tennis balls. We invite the person to hold the ball and explore its texture and feel. As thoughts arise in the mind we can bring attention gently back to the tennis ball (Gilbert and Procter, 2006).

Mindfulness can help people change their *orientation* and relationship to the flow of their thoughts, feelings and sensations – they can become more non-judgementally observant rather than caught up in them. Recall that DBT (Linehan, 1993; Marra, 2003) uses mindfulness and attention training, not so much to be one step back from them but to be fully aware and in them. Obviously, if counsellors wish to use mindfulness or DBT more fully as a therapeutic process they should become trained in these approaches.

Another way of working this way is to note that we have an 'observing self' and that we can learn to attend via the observing self. So the next time you feel angry or anxious try to see if you can sense and note that a part of you is observing. The observing self is not angry or anxious but just observes. When 'seeing though the eyes' of the observing self one may also focus on slowing the breathing rate and calming. Some people find this a helpful way of working with their attention. Try it yourself and see how you get on. Because I focus on compassionate re-focusing (see Chapter 11), my own personal practice tends to infuse the observing self with compassion.

One can also teach people to identify sources of their negative thinking. One might suggest that 'our protection strategies are often pushing for attention'. So the thought 'this won't work' or 'I am failure' and the associated 'heart-sink feeling' is my protection strategy trying to encourage me to back off. I can compassionately notice them, acknowledge them but, unpleasant though they are, I can choose to think and do something different.

We should note here that mindfulness can be more that just learning to pay attention in a particular kind of way. There is increasing evidence that mindfulness *meditation* practice can influence various physical states and affect various illnesses (Baer, 2003). It also affects brain organisation and immune functioning – that is it affects patterns in our brains and brain states (Davidson, Kabat-Zinn, Schumacher, Rosenkranz, Muller et al., 2003). Thus the effects of mindfulness cannot be restricted to its impacts on psychological processes, but using a biopsychosocial approach can be seen as a process that impacts on various interacting systems. Mindfulness *meditation* practice can be a kind of physiotherapy for the brain. Indeed, mindfulness was not developed for any particular disorder but to develop inner states of mind and body that are conducive to well-being. This may be important because, as we have noted earlier, some depressions are related to stress systems becoming overloaded by frustration and a build-up of stressors. Mindfulness may be a way of toning down this vulnerability for depressive shifts of brain states. To use this approach fully one requires training and supervision.

Self-monitoring as investigation   Self-monitoring can be used in a more *investigative* way by helping people notice the content of their thoughts and emotions and, in particular, linkages between their thoughts, memories, behaviours and feelings. Here we help people to inference chain (see Chapter 9). The thinking goes: if A then B, if B then C. Recall, though, that in our automatic reactions we do not think in a linear fashion like this. A key question is to encourage the client to ask themself 'What is my key concern or fear here?' There are now many self-help books that offer a series of questions that can help people do this for themself (see Appendix). In depression these key fears are usually loss of control, social disconnection and defeat. In standard cognitive therapy the key fears/concerns are what the (social) *world* will do, what *the self* will do or become, and how *the future* will turn out (Beck et al., 1979). In Chapter 9 we distinguished between *internal* threat and *external* threat. Helping people monitor how their threat systems easily spring into action by noting thoughts and feelings as they emerge in the mind can be very helpful. However, some depressed people find this difficult or may produce some automatic thought records just before coming to counselling to please the counsellor.

Personal diaries, logs and journals   Depressed people may not be very skilled, at least to begin with, in identifying their thoughts or even their feelings (Parkinson, Totterdell, Brinder and Reynolds, 1996). Sometimes keeping a diary is a useful procedure. The client makes a record of events, thoughts, feelings and actions at the end of the day. The person is asked to note changes in moods or feelings during the day and note how these are associated with changes in thoughts/beliefs and personal meanings. For example, Jane noted that she tended to feel more depressed in the evenings and by noting her thoughts recognised a connection between feeling low and thoughts that her boyfriend may not phone, and if he didn't this meant he didn't really care about her. Diaries can then be the source for joint exploration. It is useful to try to encourage clients to be aware of their thoughts as they actually happen (Safran and Segal, 1990) and especially those that arise in the counselling session.

Personal journals are similar to diaries but here the person writes an ongoing review of therapy and makes notes for themselves. With some clients it is helpful to suggest they write about why they think they have become depressed – to write a mini autobiography and to note repetitive themes. This does not suit all clients but some find the act of writing about themselves gives them a new insight and awareness. The client can write anything they like here from past memories to current reflections on counselling. However, it is usually *not* useful to only write about the negatives in a ruminative sort of way. Rather, this is in the service of observation and being 'curious'. Also, one encourages the person to work with their thinking, behaviour and feelings on how to change. So you might suggest: 'Try to focus your journal on developing your *compassionate* understanding and what would help you to change and grow.'

Increasing self-awareness

Non-verbal behaviour   To increase a person's self-awareness it is useful to be attentive to their non-verbal behaviour (Greenberg and Watson, 2006; Safran and Segal, 1990) – the clenched hand or jaw or the averted eyes. The counsellor can draw attention to this, for example: 'I noted, while you were talking about your girlfriend, that your jaw seemed clenched and tight. Could you focus on your jaw and explore what was going through your mind?' Or 'What is your jaw saying?' Sometimes clients are not aware of these non-verbal changes. Directing their attention to them can be helpful and illuminating.

Fantasies   A lot of what goes through our minds are plans and expectations of things that take the form of inner imagination and fantasies (see Chapter 6). Humans have natural tendencies to internally rehearse, plan for good and bad events and fantasise (Wells, 2000). These serve various functions. Fantasy can be a source of inspiration, excitement, a way of escaping reality, or our projections into the future. For example, a depressed lady with a difficult life situation would often fantasise that someone would come and rescue her, rather than her changing her situation (which she felt powerless to do). Under stress she would always have in the back of her mind: 'Never mind, one day someone will come.' As the years passed and things got worse, this fantasy could no longer sustain her. In another case, whenever a client had an argument she would simply switch off and fantasise being alone. In this way she never engaged in conflict but nevertheless was depressed by the idea: 'It's no good, I shall have to live alone. Relationships are just too difficult.' She would then spend many hours thinking about and planning how to cope with living on her own rather than trying to understand the reasons for the relationship's difficulties and deal with them. Sometimes fantasies can even be of death. Depressive fantasies often contain an 'if only' element; if only I had done X or not done Y; if only I was like this or not like that.

It is not always the case that clients will tell you of their repetitive fantasies (sometimes due to shame and sometimes due to the feeling that these are part of the deepest, inner self), and therefore one has to ask for them (e.g. 'What are your main fantasies or day dreams? When you find yourself wandering off into your inner thoughts, what kind of thoughts and images do you have or dwell on?'). As noted in Chapter 7, some clients have fantasises about their therapist.

Video play   Our natural abilities to create fantasies can be used in what can be called the video procedure. In this procedure you ask the person to make a kind of inner video of situations. For example, a person is frightened to act assertively. So you could say: 'Let's take a particular situation in which you would like to be more assertive and make an inner video. Start with being in a situation – what is happening?' The client describes a situation. 'Now run the video on to where you start to act assertively. What is happening?' As the person runs through the scenario from start to finish the counsellor obtains information about what is going through the person's mind. Let's look at an assertiveness example. Anne had difficulties in addressing her upset over her partner's behaviour of going to the pub and leaving her behind. So we did a video play. She closed her eyes and 'played the video' of events in her mind.

Anne:	I can see myself starting to tell Fred how cross I am at his going out. I feel anxious.
Counsellor:	Okay run the video on. What is happening?
Anne:	He is looking angry – like I am a pain.
Counsellor:	What are you thinking at this point?
Anne:	Oh no, he is not going to listen to me. He is just going to storm out.
Counsellor:	Okay, you see indicators that he will storm out. What are you feeling and thinking?
Anne:	I am becoming anxious and more angry. I wish he would listen.
Counsellor:	Okay, what happens next?
Anne:	I can see myself get tongue-tied, or just getting more angry. It all goes wrong. He storms out.
Counsellor:	What happens now – when he is gone?
Anne:	I feel lots of things, angry I guess and sad – let down but also that I shouldn't provoke him like this. Maybe I am a real pain to live with. Then I feel more depressed.
Counsellor:	Because you have these scenes in your mind, is this why you rarely challenge Fred?
Anne:	Yes, I guess so. It is only when I can't take it any more that I have a go at him.

This procedure allows you to gather a lot of information quickly. We learn that Anne gets angry before confronting Fred. She 'lets things' build up partly because she predicts her boyfriend will simply cut off from her if she challenges him (which he does when she is angry). Then when he is gone she feels *defeated* and alone and starts to self-blame. You are possibly already starting to formulate ideas for intervention. Could Anne learn to express her feelings in a more gentle, assertive and less angry way? Could she give up self-blame and seeing herself as a pain if Fred does walk out? Might there be other reasons that Fred storms out (e.g. that part of him feels guilty or ashamed and he cuts himself off from this)? 'Video play' can be used in many situations to obtain information on imagined or actual sequences or scenes, for example various anxieties, fears of abandonment and so forth. One can then begin to explore alternative video plays, scripting them in more helpful ways. So one might say: 'Let's imagine a different outcome. How might we get there?'

Role play   Actual role play is another powerful procedure for eliciting various forms of meaning and is a useful way of eliciting affect and demonstrating the power of automatic reactions in the counselling situation. There are a number of ways this can be done. For example, consider Anne, who is frightened of behaving assertively in many situations. She could be asked to role play an assertive sequence of behaviour. The counsellor then explores the beliefs about this (e.g. I am being unkind; Fred will think I am being selfish/unreasonable and I must maintain his approval; or, I will be embarrassed and my mind will go blank). Over time the counsellor may also introduce her to various assertive skills.

Other forms of role play can involve the re-enactment of previous painful events (e.g. arguments). Again, the counsellor can check the personal meanings about these episodes. Subsequently, they can practise alternative behaviours and cognitive responses. These include various fantasy role plays with emotional memories (Hackmann, 2005). Clients try out their new skills in real-life situations. As a rule of thumb, role play works best when the client and counsellor have developed a good working alliance. Without this the client may feel too self-conscious, not really get into the role play but just mimic it, and not really be in touch with the powerful emotions that need to be understood and worked with.

Ruminating

We noted in Chapter 6 that rumination is another spin-off from our higher level, self-conscious abilities that give rise to various meta-cognitive abilities. Rumination can often be ignited by how we respond to threats. Ed Watkins, from the University of Exeter, has done a lot of work on rumination and points out that when things go wrong the *threat* emotions of anger and fear can dominate our thinking. To use one of his examples, you have to go for an important interview. You are all dressed up but the car won't start. The ruminator panics and starts thinking: 'Oh God why does this have to happen to me and why today? This is typical of my life – things always go wrong. What's the matter with this bloody car? This car is a bastard, letting me down at the most important times!' The non-ruminator is still upset but finds ways to solve the problem: phones for a taxi and lets the interview panel know they will be late. The non-ruminator (who is more likely to have come from a secure attachment background) will expect others to be understanding while the ruminator (from an insecure background) will expect others to be condemning and unforgiving. So rumination is linked to aroused emotions, key fears and problem-solving styles.

It is now recognised that (in addition to various social problems) depressed patients tend to ruminate on why they feel so bad and the negative features of themselves, their world and their future (see pp. 119–120). Rumination plays a major role in why depression can become stuck and self-perpetuating. As we saw in Chapter 6, humans have evolved complex way of creating internal meanings with meta-cognition and self-reflection. For example, following the break-up of a relationship, one person may have a period of grief, recognise what they are going through is most unpleasant but a normal reaction, and use friends as supports. A person prone to depression, however, may personalise the break-up and feel it was due to some characteristic about them (e.g. they are boring or undesirable in some way). They then predict that they won't be able to develop meaningful, intimate relationships and are destined to be emotionally alone. They may stop going out. If these conclusions are not bad enough, they will then ruminate on how bad it will be now, given that they are going to be alone forever. In essence, the depressed person may see the break-up as a major loss of their social goals. You can explain to the person why ruminating is unhelpful by using some illustrations, for example:

> The way we think about things affects our emotions and our bodies. For instance, if you are hungry and you see a meal, this will make your mouth water. However, just *imagining* a good meal can have the same effect because your images and thoughts stimulate those areas of your brain that control your stomach acids and saliva. We often find that planning a good holiday and *just thinking* about it can give us a burst of good feeling or excitement. This is all because *our thoughts affect our bodies.* Equally, when we ruminate on stressful things we are stimulating stress hormones in our body and feel bad. So, one thing we can try to do is to keep track of our attention and, to the best of our ability, refocus our attention when we find it is ruminating on things that disturb and upset us. This may take some of the pressure off the stress system.
>
> When we get depressed it is quite natural for us to start ruminating on all the negative things in our lives, our symptoms, feelings and life difficulties. However, if possible, and to the best of your ability, try to notice when your mind is on that ruminative treadmill. We can then explore ways to refocus attention so that it is less likely to activate more stress. Some of what we will be doing together is aimed to help you get off this understandable but unhelpful ruminative treadmill. The idea in refocusing is to help break the loop between ruminating, feeling bad and ruminating.

Check that the client sees and understands this point. You can ask about their typical ruminations and ask if they think it would be helpful to reduce this rumination. One very useful way to combat rumination is with activity (see below). Also, tackling key issues (e.g. resentment, fear of change or fear of depression lasting) that can underpin rumination can be helpful. Developing a compassionate focus can also help with rumination (see Chapter 11).

Key issues 9.1   Self-monitoring and awareness training

1   As part of change the client needs to become more aware of their internal meaning-making, thoughts, beliefs and key fears/concerns and their linkages.
2   Awareness training is focused on the links between internal meaning and affective state.
3   Awareness training can take various forms such as learning mindfulness, monitoring feelings and thoughts, re-enacting events focusing on images, fantasising and being aware of non-verbal behaviour.
4   Once these meanings and cognitive styles are identified, they are subjected to progressive clarification, exposure and change.

Behavioural focusing

Behavioural experiments are now basic to many approaches to depression (Bennett-Levy et al., 2004; Martell et al., 2001). They are used for many different aspects, such as gathering more information or testing out a fear or core belief and reducing safety behaviours. A subtle point here is to focus on gaining evidence to show and *validate a positive* rather than disprove a negative. For example:

> Jane: I just can't get up in the mornings because I feel so bad.
> Counsellor: Would that help you – to get up rather than lay in bed?
> Jane: Oh yes.
> Counsellor: What would help you to have a go at this in the next day or two?
> Jane: Well I guess I could force myself out of bed.
> Counsellor: Okay, that is one way. What about trying to be kind here. Think: 'Gosh, it is hard to get up but I am going to have a go and see how far I can get. I can gently encourage myself and be understanding of how hard it is but still really try. I will probably feel better if I could.' In other words try to create warmth and understanding in your efforts.

When Jane is successful, then we can say: 'So you see actually you have a lot more courage than you have given yourself credit for. Your efforts are really impressive because you feel bad in the mornings.' Do not say: 'So you see your predictions are wrong; you can get up if you try!' You can't validate proving somebody wrong! This is central to compassion work (see Chapter 11). Behavioural experiments are worked out with the person and then tried. They can be used in a wide variety of contexts. The above is also an example of working against what our feelings entice us to do (see Chapter 4).

Independent or personal practice

Practising things covered in this and subsequent chapters is sometimes referred to as homework, although nowadays *independent practice* is regarded as a better term to avoid associations with school days. Developing a joint understanding of the value of when, why and how to engage in independent practice is important, although clients vary as to the ease in which they engage in it. Independent practice can be a key part of helping depressed people, not only for gathering more information on difficulties but mostly for beginning to develop new repertoires, skills and expectancies. It is useful to encourage the client to suggest their own ideas for things to have a go at (e.g. 'How do you think you could practise working on this difficulty?', or 'Given what we have been speaking about, what do you think would be helpful to try?'). In planning independent practice with depressed people, there are some tips to follow.

Challenging but not overwhelming   In the same way that you learn to drive, you would not go on to a motorway the first time out. So behavioural experiments and independent practice need to be realistic and approached as graded tasks (see also Dryden, 1985; Martell et al., 2001).

Chain analysis   The process of chain analysis in DBT (Linehan, 1993; Marra, 2003) helps people learn to identify key steps that have led up to a change in mood, crises or painful emotions. You can draw this out like a stepping stone diagram, trying to identify key points. Chain analysis can also be used by devising stepping stones away from the undesired outcomes. This helps to identify where a person could have acted differently to get out of 'automatic pilot' mode (e.g 'If this happens again, I could do this rather than that'). The process aids awareness that *there are* alternatives and that difficulties do not have to get caught in repetitive ruts. People can try out behavioural experiments and see what helps. Are there some stepping stones missing? Would this one be better than that?

Exposure   Exposure is also very important in behavioural work and this means accessing key emotions associated with various difficulties. As noted above, there are various ways to bring these emotions into the therapy situation (e.g. via fantasies, directed recall, role play). Here the therapist and depressed person should have agreed ways of working with these emotions when they are aroused and have an understanding of the importance of engagement and desensitisation as a way of working (Greenberg and Watson, 2006). If people are reluctant to engage with certain issues because of fears, then one might *gently* inquire: 'I wonder how you will feel if you go through therapy without addressing this?' Or 'I wonder what you might feel about me if I did not try to address this with you and left you to continue to bear it alone?' Various approaches, such as looking at advantages and disadvantages, can also help illuminate and develop awareness of key sticking points (Leahy, 2002).

Getting better by bearing discomfort   Although instilling hope is important, as therapy progresses you will share times when engaging fears or doubts and acting against depressing thoughts and avoidance behaviours may be hard to do at first (Beck et al., 1985; Leahy, 2001; Linehan, 1993). Progress can be made in steps and your encouragement and support can be crucial. People are more likely to make the efforts and bear the discomfort if they can see how and why it might be helpful to do so (Bennett-Levy et al., 2004).

Disqualifying achievements   Typical here are the ideas that 'Anyone could do that. Compared to what I used to do it is so simple.' Help clients to *imagine* that if they have fallen into a deep hole, it helps to have a ladder that they walk up rung by rung as it is not possible to jump to the top. Thus the image is on 'moving forward' rather than unrealistic expectations. The key issue is a step-by-step approach (Gilbert, 2000a).

Independent practice to please the counsellor

Sometimes clients will engage in independent practice or other therapy tasks to please the counsellor, and not because they really understand why they are doing it. This is not always problematic because if they start off like this but then learn that the practice really does help, there is a shift in motivation. Also, this can help the therapeutic relationship. However, watch out for them only saying it helps to please you or because they are fearful of telling you your therapy is not helping. Some clients write out their thought forms neatly but on exploration they lack emotional engagement. The client is writing down what they think is expected of them, not what actually helps them.

Feeling worse

If clients say that their independent work makes them feel worse the counsellor is able to use this to advantage (e.g. 'Well, this is helpful because we can look more closely at what is going on', or 'Well, this is helpful since it shows that you are really engaging in the practice'). The counsellor should be cautious of falling into the trap of expecting the client to feel better with independent practice and becoming disheartened when the client says they feel worse. The more the counsellor allows the client to feel worse from independent practice, the easier it is for the client not to fear bringing negative information to the counselling. We want to avoid the client thinking outside counselling: 'Well, I didn't like to tell my counsellor this or that because they are trying so hard and it would upset them', or 'I don't want to tell my counsellor this does not work because it upsets them and they may lose interest in helping me'. Also the counsellor should avoid setting themself up in the position of trying to get the client better. This usually leads to exhausted counsellors and problems in counselling. The process is collaboration, with agreement on the purpose of the therapeutic endeavour (see Liotti, 2007).

Some further aspects to bear in mind

Power and control

Power is different from control in that one may not be able to control an outcome as one would like, but this does not mean one is powerless. There are things one can do to exert choice over the outcome. For example, a suicidal depressed man felt very angry with how his employers had responded to his time off work – they wanted him to resign. While he was preoccupied with the unfairness of it and the need to fight them, he felt powerless, overwhelmed and subordinate to them – they were a big organisation and his union did not think he would win a case. Once he accepted that there was in reality little he could do (after talking to his union), he began to explore how he could turn it into an advantage, to see if he could get redundancy pay, which he successfully negotiated. He did not have to control the outcome in order to exert power in the situation and try to gain some advantage. Key beliefs were: 'I must not let them treat me this way. If I do, I am a weak, useless person'. The key fear was of 'being weak and the world rolling me over'.

Also involved can be *turning what is seen as a weakness into a strength*. For example, the above person had hated his job but felt he had to stay in it to prove himself. Thoughts of moving on were seen as weak, an escape and an admission of defeat. Reconstruing escape as a strength and a sign of flexibility was helpful and counteracted feelings of powerlessness. In other words, if one has tried to make something successful and it does not work out, then leaving and finding a new opportunity is useful. It is the cognitions that 'one has to prove oneself' or that leaving a difficult situation is a sign of defeat, weakness, inadequacy or inferiority, that is often inhibiting. These cognitions can produce the feelings of entrapment and depression. Much depends on the individual case, however. In some situations it may in practice be very difficult to change a situation. In other cases, a depressed client may not have really tried to make a success of a situation or relationship, thinking it would fail from the outset (see Chapter 4).

Awareness of developmental abilities and maturation

Some clients are not capable of abstract thinking but are still at a stage of more concrete thinking (McCullough, 2000; Rosen, 1989). A counsellor needs to be aware of the cognitive and conceptual abilities of the client. Sometimes one is helping this maturation process (Gilbert, 1995a). Consequently, only engage in interventions that a client will understand and is capable of achieving.

Cognitive therapy can aid maturation. This occurs because as a person changes in counselling, they are not just reprogramming themselves, but are gaining a deeper insight into the causes and origins of their self–other experiences and judgements. They may experience validation in the therapy, settle their attachment systems and develop better theory of mind skills. They may become more trusting of others and less critical of themselves. In ways that research has yet to make clear, there can be a more integrated sense of self that emerges out of the counselling experience. With maturation, attitudes and styles of thinking and responding become more flexible and varied. There is an evolution and growth of the self (Kegan, 1982). There has been a growing recognition that sometimes clients are not at a sufficiently developed stage in their maturation process to cope with complex interventions and the counsellor needs to have some awareness of this (Beck et al., 1990). Also, efforts are being made to integrate cognitive approaches with developmental concepts derived from Piaget and Erikson (see Freeman, Simon, Beutler and Arkowitz, 1989; Mahoney, 2003; Mahoney and Gabriel, 1987; McCullough, 2000). These efforts now represent different schools of cognitive counselling (e.g. the rationalists and the constructionists). Mahoney and Gabriel (1987) offer a good introduction to these issues.

Growth

Although it is painful, some clients can turn their depression into an opportunity for growth and become 'better than before' (Gut, 1989). Here the counsellor draws attention to their increased insights and understanding, their new skill for controlling depressed feelings, and so on. One may ask: 'What has your depression taught you? How have you changed?' This turns depression as a weakness (and something shameful) into depression as an opportunity. However, these aspects normally come when progress is well under way. In the early days a person may see nothing positive in being depressed and it is not a good idea to explore this too early in counselling.

Sometimes we become disturbed because we have failed to engage a developmental challenge. We cling to old ways of thinking and behaving because they seem safe. Thus change can be seen and discussed as a developmental challenge, a chance to move forward and grow. Sometimes clients come through a depression not just to return to their old premorbid styles but to change in major ways.

Painful dilemmas

As depression begins there are shifts in a range of cognitive styles, emotions, behavioural patterns and body states. We can lose focus and get trapped in negative thoughts going around and around in our heads. We can feel like rats trapped in a dark maze. Stepping into this maze and helping people to make sense of where they are, to find a way out, using the various approaches we have addressed here, is helpful to people. However, do keep in mind that depression is often centred around real-life events, difficulties and dilemmas. Behavioural work involves working with these dilemmas in a sensitive way.

Conclusion

This chapter has explored ways of engaging with the depressed person, increasing their awareness of the connections between thinking, feeling and behaviour, trying out new behaviours and working collaboratively. The formulations discussed in Chapter 9, acts as a backdrop for other 'mini' formulations and give a focus for specific types of intervention. Depressed people may find these interventions difficult at first, and thus require encouragement to practise them. The counsellor will be aware of various self-defeating thoughts, such as ideas that practice won't work. These are tackled sensitively and compassionately, by noting that they are understandable but also act as blocks, and that they can be addressed collaboratively.

In the next chapter, we will explore how to aid these interventions, specifically emphasising a compassionate focus. As for many therapies now, the idea is not so much to (just) become more rational, but to find ways that are soothing to us and that advance our personal goals and our sources of well-being.

11 Developing Self-Compassion

The last few chapters focused on ways of formulating depression, engaging, and steps out of depression. Before going into more detail on working with specific thoughts and feelings, I want to introduce you to a way of orientating your work through the lens of compassion. We first noted this idea in Chapter 7 on the therapeutic relationship. What I will suggest here is that therapy can be focused on helping a depressed (and especially self-critical) person develop *self*-compassion. By the end of this chapter I hope to have conveyed the idea that whatever 'techniques' we may use, they may work better if they are internalised as a way to nurture, care for, and be compassionate to the self.

To link this to the approach outlined here, we can remind ourselves that depression is an emergent brain state with certain psychobiological response patterns. Because of the way humans have evolved to be able to think, reflect and have self-awareness, depressed people's thinking and coping style can accentuate and maintain depressive psychobiological patterns. It therefore makes sense to help depressed people change their thinking, reduce rumination, and act in ways that engage with, rather than avoid, life difficulties and certain emotions.

Compassion-focused therapy builds on these ideas and utilises a range of cognitive behavioural and emotion-focused procedures and interventions. Although compassion-focused therapy can be linked to older systems of thought, such as Mahayan Buddhism (Gilbert, 2005a; Glaser, 2005), my own approach is rooted in evolution theory (Gilbert, 1989, 1992) and recent work on the neuroscience of emotion (Panksepp, 1998). As we have noted, depressive brain states and their psychobiological response patterns are linked to innate protection strategies that evolved for coping with loss of control over social resources, social disconnection and defeat, and can pull affect systems, thinking and behaviour in certain ways. These strategies are 'run' in the brain via a patterning of interactions between three key affect systems: *threat*, *drive* and *contentment/soothing* (see Chapters 2 and 3). As people become depressed, threat systems begin to exert more influence over processing and feeling states. Drive systems are toned down (to stop behaviour that may have low pay-offs or end in aversive outcomes) and people feel exhausted or lose energy and motivation to engage in 'doing'. Central for what we will discuss, however, is that abilities to feel socially connected, content and soothed can also be toned down. So we can direct our therapy to trying to stimulate them again, to do the work of regulating the threat and drive systems. We want to change the organising psychobiological patterns of a depressed mind.

This way of thinking about depression affects how one structures therapy. Cognitive behavioural and other focused therapies use a range of interventions to try to tone down threat processing (e.g. re-evaluating threat-focused thoughts and reducing rumination) and operate on drive systems by trying to help people increase their behaviours, especially those associated with positively reinforcing outcomes. Feelings of loss of control and entrapment can be helped with problem solving and working with dilemmas. However, while many therapies focus on self-acceptance, re-igniting a sense of social connection via the therapeutic relationship and guided social activities, compassion-focused approaches also focus on the extraordinary importance of the contentment/soothing system. We have seen that this system evolved as a regulator of threat and drive systems. Contentment tones down drive and seeking systems (Depue and Morrone-Strupinsky, 2005). Moreover, when we feel content we do not feel threatened, but safe (Gilbert, 1989). During evolution this system became used by the social affiliation and attachment system. From the first days of life, mammalian infants' psychobiological systems are regulated by experiencing the care and soothing from a parent (Carter, 1998). Children who do not receive these soothing inputs, or where parents and peers are more threatening (bullying) than soothing, become overly regulated by threat and drive systems (Perry et al., 1995). Because of these experiences a whole range of protection strategies, including those for lowered mood, become easily activated. Basically, if you do not feel safe in the world, your brain will try to go for next best options. This is why insecure attachments are so commonly linked to vulnerability to psychopathology and why secure and loving attachments can do much to reduce vulnerabilities to depression – even if you carry a genetic risk (Caspi and Moffitt, 2006; Suomi, 1999; Taylor et al., 2006).

Lacking the ability to feel safe or soothed

If you follow this way of thinking about depression, then although you may be helping people with their emotions, thinking and behaviour and to reactivate drive/engagement rather than avoidance, you will also be trying to help them activate or reactivate their soothing systems for self-organisation. In essence, you will be thinking how you might enable this basic affect soothing system to be engaged and help to regulate and tone down depressive self-protection.

I have worked with shame and self-critical depression for many years and what has struck me is just how difficult it is for sufferers to ever feel soothed, reassured or content – even at times when they are not depressed. Here are some examples of the sorts of things depressed people often say about their ability to enjoy things and feel content.

- 'I have never really felt content with my life – there always seemed so much I had to do.'
- 'Even when I was successful I could never stop to enjoy it. It was the anticipating and doing that gave me a buzz but never the actual achievement. In my heart I would always think "yes but" it is not quite good enough and I would be looking for the next thing to do or buy.'
- 'Even when I am on holiday my mind focuses on work and I think of all the problems waiting for me when I get back – it stops me enjoying the moment.'

Such views are quite consistent with ideas regarding core beliefs, assumptions and modes (Beck, 1996). They are also consistent with notions of elevated stress.

However, they point to long-lived problems in enjoyment, and being content and at peace with oneself, with difficulties in enjoying and appreciating simple things. What about the social soothing system? Here again depressed people may often have difficulties.

- 'I rarely feel safe with other people. Even if people are kind to me I don't really feel it and think that they are just pretending to be nice.'
- 'It is difficult for me to feel loved and wanted. In my head I know my partner loves me but just can't feel close to them.'
- 'If people knew the real me they would not like me.'
- 'I feel there is this wall around me and I am completely disconnected from the world and others in it.'
- 'All my life I have been bullied: at home, school and now at work. So you just have to keep people at arms' length.'

What about people's relationship with themselves? Can they derive any sense of contentment or be self-supportive?

- 'I have always had this feeling of not really being good enough. If I make a mistake, I get a sinking feeling and get really angry with myself.'
- 'I sometimes wish I was someone else – not me.'
- 'You don't get anywhere in life unless you are prepared to criticise and push yourself.'
- 'Compared to others I am so useless.'

Cognitive behavioural therapists would focus on these as indicators of core beliefs and schema, which at one level they may be. But they also reveal a lot about the person's underlying organisation of affect, sense of threat and self-protection systems, and the long-lived experience of never really feeling safe. Moreover, self-critical people and those feeling deep-seated shame do not easily feel reassured by changes in thinking (Rector et al., 2000). They may understand the logic of cognitive-focused interventions but may say 'I can see the logic but it doesn't always help me feel better'. There is a cognition-emotion mismatch.

Focusing on what is helpful

Cognitive-behavioural therapists have gradually moved away from focusing on concepts of 'logic' and 'rationality,' as a therapeutic process, important though these can be. They recognise that much of what we do – things that bring us pleasure – is not because it is rational but because it helps us to achieve valued goals, and valued goals are linked to important evolutionary outcomes such as developing helpful relationships, having families, making valued contributions and exerting control over resources. You can still find books that talk about identifying 'cognitive errors' and 'correcting faulty or distorted' thinking rather than in terms of biases (a far more shame-free term). However, many cognitive therapists now talk in terms of *helpful and unhelpful* (or anti-depressive and depressive) thinking and behaviour. The catch to this is that in order for some interventions or alternative thoughts to be helpful they have to be *felt* to be helpful. Even with something that might be difficult to do at first, if you can imagine it as being helpful, imagine how good it would feel *if you could* do it, then that will help you. It is the *experience* of helpfulness that is key.

Becoming more evidence-focused for some people is experienced as helpful and reassuring. For example, focusing on evidence against a negative view can bring things into perspective and tones down threat – it is a relief. But supposing you can't imagine certain outcomes as helpful, you don't know what it would be like to feel reassured, safe and content. Recognising that one is being illogical, and it would be better to think this or that way, may not actually change how we feel. Indeed, many depressed people know that some of their thinking is irrational and is different from how they think when not depressed. However, they can be so threat-focused that their minds keep coming up with 'yes buts'. Trying to convince someone of an alternative view using logic may become quite *unhelpful* and they may feel shame for not being able to change. So we need to understand this concept of *'helpful'* in much more detail. We need to think that maybe there is a problem in the emotion systems that give rise to the *feeling* that something is helpful, feelings of reassurance and abilities to feel safe. If this affect system is not working, then no amount of logic will help.

Although not framed in quite this way, this kind of approach has become central to working with anxiety and trauma-based problems. The therapist works directly with the fear emotions in a traumatic memory so that the person can experience *current* safeness while recalling a memory. Exposure to anxiety is designed to enable an experience of sufficient safeness (e.g. the panic did not lead to a heart attack) that changes negative beliefs and safety behaviours (Clark and Ehlers, 2004; Salkovskis, 1996a) and memory activation (Brewin, 2006; Lee, 2005). What is sometimes less acknowledged is the role of the therapist as a source of reassurance, safeness, and encouragement as people enter aversive states (Gilbert, 1989, 2007).

Some depressed people acknowledge that they may rarely have felt reassured or safe. They may have few emotional memories of such feelings. Over a number of years I have been keen to see if there are ways we could help depressed people develop self-soothing as a source of safeness; to work directly with the core *experience of helpfulness*. I have discussed these ideas (that depression is related to threat-focused protection strategies and that self-soothing may be an important quality to tone them down) with many depressed people. They have provided many fascinating insights (Gilbert and Irons, 2004). One way I do this is to draw out the three emotion circles outlined in Chapter 2 and discuss with them how our thoughts and emotions are related to these systems. The aim in therapy then becomes trying to get the different affect regulation systems into a more helpful relationship to each other. Once people understand what we are trying to do, the purpose of our intentions and efforts, they are more likely to become active collaborators in the process. Some may identify thoughts and feelings such as 'this is my threat-protection system thinking through me' or 'this is my drive system'.

Soothing

Kindness, warmth and gentleness are evolved signals that, under normal conditions, activate soothing systems in recipients (Wang, 2005). So in the mid-1990s I started to use various cognitive-behavioural interventions but asked people to hold the alternatives in mind, close their eyes and really imagine the feelings associated with the alternatives. I suggested that (once an alternative thought had been agreed as reasonable) they imagine the alternative *with the emotions of kindness and warmth* so that they could experience the alternative as soothing and helpful. I would ask them to focus on their breathing for a moment and relax, and then bring the alternative thought/idea/interpretation to mind with warmth, kindness and understanding. I would slow the process down and speak in as slow, calming and soothing a way as I could (i.e. I was trying to activate the soothing system and code this into the alternative). Sometimes it was helpful to suggest the following:

> Imagine someone who really cares about you speaking to you. Or imagine a part of yourself that is capable of kindness and care – that part of you that you might show to a child or person you care about in distress. Try to focus on that feeling and then with that feeling in mind bring your negative thoughts to mind and talk yourself through your alternative thoughts with warmth. Focus less on the words or trying to convince yourself of the alternative and more on the emotion of warmth in the alternative.

This is like a behavioural approach when one is trying to stimulate an alternative affect (like a relaxation response) to that of anxiety. It is not the logic, rationality or evidence that is key (though these are important too) but the emotional tone of self-talk and self-refection that is central. Because depressed people have the framework of the three emotion circles, they can understand the point of this. Because they are collaborators, you can ask: 'How did that work for you? How might we improve this to get more feeling into your alternative thoughts?'

Some clients quickly get the idea of 'feeling' the alternative rather than only 'thinking' it. In my discussions with clients they said that focusing on feelings of warmth and kindness first, or at the same time, made a huge difference to how they experienced their alternative thoughts – they seemed more believable and soothing. I was excited by this and tentatively introduced some of these ideas into the second edition of *Overcoming Depression* (Gilbert, 2000a). I continued (and continue) to use many interventions developed by cognitive and behavioural therapists (Socratic discussion, guide discovery, exposure and behavioural experiments) but wanted to do far more on the emotional textures of these interventions. In essence, we are facilitating a kind of *physiotherapy* for the mind (Gilbert and Irons, 2005); working a system of soothing.

Compassion can be scary

Many depressed people I work with have chronic depressions and often have a diagnosis of personality difficulties. When I began to introduce a kindness and warmth focus I ran into some major problems that were to convince me that for these people the soothing system is seriously compromised. Rather than feel relief at kindness, they began to cry and shut down. One client panicked and dissociated. When I asked them to think of feelings of kindness for someone they cared for and then, when they could imagine that feeling, to imagine it being directed at themselves, they could often do the first part, but when it came to feeling it for themselves they could not do it and noted that their feelings turned cold and harsh. They talked about feelings of self-kindness as being strange, sad and overwhelming, or just going blank.

One way of thinking about this is that the soothing system has become conditioned with threat signals. Feelings of kindness and warmth emanate from the social attachment system and when we activate these feelings we are activating this system. Recall that Ferster (1973; see also Chapter 4) pointed out that one emotion could become a condition stimulus for another. Hence children's care-eliciting feelings and desires for self-soothing (if they were frequently punished) could become conditioned to aversive emotions. It certainly seemed as if, for some people, trying to activate feelings of self-soothing triggered threat systems.

Another theme to emerge in discussion with depressed people was that when they began to acknowledge feelings of warmth, kindness and desires to feel safe this opened up a set of emotional (attachment) memories that were filled with feelings of sadness, abandonment and aloneness. These feelings produced extraordinary and powerful feelings of grief which they had spent a long time trying to keep at bay. For example, Jane had been adopted early in her life and her adopted mother was harsh and critical. When Jane began to do kindness-focused work she had a spontaneous memory of having been beaten by her mother and laying on her bed looking at the stars imagining her biological mother coming on a chariot to rescue her. Over the years she had learnt to avoid these feelings and memories because they overwhelmed her with sadness and aloneness. These kinds of experiences suggested that the soothing system, like other affect systems, can be under inhibitory control. Moreover, that inhibitory control is primarily self-protective and as you begin to work with those safety mechanisms, unprocessed feelings and memories can begin to come through. The therapist needs to have a clear view about how to handle powerful attachment fears, sadness and grief, and be able to contain them, normalise them and allow the person to tolerate feelings of sadness that they may have been avoiding (Globert, in press; Gilbert and Irons, 2005; Greenberg and Watson, 2006).

Another level with difficulties to the soothing system is related to people's *beliefs* about being kind, warm and compassionate to themselves. Some people, for example, believe that they don't deserve to be kind to themselves: it is letting them off the hook; they will become weak and vulnerable; they won't be able to 'push' themselves into achievements. One person described the beginning of compassion work as 'weak' and 'wet'. When people have negative beliefs about being compassionate the therapist always follows the threat-fear.

Jane: When I try to focus on being kind to myself, I just feel I don't deserve it.

Counsellor: Okay Jane. What is the fear in having something you do not deserve?

Jane: It will be taken away or I will be punished.

Counsellor: That feels like a frightening thing.

Jane: Yes. Thinking about it, I see it is. [Pauses.] Like someone will find me out and punish me.

Counsellor: So let's just be compassionate to the fear of punishment and note how sad that is for you.

We did not discuss the nature of deserving but the fear of having something for herself that could be taken away. At this point Jane became tearful and we explored how this fear of having things that she could be punished for, or wanting and seeking things for herself, or being kind to herself but feeling they were bad, had 'been with her a long time'. There is another example.

Sally:	This warmth feeling you are trying to help me feel – well, I don't really like it.
Counsellor:	What is it you don't like about it?
Sally:	It makes me feel vulnerable.
Counsellor:	Can you focus on that threat for you?
Sally:	I don't know, like I will be letting my guard down and then, well I don't know, I just feel something bad will happen. Something will hit me out of the blue.
Counsellor:	Okay. What if we are compassionate to the fear. Try to look at that fear – that you must not let your guard down – with kindness.
Sally:	[Looks down and becomes tearful] Oh no – not there. God that makes me feel sad, but I don't want to cry here.

As with other depressed people there was an avoidance and fear of sadness; that it would be too much, too overwhelming. Sally went on to describe how her parents were highly unpredictable and that 'you could be happily playing in the garden one minute and then mother would have one of her rages, or Dad would come home drunk and we would have to keep out of his way. You just never knew and had to stay alert.' For Sally, warmth had the feeling of letting go her vigilance, with a fear of 'allowing herself to play with not a care in the world'. Not only was this frightening, but it also brought recognition of how hard it had been for her to just be herself without fear. Later we listed the things she was sad about: always being frightened as a child, not having parents who cared for her in the way she wanted; the bullying at school; the breakdown of her marriage. This was a very moving session. Later she reflected that she had not fully realised how much sadness she had 'held inside her'. Becoming compassionate with herself allowed her to process these feelings and experiences, and brought new insights and feelings. She was also able to reflect what strengths she had developed as a result of these life events.

So we have to imagine what it is like for people attempting to use cognitive behaviour techniques but who have very little sense of warmth. I have found that their efforts to re-evaluate their negative thoughts or develop new behaviours are often done in a cold and sometimes hostile/bullying manner. It is as if the only way they know how to help themselves is by self-bullying and forcing themselves to do things. The whole idea that warmth, encouragement, support, gentleness, kindness are also ways of helping us grow and face our difficulties can seem like an anathema to them. Generally they have tried to feel better through achieving, forcing themselves to do things, staying vigilant and keeping threats at bay. However, if they cannot achieve these, then they perceive the outside world (e.g. other people around them) turning hostile and critical, and their internal world also becomes self-attacking, hostile and critical. They have nowhere to go. Depression is the shut-down protection. However, if one can help them develop a compassion focus, teach them how to generate soothing thoughts, emotions and images and offer them some 'space' when things feel overwhelming, this can provide a completely new way of being within themselves.

Developing self-compassion

We can see there are a number of good reasons for focusing on self-compassion as a therapeutic intervention. First, the contentment and soothing affect system may be relatively undeveloped or toned down in some clients and/or under inhibitory control from fear, self-criticism and negative beliefs. Second, there is increasing evidence that developing self-compassion is an important process in overcoming emotional difficulties and also facilitates well-being. Neff (2003a, 2003b; Neff, Kirkpatrick and Rude, 2007) has clarified how and why self-compassion is different from self-esteem (see also Gilbert and Irons, 2005, pp. 292–3). Self-esteem tends to focus on abilities to do, achieve and master, while self-compassion focuses on abilities to understand, empathise, acknowledge and forgive. Third, there are increasing efforts to integrate compassion into more traditional therapies (Allen and Knight, 2005; McKay and Fanning, 1992; Gilbert, 2000c; Gilbert and Irons, 2005).

Attributes of self-compassion

We discussed compassion for others, and in particular within the therapeutic relationship, in Chapter 7. We saw that compassion is a complex, multifaceted process with various qualities. These qualities evolved with the care-giving system and are designed to have a soothing impact on recipients (Gilbert, 1989, 2005a). *Self-compassion* really involves learning to direct these same qualities and talents to the self. Introducing self-compassion into standard therapies is not a new idea and different therapies have slightly different views of it. For example, McKay and Fanning (1992), who developed a cognitive-based self-help programme for self-esteem, view self-compassion as involving *understanding, acceptance* and *forgiveness*. Neff (2003a, 2003b), from a social psychology and Buddhist tradition, sees *self-focused* compassion as consisting of bipolar constructs related to kindness, common humanity and mindfulness. *Kindness* involves understanding one's difficulties and being kind and warm in the face of failure or setbacks rather than harshly judgemental and self-critical. *Common humanity* involves seeing one's experiences as part of the human condition rather than as personal, isolating and shaming. Mindful *acceptance* involves mindful awareness and acceptance of painful thoughts and feelings rather than over-identifying with them (see also Allen and Knight, 2005).

My approach to compassion is rooted in social mentality theory (Gilbert, 1989, 2000c, 2005a, 2005b). The compassion model I use suggests that compassionate behaviour evolved out of *care-giving* that first evolved in the context of maternal care for offspring and later was used for friendship formations and mutual support (Wang, 2005). To be caring requires abilities to be sensitive to the distress of others, and being motivated to promote their welfare. For the recipient, signals from others that are kind, warm and caring, and offer mutual support, stimulate the soothing and safeness system. When the mother is moved by the distress of her infant, she engages in behaviours that seek to calm the distress of her infant in a role relationship. It is this kind of relationship one seeks to create in the self-to-self relationship. So compassion utilises and *patterns* a variety of motivational,

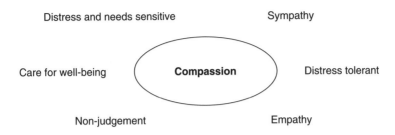

**Components of compassion
from the care-giving mentality**

Distress and needs sensitive   Sympathy

Care for well-being   **Compassion**   Distress tolerant

Non-judgement   Empathy

**Create opportunities for growth and change with
warmth**

**Figure 11.1   The compassion circle
Adapted from Gilbert 2005a: 52, reproduced with permission from Routledge**

emotional and cognitive competencies that are care-focused. For convenience, the *compassion circle*, given in Chapter 7, is reproduced here as Figure 11.1. We now are going to look at it in terms of how we try to help the client treat themself compassionately – that is develop the care-giving mentality for self-to-self relating.

Care for one's well-being and positive psychology

It may seem strange but some depressed people are very unclear about being motivated to care for, nurture and look after themselves. They may be focused on caring for other people or defending themselves and engaging in various safety behaviours to avoid bad things happening. They may also be very focused on 'achieving' to win their social place or even on narcissistic self-promotion. But genuine care and concern for their well-being is different. It is therefore useful to discuss with clients what 'care for one's well-being' means. In compassion, we focus on two key meanings: (1) empathy with and alleviation of distress, and (2) behaving in a way that facilitates one's growth, development and well-being. Therefore interventions should hold to these two basic goals and at times these may take precedence over more symptom-focused approaches.

You may recall from Chapter 7 that Fogel, Melson and Mistry (1986, p. 55) defined the core elements of nurturance as: '…the provision of guidance, protection and care for the purpose of fostering developmental change congruent with the expected potential for change of the object of nurturance'. They also outline four dimensions of care-nurturance. These are: (1) choice of object – who or what to direct care to; (2) expression of nurturant feelings; (3) motivation to nurture; and (4) awareness of nurturance. In this last dimension they suggest that: 'awareness of nurturance can be conceptualized as the degree of articulation of an individual's concepts of their own and others' developmental processes' (Fogel et al., 1986, p. 59). Depressed people may feel so bad about themselves that these ideas can be difficult. However, the key idea is that compassion-focused therapy is not just about distress alleviation, and indeed sometimes to truly care for and nurture ourselves, and develop our potential and well-being, we have to engage in things that are difficult or painful to do (e.g. learn distress tolerence, patience and acceptance).

The focus on nurturing oneself, with the aim of developing well-being and the articulation of *positive life* goals, has become increasingly recognised as a major element of change and a new orientation to therapy. In these approaches we are not just trying to reduce negative thoughts, beliefs, feelings and safety behaviours but to *actively promote feelings of well-being* – sometimes referred to as *positive psychology* (Carr, 2004). Moreover, there are now a range of different approaches that integrate positive psychology with cognitive therapy (Snyder and Ingram, 2006). The development of concern, care and compassion for self and others is regarded as a central (virtue) element within positive psychology (Peterson and Seligman, 2004). Rather than focus on negatives or deficits, positive therapies focus on developing strengths and virtues. This helps to reorganise meaning systems. In compassionate-focused therapy we do not focus on depression or negative thinking as 'deficits', but rather as the activation of protection strategies that evolved to have positive/protection functions. The fact that they often make us 'feel bad', avoid or close down is because this is precisely what they are designed to do. It is not our fault that our self-awareness systems can be focused on them and make them worse. Thus compassion-focused therapy sits comfortably in this new arena.

Distress and needs sensitivity

One of the qualities that clients may need to think about is how they can be genuinely sensitive to their own distress. For example, when one of my clients became distressed or anxious, she would simply hate herself for 'getting in this state'. Sometimes she would try to use cognitive techniques to 'control' her anxiety but this was usually in the service of being angry with herself for being anxious. The idea that she could be sensitive to her anxiety, to see it as a normal function related to basic protection strategies in her brain and that it could be treated with gentleness and kindness, engaged with rather than avoided, was a very odd idea to her. Gradually, however, she learnt how to tolerate anxiety. She used some cognitive and behavioural ideas for re-evaluating anxious thoughts and some behavioural practice/exposure techniques, but did so practising an inner voice of 'warmth and understanding'. She found that the more she was able to tolerate her anxiety, without being critical or panicked by it, and the more she was kind to herself when anxious, the easier it was to work with it.

The importance of avoidance of painful feelings has been discussed by many therapists (Hayes, Strosahl and Wilson, 2004; Linehan, 1993). Some clients engage in various levels of dissociation to avoid painful feelings. When you discuss therapy with them one of the things they will suggest is that being 'sensitive to their own distress' is sometimes the last thing they want to become. As suggested by other therapies, some of these clients will try to use therapeutic techniques to avoid dealing with key problems, memories, emotional vulnerabilities, or recognising and working on one's own needs (Greenberg and Watson, 2006; Hayes, Strosahl and Wilson, 2004). Unfortunately these do not work very well.

There are different levels to distress, however. For example, at a surface level it may be experienced as a low mood and feelings of anxiety. As you begin to explore in more detail what these emotions are about (e.g. using guided discovery and inference chains), it may be that fears of abandonment and rejection become more prominent which may be linked to pursuing one's own goals or needs (Greenberg and Watson, 2006). Taking a compassionate focus to this is to help the person stay with these (partly archetypal) fears but look at them with a compassionate and kind focus rather than a self-attacking one. This helps in the process of acceptance of difficult feelings, so that people can stay with the fears of, say, abandonment, aloneness and rejection, and process them in new compassionate ways.

Sympathy

Sympathy is the ability to be emotionally moved by the pain of others. When we have *self*-focused sympathy for our distress it means we are moved by some of the painful things that we have experienced. Sometimes clients, and indeed counsellors, can confuse sympathy with self-pity. Self-pity often has elements of contempt in it, or a sense of angry injustice. Clients may become tearful, complaining about unfairness. This is not sympathy with one's own distress. To have sympathy with one's own distress is to be genuinely moved, for example, by how awful it is to feel this depressed or how frightening it was as a child when one's mother threatened to abandon the self. This is not to ruminate on how bad it is or was in an unhelpful way but to develop compassionate understanding, validation and compassion for one's pain.

The ability to process these feelings and memories, and in particular sadness and grief, can be very important. Greenberg and Watson (2006) also note that there can be a lot of unprocessed anger in these contexts that needs to be explored and worked with too. In sympathy we allow ourselves to be moved by our history and experiences rather than shut off from them. However, while processing anger can break up the defensive, submissive aspects of helping people feel empowered rather than subordinate (Greenberg and Watson, 2006; Hackmann, 2005), it is the compassion for self (and at times for others; Allen and Knight, 2005) that is soothing. Processing anger is probably working with the threat system rather than soothing system. Thus one seeks a softening in one's anger (Greenberg and Watson, 2006).

Many times depressed people tell me that they had previously been able to 'intellectually' recognise how difficult things had been for them as a child or going through a divorce but had never really had much sympathy or kindness for those experiences. They had spent so much time in 'holding themselves together', 'protecting themselves' or 'keeping going' that they had never really had a chance to process those experiences and the pain they had been feeling. Being able to do this in a safe environment, feeling contained by the therapist and recognising that they needed to develop kindness for themselves had been important in their recovery and was a new experience for them. If you are going to develop self-compassion then one needs to be clear what one is being compassionate about.

Sympathy begins the process of acknowledging pain associated with traumatic memories. For example, John had told various therapists, in a somewhat detached way, how his father would 'throw him across the room'. The comedian Billy Connolly has also used such experiences in comedy. However, with sympathy for distress John was able to stay in this traumatic memory and begin to acknowledge just how frightened and fearful he was. This began a process of acknowledging fear, anger and intense grief. He became capable of being emotionally moved and sympathetic to his life story in a deep way. Working with trauma often requires us to be in the emotion and the sense of aloneness of it. John was able to acknowledge that in this experience there was a deep sense of aloneness in a terribly frightening and hostile world. He acknowledged that when his father became aggressive there had been no one to help him. On occasions he would hide himself in bed and on one occasion he 'wet himself' out of fear, and then was terrified of the consequences. He had become self-reliant, never expecting or wanting people to help him. This theme is brilliantly portrayed in the film *Good Will Hunting*. Working with these experiences can be very moving.

Grief for a lost past can be important too. As people with long-term depressions begin to recover you sometimes run into sadness and anger about wasted years. You need to check here that people do not have subtle self-criticisms ('I should have seen this and got over it sooner'). However, there is a reality to it too that needs to be acknowledged and worked through, and grieved over, but with a focus on tomorrow – that tomorrow is still fresh and open to possibilities – rather than on a past that is written and cannot be changed.

Distress tolerance and acceptance

Distress sensitivity and sympathy are key components for a crucial element of compassion, which is distress tolerance. Affect tolerance has been key to behavioural approaches to anxiety difficulties (Salkovskis, 1996a, 1996b). In compassion-focused therapy, however, we introduce the feelings of kindness and warmth to tolerance, so that it is *compassionate tolerance* that is the focus.

Tolerance is linked to, but not identical to, acceptance. Tolerance is the ability to stay with emotions as they happen. Acceptance can involve tolerance but it is also a deep philosophical orientation to one's difficulties and is dialectic with change (Linehan, 1993). Acceptance (including self-acceptance) also involves coming to terms with things that are as they are. A number of therapies have been focusing on distress tolerance and acceptance as a central aspect of therapy as, for example, in dialectical behaviour therapy (Linehan, 1993) and acceptance-based therapies (Hayes, Strosahl and Wilson, 2004). Acceptance is totally different from submissive resignation. In submissive resignation one feels one has to 'give in' to the inevitable and one is powerless to do anything. This is often associated with feelings of hopelessness or resentment. The spirit of acceptance is 'coming to terms' without feelings of hopelessness and resentment.

Many clients' safety behaviours, thoughts, emotions and strategies are to avoid events and feelings that they think will be overwhelmingly painful – they do not want to tolerate them or accept them. The way certain events reactivate overwhelming emotional reactions and memories from the past is one reason why tolerance can feel so difficult. For example, some clients can even feel as if certain traumas are happening again in the here and now when they recall painful memories of parental abuse. This is a particular problem with post-traumatic stress disorder (Brewin, 2006; Clark and Ehlers, 2004; Lee, 2005). Clearly, however, if clients cannot process these memories, and learn how to feel safe *in the present moment*, then their threat system will be constantly vigilant. Some clients will take various drugs or use alcohol as a distraction from painful feelings and memories. Distress tolerance, then, is the way we can begin to gently work with these safety behaviours by helping clients become distress sensitive and sympathetic rather than fearful and avoidant.

Empathy

Empathy involves both an emotional component and an ability to 'understand' and have insight into why we feel what we feel or why we have developed the safety strategies that we have (see formulation in Chapter 9). The therapist works with the formulation and various models to try to provide clients with these internal frameworks for conceptualising and understanding what is happening to them and how they can help themselves to get out of depression. As people develop their empathy and understanding of their depression (why me?, why now?), this aids them in their ability to become sensitive, sympathetic and tolerant. This empathy is both personal (linking into one's early history) but also transpersonal, via understanding the innate nature of some of our protection strategies and our common humanity. Although cognitive therapists often talk about the linkages between cognition, emotion and physiology, this should not be vague, but connect directly to the client's experiences. Explaining how protest-despair and defeat strategies work, how they are activated and can pull us into certain types of feelings and ways of thinking and experiencing the world (with a toned down soothing system) can be useful for some people. Much depends on the case, however, as to how much detail the client wants to know, is able to take on board, or is helpful.

Empathy is also an important component in the client internalising a commitment to change. Without a genuine empathic understanding of their depression, and what is likely to be helpful and why, therapy can be very much doing things because the therapist tells them. This is not always a bad thing because sometimes if a depressed person engages in more positive activities and feels better, this boosts their confidence in therapy and they become more collaborative. It is also important for the therapist to enter into the spirit of change with pleasure for the person's successes. However, submissive compliance without understanding is not usually that helpful.

Empathy can also involve beginning to understand why other people behaved in the way they did. As we have seen, depressed clients can easily take defensive self-blaming positions for other people's bad behaviour towards them (see Chapter 6). When we develop empathy we begin to open up our conceptualisations of what is going on in the mind of others, for example that parental anger may not have been because the child was bad but because the parent was themself depressed or had some other difficulties. This is a form of reattribution work but it is also more than that because it is focusing on theory of mind abilities, starting to take more complex views about how the minds of others work, and what guides their intentions, emotions, motives and actions. However, we need the emotional connection to the intellectual understanding.

Counsellor: Looking at it now and as a man yourself, what do you make of your father's rages at you?

John: I guess that there was something wrong with him.

Counsellor: So you see it was about him and his emotional problems, [*slowly*] it was not your fault.

John: Yes, I can see that.

Counsellor: [*Gently*] But can you feel it. Just stay here a while John. Look at the scenes in your mind – that it was not your fault. Really let yourself feel it – [*very slowly and gently*] that it was not your fault, John, not your fault.

Slowly John began to cry and so we sat there a while quietly together. Later he told me that he had 'kind of known' it in his head but not his heart and that after our session he felt very sad but 'strangely at peace'. So a full empathic understanding is more than an intellectual one.

Non-judgement

Key to the process of compassion is the ability to develop a non-judgemental orientation to one's depression and other difficulties in life. This is not to say that we do not have preferences but rather to say that it is the giving up of attacking and criticism that is an issue here. Mindfulness is often regarded as a helpful way of becoming aware but non-judgemental in our awareness (Allen and Knight 2005; Neff, 2003a, 2003b; Segal et al., 2002). However, in compassion-focused therapy non-judgement arises from deep empathy and understanding. Indeed, being non-judgemental of self and others also emerges out of a better (empathic) understanding of why we and others have behaved as we have. This can involve processes that underpin forgiveness (Bono and McCullough, 2006; Worthington, O'Connor, Berry, Sharp, Murray and Yi, 2005). To forgive is to let go anger and the desire for retaliation, but it is not submissive acceptance. To forgive often means acknowledging hurt and working through anger. To forgive *self* is to come to terms with our common human fragilities and needs, to acknowledge that our safety strategies were for good self-protective reasons but have *unintended* effects (Gilbert, 2000c). We can even learn forgiveness for that part of ourselves that is self-critical – rather than being angry or aggressive to it or trying to get rid of it.

Although some therapists suggest that we should become aggressive with the self-critical part of ourselves, and this may offer some relief, be cautious here. This is like a child learning from a parent that anger and aggression are the ways to resolve problems and conflict. It maintains the beliefs of good–bad, good and evil. Rather, we can develop compassion for our inner self-critic in relation to our threats and fears. This creates a new emotional tone in the self-critical system. However, because compassion is difficult (and even feared) some people find being assertive to their inner critic easier. However, over time this may not bring inner peace but further conflict. Working assertively with memories of hostile others is of course very different (Hackmann, 2005). Here assertiveness in imagery is a helpful first step to some form of reconciliation.

Developing the attributes of self-compassion

When we are teaching and using compassion to stimulate our soothing systems we call it *compassionate mind training*. We are training ourselves to be compassionate by activating different aspects and components of our brains, and strengthening these patterns – hence the physiotherapy analogy (Gilbert and Irons, 2005). This is based on the idea that our minds take on different patterns when engaged in different tasks, social roles and processing different types of signal. For example, when we are 'fighting' enemies, our interest in their welfare, our sensitivity to the distress we cause them, our tolerance and empathy are toned down. This allows the more aggressive, guilt-free behaviours to pattern our minds. To be overcome with concern or guilt would make it difficult to do what is necessary to defend ourselves or fight. Some soldiers need to practise not to feel bad about killing others (i.e. to turn off their compassionate systems) and the army has intensive training to do this. This is not to develop a schema but a brain state. In contrast, when we are trying to be caring to others it is the aggressive, self-protective systems that become toned down. Hence, rather than thinking of schemas or core beliefs, compassion-focused therapy focuses on patterns that are created in a dynamic, ever-changing mind that has to meet varied challenges, co-create social relationships and take advantage of opportunities.

To switch into a compassion-focused pattern, where different aspects of our minds (e.g. distress, sensitivity, tolerance and empathy) are being activated and brought (patterned) together, requires working with different domains of the compassion pattern. When introducing the idea of a compassion focus it is important to go back to the three circles so that clients know exactly what it is they are trying to achieve. One can then say: 'If you were to develop more compassion for yourself, what kind of qualities would you need to develop or work on?' Following this you might brainstorm together those qualities. For example, compassion might involve warmth, forgiveness and acceptance, or it might focus on sympathy. It is important for the client to become involved with this discussion. However, you can also provide guidance and a set of qualities that together you are trying to foster and develop (see Appendix).

So we have a set of qualities that we are trying to develop and part of the reason for wanting to do this is to move self-organisation and self-identity into a compassion pattern. It helps, therefore, if people are able to identify compassion as a self-identity goal rather than just a technique to use for symptom relief. It is not impossible to use compassion for those who only want to use it for symptom relief, but it is a lot easier if they begin to see how some forms of striving may (or may not) fit with a self-compassionate identity. Enabling people to see that developing compassion for self and others may become a desired self-identity can be helpful.

Processes for the development of self-compassion

We have now looked at various attributes of compassion. In this section we are going to look at how we engage with people so that they can begin to develop these attributes.

Compassion attention

Compassionate attention is learning to focus on various sensory cues, images and memories that are regarded as compassionate and soothing (Marra, 2003).

Generating certain images can be helpful and we explore compassionate imagery shortly. Compassionate attention also means focusing on one's valued qualities. Attending is a process of choosing what one will focus on to advance well-being. Thus we can focus on what would be helpful in this moment.

When clients are depressed they often exclude their positive attributes; these drop out of their attentional field. For example, a client felt bad because of anger. So we made a list of the negative attributes and hurt, and alongside made a list of her positive attributes. In the positive list were things like, 'I try to care for others. I'm a loyal person. I don't purposefully cheat others. Others often turn to me for advice. I'm approachable.' This enabled her to see that while there were things she did not like about herself, there were also things that she did value in herself and that she was disqualifying these attributes, not attending to them. Also we looked at anger as arising from disappointment. Enabling clients to attend to their more positive qualities (and not disqualify them) can be helpful, especially if they are validated by the counsellor and mirrored.

Sometimes clients see their depression as more real, that is having cognitions like: 'This is the real me.' Here it is useful to discuss the fact that we all have the potential for becoming depressed and outline the typical internal beliefs that go with depression. Depression is no more or less real than joy, happiness, love, compassion, interest, humour or other internal experiences. Humans are mosaics of possibilities and feelings. Hence the counselling changes the construct from 'this is the real me' to 'this is only one part of my inner, human potential'. So we can think through together how to keep attention balanced on the complexities of our being.

Compassionate thinking

Compassionate thinking is focused on the way in which we reason, think things through, or even ruminate; that is, it is related to meta-cognitions (Wells, 2000). Compassionate thinking is designed to be helpful, encouraging, supportive and friendly. Being evidence-focused and gaining new perspectives (as in cognitive therapy) can be very compassionate. However, we consider alternative thoughts to the negative ones, and treat our thoughts as thoughts rather than facts, not (just) because it is rational but because being like this is compassionate. Thus it is not (just) the logic that heals, but the *experience* of the helpful and nurturing nature of being like this.

One way of working with more self-supportive thoughts is with the cognitive idea of the *friend technique*. This involves helping the depressed client change their perspective on themself by considering interactions with a friend. One can use questions like 'Would you say this to a friend?' If you self-criticise and condemn (e.g. 'I failed to get the job, nobody will respect me, I'm a complete bum'), then say: 'Imagine a friend sitting in this chair. They have told you of the same event you have told me. What would you say to them?' You can help the client to see the negative impact on a friend, if they are as critical of their friend as they are of themself. Note that the key issue is to facilitate a more nurturing self-dialogue when things are not going well. Thinking how they might help a friend can help to generate alternative, helpful and supportive ideas and thoughts: 'Oh, if this happened to a friend I would be understanding. I would probably say ...'. This helps people to see that not only are self-critical thoughts unkind, but if they shift perspectives they can generate helpful and supportive thoughts and ideas. The problem is not that they cannot generate them, but rather it is in applying them to themselves and how they disqualify them. If they would say harsh things or think them about a friend, then you say: 'Well, at least you are consistent!' But then go on to explore how unhelpful that would be and what would be more helpful.

Another example of compassionate thinking is what Neff (2003a) called 'common humanity'. When we think of ourselves as inferior, alone and the only one to be incompetent or bad, we are going along with the sense of social isolation. In contrast, common humanity thinking helps us to focus on the fact that we are part of the human condition and vulnerable to a whole range of anxieties and depressions; that depressed people think remarkably similarly in terms of their negative style; that these styles can *feel* powerful and true because our emotional brains are designed to pull us to think that way and not be easily persuaded from thinking otherwise. Compassionate reasoning also helps people to think about balance in thinking and to recognise negative thinking as mostly to do with key threats. Compassionate reasoning may involve looking at our attributions and the way in which we tend to overly attribute causality to self. Many cognitive interventions (see Chapter 12) can be extremely helpful in developing compassionate reasoning, but keep your focus on 'feelings of warmth' in them.

Compassionate behaviour

Many cognitive behaviour therapists will help clients to think about 'the helpful thing to do in this situation'. As we saw in the last chapter, behavioural experiments can be very valuable here. At times this means acting against a feeling (Linehan, 1993). Compassion-focused therapy suggests exactly the same but with the focus on compassion. For example, if one has an argument with one's partner, we don't explore so much what is the rational or assertive thing to do but what would be the most helpful and compassionate thing to do. For instance, give the person you are in conflict with a chance to calm down and then explain as best as you can why you would like to sort out the problem. Think about why they might be upset like you are upset. We learn that compassion is not submissiveness. If it is getting out of bed, that is the key behaviour then we focus on this as a compassionate thing to do because it helps avoid ruminating in bed and may help us feel better in the long run. Thus (as other therapies might do) we focus on the *helpfulness* and ultimately *nurturing* aspect of encouraging ourselves to do difficult things. But we have to experience the motivation to do the behaviours as being supportive and kind, not bullying or forcing.

We also teach the importance of *putting compassion into action*. We have suggested that compassion involves both distress alleviation and the promotion of growth and well-being. Hence it is important to help clients begin to develop plans for clear actions that will help with their distress in the long term but that are also focused on developing a lifestyle that promotes their well-being. In order to do this one needs to discuss with clients their *positive* life goals, what they would like to commit to and put effort into, and what they would see as nurturing themselves. Sometimes one has to work in a motivational interviewing kind of way to help people articulate positive life goals.

Some years ago I saw an 80 year-old woman who had become physically unwell and had given up various activities, including being the church flower arranger. Although she gradually recovered from her physical illness and felt somewhat tired, she had been advised that she needed to 'slow down'. Should I help her accept this, that at her age she could not expect to do what she did when she was younger? When I saw her it was clear that part of her wanted to 'live again' and I simply advised that she should try going with that and not accept 'old age'. So she talked to the church to see if she could pick up the flower arranging, and also spent a couple of hours a day trying to do some of the things she used to do. The church was happy to have her back playing an active part and her depression quickly lifted. So there are times when to accept or change is a complex dilemma (Linehan, 1993). Of course in one sense this is a straightforward behavioural exercise and it was very helpful for her. However, the compassion focus had allowed us to acknowledge her sadness at losing her roles. It normalised the depression, taught her how to be understanding and empathic to her depression and how to act against it.

Compassionate action can be thought about as a series of actions, such as things one can do in the next day or two, over the next week, month, year or lifetime. In so far as it is focused on well-being, it may include desires to work on physical health or other aspects of one's life. In being compassionate we recognise the struggle in being human and that compassion is a way to engage with the struggle of life with gentleness. A number of clients have noted that in this work they have shifted from seeking achievement to seeking contentment.

The consequences of becoming compassionate to self and others

As noted at the end of Chapter 5, rather than think that depression is related to deficits we can see it as related to types of adaptation. Thus psychological therapies are about developing new ways of seeing and adapting to the social world and our own innate dispositions. Thus we want to explore how people can carry these new adaptations forward. So as one begins to develop the compassionate focus it can be useful to explore how this will help a person change and become more as they would like to be. One can make a list with clients on how a compassion focus will:

- affect how you feel and relate to yourself – what will be different? how will you notice this happening and build on it?
- affect how you deal with life problems – what will be different? how will you notice this happening and build on it?
- affect how you interact with other people – what will be different? how will you notice this happening and build on it?
- affect how you choose and work towards life goals – what will be different? how will you notice this happening and build on it? (Goals can be short-term – in the next few days, weeks or months – or long-term and over a lifetime.)
- affect how you deal with setbacks and life crises – what will be different? how will you notice this happening and build on it?
- affect any other life issues that are important to you – what will be different? how will you notice this happening and build on it?

Explore with them how they can build compassion into everyday life. How can we notice blocks to compassionate living and work compassionately with these? This helps us to see that we can develop compassionate living skills that offer real advantages – but that it takes attention and practice. It is worth doing this exercise for yourself and see what comes up for you. Spend time really thinking through these questions (see Appendix) These questions can also be used for personal meditations.

Compassionate imagery

As noted above, imagery can be an important aspect of compassionate attention. For many depressed people simply explaining the value of compassion and developing a warm and compassionate focus to the self is enough to get them in the swing of it. They quickly get the hang of re-examining their negative thoughts, working with painful feelings or trying new behaviours in compassionate and self-nurturing ways.

However, for some people this is a very hard and even frightening thing to do. We may be faced with having to help people experience compassion and warmth for the self for the first time and overcome fears of it. The therapeutic relationship and the gentle focusing on compassion can help, but to generate feelings of self-compassion more directly can be advanced using imagery. When some therapists first come to compassion-focused therapy they are often attracted to the imagery work. It is important to stress, however, that this therapy is nestled within other focused therapies, such as CBT and DBT, and is not a therapy in its own right. Nor is imagery its main component. Compassion-focused therapy is a way of being in and doing therapy.

In Chapter 6 we pointed out that imagination is key to so much of what humans do. Moreover, imagination can stimulate our physiological systems (Singer, 2006). If we imagine a meal when we are hungry, we can stimulate our saliva and stomach acids; if we imagine something sexual laying in our beds, we can stimulate sexual arousal. The logic behind the use of compassionate imagery is not much more complicated than that. Imagery is a powerful means of generating emotions, new insights and physiological effects (Holmes and Hackmann, 2004). Imagery is often used in fMRI research to stimulate different brain areas (George, Ketter, Parekh, Horwitz, Hercovitch and Post, 1995; Schwartz and Begley, 2002), so we know it can do this. Rein, Atkinson and McCraty (1995) explored the impact of anger imagery and compassionate imagery on a measure of immune functioning called S-IgA. Anger imagery had a negative effect on S-IgA (so keep this in mind if you are working with anger), while compassionate imagery improved it. Compassionate imagery, then, may do many things, including altering neurophysiological systems. In a recent study Gilbert, Baldwin, Irons, Baccus and Palmer (2006) asked students to engage in two forms of imagery. One was to imagine the self-critical part of self as if it were a person, note what it looked like, and how powerful and aggressive it felt. In the other imagery task students were asked to imagine a self-compassionate part of self and note what it looked like and how powerful and kind it felt. We discovered that self-critical students easily and vividly imagined a self-critical image as powerful and hostile, but struggled to imagine a compassionate part of self. For those students who were not self-critical it was the opposite – the self-critical image was not that powerful and the compassionate image was easy to generate and easy to feel warmth from. We took this to (possibly) imply that self-critical people not only have more ready access to these strong and hostile imagining and self-feelings but also have less access to self-soothing systems. Gilbert and Procter (2006) also found that their day-hospital clients had no difficulty imagining their critical selves (which were often highly hostile), but really struggled to give form or feeling to self-compassionate images (see also Gilbert and Irons, 2004). Thus there may be value in working to help self-critical people develop self-compassionate images as a way to access soothing systems.

The idea is that if we can create images that contain key signals, cues or stimuli we may be able to stimulate the soothing affiliative system. The use of imagery and fantasy generation are now major ways of working with a variety of psychological difficulties (Frederick and McNeal, 1999; Holmes and Hackmann, 2004; Singer, 2006). Indeed, for many years behaviourists have used imagery for new learning and as an aid to de-sensitisation. In compassionate imagery we are not (just) trying to tone down a threat-negative emotion system but tone up an emotional system – the soothing system. Hence we say to clients: 'When we are distressed one's attention can get pulled to negative thoughts and feelings. If these are self-critical, life can get very unpleasant because there seems to be nowhere safe or soothing for your mind to go.' 'Mindfulness' therapists would focus on helping people stay mindful of their thoughts and feelings without becoming pulled into or reacting to them (Germer et al., 2005; Segal et al., 2002). However, this can be very difficult when one is depressed and may well be easier when clients are better at self-soothing. Thus I suggest that it can sometimes be useful to practise a different focus for our attention/thinking that activates an incompatible emotional tone to that of depression and anxiety. There are two stages to this, one is 'safe place' imagery and the other is compassionate imagery.

'Safe place' imagery

This can involve relaxation training but is also more than that. With 'safe place' imagery one engages in a gentle relaxation (if the client is able to do so) and asks the client to create an image in their mind of a place that gives them a sense of safeness. You might ask people if it feels like it is inside (a certain room) or outside (on a warm sandy beach), the time of day and the feel (e.g. weather) of the day. The idea is to help direct the clients to as *many sensory cues* as possible. For example, if they imagine being on a beach by the sea, focus on the sand between their feet, the smell of the air and feel of the light sea breeze. If they choose a country garden, focus on the smell of the grass, the texture of the grass, the smell of the flowers, the sound of the birds, and so on. We call this the 'safe place' image. This should provide people with an experience of feeling safe and relaxed. You note that the mind can easily wander, and when it does, gently bring it back to the task in hand. The focus is on the effort rather than the result. Some people find images difficult so they might use a picture from a magazine and imagine themselves being there. Keep in mind that this is a collaborative approach and invite people to *discover* ways that they feel helpful and that will work for them. Singer (2006) gives examples of how to help people with using imagery.

The ideal compassionate other or inner helper

We noted above that some people find it difficult to direct compassionate feelings to themselves. However, they may find it easier to imagine compassion being directed at them from another person. So we create an internal fantasy relationship of self-in-relationship with a compassionate other. The principle is no different from other times we create fantasies of others. For example, if we want to stimulate our sexual feelings (release hormones from our pituitary) we might fantasise our ideal sexual other and imagine interacting with them. We do this because we know that fantasies can stimulate our physiological systems. Fantasising interacting with a compassionate other is designed to stimulate the soothing systems.

In Buddhist psychology there is a long history to compassionate imagery, with various images of the Compassionate Buddha that people focus and meditate on (Ringu Tilku Rinpoche and Mullen, 2005). Leighton (2003) has explored some of these images, their multiple forms, and offers the illuminating idea that they are designed to stimulate certain archetypal (innate) patterns of feelings, experiencing 'and being' within us. This fits well with the idea that different images, with different sensory cues, stimulate our physiological patterns. The Mahayana Buddhist view is also that the 'universe' is full of Bodhisattvas (those who have developed various levels of compassionate enlightenment) and one can tune into them, giving a sense of a shared journey, mutual support and a spiritual community – where all are seeking enlightenment through mindful compassion. I have no idea if such exist of course but it is a rather interesting and soothing idea, and illuminates the power of these images in many cultures.

There are also various imagery practices that are called loving kindness (Salzberg, 1995). Loving kindness meditation has been incorporated into mindful practice with good results (Shapiro, Astin, Bishop and Cordova, 2005). There are also a variety of imagery techniques that have been referred to as ego-strengthening by other types of therapist, and in working with depressed clients it can be useful to have some insight into these (e.g. see Frederick and McNeal, 1999).

In our compassion work we come at the issue from a different perspective, which does not in any way exclude spiritual aspects but is rather more mundane. For my work I want to use imagery to access the soothing systems based on affiliation rather than engage with culturally situated imagery (Gilbert and Irons, 2005). So to begin this we go back to the three circles with the depressed person and very clearly note that the point of compassionate imagery is to try to stimulate the opiate/oxytocin soothing system; and if we can get that working, and linked into ways of developing new perspectives in thinking and behaviour, this might well help.

If people agree, then they are invited to close their eyes or look at the floor or out of the window and imagine what compassion is like. The image will contain the various qualities that we have discussed above. The client is invited to 'make up' their own image, which is unique to them and represents their ideal. This is no different from having their ideal house, meal or friend – at least in fantasy. An ideal is 'ideal' to you and it contains all that *you* require of a compassionate other. Lee (2005) refers to this type of image as the 'perfect nurturer'; other therapists refer to this as the 'inner helper' or 'inner friend' (Frederick and McNeal, 1999). See what your client prefers. The terms, however, will imply slightly different things. For example, nurturer implies something different from inner guide, helper or friend – there is no reason not to have all of them if people want to (ie. more than one image). What is important is the relationship to them and our attentional focus that requires us to stimulate different parts of the brain.

Interestingly, some individuals do not like having a 'human-type image' fulfil a role of a compassionate other. This is particularly true for people who have been abused or severely let down. Their first compassionate images tend to be things like the sea, a mountain, the light of the sun, a tree or an animal. However, we ask that the image is given certain qualities because to experience compassion for self requires there to be a sense of a 'sentient' mind that is capable of understanding what it is to have a human mind. Thus, if a client has the image of an animal or the sea, these have to be somewhat supernatural because they have to have human (even superhuman) capacities for understanding our minds, with our needs and fears, and must be able to have feelings of warmth.

The ideal compassionate image also enacts the *compassion circle*, that is, the image has a complete focus on care for one's well-being; it is distress and needs sensitive; it is moved by our distress (i.e. is not cold and detached); it can tolerate any degree of distress in us; it has great empathy and wisdom (i.e. it understands that we are evolved beings with needs and are struggling as best we can); it is completely accepting of what and who we are; and, out of its empathy and understanding, it is never judgemental. These qualities are of course ideals – but that is the point (Lee, 2005). I have found that it can be useful to simplify these into four qualities in imagery exercises: wisdom, strength (as in endurance), warmth and non-judgement (see Appendix). We stress that these are creations from the compassionate part of our *own* minds.

Compassionate images can at first be difficult for clients to focus on. This is to be expected and can take some time. The key thing is to direct attention to compassion as much as to the outcome itself. Even if a person cannot create any elements an image of a wise, strong, warm, non-judging other, it is the fact that they are putting their attention and cognitive emotional systems into trying to activate such an inner system that is important. It is the effort in the moment, however small, that can be helpful. It is important to help people recognise that these images are like day-dreams and not clear 'pictures' in the mind. They tend to be fleeting fragments of images (Singer, 2006).

As fragments of images appear they can be linked to different sensory qualities, such as the appearance of the image. For example, if individuals do create a 'human' image, the image may be old with grey hair, the eyes may be sparkling blue or brown, there may be laughter lines on the face but also a sense of wisdom and age-lessness. If the sea is the chosen compassionate image, then the sea is imagined in terms of its visual and textural qualities (e.g. the client is floating in it or feeling it lapping at their feet), and of course it too has enormous wisdom, being as old as the planet itself (see Gilbert and Irons, 2005). People can have more than one image and prefer different images at different times. The gender of the image or whether it is genderless can also be explored. Ask: 'What does you compassionate image look like when it communicates with you? What does it *sound* like when communicating with you? How would you like your compassionate image to relate to you and how would you like to relate to it/him/her? (See Appendix.)

Sometimes people will have images of people they know. This is fine to begin with but these can come with other unwanted associations so the focus is on developing a *unique and ideal* image for the self. One person thought of her dead father, whom she knew loved her, but this image was always tinged with grief. Here we say that you can have this image if you wish but try also to have other images that do not have these emotions with them. The same is true for religious images. We do not suggest that a person should not use such images, but point to the fact that we want to create a unique image that is part of your own compassionate system and that does not have any other associations. People gradually get the idea of this.

When it comes to the sensory qualities, some individuals like to have something they can hold or feel that acts as a cue/stimulus to self-soothing. This is like a transitional object in Winnicott's terms or a condition stimulus in behavioural terms. These objects can be a soft cloth, toy or some other material. Sometimes clients like to associate a smell with the image, such as hand cream. Smells can be particularly helpful because they have direct access to the 'emotional brain' and can act as a powerful conditioned stimulus for the soothing system (Lee, 2005, personal communication, June 2005). So we can bring the image and compassionate feeling to mind and link them to sensory cues of sensation or smell. The key thing is to collaborate with your client, explaining in detail the point of these exercises so they become active and curious participants.

These techniques, and finding sensory cues, can be helpful for people who do not know how to soothe themselves or who may binge, drink excessively, or self-harm as ways of self-soothing. In the Gilbert and Procter (2006) study, some people found it difficult to relax or close their eyes without anxiety. So we introduced tennis balls as a mindful, sensory focus. Sensory focus is also common in DBT (Linehan, 1993). They could hold and explore the textures of the tennis balls when trying to relax and use compassionate imagery. So at times helping depressed people find and use such objects can be helpful. Keep in mind that the outcome is less the focus than the effort. This helps to avoid people trying to force images to come and then becoming disheartened if they cannot.

The compassionate reframe

If people are struggling to generate alternatives to their negative thoughts and feelings then they may first take a few breaths and bring their compassionate image to mind. They then imagine their compassionate image, inner friend or inner helper offering them alternative ideas with warmth and compassion (Gilbert, 2000c). Lee (2005) has referred to this as the compassionate reframe. These alternative ideas will focus on compassionate attention, thinking, behaviour and feeling, as noted above.

One person imagined his 'inner Buddha', and that when he worked with his negative thoughts he felt that his inner Buddha could help him 'find peace and calmness'. Another person had an image of a mixture of Buddha and an Earth Goddess that was difficult to visualise but came with the essence of warmth. The focus here is not just on creating an image but having inner *imaginary conversations*. One can imagine what this compassionate part of self would say about this situation. Getting oneself into this relational frame can make it easier to generate alternative thoughts and feel them as helpful. As with all such 'techniques' it is important to stay closely with what the person finds helpful. Not all people take to this approach, so stay with what is useful to the person you are working with.

Compassionate letter writing

Some depressed people do well with standard thought forms that help them re-evaluate their thoughts. Some of these are outlined in the Appendix. However, some people prefer a more narrative approach. Here one can encourage them to write compassionate letters to themselves (Mahoney, 2003). In the approach taken here they imagine their compassionate part of themselves communicating with them by letter. So the letter would start:

> Dear X
>
> I know you have been feeling down recently and that is very distressing for you. It is understandable you feel like this because … (empathy and validation for distress) …

The client is then encouraged to think about what kinds of messages they would like to hear that will help them. When you go through these letters with depressed people you will be looking to see if the letter is able to express care for their well-being; is distress and needs sensitive; is moved by distress (i.e. is not cold and detached); can tolerate distress; has empathy; is accepting and non-judgemental. You may find that when people first write compassion letters to themselves they can be somewhat judgemental, invalidating and commanding, with things like 'you are upset by this event but you must not let these things get to you'. So you discuss this with the client and look at alternative ways of refocusing on alternatives to negative thoughts and feelings (see Chapter 12). Letter writing is often used in constructivist approaches (Mahoney, 2003) and letters can be written to different people or from different points of view. Again, note that to do this requires a shifting of attention and focus in meta-cognitions. A fuller description of this process with a client hand-out is given in the Appendix (and see Gilbert, in press b).

Compassionate meditations

During a therapy session it can be useful to spend some time exploring the feelings associated with the various components of an image. So, for example, you might say:

> Let's for a moment close our eyes or look down and imagine what it feels like to be in contact with a part of you that is fully concerned with your well-being. Bring your compassionate image to mind and imagine that it is fully focused on your well-being and needs. What does that feel like?

Spend some time exploring the feelings and thoughts that arise from this exercise.

> Now imagine what it feels like to have this part of you sensitive to your feelings and distress. What does it feel like when you focus on wisdom for you?

Then explore 'acceptance for you', 'warmth for you' and so forth. Spend time with each element. Remember that some people may find these exercises difficult or rather emotional so go gently with them, exploring the nature of the feelings and fears. Some people may also spend time meditating on these qualities at home. In fact, therapists who use compassion-focused therapy can do this for themselves and explore these experiences so that they too learn to become compassion-focused within themselves and work on their own shame issues or other troublesome aspects. As for mindfulness, it is useful to have your own practice.

Compassion for the inner critic

One way of working with inner criticisms is to empathise with them. Thus when a person has generated some self-critical thoughts they might imagine them as coming from the self-critical part of self. Then you can ask the person to imagine this self-critical part of self as if it was a person. What does it look like? What is the emotion it is directing at you? What is its greatest fear? Then you ask the client to imagine going to the critic with your compassionate image and saying: 'I am sad that you are this frightened that you have to lash out like this. You must live in a very cold place. I can understand your fear because this (…) is what happened to us.'

When clients do this they are, in a way, automatically taking a rather superior and dominant position to the critic, as well as focusing on the fear that drives the critic. Many people find that with this approach the critical aspect of self shrinks and the images change. Moreover, the idea that their criticism is based on fear is helpful for future reference. People learn to be in touch with the fear behind the criticism and that in a way self-criticism is a frustration and panic response to errors or a set-back.

If the self-criticism is like that of an abusive parent, then say: 'You are not my father but part of my own system, me. You do not need to remind me of him nor be like him. You are free from that burden.' These are all things that clients themselves have suggested and found helpful (see Hackmann, 2005). Once people know what they are trying to achieve (to access the soothing system to reduce the sense of threat and thus use compassion to deal with the critic), they can be very inventive and find their own ways to work with their self-critics. You can see that what guides this approach are the underlying concepts of the three affect systems.

The therapeutic relationship again

The therapeutic relationship is an important source of developing self-compassion. By empathy and listening, one enables the client to experience a helpful and accepting relationship. In this way the client internalises greater self-acceptance through the acceptance and understanding of the therapist. The therapist is also clearly indicating compassion as a helpful thing to develop. Kohut (1977) stressed the importance of mirroring the client and allowing a certain idealisation. In evolutionary theory the client experiences the therapist as someone who is prepared to invest resources in them, such as time, care, energy, skill and efforts to understand and recognise their needs (Bailey, 2002; Gilbert, 1992), and this in itself can be internalised as an important source of self-validation (Gilbert, 1989, 1992). The point is, we should not underestimate the therapuetic relationship as a major source for the development of self-compassion. Hence it is useful to be attentive to various factors that may reduce the client's ability to internalise the experience of this relationship. Experiences such as strong envy of the therapist or unresolved doubts about the acceptability of the client in the eyes of the therapist (e.g. shame) can significantly block the development of self-compassion and lead to disqualifying the experience (e.g. 'It's only a job to my therapist; they are too distant/neutral to be able to understand or accept me', etc.). Unaddressed rage can also make compassion difficult.

Cautions   Keep in mind all the time that this work is collaborative, explaining each step, seeing if the person finds it helpful, moving back and forth in discussion, noting blocks, fears and problems in working compassionately with the self, being creative at helping people find their own way. As I have said, some people find this very difficult to do and it activates grief, sadness or fear. Work gently in these areas and only at the speed the depressed person is able to go. If people do not want to work this way, then do not impose it – offer it as a behavioural experiment to try and see what happens.

Keep in mind too that compassion-focused therapy is embedded in other traditional approaches such as CBT and DBT, and a lot of the time you will be working in these ways (e.g. using Socratic discussions and guided discovery, identifying distress-inducing beliefs, explaining the role of safety strategies and generating alternative ideas/thoughts, treating thoughts as theories not facts, doing behavioural experiments, developing solution-focused steps, working with traumatic memories, and using exposure). However, you will do so with a compassionate focus which is why it is called compassion focused therapy.

Conclusion

There are many aspects to compassion focused therapy that one will find in other therapies. Ideally, it is a way of working that can fit easily with other methods. However, compassionate focused therapy is based on a clear evolutionary and neuroscience model and is constantly informed by research on emotions, especially those of soothing and self-soothing. It is also a way of orientating oneself in the relationship, engaging and doing therapy. We need more research on how to target specific systems in our minds and design better interventions for them (Gilbert and Irons, 2005; Linden, 2006). Although compassion focused therapy also helps orientate people to a way of 'being in the world', to consider the value of a certain self-identity and way of organising our minds, this is related to dynamic patterns of processing in our minds. Thus they should not be reduced to the concepts of a schema or core beliefs. Moreover, as the Buddha noted, compassion needs to be skilful, which in that tradition means becoming 'mindful' and developing insight into the true nature of the mind. Psychotherapies, however, can bring other elements to bear, such as those explored in this book. For some, these may help people move on in their journey, being better placed to work mindfully if they so wish.

Key to many focused therapies is the idea that clients need to practise things outside of the session; thus they are highly task-focused. Compassionate mind training is exactly the same, with a focus on practising different compassion developing tasks outside of sessions. Keep in mind though that for some people working with compassion activates the attachment system and triggers painful and fearful emotional memories (Gilbert, in press b; Liotti, 2007).

12 Focusing Interventions with a Special Reference to Self-Criticism

Currently therapists and counsellors are enticed to link their therapeutic efforts to specific therapies and schools. However, ideally, therapies should be developed on the basis of our understanding of the complexities of depression and a range of interventions should be available for the depressed person. This idea is key to Arnold Lazarus's term of *multimodal therapy*. Recently, Lazarus (2000, p. 93) summarised this as:

> The multimodal orientation … is predicated on the assumption that most psychological problems are multifaceted, multidetermined, and multilayered, and that comprehensive therapy calls for a careful assessment of seven parameters or 'modalities': behavior, affect, sensation, imagery, cognition, interpersonal relationships, and biological processes. The most common biological intervention is the use of psychotropic drugs. The first letters from the seven modalities yield the convenient acronym BASIC I.D., although it must be remembered that the 'D' modality represents the entire panoply of medical and biological factors.

The therapeutic interventions for depression outlined previously and below can be seen in multimodal terms, or at least as interventions that address different modalities. The notion that we are dealing with patterns and activations in multiple domains is important because we must always remember we are working with 'a person' and not just treating a decontextualised neurotransmitter system or negative belief. We are using our minds (via a therapeutic relationship and our knowledge) to change something in their minds (a validating relationship, new ways of thinking and behaving, re-processing emotional memories) that changes their internal patterns. Keeping these ideas in mind we can now look at some specific interventions that target certain domains.

Targeting specific thoughts and beliefs

Socratic questioning, guided discovery, behavioural experiments, exposure, attending to behavioural avoidance and positive life planning are key to various focused therapies such as CBT and DBT. One aspect of this work is to help people appreciate that our thinking is often 'pulled' in certain ways in different states of mind. Our reasoning can be the product of emotional shifts and also cause emotional shifts. Can we use our capacities for reflection and meta-cognitive processing (that other animals do not have) to come to our aid, rather than cause more problems?

Mindfulness suggests that the act of becoming aware of our thoughts, to stand back in our attention and to see them as thoughts can itself be helpful (Segal et al., 2002). If consciousness is like a blue sky and thoughts and feelings are like clouds, we can learn to become more sky-focused than clouds-focused. We come to see that some experience depression as rippling through me creating experiences, thoughts and feelings but it is not 'me'. We learn not to identify with any state of mind that patterns experiences within self. We can *change our relationship* to our thoughts and feelings. There is increasing evidence that mindfulness-focused work with well-trained practitioners can be helpful for reducing relapse in depression (Segal et al., 2002). Mindfulness, and learning to attend in new ways to the inner patterns of thoughts and feelings flowing through us can also be incorporated in more traditional ways that enable us to work with our thoughts and feelings.

Considering evidence

Appreciating that our thinking is often 'pulled' in certain ways in different states of mind, invites us to stand back from specific thoughts and beliefs and ponder their reasonableness and accuracy. Evidence gaining and testing is a key element of cognitive therapy (Beck et al., 1979; Tarrier, 2006). This helps people 'stop, consider and re-consider' the basis of their automatic reactions and thoughts, and alter ruminations. The question, though, is how to reconsider? I have suggested that the emotional orientation for reconsidering our thoughts should be one based on warmth and compassion. So evidence-focused interventions and problem solving are contextualised as helpful thoughts, soothing thoughts, encouraging thoughts, supportive thoughts.

Is there enough information?

When seeking evidence for and against a belief it is useful to ensure that there is enough information to make judgements. Sometimes depressed people focus on small aspects of the situation and it is useful to encourage a wider exploration. For example, when Tim's girlfriend came over to see him she seemed down and distant. His thoughts were: 'Jenny seemed off me last night. I am sure that she is losing interest in me.' Note that we can see this as the *basic threat* – of rejection. Some cognitive therapists call this the 'bottom line' or catastrophe but if you keep in mind that Tim is focused on a basic threat, then it helps you keep on track with the idea we are dealing with threat-processing systems. As such, this threat will start to pull on psychobiological patterns activating a range of fears, memories and narrowing of attention. The counsellor can then explore how Jenny behaved when she met Tim last night. Did Jenny give any information about why she was quiet? Did Tim ask her? Exploring the situation may reveal information like: 'Well, actually Jenny is worried about losing her job.' This can then lead to looking at alternatives, for example 'Jenny was quiet because she felt down and worried and she tends to withdraw when she is worried.' The counsellor can then ask Tim how he might obtain information, by asking Jenny about her feelings and concerns. The counsellor might also explore the question: 'What might stop you seeking more information?' In one sense this is asking people to suspend their judgements about things when they are disappointed, rather than jump to conclusions – which is understandable but not helpful. Getting more information, including by simply asking people, is key here.

When we are depressed it is not uncommon to personalise an undesired outcome to the self. When we do this we forget that other people have issues and worries themselves that might better explain their behaviour. We lose an empathic and 'theory of mind' focus and engage in more projection (which is typical of threat processing). Becoming compassionate to self and others means recognising projection and trying to be more open to others as human beings too (Allen and Knight, 2005). This means being genuinely curious about *their* reasoning and feelings. When we are depressed (and at other times) this is not always easy to do and we have to practise it.

Looking at, or for, alternatives

Looking for, generating and considering, alternatives to negative thoughts and feelings are important aspects of helping people access different processing systems. This is because to generate and consider alternatives requires one to move out of the depressive thinking stream and use a different part of our brain. Sometimes depressed clients are convinced that there is only one way to view things. Here one teaches the client to consider *thoughts as theories* or *hypotheses*, and the more theories and hypotheses one has the better. This is similar to Kelly's (1955) view of teaching people how to treat themselves as scientists. So one explores the generation of alternative ideas/views. There are many types of Socratic question that can be used for this (see p. 197). For example, Harry, a student, gave a party in his room but some of his 'friends' did not attend. He concluded that this was because they did not like him enough to come. Again, consider Harry's basic threat.

Counsellor: Harry, you gave the party and some of the people you wanted to come did not show up. That was upsetting. One idea is that this is to do with you; that they don't like you enough. However, let's look at this idea in more detail and see if there are any other possible reasons for them not attending. Do you have any other evidence that they do not like you? For example, how do they treat you on a day-to-day basis? [*Ensure your voice tone is gentle and 'curious' and does not imply Harry is being irrational*]

Harry: Oh, day-to-day they seem friendly enough. I guess they help me with my work if I ask them.

Counsellor: Okay, what other reasons might there have been for them not attending? If you were a neutral outsider and were looking in, what other reasons may there have been for them not attending?

Harry: [*Thinks*] Well, Tom, who I wanted to come, can be unreliable. He's got a new girlfriend and maybe was out with her trying to get her into bed.

Counsellor: Anyone else?

Harry: Sally was planning to come but she was unsure if she was going to go home this weekend.

Counsellor: Could you ask these people and see if these other ideas fit? It is disappointing that they did not come to the party but not necessarily evidence of your likability – they may have had other things they wanted to do.

These are fairly simple examples for the purpose of making clear the techniques. Of course, the issues are often more complex and distressing but the principles are the same – to try to gain a balance in thinking. And if Harry were very narcissistic he might think others should give up their goals (with the girlfriend or going home for the weekend) to come to his party as proof they liked him. Or he might feel *envious* that Tom has a girlfriend and would rather be with her.

> Counsellor: I wonder if you might have felt a bit envious and resentful that they may have other things they would rather do.
>
> Harry: [*Sheepishly*] Maybe.
>
> Counsellor: Well, that is understandable. So I guess the question is how can we come to terms with our disappointment and envy without seeing it as 'they are rejecting me'?

Note that when we help people look at alternatives – in this case for the actions of others – we are also teaching people 'theory of mind skills', that is to not assume that other people's disappointing behaviour suggests negative intentions on their part. Of course in reality Harry might not be that popular and this would require us to work in a different way and help him come to terms with the fact that we cannot all be the most popular, and whether he can improve his friendship-building skills. Related to this is role reversal.

Role reversal

Helping the client think about how others might interpret events can be useful. Thus one can ask: 'How do you think others might respond to this? What accounts for the difference?' But watch out for beliefs like: 'I know others would see it differently but this just goes to show how silly I am.' The idea is that helping the client to see things from the other person's perspective helps to move the focus away from the self. Another form of role reversal helps the client to generate alternative ideas, through being encouraged to help someone else who has the same beliefs as themselves. For example, suppose a client says: 'I will never be able to succeed. I will never find the kind of relationship I need. My life is pointless and worthless.' Remember that this might be coming from an intense sense of disappointment and can be partly anger-related (see Chapter 8). The counsellor might say: 'How might you help someone else who felt disappointed and seemed trapped in this way of seeing things?' If the client attempts to do this, and is able to come up with alternative ways of thinking and looking at the problem, the counsellor may play devil's advocate and say: 'But suppose this person said, "I have tried all those things and they don't work", how would you respond to them?' In this way the counsellor avoids pitting themselves against the client and through role reversal has encouraged the client to explore alternatives to their own negative thinking by helping someone else. The counsellor might continue this with questions like: 'What do you think would stop this other person from acting on your ideas?' This enables a dialogue that helps the person to change their perspective.

Writing down

Clients often find it helpful to write things down. This helps to slow thinking down, can stop it from turning into depressing spirals of thinking and breaks up rumination. In the early stages, the counsellor and client may do this together. Later, clients do it for themselves. One simple method is with the use of two columns. In one column the depressing thoughts are written down and, in the other, various alternative thoughts. This is called the double-column technique. For example, suppose Harry had the thought 'I will never get better'.

Depressing thoughts	Helpful thoughts
I will never get better.	1. This is a distressing thought and reflects my fears and worries about my depression.
	2. Focusing on this idea is understandable because depression does that, but it makes me feel worse and I may be underselling myself.
	3. I can work on small steps towards understanding my depression and overcoming it.
	4. There are times when I do try things and sometimes feel a little better – so my depression does move a bit with what I do.
	5. I haven't always been depressed so I have shown myself I am capable of coping.
	6. Because things are difficult right now doesn't mean they will always be difficult.
Degree of belief: 75%	Degree of belief: 50%

As we work on the depression, both the degree of belief in 'I will never get better' and its frequency slowly reduce. Here is another example of Jane, who bought a dress in a hurry and when she got home found it did not fit as she would have liked.

Depressing thoughts	Helpful thoughts
I bought the wrong dress size. It bulges. I am fat and stupid.	1. How annoying – this is upsetting.
	2. It seemed to fit in the shop, but I was in a rush.
	3. I can probably take it back.
	4. Having a dress that is slightly too tight doesn't make me 'fat'.
	5. Even if I am heavier than I would like to be many millions of women feel similarly – thanks to the media!
	6. There is no link between body size and abilities.
	7. Being a rushed mother who tries hard for her family and occasionally buys things that don't fit means only that I am a rushed mother who occasionally buys things that don't fit. This is annoying – nothing more.
Degree of belief: 70%	Degree of belief: 60%

Empathy and validation for our distress

Note that the first thing we write down is empathy for our distress. For Harry this was: 'This is a distressing thought and reflects my fears and worries about my depression.' For Jane it was: 'How annoying – this is upsetting.' Some counsellors may miss this aspect and do not validate these fears, frustrations and feelings. So before we look for alternatives it is important to *acknowledge* and have empathy for our primary fears, feelings and reactions. These are spontaneous feelings, while the way we deal with these may be with more negative predictions and self-evaluations – called meta-cognitions (Wells, 2000) and secondary emotions, for example more depression and anxiety (Linehan, 1993). To have a compassionate focus requires constant attention and validation for fears and worries. Feeling that you won't get better is very frightening, but also focusing on this (although understandable because this is how depression pulls us into thinking) is unhelpful and we need to work out what would be helpful to counteract that 'pull' on our thinking.

Writing down is for the clarification it brings and acts as a focus for discussion. In the alternatives column it is important that clients recognise the thoughts and ideas as *genuine* alternatives and not as another form of instruction (this time coming from the counsellor, that is 'I believe that, but really I *ought* to believe this'). The moment the client shifts into a submissive position and feels the need to submit to the counsellor's ways of doing things, rather than it being a collaboration against the common problem of depression, one runs into resistance. Also, as noted in the last chapter, stay with an alternative in a warm frame of mind, really focus on it, until a person feels a change in emotion. Simply understanding it as logical is rarely enough. So you would ask Harry and Jane to spend time reading their alternative thoughts but to focus on feelings of 'warmth' as they read them.

Authoritarian (bullying) instructions

Watch out for what I call authoritarian instructions. Some people will generate alternative thoughts but in an *emotional tone* of anger, contempt, condemning or cold logic. For example, thoughts like: 'I am being unreasonable', 'I must look at the evidence', 'There is no need for me to feel like this', 'I am making mountains out of mole hills', 'I have let my thoughts run away with me', 'I should get out of bed and get on with things', 'I shouldn't let others get to me like this', 'I should do the work my therapist suggests', 'I should put more effort into this', etc., are examples of what can appear to be alternatives but actually are very unempathic to distress, and lack basic warmth or a focus on support, encouragement and being caring to the self. So look out for 'shoulds' and 'don't need tos'. Ask about the emotional tone in their minds when they generate alternatives.

You can check on this by asking: 'When you consider your alternative ideas and thoughts how do they feel in your mind? How do you hear them?' You may be surprised how often depressed people hear and feel their alternatives with textures of anger, of 'pull yourself together'. Jane said she thought her CBT was a mind game and while she could learn to generate alternatives they were usually cold and logical. It was very hard for her to lose the emotional tone of 'this is what I should think' or 'this is what Paul wants me to think' or 'this is the sensible thing to think and of course I have to be sensible'. So, as noted in Chapter 11, ensure the person tries to generate warmth and encouragement as the emotional tone of alternatives. Help them focus on these feelings *in* the alternative.

Spend time *feeling* the alternative

Alternative thought generation is not just a method of developing new thoughts – the thoughts must have some emotional impact. So spend time here. For example, one might suggest to Jane: 'Could you close your eyes for a moment and really focus on this alternative view? Let's explore it in detail. Really try to feel this idea that you are disappointed about the dress but this does not make you fat or that other women can feel similary. Imagine you saying this to yourself (or someone else saying it to you) with warmth and kindness. Let's stay with the idea and see if you feel something.'

If people find it hard to change the feelings associated with their thoughts, the counsellor and client need to get more evidence against a negative thought, but sometimes it is because the counsellor has not spent enough time *really letting the new ideas work themselves into the person and bed down.*

Degree of belief

To help see that our beliefs and thoughts are rarely black and white (100% this way or that) it is helpful to explore with the depressed client the degree or extent to which they believe something is true. This can be given a percentage rating. Beliefs are not always 'all or nothing' and in counselling depressed people one will see changes in the degree of a belief rather than its absolute removal. Sometimes even a 10% change is a major improvement. Some people like this kind of rating, others do not, so it is the principle that is important not the technique.

Memory prompts

Depressed clients can struggle with memories and recalling helpful things and events. This can be true in therapy too. They may forget what has happened in the last counselling session or even during a session. Therefore it is helpful for them to have prompts. This can be done by clients taking home thought records, summaries and diagrams worked through in the session. They might then make new ones or make comments on the things that have been written out to bring back to the next session. Another form of prompt can be to make a tape of the session so that the person can listen to it and make notes on it. Again, these can be brought back to the next session and discussed. Some clients like to have tapes of the session, others do not. All these help to engage the client in more independent practice.

Flash cards

Another form of prompt is to make flash cards. A flash card is a blank card about the size of a postcard. On one side of the card the client works out, with the counsellor, their thoughts, for example 'I am never able to do as good a job as I'd like. I always seem to fail. I am a useless person. What's the point of trying?' Rather than writing out these thoughts for themselves they can put a tick on the card as a thought happens. On the back, the counsellor and client work out some alternatives that the client feels are helpful. For example:

- I tend to panic and get frustrated when I fail because I am frightened of what it might lead to (e.g. criticism or rejection). I guess it brings back emotional memories from childhood (*empathy for distress*).

- However this setback is a bump in the road not a statement of me as a person. My depressed feelings may try to rubbish all I have achieved but I can stand back and look at this with kindness and see that actually I don't fail at all things – just sometimes. I have made mistakes before and it turned out okay (*refocusing attention*).
- 'Failure' is a black and white word, and in fact it's more about disappointment than abject failure. In three months' time I will have forgotten about this event. It will pass away. Everyone makes mistakes; it is only human. In fact, humans are so error-prone that we often try to makes systems that recognise this and help to reduce it (think of examples). It's what we can learn from them that is helpful and how to deal with them (*helpful thinking*).
- Right now the most helpful thing to do is... (*helpful behaviour*).

Different clients find different forms of alternatives helpful. For one client an appeal to reason is helpful, for another the appeal to self-nurturing. Sometimes clients say: 'When I looked on the back of my card I heard your voice and that was helpful.' This helps the internalisation of positive self-statements and cues emotional memory of a supportive relationship and episodes. Gradually clients learn to focus on alternatives for themselves. Sometimes we help people *tolerate* and *accept* feelings of disappointment as facts of life that are unavoidable.

Dwelling, rumination and frequency

As noted previously (see Chapter 9), it is also important to explore the frequency and extent to which a person dwells on a negative set of thoughts or ideas. As people improve they find they think less and less about them. One can also use this information to say: 'Given that such negative thoughts are stressful and distressing, can you see that if we *could* reduce their frequency this may be helpful by giving your stress system time to recover? Dwelling on negative thoughts can be like picking at a scab so that healing of your depression is harder.' Encourage people to become more attentive to their ruminations and stand back from them – noting them as 'thoughts arising in the mind'. Engaging in activities and writing thoughts down, speaking with others, considering alternatives, developing inner compassion and focusing on compassionate images can be helpful as anti-rumination processes.

Time frames

This focuses on how the person would think about this event or situation in (say) six months' time. This is appropriate for small day-to-day setbacks. Projecting forward into the future, where the client is unlikely even to remember a particular hassle or setback that has upset them, is helpful for keeping perspective. Also looking back and noting how they might have seen this, say, six months earlier, before they became depressed, can again help people recognise that some of their negative views are due to being in 'a state of depression'.

Advantages and disadvantages

This is an approach that has many uses and is used in many different therapies. It helps people develop some motivation to change. It can help to show up dilemmas and it also gives clients a clear insight into what may be blocking them from change. Write out two columns headed 'Advantages' and 'Disadvantages' (or 'Gains' and 'Losses'). Then list the ideas in each. Let's look at an example of self-blaming:

Reducing self-blaming

Advantages	Disadvantages
Would feel better.	Might become more angry.
Would take more risks.	Might become aggressive like mother (the not nice me).
Would not feel so inferior.	Might never see my faults.
Would stop hurting myself.	Others might not like me.

It is not uncommon that one of the disadvantages of changing is that the people see themselves as becoming more like a disliked (undesirable) other (i.e. an undesired self-identity). For example, in this case, the client's mother rarely blamed herself but mostly blamed the children. The client worried that by not blaming herself she might become like her (disliked) mother. Thus work focused on the type of blame (e.g. self, trait or behavioural) and helping her distinguish between blaming and responsibility.

Let's explore another example of a person who realises his perfectionistic attitudes are problematic but has trouble changing them:

Reducing perfectionism

Advantages	Disadvantages
Could relax.	Might become slapdash.
Feel less pressured.	Might make mistakes.
Could spend more time with my family.	Might miss opportunities to get on.
	Might become no better than others.
	Would lose self-respect.
	Others would reject me.

Understanding safety behaviours and beliefs

In the above case the client was sure that in becoming less of a perfectionist he would lose his self-respect. In a way he was proud to be perfectionistic and would be shamed by reducing it. Thus, although he was quite happy (supposedly) to work on his perfectionism, in fact he was not able to until it had become clear to him the potential costs, as he saw them, and worked with them. In a way this technique, in this kind of example, points to a more major issue of developing different textures to one's self-identity – and that can take time. Also note how this need to be perfect is related to various safety behaviours because it serves to ward off various fears (e.g. fears of losing self-respect and being rejected by others). So here this exploration of advantages and disadvantages helps to show up the *fears and safety behaviours that underpin the drive for perfection* (Beck et al., 1990). The counsellor would then note this with the client and explore the possible need to work on those fears.

In fact there are many 'costs to change' and the fear of change can be an important focus for counselling, for example: 'I might be abandoned. I might not like myself. God might not like me. I might become like others whom I dislike. Although things are bad now they may be worse if I change.' *Ambivalence to change is very common* and the counsellor needs to appreciate these as difficult dilemmas. While clients can agree goals in the counselling session, it is always worth running through the potential gains and losses to highlight possible losses. No client will change if somehow they sense that changing will make them worse or destabilise their self-identity. Talk about the step-by-step approach and behavioural experiments to test things out and see what helps.

If the problem is about reducing submissiveness and 'the need to please other people' beliefs and behaviours, the fears of doing so might include: 'If I give up putting others first and become more focused on my needs, then I will become selfish and unlovable.' Or even changing a basic way of thinking can relate to safety behaviours: 'If I give up black-and-white thinking then I can never be certain, and that's dangerous.' Or 'people will reject me'.

A common disadvantage in revealing a secret, like a history of abuse, an abortion, sexual or other behaviour, is 'If I tell you then you will dislike me and won't want to help me'. So again, keeping things secret can be related to various safety beliefs and behaviours.

Suppose the issue is about reducing anger at others or developing forgiveness (Worthington et al., 2005). This can be blocked because of various beliefs such as: 'If I give up my anger it is condoning what others have done to me', or 'it is saying it does not matter', or 'I will feel powerless'.

Looking at the advantages and disadvantages this way illustrates that 'techniques' are always *in the service of a process* and are not just stand-alone operations. Moreover, this way allows one to engage a *functional analysis of beliefs* which commonly are designed to ward off harms and threats – thus we call them safety behaviours and beliefs. Helping people to see that these styles are not about being irrational or distorted as such, but serve the important functions of trying to protect the person, can be very important in shifting thinking and brings the counsellor and client closer together as being engaged in working directly with the underlying fears.

By writing these down together the client is able to be clear about the dilemmas and hold them in one frame, as it were, and then there can be a new agreement to work on not just the goal, but the fears of reaching the goal, or paradoxically fear of success! Sometimes whole sessions can be given over to this one form of intervention and it is especially important in motivational interviewing.

Other people's gains?

In some cases of depression it is useful to consider the possibility of what others might gain from the client's depression. In various forms of family counselling it has been noticed that as a family member's depression reduces, other problems surface. Some years ago when I was doing some family therapy training, a colleague, Elspeth MacAdam, who was doing the training, gave the example of an adolescent girl whose mother could not decide about making a long-term commitment to a new male friend. While the daughter was depressed, the mother was able to avoid the problem. In the counselling the adolescent was offered the idea that her depression protected her mother from having to make a difficult decision. It had a remarkable effect by reframing the problem as protection of mother (see also Sloman, 2000). This was not to deny other issues, such as fear of loss if her mother focused on a new male friend, but this intervention shifts the self-identity focus.

Hence one can speculate (gently) on issues such as 'I wonder what your spouse/family gains by your being depressed and clinging on to them'. At first a client may be perplexed by such a question, but it can 'get them thinking'. This kind of question is aimed in part at illuminating the power issues that may be involved in depression, but it also helps a client to see a depression in a new light; that is, paradoxically, a depressed position can actually be *protective* of the self or of someone else. For example, if the client were not depressed they might leave a relationship. There is now growing evidence that depression acts to inhibit assertive behaviour and this can have the effect of maintaining the power of others (Gilbert, 1992). Jane felt her husband was a supportive and kind man but also shy. She had been mildly depressed when they married. Over the years her depression had got worse and had been treated with various drugs. As she recovered (with therapy) she started to want to go out with friends and maybe even train for a new job. This activated envious and jealous anger in her husband (fear that she might leave him and that he was 'not enough for her'). Thus rather than expressing joy in her recovery, there was much condemnation of the new woman she was becoming. He had little ability to see any difficulties with his own behaviour or that he was in fact insecure. She began to think that maybe her depression had kept her husband from facing his own insecurities.

This is a complex point but one can think about safety behaviour and strategies that operate at the level of the relationship rather than the individual. However, using the advantages–disadvantages process can help illuminate these themes.

Mourning the lost chance or ideal

Some safety strategies are to avoid the pain of some realities and the emotional working through needed to come to terms with them. When helping people to change it is useful to recognise that there may be a secret fantasy about what their current attitudes or behaviours may achieve if they stick with them (e.g. 'If I *could* get my performance perfect, then I would be successful. Only if I am successful will I be loved and respected. If I *could* be nice all the time, then I would be loved'). Sometimes clients find it difficult to come to terms with ordinary human failings because they wish to be superior to others in order to avoid inferiority and the possible rejections that could go with it (Gilbert, 1989, 2000a). By achieving lofty goals or high standards they think they will fulfil basic human needs for love, acceptance, respect and admiration. Our competitive societies rather feed these beliefs. Hence it often happens that overcoming resistance to changing such strivings may involve the opportunity to *mourn* these lost ideal possibilities (Gilbert and Irons, 2005). The advantages–disadvantages approach (see p. 275) can be a useful way to help explore these aspects. The client will be less likely to shift on these if the underlying ideals are not addressed. The issue here, however, is that acknowledging what we might need to soften our striving illuminates the underlying fears and emotional memories of aloneness and rejection. This can involve complex grief work.

Working with the past

It can be useful for clients to recognise that certain ways of coping may have been adaptive at one time, and are not evidence of inferiority or stupidity. Here we can use three columns.

Current belief	Contributing past experiences	Helpful alternatives
I have no control over my life.	My parents said I must always do as I was told.	I am an adult now and can choose.
	I had to change schools often due to my father's job.	I can stay where I am now if I wish.
	My parents often disliked my friends.	My choice of friends depends on my feelings and preferences.
Degree of belief: 80%	Degree of belief: 100%	Degree of belief: 45%

In the above example, it is not just a case of writing things down but using the columns to clarify meanings and experiences, such that (in this case) the person gains insight as to why it seems 'as if' they have no control (and this may have been true at one time) but they can now make changes. This involves giving up trying to please parents or fit in with others, and gaining more confidence in one's own decisions and preferences. In the above case, as counselling progressed, we saw changes in the degree of belief, with column 1 reducing and column 3 increasing. This indicates again that counselling is *a process* and rarely produces sudden change.

Further ideas for working with thoughts

The above are common forms of working with cognitive aspects but here are some additional areas that you may wish to discuss with clients (Leahy and Holland, 2000; Tarrier, Wells and Haddock, 1998):

1 Are they misunderstanding the nature of causes? Most events are multi-causal.
2 Are they confusing a thought or idea with fact?
3 Are they assuming that every situation is/will be the same?
4 How would they look at this if they were not depressed?
5 Are they confusing a high probability with a low probability?
6 Are they being honest with themselves?
7 Are they asking questions that have no answers?
8 How would they feel about this (event) in a month or a year?

Key issues 12.1   Targeting specific cognitions

1   The main focus is on the client's internal cognitions, interpretations and beliefs.
2   The counsellor aims to increase the client's awareness of these and their contribution to depression.
3   The counsellor and client try to identify typical forms of cognitive style or biases (e.g. personalisation, disqualifying the positive, black-and-white thinking).
4   Insight is important but it is not the main goal of the approach. Cognitions are treated as hypotheses and theories, not facts.
5   The counsellor and client work together to decide what are reasonable and helpful alternatives rather than just pulling ideas out of the hat.
6   The counsellor encourages the client to stay emotionally focused on alternatives until they feel some impact from that alternative.
7   The counsellor and client recognise both the advantages and the fears/disadvantages of change.
8   The counsellor continually helps the client see the safety behaviours and beliefs that can underpin various forms of thinking and behaviours and their advantages and disadvantages.

Working with the negative self-cognitions and feelings

As we saw in Chapter 6, self-criticism is a major problem in depression and is linked to shame. As Beck (1967) and many others have made clear, depression often involves negative thinking about the self. Freud used the term *superego* to describe self-attacking (Freud, 1917). Gestalt therapists suggest that there is a part of ourselves that plays top-dog and attacks and criticises, and a part that plays underdog and feels the effects of being attacked (Greenberg and Watson, 2006). Behaviourists focus on punitive self-reinforcement (Rehm, 1988). Evolution therapists focus on a dominant–subordinate self-to-self relating style (Gilbert and Irons, 2005). There is now considerable evidence that high self-criticism increases vulnerability to depression, affects expression of symptoms, elevates risk of relapse, and makes therapy more difficult (Gilbert and Irons, 2005; Zuroff, Santor and Mongrain, 2005). In this section we will look at some ways of working with self-criticism/attacking and negative thinking about the self. A more complex approach, with a review of the literature and reasons why developing self-compassion can be a key antidote to self-criticism, can be found in Gilbert (2000c), Gilbert and Irons (2005) and Gilbert and Procter (2006).

The self is a multiple system

It can be useful to explain how we are made up of different parts, motives, desires and with shifting states of mind. For some people this helps in understanding that *inner conflict is common* because we often seek different goals at the same time, for example: 'Part of me would like to play guitar and write a new song but part of me knows I need to go to work or I'll get the sack', 'Part of me would like to get my own back on the bullying boss but part of me is anxious about losing the conflict and being fired'. From here it is possible to discuss inner conflicts and aid the person to explore fully the conflict rather than try to suppress one side of it with thoughts like 'I shouldn't feel this way' or 'I shouldn't want to do this' (Gilbert, 2000c; Greenberg et al., 1993).

The inner critic and bully

Once the person has insight into the nature of different part-selves and inner conflict it is then possible to suggest that when things don't work out, or we fail in our efforts, or are not as we would like to be, we can feel a sense of disappointment and frustration. Out of this disappointment and frustration we can self-attack. Remember Jane above, who called herself fat and stupid for buying a dress in the wrong size. That is an example of self-attack. Once the person is able to verbalise the typical self-attacking thoughts, which are usually internally shaming thoughts (e.g. 'I am a failure, I will never make good, I am worthless, nobody could love me'), it is then possible to label this part of the self as the self-attacking part, or the inner shamer, the inner critic or inner bully (Gilbert, 2000c; Gilbert and Irons, 2005). Many depressed people can feel their inner shamer or critic as powerful and they usually agree with its judgements. In effect, they feel they have to submit to their own self-attacks and rarely feel able to 'fight back', challenge them or be compassionate to them (Whelton and Greenberg, 2005).

Imagining the inner critic

It can be useful to ask depressed people: 'If your critic were a person, whom you could see, what would they look like?' (i.e. use visualisations). Sometimes they seem like a real person; at other times no clear image comes but they have a sense of the inner bully. Sometimes they can identify it as the voice of a parent or other person who has put them down. Commonly, depressed people find this easy to do and use descriptions such as: big, powerful, dark, looming, with an angry face, or sadistic smile (Gilbert, 2000c; Gilbert and Irons, 2005). To focus on the emotional tone of the critical thoughts, you can ask: 'If you run those critical thoughts through in your mind, what emotions do they have when they put you down? What emotion is your inner critic directing at you? What emotion does it have for you?'

These turn out to be mostly angry, aggressive or contemptuous. One might then say: 'Given these qualities, it is easy to see how you would struggle to not feel beaten down by it.' You might also decide to name it so that these aspects of self can be externalised. I tend to go with simple names like inner critic, shamer or bully because I point out that self-attacks in depression usually seek submission and cause more depression and anxiety, just like any other real bully does. As noted in Chapter 11, we can develop understanding and compassion for this part of self because it can be an automatic reaction to threat and frustration.

Functional analysis

It is important to explore the functions of self-criticism because there are many different functions, forms and sources for self-criticism and it should not be seen as one process (Gilbert, Clarke, Kempel, Miles and Irons, 2004). Typical functions include: 'I criticise myself because it keeps me on my toes and stops me making mistakes; it drives me on and thus increases the chances of my success; it makes me responsible.' These are what we call self-improving self-criticism. These forms of self-criticism can be used as a *warning:* 'If you don't improve then others will reject you.' 'If you don't stop eating you will get fat and out of control.' 'If you are not more assertive others are just going to walk all over you.' They are commonly triggered by frustration and making errors, and are full of frustrated anger: 'You stupid person – why did you do that?'

A different function is related to self-disgust and hatred. Here the person criticises themselves, not to improve themselves, but because there are things about them they dislike or hate and want rid of or even to destroy: 'I criticise my weight because I am fat and disgusting and I know I am weak not to do anything about it.' 'I criticise myself because after my abuse I feel there is something bad in me and I have a sense of disgust with my body.' To 'hate' something about the self is very different from the drive to improve and make good. This type is more common when people have had abusive experiences.

These two types are by no means mutually exclusive, although they can have their origins in different types of experience. The degrees of frustration, anger and hatred in the self-to-self relationship can be linked to the degree of depression and other complexities, such as personality difficulties. People suffering borderline personality disorders can have very vicious self-critical styles, while mild depressives have more disappointed-in-self, self-critical styles.

The two chairs

One procedure for increasing awareness of the power of self-criticism, and its emotive effects, is the two chairs procedure (Greenberg et al., 1993; Whelton and Greenberg, 2005). In this situation the counsellor elicits the negative dialogue in the form of an inference chain. For example, as noted above, Jane bought a dress which, when she tried it on again at home, she felt did not fit. Her thoughts were: 'I bought the wrong size dress. I bulge all over the place. I am fat and stupid.' This was written on a card and placed on one chair. She was then invited to sit in this chair and read the card to the chair opposite saying out loud: 'You bought the wrong size dress. It bulges all over the place. You are fat and stupid.' We can call this the attacking or critical chair. When a certain level of affect had been put in to this, she changed back and sat in the chair at which the attack was directed. She was then asked to explore her feelings about this attack being levelled against her. In the attacking chair she felt angry and annoyed with herself but in the other chair her feelings were of passive acceptance of the attack, sadness and helplessness. Greenberg et al. (1990) pointed out that people often get depressed because they cannot defend themselves against their self-criticism. In essence their own self-criticisms direct contempt or hostility at the self. It bullies and beats them down and then they feel defeated.

Here we note that Jane can be encouraged to see the self-criticisms coming from a sense of disappointment, shame-like thoughts (I have let myself go) and a fear others will not like her if she does not look nice. So her self-criticism is related to *basic threats* to the self. These feelings are understandable and so Jane could validate her feelings and may think: 'I can see this self-criticism is related to my disappointment and fears but is not a reflection of me as a person.' Greenberg and Watson (2006) suggest that enabling a dialogue between the critical part of the self and the part that feels the criticism can soften it. I have found that being compassionate to the criticisms is also helpful: 'I am so sorry you feel this upset and frightened that you have to lash out at me like this. However, it does not have to be this way.' Then bring in the compassionate alternatives.

Some therapists suggest trying to get rid of or even imagining trying to shoot the self-critic. I do not advocate this because we are trying to work with threats and develop self-soothing for self-criticism. You do not want to demonstrate that dealing with self-criticism is about aggressive power and becoming angry with the self-criticism. This may simply maintain anger affect systems. So we develop empathy for self-criticism. This is why we switch to a compassionate stance and invite the person to say to their self-critic: 'I am so sorry you feel so threatened that all you can do is lash out like this. You must feel very threatened to say this to me.' This produces an automatic distancing from the self-criticism and activates a different affect system. Then we explore compassionate attention, thinking behaviour and feeling. What this does, in essence, is to by-pass the self-critic. What we are suggesting is that you can listen to your critical voice, which comes from your threat system, but you can learn to attend more to your compassionate voice. In this way we are simply building up alternative ways of learning to cope with setbacks and threats. As people learn to do this they become less threatened by setbacks and thus the self-criticism automatically shrinks. Nowadays I do not directly engage in argument and counter-argument with the self-critical. This is to perpetuate conflict (trying to defeat a part of self) and I suspect maintains amygdala processing. So we note its voice and the threat nature of it, but we want to activate soothing affects, not conflictual ones. I have found that depressed people find this much easier to do rather than just trying to contradict their critical self with alternative evidence. You may use evidence, of course, in the alternatives, but the key is to focus on the compassionate feel of it.

Recall Jane, whose dress did not fit. We could invite her to develop self-compassion and warmth that is linked to thoughts like: 'The dress not fitting is a disappointment (empathy for the distress), but this does not make me fat or stupid – thinking like that is because I feel (understandably) frustrated and cross. I wouldn't be the first woman...' and so on, as above. So here we accept the disappointment as a disappointment, recognise we are not alone in feeling such disappointment and then focus on a coping behaviour. We work to hear the tone of these thoughts as validating, warm and supportive. Working on the deeper shame issue will emerge over time.

One client (we will call Bob) failed to get the job he wanted. When he sat in the critical chair he blamed himself and labelled himself as 'a bum'. When he switched chairs he was able to see that some of his attacks were because he was upset and disappointed and these attacks were a 'bit over the top'. He had not really appreciated how aggressive he was with himself. In the two chairs he was able to give himself the message: 'Many people fail to get the jobs they want. Maybe they were looking for someone with different skills. Failing to get a job is evidence of problems in the job market, not of being a bum.' He was able to empathise with the disappointment and sadness of not getting the job and reduce the self-attacking.

Working with self-criticism often involves developing alternative 'inner voices, thoughts and images' that are warm *and compassionate* ones and the person can practise refocusing on these. So, for example, sometimes the client is *first* encouraged to imagine feelings of warmth and caring, as if they were speaking to a friend or someone they cared for, and focus on those feelings for a moment. Or they might focus on their compassionate image and do a compassionate reframe (see pp. 263–264). When they have brought those feelings to mind they then focus on those feelings and in a warm voice might say: 'I know I didn't get the job and that is very disappointing. I guess it is only natural to be upset about this. But I have got jobs in the past and if I keep trying I have a fair chance in the future. Not getting the job is evidence of how hard it is to get jobs nowadays, not evidence of bum-hood.'

Working with different sources of self-criticism

Sometimes people can identify the source of their self-criticism as coming from childhood, such as a parent. One can ask: 'Did that type of self-criticism remind you of anyone?' If it turns out to be a parental figure, this may elicit important feelings and memories and the counsellor needs to be sensitive to allow these to emerge and work gently with them. We might acknowledge how hard it would be not to become self-critical if someone was putting you down a lot. You might say:

> When we are children we tend to see ourselves as others treat us. If they treat us nicely, then we learn to treat ourselves that way, but if they are harsh then we can see ourselves *that* way. It is almost impossible for us to not be affected by others' judgements, especially as children. But maybe the time has come to think: 'If I could go back and parent myself with love and kindness, what would I like to say to me as a child?' You see, we may never have given ourselves a chance to heal because we stay trapped with all those other voices and memories in our heads.

There are many ways you can work with critics that come from the past. For example, Lee (2005) has shown how you can identify the voice of the critic, say as a mother, and then look *at the credentials* of, say, the mother as a critic. For one of her patients, who heard the critical voice of her mother, she was able to see that far from being a loving, caring and calm mother, she was a tense, irritable, self-centred woman from a difficult background herself, who constantly worried about appearances. Thus, maybe her mother's judgements are not that reliable.

Gilbert and Irons (2005) have pointed out that some people are very anxious about seeing this kind of 'truth'. They may feel they are being disloyal to their family, or might discover aggressive feelings, or have guilt feelings. To begin to realise that one's parents may not have been able to care for them in the way they needed can be frightening and sad, especially if people have worked hard to try to earn their parents' love. Thus we need to understand the complexities associated with *rebellion* to parental views of self. As noted elsewhere (Gilbert and Irons, 2005), rebellion is the first step to changing the negative 'voices' in our heads. It can go through stages that include:

- beginning *inner doubt* – beginning to doubt the validity of the others' judgements about the self;
- *externalisation of doubt* – giving voice to that doubt and clarifying the reasons for doubting;

- *active dissent and 'disobedience'* – beginning to think *and act* in ways that fulfil self-nurturing goals even if (past) others would not approve of them (i.e. to act against the dictates of the parent and learn to adopt new values). This may involve distancing oneself. For example, one depressed person found telephone conversations with her mother stressful because her mother constantly criticised her for not doing enough. So she explained to her mother that she could not continue to take the calls if she was going to be critical. This act of rebellion took a lot of courage but brought great relief too.

Hackmann (2005) has noted that sometimes it can be useful to engage in imaginary assertiveness. For example, one of her patients imagined a critical event when her parents were not there for her (being in hospital). She re-played the scene in her mind but explained assertively how disappointed she was with them. In this way the inner construction changes from passive, submissive acceptance to one of assertiveness.

More ways of working with self-critical thoughts

When it comes to compassionate attention, thinking, behaviour and feeling it is useful to have some idea of how to work on these. Let's look at some, but keep in mind that it is always a collaborative process and depressed people need to *feel* these to be helpful. So you should not get into a conflict where you are trying to force people to see things your way, and imply (unintentionally) that they are daft, difficult or resistant if they don't. Force of argument is no alternative to a therapy that understands that people can be frightened of change.

Thinking in blends, shades or dimensionally

A common difficulty in depression (and self-criticism) is dichotomous thinking or thinking in black and white (Beck et al., 1979). In psychodynamic theory this is called 'splitting' (Gilbert, 1992). There are two aspects here: basic black-and-white thinking and coping with ambivalence (Gilbert, 2000c). For basic black-and-white thinking there are various ways to explore this. One is to draw a straight line with a bipolar construct. For example, suppose a client says 'My performance was a complete failure', the counsellor may draw a line like this:

```
Failure ------------------------------------------------- Success
Bad ------------------------------------------------------ Good
Terrible ------------------------------------------------- Wonderful
```

The client then places an X on the line to show the degree of success or failure they think applies to them. Often this is put close to the failure end of the line. The counsellor then discusses various other behaviours that might rate as greater failures to illuminate how the person's construct is rather narrow. For example, suppose someone places a mark at the end of the bad–good line, indicating they feel totally bad. One might then ask: 'So where would you put Hitler?' Use gentle humour. The idea here is (a) to help people understand how, in depression, it is so easy to lose perspective and the importance of working hard to regain it, (b) how the inner bully is often a crude black-and-white thinker and labeller – because that is how threat systems think (c) that disappointments can stimulate our threat systems and we can 'panic' and become angry as a result. One can talk in terms of focusing on the achievements or the failures, the glass that is half-full or half-empty. Again the technique is to help the client understand the nature of their absolutistic thinking, and a great deal of discussion is also involved in a gentle and sometime humorous way. Keep in mind that gentle humour is also inducing a new emotion, a kind of playfulness that can create new emotional textures to thoughts.

Distinguishing self-rating from behavioural rating

This is a very common problem in depression and is often reinforced culturally. Basically, it is 'if my performance is poor then "I" (as a person) am a failure' (Ellis, 1977a, 1977b). Here again one focuses on the feelings of disappointment (empathy for distress) and then explores the problems of global self-rating and negative self-labelling. We note how, when we feel disappointed, this can feel *as if* the self is a failure, but we can spot these tendencies in ourselves (which may include emotional memories), stand back and take a more balanced view.

You can use the *part–self* approach to talk about there being many aspects of self that one can call 'little i's' rather than one big or global 'I'. This aids in illustrating how a client may be making global generalisations about themself from single events. Sometimes we call this kind of self-rating from performance outcomes the IT–ME confusion. I only accept ME if I do IT well. Or I only like myself if I am succeeding at X. IT–ME confusions often lie behind ideas of worth (lessness) and also self-labelling. Hence we try to teach self-understanding and acceptance, and again much discussion can be given over to this issue (Gilbert, 2000c).

IT–ME confusions are part of western culture. They are very common, and the counsellor should be clear in their own mind about this. As Fennell (1989) says, this is a case of 'physician heal thyself'. In training therapists and counsellors I have found that many find this a basic problem: 'But surely your worth is dependent on how competent you are!' they say to me. Counsellors who have this basic belief may have problems in helping their clients change such beliefs (see Bennett-Levy and Thwaites, 2007).

Reattribution training

In depression there can be much personalisation for bad outcomes. The inner critical part of self often goes in for a lot of blaming: 'It's my fault that Fred/Sally left me.' Simple interventions can involve looking at the evidence for and against the attribution. Another technique is to draw a circle and allocate various aspects of causality to slices of the circle (see Gilbert, 2000a, p. 141). In this way one derives a picture of how events often have many causes. However, again there can be complications. For example, a depressed client may say: 'If I blame others then I would be in a rage and that makes me feel bad about myself.' Hence self-blame can have a protective function (see above). Indeed, the way self-blame stops one expressing anger at others can be explored in many ways (e.g. as defensive exclusion: as a child the client has learnt not to be critical of others and therefore ignores other people's bad behaviour towards them; Gilbert and Irons, 2005). So when self-blame arises it is always useful to keep in mind whether this is concerned with interpersonal events or not, the former being more complex. The advantages–disadvantages approach can also be used to explore the issue of 'not taking the blame' (see above and Gilbert, 2000a).

The other distinction to be aware of is attribution for causes and attributions for changes or solutions. For example, people can feel ashamed of depression because they attribute the cause to themselves. Cause and solution can be linked in the following ways:

1 It is not my fault I am depressed and there is nothing I can do to change.
2 It is my fault I am depressed and there is nothing I can do to change.
3 It is my fault I am depressed and I can take steps to change.
4 It is not my fault I am depressed but I can take steps to overcome depression.

The causes of depression, and vulnerability to it, can arise from many sources (e.g. post-viral infections, hostile marriages, poor early experiences, etc.) Getting caught up in self-blaming for causing depression is not helpful. Thus we can endorse a multi-factor causal model. Nevertheless, helping clients recognise that by putting themselves down they may maintain and worsen their depression is not to be taken as evidence of personal blame for depression. The match between client and counsellor attribution for depression can be a source of difficulty that interferes with therapeutic work (for an illuminating discussion, see Jack and Williams, 1991; and Leahy, 2007).

The other distinction that can be made in attributions, which is similar to the IT–ME confusion, is the distinction between blaming one's character and blaming one's behaviour. Generally, character (personal attributes and qualities) self-blame is more depressogenic than behavioural self-blame (Janoff-Bulman, 1979; Janoff-Bulman and Hecker, 1988). For example, Janoff-Bulman found that, in women who had been raped, character self-blame ('it was something about me that invited it') was more commonly associated with depression than behavioural self-blame ('it was something I did, such as walk in the wrong part of town'). Andrews (1998) gives a very good review of this work in relation to shame and depression. Dryden (1989d) suggests that there are three levels of self-blame: blaming self, blaming traits and blaming behaviour. These vary in terms of the global qualities of self-blame. I suggest that self-blame is rarely helpful (because it is not far from accusing and condemning). So I encourage people to think non-judgementally of 'what was my contribution to this difficulty and how might I change that in the future'. We are all part of dynamic, reciprocal interactions and it is understanding these patterns that is key, rather than blaming or accusing.

Attitudes to feelings

Sometimes in depression there is much resentment, envy and anger under the surface (Gilbert, 1992, 2000a) but the person has difficulty in coping with these feelings because they see them as evidence of a bad self (i.e. they are ashamed of these feelings – the inner critic tells them it is bad to feel these things). Some people feel that they do not have the right to be angry, while others feel that anger makes them unlovable; thus anger cues an internal attack and the client takes a defensive position to it (e.g. I am a horrible or ungrateful person to feel this kind of anger). In Chapter 11 we noted that negative beliefs and fears of emotions acted as blocks to compassion (see also Leahy, 2002).

The counsellor helps the client accept their resentment or other feelings and to recognise that very often they relate to painful disappointment. In many cases I have found a cycle of disappointment cuing anger, anger cuing bad self-experience, and bad self-experiences cuing fears of abandonment and loss (see the case of Peter in Chapter 8). This goes around in the person's mind, leading to much confusion and distress. An empathic counsellor always has an ear open for disappointment, whether this be of an ideal self or a hoped for outcome/event, and allows the grief and anger to be explored. Generally, it is useful to explore what ignites negative feelings, and especially the beliefs that are involved. The counsellor then tries to de-shame them, and explores how the issues that generate strong negative emotions (like anger) can be tackled in different ways, such as via assertiveness training. Sometimes irritability is part of being stressed or becoming depressed, and some women feel it is related to their menstrual cycle. Sometimes it may even be related to medication. So it is important to explore the origins of anger (and other negative affects), for example: Is increased anger arousal new? Does it seem related to life events or mood change? In working with attitudes to feelings much depends on the person and situation.

Here's a complex (but not uncommon) example that illustrates how to break problems down, empathise with unspoken feelings, de-shame anger and reduce guilt. Having spoken with Oliver, I had a view of his marital conflicts.

Oliver: We have been married over twenty years and I love my wife but she fusses around me and wants me to go out more. I just get angry with her and then feel guilty. She is only trying to help but sometimes the atmosphere is tense. It's all my fault.

Counsellor: There seems to be a number of different things happening here. First, you say your wife feels that if you could do more, that might be helpful. She might be right about that. However, you resent the suggestion and feel that she thinks you are not making enough effort. You then feel shamed and angry, and then guilty for being angry?

Oliver: Yes. That is a typical way it goes.

Counsellor: Okay, well first I think depressed people will only do more if they can see that in the long run it will help and I am not sure that you do. So we will need to work together on that to see what kinds of things *you* think will be helpful. [*Counsellor thinks here of using the advantages–disadvantages approach*]. If it is helpful, we could invite your wife to a meeting or two to explore this. The problem here may be that you feel you have to do things to please the other person and not because you yourself really want to. If you go along with her suggestions you feel you are merely submitting to her requests and you resent that?

Oliver: I guess that's true. I do feel I ought to give in and do what she says. I am sure she is being very sensible but I meant it.

This is a typical issue in depression. Helpful suggestions by others may or may not be seen as helpful but as things the depressed person feels they should *submit* to in order to please or placate the other person. This issue needs to be clarified (see Chapter 5) because feeling one needs to submit invariably produces anger and resentment.

> Counsellor: Feeling that you have to submit although you don't want to will naturally produce resentment and resistance. This is true for most people, including me [*smiles*]. Without wanting to, it can become a clash of wills. There is nothing bad about you for feeling like this but of course it does produce an undesirable effect – the bad atmosphere. So what we can do here is explore with both of you when it would be helpful to encourage you more and when not. As to when to do more, this can be explored here in our therapy together (e.g. by using activity scheduling). Secondly, both you and your wife are angry with the depression – and that too is only natural. The trick is how to form a bond against the common problem – the depression – rather than against you or each other. Do you have any thoughts about that?
>
> Oliver: Well I guess I need to talk to her more about my depression and how I feel. I do tend to shut her out. I just feel I should pull myself out of this and stop being such a pain and worry to her.
>
> Counsellor: Sharing your feelings with your wife and 'not shutting her out' would certainly be worth exploring. Also, you know, your anger could be seen as a kind of resistance that is actually about you trying to hold to your self-integrity and not simply do what others want. Sure, it does not produce the effects you want, but at least it shows you are no push-over?
>
> Oliver: [*After some thought*] Hm. I suppose that's true. There is a part of me that thinks I don't want to be pushed around any more.

Oliver also felt others were ready with advice but did not listen to him. No client will change if they see disadvantages in changing. Also, note how there is a lot of defending a self-identity here: 'I don't want to be pushed around any more'. Let's look, then, at Oliver with the advantages–disadvantages technique. One of the disadvantages of 'doing more' was that he saw it as simply evidence that he submits to what others want him to do.

Doing more: e.g. going out

Advantages	Disadvantages
Might feel better.	Only doing what I am told/submissive.
Regain old enjoyments.	Feel tired and anxious.
Could spend more time with wife.	Probably boring to be with.
	Not much of a conversationalist when out these days.
	Feel under pressure to have interesting conversations and then I feel worse.

This helped Oliver gain more insight to how his resistance to change was rooted in a desire not to submit and simply to do what he was told or to be treated like a child. I had to be careful of this when working with him as what I thought was collaborative he sometimes took as me suggesting what he should do and him having to go along with it. Also note that going out activated fears of having to make interesting conversation or show he was enjoying himself – 'putting a face on' – which again felt to him like a submission. So we need to validate the 'I don't want to submit anymore' as a sign of strength and, indeed, foster that. But this can have unfortunate consequences if done in certain ways and one can end up cutting one's nose to spite one's face. There are other ways to be assertive.

In a joint session with his wife we explored how the depression would take some time to change in a step-by-step way, that scheduling activities would be done in the therapy and how they could share feelings without each feeling ashamed and resentful. Helping his wife feel less 'shut out', clarifying the nature of depression, improving communication while relieving her of responsibility to help Oliver change, and acknowledging that resentment and anger are often part of the frustrations of being depressed, did much to ease the tensions at home. It enabled Oliver to start to take more control over his depression rather than feeling he had to do what his wife said (submit) to please her. And by understanding the nature of his anger he became less ashamed and guilty of it. In fact, his anger was re-labelled as a kind of strength to resist submitting.

Of course these snippets of interaction are actually part of an ongoing relationship, and I was able to make these kinds of intervention because I knew Oliver had had ongoing life difficulties of feeling 'he had to submit', and 'not being heard' going right back to a dominant mother. But I hope they give some insight into working with conflicts and emotions in relationships.

Identifying the shoulds, oughts and musts

Self-critical thoughts are usually (like the superego) full of 'shoulds' and 'oughts'. They issue instructions. There are many forms of 'must' that can 'surface' as people become depressed: I have to be loved, I must be perfect, or, as in Oliver's case, 'I must not feel angry with people who are only trying to help me'. The main concern here is to change a 'must', 'ought' or 'should' into an 'I'd like/prefer to'. Hence it is changing *commands* or *demands* into *preferences*. One can engage the depressed client in discussion of their 'life's rule book' or our 'personal contracts with life', pointing out that 'musts' lead to certain feelings of compulsion and lack of freedom. Or one can simply ask: 'Why do you think you *must* be loved?' In this way you can elicit an underlying belief and fear such as 'Without love I'm worthless'. Hence, the worthless idea leads to the compulsion to be loved. You can also relate this to basic fears of aloneness (see chapter 5). Thus 'oughts', 'shoulds' and 'musts' are often driven by some underlying self-evaluative concept and basic fear. However, in this kind of situation it is important that the counsellor does not convey the view that there is something unacceptable in the *strong desire* to have a loving relationship, or control one's anger – far from it. Rather, the focus is on the sense of worthlessness (the inner attack), not the desire. Indeed, counselling may involve helping the person acquire skills that make it more likely they can form intimate and meaningful relationships – that may be a counselling goal!

Also, the idea that life would be meaningless without success or love can be an issue. Here again, one does not suggest that the goal is undesirable, and one can discuss the evolutionary importance of it. So the focus is on the global evaluations and the dismissal of other sources of positive rewards. In such cases mourning may be involved as counselling unfolds, especially if these desires are highly idealised (Gilbert, 2000a, 2000c).

The counsellor will also use their empathy to recognise when a client is using the words 'should', 'ought' or 'must' in a relative way or in an absolute way. We often use 'should' and 'ought' words in normal, everyday language, but this does not mean we 'feel' them as absolute 'musts'. Thus clients can be asked to rate the degree of belief in their 'musts' and 'shoulds'.

Key issues 12.2   Working with negative self-cognitions and feelings

1   Identify the typical feelings associated with self-criticism and self-attacking (e.g. anger, contempt, hostility).
2   Clarify the stress-inducing and mood-depressing effects of these thoughts and feelings.
3   Teach the nature of 'part-selves' such that the client can identify the 'voice of' their internal critic or shamer.
4   Use visualisation as appropriate.
5   Use compassionate focusing to see the fear behind the self-criticism and also to develop self-compassion.
6   Intergrate various of the cognitive-behavioural interventions to address self-criticism in a compassionate way.

Conclusion

This chapter has explored various ways that you can work with negative thinking and self-attacking, and introduce more positive tones into a client's thinking styles. These are in the spirit of *reducing the negative* and *increasing the positive* and regaining perspective. On the 'rational' side, one looks at the evidence for and against a particular belief or view, and helps the person generate alternative views, reattribute causes, and develop new coping options. However, it is also important to help people develop more inner warmth, especially in the ways they cope with frustrations and setbacks. Warm and supportive inner signals are more likely to be emotionally and physiologically soothing and it is important to share these ideas so that people understand the purpose of the exercise. It is important, then, to help clients *generate alternatives in a warm, supportive and compassionate way.* This is especially so when it comes to self-criticisms. One might ask: 'How does this alternative view *sound* to you when you run it through in your mind? Does it seem warm and reassuring or cold, rational, aloof, distant or angry?' The more you can help clients develop inner warmth in their inner world the more likely they are to soften their depression.

So, as emphasised all the way through, if you are new to counselling try not to be so mesmerized or worried by techniques that you lose sight of the basic counselling skills. Counselling is a process where the relationship you form with your client is paramount.

13 Working with Specific Difficulties I: Approval, Achievement, Assertiveness and Rebellion

This chapter, and the next, explores ideas for working with specific difficulties that are common in depression. Previous chapters have outlined models for thinking about depression and a variety of focused interventions (e.g. by focusing on thoughts, feelings and behaviours, and developing self-compassion). First, let's note that at the beginning of each session there are a few things that it is often useful to do.

1 Check on mood at the beginning of each session. Has it got worse, stayed the same or improved?
2 The therapist will review independent work that the depressed person has been trying outside session, such as working on thoughts, behavioural enactments, experiments or new social roles.
3 The therapist will check for any critical events between sessions.
4 Feelings and ideas about previous sessions will be explored (e.g. 'Did you have any new thoughts this week arising from our last meeting?').
5 Together, therapist and client will then set an agenda and priorities for the session (e.g. ask 'what would you like to focus on today?').

The above occurs (usually) in the first ten minutes or so of the session. The structure should not be overly prescribed, however, as this may allow the client to avoid key themes. A clue to this problem can be noted if the client tends to leave the important material to the last five minutes. As counselling progresses, more information will arise as to the key interpersonal areas that are problematic and these will tend to present as repetitive themes (e.g. need for approval/recognition, assertiveness, etc.). This chapter will explore how to work with some of these core beliefs and safety strategies, beginning with approval.

Approval-seeking

Many theories of depression see the need for approval as playing a central role in vulnerability to and the maintenance of depression (see Chapters 5 and 6). When approval-seeking relates to an intimate domain, this often takes the form of needs to confirm one's lovability, to stay in a close relationship with another and/or feel protected (Beck, 1983; Bowlby, 1980). When approval needs operate in a less intimate domain, social approval needs are focused on recognition of talent and ability, and social belonging. These are, however, not mutually exclusive. Loss of needed, intimate relationships often involves the feelings of yearning and proximity-seeking. Those focused on more social domains do not involve the same yearning for proximity. In dealing with dependency, the therapist should be clear about the distinction between genuine emotional dependency and other forms (e.g. economic). Often dependency is secondary to a feeling of inferiority. The example below looks at Sally's problems in intimate relating. This was presented in the first edition of this book.

On the surface, Sally seemed to have a need for intense relationships with men and much reassurance once in them. She had become depressed when a long-standing relationship (with Fred) had broken down. She understood the basis of the cognitive approach and had made some early gains in her counselling. Nevertheless, on core issues she seemed rather stuck. At this point we used the advantages (gains) and disadvantages (losses) procedure to help articulate the difficulty. The following dialogue highlights how the therapist can use a 'technique' but must stay open to the affective changes that occur in the session.

Sally:	I just never seem to be able to make a success of relationships. I mean, I thought that Fred and I were doing okay but it ended like all the others.
Therapist:	Did Fred tell you why he was breaking up?
Sally:	Well, he mentioned that maybe I was too intense. Like I needed too much reassurance. I wanted to be with him all the time. This seemed to me how lovers should be. I didn't like him looking at other women and, like I said before, we did sometimes have rows over this.

The therapist might note the possibility of black-and-white thinking here, that is 'Either I am with a lover all the time or we don't have a loving relationship.' This is implied, if not stated clearly. For Sally, working on black-and-white thinking has only been marginally helpful.

Therapist:	Do you think Fred had a point?
Sally:	Probably. Yes.
Therapist:	Is that something we might continue to work on?
Sally:	Maybe, but I don't think I can be any different. I have tried really, but I just seem to get taken over by the relationship, like it is everything to me.
Therapist:	Sounds like there are some basic ideas about changing and not being able to. What about if we look at the advantages and disadvantages of changing, or if you like, the gains and losses. Perhaps we can get a clearer idea of what this is about. I'm going to draw two columns and call one 'advantages' and the other 'disadvantages'. Okay? [*Sally nods*] Now, what would be the advantages of changing, becoming less intense and needy in the relationship?
Sally:	Well, it would certainly make things easier I guess.
Therapist:	Okay, that's our first advantage. It would make things easier. Anything else?
Sally:	I might hold on to my man. [*The therapist notes the words 'hold on to'. Key words can be markers for underlying basic beliefs and felt needs*]
Therapist:	You might hold on to a man. Any other advantages?

Sally:	[*Thinks*] No, can't think of any.
Therapist:	Fine, let's just stop here for a moment. Suppose you did find it possible to be less intense and needy, how would that affect you? I mean, what would be the benefits for you? How would you be different, like inside you? [*Here the therapist is helping to focus more on the internal self-experience.*]
Sally:	I wouldn't get so jealous.
Therapist:	Would that feel better?
Sally:	Oh yes. I hate feeling jealous, it really cuts me up you know.
Therapist:	Okay, so becoming less jealous might be a help. Anything else, like how your thoughts or fantasies might go? [*Note how the therapist is having to draw out advantages with questions*]
Sally:	Oh, yeah, that. Yeah, I wouldn't spend so much time fantasising or worrying about the relationship. Like I told you before, they kind of take me over and I spend all my time thinking about the relationship, mainly if it's going to work out and what will happen if it doesn't.
Therapist:	So if you became less intense and needy then you might have less worrying thoughts about the relationship. What about you? I mean how might you come to think about yourself – your own person-ness.
Sally:	Hmm, I've been thinking about that since I saw you and talked to Jackie about it. I do feel bad about myself when things don't work out, like I've put so much effort into it and it goes wrong, so maybe it's me. I get confused with that.
Therapist:	What kinds of ideas do you have about you?
Sally:	It's difficult to put into words but somewhere I feel I must be unlovable. [*Note how the therapist has had to ask more than once to help Sally get to her beliefs about herself when the relationship does not work. Then comes the idea 'maybe I'm not lovable'.*]
Therapist:	Are there any other thoughts or feelings about yourself?
Sally:	I guess I'm angry with myself. I look back and see what I did wrong. I think of how I was jealous and at times demanding, and wish I could be more relaxed, not so needy you know. Part of me would like to be more independent. [*After further discussion on these general themes the therapist summarises*]
Therapist:	Let's go over some of the advantages of becoming less intense. The relationship might be easier. You'd feel less jealous. You might be able to maintain the relationship. You might get less angry with yourself and feel better about yourself. You may become more independent. How does that sound?
Sally:	Well, when you lay it out like that it sounds silly to get so involved and I suppose I do lose something.
Therapist:	[*Smiling*] I think I see a 'but' on your face though.
Sally:	You make it sound so logical but I can't help it. It's my heart that rules me.

Here Sally acknowledges the logic of change, yet is not convinced. Therapists should not be at all discouraged by this. Thus we must move to the disadvantages. Indeed, in working with depressed people, helping them see the advantages of change may be less important than working with the disadvantages. *Be prepared for ambivalence as this is common in trying to change even when the advantages seem very positive.* The chances are there are some threat and safety strategies that are holding her back. Thus spending more time looking at the disadvantages may be valuable. This turned out to be important in Sally's case.

> *Therapist*:   [*Smiles*] You're right, of course. We are approaching the issue in a reasonably logical way but our feelings don't always obey logic. Still, maybe as you say, you can see that it is not all gains in having an intense relationship. Anyhow we can come back to this. Let's focus on the aspect that you mention here again about being taken over by the relationship.

Now the therapist has already explored inference chains on relationships and found that Sally's sense of feeling good about herself is very much related to having a man love her (i.e. close intimate relationships). She is also *competitive* in love, hence her jealousy. She has beliefs such as 'If a man loves me I must be as good or better than other women'. So there will be an issue of feeling defeated if she loses in the 'love competition'. At the same time, however, she often feels vulnerable because her 'good sense of self' can be taken away from her if the relationship fails. Sally has not been able to make a lot of progress with simple alternative thinking so the problem can be approached from a different direction and we can try to engage Sally more fully in understanding the benefits and losses (threats) to her of changing her basic style.

> *Therapist*:   So far we have looked at a few advantages of becoming less intense in relationships with men, but now let's think about the disadvantages. What would you lose?
>
> *Sally*:   [*Thinks*] The first thing that springs to mind, even as we were going through the advantages, was that it wouldn't be natural.
>
> *Therapist*:   Natural?
>
> *Sally*:   It wouldn't be me, like I'd either be pretending or that I didn't care that much.
>
> *Therapist*:   So it's the intense feeling that makes it seem real and natural?
>
> *Sally*:   Yes.
>
> *Therapist*:   Okay, what other disadvantages are there?
>
> *Sally*:   I wouldn't be sure if this was the right man for me. Like I'd be wasting my time. [*The therapist thinks about the statement 'right man for me', and considers the possibility of looking at the evidence that emotions are the best way to make such judgements. He wonders what the fear might be in 'not getting the right man'? However, at this point he decides to focus on internal feelings.*]
>
> *Therapist*:   How would you feel inside?
>
> *Sally*:   [*Thinking*] Kind of empty about it, I guess.
>
> *Therapist*:   Empty. Without the intensity it would feel empty?
>
> *Sally*:   I think so.
>
> *Therapist*:   How about you? What would your experience of you be? [*Again, note how the therapist returns to the internal self-evaluation and experience.*]
>
> *Sally*:   The same empty feeling.

At this point the Sally touches affect and her mood seems to become more sad. This is picked up in her non-verbal behaviour and slowed speech. It is important to stay with these affective pointers (Greenberg and Safran, 1987; Greenberg and Watson, 2006). So even though we are using a fairly structured technique we remain sensitive to the affective changes in the session. We also want to explore if these feelings are coming from some aroused schema and/or emotional memories – what has caused this shift in affect.

> *Therapist*: That's interesting, Sally. Without the intense feeling in the relationship it feels empty and you feel empty in it. Can you remember having these feelings before, like in childhood? [*This question 'can you remember?' is the link to the past and for emotional memories*].
>
> *Sally*: [*Speech rate slows down and talks more deliberately*] As I think about it, it reminds me of my Dad. Poor old Dad, he had to work long hours and was often away from home. I just got this image of waiting at the window for him to come home and then mother would say I'd have to go to bed or he wasn't coming home that night. I really used to miss him 'cos on the occasions when he was there he would spend a lot of time with me and it was really good, like *really* good and exciting. He'd take me out, unlike Mum. I hated him going away again, life seemed more dull. Later, they got divorced and secretly I really hoped I could go and live with him but Mum wanted us to stay with her. She needed us I suppose, but I wanted to be with Dad.

In attachment theory Dad had been 'exciting but abandoning,' linking strong feelings in Sally of 'wanting closeness' to fear of, and feelings of, 'loss.' Sally has spontaneously made a link with the past, noting various memories. Safran and Segal (1990) suggest that working with historical data is important, especially if explored in the course of counselling, in the presence of affect, and when it emerges spontaneously. Thus, we cannot let this opportunity go by.

> *Therapist*: Sounds like he really liked being with you when he was home?
> *Sally*: Sometimes I thought he enjoyed being with me more than Mum. They didn't get on at all. He didn't talk about it much but I always felt on his side.
> *Therapist*: Against Mum?
> *Sally*: Yeah, perhaps.

In addition to noting father as exciting but abandoning relationship, the therapist notes the possible *competition* with mother for father's affection. It runs through his mind that this might have something to do with Sally's competitive style and preparedness to drop female friends whenever a man came along. But since the focus is on the need for intensity we stay with this theme.

> *Therapist*: Sounds like you longed for that intensity to be there all the time; to be with Dad.
> *Sally*: [*Nods sadly*]
> *Therapist*: Do you think those experiences might have anything to do with what happens with you today in relationships?
> *Sally*: I'd never thought of that. [*Pause*] I can see that.
> *Therapist*: You look sad.
> *Sally*: I was just remembering how lonely I used to feel and how much I wished he'd come home.

At this point, while using an advantages–disadvantages approach, we have tapped into an underlying emotional memory of a need for intensity and closeness, and how there is both a desire to recapture closeness, and also a fear of losing it. In attachment theory (see Chapter 5), this might be seen as an anxious attachment to father that has set a template for anxious attachment to men. However, the point is, there do seem to be some early experiences here and these are going to need work to help Sally change her interpersonal style with lovers.

It is important then that the therapist does not use the techniques of counselling simply as 'techniques' but crafts them into a therapeutic relationship. They are a recipe not only to help people understand at a rational level the nature of their difficulties, but also to engage *emotional experience*. So one wants to try to bring this emotional experience into the list of disadvantages.

> *Therapist*:   Okay, Sally, perhaps we can see how this need for intensity may have something to do with your past experience with Dad. But I guess that this may turn out to be an advantage. I mean if some of the need for intensity is coming from a disappointing relationship with Dad, then it might be helpful to try to deal with this disappointment rather than you carrying it from one relationship to another. [*Here the therapist is directing attention to Sally's interpersonal style*]
>
> *Sally*:   I hadn't seen that, but sitting here it makes sense. Are you saying that I am trying to recapture something?
>
> *Therapist*:   What do you think?
>
> *Sally*:   I think I have known that but yet haven't been aware of it. [*Pause*] Oh, that sounds silly doesn't it?
>
> *Therapist*:   [*Gently*] I wouldn't say silly at all. It seems more about making connections. Something we feel but it's like it is in the background, not clear.
>
> *Sally*:   Yes, that's how it is, in the background, not clear.

Sally makes the observation of having an awareness of the problem but not being consciously able to connect things in her mind and articulate them clearly. When people do make the connections it makes emotional sense and feels 'right'. This is one of the processes of therapy. So we then had a discussion of what we mean by 'being in the background' and how some of our ideas and feelings get connected within us without us consciously recognising it. In essence, Sally had a belief which said 'I must have a close relationship with a man to be happy'. This came from a real experience (emotional memories) of being happy when she was close to her father and craving and yearning for it when he wasn't. Her jealousy was partly related to the external threat of losing contact with the 'wanted other' and partly to the internal threat of feeling alone again, as she did as a child – the reactivation of painful emotional memories.

> *Therapist*:   So we are saying that a disadvantage of giving up the need for intensity may mean that you feel less able to 'recapture something', to use your words.

We spent about twenty minutes in emotional discussion around this theme, trying to clarify it and articulate the basic fears and beliefs. The focus remained the disadvantage of losing intensity in relationships with men. It is not only the connection with the past that was important here, but the link with the memory of intense emptiness and loss. At the end of this part of the session the therapist returned to the basic task. They had both gained more insight into the feared losses associated with changing and giving up intensity. At times Sally's sadness was intense.

Therapist: Okay, Sally, let's look on our paper and see what we've got here. First, you see that intensity in relationships is not all good now. Therefore you recognise some potential benefits from becoming less intense. However, there are many disadvantages in making this change. First, it may make the relationship feel unnatural or unreal and this links to a feeling of emptiness. That in turn reminds you of your relationship with your father. So, although at a logical level, you can understand that there are advantages to becoming less intense and needy, at an emotional level it does not feel like a gain, but a pretty big loss. Now nobody will change if they feel inside they are heading for a loss.

Sally: [*Slightly tearful*] Yeah, I must say I have been trying to follow through in therapy but that has been the feeling. I know I want to change and part of me knows what we've been doing is sensible but inside I don't want to change, like I am leaving something important behind.

Therapist: Do you think you are clearer about what you might be leaving behind?

Sally: The kind of relationship I wanted with Dad. [*Cries gently*]

At this point I am silent, allowing Sally to be aware of the pain of the insight. As therapy progressed, Sally began to reach a certain anger at her father, whom she had idealised. She had not been able to contact this before because her positive feelings for him had been special and an important source of self-esteem. Now this is not at all uncommon in idealised relationships when there has actually been considerable loss and distance. Making contact with the anger can be helpful (Greenberg and Watson, 2006). It helped Sally understand that often, in intimate relationships, she also felt resentful without really knowing why. She began to explore the fear of being alone and left behind. Without intensity, she might be left like mother, alone and somewhat bitter. So again the techniques of therapy were ways of helping her gain insight and make important changes in self-understanding and interpersonal relationships. One of her out-of-session tasks was to try to look at ordinary friendships with men and the feelings she had about them. We also looked at other ways of evaluating what kind of relationship she wanted with a man (e.g. honesty, respect, sharing pleasant activities, etc.). As therapy progresses one is gradually weaving together various themes and illuminating basic beliefs and memories, such that they become available for reworking in the present situation.

Achievement

The need for achievement and social recognition is also common in depression (see Chapters 5 and 6). Let's look at Dan, who showed this strongly. Dan had a need for approval, but it did not manifest as intimate or proximity needs as did Sally's. Rather, it was a need to be recognised as talented and able. Let us now consider Dan using the same technique of advantages–disadvantages (gains–losses).

Therapist:	You were saying earlier, Dan, that you felt a great need to achieve things and felt that much of your life had been a failure. Over the past few sessions we have looked at the evidence for this and also how you would talk to a friend. Has that changed things?
Dan:	I can see what you are driving at and it sort of makes sense. I do punish myself a lot but it's so automatic that it's difficult to change.
Therapist:	Well, let's look at this from a different perspective for a moment. We can make a list of the gains and losses of changing the need for success. I'll come and sit next to you and we can write them out together. [*Does so*] Now, let's look at the advantages first. What might be the advantages of changing this drive for success?
Dan:	I would be more relaxed about things and less anxious.
Therapist:	Anything else?

The following advantages were then elicited. 'I'd be less hard on myself. I'd be easier to live with. If I was less tense, I might get less depressed. Life might be more fun.'

Therapist:	Okay, let us now look at the disadvantages.

Recall that disadvantages are also the *threats* of change and this is what maintains the status quo and safety strategies. These were the disadvantages: 'I might become sloppy. I might end up lazy. I might lose respect [He took a secret pride in others calling him a perfectionist. He also took a secret pride in feeling superior to others]. I might lose my purpose in life and life would become empty and pointless.'

Therapist:	It is understandable why you would find it difficult to change if these are the likely consequences. Therapy must seem a bit confusing to you if you think that by changing your style you are going to feel worse, like empty and pointless.
Dan:	[*Long pause as Dan looks over the list*] Yes. That makes sense. I kind of know what you are saying but it has never seemed a right fit for me, like I was frightened of letting go of something. I have felt confused really.

From here therapy began to work more closely with the fears and the sense of superiority that Dan maintained from his perfectionism, and the fear of letting go. There was some *mourning* of the failure of recognition of early life and a movement to look at life with regard to more pleasurable activities. Black-and-white thinking was explored many times in terms of a fear of becoming more sloppy and losing respect. Each time we were able to keep in mind the *fear* of change.

In these cases the therapist needs to empathise with the (sometimes desperate) feelings of the need for recognition and to be valued. In cognitive terms these are the 'I must' beliefs. It is not the case that these clients want to be cared for or necessarily crave an intense intimate relationship. More often they are seeking a sense of personal value that will help them feel heard, listened to, valued and connected, and have worked out various tactics for trying to achieve that. If the therapist does not recognise this need for value and moves too quickly to try to change the client's thinking, the client can feel misunderstood. Further, the therapist should be alert to the *disappointment and grief* of not having felt valued which goes with these themes. Therapists can sometimes miss the difficult struggle for respect and a sense of personal value that have often been important life goals (see Chapters 5 and 6).

In both Sally's and Dan's cases the therapist often returns to self-evaluation. The key is helping the person to avoid self-attacking or self-downing if their goal does not come about. If one can stop the self-attacking and maintain a reasonably stable self-relationship, then depression might be less likely. Today I would use a more compassion-focused approach to help this, but Dan did okay because he could work with his feelings. Let us now review our thoughts about one of the most commonly used techniques: advantages–disadvantages.

Key issues 13.1   Working on advantages–disadvantages

1   The therapist may have to draw out the advantages and help people to list these.
2   The therapist uses questions to help clients articulate how they might think about themselves differently through changing.
3   It is common, however, that working with the advantages of change is not always helpful. People often know what might be in their best interests, but do not do it.
4   Consequently, looking at the disadvantages of change can be more powerful because it illuminates the threats and helps to clarify how part of the problem is linked to safety strategies.
5   Thus the therapist can draw out the negative self-beliefs, self-experiences and basic fears and losses that might arise from change.
6   If clients spontaneously report memories or images from the past that are linked with negative emotions, the therapist should explore these. Sometimes the advantages–disadvantages process is the focus for the whole session or number of sessions.

Assertiveness

There is good evidence that low assertiveness is often a problem in some depressions (Arrindell et al., 1988). In my self-help book (Gilbert, 2000a), there are two chapters devoted to anger and assertiveness. Commonly, depressed people with anger and assertiveness problems will either carry considerable resentment and then label themselves as bad for feeling resentful, or feel weak for not standing up for themselves and/or they may have explosions of anger and then feel guilty and even more depressed and inhibited. Obviously, assertiveness is an interpersonal style that has various social outcomes, and of course these days I focus on *compassionate* assertiveness. Why are depressed clients not more assertive? It can be a basic skill problem and this requires education in line with normal social skills training. However, there can also be a number of perceived disadvantages to becoming more assertive, most often loss of approval or abandonment (see also Leahy, 2002). In some cases low assertiveness has been the source of positive self-esteem (I am good because I'm not pushy). In fact, we can identify a number of basic themes that maintain a person in a submissive, non-assertive state. Thus, the therapist can explore the various reasons (key fears) for inhibited assertiveness in depression. Again, these can emerge by exploring the disadvantages and noting how they are often threat- and fear-focused. Below are listed some typical reasons.

Fear of counterattack and shame

Here the person is fearful of being overwhelmed by the counter-response from another person. There may be a fear that they will then become tongue-tied, that their mind will go blank, that they will look silly or forget what they want to say, that others may overpower them, or be quicker, etc. There can be a fear of loss of poise, or of 'asserting themselves badly' and being subject to feelings of *shame*. Also there can be a fear of harsh put-down, rejection or even injury by a more powerful other. Hence the basic fear is that they will come off worst.

Fear of loss of control

Assertiveness can be physiologically arousing and some clients become fearful of this arousal in themselves. They may worry that they will lose control or say something extreme or shameful. Hence internal physiological cues can act as assertiveness inhibitors.

Fear of abandonment

Clients fear that others may come to dislike them or abandon them if they are assertive. This normally applies to more intimate and friendship-type relationships. Further, this is associated with ideas that they would not be able to cope alone, that they would become worthless, unlovable or incapable.

Rights

Some clients are unclear about their personal rights. They are apt to make various excuses for others' bad behaviour towards them or take the attitude 'others are more important than me'. They feel guilty at putting themselves first or owning their own needs. They can have a (superficially) over-caring attitude to others, but this is not always without a certain resentment that others do not (without them having to ask) recognise their needs. Although they allow themselves to be treated as doormats, they would like others to respect them without having to assert themselves.

Self-blame

It is not uncommon that clients blame themselves for conflicts in some situations. Even women who are suffering from abuse at home may still blame themselves for it (see Chapter 6). As we have noted a number of times, self-blame can be a highly protective strategy for it reduces the chances of retaliation but it also increases depression.

Positive self and competitiveness

Some clients suggest that they do not like assertive people and regard them as selfish. Hence they can feel good about themselves if they refrain from behaving like those 'selfish others'. In a way the lack of assertiveness is taken as evidence of a good self and a caring non-selfishness. To become more assertive threatens becoming similar to people they do not like, and losing a certain satisfaction with self that they are nicer than other people.

In any one case, each or all of these possibilities can be present. The client might also feel anger at what they see as other people's selfishness. They may have beliefs such as: 'Others should not behave like that, they should know that it is wrong. I expect/demand people to behave as I think is right.' In the latter case this is using projection rather than theory of mind. Clients might also have a wish for revenge. The advantages–disadvantages procedure usually reveals which themes are most problematic and therapy can be tailored accordingly. It can also be useful to role play situations so that clients can learn the behaviours associated with helpful and compassionate assertiveness and deal with negative cognitions that may arise. This can also be handled in structured assertiveness groups. Many women who have been depressed attest to the benefits of these groups (see Dickson, 1982).

Assertiveness, attractiveness and initiation

A particular problem with some depressed clients is that they do not initiate things that are positively reinforcing. In a factor analysis, Arrindell et al. (1988) found that assertiveness had at least four components: (1) display of negative feelings, involving standing up for oneself and engaging in conflict; (2) expression of and dealing with personal limitations, involving a readiness to admit mistakes and deficits; (3) initiating assertiveness, involving making one's opinion known; (4) praising others and accepting praise.

One of the clear findings from research is that depressed clients are not much fun to be with (Segrin and Abramson, 1994). This is, in part, because they do not initiate positive interactions. There are various reasons for this, for example fear of rejection or attracting too much attention. Another reason may be high self-focused attention (e.g. see Pyszczynski and Greenberg, 1987). Resentment may also be important. For example, it is not uncommon to find that an individual does not initiate sex out of resentment towards the partner. Complying with sex, on the other hand, can give a sense of power and being needed. But initiation is an important social skill and our flow of positive social interaction depends on it. We could call this enthusiasm. Some therapies focus on these social behavioural aspects of depression (McCullough, 2000).

John was rather anxious about initiating social interactions. His wife found him difficult. He would sometimes sulk about the house and expect her to be sensitive and talk to him about what was on his mind (usually some minor grievance). If she made an enquiry, there would have to be a little ritual of denial that there was anything wrong followed by his wife insisting that there was. He would play the game of making her 'force it out of him'. When his wife tired of this 'game' he became more resentful, attributing it to lack of care. Sulking can be quite a problem in some cases of depression (Dryden, 1992). This pattern can be picked up in childhood.

In sexual relationships it was a similar story. He would prefer his wife to initiate sexual contact and had to have clear signals that she desired sex. This again put a burden on his wife. Work out of session involved: (a) learning to give up the game of 'You have got to make me speak of my grievance as a test of your care'; (b) initiating at least one positive interaction per day; and (c) making his desire for sexual contact clear and 'up front'. For this John's wife was invited to counselling and he was surprised to learn how much she resented having to do all the emotional work. Of course exploration is also needed on the disadvantages of making these changes – what is the threat from change? As I recall, one of John's difficulties was that he could not cope with ambivalence and owning his annoyances openly. So he was fearful of change (or at least the process of change) because he would have to face these, acknowledge he carried a lot of anger from his past, and often felt pushed into things and then resentful with himself and others. Yet of course what he really wanted was to feel loved and validated and to feel himself as a kind, loving person. He could see no way to reconcile these two (Jekyll and Hyde) aspects of himself. So we did a lot of empathising with this struggle and his fears – that we cannot 'rid' ourselves of our Mr Hyde sides (that was the point of the original story) but that we can work with it and understand it in a non-shaming way, and then it changes. Also, of course, we worked on becoming more socially engaged in a helpful way.

Socially explorative behaviour shows itself as taking an interest in, and showing appreciation of, others. If one is initiating questions, ideas (or even sex) and generally exploring another person's viewpoint, then one is showing interest (see Heard and Lake, 1986 for a discussion of the importance of this mutual, valuing interactional style). Being the recipient of interest is positively rewarding. It is not uncommon to find that rather passive individuals have histories of authoritarian parenting. A lack of socially explorative behaviour is unattractive, but too much initiation (e.g. sexual advances) and following one's own agendas/goals is also unattractive and is seen as dominating. Too much interest in another can be intrusive. So it is a tricky balance and clients need to learn how to be sensitive to their partners (e.g. to accept a refusal of sexual contact gracefully without building up resentment or ideas like 'Right that's the last time I am going to make a pass at you').

It is, however, common to find that significant others in the client's life are not valuing or appreciating of the client. Some depressed clients (especially women) may be living with emotionally neglectful or domineering partners. Interpersonal and evolutionary theory (Gilbert, 1992) suggests that we are not socially decontextualised beings, and all of us need at least some degree of positive signals of value from others. This is why social support comes out so strongly as a factor in both depression and recovery. Criticism by a spouse is a predictor of relapse (Hooley and Teasdale, 1989).

> **Key issues 13.2   Assertiveness**
>
> 1   Assertiveness is much more than just standing up for oneself in situations of conflict. It involves also positive initiations.
> 2   The therapist can recognise that the client may have various fears of assertiveness (e.g. of the counterattack or fear of rejection). These need to be made clear.
> 3   Lack of assertive behaviour often leads to resentment and needs to be acknowledged.
> 4   Part of adaptive assertive behaviour is the ability to initiate positive behaviours and state clearly one's preferences. Sometimes depressed clients see this as selfish and think that they should do what others want.
> 5   Sulking can be a problem in depression and may be associated with a fear of open assertive behaviour, and for a sense of power that can be gained from withholding.
> 6   Therapists may offer role play exercises to help clients explore their negative thoughts while enacting assertive and more positive roles.

Rebellion

Joe was diagnosed with a chronic but not severe depression. He had seen a number of therapists. He presented as a superficially pleasant and compliant man who appeared to do the independent tasks agreed in therapy. On the surface he should have progressed well, but did not. In fact, he feigned agreement but had a passive-aggressive style and was full of 'yes buts'. Previous therapists had become frustrated with him. He could not understand why others eventually got angry or lost interest in helping him. Thus, we focused at an early stage on issues of compliance. I noted that when Joe spoke of minor rebellions at school his eyes lit up and he become more 'emotionally expressive' during counselling.

I pointed this out. Could that spark be used to engage Joe? It was agreed that Joe should begin to argue during our therapy on why he should not do work outside the session. It was agreed he would work on non-compliance. Once permission had been given for this 'rebellion', Joe took to counselling with vigour. The focus became his ability to resist others, including the therapist.

Therapist: We agreed that you would monitor some of your thoughts about doing jobs about the house. Is it likely that you will?

Joe: [*With a slight smile*] I might, but knowing me I probably won't.

Therapist: Good, so you will rebel. How does that feel?

Joe: [*Pause, then cautiously*] I guess I feel a little bit stronger than you.

Therapist: Is that okay or does that feeling worry you at all?

Joe: I know you say it is alright for me to rebel if I want to, but I think you will reject me if I go on like this. Sooner or later I am going to have to give in, aren't I, and work at counselling?

Therapist: Hmm. [*Pause, watching Joe's non-verbal behaviour*] You look puzzled.

Joe: I can't believe you are encouraging me to rebel against this therapy. The other therapists told me I had to work in the therapy or I wouldn't get better and you're telling me I don't have to.

Therapist: It is not so much whether you work or not but *how we work together*. When you rebel I see you struggling to stay you. I would like to work with the rebel inside you not against it. Would you like to talk to the rebel inside?

After some discussion Joe agreed, just for the 'hell of it'. At this point we wrote on a card the typical thoughts the 'rebel' had. 'They can't make me do things. They will never get to me. They don't really understand – all smart arses every one.' (I think he included me here.)

The tone of therapy at this point was like a game, sort of safely playful, but nevertheless with the serious intent of eliciting basic beliefs and attitudes. Also, you will note that there were various envy elements in this theme. Joe was then encouraged to answer back at the rebel part of him. 'Okay, maybe others have put me down but aren't I cutting off my nose to spite my face? I mean I might be able to resist others but that's not much fun in the end.' The therapist also helped Joe to see the positive side of the rebel and talked openly that rebels had (sometimes) important uses, but they had to be part of the self and not running the whole show. Today I would concentrate far more on compassionate focusing and that underneath Joe was a rather frightened and lonely person.

Whether Joe was convinced by 'the technique' or not, it changed his attitude to therapy. By validating the rebel and bringing it into sessions, he began gradually to be more open and hard-working on his anger and envy. Had the rebel in him not been acknowledged, then therapy may have been difficult. Still this was a slow process. One could easily see how his rebellious attitude would elicit anger in others and this in turn would reinforce his need to rebel, to hang on to his sense of self. His depression was of a passive-aggressive kind, but also a safety strategy to not face the fear of being out of control or controlled by others. The two chair technique could have been explored.

Much discussion focused on Joe's sense of strength and renewed vigour in being encouraged to rebel. Out-of-session work and other procedures were seen as vehicles to help Joe internalise a stronger sense of self. Rebelling at therapy became 'doing it his way'. Slowly, Joe began to give up his pleasant but passive resistance and engaged in more collaborative work. This case is cited to help therapists see that one should try to work with their clients' internal experience and not apply techniques because they seem logical or the correct way to do things. It is not unusual that openly helping clients rebel and become assertive is an important factor in change and here the therapist may need to facilitate a certain degree of rebellion in the therapy which is safe and does not result in rejection. For some, however, rebellion is frightening (Gilbert and Irons, 2005; see also pp. 283–284 in this volume).

Bingeing

Another area where it is important to 'enable the rebel to speak' is in binge problems. Depressed clients who binge drink or binge eat are often trying to cope with unpleasant feelings. Often the trigger is disappointment, frustration or the feeling of being put down or marginalised, which is associated with rage. The thoughts associated with bingeing may be: 'Sod it. I've had enough. I'll show them. What do I care? They can't make me do XYZ. I'll make them feel bad – look what they made me do', etc. At these times therapists should be very cautious not to be punitive. Also, be sensitive to the shame that might follow when the patient is sober or out of the binge state. Try to enable the client to verbalise their flow of thoughts and feelings associated with frustration and anger (the 'f..k you' thoughts) as the trigger – their desire to rebel and 'break out' – try to work out alternative behaviours for such anger, to recognise disappointment, and to help the client recognise that the inner rebel may be working against them rather than for them.

Conclusion

This chapter has looked at various interpersonal themes and issues, and how the cognitive-behavioural 'techniques' of earlier chapters can be integrated with an understanding of the client's interpersonal style and key fears. The self-experience remains a central focus but there is also a focus on how the client acts in their social world. When using techniques, try to stay with the client's emotional experience, and elicit affect where appropriate.

It is particularly appropriate to work with the *fears and threats* (disadvantages) of changing. If clients are given the opportunity to really explore these fears and disadvantages they may move more easily through the process of change. Some forms of passive resistance can be difficult and this is why clarifying this and the way a rebellious attitude can be linked to self-identify can be helpful. Usually resistance is related to unaddressed fears or dilemmas of changing (e.g. addressing anger). Most important is to avoid shaming or blaming people for their resistance or passivity (Leahy, 2001). Try to explore the *functions* of these behaviours *with an open curiosity*. A compassionate focus can help.

14 Working with Specific Difficulties II: Shame, Guilt, Ideal and Envy

In this chapter we will take a few more examples of difficulties and explore them in detail, bringing together the themes we have discussed in this book so far. We start with a key issue in depression – that of shame.

Working with shame

In Chapter 6 we saw that shame can be central to many aspects of depression. A typical shame problem can be in revealing the intensity of internal feelings or allowing oneself to be in touch with feelings (thus emotional avoidance and poor affect tolerance). Mary found it extremely difficult to cry in counselling. When she did so, she would cover her face with both hands and push back her tears. It was difficult to work with emotional material because she was deeply shame-prone about her feelings. The focus in the early counselling was one of listening and trying not to engage her shame too quickly, on the assumption that before an empathic relationship had developed she might find it overwhelming and avoid therapy altogether. Gradually, however, I felt able to draw attention to the shame aspect.

> Therapist: I note that you try to push back your tears at times.
> Mary: [*Slightly angrily*] I have cried so much and don't want to cry here.

Because of the feelings generated (she had a very angry presentation) in previous sessions, I felt if I drew further attention to it I might be almost persecuting her in some way. Also I felt pushed out from her pain. This countertransference persecutory feeling in the therapist can arise in severe shame cases.

> Therapist: [*Gently*] Could we think about that a moment. What would crying here mean to you; I mean really letting go?
> Mary: I would feel vulnerable and exposed. It's a stupid thing to do and doesn't do any good.
> Therapist: Stupid?

The fear of revealing powerful feelings is a common problem in some depressions and can say much about the internal self-structure and self–other schema. Many questions arise in the therapist's mind at this point. Has the person been punished in the past for showing strong feelings of distress? In Mary's case the answer was almost certainly 'yes'. Is the person angry with herself for having such feelings and is she trying to deny them? How does she use anger (as a safety strategy) to keep well away from processing deep sadness? Does crying make her feel small/inferior in the eyes of the therapist and in her own eyes?

From a 'technique' point of view the therapist tries to explore the disadvantages of crying and letting go of feelings; that is, the meaning of sharing feelings, but in a less structured way than discussed earlier. Here the therapist has a choice of focus: (a) to reflect 'doesn't do any good'; or (b) the issue of vulnerability and exposure. If the former is chosen the discussion might become intellectualised. Alternatively, it might lead to a discussion of previous experiences of being rejected. Hence, when a client gives two messages like this, the therapist uses their judgement as to which aspect to focus on. 'Stupid' felt like a more self-evaluative shame concern and therefore this was the choice for reflection.

> *Mary*:   [*Crying*] I can't stand to feel like this.
> *Therapist*:   Because you feel exposed?
> *Mary*:   [*Nods*]
> *Therapist*:   [*Gently*] Could you say more about feeling exposed?

This enables the client to talk more about the feelings and attitudes to crying rather than going into what the tears may be about and is therefore (possibly) less threatening. From an evolutionary point of view we would guess they are about feeling lonely and wanting comfort but also being frightened to acknowledge that.

> *Mary*:   [*Silence and then*] I feel it is somehow a weakness.
> *Therapist*:   [*Gently*] Why are tears and distress a weakness?
> *Mary*:   Because others can hurt you if they know your weakness. They might appear concerned but inside you know they are thinking you are pathetic.

Here Mary articulates her ideas about 'what is in the minds of others' (which is an external shame issue) and how they would respond to her distress. She cannot trust empathy responses from others, even if they are given. Does this apply to the therapeutic relationship? If it does it will make her ability to deal with high levels of distress very difficult. So we need to check this out.

> *Therapist*:   Would that be the same here, like I might see you as pathetic?
> *Mary*:   I don't know. [*Looks up and sideways*] Why wouldn't you? You must get lots of stupid females bawling their eyes out.

Here the client reveals a desire not to be like those 'other bawling females', not to appear weak and stupid. How can the therapist help here? Because the session has been moving to the discussion of emotionally painful material, emotion is activated in both therapist and client. Can the therapist contain it and not get defensive or feel persecutory? At this point, containment is just about staying with Mary and not pushing too hard. At the same time the therapist wants to try to convey a recognition of pain and inner conflict and, if possible, focus on the underlying negative self-evaluation and shame. I know Mary has difficulties coping with the feelings of shame (e.g. from crying in front of me) because she has told me that she can and does cry on her own. There also appears to be an increasing emergence of a rage–shame spiral (e.g. her somewhat aggressive statement of 'Why wouldn't you?')

> Therapist: [Gently] I sense these painful feelings have been with you for a long time and they are deeply powerful for you. Maybe you are beginning to explore and understand them a little. Do they remind you of anything?
>
> Mary: [Beginning to cry more openly but also angry] My father used to tease me if I cried. He'd call me poor little baby face or cry baby. I hated him for that. I really hated him. Nobody seemed to care why I cried and I just couldn't do anything.

Linking with the past had opened the opportunity to direct attention away from the present, and focus on painful memories.

> Therapist: Hmm, so it is horrible when people don't recognise your feelings for care and put you down. That feels a very lonely place to be. [Pause, then gently] Mary, these feelings are painful to you because maybe you have never been able to share them before. But you are a human being and can feel hurt, deep hurt, and that doesn't make you weak, it makes you a feeling human being.

Here the therapist has tried to empathise with her experience and gives her a positive construction of feelings – being a feeling human being. It is an attempt to rescue the self from internal attack and rage. More importantly, the therapist truly believes this and it is not said 'matter of fact'. Mary was able to listen to this intervention and after a long pause of quiet crying with hands over her face said:

> Mary: I guess you are the only person that thinks so. [Looks at the therapist] I think most of the time I hold back on feelings. Some think I'm cold maybe, but I'm not. I just find it hard to show my feelings. It wasn't done in our family.

Mary then went on to talk in more depth about her family experience, as I quietly listened. A history of emotional neglect began to come through. Here the affect remained high but not overwhelming. At the end of the session I repeated the positive statement of feelings.

> Therapist: Well, Mary, given what you have said it is more than understandable why you have difficulty showing your feelings and yet in your heart you do feel things intensely. Perhaps as we work together we can see this and help you reclaim those emotional bits that you had to bury.
>
> Mary: [Softly] Yes, I've done a lot of burying of things.

This is a recognition of her experience of hiding, concealing or splitting off, even from herself. Such an acknowledgement is an important change.

> Therapist: And this was because you viewed them as bad and weak. You have labelled yourself bad when you have strong feelings. Almost like your

father did. Also you did not want to be in a position where you could be
hurt or feel small. Keeping away from feelings like this and being angry
has protected you. [*Notice how we direct attention to self-protection*]

Mary: Yes, that is how it has been.
Therapist: Do you think it is time for you to have another look at this? As a child,
            burying feelings was self-protective and helpful. But maybe things can
            be different now.

Here the therapist points to the fact that at one time her coping behaviour may
have been adaptive and again is not a sign of weakness or stupidity.

Mary: Hmm.
Therapist: So the first person to focus on is you and how you down yourself when
            you think about having strong feelings.

One might gently say to her 'this is not your fault' three or four times. Despite the
anger and the pushing others away, many depressed people with these kinds of
problems feel that it is 'all their fault', or there *is* something wrong with them.
When you say 'this is not your fault' softly, it can elicit tears and reveals these fears
which they have previously not expressed.

Deep shame is never easy to work with. Sometimes it lies behind emotional
avoidance noted by clients' statements 'it's too painful to think about', although
not all emotional avoidance is shame-based. So we can only offer a few guidelines. First, shame clients can stir up various feelings in the therapist as a result
of their need to conceal, and especially if this is associated with rage. Clients can
have a certain prickliness about them. However, the therapist needs to clearly
recognise these as part of the shame experience and think about the rage, loneliness and the fear of rejection that goes with the shame experience. Second, the
therapist needs to convey to the client that they sense, and are trying to understand the struggle and the risk, which the client feels is great. Third, the therapist tries to make contact with the loneliness and emptiness of the client. If the
therapeutic relationship is good, the recognition of loneliness can form a bridge
to the shame issue. Finally, the therapist is aware of the self-dislike and self-
blame that are part of shame and these will be a source of work later in therapy.
However, these points are only guides and there is much in this case that could
take us through many chapters.

Distinguishing external and internal shame

Chapter 6 explained in detail the importance of distinguishing external threats (as
things that arise in the outside world that are coming towards you) from internal
threats (things that emerge from within you). In shame the external threat is what
other people feel and think and what they are likely to do as a result. When you
are doing your inference chains it is therefore very useful to separate internal from
external shame. This can be written in a single column or as two columns. Let's
look at the example of Mary, who has shame about expressing emotions, especially those of sadness. In the 1992 edition I did not clearly articulate this but this
is one way we could have worked together.

External shame	Internal shame
If I show my feelings other people will be critical and see me as foolish.	Having certain feelings may get out of control.
If they see me as foolish they will ridicule me or distance themselves from me.	I will become confused and vulnerable.
They will know my vulnerabilities and will be able to get the better of me.	I will be pathetic.
My key fear is that others will hurt and abandon me. (Reactivation of childhood memory of experience of others).	*My key fear* is falling apart and having no way to recover; being alone and miserable (reactivation of childhood memory of inner experience of self).

Because compassion-focused therapy *always follows the fear,* this helps to illuminate two very different types of fear. One is what the outside world will think and do, and the other is what will happen and emerge inside oneself. We can see again that with this kind of experience both the inside world and the outside world become very threatening. There is yet a third form of internal threat, which is the self-criticism for allowing oneself to 'get into this state'. In other words, rather than feeling compassionate and empathic to these fears and terrors, the self launches an attack. In Mary's case it was telling her she was stupid and she should pull herself together. If one explores this then it can help Mary see that her self-criticism is threat-based; it emerges from a kind of panic of these negative events happening and trying to *force* herself to stay in control.

This points to a process for intervention by being compassionate to these fears as understandable and not Mary's 'fault'. It is very important when working with shame that one does not imply people are being irrational, because this does not help them appreciate the power of emotional memory and *conditioned emotional responses.*

Making the changes

So a lot of Mary's thinking was on the self-criticism and not being able to be compassionate to her underlying fears. No one had been compassionate to her so she did not know how to be compassionate to herself. In the therapy these thoughts were: 'You should control your feelings. It's weak to cry, bad to feel rage. Paul will think you are pathetic. You are pathetic when you cry.'

However, working with the focus on the fear and safety behaviours Mary gradually began to identify how paralysed she felt under this kind of attack; how this was the same feeling she had as a child. She became able to verbalise her feelings of helplessness and anger at this internal experience. She practised arguing with her father in role play. It was also possible to write some flash cards that she felt helped her with these feelings. Now as I have mentioned, we are using case examples to make points, so Mary is something of a mixture of people and today we can work in a more compassionate-focused way than I did for previous editions of this book. So, we could now work with:

Empathy and validation for one's distress   It is very frightening and sad to be so worried about one's own human feelings and be in touch with one's own sadness and vulnerability. Crying is a sign of hurt not weakness.

Compassionate attention   In my heart I know I am not without feelings and vulnerabilities but also I have been able to regulate my feelings when I have needed to – it is a question of balance. I can focus on my caring-nurturing self-image and contact that part of me that would like to be compassionate. Breathe slowly and focus on the sense of a compassionate self or image.

Compassionate thinking   If friends cry I would try to offer them comfort. Actually what I needed as a child was what every child needed – comfort and being listened to when distressed. I can learn to focus on thoughts that are helpful and supportive when I have these fears by recognising them as understandable but they may not be helpful now. My father told me not to cry but I don't have to treat myself like he treated me. Although I am worried that Paul might see me the same way, it is possible that he doesn't and it would be helpful to try to explore that.

Compassionate behaviour   I have used anger a lot in my life to hide what I feel. Let's see if I can try out using compassion to learn to tolerate and be with my feelings.

When helping people work through these alternatives they need to feel them, so Mary would have to go through these slowly and create an inner 'warm voice' and to really focus on the warmth, understanding and support in these alternatives. They mustn't just stay at the level of evidence or logical alternatives. Another technique we can use employs imagery. When Mary is in touch with some of her feelings of shame coming from early childhood, she can imagine herself as the child coming into the room saying 'Dad has been horrible to me'. Mary could imagine herself putting her arm around the child and comforting her. In this way she may be able to begin to activate a more nurturing mentality to herself. Of course, this is only an aspect of the work on her difficulties but it can provide for a more self-accepting attitude to herself and allow work on very emotional material. Working like this with a similar case to Mary, the person found that as she was able to express her feelings in the therapy she cried less on her own. As for Mary, although we did not then do the compassionate work we do now, over the year in counselling, the rather depressed, brittle, angry and at times silent woman who came through the door on her first day, softened.

The black hole of shame

Shame can paralyse our thinking (mind goes blank) and behaviour and all we want to do is run away or hide – we wish the ground would open up and we could slip away. In some cases of shame a client may fall into a state that can be described as a 'black hole'. For example, Jane had serious shame about her physical appearance, especially the shape of her body. This was an issue she wanted to discuss but each time we approached it her mind went blank and she began to feel highly scrutinised and very aware of being looked at. So overwhelming was this feeling that she felt paralysed. Her head would go down and she simply could not speak, while her main impulse was to run from the room. Ideas rushed through her mind, few of which she could focus on. These are intense states of inhibition.

This difficulty in verbalising feelings might, by some therapists, be seen as a problem of very early schema of the self which formed before language (e.g. Young et al., 1993), thus making articulation of feeling difficult. However, it is equally possible that it results from high levels of internal inhibition (Gilbert, 1992, 1998c, 2003). Therapists sometimes wonder whether it is helpful to speak or remain silent in these situations. In my view the therapist has to use empathic awareness to decide if a client is gradually working out of the state of inhibition or whether they are lost in it. In the latter case, the therapist may need to do the work, for sometimes these states are not easy to get out of and sitting waiting for the client to speak tends to push the silence into an unhelpful position. (Gilbert, 2007). Equally, going too quickly after self-evaluations can miss contact with the internal experience and the client simply switches off (see Chapter 7).

With these kinds of problem the therapist can separate the first from subsequent occasions. Sometimes one can be taken by surprise when the 'black hole' of shame appears. Here the therapist walks a difficult line between helping the client out of the black hole, and yet not interfering in a potentially important self-helping or self-recovery process. The empathic response can be helpful when it first appears.

Jane had sat in her chair for a long time unable to respond to the therapist.

Therapist: This feels like a very painful state for you, Jane, especially with me sitting here looking at you. Maybe you are frightened of what I'm thinking.

Jane: [*Makes a slight head movement and half shrug*]

Therapist: [*Softly*] Okay, Jane. Now I am going to talk to you a little. What I am thinking is that you are in a lot of pain right now. Perhaps you have different emotions of anger, fear, loneliness, feeling cut off. I would like to help you out of that position. But maybe first it would be helpful if we had a better idea of what is going on in your mind and why. Would you allow me to try to explain some things about what we call shame and see if this helps?

Jane: [*Nods*]

Therapist: Like I said, you may be experiencing a deep shame experience. This can come for all kinds of reasons. For example, it may be that people have put us down in the past, and we can become anxious about saying the right thing or sounding silly or simply being confused and not knowing what to say. When this comes over us we can have all kinds of feelings, including feeling just 'shut down' inside. We may wish to run away, or feel anger at ourselves and others, even the therapist for being here.

Knowledge of shame is sometimes helpful because the person can see that it is a symptom of pain and fear and not a specific abnormality about them; they are not stupid or weak, etc. You can explain it as a protection strategy that can be *automatic* and shuts us down (or sometimes produces rage) and that this is 'not their fault'. Also, if your empathy is on track, clients can feel very relieved that you understand what is going on in their minds and why they suddenly feel so paralysed. After discussion of the shame experience, the client and therapist may then discuss how they should collaborate and work together if this state re-emerges during therapy sessions. This is designed to help the client have more understanding and control in these situations. Thus some clients can indicate to the therapist that they feel they are falling into the black hole and then the coping options worked out between them can be put into place. One client said: 'It's been a great help knowing you understand my feelings and helping me understand what happens to me. I never realised what was happening. It just took me over.' Some clients are able to say that they are 'starting to get lost' and 'shut down'.

When severe shame feelings do arise, on later occasions, the therapist might say something like: 'Your feelings are trying to stop you from speaking. Maybe they are trying to protect you from ridicule and hurt perhaps.' However, as we talked about before, you can say to these feelings: 'Thank you for your concern but I do not need your protection right now. I can gradually begin to explore these things now.' If you think the black hole is getting too dark, just stop for a moment, let's take stock and relax ourselves.

In a sense this is a form of *de-sensitisation* to the emotions of deep shame via gradual exposure. Thus one is enabling a client to be less paralysed or over-whelmed by shame. Sooner or later, however, the client will usually need to talk about what it is they feel ashamed about. Fears may include previous sexual abuse, an abortion, homosexual feelings, aggressive feelings to children or to the therapist, and so forth. One of my patients, for example, struggled to tell me that he was having an affair which was related to great conflict and the source of his depression. If there is a good therapeutic relationship, then usually the client has a wish to reveal and the therapist can use this.

> *Therapist*:   I might be wrong about this but I sense there is something that you would like to discuss but are frightened to. Now I don't want to push you or anything, I just want you to know that this is how it seems to me.

Silence and other non-verbal signals to this statement can suggest to the therapist that they are on the right lines. Often the client will agree and then it is possible to explore further, but sometimes clients remain silent. The therapist may then ask about fears of revealing (e.g. confidentiality or therapist rejection). Just enabling the client to talk around the issue is helpful, but again this should not be under-taken without a good therapeutic relationship.

> *Therapist*:   I sense that there is a great risk for you, but we don't have to explore it all in one go. Is there some aspect of it that you could discuss and share here?

If sexual abuse is suspected, the therapist might say:

> *Therapist*:   You know, sometimes when we are young, people we trust do things to us that we sense is wrong or leaves us feeling ashamed. Maybe they interfere with us in some way. Has anything like that happened to you?

By careful and sensitive questioning that conveys an empathic awareness of the risks, the client can be helped to feel safe enough to reveal. Jehu (1988, 1989) has indicated how the cognitive approach can be used in cases of abuse. Family mem-bers in abuse cases may have used shame-invoking to inhibit the child from revealing to others, including telling the child that it was their fault or even deny-ing that it happened at all. In one case the mother had not only denied the abuse, but had accused her daughter of being disgusting/terrible even to think that her father could have done such a thing. The experience of being disbelieved can be a powerful inhibitor of sharing feelings in therapy and is associated with feelings of shame and guilt in revealing, and also disgust at self.

Also, as we discussed earlier, when shame relates to what other people have done, particularly family members, there can be a sense of betrayal and it is this sense of betrayal of breaking the 'secret' that can feel shameful and an act of betrayal (Gilbert and Irons, 2005; see also pp. 283–284 in this volume).

Key issues 14.1 Shame

1 Shame is one of the most important affects to understand in therapy, especially with depressed people.
2 Shame is focused on two types of threat. How the outside world will see the self and respond to the self and what will emerge inside of the self.
3 Shame usually motivates concealment and hiding (and sometimes rage). If not completely so, then clients will put a spin on their story, tell half-truths or tell it in a way that in their hearts they know it is not entirely accurate.
4 Very powerful shame paralysis can occur in therapy and these feelings can be difficult to control. The person experiences their mind going blank or has panic-like feelings of wanting to run away and hide.
5 People can have shame about revealing things in the past; about their emotional reactions to things; about how they are coping with their feelings currently (e.g. ashamed of feeling tearful and vulnerable); and about how the therapist may see them and what they may trigger in the therapy.
6 The therapist works with shame as basically a fear problem and tries to make an empathic connection to shame states.

Guilt

Guilt, like shame, is a powerful human emotion (Baumeister, Stillwell and Heatherton, 1994). It is often confused with shame, and clients may use the words 'shame' and 'guilt' interchangeably (Gilbert, 2003). But shame and guilt can be conceptualised as very different psychological processes. Unlike shame, the focus of guilt is on harm done to others and sometimes the self. Guilt tends to be focused on specific behaviours rather than global evaluations of the self as 'bad and flawed' (Tangney and Dearing, 2002). Anger at others is rare or non-existent and disgust has never been associated with guilt, but is often associated with shame. Guilt can be associated with anxiety, however, especially anxiety of doing harm. Importantly, guilt motivates desires to repair and atone for harm done rather than concealing, hiding, covering up and running away – as is the case for shame. There is also a difference in the power relationship. In shame, others are seen as more powerful and capable of rejecting the self. In guilt, it is we who have used our power unwisely to hurt or let others down. Shame is about blame, guilt is about resposibility.

Guilt and shame can co-exist, as in the case when one's harmful behaviour might become known to another, thus making one an object of rejection, scorn and put-down. Guilt usually involves ideas of 'I should not have done this', where the focus is on a specific behaviour rather than the self (Tangney and Dearing, 2002). Guilt as a 'should not' attitude often relates to moral dilemmas. There are many types of guilt, two of which are:

1   Guilt about breaking one's own standards when these actions have little to do with other people (e.g. breaking a diet regime, spending money on oneself, having fantasies that break moral codes). Yalom (1980) talks of existential guilt – the guilt that comes from believing one has not supported oneself or has lived inauthentically.
2   Guilt about actions that affect other people which break down into acts of commission and acts of omission. Acts of commission are doing things that hurt another (e.g. having an affair with a married person, hitting children, etc.). Acts of omission are things that one feels one could have done to be helpful, but did not do. Not caring enough is a common guilt scenario.

Strong guilt feelings often act as entrapments (Gilbert, Gilbert and Irons, 2004). For example, the person who stays in a marriage out of guilt (because they do not want to hurt their partner or leave their children) may feel trapped in the marriage and resentful and hopeless. At the same time they may feel needed, which gives them some sense of self-esteem and power. Dickson (1982) calls this the compassion trap, for individuals who have assertiveness problems associated with guilt. Dickson's book can be recommended reading for such difficulties.

Lynn O'Connor, in San Francisco, has also pointed out that people can feel guilt because they are better off than others (O'Connor, 2000). For example, survivors of disasters may feel guilty because they survived but others died or were hurt. Imagine you and a friend enter a beauty contest and you are both really keen. You win and your friend comes last! Your feelings of disappointment for your friend could lead to guilt. Sometimes people may even inhibit themselves so as not to hurt others (e.g. knowing that your friend will feel badly if you win, you don't enter). And guilt-inducing reactions (e.g. a parent constantly claiming how hurt they have been by a child's action) can lead to hyper-sensitivity to others' feelings to the point where one is not able to acknowledge or be assertive about one's own needs. People who always *have to* put the needs of others first are often susceptible to strong guilt feelings or shame-fears that others won't like them if they do put their own needs first. So guilt is this sensitivity to other people's feelings but it is easily fused with shame and it is the shame aspects linked with guilt that are most pathogenic (Tangney and Dearing, 2002).

There are other problems that can arise from harm (to others) avoidance, guilt and a heightened sense of responsibility. For example, in some psychotic depressions people can have delusions of having caused harm. Some obsessional disorders have been related to fears of harming others (e.g. by contaminating others or not taking enough care or checking things) and an inflated sense of responsibility (Wroe and Salkovskis, 2000). Some people can have exaggerated feelings of responsibility for the welfare of others (O'Connor, 2000).

Working with guilt

Doris's father came to live with her when her mother died. At first Doris was pleased to be able to help, but weeks turned to months and there was no sign that her father was making plans to get his own place. Also, he gave her little money to cover his living expenses and she felt that she could not ask him for more because it was his 'pension'. Doris tried to make hints that her father should move out but he turned things around by saying: 'When you were in need we looked after you. I don't think I can cope on my own at the moment. Of course, if ever I thought you didn't want me any more then I would go.' Trying to induce guilt in others so that they will care for one in the way one wants is a common interpersonal tactic (Baumeister et al., 1994). Doris felt helpless to confront her father because she felt terribly guilty at 'wanting to push him out' and feeling responsible for him.

Guilt (and shame) links with cultural values. For example, for obvious financial reasons the governments of the past twenty years have encouraged people to care for their elderly parents. The fact that people now live much longer than they did a few hundred years ago (thanks to modern medicine) is not acknowledged. Some feel guilty at not wishing to carry this burden. Thus, cultures vary in terms of their guilt- and shame-inducing tactics (Murphy, 1978). Feminists have suggested that women have been so indoctrinated in the caring-loving role that guilt is a common problem.

Guilt, shame, entrapment and escape

Guilt and shame can often give rise to a sense of entrapment and desire to escape (see Chapter 3). In serious depression, for example, people may feel they are being a burden to others and the best way out is to kill themselves. When Tim lost his job he became depressed and felt he was letting his family down. He spent days just lying in bed or staring at the television. He became convinced that although his family would be sad for a while if he died, they would get over it and be much better off without him. The pain of his depression and guilt for being 'a let down' and a burden to them fuelled his suicidal escape feelings. Clearly, there was much else besides, including shame, anger over his lost job and a loss of self-confidence, but guilt (responsibility) was also a key issue for him. Luckily his guilt over leaving his children also acted to stop him. So guilt is a double-edged sword. It can keep us in relationships (guilty about leaving) but it can also motivate strong desires to escape because the relationship(s) often seems to activate strong feelings of not being good enough or being a burden in some way.

Affect toleration   Although shame and guilt (like any emotion) can become problematic, it is also the case that at times we simply have to learn to tolerate them. It is not possible to live a shame- or guilt-free life. These are part of normal human experience. Just as people with anxiety disorders may have to learn how to tolerate anxiety without taking immediate flight, the same can be true of guilt and shame (or indeed any negative emotion). For Doris, for example, being honest with her father did induce guilty feelings which she had to learn to tolerate. She had to learn not to be overly inhibited by such feelings. We often have to do things that we feel bad about but know we need to do them anyway. For example, having to discipline a colleague at work is rarely easy. So we sometimes have to tolerate and accept shame and guilt feelings. Indeed, in small measure, the ability to tolerate shame and guilt is helpful and those who cannot tolerate them can be either very socially anxious, inhibited or even aggressive. Assertiveness is helpful in being able to tolerate feelings of guilt and shame.

Forgiveness   Perhaps one of the things that allow us to tolerate shame and guilt is some kind of inner forgiveness (Worthington et al., 2005). This is also related to the ability to be self-soothing and compassionate. If we have made a mistake or done harm to others we need to be able to tolerate those feelings without launching major self-attacks. So, self-forgiveness is an important quality of inner caring and compassion. When people find self-forgiveness difficult they often use the concept of 'don't deserve'. There has been growing attention to the importance of a forgiveness triad (Enright, 1996). The triad involves being able to forgive others rather than ruminate on vengeful and often impotent rage; being able to be helped by receiving the forgiveness of others (e.g. not disqualifying it); and self-forgiveness (see also Freedman and Enright, 1996; McCullough, Worthington and Rachal, 1997). So the process of forgiveness, which obviously is very different from denial or other defensive manoeuvres, is a key process in developing self-compassion.

Key issues 14.2   Guilt and forgiveness

1   Guilt in depression is often about a sense of responsibility and trying to avoid harming or recognising that in recovery one has to become more self-focused and this may bring one into conflict with others.
2   What type of guilt does the person suffer:

    (a) about the self?
    (b) about acts of commission or omission?

3   Look for the 'shoulds', 'should nots', and the 'musts' in beliefs and attitudes.
4   Guilt can be a trap and lead to resentment (e.g. the compassion trap).
5   Explore cultural or social values that are maintaining guilt and discuss these with the client.
6   Explore the capacity to 'tolerate guilt' and use self-forgiveness and self-acceptance techniques.

Ideals

Ideals are often powerful in depression, and unrealistic (Bibring, 1953; Moretti, Higgins and Feldman, 1990). Humans are future-orientated. They plan with hopes, expectations and ideals related to positive outcomes. Our ideals involve a kind of matching to some internal standard, fantasy or template, and can be the source of our 'shoulds', 'oughts' and 'musts'. They provide the source of information for how we would like things to be. They are the focus of various dysfunctional attitudes. We can have various types of ideals:

1   Ideals about how others should be, that is, our friends, lovers, spouse (e.g. understanding, fun, loving, accepting).
2   Ideals about how we should be (e.g. able, strong, anxiety-free, competent, respected).
3   Ideals about how we should experience the world (e.g. fun, open, helpful).

Bibring (1953) based his early ego analytic theory of depression on the notion of ideals. Bibring suggested three types of ideals and aspirations which the (pre)depressive may seek:

1   The wish to be worthy and loved, and to avoid inferiority and unworthiness.
2   The wish to be strong, superior, secure, and to avoid being weak and insecure.
3   The wish to be loving and good and not aggressive, hateful or destructive.

In the last case, Bibring suggests that the awareness of internal aggressive impulses deals a blow to self-esteem. Bibring (1953, pp. 25–6) suggests that 'depression can be defined as the emotional correlate of a partial or complete collapse of the self-esteem of the ego, since it feels unable to live up to its aspirations ... while they are strongly maintained'. As we have seen, however, shame is probably a better way to think about this and in particular that it is not loss of ideals but becoming the undesired self that is crucial (see Chapter 6).

Becker (1979, p. 324) points out that vulnerability to depression according to this model has a number of causes, which include: 'constitutional intolerance of persistent frustration, severe and prolonged helplessness, and developmental deficiencies in skill acquisition. These deficiencies are enhanced by the ego ideals which tend to be high and rigidly adhered to by depressives'. Abramson, Metalsky and Alloy (1989) developed a theory of what they call *hopelessness depression* derived from the perceived failure to be able to reach goals, standards or ideals.

The problem with strong ideals is that they activate our old friend 'disappointment' when outcomes or events fall too far below the ideal. Some try to defend against this with mottoes such as, 'Don't expect too much and you won't be disappointed'. The empathic response to failed ideals and hopes tunes into the experience of disappointment. However, as noted a number of times, disappointment in itself need not be a problem if it does not activate self- or other-attacking, but for some this is exactly what happens. Also keep in mind that running with disappointment can be bigger fears of rejection or criticism from others.

Working with ideals

Ken was in his forties when I first saw him. He had been known to the psychiatric services for thirty years. When he was eight his parents moved to another part of the country. Although he felt he had been popular in his old school, things turned out differently in his new junior school. His accent marked him as different and he had trouble understanding the teachers. His elder brother (by five years), on the other hand, did well in his new senior school, quickly became integrated, went on school trips and played various sports for the school teams. Their adaptation could not have been more different. Ken developed panic attacks and spent a lot of time away from school. He was eventually sent to a school for children with emotional difficulties. Here also he felt he did not fit in. A strong theme in his life was that of the outsider.

Ken had developed a strong fantasy that if someone could 'cure' his anxiety then he would be able to be like others, especially more like his brother, who was successful both socially and in business. He idealised the medical profession but also had great rage at the way he thought he had been treated by them. When he was referred, he was having panic attacks at home and spending days in bed, and saying he would kill himself, it was all pointless. Electroconvulsive Therapy (ECT) was considered.

At first the therapist listened to the story for Ken was too angry to start exploring his own attitudes and felt that no one had understood him. The panics were fairly classic and focused on fears of being unable to breathe and dying. These responded to basic cognitive behavioural interventions of breathing control, hyperventilation, gradual exposure and re-education (Clark, 1999). He did so well in therapy that he bought a new car and went on a trip to the continent. But when he came back he went to bed, got depressed and became very angry.

The relapse was formulated as a problem of unrealistic ideals. Ken had the fantasy that if his anxiety was cured he would become 'turbo charged' and would make up for many lost years. For many years he had developed a fantasy of what it would be like to be anxiety-free and not an outsider. In this fantasy he would be like others, able to travel, able to be successful, and in his words 'rejoin the human race at last'. He imagined that normal people never suffered from anxiety. Also he had a hope that there would be some magic answer that would take the anxiety away, and that 'once good it should stay good'. At this session he explained his trip to the continent. He had suffered anxiety on the trip but had kept this under control.

We drew out two boxes that captured this situation. Ideal me = me without anxiety. Actual me = how I am now.

Ideal me	Actual me
Like others.	Not like others/different.
Able to enjoy life.	Life is miserable.
Confident/successful.	A failure.
Explorative.	Frightened.

I refer to the difference between these two as the 'disappointment gap' (Gilbert, 2000a). When depression-prone people suffer severe disappointment, their anger is often directed at themselves (self-criticism for failing) or at others (e.g. for letting them down). They can become so disheartened they give up. Let's look at how Ken dealt with his trip.

Therapist:	As we have been talking it seems like you did quite a lot on your trip, but you feel disappointed with it. What happened when you got back?
Ken:	I started to look back on it and thought, 'Why does it have to be so hard for me, always fighting this anxiety?' I should have enjoyed it more after all the effort I put into it. I should have done more. It's been a struggle. So I just went to bed and brooded on how bad it all was and what's the point. [*We see how rumination/brooding is a problem that will need working with but for moment we stay with the ideals aspect.*]
Therapist:	From what we have discussed before it sounds like your experience did not match your ideal.
Ken:	Oh yeah, it was far from that.
Therapist:	Okay, what went through your mind when you found that the trip was not matching your ideal?
Ken:	I started to think I should be enjoying this more. If I were really better I would enjoy it more. If I felt better I would do more. I'll never get on top of this. It's all too late and too much effort.

Therapist:	That sounds like it was very disappointing to you.
Ken:	Oh yes, very, terribly, but more so when I got back.
Therapist:	What did you say about you?
Ken:	I've failed again. I just felt totally useless. After all the work we've done nothing has changed.
Therapist:	Let's go back to our two boxes for a moment and see if I have understood this. For many years you've had the fantasy of how things would be if you were better. [*Points to ideal box*] But getting there is a struggle and this is disappointing to you. When you get disappointed you start to attack yourself saying that you are a failure and it's too late and it is all hopeless. That makes the actual you seem unchanged. Is that right?
Ken:	Yes, absolutely.
Therapist:	Can we see how the disappointment of not reaching the ideal starts up this internal attack on yourself, and the more of a failure you feel the more anxious, angry and depressed you get?
Ken:	Hmm, yes.

In Ken's case we were able to work with the link joining the ideal, the disappointment and the self-attack. You can see also that there is thirty years of disappointment in these experiences. Later in the session we were able to explore the successes that had taken place on the trip and explore how Ken would disqualify the positives if they did not match up to an ideal. He saw it as 'destroying and ripping up the good things that happened to him'.

There were other issues, such as the new self-identity of being able to travel and no longer being a victim to anxiety. His new sense of self was 'strange' to him and he worried that if they became well others would not be so interested in helping him. He also felt that it would be letting go of his past in which he felt 'very rooted'. However, slowly Ken began to modify his ideal and gradually mourn lost opportunities. He had to do a lot of work with sadness which his anger tended to cover up. This took a long time and therapy lasted well over a year. Over the years I have seen Ken for small relapses and 'booster' sessions.

So, 'shoulds' often point to ideals. The self-attacks come from the disappointment and this makes the person feel further away from the ideal. Unfortunately, these attacks, consequent to disappointment, and the failure of others to fulfil various needs for the client, can also fuel aggression. In one case a young man had very unrealistic fantasies of how a loving relationship would be (he was highly egocentric). When his lovers did not live up to his ideal image, he expressed his disappointment in violence. He had a lot of difficulty in giving up the ideal ('they should be ...' thoughts) as his needs for constant attention were great.

Thus, therapy explores the 'shoulds', 'oughts' and 'musts' implicit in high ideals. It is helpful to be aware of the experience of disappointment that is consequent upon failing to reach high ideals. Type A personalities (those rather competitive and time-urgent folk) can also have difficulty in changing their standards because this may mean that they will not be able to get to their ideal of being more special or superior to others (Gilbert, 1989). In these cases the advantages–disadvantages technique of changing ideals can be helpful (see Chapter 12). Thus, in counselling a certain working through of disappointment is often necessary.

There is a lot in positive psychology which is about helping people articulate their goals and ideals and how to reach them. Sometimes this is presented in a fairly neutral way but in reality the therapist will be directing these so that they are realistic, achievable and socially appropriate. One of the problems with depression is that ideals are not just ideals but are given enormous emotional significance because they are associated with recovery from distress, overcoming a depression, or a hoped-for self-identify. Very often we need to make clear that reaching one's ideals won't necessarily lead to a happy life and it is in fact a myth of western societies that it would. There are certain things that are conducive to happiness and certain things that are not (Carr, 2004). So when working with ideals recognise the way in which people use them, strive for them and their implied functions. Clearly, the issue of tolerance and acceptance of disappointment is also important (see Chapter 4).

Key issues 14.3   Ideals

1   Ideals represent our hopes and aspirations of how we would like things to be. These can be drawn out by the therapist with questions such as: 'How would you like things to be? How would you like yourself to be?'
2   Depressed clients can have unrealistic ideals and feel a strong sense of disappointment when ideals are not achieved. This is partly because their ideals are not just about good things but are linked to having almost magical curative properties. Failure to reach 'ideals' can also trigger key fears.
3   At times, depressed people are so disappointed by failing to reach their ideals that disappointment spills over into anger and they disqualify or destroy the positive aspects of their lives.
4   Helping clients recognise the thoughts, feelings and key fears that are triggered by the disappointment is a key to working with ideals.

Envy

Envy is different from jealousy and arises from feeling that others are better off than oneself (Parrott and Smith, 1993; Smith and Kim, 2007). Envy, like shame, arises out of self–other comparisons, and where the person feels they are in some sense inferior. Parrott and Smith (1993) found that envy involves feeling inferior to the envied, longing, and resentment, but also disapproval of the emotion. Indeed, acknowledging envy can feel shameful, so clients may not acknowledge this openly in therapy. In competitive cultures which stress individualism, envy is unfortunately rife (Gilbert, 1989, 1992). Smith, Parrott, Ozer and Moniz (1994) found that the hostile feelings of envy tend to relate to a sense of injustice – that the envied person has an *unfair* advantage. The depressive elements are related to the fact that those who have more of something or are seen to be superior in some way show up one's own inferiority – it is the negative social comparison and self-evaluations of envy that seem to be depressing (Gilbert, 1992). There are various forms of envy.

Fear of one's own envy

Anne's depression was related, she thought, to the menopause. She was angry that 'her hormones were giving her such a hard time'. She also had thoughts of wanting to bring other people down because she felt people didn't understand how bad she felt – she was fed up with being given advice by friends of how 'they had coped with the menopause'. 'If only I can make them feel like I do, that would wipe the smile off their faces', she'd say. There were also various aggressive fantasies. But then she'd add: 'Oh, but I shouldn't think like that, should I? I feel terrible about it.' So these feelings made her feel more isolated and she took them as being evidence of a bad, unlovable self (i.e. a source of shame).

Anne:	Until I got this depression, I never realised I could feel so vengeful. I see my friends having fun and I think 'I used to be like that'. Why me? Why not them? I actually hate them for being happy. It's terrible. Perhaps I deserve this because inside I'm so nasty.
Therapist:	So you have two issues. One is your vengeful feelings, and the other is that you see this as evidence of you being nasty?
Anne:	Yes. I hate to feel this burning resentment when I am with others.
Therapist:	So your resentment makes you feel different, not like others?
Anne:	Oh yes, and so does my depression. I used to be like them. I rarely had time for depressed people. I know what they must be thinking about me now. But, of course, I try to hide it.

At this point Anne talked at length about the loss of her old self, and her anger at what had 'happened to her'. As we moved back to envy again, the therapist tried to focus on the experience of envy, negative self-beliefs and loss of the 'happy self'.

Therapist:	Okay, let's think about envy for a moment. Suppose you could allow yourself to feel envy without saying this means you are nasty?
Anne:	But it is nasty, Paul. It's so destructive. I don't want to feel this. I want to be well again.
Therapist:	Yes, that is our goal, but on the way we are trying to explore your negative ideas about yourself, which right now focus on envy.
Anne:	Hmm, I don't want to feel envy.
Therapist:	Well, let's draw it out.

The therapist then draws a circle with the links: feel envy at being depressed, this means I'm nasty, feel worse about myself, leading to more depression and more envious feelings.

Therapist:	You see, if we could work on the 'this means I'm nasty', that may help you feel less negative about yourself. It is a rather global judgement which gives you the feeling of a lost good self that you had previously.
Anne:	If I'm not nasty, then what am I?
Therapist:	Well, let's think about alternatives? In general, why are people envious – oh, apart from being nasty? [*Client smiles*]
Anne:	[*Thinks*] Hmm, I guess they feel one down or in need like we said before.
Therapist:	Does that seem reasonable, that people can feel envy when inside they feel needing of something?
Anne:	Yes, I think so.
Therapist:	So supposing we applied those judgements to you and said your envious feelings reflect a need to be well and like others again, rather than as evidence of a nasty self?

Anne:	I'd have to think about this.
Therapist:	Fine. [*Smiles*] Let's think about it.

We then worked with changing the self-judgement such that she began to reconsider envy in terms of feelings of need and being different from others and not as evidence of a nasty person. Envy became an unpleasant affect that was understandable rather than an internal experience that made her feel bad about herself. Gradually, as Anne began to accept her envy and other destructive feelings without attacking herself, she was able to talk more to her friends about her depression and gradually recovered. Later, she also revealed that my approach to her envy and my refusal to see it as evidence of her nastiness had helped her accept it and work it through. As with other examples, today we might do more on compassionate acceptance.

Envy of the therapist

Sometimes clients will feel intense envy of the therapist and have various ideas that the therapist has a relatively easy and pain-free life – and compared to our clients there may be some truth to this, although for some therapists less than might be supposed. It is important that therapists don't get defensive about this or try to show the client that 'my life is not so hot for me you know'. Rather, it is useful to bring these feelings into the therapy and avoid shaming them, but at the same time to explore how they can be destructive of collaborative work. For example, Dean was struggling to do various aspects of work out of session and I was trying to help him through it a step at a time. Our conversation went something like this:

Dean:	Look, it's easy for you – you understand these things, you got degrees and all. But I don't. My life is tough – not like yours.
Therapist:	Hmm. Sounds like you feel disappointed you can't do it as you'd like and resentful that things seem tougher for you than for others. And it's easy for me.
Dean:	Oh sure. I never get the breaks. It always seems so much easier for others. Like when I was at school. If only I had been brighter and not seen as a dumbo.

By depersonalising the attack to a more general feeling of envy (resentment) we were able to explore this long-lived feeling of being less able than others (which we had met before in our work together). By empathising with the disappointment, I was then able to gradually work around to exploring the envy. I also tried to show I could cope with his envious attacks and not shame him for them. I had to be mindful of how he could stir up defensive and aggressive feelings in me – I had to note them but try to stay compassionate, curious and empathic.

Therapist:	I wonder how much your thoughts that 'it is easier for me' stops you from really taking from here things that might be useful to you?
Dean:	Maybe.
Therapist:	Okay, maybe it's true it is easier for me – so what would you need from me to make things easier for you? I mean how could you use me more to your advantage?

Dean:	[*Looks surprised*] I don't know. [*Pauses*] I guess I'd never thought of me being able to use you.
Therapist:	Sounds to me you have a choice. Either you can stay feeling envious and resentful, that I seem able to understand these things and you don't, or you can say 'I am going to make that therapist show me too'.

Noting a change in Dean's mood, I smiled and added: 'You could say hey, I am going to make that therapist really work for his money!' At this Dean gave a short smile. We had these sorts of conversations a number of times but I tried not to be defensive to his attacks but focus Dean on how he could use what was on offer, work collaboratively and tried to empower him in the therapy. It was a difficult therapy and Dean remained somewhat envious and distrustful of those in authority but he did become less depressed and able to focus on what he could do rather than on what he couldn't. He also became more aware of his own shame (feeling inwardly a 'dumbo') and did a lot of work on healing that. By the end of therapy he was more affiliative, relaxed and able to acknowledge that 'on the whole the therapy had been a helpful experience' for him – and he was genuinely sad to leave it. I offer this snippet of a case of envy to alert therapists to it. However, working with very envious people can be hard work and you'll need good supervision (see Horner, 1989 for a further discussion of envy in therapy).

Fear of igniting other people's envious attacks

Some years before starting counselling Ken bought a new car but sold it three months later. When asked why, he said that while driving around he had the idea that others were looking at him thinking: 'Where the hell did he get the money from to buy that? Who does he think he is?' Thus, Ken had an acute sense of external persecution. His family history revealed much envy as part of the family dynamics.

Therapist:	Even if it is true that others would be envious of you, why would that mean you had to sell the car?
Ken:	I wouldn't want them to think like that. They would try to put me down.
Therapist:	But suppose we said, look, envy is part of life and we have to learn to cope with it rather than hide from that. What would you say?
Ken:	Hmm, I am not sure about that.
Therapist:	Okay, let's look at the advantages and disadvantages of accepting other people's envy.

This revealed many advantages: 'I would be free to have what I want (cars, clothes, etc.). I would feel more in control of my life, not having to look over my shoulder. I would feel better and more hopeful.' However, the disadvantages were many: 'Others would think I was above my station. They might try to hurt or pull me down. They will think I'm okay and don't need help. They wouldn't want to help me if I needed it. They might take pleasure in seeing me fall. I might become even more of an outsider.'

Therapist:	It sounds like you actually have a certain terror of success and changing.
Ken:	Written down like that I see it. I do get very anxious about what others think if good things happen to me.

Therapist: Yeah, but it's more than that, it's a belief that others will pull you down, won't help you and that you would not be able to cope with that.

Exploration of his history had revealed a father figure who had rarely praised Ken, in part because he was never as good as his brother and in part because, while the brother was seen as advancing the family and giving it pride, the father had not taken that view of Ken. Thus, when Ken had bought this new car and proudly shown it to his father, his father had simply commented that he could not see the point of Ken having a car like that in his situation. Also, the father had seemed mildly angry that this son, who had been anxious and depressed for many years, should have a new car.

Much discussion was given over to these aspects, with the therapist acting in an encouraging way (or, in self-psychology terms (Wolf, 1988), a mirroring self-object) (see pp. 120–124). Thus, one thing to try out of session was for Ken to begin to look at new cars and eventually buy one, which he did. Also, he openly discussed his feelings with friends and many of them said: 'Good luck mate, if you can afford it.' One of his friends said 'There's no pockets in shrouds', and this motto stuck. Thus, he sought out other sources of evidence. In some ways the fear of other people's envy can be seen as a form of need for approval. However, in envy it is not only disapproval that is feared but actual attacks, subsequent refusals of help and becoming isolated. In Ken's case there was a clear conflict between being seen as injured and needy, and being successful and contented.

Key issues 14.4   Envy

1   Envy relates to powerful feelings and beliefs about being different from others and less than others in some way.
2   Envious feelings themselves often increase the sense of difference and of being an outsider.
3   The therapist helps the client accept their envy, and recognise that it is often related to some feelings and beliefs about need rather than evidence of a bad or nasty self.
4   In some depressions, experiences of envy can be destructive of therapy if they are not acknowledged. At times, a client might feel envious of the therapist (or the therapist's lifestyle) and have difficulty working in an alliance.

Conclusion

This and the previous chapter explored various key themes which focus on how clients sees themselves in relation to others. Shame, guilt, unrealistic ideals, unfavourable social comparisons and envy are all powerful emotions and cognitions which can be very disruptive to all kinds of relationship, including therapy. Behind many of these negative emotions and cognitions, which are liable to make depression worse, are self-attacks, avoidance, blocking and resistance.

When working with these interpersonal themes remember that they can impinge on the therapy relationship. As in all such work, acting non-defensively and ensuring that you do not go beyond the limits of your expertise and experience is important. Therapists can learn how to avoid activating resistance by not themselves behaving in a shaming, critical, defensive and patronising manner. You can rarely predict in advance what kind of issues you will illuminate as you begin your work, so it is important that you are able to recognise these kinds of issues. And if you find you are struggling with your work, do seek advice and supervision and be prepared to pass clients to more experienced colleagues. However, we can be realistic here. It is only human to get defensive from time to time, but if we are compassionate to that, and openly try to work with therapeutic ruptures, this can be helpful for people (see Gilbert and Leahy, 2007).

15 Overview, Saying Goodbye and Personal Reflections

We started this book by thinking about the origins of depression and how far back in evolution we could detect it. The answer seems to be that the potential to tone down positive affect and tone up negative affect goes back a very long way. These potential brain states have evolved because they are part of the way animals defend themselves from various types of threat and harm. So our explorations into depression have examined depression as a form of threat-sensitivity and protection. This is at the core of how we empathise with the depressed person, as being in the grip of powerful defensive, evolved strategies. Humans are something of a tragic species because we have also evolved a range of abilities for certain kinds of self-awareness and thinking. We don't just fight with others we are in conflict with, but can plan how to fight and build bombs to drop on people. We can be gripped by desires for revenge with terrible cost. Our thinking abilities have given us new ways to see and understand the world but can also be a means to greatly accentuate more primitive motives and protection strategies.

The depressed mind, therefore, is one where we can be dragged into primitive forms of protective shutting-down. To experience our mind doing this is to experience acute emotional pain and darkness. Then we can become trapped because our thoughts and behaviours can maintain and worsen these states. Our vulnerabilities to these may lie in our genes, early experiences and their interactions (Caspi and Moffitt, 2006; Taylor et al., 2006), our emotional memories and their brain states (Brewin 2006; Gilbert, 1984), and the internal working models or self–other schema we develop (Baldwin, 2005; Beck et al., 1979; Bowlby, 1980).

Yet our evolution of the ability to relate to others in caring ways, to feel safe, and to be influenced by the minds of others, can be a source of our liberation, because when we feel safe many things change. Moreover, the very processes of thoughts, meta-cognitions, types of self-awareness that just take us down can, when focused in different ways, release us. This was an insight of the Buddha nearly 3000 years ago. Life involves suffering but it is *how* we suffer that is important. In the western world we have found also that once we know how unruly our minds can be, and once we have insight into the way our behaviours and thoughts (directed at the external and internal world) can make us worse, we are better placed to work to help ourselves. There are ways we can attend to the inner 'pullings' of our minds, not take our thoughts at face value, engage with rather than avoid the things that we fear, and act against the shut-down and withdrawal tendencies of depression. We may need another mind (person) to guide us, and to help us feel safe enough and contained enough to do this, but we can do it. The research shows that for many people these are ways to turn off depressive protection strategies.

Looked at this way, depression is neither a deficit (though deficits arise) nor dysfunction (though dysfunctions arise) nor an error (though errors arise), but an adaptation at both a genetic and a phenotypic level. Whether we look at the way our brains are affected by early abuse or neglect, or how some of us with certain temperaments cope with bullying, or how some of us strive to earn our place in the world and drive ourselves through harsh self-criticisms, what we are observing is that we are trying as best we can to adapt to threats and challenges upon us. Having a brain that has, say, reduced functioning in the frontal cortex due to abuse, so that trust and feeling safe is difficult, may be adaptive for highly hostile environments where life might have been short. The ways our brains (and different phenotypes) adapt to different environments may turn out to be harmful and maladaptive, especially if environments change (and given our human capacities for certain types of thinking), but that is not our fault – it is to do with having the kinds of brain, with the kinds of needs that we have.

In my view, this is why biopsychosocial approaches are so important. They allow us not only to think about the complexities of interactions, but also to move beyond 'schools of therapy' and begin to focus our interventions for specific kinds of difficulty. Indeed, this is exactly where modern research and therapy are going. We assess a person's difficulties carefully and then use evidence-based approaches to target specific difficulties. Thus we address avoidance behaviour, coping with interpersonal conflicts, unprocessed emotions or memories, rumination, attention focusing, styles of thinking and interpreting situations, ways to be compassionate to self rather than harshly self-critical. In essence, we use our increasing psychological science and research findings to develop scientifically based interventions. Not only this but we are increasingly moving towards considering how to develop psychological interventions that target specific neurophysiological processes (Cozolino, 2002; Linden, 2006). If someone has problems in certain brain pathways, such as the frontal cortex or soothing systems, what kinds of intervention can help, since we now know that the brain is far more plastic and changeable than previously thought (Schwartz and Begley, 2002). How does compassion work help here? We need to do the research. So the above is the basis for the therapy interventions that have been discussed here. We can now briefly review our thoughts on these interventions

Overview

When people come for help for depression they usually have a complex mixture of different problems. These problems are related to external difficulties and threats and also internal difficulties and threats. For the psychotherapist and counsellor, whatever the source of the depression, the experience of emotional disconnection and being internally closed down, often with strong desires to escape, can be key to the experience. Figure 15.1 offers a brief overview and a conceptual map for assessment and intervention.

Thinking about the body

Depression affects us biologically as much as psychologically and these aspects constantly interact. For example, there is now good evidence that depressed states

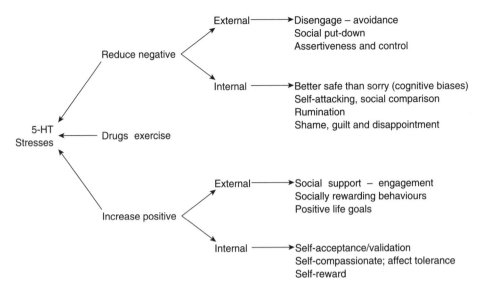

Figure 15.1   Biopsychosocial intervention strategies

vary, and represent complex psychobiological patterns associated with heightened activity in various stress systems (e.g. amygdala and HPA). These produce dysregulations in body rhythms, including sleep patterns and dream content. In very general terms, negative signals such as losses and threats tend to increase stress and can adversely affect 5-HT, and other neurotransmitters, whereas positive signals (approval, love) tend to reduce stress (e.g. cortisol), increase 5-HT and the opiates. There are, of course, many complications to such general rules, but a useful rule of thumb in working with depression is to try to *reduce the negative and increase the positive*. In this book we have noted two types of positive emotion systems: drive and contentment/soothing, and how to work with both.

As to whether people will use medication, that is normally something discussed elsewhere with medically qualified people, but we remain collaborative and open to discuss thoughts and feelings about medications (Burns, 1980). Medications will be an important component of successful treatment for some people and many studies suggest that for severe and chronic depression combined treatments can work well (e.g. Dimidjian et al., 2006; Klein et al., 2004). Medications can be helpful when depressed people are exhausted by their depression, are sleep disturbed and anhedonic. A problem with anti-depressants for some people, however, is side-effects. There are large individual differences in how people physiologically respond to drugs that are little to do with the disorder (Healy, 2001). Think of how different people respond to alcohol, for example. Also drugs are only one way to directly affect physiological systems. Exercise can also be useful for depression, and can be suggested after discussion with the general practitioner, who may know of physical reasons to be cautious. Recently, there has also been interest in the herb St John's Wort and also Omega 3. Diet change and massage can be helpful for some people. The point is that we should not neglect the 'body aspects' of depression, including the importance of sleep and getting a restorative sleep pattern (Moldofsky and Dickstein, 1999). So, on these matters we work closely with the client's doctor to collaborate and plan good quality care and interventions, that is we work on the depression from many angles.

Think about your model

There are many 'models and theories' about depression. Even within cognitive behaviour therapy there are many varieties. There is increasing concern about this. One way around this difficulty is to try to be science-based so that we understand the processes involved in depression and develop therapeutic interventions for those processes. The evidence is that focused therapies that identify specific difficulties, such as negative thinking styles, rumination, unresolved traumatic memories, behavioural-avoidance, and target interventions to those difficulties, are most effective. This does not mean that one becomes a technician and not focused on issues such as the therapeutic relationship, and guided discovery. Far from it. Nonetheless, it is useful for you to have a model in your mind that you will be able to discuss with depressed people. We can think about how we will de-shame depression, normalise the experience of human suffering, while at the same time recognising that some depressions may well be intense and chronic activations of protection strategies (loss of control, protest-despair and defeat) fuelled by styles of thinking and behaving. Our ability to de-shame depression and the processes involved in recovery will enable people to tell their stories and begin the journey of guided discovery of causes and roads out of depression. We can think about how to discuss with them the nature of depression (e.g. as exhaustion and threat-focused), and develop a working collaboration. We are thus attentive to the therapeutic relationship.

We should be attentive to the use of our language and try to avoid concepts such as 'cognitive error', 'thinking deficits', 'faulty thinking', 'maladaptive beliefs', 'distorted thinking', etc. This is not because these may or may not be the case, but because this is potentially shaming language. Hence, we can focus more on understanding biases in thinking, 'better safe than sorry' thinking and safety protective behaviours, all of which can lead to unintended consequences. It is not becoming rational that makes us happy, rather it is thinking and behaving in ways that are experienced as helpful, supportive and encouraging (rationality is only a means to those ends). Happiness lies in securing important evolutionary goals, especially social ones.

Reducing the negative

Depressed clients will often have a number of different external issues, which increases the flow of negative signals to them. In these contexts depressed people may need to engage with those difficulties rather than avoid them and this is, of course, key to the behavioural approach (see Chapter 4). Activity planning can be a way in which people begin to engage with some of their life difficulties and avoidance behaviours.

Disengage and create personal space

A key domain is the degree to which individuals feel trapped, or caged, and have a strong wish to escape (Chapter 3). Some clients can feel very overwhelmed by responsibilities and demands; others can be subject to high levels of criticism or even abuse if they try to actualise their individuality. Some individuals are simply unable to get enough help to allow them some respite from caring roles. At times counselling will focus on helping people to disengage or at least space themselves sufficiently to give themselves opportunities for respite. This can often involve providing an opportunity to explore various dilemmas about taking 'time out'. There is also increasing concern that our western lifestyles of life are simply exhausting us with our hectic and competitive work places and role strains. The key issue here is to explore how the depressed person might like to reduce negative signals in their environment by the use of 'space'. The idea of resting and allowing the body to recuperate from stress is a rather old-fashioned but nevertheless an important idea. It is often the lack of opportunities or the inability to do that, or intrusive ruminations when people try, which can be a problem.

Social put-down

There is good evidence now that onset and relapse for some people is related to partner or family criticism (Wearden et al., 2000). It is important, therefore, to explore the degree to which people are subject to criticism, put-down, or bullying, and of course various forms of physical intimidation and abuse, although note that people may feel ashamed to admit this in the first instance. Not only does shaming and intimidation take place in families, but increasingly we are aware that this can take place at work. People can feel trapped in not being able to give up their jobs because they need the money. Sometimes people stay in unrewarding or abusive situations/relationships out of guilt of leaving or negative beliefs that this is the best they can achieve. So we can explore the kinds of negative situations people are subjected to and what stops them from moving on or away from them. This involves careful discussion of dilemmas, problem solving, behavioural experiments, and relationship focused interventions.

Assertiveness and control

When people are depressed they may engage in unhelpful forms of social avoidance and/or harbour brooding resentments. Some people may be very socially anxious. In these cases it is useful to work with their social anxiety or anger. So at times one might help people *reduce* escape and avoidance behaviours. Although spacing, escaping, respite and resting can be important, it is also often the case that depressed people may be helped by exerting more control over situations. Developing assertiveness can be an important intervention for some depressed people, although people may have fear-based beliefs of being disliked or abandoned, shame, guilt or fears of others becoming more aggressive.

Learning to exert more control over negative life events and situations may also be aided by problem-solving approaches where people learn to break problems down rather than feeling overwhelmed. Remember that when depressed, people may not be able to think things through clearly because of the brain state of depression. So the key message is that while at times people may need to explore how to space themselves from negative situations, at other times they can learn how to engage negative situations and cope with them. This is key to behavioural approaches (see Chapter 4).

Internal negative signals

As discussed, internal signals can operate on the brain, like external signals. Negative thinking about oneself or one's future can therefore be detrimental to recovering from stress or boosting mood. In the spirit of reducing the negative and boosting the positive, we can be attentive to, and intervene in, internal negative thinking.

Better safe than sorry

When people become depressed they become more attentive to, and affected by, negative events and situations. It is useful to talk to clients about how cognitive biases spring up so easily and are related to safety strategies (Gilbert, 1998b). Basically, under stress the brain is designed to look out for the negatives/threats. Also, under stress we need to react quickly rather than logically – logic would take time. So cognitive biases can arise from both reactivation of early schema memories and conditioned emotions, but also because of the brain's natural tendency to assume the worst in stressful situations. Of course, all this is rule of thumb and there are many exceptions, but I think it helps depressed people avoid assuming they are 'stupid' or being irrational. It emphasises the importance of taking account of the way the brain functions and it highlights the importance of *practice* to counteract these tendencies. This is, of course, the basis of Buddhist psychology too.

Negative thinking, shame and social comparison

As we have seen, shame and feeling inferior to others are major issues in many depressions. However, remember that shame issues are not easily revealed and you may need to develop your therapeutic relationship before you can work in this area. Part of what makes failures, setbacks and disappointments difficult to cope with is that they are linked to self-identity and external threats (e.g. 'If I fail I am stupid and people will reject me or look down on me'). A motto I use is that 'the secret of success is the ability to fail' (Gilbert, 2000a). The self-attacking aspects of shame can have very serious effects on people's mood and physiology, and can operate like constant harassment.

Rumination

We know that when people become depressed they tend to ruminate about their difficulties. They find their mind wandering back over the negatives. This has an impact on mood and also stress. Identifying and developing ways to reduce rumination with activities such as mindfulness, distraction, focused activities and generating compassionate alternatives to focus on can help.

Affect toleration

Sometimes people become depressed because they are not able to tolerate negative emotions and try to avoid them. This can be true for anger, anxiety, shame, and guilt. Helping people learn to work through their negative emotions and tolerate them can be very important (Greenberg and Watson, 2006).

Trauma memory

Difficulties with affect regulation can be related to unprocessed trauma memories. People with abusive or other painful experiences in their lives may have unprocessed memories that may need addressing. The way of dealing with this can be similar to working with traumatic memories and, as we have seen, there is growing evidence for how to do this (Brewin, 2006; Clark and Ehlers, 2004).

Conflicts are common

Many depressed people have a range of conflicts that are upsetting and stressful. These can be approach-avoidance conflicts, life dilemmas, and conflicts between emotions and thoughts. Help people to recognise these by carefully outlining them, accepting them as (often) a part of life and may take time to work through.

Increasing the positives

Not only is it important to reduce the negatives but also to increase the positives. Many depressed clients have lost the ability to experience much joy in their lives, create positive life goals and plans, elicit supportive relationships or be self-accepting. In fact, there are now major efforts to link therapy to the development of positive life goals and developing a commitment to change in pursuit of these goals (Karwoski, Garratt and Ulardi, 2006; Riskin, 2006; Snyder and Ingram, 2006). In this book we have argued that positive experiences are related to two different types of affect system. If you keep these two affect systems in mind it will help you think more clearly about which aspects of the 'positives' you are trying to achieve. It is important not to be over-focused on achievement, such that people don't actually learn the importance of mindfulness, compassion and peaceful contentment. Happiness is not just about doing and achieving goals all the time.

Instil hope

We can instil hope through our open and supportive therapeutic relationship, which enables people to know that you will listen to them, give them time to tell their stories, and that you are familiar with depression. Normalise some of the experiences of depression as related to, say, exhaustion. De-shaming and addressing the sense of blame, fault or weakness for being depressed can be helpful, be a relief and instil hope.

Gaining support

For some depressed people it is important to look at the external environment and to engage in socially supportive endeavours. Some depressed people are very socially isolated and linking them with supportive self-help groups and other support agencies can be helpful. It is also important to explore with people how they can increase socially rewarding behaviour (see Martell et al., 2001; McCullough, 2000; Milne, 1999). This can be done by planning positive activities. We should not underestimate the role of positive, enjoyable environmental inputs for some depressed clients. Check if there are others who are threatened by the depressed person doing enjoyable things, such as going out with friends (e.g. jealous partners).

Time scales

Positive goals can be short- and long-term. Short-term goals are the things that one might try to achieve over a couple of days or maybe weeks. Long-term goals focus on trying to (appropriately and realistically) create or develop a path towards the kind of life one would like, and the kind of self-identity one would like. What can the person realistically work for and commit to, even if getting there might be hard at first? If confidence is an issue, then this can be worked with and the counsellor helps to inspire and validate the person's efforts.

Developing inner compassion for self

As indicated throughout this book, treating depression is not only about reducing avoidance and negative thinking. It is also about increasing compassionate and warm thinking. When people have self-critical thoughts, these thoughts are often delivered in an angry, aggressive, contemptuous, powerful and hostile way. Even generating alternatives may not be done in a warm way. Therefore, it is important to find ways that counteract inner hostility, and also generate feelings of compassionate acceptance and warmth (see Chapter 11).

The idea here is that the client learns to become empathic and validating of their distress and generate alternatives to the negative thoughts and feelings, by practising generating an inner warm voice. This is not self-love as such; there may be many things we won't necessarily like about ourselves, but it is about compassionate self-acceptance. It is also about trying to help clients generate internal signals that are potentially biologically powerful. However, keep in mind that some depressed people can be frightened and avoidant of self-compassion at first.

Self-reward

Depressed people have often had a history where their negative behaviours have been punished and their positive behaviours have been ignored. Even their efforts at self-improvement can at times be criticised by those who have vested interests in maintaining the person in a subordinate position. It is therefore important to begin to institute self-rewarding and self-validating strategies for depressed people. This involves showing them how to take pleasure in the small achievements of everyday life, to focus on what they have done and can do rather than on what they cannot. The practice of self-reward can be anything from giving themselves mild praise or a smile to an actual reward, such as buying themselves a small present, an item of clothing or whatever is rewarding. Both developing inner warmth and taking (mindful) pleasure in small things can help to create a feeling of contentment.

Time to say goodbye

For most mild to moderate depressions therapy will be time limited and provide clients with life skills to help them with subsequent stresses in their lives. With more severe and chronic cases, however, things take longer. For some of my clients I offer an 'open door' access, especially if they have had a chronic relapse in their depression. A few booster sessions at key points, as well as the ability to 'touch base' can be very helpful in heading off relapse. Nonetheless there are some general principles to follow when coming to the end of counselling with the depressed client (Ward, 1989). These general points can be relevant not only to the ending phase but throughout counselling.

Normal sadness

In any relationship where there has been emotional sharing, support and encouragement, there can be sadness and reluctance at saying goodbye. The counsellor may be the first person with whom the client has shared certain aspects of their life, and their deeper thoughts. So we normalise this.

Reactivating emotional memories

Approaching the end of therapy can be a time when the client may re-experience fears of abandonment or coping alone. These issues need to be addressed not in order to prolong counselling, but to give the client new opportunities to work with the affects and beliefs of leaving and separating. Sometimes 'open door' access is important. For example, one of my depressed clients had been in and out of care and had never had a stable base, and so once the current episode of depression had been resolved we agreed that she was free to come and see me from time to time. Over the years the contact gradually faded away. I get a postcard from her occasionally. In her view this has been an important support in preventing relapse. The evidence on such work needs to be developed, of course, but with complex depressions we must avoid over medicalising them and seeing therapy as a kind of 'surgery'. Our aim should be to help people become well and stay well.

Ending as a process

Preparing to leave is a process not a sudden cessation of counselling and therefore needs to be discussed before it actually occurs. Ending is a stage in a process and is planned (Egan, 2002; Hardy et al., 2007). The client's thoughts and feelings about 'life beyond therapy' are explored. In some short-term therapies, the ending is an issue discussed right at the start as the counsellor negotiates the number of sessions.

Follow-up

With many depressed clients it may be appropriate to gradually space the counselling sessions, for example, moving from, say, weekly to fortnightly to monthly and then to a six-monthly follow-up. If clients have chronic problems or have had severe episodes, it is inappropriate to terminate without this gradual process (McCullough, 2000). Some depressed clients show what is called 'a flight in health' but can relapse subsequently. This kind of gradual tailoring off may help avoid sudden relapses. It also allows the client to move from an intense working relationship to a less intense working relationship. Clients benefit from having the opportunity for a general review at some point distant to the intense period. Frank, Kupfer and Perel (1989) compared drug treatment and interpersonal counselling for depression, and found that interpersonal counselling (only once a month) was the best predictor of length of interval to a relapse (i.e. the clients receiving it stayed well longer) (see also Klein, Santiago, Dina et al., 2004.)

Booster sessions

A counsellor can negotiate with the client the possibility of booster sessions. These may be either on an 'if and when' basis or planned into a follow-up. One needs to be aware of cultural attitudes towards independence, which can result in ideas that once a client has left counselling they should never need help again. However, it is wise to make clear that booster sessions are not the same as re-entering counselling, and usually they are only one or a few in number. Of course, if a client has had a major relapse into depression, then re-entering counselling may be appropriate, along with considerations of other treatment possibilities.

Unrealistic ideals

One aspect counsellors have to face is unrealistic ideals about what the counselling could/should achieve. Both counsellors and clients can have understandable but unrealistic views about what therapy can achieve. Life for many people remains difficult even after therapy. Thus, as indicated earlier, the counsellor and the client should discuss the aims and expectations of the counselling enterprise. Also clients and counsellors should be aware that in a sense one never stops the process. Self-monitoring and treating self and others with compassion and respect are things that one continues to struggle with throughout life. My wife comments that I can still be 'a grumpy old man', so I need more practice.

Questions about saying goodbye

There are certain obvious questions about ending therapy. These include:

- Does the client feel better?
- Has the client changed in the styles of thinking and relating?
- Has the client's sense of self improved?
- Can the client cope better with major life events? (Egan, 2002; Ward, 1989).

Some people leave therapy early because they have got better within a few sessions (Stiles, Leach and Barkham, 2003). For some people withdrawing from treatment is another style of avoidance or feeling that the therapy can't help them. However, people might drop out of therapy due to external pressures (e.g. the family is resistant to the client's attendance or there are financial or time constraints, or childcare problems). There can also be problems from the service delivery side, where an increasing focus on costs put pressures on clinicians to complete therapy quickly. Even in medical treatments there have been a number of disturbing reports of clients being discharged too early from hospital. This is a difficult balance. These issues need to be addressed openly and ways to cope with them negotiated.

Premature ending of counselling is normally defined as occurring when a client has an appointment but, without notice, does not attend further. In my practice, I normally try to contact the client and discuss their reasons for non-attendance – obviously not in an accusing way but to explore with the client potential difficulties. If a client is very depressed, is drinking heavily or may be a suicide risk, then other agencies need to be contacted (e.g. the general practitioner). Where possible, I leave it open for clients to attend while at the same time respecting their wishes. I make it clear that I would *like* them to return. A number of clients have mentioned that that had been helpful because no one had been that bothered with them before. It is an interesting question of how one balances enabling people to come to their own choices and decisions but not to be so detached that clients feel you are relatively indifferent to them turning up or not. One has to make the balance between caring for the conflicts of the client in attending and not being coercive. So, although not for every case, I have the impression that contacting clients is helpful. However, the psychology of this may be different in a free system like the British National Health Service from a private service where people have to pay. Sometimes shame is a factor in non-attendance. On the telephone the client may verbalise thoughts such as: (a) 'It's been a terrible week and I thought you'd get fed up with me'; (b) 'I just couldn't face you after what we talked about last week'; (c) 'I was too depressed to get out of bed and was too ashamed to call you'; and even (d) 'I wanted to feel better before I saw you'. You also sometimes enable people to say more negative things about you or the therapy on the phone, so validate these fears and work these through.

Where to now?

We are gradually moving away from schools of psychotherapy (although clinical trials are still set up to gather evidence from different schools/approaches) to processes in psychotherapy. As our assessments get better we will be able to target therapies better. Work in anxiety and post-traumatic stress disorder (Clark and Ehlers, 2004), show the benefits of this focused approach. When it comes to working with complex imagery, different memory systems or affect processing systems it is probably difficult to 'shoe horn' these into one model and it would be better to think of them as evidence-based, focused psychological interventions. The same is beginning to happen in depression. Increasingly, clinicians are suggesting that for the more complex depressions at least, one cannot be a therapeutic 'one-club golfer' (Karasu, 1990).

The other exciting developments are related to better integration of psychological and physiological processes in depression. This allows us to better target psychological therapies to stimulate and activate different types of processing systems (Linden, 2006). There is good evidence now that psychological therapies have physiological effects (Cozolino, 2002). So in this book integration has focused on 'integrating our biopsychosocial knowledge' about depression-linked processes and focusing on evidence-based interventions.

Training and supervision

Counsellor skill and abilities to form good therapuetic relationships are factors that are highly related to outcome. Thus it is important that we should have access to good training opportunities. However, given the epidemic of mild-moderate depression in our communities, various professional groups are developing basic skills in cognitive behavioural approaches. This includes people who may not have direct training in psychopathology. Currently, these approaches are under research and we await to see the long-term benefits of them. When it comes to more complex, chronic and relapsing conditions, one needs to have rather more experience both with the disorder itself and the complexity of its treatment. Hence, counsellors working with depressed clients should be familiar with the different theories of depression (Beckham and Leber, 1995; Gotlib and Hammen, 2002; Power, 2004).

The importance of understanding how to use a focused intervention technically 'correctly' is obviously key to success. This will require supervision in the practice of the therapy. Moreover, it is noted that the ability to weave these technical elements into a therapeutic process that engages the person is a skill (see Chapter 7). The role of personal counselling for the counsellor is a complex one, but many agree that some kind of personal experience may be helpful in achieving this blending (Bennett-Levy and Thwaites, 2007; Dryden, 1991).

We should be aware of some of our own beliefs that can make counselling difficult and also be a source of negative feelings. Some common, unhelpful beliefs are as follows.

Beliefs about technique:

1   If a client isn't getting better my technique is wrong.
2   To help clients improve I must get to my techniques quickly.
3   I don't know my techniques well enough, therefore I can't help clients.
4   I don't seem to know what is going on with this client, therefore the counselling can't be helpful.
5   I must be able to help this person (or all clients) in order to regard myself as a good counsellor or even a good person.

6   If I can't help people then I am a no good person.
7   I must never feel anxious or angry with a client (with heart rate going up, etc.).
8   I must like my clients.
9   I must never be moved to tears with a client.
10   I must never show a client I am confused and ask for clarity (i.e. I must cover my thoughts). Shame in the counsellor is an unacknowledged problem in my view (Pope et al., 2006).
11   I must constantly challenge clients' 'irrational' thoughts.

Beliefs about the client:

1   Empathy and being with a client are not enough; they have to do some work.
2   If the client can't understand the techniques (or work with them) they won't get better.
3   If clients can't articulate their thoughts they won't get better.
4   If clients don't change quickly they won't change at all.
5   This client likes being depressed.
6   This client is not motivated to get well.
7   Depressed people are basically weak people.
8   I could never get that depressed myself.
9   This client is manipulative.

And, finally, 'If I have any of the above beliefs I am a bad person. I shouldn't have these beliefs – the book says so.' Frankly, we all have automatic thoughts like these at times. But if we can stay open, check them out, allow them to come into our awareness, talk them over with a colleague, rather than turning a blind eye to them, then we can be more helpful to ourselves and our clients. In essence, this is about being in tune with the countertransference (Pope et al., 2006; Katzow and Safran, 2007; Watkins, 1989b).

There are many other beliefs one can have in counselling and we can make it a point of interest, rather than fear and dread, to try to find them. How many negative thoughts did you have in your work today? If we treat ourselves with compassion and honesty and do not demand that we are always a perfectly nice counsellor with perfectly pure thoughts, then we may become less anxious or demoralised with depressed clients.

To be proficient and stay proficient requires an open capacity to learn through reading, studying, taking refresher courses, supervision, and discussions with other counsellors (Dryden, 1991). The therapist and counsellor remain open and know that at all times there is more to be learnt, that counselling itself is a process and if we find that at times we are stumped or lost or make mistakes we can take this as a challenge rather than as a self-rebuke. Never put your own self-evaluations on the line in counselling, for this may lead to defensiveness and the need for the client to get better to prove to yourself how good you are. Skovholt and Rønnestad (1992) have published a fascinating study of how therapists change over time. Becoming less focused on a need to change 'the client' is a major part of professional development. Some clients remain hard to help despite our best efforts. You may not be able to help everyone who walks through your door. Some will require different types of intervention, and some clients with chronic difficulties tax all therapies of whatever type.

Personal reflections

My own approach to therapy reflects my evolutionary view that we are evolved beings in this vast universe. The sources of our passions, drives, cruelties, anxieties and depressions are rooted in the painful road by which we got here. This is not everybody's cup of tea, but I think we do need to keep in mind some of the political implications of cutting humans away from their emotional and social bases. We cannot simply see the mind as a collection of rarefied thoughts and beliefs. Although it may be politically expedient to suggest that a few tweaks here and there in people's thinking styles will relieve people of their depression, this is problematic. A lot of depression relates to how people cope with poverty, social isolation and insufficient care early in life. Our therapies should also reflect these realities, hence my personal interest in biopychosocial approaches to therapy.

Although some therapists, who have a political view about therapy, can see therapy as a kind of sticking plaster for major social ills, we must be cautious here. Some, for example, who have taken the political route, have poured scorn on therapy. In my view, this is like saying to a man who has just had a heart attack 'I'm sorry we won't help you because you are a victim of the food and smoking industry'. The issue is not so much the provision of individual therapies for people who suffer but the question of prevention. On this, once again, our theories matter a lot. If we have a biopsychosocial view which sees a key role for social connectedness and compassion in relationships, that will have an impact for the kind of prevention strategies we might try to develop.

Conclusion

This book has presented a particular view of depression in relation to the activation of primitive protection strategies. These strategies involve the toning down of two types of positive affect and toning up of negative affect. These protection strategies can be highly sensitised as a result of childhood adversities. When activated, they pull our thinking and feelings in particular ways and various emotional memories and brain state patterns can ripple through the brain. In a sense, then, to be depressed is to be caught in something archetypal and common to our humanity, to feel a change within one's head and at times to feel 'ill'. Therapists who can empathise with this experience and gradually hold the lantern of hope via their knowledge of behaviour change, cognitive interventions and emotional working, are likely to be highly effective. Compassion-focused approaches may aid this endeavour. Keep in mind that for some people experiencing compassion in the therapist can re-activate the soothing and attachment systems. This can trigger emotional memories of neglect, aloneness, fear and/or anger that can be overwhelming and confusing (see pp. 245–7 in this volume and Gilbert, in press b). So work with these openly and slowly and seek advice from those who work with early trauma. Good luck and listen to your compassionate heart.

Appendix 1   Formulation and Case Conceptualisation

There are many ways to develop a formulation depending on the model of working one adopts and the functions and purpose of the formulation. Standard CBT formulations are different from those of behavioural activation or dialectical behavioural ones, which are totally different from psychodynamic ones. However, what focused therapists have in common is that they try to develop shared overviews with people that usually are written down. The formulation might start by focusing on certain specific problems and small steps and build up to a larger formulation that includes background, the way the background has influenced the person's feelings, beliefs and behaviours, current difficulties and current symptoms that guide the treatment plan and focus. Formulation is to help the person make sense of depression, and be a source for reflection and intervention. Increasingly, counsellors and therapists are writing letters to their clients. Some aspects of these may form part of clinical letters. In the NHS now clinicians are advised to copy clinical letters to their clients.

Formulation 1 offers a fairly straightforward and standard formulation. Formulation 2 offers one that is more focused on a safety strategies approach. These are not mutually exclusive. Different overviews, reviews and types of formulation can be used at different stages of therapy.

Case Formulation 1: Cognitive-focused formulation (see p. 216)

Early history (key relationships, experiences, life events and meanings given to them)

Sees self as   **Sees others as**

Depressive rules for living and core beliefs

Key social behaviours
(that can maintain depression and/or increase vulnerability)

Current life events and triggers

Typical automatic depressive thoughts and thinking styles

Current symptoms

Case formulation 2: Threat/safety strategies formulation (see p. 218)

Historical influences	Key fears	Safety/defensive behaviours	Unintended consequences
(Emotional memories) Self as .... Other as		Self-to-self relating	

Pointers

Try to stay simple to start with. Focus on sharing and understanding together; encourage the depressed person to reflect and develop their own formulation. Part of the focus is understanding our difficulties in a 'not your fault' way.

Avoid language of cognitive *distortion* or *maladaptive* schema as this can be shaming for high-shame patients.

Focus on 'your defence system has tried to keep you safe; better safe than sorry', etc. One's defences and safety strategies are natural efforts to adapt to challenges and threats but with unintentional drawbacks/consequences (e.g. little new learning, not able to disconfirm basic threat beliefs, few opportunities for exploration).

Key questions

What do you see as key background experiences to your depression? What key fears and concerns do you think these created for you? (Keep in mind to explore external fears and internal ones.) Looking back, how do you think your mind has tried to protect you (again think about protecting self from *external* threats such as rejection and also *internal* ones such as overwhelming feelings). Recognise that some people may close down on threat and may not be able to reflect on painful experiences or memories; they simply are unable to or don't want to 'go there' and don't want to 'go there'. Spend time enabling people to be empathic to their safety strategies as 'best efforts'. What have been the unintended consequences (disadvantages) of these safety strategies? What do you think about yourself when you run into these unintended consequences?

Appendix 2   Behavioural Scheduling

Helping people work directly on their behaviour can be a very helpful way of engaging and starting the process of reactivation in depression. It is important that you discuss with your clients the point of it (see p. 69). For example, that when we are depressed part of the state of depression is to affect the way in which our brains work. Depression can reduce drive and makes concentration and clear step-by-step thinking difficult. To help us we can write down and plan activities in a step-by-step fashion. It is like using a walking stick when we have broken a leg and are getting fit again. If we can follow the plan, this can be helpful.

Another way that activity scheduling can be used is for the counsellor to agree on helpful key activities between sessions. Because people tend to put things off it is important to identify the day and time of an activity. The client can then tick it off when it is done.

Another way that activity scheduling can be used is to focus on specific types of activity. For example, you may say: 'can we see if you could keep an activity record of how much you were able to practise (for example) compassionate mind focusing or going to the gym or spending time on an enjoyable activity?'

So, behavioural scheduling and these types of form can be used in all kinds of ways. Once again it is important to understand the principles of what you are trying to do and adapt your forms to the needs of your clients – what helps people best.

Activity scheduling

Activity monitoring	Morning	Afternoon	Evening
Monday			
Tuesday			
Wednesday			
Thursday			
Friday			
Saturday			
Sunday			

The idea of activity scheduling is to help you focus on increasing your activities rather than avoiding or withdrawing. When we get depressed it is very easy to get stuck. So let's see what happens if we try to plan things in advance (e.g. work out a plan for the day and see how you do).

Remember, if things don't work out as you would like, try to be compassionate and understanding rather than critical. Focus on what you did try to do. When you have done something, reflect on the degree to which you are pleased that you were able to do it. If it is something that was designed to be enjoyable, try to see if there was any degree of enjoyment no matter how small. It is learning to focus on these aspects that can get our positive feelings moving again.

Appendix 3　Working with People's Thinking

(Information sheets like this can be given to clients)

Typical depressive styles of thinking

When people become depressed they tend to see themselves in negative ways. They may see themselves as failures, inferior or worthless, their relationships as unfulfilling and the future as rather black. These thoughts and beliefs are often maintained by mood shifts and emotional memories, producing a spiral further into depression. When we are depressed we look on the black side of things and can overestimate dangers and setbacks. This is because depression is linked to feelings of loss and threat in the world. It is in the very nature of depression to pull our thinking to focus on threats and losses. This is not your fault but it is useful to notice how depression gets us thinking in certain ways. Some of the more common depression thinking styles include the following:

Jumping to conclusions
When we are depressed we tend to jump to conclusions easily, particularly negative conclusions. For example, a friend is in an irritable mood so we might conclude that this is because she doesn't like us. The shop assistant gives the wrong change and we conclude they take us for a 'soft touch', rather than she made an honest mistake.

Emotional reasoning
Emotional reasoning is related to jumping to conclusions. This is when we go for gut reactions to things: it is our first immediate emotional response. So if we get the 'feeling' that somebody doesn't like us, we assume that it is true rather than test the evidence for it. To act against both jumping to conclusions and emotional reasoning it can be helpful to practise generating alternatives. Unfortunately, given the way our brains work, we cannot assume that our emotions have necessarily given us an accurate view of the world, or point to helpful behaviours.

Discounting the positive
When we get depressed it is very easy to discount our positives. We are not able to focus on things we do or have. Rather, we focus on those things that we cannot do or don't have. Discounting positives is often related to disappointment in not being able to achieve what one wants. When people who are depressed achieve

things they tend to discount it with the idea that 'anyone could do that' or 'I used to do so much more when I wasn't depressed'. However, remember that over-coming depression is a step-by-step process and if we continually discount our positives it is going to be difficult to start moving up the ladder.

Disbelieving others

When we become depressed it is very common to believe that others are only being nice because they want to appear good themselves. Depressed people some-times believe that individuals have one set of thoughts that they express outwards and a set of thoughts that they keep private. Of course, this can often be true. However, depressed people and socially anxious people worry that the private thoughts of others are very negative towards them. So it is important to explore this and not take these negative ideas for granted.

Black and white thinking

When we become depressed it becomes less easy for us to think about life in complex ways. This is partly to do with the fact that stress interferes with our logical step-by-step thinking. Therefore we may become very black and white in our thinking: either we are a success or we are a failure; either this relationship is good or it is a complete failure. It is useful to remind ourselves that most things in life are a bit of this, a bit of that; bit of good, bit of less good, rather than absolutes. When we become depressed we can forget this. So try thinking in shades of things: a bit of this, a bit of that. If you are thinking about relationships, focus on the things that you like about them and things that you prefer, as well as the things you dislike. Try to conceptualise this as a complex mixture of different things rather than all good or all bad.

Self-criticism

We may become depressed because we are disappointed in the way things have gone, for example how we look, or maybe achievements haven't worked out, or relationships haven't gone so well. We can become quite frustrated. This frustra-tion can sometimes turn in on the self as if we believe that 'if only I had been dif-ferent, looked different or behaved differently then everything would have worked out fine'. Self-criticism often generates negative emotions, particularly anger towards the self, and this increases the 'stress' on our stress system. That in turn will continually fuel the depression. This is why learning to recognise your tendencies for self-criticism (but also deciding and choosing that perhaps being compassionate to yourself would help more) is important.

Appendix 4 Some Useful Things to Reflect on in Regard to Working with Depressing Thoughts

When considering alternatives to depressing styles of thinking it is useful to keep in mind that you will want to *avoid* pitting yourself against your clients or getting into unhelpful debates. So you will need to explore with your clients ways in which they come to reflect on and question their own thinking. It is always about collaboration and exploring what they would find helpful. If you find yourself becoming slightly frustrated because the client is not 'seeing it as you want them to see it', you have dropped out of collaborative mode. Here are some pointers:

Step 1

Help the person validate and be empathic to the distress that life events and thoughts can trigger. Help the client reflect on 'it is understandable that I feel like this because …'. Then help the client recognise that their thinking can be 'pulled' by their feelings and core beliefs, so it is useful to stand back and explore alternatives, take a wider view, break out of the funnelled view of negative feelings.

One aspect of this can be to recognise how anger can stop us even wanting to change our thoughts, so we can ask: 'Do you feel so angry/frustrated you do not want to change your thoughts, at least not yet?' For other clients the blocks may relate to the lack of motivation or energy. If people are very depressed, then working on more behavioural tasks may be important before addressing people's thinking. The helpful thing about a behavioural task is that one simply needs to do it and see what happens.

Step 2

Say to the client that 'it can be useful to try to expand the focus here, let's see if we can think of some ways of looking at this situation afresh. One way of doing this is to stand back and ask ourselves some questions and truly think about how we might answer them.' This enables us to balance our own thoughts.

- How would you typically see this if you were not stressed or depressed (i.e. in a different state of mind)?
- Can you bring to mind other times things have seemed difficult and you got through?
- Are you underestimating your courage and coping abilities?
- How might you see this in six months' time?
- If a friend was trying to be supportive and helpful, what is it they are likely to say to you?

- What would you say to a friend in this situation?
- When you try to help a friend, what happens in your mind? How do you think?
- If you were to apply that to yourself, how would it be?
- If you were honest, and to take a generally fair and balanced view, what would it be?
- If we could brainstorm alternatives what might they be?
- Which aspect of this would it be helpful to focus on?
- If we take a deep breath and focus on coping in this moment, what would be helpful?
- In what way may these thoughts and feelings actually be unreliable sources of information for you?
- Suppose you were able to think about this differently, how would that be? (Just stay with this, allowing the patient to experience those feelings.)

On the next pages we have outlined some very simple thought forms, which have some key headings and then at the bottom some questions. Some people find these thought forms very helpful, other people less so. They can be done in a fairly straightforward manner or they can be made a little more complicated. It is very easy nowadays to develop these forms using word-processing programs. The key thing is to understand the principles and tailor your forms to the abilities and needs of your clients so that sometimes you might only have two columns and other times you may have more. When alternative ideas and thoughts are generated explore if the person feels they are reasonable and what might be a 'yes but'. Help the client stay focused on the alternative and let it 'filter' through their mind. Allow time to feel a change in emotion by 'staying with' an alternative thought, and use imagery if this helps. Be very cautious of just relying on people seeing alternatives as 'logical or sensible' as that may not change feelings. Talk in terms of 'bringing balance' to our thoughts, developing an open mind or wisdom rather than 'correcting errors in thinking'. Acknowledge possible fear of 'believing' the alternative thoughts, e.g. ask 'What would your fear be in really allowing yourself to believe this alternative?' Empathise with that fear and brain storm ways to work with that fear. Maintain a gentle but firm focus and avoid an argumentative or frustrated stance. Remember you are not responsible for 'making someone change' – you are trying to create conditions and dialogues that enable change.

Form for exploring unhelpful thoughts and generating helpful alternative thoughts and ideas

Triggering events, thoughts, feelings or images	Depressing or upsetting thoughts	Feelings	Helpful alternative ideas
Key questions to help you identify your thoughts.	*What actually happened?* *What went through your mind?* *What are you thinking about yourself?* *What are you thinking others are thinking about you?* *What are you saying about your future?*	*What are your main feelings?*	*What would you say to a friend?* *What alternatives might there be?* *What might a more balanced view be?*

Form for exploring unhelpful thoughts and generating helpful alternative thoughts and ideas: worked example (1)

Triggering events, thoughts, feelings or images	Depressing or upsetting thoughts	Feelings	Helpful alternative ideas
Bought the wrong size dress.	I should have known that this dress would not fit me. It bulges all over the place. I am fat and stupid. (Believe 70%)	Depressed, disheartened.	How annoying! It is understandable why I feel like this as I am quite rushed at the moment. It seemed to fit in the shop but I was in a rush. I can probably take it back and change it. Having a dress that is slightly too tight is disappointing but doesn't make me stupid! Even if I am heavier than I would like to be, many millions of women feel similar thanks to the media. There is no link between body size and abilities. Being a rushed mother who tries hard for her family and occasionally buys things that don't fit means only that I am a rushed mother who occasionally buys things that don't fit – nothing more. (Believe 60%)
Key questions to help you iden-tify your thoughts.	*What actually happened?* *What went through your mind?* *What are you thinking about yourself?* *What are you thinking others are thinking about you?* *What are you saying about your future?*	*What are your main feelings?*	*What would you say to a friend?* *What alternatives might there be?* *What might a more balanced view be?*

Form for exploring unhelpful thoughts and generating helpful alternative thoughts and ideas: worked example (2)

Triggering events, thoughts, feelings or images	Depressing or upsetting thoughts	Feelings	Helpful alternative ideas
Unsuccessful at job.	Didn't want me for the job. Obviously didn't interview well. Don't have the skills required. Never going to get a new job. Will end up just a bum. (Believe 80%)	Depressed, hopeless.	It is disappointing not to obtain the job I wanted. However, the interview did not go all badly. It may be true that on this occasion there was somebody that they preferred over me but the job market is very tight right now. I know many people who have been for jobs and didn't get them but went on to get a job later. Even if I am unsuccessful in getting the job, this means the job market is difficult but this does not make me a bum. Because getting a job is difficult doesn't mean I have to run myself down. I can focus on what I can do rather than what I can't. (Believe 50%)
Key questions to help you identify your thoughts.	*What actually happened?* *What went through your mind?* *What are you thinking about yourself?* *What are you thinking others are thinking about you?* *What are you saying about your future?*	*What are your main feelings?*	*What would you say to a friend?* *What alternatives might there be?* *What might a more balanced view be?*

Different type of thought form that focuses on a number of thoughts and their alternatives

Triggering events, feelings or images	Depressing or upsetting thoughts	Feelings	Alternative helpful ideas	Degree of feeling change
Key questions to help you identify your thoughts: What actually happened?	What went through your mind? What are you thinking about yourself and your future? What are you thinking about others? Rate degree of belief 0–100	What are your main feelings and emotions? Rate degree of feelings 0–100	What would you say to a friend? What alternatives might there be? What is the evidence against this view? How would you see this if you were not depressed? Rate degree of belief in alternatives 0–100	Write down any degree of change in the feelings you now feel.
Example 1 Friend at work snubbed me.	She doesn't like me. Sees me as inadequate. 70%	Upset, hurt, angry. 60%	Probably nothing to do with me at all. Friend can be quite moody and I have seen her do this to others. 50%	Calmer. 20%
Example 2 Forgot to take important file to work.	This is typical me. I am useless and a failure. 80%	Frustrated, angry. 90%	I am bound to be frustrated at this because it will hold up my work today. However, this does not make me useless. I won't even remember this event in three months' time. I can accept my frustrations and try to relax. 70%	Calmer. 40%
Example 3 Just feeling down today.	I am always going to be depressed. Nothing will ever work for me. 70%	Depressed, fed up. 80%	Moods do go up and down. This is normal. However, I have had better days than today. I am disappointed but I can see the sense of working with my thoughts and in my heart I know if I keep going I'll feel better. 30%	Calmer. 20%

Appendix 5   Compassion-Focused Therapy

Developing qualities of inner compassion (client handout)

As we have seen from our work together, being self-critical can be very stressful and make us feel worse. One way of coping with disappointment and our 'inner bully' is to learn to be compassionate with ourselves. This requires a number of things of us:

1. Valuing Compassion. Some people are worried that if they are compassionate with themselves they may somehow be weak or lack the drive to succeed. Thus, they don't really value compassion. However, if we think about people who are renowned for their compassion, such as Buddha, Jesus, Gandhi, Mother Teresa, Florence Nightingale, and Nelson Mandela, they can hardly be regarded as weak or 'unsuccessful'. Learning to be compassionate can actually make us stronger and feel more confident.

2. Empathy. Empathy means that we can understand how people feel and think, and can see things from their point of view. Similarly, when we have empathy *for ourselves* we can develop a better *understanding* for some of our painful feelings of disappointment, anxiety, anger or sadness. This can mean we may need to learn when to be *gently sensitive to our* feelings and distress – rather than try not to notice them or avoid them. Sometimes we tell ourselves that we shouldn't feel or think as we do, and try to deny our feelings rather than working with them. The problem with this is that we don't explore them to understand them and then they can be frightening to us.

3. Sympathy. Sympathy is less about our understanding and more about feeling and wanting to care, help and heal. When we feel sympathy for someone, we can feel sad or distressed with them. Learning to have sympathy for *ourselves* means that we can learn to be sad, without being depressed, for example without telling ourselves that there is something wrong or bad about feeling sad. We can also focus on feelings of *kindness in our sympathy.*

4. Forgiveness. Our self-critical part is often very unforgiving, and will usually see any opportunity to attack or condemn as an opportunity not to be missed! Learning the art of forgiveness, however, is important. Forgiveness allows us to learn how to change; we are open to our mistakes and learn from them.

5. Acceptance/tolerance. There can be many things about ourselves that we might like to change, and sometimes it is helpful to do that. However, it is also important to develop acceptance of ourselves as human beings, 'as we are' with a full range of positive and negative emotions. Acceptance isn't passive resignation, such as feelings of being defeated, or not bothering with oneself. It is an *open-heartedness* to all our fallibilities and efforts. It is like having the flu and accepting that you have to go to bed perhaps, but also doing all you can to help your recovery.

6. Developing feelings of warmth. This requires us to begin to experience and practise generating *feelings* of warmth for ourselves. To do this we can use images and practise feeling warmth coming into us. When we are depressed this feeling may be very toned down and hard to generate, so we will have to practise. It can seem strange and sometimes even frightening, so we can go one step at a time.

7. Growth. Compassion is focused on helping people grow, change and develop. It is life-enhancing in a way that bullying is not. When we learn to be compassionate with ourselves, we are learning to deal with our fallible selves, such that we can grow and change. Compassion can also help us face some of the painful feelings we wish to avoid.

8. Taking responsibility. One element of compassionate mind work is taking responsibility for one's self-critical thinking. We can learn to understand how and why we became self-critical, often because we felt threatened in some way. Becoming empathic means coming to see the threats that lay behind self-criticism. To do this we can learn to recognise when it's happening and then use our compassionate side to provide alternative views and feelings.

9. Training. When we attack ourselves we stimulate certain pathways in our brain but when we learn to be compassionate and supportive to our efforts we stimulate different pathways. Sometimes we are so well practised at stimulating inner attacks/criticisms that our ability to stimulate inner support and warmth is rather under-developed. Hence, now that we have seen how we can generate alternatives to our self-attacking thoughts, we can explore ways to help them have more emotional impact. It does not take away painful realities but it can help us to cope in a different way. The training part can be like going to a physiotherapist, where you learn to do exercises and build up certain strengths. The compassion systems in your brain are the ones we are trying to strengthen with our exercises.

Appendix 6   Building a Compassionate Image (Client Handout)

This exercise is to help you *build* up a compassionate image for you to work with and develop (you can have more than one if you wish, and they can change over time). Whatever image comes to mind, or you choose to work with, note that it *is* *your* creation and therefore your own personal ideal – what you would really like from feeling cared for and cared about. Therefore, in this practice it is important that you try to give your image certain qualities. These will include:

Wisdom, Strength, Warmth and Non-judgement

So in each box below think of these qualities (wisdom, strength, warmth and non-judgement) and imagine what they would look, sound or feel like.

If possible we begin by focusing on our breathing, finding our calming rhythm and making a gentle, warm smile. Then we can let images emerge in the mind – as best we can. Do not try too hard. If nothing comes to the mind, or the mind wanders, just *gently* bring it back to the breathing and practise compassionately accepting. Your images will not be like clear pictures or photographs in the mind but more like daydreams, with fragments of scenes or fleeting impressions.

Here are some questions that might help you build an image: would you want your caring/nurturing image to feel/look/seem old or young; male or female (or non-human looking, for example an animal, the sea or light)? What colours and sounds are associated with the qualities of wisdom, strength, warmth and non-judgement? Remember, your image brings compassion to you and for you.

How would you like your ideal caring-compassionate image to look (e.g. visual qualities)?
How would you like your ideal caring-compassionate image to sound (e.g. voice tone)?
What other sensory qualities can you give to it?
How would you like your ideal caring-compassionate image to relate to you?
How would you like to relate to your ideal caring-compassionate image?

Appendix 7   Using Compassion to Change our Minds (for Therapists)

In helping people work with distressing thoughts, feelings and behaviours, compassion–focused approaches, and compassionate mind training (CMT), follows a fairly standard CBT format in some ways. One helps clients to identify triggering events, explore current feelings and then the meanings and thoughts associated with them. However, compassionate mind work also varies in a number of ways.

1. CMT suggests that negative automatic thoughts are related to threat-focused automatic reactions. For thoughts associated with negative moods CMT distinguishes between *external* and *internal* threats. External threats are what the world and/or people in it will do to the self; internal threats are related to thoughts and feelings that arise within the self. People can, of course, then worry that they will be criticised or shamed for those internal reactions. Thus, thought forms will reflect this, as in the compassionate form (see below). However, the one we provide here is quite complicated and is used for demonstration (see pp. 360–1). Whether or not you would need to have a much simpler form, but one which captures the essence of the compassionate approach, is a clinical judgement.

2. Not only can people feel frightened by the emergence of powerful feelings, but they can experience their own self-evaluations in a frightening way. Thus in CMT we focus on the *emotions* that can be generated within a self-critical or self-attacking sequence. The consequences of feeling attacked by one's own negative thoughts may be to feel beaten down. So CMT spends time exploring the *emotions of the self-attack*, for example, frustration, anger, or aggressive or submissive contempt. We explore the *function* of the self-attacking, its possible *origins* and why we *submit/agree* with it (e.g. is it a habit or is it fear-based?). The client can be asked to imagine the self-attacking part as if it were a person: 'What would it look like?' 'What emotions would it be directing at you?' This can help people recognise the power of their self-critical side.

3. CMT helps people recognise self-attacking as a component of their *threat* systems. Commonly, when people become threatened about making mistakes or being shamed, there is a kind of inner panic and frustration which becomes weaved into a self-attacking focus. Sometimes, however, the self-criticism is a memory of being attacked and one can identify the critical 'voice' as the voice of a parent or authority figure. When the client plays this in their mind they may adopt the same submissive postures as they did as a child. Either way threat powers the self-attacking system. One can work on that by revisiting the authority, credentials or legitimacy of the critic. This helps people to see that they often maintain this bullying out of fear of change rather than logic.

The new emotional experience

4. Mindfulness approaches work by helping people become better observers and more attentive to the flow of their thoughts rather than being rushed along with them. The idea is to change the relationship with the thoughts, rather than the thoughts themselves. CMT utilises this approach but suggests that some people may find it easier, at least in the early stages, if they can deliberately re-focus their attention in a compassionate way to be with themselves.

5. Some cognitive-based approaches are focused on trying to generate alternative evidence to counteract negative thoughts. CMT does this too but suggests that focusing on evidence may not necessarily be sufficient to help people change. Rather, we need to get 'processing' from a different emotional source and create a new emotional experience in one's thinking that counteracts the emotional experience of their frustration, anger or contempt of the self-criticism. Rational and evidence-based re-evaluations are useful in so far as they help to do this.

The first steps

6. The first movement into change is developing *empathy for one's own distress*. This is directing the person's attention to why this distress is understandable (though obviously undesirable). This does require understanding with acceptance. Many clients have a sense of shame and feeling that they are not coping because of their distress. Empathy for one's distress can take a lot of work therapeutically, but it is key for the person to begin to work with their distress rather than avoid it. Explore how clients think and feel when they do this. Empathic understanding can also be extended to self-criticism because we can see it as threat-based.

7. CMT will then try to recruit attention, memory, meta-cognitive reasoning, behaviour and emotion systems in the service of being nurturing and caring of oneself. CMT tries to integrate these different elements and focus them all on developing compassion.

   Compassionate attention involves the way in which we focus our minds, what we choose to attend to. The exact focus of attention will be worked out with the client but it may involve a focus on a compassionate image, an object, a smell, a smiling face of someone who was caring, a compassionate memory. Compassionate attention focuses on the sensory modalities.

   Compassionate thinking is related to the process of reasoning and meta-cognition. It will focus on many cognitive therapy elements, such as bringing balance to thinking, de-personalising and de-shaming, developing multi-causal ideas of responsibility, seeing each event as unique rather than over-generalising, and 'common humanity thinking' (to tackle negative social comparisons). When compassionate thinking is fused with compassionate feeling we move towards the position of wisdom. Wisdom emerges because we have deep insight into the nature of things.

   Compassionate behaviour focuses on what people feel would be the most helpful, nurturing, supportive or encouraging thing to do. As noted in the behavioural approaches, actions are important. There needs to be clarity on the distinction between compassionate behaviour and submissiveness. Compassionate behaviour is also more than being 'nice to oneself'. It will focus on the quality for growth, development and flourishing. Compassionate behaviour can focus on immediate behaviours or on longer-term goals.

Compassionate emotion focuses on trying to generate a certain emotional tone in the whole process of change and growth. The emotions that we are interested in are therefore warmth, kindness, gentleness and soothing. Hence when we create alternative thoughts in our mind we deliberately try to make them warm, gentle and soft in tone. Of course this does not in any way preclude more exciting emotions and feelings of joy when we succeed, or our children succeed, at certain things. Joy is a part of compassion too, although probably has more activation in it. The key of the compassionate emotions is that they are focused on well-being and flourishing.

Example

I am going to offer a rather complex thought form that you would simplify for certain people. Certainly for very depressed people this may be a bit much, although if you go through it with them and do the writing for them it can be useful for them to have as an overview in later sessions. You will need to use your clinical sensitivity and judgement here. The idea is to give you a certain flavour of the whole thing put together. You will note that we include images and functions of self-criticisms and the images and functions of self-compassion. Various thought forms can be used, but ideally these should be quite simple. So these types of thought form should be completed first with the therapist, gradually building up understanding and knowledge. They may be simplified to one or two columns. Independent work should be straightforward and understandable.

The person with whom we will develop our example was a high executive who then became very depressed and had to have time off work. However, he was quite capable of understanding the concepts and found them helpful and important for him. The situation was basically that he became overloaded with too much work, started to miss things and one day forgot an important meeting. So, his key worry became 'not getting work finished'. As this built up he had more and more self-critical thoughts and feelings. We did a lot of normalising of the way in which stress does affect concentration and abilities, and the need for recuperation and time out. However, that recuperation will be compromised if he ruminates in a self-critical way. I think our competitive society is producing more and more people who suffer like this. You will see that he came from a 'high-flying' family who were also relatively emotionally distant and he had been at boarding school from a young age. You will also notice in your compassionate thinking that part of him is also quite angry at having been put under this level of strain, which at one level he thought was very unfair. He is rather inhibited in this anger, however, because he feels others have coped with the work pressures (negative social comparison), although in reality they may have been less conscious of needing to prove themselves.

Form for exploring unhelpful thoughts and generating compassion-focused alternative thoughts and ideas

Triggering events, feelings or images	Depressing or upsetting thoughts	Feelings	Compassion-focused alternatives to self-critical thoughts	Understanding and change in feelings
Key questions to help you identify your thoughts: *What actually happened? What was the trigger?*	*What went through your mind? What are you thinking about others and What are their thoughts about you? What are you thinking about yourself and your future?*	*What are your main feelings and emotions?*	*What would you say to a friend? What compassionate alternatives might there be? What is the evidence for a new view? How are these examples of compassion, care and support? Can you think these through with warmth?*	*Write down any change in your feelings*
Not getting work finished	**External shame (what I think others think about me)** People will think I am losing it. Disappointed in me – see me as no longer up to it – sad but dead wood. Overstretched myself. **Key feared consequences** Disconnect – they will look for, prefer someone else. Wish I was not on the team.	World feels very unsafe. Anxious and hurried and angry.	**Empathy for own distress** Understandable, because I felt safe if I could do things well and others valued me. However I felt isolated as a child at boarding school, envious attacks from class bully, teacher and, to some degree, father if I did well or showed high ambition. My thoughts are echoes of these fears and early experiences. Breathing and just allowing them to be there. Compassionate to the fears I have as in part coming from my past. **Compassionate attention** Although understandable to focus on threat, I can also attend to work I have done and people's reactions. Specific memory is – I developed a new procedure and can remember boss's face of pleasure. Wife and children have shown genuine concern for me. Some work colleagues have shown concern.	Feel calmer and able to refocus my feelings towards being warm with self. In my heart I know I can get through this if I can accept and work with my fatigue and anger.

Continued

Triggering events, feelings or images	Depressing or upsetting thoughts	Feelings	Compassion-focused alternatives to self-critical thoughts	Understanding and change in feelings
	Internal shame (what I think about me) Lost the plot. Took on too much – typical – always trying to impress people. Big ambition, small brain. **Key feared consequences** Failure, end up alone.	Stress with physical changes, ruminating and sleep problems. Fatigue, loss of motivation, concentration.	**Compassionate thinking** Has been a lot of work recently and many of us have felt stressed. Not my fault as have been trying my best hence problems related to overload not 'big ambition, small brain'. Probably true I haven't been looking after myself in terms of time out and sharing problems with others, which I can work on. Anger is part of the stress and also others feel like this. **Compassionate behaviour** Consider who to share problems with, be honest about my limitations and abilities. Talk to boss openly. Develop more pleasurable activities. Practice compassionate imagery and using a compassionate focus.	
	Image and emotion Male, father's age, gloating 'too cocky for your own boots', contempt, pleased to see me fail. Memories of boarding school.		**Image and emotion** Kind, elderly man, who has seen it all before. Laid back. Concerned for me and values me.	
	Function Stop me trying to getting ahead.		**Function** To help me cope with a difficult situations and the return of my fears. Helps me feel supported, keep it in perspective.	

Appendix 8   Compassionate Letter Writing

Therapist note

The idea behind compassionate mind letter writing is to help depressed people engage with their problems with a focus on understanding and warmth. We want to try to bring this emotional system into helping with the depression. It is from a position of compassionate understanding that you can then integrate the various cognitive, behavioural and emotional interventions and alternatives that we looked at in this book. Focusing on the warmth system helps to reduce the likelihood that alternative thoughts and behaviours are done in a cold or aggressive manner. Also, you are teaching your clients to begin to develop a new type of relationship with themselves. Explain the idea of compassionate letter writing and explore their thoughts about it, so that it is a collaborative exercise and experiment.

You can then use various ideas to try to help people put themselves in a *compassionate frame of mind.* For example, if you have worked on the compassionate ideal, and they have various images of that, they can take a few slow breaths, bring the image to mind and then write the letter as from that point of view – e.g., imagine this image talking to them, which they write down. Alternatively the client may imagine their ideal compassionate self – the kind of caring person they would like to be. This is the focus that we will use in the client handout below.

The content of the letter should show clear empathy for distress with phrases such as 'it is understandable you feel x because …'. In other words you are helping people to write about and be clear about the nature of their distress rather than just being self-critical.

Look to see if they can focus on compassionate attention, compassionate thinking and compassionate behaviour. This is how the person brings their work on generating alternative thoughts, reflecting and really focusing on those behaviours that are likely to be helpful to them. Compassionate behaviours are not just things such as doing nice things for oneself but need to be focused on the problem at hand. Commonly, this may be focused on help-seeking behaviour or even learning to be compassionately assertive. You can write letters in session with them, or you can suggest that you leave the client for five minutes or so and let them write one, or it can be between sessions. When they bring the letter back they can read it to you, trying to put as much warmth in their voice as possible. Also it can be helpful if you read their letters back to them, again speaking slowly and with as much warmth inflection in your voice as you can manage – but this needs to be genuine and not 'sickly or false'. Explore their feelings and the degree to which their alternative thoughts in the letter are believable, acceptable and helpful.

Keep to the spirit of the exercise, rather than getting caught up in technique. Constantly collaborate with your client, which will mean at times going back to the three circles, so that there is clarity as to what together you are trying to achieve. Always invite your client to think how they could improve on the procedures, so that they become their own best guides.

Below is a client hand-out, which offers some guides for letter writing. When you give this to your client check out that they understand the point and they would find it helpful. Remind them that this is, in part, an experiment and not about doing things, right or wrong. Also note that it may take some practice to get the hang of it but that, of course, is the point. If people are struggling with the *fear* of being compassionate then acknowledge that compassionately, go back to the three circles and 'brain storm' how you can move forward and what would be helpful. Sometimes the client will need more compassionate interactions and reflections from you before they can internalise it enough to be able to develop this attitude to themselves. Keep in mind that avoidance of feelings of warmth can be a form of safety behaviour.

The client handout below is only a guide.

Client handout

The idea of compassionate letter writing is to help you refocus your thoughts and feelings on being supportive, helpful and caring of yourself. In *practising* doing this it can help you access an aspect of yourself that can help tone down more negative feelings and thoughts.

To start your letter, try to feel that part of you that can be kind and understanding of others; how you would be if caring for someone you like. Consider your general manner, facial expressions, voice tone and feelings that come with your caring self. Think about that part of you as the type of self you would like to be. Think about the qualities you would like your compassionate self to have. It does not matter if you feel you are like this – but focus on the *ideal* you would like to be. Spend a few moments really thinking about this and trying to feel in contact with that 'kind' part of you.

As you write your letter, try to allow yourself to have *understanding and acceptance* for your distress. For example, your letter might start with 'I am sad you feel distressed; your distress is understandable because…'. Note the reasons, realising your distress makes sense. Then perhaps you could continue your letter with: 'I would like you to know that…' (e.g. your letter might point out that as we become depressed, our depression can come with a powerful set of thoughts and feelings – so how you see things right now may be the depression view on things). Given this, we can try to 'step to the side of the depression' and write and focus on how best to cope, and what is helpful.

Ideas

There are a number of ideas that you might consider in your letter. Do *not* feel you have to cover them all. In fact you might want to try different things in different letters to yourself. With all of these ideas, although it can be difficult, try to avoid telling yourself what you should or should not think, feel or do. There is no right or wrong, it is the process of trying to think in a different way that is important.

Standing Back: Once you have acknowledged your distress and not blamed yourself for it, it is useful if your letter can help you stand back from the distress of your situation for a moment. If you could do that, what would be helpful for you to focus on and attend to?

For example, you might think about how you would feel about the situation in a couple of days, weeks or months, or you might recall that the depression can lift at certain times and remember how you feel then. It can be helpful to recall in your letter, and bring to your attention, times that you have coped with difficulties before; bring those to mind. If there are any tendencies to dismiss them, note them, but try to hold your focus on your letter. Your letter can focus on your efforts and on what you *are* able to do.

Your compassionate side might gently help you see things in a less black-and-white way. Your compassionate side is never condemning and can help you reduce self-blaming. Remember your compassionate side can help you with kindness and understanding. Here are some examples: If someone has shunned you and you are upset by that, your compassionate side will help you recognise your upset but also that thoughts such as 'the person doesn't like me, or that I am therefore unlikable,' maybe very unfair. Perhaps a more balanced view would be that the person who shunned you can do this to others and has difficulties of their own; your compassionate side can remind you that you have other friends who don't treat you this way. As another example if you have forgotten to do something, or have made a mistake and are very frustrated and cross with yourself, your compassionate side will understand your frustration and anger but help you see that the mistake was a genuine mistake and is not evidence of being stupid or useless. It will help you think about what is the most compassionate and helpful thing to do in these circumstances.

Not alone: Depression often makes us feel that we are different in some way. However, rather than feeling alone and ashamed remember many others can feel depressed with negative thoughts about themselves, the world or their future. In fact 1 in 20 of us, or more, can be depressed at any one time, so the depression is very sad but is far from uncommon. Your depression is *not* a personal weakness, inadequacy, badness or failure.

Self-criticism: If you are feeling down, disappointed or are being harsh on yourself, in your letter, note that self-criticism is often triggered by disappointment (e.g. making a mistake or not looking like we would like to), loss (e.g. of hoped for love) or fear (e.g. of criticism and/or rejection). Maybe being self-critical is a way you have learned to cope with these things or take your frustration out on yourself, but this is not a kind or supportive thing to do. Understandable perhaps, but it does not help us deal with the disappointment, loss or fear. So we need to acknowledge and be understanding and compassionate about the disappointment, loss or fear. Allow yourself to be sensitive to those feelings.

Compassionate behaviour: It is useful to think about what might be the compassionate thing *to do* at this moment or at some time ahead – how might your compassionate part help you do those things? So in your letter you may want to think about how you can bring compassion into action in your life. If there are things you are avoiding or finding difficult to do, write down some small steps to move you forward. Try to write down steps and ideas that encourage you and support you to do the things that you might find difficult. If you are unsure what to do maybe try to brain storm as many options as you can and think which ones appeal to you.

Dilemmas: If you are in a dilemma about something, focus on the wise, gentle, compassionate voice inside you and write down the different sides of the dilemma. Note that dilemmas are often difficult, and at times there are hard choices to be made. Therefore, these may take time to work through. Talking through with others might be a helpful thing to do. Acceptance of the benefits and losses of a decision can take time.

Compassion for feelings: Your compassionate side will have compassion for your feelings. If you are having powerful feelings of frustration, anger or anxiety, then compassionately recognise these. Negative emotions are part of being human and can become more powerful in depression but they do not make you a bad person – just a human being trying to cope with difficult feelings. We can learn to work with these feelings as part of our 'humanness' without blaming or condemning ourselves for them. Your compassionate mind will remind you that we often don't choose to feel negatively and these feelings can come quite quickly. In this sense it is not our fault, although we can learn how to work with these difficult feelings.

Loss of positive feelings: If you are feeling bad because you have lost positive feelings then we can be compassionate to this loss – it is very sad to lose positive feelings. Sometimes we lose loving feelings because a relationship has run its course, or we are just exhausted, or depression can block positive emotion systems. As we recover from the depression these positive systems can return. Your compassionate letter can help you see this without self-blaming.

What is helpful: Your letter will be a way of practising how to really focus on things that you feel help you. If thoughts come to mind that make you feel worse, then notice them, let them go and refocus on what might be helpful – remember there are no 'I shoulds'.

Warmth: Now try to focus on the feelings of warmth and genuine wish to help in the letter as you write it. Spend time breathing gently and really try, as best you can, to let feelings of warmth be there for you. When you have written your letter, read it through slowly, with as much warmth as you can muster. If you are writing to somebody else would you feel your letter is kind and helpful? Could you change anything to make it more warm and helpful?

Remember that this is an *exercise* that might seem difficult to do at times but with practice you are exercising a part of your mind that can be developed to be helpful to you. Some people find that they can rework their letters the next day so they can think through things in a different way. The key of this exercise is the desire and effort of becoming inwardly gentle, compassionate and self-supportive. The benefits of this work may not be immediate but like 'exercising to get fit' can emerge over time with continued practice. Sometimes people find that even though they are depressed they would very much like to develop a sense of self that can be wise and compassionate to both themselves and others. You can practice thinking about how, each day, you can become more and more as you wish to be. Spend time imagining your postures and facial expressions, thoughts and feelings that go with being compassionate and practise creating these inside you This means being open with our difficulties and distress, rather than just trying to get rid of them.

Appendix 9 The Consequences of Becoming Compassionate to Self and Others

As one begins to develop the compassion focus it can be useful to explore how this will help you change and become more as you would like to be. List down how a compassion focus will:

1. Affect how you feel and relate to yourself – what will be different? How will you notice this happening and build on it?

2. Affect how you deal with life problems – what will be different? How will you notice this happening and build on it?

3. Affect how you interact with other people – what will be different? How will you notice this happening and build on it?

4. Affect how you choose and work towards life goals – what will be different? How will you notice this happening and build on it? (Goals can be short-term – in the next few days, weeks or months – or long-term and over a lifetime.)

5. Affect how you deal with setbacks and life crises – what will be different? How will you notice this happening and build on it?

6. Affect any other life issues that are important to you – what will be different? How will you notice this happening and build on it?

How can we build compassion into everyday life? How can we notice blocks to compassionate living and work compassionately with these?

Appendix 10   Self-Help Material and Useful Websites

There are a number of self-help materials that can be useful to consider for people as part of your work together.

Brantley, J. (2003). *Calming Your Anxious Mind: How Mindfulness and Compassion Can Free You from Anxiety, Fear and Panic.* New York: Harbinger. This comes with a CD that is very useful.

Fennell, M. (2006). *Overcoming Low Self-Esteem: A Self-Help Course.* A three-part programme based on cognitive behavioural techniques. London: Robinson. A very useful, clear, step-by-step approach with lots of simple, basic and practical experiences to try. You will find a whole number of thought-recording forms here if that is an approach you feel comfortable with.

Gilbert, P. (2000a). *Overcoming Depression: A Self-Guide Using Cognitive Behavioural Techniques* (rev. edn). London: Robinson and New York: Oxford University Press. This uses a more narrative approach than many self-help books but contains exercises. It is slightly bigger because there are many case examples for people to read. This helps depressed people to see that they are not alone and there are things that can be done to help depression. It also introduces the importance of self-compassion.

Leahy, R.L. (2000). *The Worry Cure.* New York: Piatkus

Leahy, R.L. and Holland, S.J. (2000). *Treatment Plans and Interventions for Depression and Anxiety Disorders.* New York: Guilford Press. This is an excellent text. It also comes with a CD and you can print out various forms and exercises for your clients.

Marra, T. (2003). *The Dialectical Behavior Therapy Workbook for Overcoming Depression and Anxiety.* Oakland, CA: New Harbinger Publications. This is a very useful workbook that you can share with your clients. It gives a good overview of the structure and steps for dialectical behaviour therapy. You will see that compassion-focused approaches can sit quite comfortably within DBT.

Padesky, C. and Greenberg, D. (1995). *Clinicians' Guide to Mind over Mood.* New York: Guilford Press. There is also a patient workbook to go with this. Many counsellors who follow the cognitive approach have found this useful. Again, there are various exercise and work forms.

Useful websites

For information about depression see the National Institute for Clinical Excellence (NICE) website: www.NICE.org.uk

This website gives information on the management of depression in primary and secondary care, computerised self-help, and depression in children and adolescents.

Self-help

An important self-help website is the Australian site 'Beyond Blue': www.beyondblue.org.au
This is a government-backed website and is regarded as a world leader.
The Five Areas Approach websites, including workbooks, are available at the free NHS-funded CBT life skills website: www.livinglifetothefull.com

Therapy websites

The American Institute of Cognitive Therapy: www.CognitiveTherapyNYC.com
Robert L. Leahy is the President of the American Institute of Cognitive Therapy and more information can be found here, including how to become a member and receive the society's journal, the *Journal of Cognitive Psychotherapy, an International Quarterly*

The Beck Institute of Cognitive Therapy: www.beckinstitute.org
Information on the Beckian developments in cognitive therapy can be found at this website.

The Institute of Psychiatry: www.iop.kcl.ac.uk
Cognitive approaches and training can be accessed at the Institute of Psychiatry in London.

Oxford Cognitive Therapy Centre: www.octc.co.uk
Cognitive approaches and training can be accessed at the Oxford Cognitive Therapy Centre.

Emotion-focused Therapy: www.EmotionFocusedTherapy.org and www.psych. yorku.ca/greenberg
This approach has been pioneered by Lesley Greenberg in Canada.

Commitment Acceptance Therapy: www.acceptanceandcommitmenttherapy. com, www.relationalframetheory.com and www.contextpress.com
This approach has been pioneered by Steve Hayes. For information on Commitment Acceptance Therapy (Steve Hayes) see any of the above websites.

Dialectical Behavioural Therapy: www.faculty.washing.edu/linehan
This approach has been pioneered by Marsha Linehan. For more information on DBT see the above website.

Self-psychology: www.selfpsychology.com
This approach has been pioneered by Heinz Kohut.
The International Council for Psychoanalytic Self-psychology can be accessed at: www.psychologyoftheself.com

Interpersonal schema studies

Studies exploring the non-conscious effects on processing of certain types of interpersonal schema can be found at the web addresses below. This is work pioneered by Mark Baldwin. In addition, Mark is developing computer games to stimulate certain kinds of social emotional processing system. Do visit his website and have a go on the games.

www.selfesteemgames.mcgill.ca

The research itself reported at: www.selfesteemgames.mcgill.ca/research/index.htm

Mindfulness websites

There are a large range of websites now for mindfulness but I am not able to comment on these, but here are a few of interest.

www.mindfultherapies.com

www.bangor.ac.uk/mindfulness/

www.mindfulness.com/

http://en.wikipedia.org/wiki/Mindfulness

www.budsas.org/ebud/mfneng/mind0.htm

www.priory.com/psych/mindfulness.htm

www.psychiatry.ox.ac.uk/csr/mbct.html

www.jimhopper.com/mindfulness/

Compassion-focused Therapy

You can look up our Compassionate Mind Foundation at: www.Compassionatemind.co.uk

My website is: www.derby.ac.uk/schools/sehs/research/mhru/

Kristen Neff has a website for her work on self compassion at www.self-compassion.org

The Dalai Lama has developed relationships with western scientists to develop more compassionate living. More information on this can be found at: www.mindandlife.org

Bibliography

Abbott, D.H., Keverne, E.B., Bercovitch, F.B. et al., (2003). Are subordinates always stressed? A comparative analysis of rank differences in cortisol levels among primates. *Hormones and Behavior*, 43, 67–82.

Abbott, P. and Williamson, E. (1999). Women, health and domestic violence. *Journal of Gender Studies*, 8, 83–102.

Abramson, L.Y., Metalsky, G.I. and Alloy, L.B. (1989). Hopelessness: A theory-based subtype of depression. *Psychological Review*, 96, 358–72.

Ahmed, E. and Braithwaite, V. (2004). 'What, me ashamed?' Shame management and school bullying. *Journal of Research in Crime and Delinquency*, 41, 269–94.

Akiskal, H.S. and McKinney, W.T. (1973). Depressive disorders: Toward a unified hypothesis. *Science*, 182, 20–9.

Akiskal, H.S. and McKinney, W.T. (1975) Overview of recent research in depression: Integration of ten conceptual models into a comprehensive frame. *Archives of General Psychiatry*, 32, 285–305.

Aldridge, D. (2000). *Spirituality, Healing and Medicine*. London: Jessica Kingsley.

Allan, S. and Gilbert, P. (1997). Submissive behaviour and psychopathology. *British Journal of Clinical Psychology*, 36, 467–82.

Allen, N.B. and Badcock, P.B.T. (2003). The social risk hypothesis of depressed mood: Evolutionary, psychosocial, and neurobiological perspectives. *Psychological Bulletin*, 129, 887–913.

Allen, N.B. and Knight, W.E.J. (2005). Mindfulness, compassion for self and compassion for others: Implications for understanding the psychopathology and treatment of depression. In P. Gilbert (ed.), *Compassion: Conceptualisations, Research and Use in Psychotherapy* (pp. 239–62). London: Brunner-Routledge.

Alloy, L.B., Abramson, L.Y., Whitehouse, W.G., Hogan, M.E., Panzaralla, C. and Rose, D.T. (2006). Prospective incidence of first onsets and recurrences of depression in individuals at high and low cognitive risk for depression. *Journal of Abnormal Psychology*, 115, 145–56.

Andrews, B. (1998). Shame and childhood abuse. In P. Gilbert and B. Andrews (eds), *Shame: Interpersonal Behavior, Psychopathology and Culture* (pp. 176–90). New York: Oxford University Press.

Andrews, B. and Brewin, C.R. (1990). Attributions of blame for marital violence: A study of antecedents and consequences. *Journal of Family and Marriage*, 52, 757–67.

Apter, A., Horesh, N., Gothelf, D., Graffi, H. and Lepkifker, E. (2001). Relationship between self-disclosure and serious suicidal behaviour. *Comprehensive Psychiatry*, 42, 70–5.

Argyle, M. (1984). *The Psychology of Interpersonal Behaviour* (4th edn). Harmondsworth: Penguin.

Arieti, S. and Bemporad, J. (1980a). The psychological organization of depression. *American Journal of Psychiatry*, 137, 1360–5.

Arieti, S. and Bemporad, J. (1980b). *Severe and Mild Depression: The Psychotherapeutic Approach*. London: Tavistock.

Arrindell, W.A., Sanderman, R., Van der Molen, H., Van der Ende, J. and Mersch, P.P. (1988). The structure of assertiveness: A confirmatory approach. *Behaviour Research and Therapy*, 26, 337–9.

Arrindell, W.A., Steptoe, A. and Wardle, J. (2003). Higher levels of depression in masculine than in feminine nations. *Behaviour Research and Therapy*, 41, 809–17.

Ashby, F.G., Isen, A.M. and Turken, A.U. (1999). A neuropsychological theory of positive affect and its influence on cognition. *Psychological Review*, 106, 529–50.

Babiker, G. and Arnold, L. (1997). *The Language of Injure: Comprehending Self-Mutilation*. Leicester: British Psychological Society.

Baer, R.A. (2003). Mindfulness training as a clinical intervention: A conceptual and empirical review. *Clinical Psychology: Science and Practice*, 10, 125–43.

Bailey, K.G. (2002). Recognizing, assessing and classifying others: Cognitive bases of evolutionary kinship therapy. *Journal of Cognitive Psychotherapy: An International Quarterly*, 16, 367–83.

Baker, H.S. and Baker, M.N. (1988). Arthur Miller's 'Death of a Salesman': Lessons for the self psychologist. In A. Goldberg (ed.), *Progress in Self Psychology* (vol. 4). Hillsdale, NJ: The Analytic Press.

Baldwin, M.W. (1992). Relational schemas and the processing of social information. *Psychological Bulletin*, 112, 461–84.

Baldwin, M.W. (ed.) (2005). *Interpersonal Cognition*. New York: Guilford Press.

Baldwin, M.W. and Dandeneau, S.D. (2005). Understanding and modifying the relational schemas underlying insecurity. In M.W. Baldwin (ed.), *Interpersonal Cognition* (pp. 33–61). New York: Guilford Press.

Baldwin, M.W. and Holmes, J.G. (1987). Salient private audiences and awareness of the self. *Journal of Personality and Social Psychology*, 52, 1087–98.

Banai, E., Shaver, P. and Mikulincer, M. (2005). 'Self objects' in Kohut's self psychology: Links with attachment, affect regulation, and adjustment. *Psychoanalytic Psychology*, 22, 224–60.

Bandura, A. (1977). *Social Learning Theory*. Englewood Cliffs, NJ: Prentice-Hall.

Bateman, A. and Fonagy, P. (2004). *Psychotherapy for Borderline Personality Disorder: Mentalization Based Treatment*. Oxford: Oxford University Press.

Bates, A. and Clark, D.M. (1998). A new cognitive treatment for social phobia: A single case study. *Journal of Cognitive Psychotherapy: An International Quarterly*, 12, 289–302.

Baumeister, R.F. (1990). Suicide as escape from self. *Psychological Review*, 97, 90–133.

Baumeister, R.F., Bratslavsky, E., Finkenauer, C. and Vohs, K.D. (2001). Bad is stronger than good. *Review of General Psychology*, 5, 323–70.

Baumeister, R.F. and Leary, M.R. (1995). The need to belong: Desire for interpersonal attachments as a fundamental human motivation. *Psychological Bulletin*, 117, 497–529.

Baumeister, R.F., Stillwell, A. and Heatherton, T.F. (1994) Guilt: An interpersonal approach. *Psychological Bulletin*, 115, 243–67.

Baumeister, R.F., Tice, D.M. and Hutton, D.G. (1993). Self-presentation motivations and personality differences in self-esteem. *Journal of Personality*, 57, 547–79.

Beach, S.R.H., and Jones, D.J. (2002). Marital and family therapy for depressed adults. In I.H. Gotlib and C.L. Hammen (eds), *Handbook of Depression* (pp. 422–40). New York: Guilford Press.

Bebbington, P. (2004). The classification and epidemiology of unipolar depression. In M. Power (ed.), *Mood Disorders: A Handbook of Science and Practice* (pp. 3–27). Chichester: Wiley and Sons Ltd.

Bebbington, P., Katz, R., McGuffin, P., Tennant, C. and Hurry, J. (1989). The risk of minor depression before age 65: Results from a community survey. *Psychological Medicine*, 19, 393–400.

Beck, A.T. (1967). *Depression: Clinical, Experimental and Theoretical Aspects*. New York: Harper & Row.

Beck, A.T. (1976). *Cognitive Therapy and the Emotional Disorders*. New York: International Universities Press.

Beck, A.T. (1983). Cognitive therapy of depression: New perspectives. In P.J. Clayton and J.E. Barrett (eds), *Treatment of Depression: Old Controversies and New Approaches* (pp. 265–90). New York: Raven Press.

Beck, A.T. (1987). Cognitive models of depression. *Journal of Cognitive Psychotherapy: An International Quarterly*, 1, 5–38.

Beck, A.T (1996). Beyond belief: A theory of modes, personality and psychopathology. In P. Salkovskis (ed.), *Frontiers of Cognitive Therapy* (pp. 1–25). London: Guilford Press.

Beck, A.T., Emery, G. and Greenberg, R.L. (1985). *Anxiety Disorders and Phobias: A Cognitive Approach*. New York: Basic Books.

Beck, A.T., Freeman, A. et al. (1990). *Cognitive Therapy of Personality Disorders*. New York: Guilford Press.

Beck, A.T., Rush, A.J., Shaw, B.F. and Emery, G. (1979). *Cognitive Therapy of Depression*. New York: Wiley.

Becker, J. (1979). Vulnerable self-esteem as a predisposing factor in depressive disorders. In R.A. Depue (ed.), *The Psychobiology of the Depressive Disorders: Implications for the Effects of Stress* (pp. 317–34). New York: Academic Press.

Beckham, F.E. and Leber, W.R. (eds) (1995). *Handbook of Depression* (2nd edn). New York: Guilford Press.

Beidel, D.C. and Turner, S.M. (1998). *Shy Children, Phobic Adults: Nature and Treatment of Social Phobia*. Washington, DC: American Psychology Press.

Belsher, G. and Costello, C.G. (1988). Relapse after recovery from unipolar depression: A critical review. *Psychological Bulletin*, 104, 84–6.

Belsky, J., Steinberg, L. and Draper, P. (1991). Childhood experiences, interpersonal development, and reproductive strategy: An evolutionary theory of socialization. *Child Development*, 62, 647–70.

Bennett-Levy, J., Butler, G., Fennell, M., Hackmann, A., Mueller, M. and Westbrook, D. (2004). *Oxford Guide to Behavioural Experiments in Cognitive Therapy*. Oxford: Oxford University Press.

Bennett-Levy, J. and Thwaites, R. (2007). Self and self-reflection in the therapeutic relationship: A conceptual map and practical strategies for the training, supervision and self-supervision of interpersonal skills. In P. Gilbert and R. Leahy (eds), *The Therapeutic Relationship in the Cognitive Behavioural Psychotherapies* (pp. 255–81). London: Routledge.

Bering, J.M. (2002). The existential theory of mind. *Review of General Psychology* 6, 3–34.

Berndt, D.J. (1990). Inventories and scales. In B.B. Wolman and G. Stricker (eds), *Depressive Disorders: Facts, Theories and Treatment Methods* (pp. 255–74). New York: Wiley.

Bibring, E. (1953). The mechanism of depression. In P. Greenacre (ed.), *Affective Disorders* (pp. 14–47). New York: International Universities Press.

Bieling, P.J. and Kyken, W. (2003). Is cognitive case formulation science or science fiction? *Clinical Psychology: Science and Practice*, 10, 52–69.

Bifulco, A. and Moran, P. (1998). *Wednesday's Child: Research into Women's Experiences of Neglect and Abuse in Childhood, and Adult Depression*. London: Routledge.

Birtchnell, J. (2003). *The Two of Me: The Relational Outer Me and the Emotional Inner Me*. London: Routledge.

Blackburn, I.M. and Davidson, K. (1995). *Cognitive Therapy for Depression and Anxiety* (2nd edn). Oxford: Blackwell.

Blackburn, I.M. and Twaddle, V. (1996). *Cognitive Therapy in Action*. London: Souvenir Press.

Blatt, S. and Zuroff, D. (1992). Interpersonal relatedness and self-definition: Two prototypes for depression. *Clinical Psychology Review*, 12, 527–62.

Blatt, S.J., Quinlan, D.M., Chevron, E.S., McDonald, C. and Zuroff, D. (1982). Dependency and self criticism: Psychological dimensions of depression. *Journal of Consulting and Clinical Psychology*, 50, 113–24.

Bono, G. and McCullough, M.E. (2006). Positive responses to benefit and harm: Bringing forgiveness and gratitude into cognitive psychotherapy. *Journal of Cognitive Psychotherapy: An International Quarterly*, 20, 147–58.

Book, H.E. (1988). Empathy: Misconceptions and misuses in psychotherapy. *American Journal of Psychiatry*, 145, 420–4.

Bordin, E. (1979). The generalizability of the psychoanalytic concept of the working alliance. *Psychotherapy: Theory, Research and Practice*, 16, 252–60.

Bowlby, J. (1969). *Attachment: Attachment and Loss* (vol. 1). London: Hogarth Press.

Bowlby, J. (1973). *Separation, Anxiety and Anger: Attachment and Loss* (vol. 2). London: Hogarth Press.

Bowlby, J. (1980). *Loss: Sadness and Depression: Attachment and Loss* (vol. 3). London: Hogarth Press.

Brantley, J. (2003). *Calming Your Anxious Mind: How Mindfulness and Compassion Can Free You from Anxiety, Fear and Panic*. New York: Harbinger.

Bremner, J.D. (2002). *Does Stress Damage the Brian?* New York: W.W. Norton.

Brewin, C.R. (2006). Understanding cognitive behaviour therapy: A retrieval competition account. *Behaviour Research and Therapy*, 44, 765–84.

Brewin, C.R., Andrews, B. and Gotlib, I.H. (1993). Psychopathology and early experiences: A reappraisal of retrospective reports. *Psychological Bulletin*, 113, 82–98.

Brewin, C.R. and Furnham, A. (1986). Attributional and pre-attributional variables in self-esteem and depression: A comparison and test of learned helplessness theory. *Journal of Personality and Social Psychology*, 50, 1013–20.

Brown, G.W. (1989). Depression: A radical social perspective. In K. Herbst and E. Paykel (eds), *Depression: An Interactive Approach*. Oxford: Heinemann Medical Books.

Brown, G.W., Adler, W.Z. and Bifulco, A. (1988). Life events, difficulties and recovery from chronic depression. *British Journal of Psychiatry*, 152, 487–98.

Brown, G.W. and Harris, T.O. (1978). *The Social Origins of Depression*. London: Tavistock.

Brown, G.W., Harris, T.O. and Hepworth, C. (1995). Loss, humiliation and entrapment among women developing depression: A patient and non-patient comparison. *Psychological Medicine*, 25, 7–21.

Brugha, T. (ed.) (1995). *Social Support and Psychiatric Disorder: Research Findings and Guidelines for Clinical Practice*. Cambridge: Cambridge University Press.

Buchbinder, E. and Eisikovits, Z. (2003). Battered women's entrapment in shame: A phenomenological study. *American Journal of Orthopsychiatry*, 73, 355–66.

Burns, D.D. (1980). *Feeling Good*. New York: Morrow.

Buss, D.M. (2003). *Evolutionary Psychology: The New Science of Mind* (2nd edn). Boston: Allyn and Bacon.

Buunk, B.P. and Gibbons, F.X. (eds) (1997). *Health, Coping and Well-Being: Perspectives from Social Comparison Theory*. Mahwah, NJ: Lawrence Erlbaum Associates.

Byrne, R.W. (1995). *The Thinking Ape*. Oxford: Oxford University Press.

Byrne, R.W. (1999). Human cognitive evolution. In M.C. Corballis and S.E.G. Lea (eds), *The Descent of Mind: Psychological Perspectives on Humanoid Evolution* (pp. 71–87). New York: Oxford University Press.

Cacioppo, J.T., Berston, G.G., Sheridan, J.F. and McClintock, M.K. (2000). Multilevel integrative analysis of human behavior: Social neuroscience and the complementing nature of social and biological approaches. *Psychological Bulletin*, 126, 829–43.

Cacioppo, J.T., Hawkley, L.C., Rickett, E.M. and Masi, C.M. (2005). Sociality, spirituality, and meaning making: Chicago health, aging and social relations study. *Review of General Psychology*, 9, 143–55.

Carr, A. (2004). *Positive Psychology: The Science of Happiness and Human Strengths*. Hove: Brunner-Routledge.

Carter, C.S. (1998). Neuroendocrine perspectives on social attachment and love. *Psychoneuroendocrinology*, 23, 779–818.

Carver, S.A., Weintraub, K.J. and Schierer, F.M. (1989). Assessing coping strategies: A theoretically based approach. *Journal of Personality and Social Psychology*, 56, 267–83.

Caspi, A. and Moffitt, T.E. (2006). Gene-environment interactions in psychiatry: Joining forces with neuroscience. *Nature Reviews: Neuroscience*, 7, 583–90.

Caspi, A., Sugden, K., Moffitt, T.E., Talyor, A., Craig, I.W., Harrington, H., McClay, J., Will, J., Braithwaite, A. and Poulton, R. (2003). Influence of life stress on depression: Moderation by a polymorphism in the 5-HTT gene. *Science*, 301, 386–98.

Cassidy, J. and Shaver, P.R. (eds) (1999). *Handbook of Attachment: Theory, Research and Clinical Applications*. New York: Guilford Press.

Champion, L. and Power, M. (1995). Social and cognitive approaches to depression: Towards a new synthesis. *British Journal of Clinical Psychology*, 34, 485–503.

Chartrand, T.L., van Baaren, R.B. and Bargh, J.A. (2006). Linking automatic evaluation to mood and information processing style: Consequences for experienced affect, impression formation, and stereotyping. *Journal of Experimental Psychology: General*, 135, 70–7.

Cheung, M.S.P., Gilbert, P. and Irons, C. (2004). An exploration of shame, social rank and rumination in relation to depression. *Personality and Individual Differences*, 36, 1143–53.

Clark, D.M. (1999). Anxiety disorders: why they persist and how to treat them. *Behaviour Research and Therapy*, 37, 5–27.

Clark, D.M. and Ehlers, A. (2004). Posttraumatic stress disorder: From cognitive theory to therapy. In R.L. Leahy (ed.), *Contemporary Cognitive Therapy: Theory, Research and Practice* (pp. 141–60). New York: Guilford Press.

Clarkin, J.F., Haas, G.L. and Glick, I.D. (1988). *Affective Disorders and the Family: Assessment and Treatment*. New York: Guilford Press.

Cleare, A.J. (2004). Biological models of unipolar depression. In M. Power (ed.), *Mood Disorders: A Handbook of Science and Practice* (pp. 29–46). Chichester: Wiley and Sons Ltd.

Cochran S.V. and Rabinowitz, F. (2000). *Men and Depression: Clinical and Empirical Perspectives*. New York: Academic Press.

Collins, N.L. and Read, S.J. (1990). Adult attachment, working models, and relationship quality in dating couples. *Journal of Personality and Social Psychology*, 58, 644–63.

Conway, M.A. and Pleydell-Pearce, C.W. (2000). The construction of autobiographic memories in the self-memory system. *Psychological Bulletin*, 107, 261–88.

Coon, D. (1992). *Introduction to Psychology: Exploration and Application* (6th edn). New York: West Publishing Company.

Cozolino, L. (2002). *The Neuroscience of Psychotherapy: Building and Rebuilding the Human Brain*. New York: W.W. Norton.

Cukrowicz, K.C., Otamendi, A., Pinto, J.V., Bernert, R.A., Krakow, B. and Joiner, T.E. (2006). The impact of insomnia and sleep disturbances on depression and suicidality. *Dreaming*, 16, 1–10.

Dalenberg, C.J. (2004). Maintaining the safe and effective therapeutic relationship in the context of distrust and anger: Countertransference and complex trauma. *Psychotherapy, Theory, Research, Practice, Training*, 41, 438–47.

Dalgleish, T. (2004). Cognitive approaches to posttraumatic stress disorder: The evolution of multirepresentation theorizing. *Psychological Bulletin*, 130, 228–60.

Dalgleish, T., Rosen, K. and Marks, M. (1996). Rhythm and blues: The assessment and treatment of seasonal affective disorder. *British Journal of Clinical Psychology*, 35, 163–82.

Davidson, R.J. and Harrington, A. (eds) (2002). *Visions of Compassion: Western Scientists and Tibetan Buddhists Examine Human Nature*. New York: Oxford University Press.

Davidson, R.J., Kabat-Zinn, J., Schumacher, J., Rosenkranz, M., Muller, D. et al. (2003). Alterations in brain and immune function produced by mindfulness meditation. *Psychosomatic Medicine*, 65, 564–70.

Davidson, R.J., Pizzagalli, D. and Nitschke, J.B. (2002). The representation and regulation of emotion in depression. In I.H. Gotlib and C.L. Hammen (eds), *Handbook of Depression* (pp. 219–44). New York: Guilford Press.

Davies, R.N. and Nolen-Hoeksema, S. (2000). Cognitive inflexibility among ruminators and non-ruminators. *Cognitive Therapy and Research*, 24, 699–711.

Decety, J. and Jackson, P.L. (2004). The functional architecture of human empathy. *Behavioral and Cognitive Neuroscience Reviews*, 3, 71–100.

Deitz, J. (1988). Self-psychological interventions for major depression. *American Journal of Psychotherapy*, XLII, 597–609.

Depue, R.A. and Morrone-Strupinsky, J.V. (2005). A neurobehavioral model of affiliative bonding. *Behavioral and Brain Sciences*, 28, 313–95.

de Waal, F.B.M. (1996). *Good Natured: The Origins of Right and Wrong in Humans and Other Animals*. London: Harvard University Press.

Dickerson, S.S. and Kemeny, M.E. (2004). Acute stressors and cortisol response: A theoretical integration and synthesis of laboratory research. *Psychological Bulletin*, 130, 335–91.

Dickson, A. (1982). *A Woman in Your Own Right* (rev. edn). London: Quartet Books.

Diener, E., Lucas, R.E. and Scollon, C.N. (2006). Beyond the hedonic treadmill: Revising the adaptation theory of well-being. *American Psychologist*, 61, 305–14.

Dimidjian, S., Hollon, S.D., Dobson, K.S. et al. (2006). Randomized trial of behavioral activation, cognitive therapy, and anti-depressant medication in the acute treatment of adults with major depression. *Journal of Consulting and Clinical Psychology*, 74, 658–70.

Dixon, A.K. (1998). Ethological strategies for defence in animals and humans: Their role in some psychiatric disorders. *British Journal of Medical Psychology*, 71, 417–45.

Dreher, M., Mengele, U., Krause, R. and Kämmerer, A. (2001). Affective indicators of the psychotherapeutic process: An empirical case study. *Psychotherapy Research*, 11, 99–117.

Driscoll, R. (1989). Self-condemnation: A conceptual framework for assessment and treatment. *Psychotherapy*, 26, 104–11.

Dryden, W. (1985). Challenging but not overwhelming: A compromise in negotiating homework assignments. *British Journal of Cognitive Therapy*, 3, 77–82.

Dryden, W. (ed.) (1989a). *Key Issues for Counselling in Action*. London: Sage.

Dryden, W. (1989b). The therapeutic alliance as an integrating framework. In W. Dryden (ed.), *Key Issues for Counselling in Action* (pp. 1–15). London: Sage.

Dryden, W. (1989c). The use of chaining in rational-emotive therapy. *Journal of Rational-Emotive Therapy*, 7, 59–66.

Dryden, W. (1989d). Attributions, beliefs and constructs: Some points of comparison. In D. Lane (ed.), *Attributions, Beliefs and Constructs in Counselling Psychology*. Leicester: British Psychological Society.

Dryden, W. (1991). *Dryden on Counselling*. Vol. 3: *Training and Supervision*. London: Whurr.

Dryden, W. (1992). *The Incredible Sulk*. London: Sheldon Press.

Duan, C. and Hill, C.E. (1996). The current state of empathy research. *Journal of Counselling*, 43, 261–74.

Dunkley, D.M., Zuroff, D.C. and Blankstein, K.R. (2003). Self-critical perfectionism and daily affect: Dispositional and situational influences on stress and coping. *Journal of Personality and Social Psychology*, 84, 234–52.

Dunkley, D.M., Zuroff, D.C. and Blankstein, K.R. (2006). Specific perfectionism components versus self-criticism in predicting maladjustment. *Personality and Individual Differences*, 40, 665–76.

Dykman, B.M. (1998). Integrating cognitive and motivational factors in depression: Initial tests of a goal orientation approach. *Journal of Personality and Social Psychology*, 74, 139–58.

Egan, G. (2002) *The Skilled Helper* (7th edn). Pacific Grove, CA: Brooks/Cole.

Ehlers, A., Maercker, A. and Boos, S. (2000). Posttraumatic stress disorder following imprisonment: Role of mental defeat, alienation, and perceived permanent change. *Journal of Abnormal Psychology*, 109, 45–55.

Eisenberg, L. (1986). Mindlessness and brainlessness in psychiatry. *British Journal of Psychiatry*, 148, 497–508.

Eisenberg, N. (1986). *Altruistic Emotion, Cognition and Behavior: A New View*. Hillsdale: NJ: Lawrence Erlbaum Associates.

Eisenberg, N. (2002). Empathy-related emotional responses, altruism, and their socialization. In R. Davidson and A. Harrington (eds), *Visions of Compassion: Western Scientists and Tibetan Buddhists Examine Human Nature* (pp. 31–164.) New York: Oxford University Press.

Ellenberger, H.F. (1970). *The Discovery of the Unconscious: The History and Evolution of Dynamic Psychiatry*. New York: Basic Books.

Ellis, A. (1977a). Characteristics of psychotic and borderline psychotic individuals. In A. Ellis and R. Grieger (eds), *Handbook of Rational Emotive Therapy*. New York: Springer.

Ellis, A. (1977b). A rational approach to interpretation. In A. Ellis and R. Grieger (eds), *Handbook of Rational Emotive Therapy*. New York: Springer.

Enright, R.D. (1996). Counselling within the forgiveness triad: On forgiving, receiving forgiveness, and self-forgiveness. *Counselling and Values*, 40, 107–26.

Epstein, S. (1994). Integration of the cognitive and the psychodynamic unconscious. *American Psychologist*, 49, 709–24.

Epstein, S., Lipson, A., Holstein, C. and Huh, E. (1992). Irrational reactions to negative outcomes: Evidence for two conceptual systems. *Journal of Personality and Social Psychology*, 62, 328–39.

Espie, C.A. (2006) *Overcoming Insomnia and Sleep Problems*. London: Robinson.

Etcoff, N. (1999). *Survival of the Prettiest: The Science of Beauty*. New York: Doubleday.

Fazaa, N. and Page, S. (2003). Dependency and self-criticism as predictors of suicidal behavior. *Suicide and Life Threatening Behavior*, 33(2), 182–5.

Fennell, M.J.V. (1989). Depression. In K. Hawton, P.M. Salkovskis, J. Kirk and D.M. Clark (eds), *Cognitive Behaviour Therapy for Psychiatric Problems* (pp. 169–234). Oxford: Oxford University Press.

Ferguson, B. and Tyrer, P. (1989). Rating instruments in psychiatric research. In C. Freeman and P. Tyrer (eds), *Research Methods in Psychiatry: A Beginner's Guide*. London: Gaskell/The Royal College of Psychiatrists.

Ferster, C.B. (1973). A functional analysis of depression. *American Psychologist*, 28, 857–70.

Ferster, C.B. (1974). Behavioral approaches to depression. In R.J. Friedman and M.M. Katz (eds), *The Psychology of Depression: Contemporary Theory and Research*. New York: Winston Wiley.

Field, T. (2000). *Touch Therapy*. New York: Churchill Livingstone.

Fogel, A., Melson, G.F. and Mistry, J. (1986). Conceptualising the determinants of nurturance: A reassessment of sex differences. In A. Fogel and G.F. Melson (eds), *Origins of Nurturance: Developmental, Biological and Cultural Perspectives on Caregiving* (pp. 53–67). Hillsdale, NJ: Lawrence Erlbaum Associates.

Fombonne, E. (1999). Time trends in affective disorders. In P. Cohen, C. Slomkowski and L.N. Robins (eds), *Historical and Geographical Influences on Psychopathology* (pp. 115–40). Mahwah, NJ: Lawrence Erlbaum Associates.

Fonagy, P. and Target, M. (2006). The mentalization-focused approach to self pathology. *Journal of Personality Disorders*, 20, 544–76.

Forrest, M.S. and Hokanson, J.E. (1975). Depression and autonomic arousal reduction accompanying self-punitive behavior. *Journal of Abnormal Psychology*, 84, 346–57.

Fournier, M.A., Moskowitz, D.S. and Zuroff, D.C. (2002). Social rank strategies in hierarchical relationships. *Journal of Personality and Social Psychology*, 83, 425–33.

Frank, E., Kupfer, D.J. and Perel, J.M. (1989). Early recurrence in unipolar depression. *Archives of General Psychiatry*, 46, 397–400.

Frederick, C. and McNeal, S. (1999). *Inner Strengths: Contemporary Psychotherapy and Hypnosis for Ego Strengthening*. Mahwah, NJ: Lawrence Erlbaum Associates.

Fredrickson, B.L. (1998). What good are positive emotions? *Review of General Psychology*, 2, 300–19.

Fredrickson, B.L., Tugade, M.M., Waugh, C.E. and Larkin, G.R. (2003). What good are positive emotions in crises? A prospective study of resilience and emotions following the terrorist attacks on the United States on September 11, 2001. *Journal of Personality and Social Psychology*, 84, 365–77.

Freedman, S.R. and Enright, R.D. (1996). Forgiveness as an intervention goal with incest survivors. *Journal of Consulting and Clinical Psychology*, 64, 983–92.

Freeman, A. and McCloskey, R.D. (2003). Impediments to psychotherapy. In R.L. Leahy (ed.), *Roadblocks in Cognitive-Behavioral Therapy: Transforming Challenges into Opportunities for Change* (pp. 24–48). New York: Guilford Press.

Freeman, A., Simon, K.M., Beutler, L.E. and Arkowitz, H. (eds) (1989). *Comprehensive Handbook of Cognitive Therapy*. New York: Plenum.

Freud, S. (1917). Mourning and Melancholia. In *Complete Psychological Works*, Vol. 14 (Standard Edition). Translated and edited by J. Strachey. London: Hogarth Press.

Geary, D.C. (2000). Evolution and proximate expression of human parental investment. *Psychological Bulletin*, 126, 55–77.

George, M.S., Ketter, T.A., Parekh, P.I., Horwitz, B., Hercovitch, P. and Post, R.M. (1995). Brain activity during transient sadness and happiness in healthy women. *American Journal of Psychiatry*, 152, 341–51.

Gerhardt, S. (2004). *Why Love Matters: How Affection Shapes a Baby's Brain*. London: Routledge.

Germer, C.K., Siegel, R.D. and Fulton, P.R. (2005). *Mindfulness and Psychotherapy*. New York: Guilford Press.

Gibb, B.E., Abramson, L.Y. and Alloy, L.R. (2004). Emotional maltreatment from parent, verbal peer victimization, and cognitive vulnerability to depression. *Cognitive Therapy and Research*, 28, 1–21.

Gilbert, P. (1984). *Depression: From Psychology to Brain State*. London: Lawrence Erlbaum Associates.

Gilbert, P. (1989). *Human Nature and Suffering*. London: Lawrence Erlbaum Associates.

Gilbert, P. (1992). *Depression: The Evolution of Powerlessness*. Hove: Lawrence Erlbaum and New York: Guilford Press.

Gilbert, P. (1993). Defence and safety: Their function in social behaviour and psychopathology. *British Journal of Clinical Psychology*, 32, 131–54.

Gilbert, P. (1995a). Biopsychosocial approaches and evolutionary theory as aids to integration in clinical psychology and psychotherapy. *Clinical Psychology and Psychotherapy*, 2, 135–56.

Gilbert, P. (1995b). Attachment, co-operation and rank: The evolution of the need for status and support. In T. Brugha (ed.), *Social Support and Psychiatric Disorder: Research Findings and Guidelines for Clinical Practice* (pp. 117–41). Cambridge: Cambridge University Press.

Gilbert, P. (1997). The evolution of social attractiveness and its role in shame, humiliation, guilt and therapy. *British Journal of Medical Psychology*, 70, 113–47.

Gilbert, P. (1998a). What is shame? Some core issues and controversies. In P. Gilbert and B. Andrews (eds), *Shame: Interpersonal Behavior, Psychopathology and Culture* (pp. 3–38). New York: Oxford University Press.

Gilbert, P. (1998b). The evolved basis and adaptive functions of cognitive distortions. *British Journal of Medical Psychology*, 71, 447–64.

Gilbert, P. (1998c). Shame and humiliation in complex cases. In N. Tarrier, G. Haddock and A. Wells (eds), *Treating Complex Cases: The Cognitive Behavioural Approach* (pp. 241–71). Chichester: Wiley.

Gilbert, P. (2000a). *Overcoming Depression: A Self-Guide Using Cognitive Behavioural Techniques* (rev. edn). London: Robinson and New York: Oxford University Press.

Gilbert, P. (2000b). Varieties of submissive behaviour: Their evolution and role in depression. In L. Sloman and P. Gilbert, (eds), *Subordination and Defeat: An Evolutionary Approach to Mood Disorders* (pp. 3–46). Hillsdale, NJ: Lawrence Erlbaum Associates.

Gilbert, P. (2000c). Social mentalities: Internal 'social' conflicts and the role of inner warmth and compassion in cognitive therapy. In P. Gilbert and K.G. Bailey (eds), *Genes on the Couch: Explorations in Evolutionary Psychotherapy* (pp. 118–50). Hove: Brunner-Routledge.

Gilbert, P. (2001a). Evolutionary approaches to psychopathology: The role of natural defences. *Australian and New Zealand Journal of Psychiatry*, 35, 17–27.

Gilbert, P. (2001b). Depression and stress: A biopsychosocial exploration of evolved functions and mechanisms. *Stress: The International Journal of the Biology of Stress*, 4, 121–35.

Gilbert, P. (2002). Evolutionary approaches to psychopathology and cognitive therapy. In P. Gilbert (ed.), *Journal of Cognitive Psychotherapy: An International Quarterly* (Special Edition: Evolutionary Psychology and Cognitive Therapy), 16, 263–94.

Gilbert, P. (2003). Evolution, social roles, and differences in shame and guilt. *Social Research: An International Quarterly of the Social Sciences*, 70, 1205–30.

Gilbert, P. (2004). Depression: A biopsychosocial, integrative and evolutionary approach. In M. Power (ed.), *Mood Disorders: A Handbook of Science and Practice* (pp. 99–142). Chichester: J. Wiley and Sons.

Gilbert, P. (2005a). Compassion and cruelty: A biopsychosocial approach. In P. Gilbert (ed.), *Compassion: Conceptualisations, Research and Use in Psychotherapy* (pp. 9–74). London: Brunner-Routledge.

Gilbert, P. (2005b). Social mentalities: A biopsychosocial and evolutionary reflection on social relationships. In M.W. Baldwin (ed.), *Interpersonal Cognition* (pp. 299–335). New York: Guilford Press.

Gilbert, P. (2006a). Evolution and depression: Issues and implications (invited review). *Psychological Medicine*, 36, 287–97.

Gilbert, P. (2006b). Old and new ideas on the evolution of mind and psychotherapy. *Clinical Neuropsychiatry: Journal of Treatment Evaluation*, 3, 139–53.

Gilbert, P. (2007). Evolved minds and compassion in the therapeutic relationship. In P. Gilbert and R. Leahy (eds), *The Therapeutic Relationship in the Cognitive Behavioural Psychotherapies* (pp. 106–42). London: Routledge.

Gilbert, P. (in press a). The evolution of shame as a marker for relationship security. In J. Tracy, R. Robins, and J. Tangney (eds), *Self-Conscious Emotions: Theory and Research*. New York: Guilford Press.

Gilbert, P. (in press b). Evolved minds and compassion focused imgery in depression. In L. Stopa (ed.), *Imagery and the Threatened Self: Perspectives on Mental Imagery in Cognitive Therapy*. London: Routledge.

Gilbert, P. and Allan, S. (1998). The role of defeat and entrapment (arrested flight) in depression: An exploration of an evolutionary view. *Psychological Medicine*, 28, 584–97.

Gilbert, P., Allan, S., Ball, L. and Bradshaw, Z. (1996). Overconfidence and personal evaluations of social rank. *British Journal of Medical Psychology*, 69, 59–68.

Gilbert, P., Allan, S., Brough, S., Melley, S. and Miles J. (2002). Anhedonia and positive affect: Relationship to social rank, defeat and entrapment. *Journal of Affective Disorders*, 71, 141–51.

Gilbert, P. and Andrews, B. (eds) (1998). *Shame: Interpersonal Behavior, Psychopathology and Culture*. New York: Oxford University Press.

Gilbert, P., Baldwin, M., Irons, C., Baccus, J. and Palmer, M. (2006). Self-criticism and self-warmth: An imagery study exploring their relation to depression. *Journal of Cognitive Psychotherapy: An International Quarterly*, 20, 183–200.

Gilbert, P., Birchwood, M., Gilbert, J., Trower, P., Hay, J., Murray, B., Meaden, A., Olsen, K. and Miles, J.N.V. (2001) An exploration of evolved mental mechanisms for dominant and subordinate behaviour in relation to auditory hallucinations in schizophrenia and critical thoughts in depression. *Psychological Medicine*, 31, 1117–1127.

Gilbert, P., Cheung, M., Irons, C. and McEwan, K. (2005). An exploration into depression focused and anger focused rumination in relation to depression in a student population. *Behavioural and Cognitive Psychotherapy*, 33, 1–11.

Gilbert, P., Cheung, M., Wright, T., Campey, F. and Irons, C. (2003). Recall of threat and submissiveness in childhood: Development of a new scale and its relationship with depression, social comparison and shame. *Clinical Psychology, and Psychotherapy*, 10, 108–15.

Gilbert, P., Clarke, M., Kempel, S., Miles, J.N.V. and Irons, C. (2004). Criticizing and reassuring oneself: An exploration of forms, styles and reasons in female students. *British Journal of Clinical Psychology*, 43, 31–50.

Gilbert, P. and Gelsma, C. (1999). Recall of favouritism in relation to psychopathology. *British Journal of Clinical Psychology*, 38, 357–73.

Gilbert, P. and Gilbert, J. (2003). Entrapment and arrested fight and flight in depression: An exploration using focus groups. *Psychology and Psychotherapy: Theory Research and Practice*, 76, 173–88.

Gilbert, P., Gilbert, J. and Irons, C. (2004). Life events, entrapments and arrested anger in depression. *Journal of Affective Disorders*, 79, 149–60.

Gilbert, P., Hughes, W. and Dryden, W. (1989). The therapist as the crucial variable in psychotherapy. In W. Dryden and L. Spurling (eds), *On Becoming a Psychotherapist* (pp. 3–13). London: Routledge.

Gilbert, P. and Irons, C. (2004). A pilot exploration of the use of compassionate images in a group of self-critical people. *Memory*, 12, 507–16.

Gilbert, P. and Irons, C. (2005). Focused therapies and compassionate mind training for shame and self-attacking. In P. Gilbert (ed.), *Compassion: Conceptualisations, Research and Use in Psychotherapy* (pp. 263–325). London: Brunner-Routledge.

Gilbert, P. and. Leahy, R. (eds) (2007). *The Therapeutic Relationship in the Cognitive Behavioural Psychotherapies*. London: Routledge.

Gilbert, P. and McGuire, M. (1998). Shame, social roles and status: The psycho-biological continuum from monkey to human. In P. Gilbert and B. Andrews (eds), *Shame: Interpersonal Behavior, Psychopathology and Culture* (pp. 99–125). New York: Oxford University Press.

Gilbert, P. and Miles, J. (2000). Sensitivity to put down: Its relationship to perceptions of shame, social anxiety, depression, anger and self–other blame. *Personality and Individual Differences*, 29, 757–74.

Gilbert, P. and Miles, J. (eds) (2002). *Body Shame: Conceptualisation, Research and Treatment*. Hove: Brunner-Routledge.

Gilbert, P., Price, J.S. and Allan, S. (1995). Social comparison, social attractiveness and evolution: How might they be related? *New Ideas in Psychology*, 13, 149–65.

Gilbert, P. and Procter, S. (2006). Compassionate mind training for people with high shame and self-criticism: Overview and pilot study of a group therapy approach. *Clinical Psychology and Psychotherapy*, 13, 353–79.

Giles, D., Jarrett, R., Biggs, M., Guzick, D. and Rush, J. (1989). Clinical predictors of reoccurrence in depression. *American Journal of Psychiatry*, 146, 764–7.

Gilmore, D.D. (1990). *Manhood in the Making: Cultural Concepts of Masculinity*. New Haven, CT: Yale University Press.

Glaser, A. (2005). *A Call to Compassion: Bringing Buddhist Practices of the Heart into the Soul of Psychotherapy*. Berwick, ME: Nicolas-Hays.

Goldstein, A.P. and Michaels, G.Y. (1985). *Empathy: Development, Training and Consequences*. Hillsdale, NJ: Lawrence Erlbaum Associates.

Goodman, S.H. (2002). Depression and early life adverse experiences. In I.H. Gotlib and C.L. Hammen (eds), *Handbook of Depression* (pp. 245–67). New York: Guilford Press.

Gotlib, I.H. and Colby, C.A. (1987). *Treatment of Depression: An Interpersonal Systems Approach*. New York: Pergamon Press.

Gotlib I.H. and Hammen C.L. (eds) (2002). *Handbook of Depression*. New York: Guilford Press.

Goudsmit, F.M. and Gadd, R. (1991). All in the mind? The psychologisation of illness. *The Psychologist: Bulletin of the British Psychological Society*, 4, 449–53.

Gray, J.A. (1979). *Pavlov*. London: Fontana.

Gray, J.A. (1987). *The Psychology of Fear and Stress* (2nd edn). London: Weidenfeld and Nicolson.

Greenberg, D. and Padesky, C. (1995). *Mind Over Mood*. New York: Guilford Press.

Greenberg, L.S. (1979). Resolving splits: Use of the two-chair technique. *Psychotherapy, Theory, Research and Practice*, 16, 316–24.

Greenberg, L.S. (2002). Evolutionary perspectives on emotions: Making sense of what we feel. *Journal of Cognitive Psychotherapy: An International Quarterly*, 16, 331–47.

Greenberg, L.S. (2007). Emotion in the therapeutic relationship in emotion focused therapy. In P. Gilbert and R. Leahy (eds), *The Therapeutic Relationship in the Cognitive Behavioural Psychotherapies* (pp. 43–62). London: Routledge.

Greenberg, L.S., Elliott, R.K. and Foerster, F.S. (1990). Experiential processes in the psychotherapeutic treatment of depression. In C.D. McCaan and N.S. Endler (eds), *Depression: New Directions in Theory, Research and Practice* (pp. 157–85). Toronto: Wall and Emerson.

Greenberg, L.S., Rice, L.N. and Elliott, R. (1993). *Facilitating Emotional Change: The Moment-by-Moment Process.* New York: Guilford Press.

Greenberg, L.S. and Safran, J.I. (1987). *Emotion in Psychotherapy.* New York: Guilford Press.

Greenberg, L.S. and Watson, J.C. (2006). *Emotion Focused Therapy for Depression.* Washington, DC: American Psychological Association.

Grollman, E.A. (1988). *Suicide: Prevention, Intervention and Postintervention* (2nd edn). Boston: Beacon Press.

Guidano, V.F. and Liotti, G. (1983). *Cognitive Processes and Emotional Disorders.* New York: Guilford Press.

Gut, E. (1989). *Productive and Unproductive Depression: Success or Failure of a Vital Process.* London: Routledge and Kegan Paul.

Hackmann, A. (1997). The transformation of meaning in cognitive therapy. In M. Power and C. Brewin (eds), *The Transformation of Meaning in Psychological Therapies* (pp. 125–40). Chichester: Wiley.

Hackmann, A. (2005). Compassionate imagery in the treatment of early memories in axis I anxiety disorders. In, P. Gilbert (ed.), *Compassion: Conceptualisations, Research and Use in Psychotherapy* (pp. 352–68). London: Brunner-Routledge.

Haidt, J. (2001). The emotional dog and its rational tail: A social intuitionist approach to moral judgment. *Psychological Review,* 108, 814–34.

Hammen, C., Henry, R. and Daley, S.E. (2000). Depression and sensitization to stressors among young women as a function of childhood adversity. *Journal of Clinical and Consulting Psychology,* 68, 782–7.

Hanh, T.N. (1991). *The Miracle of Mindfulness.* London: Rider.

Hankin, B.L. and Abramson, L.Y. (2001). Development of gender differences in depression: An elaborated cognitive vulnerability-transactional stress theory. *Psychological Bulletin,* 127, 773–96.

Hardy, G., Cahill, J. and Barkham, M. (2007). Active ingredients of the therapeutic relationship that promote client change: A research perspective. In P. Gilbert and R. Leahy (eds), *The Therapeutic Relationship in the Cognitive Behavioural Psychotherapies* (pp. 24–42). London: Routledge.

Harper, L.V. (2005). Epigenetic inheritance and the intergenerational transfer of experience. *Psychological Bulletin,* 131, 340–60.

Harvey, A., Watkins, E., Mansell, W. and Shafran, R. (2004). *Cognitive Behavioural Processes across Psychological Disorders: A Transdiagnostic Approach to Research and Treatment.* Oxford: Oxford University Press.

Hassin, R.R., Uleman, J.S. and Bargh, J.A. (2005). *The New Unconscious.* New York: Oxford University Press.

Hawker, D.S. and Boulton, M.J. (2000). Twenty years' research on peer victimisation and psychosocial maltreatment: A meta-analytic review of cross-sectional studies. *Journal of Child Psychology and Psychiatry and Allied Disciplines,* 41, 441–55.

Hawton, K. (1987). Assessment of suicide risk. *British Journal of Psychiatry,* 150, 145–53.

Hawton, K. and Catalan, J. (1987). *Attempted Suicide: A Practical Guide to its Nature and Management.* Oxford: Oxford University Press.

Hayes, S.C., Follette, V.M. and Linehan, M.N. (2004). *Mindfulness and Acceptance: Expanding the Cognitive Bahavioral Tradition.* New York: Guilford Press.

Hayes, S.C., Strosahl, K.D. and Wilson, K.G. (2004). *Acceptance and Commitment Therapy: An Experiential Approach to Behavior Change*. New York: Guilford Press.

Hayes, S.C., Wilson, K.G., Gifford, E.V., Follette, V.M. and Strosahl, K. (1996). Experiential avoidance and behavioral disorders: A functional approach to diagnosis and treatment. *Journal of Consulting and Clinical Psychology*, 64, 1152–68.

Healy, D. (2001). The dilemmas posed by new fashionable treatments. *Advances in Psychiatric Treatment*, 7, 322–7.

Heard, D.H. and Lake, B. (1986). The attachment dynamic in adult life. *British Journal of Psychiatry*, 149, 430–8.

Heinrichs, M., Baumgartner, T., Kirschbaum, C. and Ehlert, U. (2003). Social support and oxytocin interact to suppress cortisol and subjective response to psychosocial stress. *Biological Psychiatry*, 54, 1389–98.

Higley, J.D., Mehlman, P.T., Higley, S., Fremald, B., Vickers, J., Lindell, S.G., Taub, D.M., Suomi, S.J. and Linnoila, M. (1996). Excessive mortality in young free-ranging male nonhuman primates with low cerebrospinal fluid 5-hydroxyindoleacetic acid concentrations. *Archives of General Psychiatry*, 53, 537–43.

Hobfoll, S.E. (1989). Conservation of resources: A new attempt at conceptualizing stress. *American Psychologist*, 44, 513–24.

Hofer, M.A. (1994). Early relationships as regulators of infant physiology and behavior. *Acta Paediatiricia Supplement*, 397, 9–18.

Hollon, S.D., DeRubeis, R.J. and Seligman, M.E.P. (1992). Cognitive therapy and the prevention of depression. *Applied and Preventative Psychology*, 1, 89–95.

Hollon, S.D. and Kriss, M.R. (1984). Cognitive factors in clinical research and practice. *Clinical Psychology Review*, 4, 35–76.

Holmes, E.A. and Hackmann, A. (eds) (2004). Mental Imagery and Memory in Psychopathology. A special issue of *Memory*, 12(4). Hove: Psychology Press.

Holmes, J. (2001). *The Search for the Secure Base: Attachment Theory and Psychotherapy*. London: Brunner-Routledge.

Honos-Webb, L., Stiles, W.B. and Greenberg, L.S. (2003). A method of rating assimilation in psychotherapy based on markers of change. *Journal of Consulting and Clinical Psychology*, 50, 189–98.

Hooley, T.M. and Teasdale, J.D. (1989). Predictors of relapse in unipolar depressives: Expressed emotion, marital distress and perceived criticism. *Journal of Abnormal Psychology*, 98, 229–35.

Horner, A. (1989) *The Wish for Power and the Fear of Having It*. Northvale, NJ: Jason Aronson.

Iacoviello, B.M., Alloy, L.B., Abramson, L.Y., Whitehouse, W.G. and Hogan, M.E. (2006). The course of depression in individuals at high and low cognitive risk for depression: A prospective study. *Journal of Affective Disorders*, 93, 61–9.

Irons, C., Gilbert, P., Baldwin, M.W., Baccus, J. and Palmer, M. (2006). Parental recall – attachment relating and self-attacking/self-reassurance: Their relationship with depression. *British Journal of Clinical Psychology*, 45, 297–308.

Ivey, A.E. and Ivey, M.B. (2003). *Intentional Interviewing and Counselling: Facilitating Client Change in a Multicultural Society* (5th edn). Pacific Grove, CA: Brooks/Cole.

Izard, C.E. (2002). Translating emotion theory and research into preventative interventions. *Psychological Bulletin*, 128, 796–824.

Jack, R.L. and Williams, J.M.G. (1991). Attribution and intervention in self-poisoning. *British Journal of Medical Psychology*, 64, 345–58.

James, O. (1997). *Britain on the Couch: Why We're Unhappier than We Were in the 1950s – Despite Being Richer: Treating a Lower Serotonin Society*. London: Century.

Janoff-Bulman, R. (1979). Characterological versus behavioral self-blame: Inquiries into depression and rape. *Journal of Personality and Social Psychology*, 37, 1798–809.

Janoff-Bulman, R. and Hecker, B. (1988). Depression, vulnerability, and world assumptions. In L.B. Alloy (ed.), *Cognitive Processes in Depression* (pp. 177–92). New York: Guilford Press.

Jehu, D. (1988). *Beyond Childhood Abuse: Therapy for Women Who Were Childhood Victims*. Chichester: Wiley.

Jehu, D. (1989). Mood disturbances among women clients abused in childhood: Prevalence, etiology and treatment. *Journal of Interpersonal Violence*, 4, 164–84.

Kahn, E. (1985). Heinz Kohut and Carl Rogers: A timely comparison. *American Psychologist*, 40, 893–904.

Kahn, E. (1989). Heinz Kohut and Carl Rogers: Towards a constructive collaboration. *Psychotherapy*, 26, 555–63.

Karasu, T.B. (1990). Toward a clinical model of the psychotherapy for depression, II: An integrative and selective treatment approach. *American Journal of Psychiatry*, 147, 269–78.

Karwoski, L., Garratt, G. and Ulardi, S.S. (2006). On the integration of cognitive-behavioural therapy for depression and positive psychology. *Journal of Cognitive Psychotherapy: An International Quarterly*, 20, 159–70.

Kasper, S. and Rosenthal, N.E. (1989). Anxiety and depression in seasonal affective disorder. In P.C. Kendall and D. Watson (eds), *Anxiety and Depression: Distinctive and Overlapping Features*. New York: Academic Press.

Kasser, T. (2002). *The High Price of Materialism*. Cambridge, MA: MIT Press.

Katakls, C.D. (1989). Stages of psychotherapy: Progressive reconceptualisation as a self-organizing process. *Psychotherapy*, 26, 484–93.

Katz, K., Shaw, B.F., Vallis, T.M. and Kaiser, A.S. (1995). The assessment of severity and symptom pattern in depression. In F.E. Beckham and W.R. Leber (eds), *Handbook of Depression*, (2nd edn, pp. 61–85). New York: Guilford Press.

Katzow, A.W. and Safran, J.D. (2007). Recognizing and resolving ruptures in the therapeutic alliance. In P. Gilbert and R. Leahy (eds), *The Therapeutic Relationship in the Cognitive Behavioural Psychotherapies*. London: Routledge.

Kaufman, G. (1989). *The Psychology of Shame*. New York: Springer.

Kegan, R. (1982). *The Evolving Self: Problem and Process in Human Development*. Cambridge, MA: Harvard University Press.

Keller, M.B., McCullough, J.P., Klein, D.N. et al. (2000). A comparison of nefazodone, the cognitive behavioral analysis system of psychotherapy and their combination for the treatment of chronic depression. *New England Journal of Medicine*, 32(342), 1462–70.

Keller, M.C. and Nesse, R.M. (2005). Subtypes of low mood provide evidence of its adaptive significance. *Journal of Affective Disorders*, 86, 27–35.

Keller, M.C. and Nesse, R.M. (2006). Significance of depressive symptoms: Different adverse situations lead to different depressive symptom patterns. *Journal of Personality and Social Psychology*, 91(2) 316–30.

Kelly, G. (1955). *The Psychology of Personal Constructs*. New York: W.W. Norton.

Keltner, D., Gruenfeld, D.H. and Anderson, C. (2003). Power, approach and inhibition. *Psychological Review*, 110, 265–84.

Keltner, D. and Harker, L.A. (1998). The forms and functions of the nonverbal signal of shame. In P. Gilbert and B. Andrews (eds), *Shame: Interpersonal Behavior, Psychopathology and Culture* (pp. 78–98). New York: Oxford University Press.

Kendler, K.S., Hettema, J.M., Butera, F., Gardner C.O. and Prescott, C.A. (2003). Life event dimensions of loss, humiliation, entrapment, and danger in the prediction of onsets of major depression and generalized anxiety. *Archives of General Psychiatry*, 60, 789–96.

Kessler, R.C. and Magee, W. (1993). Childhood adversities and adult depression: Basic patterns of association in a US national survey. *Psychological Medicine*, 23, 679–90.

Kirschenbaum, H. and Jourdan, A. (2005). The current status of Carl Rogers and the person-centred approach. *Psychotherapy, Theory, Research, Practice, Training*, 42, 37–51.

Klein, D.N., Santiago, N.J., Dina, V. et al. (2004). Cognitive-behavioural analysis system of psychotherapy as a maintenance treatment of chronic depression. *Journal of Consulting and Clinical Psychology*, 4, 581–688.

Klerman, G.L. (1988). The current age of youthful melancholia: Evidence for increase in depression among adolescents and young adults. *British Journal of Psychiatry*, 152, 4–14.

Klerman, G.L., Weissman, M.M., Rounsaville, B.J. and Chevon, E.S. (1984). *Interpersonal Psychotherapy of Depression*. New York: Basic Books.

Klinger, E. (1975). Consequences and commitment to aid disengagement from incentives. *Psychological Review*, 82, 1–24.

Klinger, E. (1993). Loss of interest. In C.G. Costello (ed.), *Symptoms of Depression* (pp. 43–62). New York: J. Wiley.

Kohut, H. (1971). *The Analysis of the Self*. New York: International Universities Press.

Kohut, H. (1977). *The Restoration of the Self*. New York: International Universities Press.

Koren-Karie, N., Oppenheim, D., Dolev, S., Sher, S. and Etzion-Carasso, A. (2002). Mothers' insightfulness regarding their infants' internal experience: Relations with maternal sensitivity and infant attachment. *Developmental Psychology*, 38, 534–42.

Kuehlwein, K.T. and Rosen, H. (1993) *Cognitive Therapies in Action: Evolving Innovative Practice*. San Francisco: Jossey-Bass.

Kumashiro, M. and Sedikides, C. (2005). Taking on board liability-focused information: close positive relationship as a self-bolstering resource. *Psychological Science*, 16, 732–9.

Laidlaw, K. (2004). Depression in older adults. In M. Power (ed.), *Mood Disorders: A Handbook of Science and Practice* (pp. 337–51). Chichester: Wiley and Sons.

Lazarus, A. (2000). Mutlimodal replenishment. *Professional Psychology: Research and Practice*, 31, 93–4.

Lazarus, R.S. (1994). *Coping and the Self-Management of Emotion*. New York: Oxford University Press.

Lazarus, R.S. (1999). *Stress and Emotion: A New Synthesis*. London: Free Association Press.

Leahy, R.L. (2001). *Overcoming Resistance in Cognitive Therapy*. New York: Guilford Press.

Leahy, R.L. (2002). A model of emotional schemas. *Cognitive and Behavioral Practice*, 9, 177–90.

Leahy, R.L. (ed.) (2004). *Roadblocks in Cognitive-Behavioral Therapy: Transforming Challenges into Opportunities for Change*. New York: Guilford Press.

Leahy, R.L. (2005). A social-cognitive model of validation. In P. Gilbert (ed.), *Compassion: Conceptualisations, Research and Use in Psychotherapy* (pp. 195–217). London: Brunner-Routledge.

Leahy, R.L. (2007). Schematic mismatch in the therapeutic relationship: A social-cognitive model. In P. Gilbert and R. Leahy (eds), *The Therapeutic Relationship in the Cognitive Behavioural Psychotherapies* (pp. 229–54). London: Routledge.

Leahy, R.L. and Holland, S.J. (2000). *Treatment Plans and Interventions for Depression and Anxiety Disorders*: New York: Guilford Press.

Leary, M.R. (1995). *Self-Presentation: Impression Management and Interpersonal Behavior*. Madison, WI: Brown and Benchmark.

Leary, M.R., Tambor, E.S., Terdal, S.K. and Downs, D.L. (1995). Self-esteem as an interpersonal monitor: The sociometer hypothesis. *Journal of Personality and Social Psychology*, 68, 519–30.

Leary, M.R. and Tangney, J.P. (eds) (2003). *Handbook of Self and Identity* (pp. 367–83). New York: Guilford Press.

LeDoux, J. (1998). *The Emotional Brain*. London: Weidenfeld and Nicolson.

Lee, D.A. (2005). The perfect nurturer: A model to develop a compassionate mind within the context of cognitive therapy. In P. Gilbert (ed.), *Compassion: Conceptualisations, Research and Use in Psychotherapy* (pp. 326–51). London: Brunner-Routledge.

Lee, D.A., Scragg, P. and Turner, S.W. (2001). The role of shame and guilt in reactions to traumatic events: A clinical formulation of shame-based and guilt-based PTSD. *British Journal of Medical Psychology*, 74, 451–66.

Leighton, T.D. (2003). *Faces of Compassion: Classic Bodhisattva Archetypes and Their Modern Expression*. Boston: Wisdom Publications.

Lerner, J.S. and Keltner, D. (2001). Fear, anger and risk. *Journal of Personality and Social Psychology*, 81, 146–59.

Levitan, R., Hasey, G. and Sloman, L. (2000). Major depression and the involuntary defeat strategy: biological correlates. In L. Sloman and P. Gilbert, (eds), *Subordination and Defeat: An Evolutionary Approach to Mood Disorders and Their Therapy* (pp. 95–114). Mahwah, NJ: Lawrence Erlbaum Associates.

Lewis, M. (1992). *Shame: The Exposed Self*. New York: The Free Press.

Lewis, M. (2003). The role of the self in shame. *Social Research: An International Quarterly of the Social Sciences*, 70, 1181–204.

Linden, D.E.J. (2006). How psychotherapy changes the brain – the contribution of functional neuroimaging. *Molecular Psychiatry*, 11, 528–38.

Lindisfarne, N. (1998). Gender, shame, and culture: An anthropological perspective. In P. Gilbert and B. Andrews (eds), *Shame: Interpersonal Behavior, Psychopathology and Culture* (pp. 246–60). New York: Oxford University Press.

Lindsay-Hartz, J., de Rivera, J. and Mascolo, M.F. (1995). Differentiating guilt and shame and their effects on motivations. In J.P. Tangney, and K.W. Fischer (eds), *Self-Conscious Emotions: The Psychology of Shame, Guilt, Embarrassment and Pride* (pp. 274–300). New York: Guilford Press.

Linehan, M. (1993). *Cognitive Behavioral Treatment of Borderline Personality Disorder*. New York: Guilford Press.

Liotti, G. (1988). Attachment and cognition: A guide for the reconstruction of early pathogenic experiences in cognitive therapy. In C. Perris, L.M. Blackburn and H. Perris (eds), *Handbook of Cognitive Psychotherapy*. New York: Springer.

Liotti, G. (2000). Disorganised attachment, models of borderline states and evolutionary psychotherapy. In P. Gilbert and B. Bailey (eds), *Genes on the Couch: Explorations in Evolutionary Psychotherapy* (pp. 232–56). Hove: Brunner-Routledge.

Liotti, G. (2002). The inner schema of borderline states and its correction during psychotherapy: A cognitive evolutionary approach. *Journal of Cognitive Psychotherapy: An International Quarterly*, 16, 349–65.

Liotti, G. (2007). Internal models of attachment in the therapeutic relationship. In P. Gilbert and R. Leahy (eds), *The Therapeutic Relationship in the Coginitve Behavioural Psychotherapies* (pp. 143–61). London: Routledge.

Lock, A. (1999). On the recent origin of symbolically-mediated language and its implications for psychological science. In M.C. Coballis and M.E.G. Lea (eds), *The Descent of Mind: Psychological Perspectives on Humanoid Evolution* (pp. 324–55). New York: Oxford University Press.

Loewenstein, G.F., Weber E.U., Hsee, C.K. and Welsch, N. (2001). Risk as feelings. *Psychological Bulletin*, 127, 267–86.

Lovibond, P.F. and Lovibond, S.H. (1995). The structure of negative emotional states: Comparison of the Depression Anxiety Stress Scales (DASS) with the Beck Depression and Anxiety Inventories. *Behaviour Research and Therapy*, 33, 335–43.

Lynch, T.R., Chapman, A.L., Rosenthal, M.Z., Kuo, J.R. and Linehan, M.M. (2006). Mechanism of change in dialectical behaviour therapy. *Journal of Clinical Psychology*, 62, 459–80.

MacDonald, G. and Leary, M.R. (2005). Why does social exclusion hurt? The relationship between social and physical pain. *Psychological Bulletin*, 131, 202–23.

MacDonald, K. (1992). Warmth as a developmental construct: An evolutionary analysis. *Child Development*, 63, 753–73.

MacLean, P. (1985). Brain evolution relating to family, play and the separation call. *Archives of General Psychiatry*, 42, 405–17.

MacLeod, A.K. (2004). Suicide and attempted suicide. In M. Power (ed.), *Mood Disorders: A Handbook of Science and Practice* (pp. 319–35). Chichester: Wiley and Sons.

Mahoney, M.J. (2003). *Constructivist Psychotherapy: A Practical Guide*. New York: Guilford Press.

Mahoney, M.J. and Gabriel, T.J. (1987). Psychotherapy and cognitive science. *Journal of Cognitive Psychotherapy: An International Quarterly*, 1, 39–60.

Malik, K. (2000). *Man, Beast and Zombie: What Science Can and Cannot Tell about Human Nature*. London: Weidenfeld and Nicolson.

Malle, B.F. and Hodges, S.D. (eds) (2005). *Other Minds: How Humans Bridge the Divide Between Self and Others*. New York: Guilford Press.

Margulies, A. (1984). Toward empathy: The uses of wonder. *American Journal of Psychiatry*, 141, 1025–33.

Markowitz, J.C. (2004). Interpersonal psychotherapy of depression. In M. Power (ed.), *Mood Disorders: A Handbook of Science and Practice* (pp. 183–200). Chichester: Wiley and Sons.

Markowitz, J.C. and Weissman, M.M. (1995). Interpersonal psychotherapy. In F.E. Beckham and W.R. Leber (eds), *Handbook of Depression*, (2nd edn, pp. 376–90). New York: Guilford Press.

Marks, I.M. (1987). *Fears, Phobias, and Rituals: Panic, Anxiety and their Disorders*. Oxford: Oxford University Press.

Marra, T. (2003). *The Dialectical Behavior Therapy Workbook for Overcoming Depression and Anxiety*. Oakland, CA: New Harbinger Publications.

Martell, C.R., Addis, M.E. and Jacobson, N.S. (2001). *Depression in Context: Strategies for Guided Action*. New York: W.W. Norton.

Martin, Y., Gilbert, P., McEwan, K. and Irons, C. (2006). The relation of entrapment, shame and guilt to depression, in carers of people with dementia. *Aging and Mental Health*, 10, 101–6.

Masten, A.S. (2001). Ordinary magic: Resilience processes in development. *American Psychologist*, 56, 227–38.

McCann, I.L., Sakheim, D.K. and Abrahamson, D.J. (1988). Trauma and victimization: A model of psychological adaptation. *The Counselling Psychologist*, 16, 531–94.

McCullough, J.P. Jr (2000). *Treatment for Chronic Depression: Cognitive Behavioral Analysis System of Psychotherapy*. New York: Guilford Press.

McCullough, M.E., Worthington, E.L. Jr. and Rachal, K.C. (1997). Interpersonal forgiving in close relationships. *Journal of Personality and Social Psychology*, 73, 321–36.

McGregor, I. and Marigold, D.C. (2003). Defensive zeal and the uncertain self: What makes you so sure? *Journal of Personality and Social Psychology*, 85, 838–52.

McGuire, M.T. and Troisi, A. (1998a). *Darwinian Psychiatry*. New York: Oxford University Press.

McGuire, M.T. and Troisi, A. (1998b). Prevalence differences in depression among males and females: Are there evolutionary explanations? *British Journal of Medical Psychology*, 71, 479–92.

McKay, M. and Fanning, P. (1992). *Self-Esteem: A Proven Program of Cognitive Techniques for Assessing, Improving, and Maintaining Your Self-Esteem* (2nd edn). Oakland, CA: New Harbinger Publishers.

Melzer, D., Fryers, T. and Jenkins, R. (2004). *Social Inequalities and the Distribution of the Common Mental Disorders*. Hove: The Psychology Press.

Mikulincer, M. and Shaver, P.R. (2004). Security-based self-representations in adulthood: Contents and processes. In N.S. Rholes and J.A. Simpson (eds), *Adult Attachment: Theory, Research, and Clinical Implications* (pp. 159–95). New York: Guilford Press.

Mikulincer, M. and Shaver, P.R. (2005). Mental representations of attachment security: Theoretical foundations for a positive social psychology. In M.W. Baldwin (ed.), *Interpersonal Cognition* (pp. 233–66). New York: Guilford Press.

Miller, I.J. (1989). The therapeutic empathic communication (TEC) process. *American Journal of Psychotherapy*, 43, 531–45.

Miller, S.B. (1996). *Shame in Context*. Hillsdale, NJ: The Analytic Press.

Milne, D.L. (1999). *Social Therapy: A Guide to Social Supportive Interventions for Mental Health Practitioners*. Chichester: Wiley.

Miranda, R. and Anderson, S. (2007). The therapeutic relationship: Implications from social cognition and transference. In P. Gilbert and R. Leahy (eds), *The Therapeutic Relationship in the Cognitive Behavioural Psychotherapies* (pp. 63–89). London: Routledge.

Mithen, S. (1996). *The Prehistory of the Mind: A Search for the Origins of Art and Religion.* London: Thames and Hudson.

Moldofsky, H. and Dickstein, J.B. (1999). Sleep and cytokine-immune functions in medical, psychiatric and primary sleep disorders. *Sleep Medicine Reviews*, 3, 325–37.

Monroe, S.M. and Harkness, K.L. (2005). Life stress, the 'kindling' hypothesis, and the recurrence of depression: Considerations from a life stress perspective. *Psychological Review*, 112, 417–45.

Moretti, M.M., Higgins, E.T. and Feldman, L.A. (1990). The self-system in depression: Conceptualization and treatment. In C.D. McCarn and N.S. Endler (eds), *Depression: New Directions in Theory, Research and Practice.* Toronto: Wall and Emerson.

Morgan S.P. (2005). Depression: Turning towards life. In C.K. Germer, R.D. Siegel and P.R. Fulton (eds), *Mindfulness and Psychotherapy* (pp. 130–51). New York: Guilford Press.

Morrison, A.P. (1984). Shame and the psychology of the self. In P.E. Stepansky and A. Goldberg (eds), *Kohut's Legacy: Contributions to Self Psychology.* New York: Analytic Press/Lawrence Erlbaum Associates.

Morriss, R.K. and Morriss, E.E. (2000). Contextual evaluation of social adversity in the management of depressive disorder. *Advances in Psychiatric Treatment*, 6, 423–31.

Murphy, H.B.M. (1978). The advent of guilt feelings as a common depressive symptom: A historical comparison on two continents. *Psychiatry*, 41, 229–42.

Murphy, J.M., Nierenberg, A.A., Monson, R.R., Laird, N.M., Sobol, A.M. and Leighton, A.H. (2002). Self-disparagement as a feature and forerunner of depression: Findings from the Stirling County study. *Comprehensive Psychiatry*, 43, 13–21.

Murray, S.L., Griffin, D.W., Rose, P. and Bellavia, G. (2006). For better or worse? Self-esteem and the contingencies of acceptance in marriage. *Personality and Social Psychology Bulletin*, 32, 866–80.

Nassbaum, M.C. (2003). *Upheavals of Thought: The Intelligence of Emotions.* Cambridge: Cambridge University Press.

Nathanson, D.L. (ed.) (1987). *The Many Faces of Shame.* New York: Guilford Press.

Neff, K.D. (2003a). Self-compassion: An alternative conceptualization of a healthy attitude toward oneself. *Self and Identity*, 2, 85–102.

Neff, K.D. (2003b). The development and validation of a scale to measure self-compassion. *Self and Identity*, 2, 223–50.

Neff, K.D., Kirkpatrick, K.L. and Rude, S.S. (2007). Self-compassion and adaptive psychological functioning. *Journal of Personality*, 41, 139–54

Nesse, R.M. (1990). Evolutionary explanations of emotions. *Human Nature*, 1, 261–89.

Nesse, R.M. (1998). Emotional disorders in evolutionary perspective. *British Journal of Medical Psychology*, 71, 397–416.

Nesse, R.M. (2000). Is depression an adaptation? *Archives of General Psychiatry*, 57, 14–20.

Nesse, R.M. and Jackson, E.D. (2006). Evolution: Psychiatry's nosology's missing biological foundation. *Clinical Neuropsychiatry: Journal of Treatment Evaluation*, 3, 121–31.

Nesse, R.M. and Williams, G.C. (1995). *Evolution and Healing.* London: Weidenfeld and Nicolson.

Nezu, A.M., Nezu, C.M., McClure, K.S. and Zwick, M.L. (2002). Assessment of depression. In I.H. Gotlib and C.L. Hammen (eds), *Handbook of Depression* (pp. 62–85). New York: Guilford Press.

NICE (National Institute for Clinical Excellence) (2004). *Depression: Management of Depression in Primary and Secondary Care.* London: National Institute for Clinical Excellence.

Nickerson, R.S. (1999). How we know – and sometimes misjudge – what others know: Inputting one's own knowledge to others. *Psychological Bulletin*, 125, 737–59.

Nijenhuis, E.R.S., van der Hart, O. and Steele, K. (2002). The emerging psychobiology of trauma-related dissociation and dissociative disorders. In H. D'haenen, J.A. van de Boer and P. Willner (eds), *Biological Psychiatry* (pp. 1–19). Chichester: J. Wiley and Sons.

Nolen-Hoeksema, S. and Davis, C.G. (1999). 'Thanks for sharing that': Ruminators and their social support networks. *Journal of Personality and Social Psychology*, 77, 801–14.

Nolen-Hoeksema, S., Grayson, C. and Larson, J. (1999). Explaining the gender difference in depressive symptoms. *Journal of Personality and Social Psychology*, 77, 1061–72.

Nolen-Hoeksema, S., Marrow, J. and Fredrickson, B.L. (1993). Response styles and the duration of episodes of depressed mood. *Journal of Abnormal Psychology*, 102, 20–8.

Norcross, J.C. (2002). *Psychotherapy Relationships that Work*. New York: Oxford University Press.

Numeroff, C.B. (1998). The neurobiology of depression. *Scientific American*, June, 28–35.

O'Connell, S. (1997). *Mind Reading: How We Learn To Love and Lie*. London: Arrow Books.

O'Connor, L.E. (2000). Pathogenic beliefs and guilt in human evolution: Implications for psychotherapy. In P. Gilbert and K.G. Bailey (eds), *Genes on the Couch: Explorations in Evolutionary Psychotherapy* (pp. 276–303). Hove: Brunner-Routledge.

Ogilvie, D.M. (1987). The undesired self: A neglected variable in personality research. *Journal of Personality and Social Psychology*, 52, 379–88.

Ornstein, R. (1986). *Multimind: A New Way of Looking at Human Beings*. London: Macmillan.

Osherson, S. and Krugman, S. (1990). Men, shame, and psychotherapy. *Psychotherapy*, 27, 327–39.

Ostler, K., Thompson, C., Kinmonth, A.L.K., Peveler, R.C., Stevens, L. and Stevens, A. (2001). Influence of socio-economic deprivation on the prevalence and outcome of depression in primary care: The Hampshire Depression Project. *British Journal of Psychiatry*, 178, 12–17.

Padesky, C. and Greenberg, D. (1995). *Clinicians' Guide to Mind over Mood*. New York: Guilford Press.

Panksepp, J. (1998). *Affective Neuroscience*. New York: Oxford University Press.

Panskepp, K. (2005). Why does separation distress hurt? Comment on MacDonald and Leary (2005). *Psychological Bulletin*, 131, 224–30.

Parkinson, B., Totterdell, P., Brinder, R. and Reynolds, S. (1996). *Changing Moods: The Psychology of Mood and Mood Regulation*. London: Longman.

Parrott, W.G. and Smith, R.H. (1993). Distinguishing the experiences of envy and jealousy. *Journal of Personality and Social Psychology*, 64, 906–20.

Paykel, E. (1989). The background: Extent and nature of the disorder. In K. Herst and E. Paykel (eds), *Depression: An Integrative Approach*. Oxford: Heinemann Medical Books.

Peck, D. (2004). Current approaches to the assessment of depression. In M. Power (ed.), *Mood Disorders: A Handbook of Science and Practice* (pp. 307–17). Chichester: Wiley and Sons.

Pennebaker, J.W. (1988). Confiding traumatic experiences and health. In S. Fisher and J. Reason (eds), *Handbook of Life Stress, Cognition and Health*. Chichester: Wiley and Sons.

Pennebaker, J.W. (1997). *Opening Up: The Healing Power of Expressing Emotions*. New York: Guilford Press.

Pennebaker, J.W. and Becall, S.K. (1986). Confronting a traumatic event: Toward an understanding of inhibition and disease. *Journal of Abnormal Psychology*, 95, 274–87.

Perrez, M. and Reicherts, M. (1992). *Stress, Coping and Health: A Situation-Behavior Approach, Theory, Methods and Applications*. Bern: Hogrefe and Huber.

Perry, B.D., Pollard, R.A., Blakley, T.L., Baker, W.L. and Vigilante, D. (1995). Childhood trauma, the neurobiology of adaptation and 'use – dependent' development of the brain: How 'states' become 'traits'. *Infant Mental Health Journal*, 16, 271–91.

Peterson, C., Maier, S.F. and Seligman, M.E.P. (1993). *Learned Helplessness: A Theory for the Age of Personal Control*. New York: Oxford University Press.

Peterson, C. and Seligman, M.E.P. (2004). *Character Strengths and Virtues: A Handbook and Classification*. New York: Oxford University Press.

Pinel, E.C. (1999). Stigma consciousness: The psychological legacy of social stereotypes. *Journal of Personality and Social Psychology*, 76, 114–28.

Pope, K.S., Sonne, J.L. and Greene, B. (2006). *What Therapists Don't Talk About and Why: Understanding Taboos That Hurt us And Our Clients*. Washington DC: American Psychological Association.

Porter, R. (2002). *Madmen: A Social History of Madhouses, Mad-Doctors & Lunatics*. Stroud, Gloucestershire: Tempus.

Posternak, M.A. and Miller, I. (2001). Untreated short-term course of major depression: A meta-analysis of outcomes from studies using wait-list control groups. *Journal of Affective Disorders*, 66, 139–46.

Posternak, M.A. and Zimmerman, M. (2002). Partial validation of the atypical features subtype of major depressive disorders. *Archives of General Psychiatry*, 59, 70–6.

Power, M. (ed.) (2004). *Mood Disorders: A Handbook of Science and Practice*. Chichester: Wiley and Sons.

Power, M. and Dalgleish, T. (1997). *Cognition and Emotions: From Order to Disorder*: Hove: The Psychology Press.

Price, J.S. (1972). Genetic and phylogenetic aspects of mood variation. *International Journal of Mental Health*, 1, 124–44.

Price, J.S. (2000). Subordination, self-esteem and depression. In L. Sloman and P. Gilbert (eds), *Subordination and Defeat: An Evolutionary Approach to Mood Disorders and Their Therapy* (pp. 165–77). Mahwah, NJ: Lawrence Erlbaum Associates.

Price, J.S. and Sloman, L. (1987). Depression as yielding behaviour: An animal model based on Schjelderup-Ebb's pecking order. *Ethology and Sociobiology*, 8 (Suppl.), 85–98.

Price, J.S., Sloman, L., Gardner, R., Gilbert, P. and Rohde, P. (1994). The social competition hypothesis of depression. *British Journal of Psychiatry*, 164, 309–15.

Prince, S.F. and Jacobson, N.S. (1995). Couple and family therapy in depression. In F.E. Beckham and W.R. Leber (eds), *Handbook of Depression*, (2nd edn, pp. 404–24). New York: Guilford Press.

Pyszczynski, T. and Greenberg, J. (1987). Self-regulatory preservation and the depressive self-focusing style: A self-awareness theory of reactive depression. *Psychological Bulletin*, 102, 122–38.

Rector, N.A., Bagby, R.M., Segal, Z.V., Joffe, R.T. and Levitt, A. (2000). Self-criticism and dependency in depressed patients treated with cognitive therapy or pharmacotherapy. *Cognitive Therapy and Research*, 24, 571–84.

Rehm, L.P. (1988). Self-management and cognitive processes in depression. In L.B. Alloy (ed.), *Cognitive Processes in Depression* (pp. 143–76). New York: Guilford Press.

Rein, G., Atkinson, M. and McCraty, R. (1995). The physiological and psychological effects of compassion and anger. *Journal for the Advancement of Medicine*, 8, 87–105.

Reinders, A.A.T.S., Nijenhuis, E.R.S., Paans, A.M.J., Korf, J., Willemsen, A.T.M. and den Boer, J.A. (2003). One brain, two selves. *NeuroImage*, 20, 2119–25.

Reite, M. and Field, T. (1985). *The Psychobiology of Attachment and Separation*. New York: Academic Press.

Reynolds, M. and Brewin, C.R. (1999). Intrusive memories in depression and posttraumatic stress disorder. *Behavior Research and Therapy*, 37, 201–15.

Riley, W.T., Treiber, F.A. and Woods, M.G. (1989). Anger and hostility in depression. *Journal of Nervous and Mental Disease*, 177, 668–74.

Ringu Tilku Rinpoche and Mullen, K. (2005). The Buddhist use of compassionate imagery in Buddhist mediation. In P. Gilbert (ed.), *Compassion: Conceptualisations, Research and Use in Psychotherapy* (pp. 218–38). London: Brunner-Routledge.

Riskin, J.H. (2006). Links between cognitive-behavioral hope-building and positive psychology: Applications to a psychotic patient. *Journal of Cognitive Psychotherapy: An International Quarterly*, 20, 171–82.

Rogers, C. (1957). The necessary and sufficient conditions of therapeutic change. *Journal of Consulting Psychology*, 21, 95–103.

Rohner, R.P. (1986). *The Warmth Dimension: Foundations of Parental Acceptance–Rejection Theory*. Beverly Hills, CA: Sage.

Rohner, R.P. (2004). The parent 'acceptance–rejection syndrome': Universal correlates of perceived rejection. *American Psychologist*, 59, 830–40.

Rosen, H. (1989). Piagetian theory and cognitive therapy. In C. Freeman and P. Tyrer (eds), *Research Methods in Psychiatry: A Beginner's Guide*. London: Gaskell/The Royal College of Psychiatrists.

Rosen, J.B. and Schulkin, J. (1998). From normal fear to pathological anxiety. *Psychological Bulletin*, 105, 325–50.

Rottenberg, J. and Gotlib, I.H. (2004). Socioemotional functioning in depression. In M. Power (ed.), *Mood Disorders: A Handbook of Science and Practice* (pp. 61–77). Chichester: Wiley and Sons.

Russell, G.A. (1985). Narcissism and narcissistic personality disorder: A comparison of the theories of Kernberg and Kohut. *British Journal of Medical Psychology*, 58, 137–48.

Ryle, A. (1990). *Cognitive-Analytic Therapy: Active Participation in Change*. Chichester: Wiley.

Sacco, W.P. and Beck, A.T. (1995). Cognitive theory and therapy. In F.E. Beckham and W.R. Leber (eds), *Handbook of Depression* (2nd edn, pp. 329–51). New York: Guilford Press.

Safran, J.D. (1998). *Widening the Scope of Cognitive Therapy: The Therapeutic Relationship, Emotion, and the Process of Change*. San Francisco: Jossey-Bass.

Safran, J.D. and Segal, Z.V. (1990). *Interpersonal Process in Cognitive Therapy*. New York: Basic Books.

Salkovskis, P.M. (1996a). The cognitive approach to anxiety: Threat beliefs, safety-seeking behavior, and the special case of health anxiety and obsessions. In, P.M. Salkovskis (ed.), *Frontiers of Cognitive Therapy* (pp. 48–74). New York: Guilford Press.

Salkovskis, P.M. (1996b). Avoidance behavior is motivated by threat beliefs: A possible resolution of the cognitive behavioural debate. In P.M. Salkovskis (ed.), *Trends in Cognitive and Behavioural Therapies* (pp. 25–42). Chichester: Wiley.

Salzberg, S. (1995). *Loving-Kindness: The Revolutionary Art of Happiness*. Boston: Shambhala.

Santor, D. and Walker, J. (1999). Garnering the interests of others: Mediating the effects among physical attractiveness, self-worth and dominance. *British Journal of Social Psychology*, 38, 461–77.

Santor, D. and Zuroff, D. (1997). Interpersonal responses to threats to status and interpersonal relatedness: Effects of dependency and self-criticism. *British Journal of Clinical Psychology*, 36, 521–41.

Sapolsky, R.M. (1989). Hypercortisolism among socially subordinate wild baboons originates at the CNS level. *Archives of General Psychiatry*, 46, 1047–51.

Sapolsky, R.M. (1994). *Why Zebras Don't Get Ulcers: An Updated Guide to Stress, Stress-Related Disease, and Coping*. New York: Freeman.

Sapolsky, R.M. (2000). Glucocorticoids and hippocampus atrophy in neuropsychiatric disorders. *Archives of General Psychiatry*, 57, 925–35.

Schore, A.N. (1991). Early superego development: The emergence of shame and narcissistic affect regulation in the practising period. *Psychoanalysis and Contemporary Thought: A Quarterly of Integrative and Interdisciplinary Studies*, 14, 187–250.

Schore, A.N. (1994). *Affect Regulation and the Origin of the Self: The Neurobiology of Emotional Development*. Hillsdale, NJ: Lawrence Erlbaum Associates.

Schore, A.N. (1998). Early shame experiences and infant brain development. In P. Gilbert and B. Andrews (eds), *Shame: Interpersonal Behavior, Psychopathology and Culture* (pp. 57–77). New York: Oxford University Press.

Schore, A.N. (2001). The effects of early relational trauma on right brain development, affect regulation, and infant mental health. *Infant Mental Health Journal*, 22, 201–69.

Schwartz, J.M. and Begley, S. (2002). *The Mind and the Brain: Neuroplasticity and the Power of Mental Force*. New York: Regan Books.

Scott, J. (1988). Chronic depression. *British Journal of Psychiatry*, 153, 287–97.

Scott, J.C. (1990). *Domination and the Arts of Resistance*: New Haven, CT: Yale University Press.

Segal, Z.V., Kennedy, S., Gemar, M., Hood, K., Pedersen, R. and Buis, T. (2006). Cognitive reactivity to sad provocation and the prediction of depressive relapse. *Archives of General Psychiatry*, 63, 749–55.

Segal, Z.V., Williams, J.M.G. and Teasdale, J. (2002). *Mindfulness-based Cognitive Therapy for Depression: A New Approach to Preventing Relapse.* New York: Guilford Press.

Segrin, C. and Abramson, L.Y. (1994) Negative reactions to depressive behaviours: A communication theories analysis. *Journal of Abnormal Psychology,* 103, 655–68.

Seligman, M.E.P. (1975). *Helplessness: On Depression, Development and Death.* San Francisco: Freeman.

Shahar, G., Blatt, S.J., Zuroff, D.C., Kupermine, G.P. and Leadbeater, B.J. (2004). Reciprocal relationship between depressive symptoms and self-criticism (but not dependency) among early adolescent girls (but not boys). *Cognitive Therapy and Research,* 28, 85–103.

Shahar, G., Henrich, C.C., Blatt, S.J., Ryan, R. and Little, T.D. (2003). Interpersonal relatedness, self-definition and their motivational orientation during adolescence: A theoretical and empirical integration. *Developmental Psychology,* 39, 470–83.

Shapiro, S.L., Astin, J.A., Bishop, S.R. and Cordova, M. (2005). Mindfulness-based stress reduction for health care professionals: Results from a randomised control trial. *International Journal of Stress Management,* 12, 164–76.

Sharhabani-Arzy, R., Amir, M. and Swisa, A. (2005). Self-criticism, dependency and posttraumatic stress disorder among a female group of help-seeking victims of domestic violence. *Personality and Individual Differences,* 38, 1231–40.

Sholomskas, D.E. (1990). Interviewing methods. In B.B. Wolman and G. Stricker (eds), *Depressive Disorders: Facts, Theories and Treatment Methods.* New York: Wiley.

Siegel, D.J. (2001). Toward an interpersonal neurobiology of the developing mind: Attachment relationships, 'mindsight' and neural integration. *Infant Mental Health Journal,* 22, 67–94.

Siegle, G., Carter, C.S. and Thase, M.E. (2006). Use of fMRI to predict recovery from unipolar depression with cognitive behaviour therapy. *American Journal of Psychiatry,* 163, 735–8.

Singer, J.L. (2006). *Imagery in Psychotherapy.* Washington DC: American Psychological Association.

Skovholt, T.M. and Rønnestad, M.H. (1992). *The Evolving Professional Self: Stages and Themes in Therapist and Counsellor Development.* Chichester: Wiley.

Sloman, L. (2000). The syndrome of rejection sensitivity: An evolutionary perspective. In P. Gilbert and K. Bailey (eds), *Genes on the Couch: Explorations in Evolutionary Psychotherapy* (pp. 257–75). Hove: Brunner-Routledge.

Sloman, L. and Gilbert, P. (eds) (2000). *Subordination and Defeat: An Evolutionary Approach to Mood Disorders* (pp. 3–46). Hillsdale, NJ: Lawrence Erlbaum Associates.

Sloman, L., Gilbert, P. and Hasey, G. (2003). Evolved mechanisms in depression: The role and interaction of attachment and social rank in depression. *Journal of Affective Disorders,* 74, 107–21.

Smith, P.K. and Trope, Y. (2006). You focus on the forest when you're in charge of the trees: Power priming and abstract information processing. *Journal of Personality and Social Psychology,* 90, 578–96.

Smith, R.H. and Kim, S.H. (2007). Comprehending envy. *Psychological Bulletin,* 133: 46–64.

Smith, R.H., Parrott, W.G., Ozer, D. and Moniz, A. (1994). Subjective injustice and inferiority predictors of hostile and depressive feelings in envy. *Personality and Social Psychology Bulletin,* 20, 705–11.

Snyder, C.R. and Ingram, R.E. (2006). Special issue on positive psychology. *Journal of Cognitive Psychotherapy: An International Quarterly,* 20, 115–240.

Stern, D.N. (2004). *The Present Moment in Psychotherapy and Everyday Life.* New York: W.W. Norton.

Stiles, W.B., Leach, C. and Barkham, M. (2003). Early sudden gains in psychotherapy under routine clinical conditions: practiced-based evidence. *Journal of Consulting and Clinical Psychology,* 71, 14–21.

Sturman, E.D. and Mongrain, M. (2005). Self-criticism and major depression: An evolutionary perspective. *British Journal of Clinical Psychology,* 44, 505–19.

Suddendorf, T. and Whitten, A. (2001). Mental evolutions and development: Evidence for secondary representation in children, great apes and other animals. *Psychological Bulletin*, 127, 629–50.

Suomi, S.J. (1999). Attachment in rhesus monkeys. In J. Cassidy and P.R. Shaver (eds), *Handbook of Attachment: Theory, Research and Clinical Applications* (pp. 181–97). New York: Guilford Press.

Swallow, S.R. and Kuiper, N.A. (1988). Social comparison and negative self-evaluation: An application to depression. *Clinical Psychology Review*, 8, 55–76.

Swann, W.B., Rentfrow, P.J. and Guinn, (2003). Self-verification: The search for coherence. In M.R. Leary and J.P. Tangney (eds), *Handbook of Self and Identity* (pp. 367–83). New York: Guilford Press.

Tangney, J.P. and Dearing, R.L. (2002). *Shame and Guilt*. New York: Guilford Press.

Tangney, J.P. and Fischer, K.W. (eds) (1995). *Self-Conscious Emotions: The Psychology of Shame, Guilt, Embarrassment and Pride*. New York: Guilford Press.

Tangney, J.P., Wagner, P.E., Barlow, D.H., Marschall, D.E. and Gramzow, R. (1996). Relation of shame and guilt to constructive versus destructive responses to anger across the lifespan. *Journal of Personality and Social Psychology*, 70, 797–809.

Tarrier, N. (ed.) (2006). *Case Formulation in Cognitive Behaviour Therapy: The Treatment of Challenging and Complex Cases*. London: Routledge.

Tarrier, N., Wells, A. and Haddock, G. (1998). *Treating Complex Cases: The Cognitive Behavioural Therapy Approach*. Chichester: Wiley.

Taylor, C. (1989). *Sources of the Self: The Making of the Modern Identity*. Cambridge: Cambridge University Press.

Taylor, S.F. and Brown, J.D. (1988). Illusion and well being: A social psychological perspective on mental health. *Psychological Bulletin*, 103, 193–210.

Taylor, S.E., Way, B.M., Welch, W.T., Hilmert, C.J., Lehman, B.J. and Eisenberger, N.I. (2006). Early family environment, current adversity, the serotonin transporter promoter polymorphism, and depressive symptomatology. *Biological Psychiatry*. 60: 671–676.

Teasdale, J.D. (1997). The transformation of meaning: The interacting cognitive subsystems approach. In M. Power and C.R. Brewin (eds), *The Transformation of Meaning in Psychological Therapies: Integrating Theory and Practice* (pp. 141–56). Chichester: Wiley.

Teasdale, J.D. and Barnard, P.J. (1993). *Affect, Cognition and Change: Remodelling Depressive Affect*. Hove: Lawrence Erlbaum Associates.

Teasdale, J.D. and Dent, J. (1987). Cognitive vulnerability to depression: An investigation of two hypotheses. *British Journal of Clinical Psychology*, 26, 113–26.

Teicher, M.H. (2002). Scars that won't heal: The neurobiology of the abused child. *Scientific American*, 286(3), 54–61.

Teicher, M.H., Samson, J.A., Polcari, A. and McGreenery, C.E. (2006). Sticks and stones and hurtful words: Relative effects of various forms of childhood maltreatment. *American Journal of Psychiatry*, 163, 993–1000.

Thase, M.E. and Howland, R.H. (1995). Biological processes in depression: An updated review and integration. In F.E. Beckham and W.R. Leber (eds), *Handbook of Depression* (2nd edn, pp. 213–79). New York: Guilford Press.

Thase, M.E., Jindal, R. and Howland, R.H. (2002). Biological aspects of depression. In I.H. Gotlib and C.L. Hammen (eds), *Handbook of Depression* (pp. 192–218). New York: Guilford Press.

Thwaites, R. and Freeston, M.H. (2005). Safety-seeking behaviours. Fact or Fiction: How can we clinically differentiate between safety behaviours and additive coping strategies across anxiety disorders. *Behavioural and Cognitive Psychotherapy*, 33, 177–88.

Timberlake, W. (1994). Behavior systems, associationism, and pavlovian conditioning. *Psychonomic Bulletin and Review*, 1, 405–20.

Tobena, A., Marks, I. and Dar, R. (1999). Advantages of bias and prejudice: An exploration of their neurocognitive templates. *Neuroscience and Behavioral Reviews*, 23, 1047–58.

Trevarthen, C. and Aitken, K. (2001). Infant intersubjectivity: Research, theory, and clinical applications. *Journal of Child Psychology and Psychiatry*, 42, 3–48.

Trower, P., Sherling, G., Beech, J., Horrop, C. and Gilbert, P. (1998). The socially anxious perspective in face-to-face interaction: An experimental comparison. *Clinical Psychology and Psychotherapy: An International Journal of Theory and Practice*, 5, 155–66.

Uväns-Morberg, K. (1998). Oxytocin may mediate the benefits of positive social interaction and emotions. *Psychoneuroendocrinology*, 23, 819–35.

Vasile, R.G., Samson, J.A., Bemporad, J., Bloomingdale, K.L., Creasey, D., Fenton, B.T., Gudeman, J.E. and Schildkratit, J.J. (1987). A biopsychosocial approach to treating patients with affective disorders. *American Journal of Psychiatry*, 144, 341–4.

Verrier, N.N. (1997). *The Primal Wound: Understanding the Adopted Child*. Baltimore, MD: Gateway Press.

Völlm, B.A., Taylor, A.N.W., Richardson, P., Corcoran, R., Stirling, J., McKie, S., Deakin, J.F.W. and Elliott R. (2006). Neuronal correlates of theory of mind and empathy: A functional magnetic resonance imaging study in a nonverbal task. *NeuroImage*, 29, 90–8.

Vonk, R. (1998). The slime effect: Suspicion and dislike of likeable behavior toward superiors. *Journal of Personality and Social Psychology*, 74: 849–64.

Wang, S. (2005). A conceptual framework for integrating research related to the physiology of compassion and the wisdom of Buddhist teachings. In P. Gilbert (ed.), *Compassion: Conceptualisations, Research and Use in Psychotherapy* (pp. 75–120). London: Brunner-Routledge.

Ward, D.E. (1989). Termination of individual counselling: Concepts. In W. Dryden (ed.), *Key Issues for Counselling in Action* (pp. 97–110). London: Sage.

Watkins, C.E. (1989a). Transference phenomena in the counselling situation. In W. Dryden (ed.), *Key Issues for Counselling in Action* (pp. 73–84). London: Sage.

Watkins, C.E. (1989b). Countertransference: Its impact on the counselling situation. In W. Dryden (ed.), *Key Issues for Counselling in Action* (pp. 85–96). London: Sage.

Wearden, A.J., Tarrier, N., Barrowclough, C., Zastowny, T.R. and Rahil, A.A. (2000). A review of expressed emotion research in health care. *Clinical Psychology Review*, 5, 633–66.

Weiss, J.M., Demetrikopoulos, M.K., McCurdy, P.M., West, C.H.K. and Bonsall, R.W. (2000). Depression seen through an animal model: An expanded hypothesis of pathophysiology and improved models. In R.J. Davidson (ed.), *Anxiety, Depression and Emotion* (pp. 3–35). New York: Oxford University Press.

Weissenburger, J.E. and Rush, A.J. (1996). Biology and cognitions in depression: Does the mind know what the brain is doing? In P.M. Salkovskis (ed.), *Frontiers of Cognitive Therapy* (pp. 114–34). New York: Guilford Press.

Wells, A. (2000). *Emotional Disorders and Metacognition: Innovative Cognitive Therapy*. Chichester: Wiley.

Whelton, W.J. and Greenberg, L.S. (2005). Emotion in self-criticism. *Personality and Individual Differences*, 38, 1583–95.

Whiten, A. (1999). The evolution of deep social mind in humans. In M.C. Corballis and S.E.G. Lea (eds), *The Descent of Mind: Psychological Perspectives on Humanoid Evolution* (pp. 173–93). New York: Oxford University Press.

Wilkinson, R.G. (1996). *Unhealthy Societies: The Afflictions of Inequality*. London: Routledge.

Williams, C.J. (2001). *Overcoming Depression: A Five Areas Approach*. London: Arnold.

Williams, J.M.G. and Wells, J. (1989). Suicide patients. In J. Scott, I.M.G. Williams and A.T. Beck (eds), *Cognitive Therapy in Clinical Practice: An Illustrative Casebook Practice*. London: Routledge.

Williams, M. (1997). *Cry of Pain*. London: Penguin Books.

Wilson, D.R. (1998). Evolutionary epidemiology and manic depression. *British Journal of Medical Psychology*, 71, 375–95.

Wolf, E.S. (1988). *Treating the Self Elements of Clinical Self Psychology*. New York: Guilford Press.

Wolfe, R.N., Lennox, R.D. and Cutler, B.L. (1986). Getting along and getting ahead: Empirical support for a theory of protective and acquisitive self-presentation. *Journal of Social and Personality Psychology*, 50, 356–61.

Wolpe, J. (1971). Neurotic depression: Experimental analogue, clinical syndromes and treatment. *American Journal of Psychotherapy*, 25, 362–8.

Wolpe, J. (1979). The experimental model and treatment of neurotic depression. *Behaviour Research and Therapy*, 17, 555–65.

Wolpert, L. (1999). *Malignant Sadness: The Anatomy of Depression*. London: Faber and Faber.

Wong, P.T.P. (2006). Existential and humanistic theories. In C. Thomas and D.L. Segal (eds), *Comprehensive Handbook of Personality and Psychopathology Vol 1: Personality and Everyday Functioning* (pp. 192–211). New York: Wiley.

Worthington, E.L., O'Connor, L.E., Berry, J.W., Sharp, C., Murray, R. and Yi, E. (2005). Compassion and forgiveness: Implications for psychotherapy. In P. Gilbert (ed.), *Compassion: Conceptualisations, Research and Use in Psychotherapy* (pp. 168–92). London: Routledge.

Wright, B., Williams, C. and Garland, A. (2002). Using the five areas cognitive-behavioural therapy model with psychiatric patients. *Advances in Psychiatric Treatment*, 8, 307–15.

Wroe, A.L. and Salkovskis, P.M. (2000). Causing harm and allowing harm: A study of beliefs in obsessional problems. *Behaviour Research and Therapy*, 38, 1141–62.

Yalom, I.D. (1980). *Existential Psychotherapy*. New York: Basic Books.

Young, J.E., Beck, A.T. and Weinberger, A. (1993). Depression. In H.D. Barlow (ed.), *Clinical Handbook of Psychological Disorders* (pp. 240–77). New York: Guilford Press.

Young, J.E. and Klosko, J.S. (1993). *Reinventing Your Life*. New York: Dutton-Penguin.

Zuroff, D.C. and Blatt, S.J. (2006). The therapeutic relationship in the brief treatment of depression: Contributions to clinical improvement and enhanced capacities. *Journal of Consulting and Clinical Psychology*, 74, 130–40.

Zuroff, D.C., Koestner, R. and Powers, T.A. (1994). Self-criticism at age 12: A longitudinal study of adjustment. *Cognitive Therapy and Research*, 18, 367–85.

Zuroff, D.C. Moskowitz, D.S. and Cote, S. (1999). Dependency, self-criticism, interpersonal behaviour and affect: Evolutionary perspectives. *British Journal of Clinical Psychology*, 38, 231–50.

Zuroff, D.C., Santor, D. and Mongrain, M. (2005). Dependency, self-criticism, and maladjustment. In J.S. Auerbach, K.N. Levy and C.E. Schaffer (eds), *Relatedness, Self-Definition and Mental Representation: Essays in Honour of Sidney J. Blatt* (pp. 75–90). London: Routledge.

Index

Note: Page numbers in *italics* denote figures